Ulick Joseph Bourke

Easy Lessons

Or Self-Instruction in Irish

Ulick Joseph Bourke

Easy Lessons
Or Self-Instruction in Irish

ISBN/EAN: 9783744738033

Printed in Europe, USA, Canada, Australia, Japan

Cover: Foto ©Paul-Georg Meister /pixelio.de

More available books at **www.hansebooks.com**

EASY LESSONS:

OR,

SELF-INSTRUCTION IN IRISH.

BY THE

REV. ULICK J. BOURKE,

President, St. Jarlath's College, Tuam.

———

A KEY IS ANNEXED TO THE END OF EACH PART.

NEW YORK:

P. M. HAVERTY, No. 9 BARCLAY STREET.

1873.

SELF-INSTRUCTION IN IRISH.

We commence our Easy Lessons in the Irish Language. We have, as will be manifest to those intimately acquainted with it, made it our special endeavour to be as simple and concise as possible, consistent with a proper elucidation of the subject-matter.

FIRST LESSON.

THE IRISH LETTERS—THEIR SOUNDS:

THE VOWELS.

There are seventeen letters in the Irish Alphabet. Of these seventeen five are vowels, the remaining twelve are consonants.

THE IRISH ALPHABET.

Cap.	Small.	PRONUNCIATION.
Ⰰ	ᴀ	*a* French or *aw* English
b	b	
C	c	*c* hard, or *k;* never at all pronounced like *s* or *ch* soft.
Ⱁ	ꝺ	*dh*
e	e	*e* (as *é* in *thére*).
Ϝ	ꝼ	*f*
Ʒ	ʒ	*g* hard, as *g* in *get;* never sounded soft, like *g* in *gin.*
]	ı	*i* French, *ee* English.
Ⱡ	l	*l* generally as the first *l* in *William.*
Ⰿ	m	*m*
N	n	*n*
O	o	*o*
p	p	*p*
R	ɼ	*r*
S	ꝩ	*s*
Ꞇ	ꞇ	*t* Italian, or *th* Eng.
U	u	*u* Italian, *oo* English. or *u* in *bull;* never sounded as *u* (*you*).

We omit denominating the letters by their Irish names, *Ailm*, *Beith*, &c., so called just as the letters in Greek are called *Alpha*, *Beta*, or in Hebrew, *Aleph*, *Beth*, &c., to distinguish them one from the other, and from those of any other language—partly because they are, at present, seldom or never called by their names, and partly because some persons mistake the name for the sound of the letter.

With regard to the pronunciation of the letters in Irish, and of the language generally, the fullest, the most open enunciation is required. The vowels must be sounded as in Italian or French; the consonants as in German or Spanish. This open, full sounding of the vowels and con sonants enables foreigners to learn to speak Irish more cor rectly and more readily than English-speaking people can ever acquire. Of all the languages spoken throughout the globe, the pronunciation of English is the most opposed to that of Irish ; and this is very likely one of the reasons why English-speaking Irishmen feel such a distaste for the broad pronunciation of their mother-tongue

Obs. 1.—The letter S, ſ, is always sounded like *sh* whenever it goes before or comes after the vowels e or ı, as ſın-ne, *us*, pronounced *shinné*, and not *sinné*. There is one exception to this rule, the word ıſ, *is* ; the third person singular present, indicative of the assertive form of the verb *to be*, which is pronounced *is*, and not *ish*.

Again, S, ſ, before or after a, o, u, is sounded simply like *s* in *soon* ; as ſuıl, *the eye*—pronounced *soo-ill*, and not *shoo-ill*. To the second part of the Obs. the demonstrative pronoun ſo, *this*, is in Connaught an exception, being pronounced *sho* in that province; but in Munster *so*, agreeably to the general rule here laid down.

Obs. 2.—The form or shape of each of the Irish letters is substantially the same as that of the Roman character of the same sound and name—small (ɲ) *r* and small (ſ) *s* excepted ;—but their form is easily distinguished, ɲ being very like the written *e* in the Roman character, and ſ not unlike the printed *r*, but with a longer stem.

SOUNDS OF THE VOWELS.

á, long, as *a* in the word *wall.* Example, áꞃꝺ, *high*, pronounced *awrd*, answering to the *broad* sound of *a* in English

 á *short,*   ...   *a* in *bat;*   ...   aɲaṁ, *a soul.*

There is a third sound of á, very common in the West and South of Ireland—just the same as the short sound of bread *a* in English, as *a* in *what, quadrant.* Example, ꞡaꞃ, *near;* ꞇaꞃꞇ, *thirst;* maꞃꞇ, *a beef.*

é, long,	*e* in *where;*	cꞃé, *clay;* ꞡé, *a goose.*
e, short,	*e* in *when;*	baile, *a town.*
í, long,	*ee,* or *i* in pique;	mín, *fine.*
ı, short,	*i,* in *pick;*	mın, *meal.*
ó, long,	*o* in *told;*	ól, *drinking.*
o, short,	*o* in *other;*	coꞃp, *a body.*
ú, long,	*u* in *rule;*	úꞃ, *fresh.*
u, short,	*u* in *full;*	ucꞇ, *breast.*

Oʙs. 1.—The *grave* accent ('), which is the same in form as the *acute* of the Greeks, shows that the vowel over which it is placed is to be sounded long

The absence of the accent (') does not *always* indicate that the vowel is to be sounded short; because when the language was commonly spoken by the people, they re quired no such phonographic aid. For this reason some writers have at times not made use of it.

Oʙs. 2.—The vowels are divided into *broad* and *slender.* The *broad* are a, o, u; the *slender* are e, ı.

The reason of this division and its utility shall be shown in a subsequent Lesson.

VOCABULARY

aꞡuꞃ, and.
aṁ, time.
áꞃ, slaughter.
báɲ, white.
báꞅ, death.
bıɲɲ, harmonious.
boꞅ, fist, the palm.
bꞃaꞇ, cloak, garment.
bꞃóɲ, sorrow.
cab, mouth; the closed lips.
claꞃ, a board, a table; a chapter, the forehead.
caꞃa, a friend; Latin, *charus.*
coꞅ, foot; Lat. *pes;* Gr. πους, *pous.*
ꝺáɲ, a poem.
ꝺoꞃɲ, the fist clenched; a blow given with the fist.
ꞡoꞃm, blue.

ꞡoꞃꞇ, hunger; a field; an orchard.
ım, butter.
lá, day.
mac. a son.
máꞅ, thigh, flank.
mí, or mıoꞅ, a month; Lat. *mensis.*
mıl, honey; Lat. *mel;* Gr. μέλι. *meli.*
mılıꞅ, sweet.
olc, bad.
óꞃ, gold.
puꞅ, lip.
ꞃóꞅ, a rose; Latin, *rosa.*
ꞃúɲ, secret, dear, beloved.
ꞃal, filth.
ꞃál, heel.
ꞅlaꞇ, rod, yard, (a measure.)
ꞇꞃom, heavy.
úꞃ, fresh.

EXERCISE I.

1. Am agus ór. 2. án agus bár. 3. bos agus cos. 4 bán agus gorm. 5. brat agus slat 6. mac agus nún. 7. már agus sál. 8. mil agus ór. 9. úr agus olc. 10. bos agus donn. 11. pus agus cab. 12. bán binn. 13. gort agus brón. 14. im agus mil. 15. lá agus mí. 16. mí olc; gort bán; ór trom; min mín, milis. 17. brat gorm; im úr, agus bán binn. 18. clár bán, brón trom, agus bár olc. 19. anam agus corp 20. slat agus ór; cré mín, agus min úr.

Obs.—The position of the adjective is *always* AFTER the noun with which it agrees

VOCABULARY.

aill, a clift.
al, a brood.
ala, swan.
an, the (the definite article).
ard, high.
at, swelling.
bád, a boat.
barr, top.
bó, a cow; Lat. bos; Gr. βους, bous.
bog, soft.
bolg, belly, pouch, paunch, bellows.
cam, hooked, bent.
cás, case.
dall, blind.
dil, fond; and dílis, fond, loving.
dubh, black (pr. duv).
fada, long.
gann, scarce.
gar, near.
gas, stalk.

glan, clean.
glas, green.
lán, full.
long, ship.
lorg, track.
mall, late.
mam, mother.
mór, great, large.
mós, manner; Latin, mos.
muc, pig.
nós, fashion.
óg, young.
onc, prince.
ord, order; Latin, ordo.
pis, pease, pr. *pish*; see Obs. 1 p. 2.
port, harbour; a tune.
rí, pr. *ree*, king; Italian, *re*; Spanish, *rey*.
rosg, eye.
tonn, wave.

EXERCISE II.

1. al óg. 2. ala bán. 3. at ard. 4. bolg mór. 5. bó dubh. 6. cás cam. 7. barr glas. 8. bád fada 9. onc dall. 10. mam dil. 11. gar gann. 12. long mór. 13. long glan 14. rosg gorm. 15. rí óg. 16. ord gann. 17: tonn mór.

18. ᵹaʁ boᵹ.   19. poʁc biɲɲ.   20. coɲɲ áʁʊ, aᵹuʁ ac móʁ.
21. muc ʊuḃ aᵹuʁ bó ᵹlaʁ.   22. poʁᵹ boᵹ, aᵹuʁ bolᵹ móʁ.
23. ala mal, aᵹuʁ al ᵹaɲɲ.   24. ᵹaʁ báɲ, aᵹuʁ baʁʁ boᵹ.
25. piʁ láɲ, aᵹuʁ ᵹaʁ cam.   26. ʁoʁ úʁ, aᵹuʁ óʁ cʁom.

VOCABULARY.

ball, a member.	cʁom, crooked.
blaʁ, taste.	cúl, back.
boɲʊ, table.	cú, hound.
bʁoc, badger.	ʊoɲɲ, brown.
bun, the foundation, bottom.	ʁuʁ, wood.
cac, cat.	ʁʁóɲ, nose
cill, church, graveyard.	cá, am, is, are.
claɲ, children.	ciɲɲ, sick, sore, unwell.
clé, left-handed.	cíʁ, country.
cló, nail, type, defeat; Fr. clou.	coʁ, tower.
clú, fame.	coʁʊ, silence.
coʁɲ, goblet.	cúʁ, beginning.

EXERCISE III.

1. cá aɲ ball ciɲɲ.   2. aɲ cac aᵹuʁ aɲ bʁoc.   3. cá aɲ
boʁ clé ciɲɲ.   4. cá aɲ cíʁ báɲ.   5. cá aɲ cló ʊuḃ.   6. cá
aɲ coɲɲ ᵹoʁɲ.   7. cá aɲ cac ʊoɲɲ.   8. cá aɲ mac óᵹ.   9.
cá aɲ lá ʁaʊa.   10. cá aɲ coʁ áʁʊ.   11. cá aɲ ʁm úʁ :
12. cá aɲ boɲʊ áʁʊ.   13. cá aɲ coʁɲ cʁom.

EXERCISE IV.

1. Honey and butter.   2. Top and bottom.   3. Hand
and thigh.   4. Blue and white.   5. Gold and country.
6. The day is long.   7. The land is brown.   8. The king
is young.   9. The prince is tall.   10. The friend and the
beloved.   11. The day and the month.   12. The son and
the children.   13. The clay is fresh.   14. The stalk is
green.   15. The goblet is high.   16. The eye is blue.
17. The wave is large.   18. The son and the mother.
19. Bad and fresh.   20. The meal is fine.   21. The
stronghold is high.   22. The foot is long.   23. The beginning is near.   24. The table is large and high, and the
children are young and fond.   25. A brown hound, a
white cat.   26. The butter is fresh ; a secret is sweet.
27. The fashion is new.   28. Gold is scarce.   29. Death
s late.   30. A friend and gold are near.

SECOND LESSON.

OF THE UNION OF TWO OR MORE VOWELS, AND OF THEIR SOUNDS.

Two vowels coming together form a diphthong. Three coming together form a tripthong. In Irish there are thirteen diphthongs ; five triphthongs. The chief use in treating of them at any length at so early a stage in our instructions, is to know their sounds clearly.

Of the thirteen diphthongs six are always long, or naturally so ; seven are naturally short, but become long when marked with the accent. The long diphthongs do not require, as they are always long, any notation of the accent. The seven naturally short do require the presence of the accent to show that their sound is, in the case so noted, to be pronounced long.

The long are:—ᴀe, ᴀo, eo, eu, ĵᴀ, uᴀ : ĵu (see Third Lesson, p. 13) has not yet been ranked amongst the long diphthongs.

Sounds of the six long Diphthongs.

ᴀe, like *ae* in *Musæ,*   ex. ᵑᴀe,   *yesterday.*
ᴀo, ... *ee* in *queer :*—in Munster, like the first *e* in the word *there.*
                              bᴀoᵱ, *dear ;* ᵲᴀoᵱ, *cheap.*
eo, ... *eo* in *Keon,*   ceol, *music.* It is short in the five following words : eoċᴀᵱ, *a key ;* beoċ, *a drink ;* Coċᴀᵭ, *a man's name ;* ᵲeo,* *this ;* ᵲeoċ, *apart.*
eu, long, like *ai* in *wail,*   beul, *mouth ;* ᵲᵹeul, *story.*
ĵᴀ, like *ee* in *teem,*   pĵᴀᵑ,   *pain.*
uᴀ, like *ooe* in *wooer,*   ᵲuᴀᵑ,   *rest.*

This sound is easy, if it be kept in mind that *u* is always sounded as in the Continental languages, *oo,* and not "*you.*"

---

* *So,* and ᵲeo, *this,* are the same pronoun ; e is, by some, inserted before o, in order that ᵲ in ᵲo might, according to the general rule (see Obs. 1, p. 2), receive the sound of *sh*—a sound which, be it remembered, it always has when placed before or after e or ĵ.

VOCABULARY.

ae.

ᴀeṗ, air.

ʒᴀe, of an arrow ; possessive case of ʒᴀ, an arrow, a ray, a javelin.

lᴀe, of a day ; poss. of lᴀ, a day.

ṗᴀe, yesterday ; ṗᴀe, the moon.

ᴀɩʒ, at, to ; le, with ; ó, from.

ᴀʒᴀṁ, to me ; ᴀʒᴀꝺ, to thee ; ᴀɩʒe, to him.

ᴀṗṗ, in ; ᴀṗ, the ; ᴀṗ, whether (Latin, *anne*).

ᴄu, thou, second person sing.

ṗɩḃ (*shiv*), you, second person plural, is never, in Irish, employed for the second person singular.

ᴀo.

ᴀol, lime.

ᴀoṗ, one, any ; Fr. un ; Gr. ἔν, (*en*); Lat. unum.

ᴀoṛ, age.

blᴀoṛʒ, shell.

bṛᴀoṗ, drop.

cᴀol, slender.

cᴀoṛ, berry, a burning coal.

ꝺᴀoṛ, dear.

ṗᴀoṗ, weak, pining, feeble.

ṁᴀol, bald.

mᴀoṛ, a steward.

ṛᴀob, rend (to) *v.*

ṛᴀoṛ, cheap, free ; a workman.

ᴄᴀoṁ, a fit, rage.

ṛᴀoṛ, dough.

mᴀṛ, as, like.

ṗɩ, not.

ḃ-ṗuɩl (pr. *will*), is ?

eo.

beo, alive.

ceo, fog, vapour.

ceol, music.

ꝺeol, suck.

ꝺeoṛ, a tear, a drop.

leoṛ, enough.

ṛeol, a sail.

ᴄṛeoṛ, a guide.

oṛm, on me.

oṛᴄ, on thee.

ᴀṛ, on him.

EXERCISE V.

1. ḃ-ṗuɩl ᴀṗ ᴄ-ᴀeṗ ᴀṗꝺ? 2. ᴄᴀ ᴀṗ ᴄ-ᴀeṗ ᴀṗꝺ. 3. ḃ-ṗuɩl ᴀṗ lᴀ ṗᴀꝺᴀ? 4. ᴄᴀ ᴀṗ lᴀ ṗᴀꝺᴀ. 5. ḃ-ṗuɩl ᴀṗ mᴀc ᴄɩṗṗ ó ṗᴀe? 6. ᴄᴀ ᴀṗ mᴀc ᴄɩṗṗ ó ṗᴀe. 7. ḃ-ṗuɩl ᴀṗ ṗᴀe bᴀṗ? 8. ᴄᴀ ᴀṗ ṗᴀe bᴀṗ. 9. ḃ-ṗuɩl bᴀṗṛ ᴀṗ ʒᴀe ʒᴀṗʒ? 10. ᴄᴀ bᴀṗṛ ᴀṗ ʒᴀe ʒᴀṗʒ. 11. ᴄᴀ ᴀṛᴀṗ (bread) ṛᴀoṗ. 12. ḃ-ṗuɩl ᴀol ꝺᴀoṗ? 13. ᴄᴀ ᴀol ꝺᴀoṗ. 14. ḃ-ṗuɩl ᴀoṗ blᴀoṛʒ ᴀʒᴀꝺ? 15. ᴄᴀ blᴀoṛʒ ᴀʒᴀṁ. 16. ḃ-ṗuɩl ᴀoṗ bṛᴀoṗ ᴀʒᴀꝺ? 17. ᴄᴀ bṛᴀoṗ ᴀʒᴀṁ. 18. ḃ-ṗuɩl ᴄᴀoṁ oṛᴄ? 19. ᴄᴀ ᴄᴀoṁ oṛm. 20. ḃ-ṗuɩl ᴀṗ mᴀc ṗᴀoṗ? 21. ᴄᴀ ᴀṗ mᴀc ṗᴀoṗ. 22. ḃ-ṗuɩl ᴀṗ bó beo? 23. ᴄᴀ ᴀṗ bó beo. 24. ḃ-ṗuɩl ᴀṗ mᴀoṛ ᴄɩṗṗ? 25. ᴄᴀ ᴀṗ mᴀoṛ ᴄɩṗṗ. 26. ᴄᴀ ᴀṗ ᴄᴀoṛ ꝺᴀoṗ. 27. ᴄᴀ ceol ᴀɩʒe. 28. ḃ-ṗuɩl ᴀoṗ ꝺeoṛ ᴀʒᴀꝺ? 29. ᴄᴀ ceo ᴀṗṗ. 30. ḃ-ṗuɩl eoᴄᴀɩṛ ᴀʒᴀꝺ? 31. ᴄᴀ ꝺeoᴄ ᴀʒᴀṁ ᴀṗṗ ṛeo.

EXERCISE VI.

1. Is the cow white? 2. The cow is white. 3. Is the son tall? 4. The son is tall. 5. Is the day long? 6. The

·lay is not long.   7. Have you a berry?   8. I have not a berry.   9. Is the steward alive?   10. The steward is not alive.   11. The steward was alive yesterday.   12. He was not alive yesterday.   13. He was sick yesterday.   14. Are you sick?   15. No; I am not.   16. Time is like a vapour. 17. Is music melodious?   18. Yes ; music is melodious. 19. He tore a string of the harp (cᚱuᚔᚈ).   20. Music is cheap.   21. He tore the sail with the top of the arrow.

Obs. 1.—There are at present very few words spelled with the diphthong ᚐe, in fact only one or two more besides those given here ; as, ᚠᚐeᚈeᚐᚘ, *smiling :* in modern Irish, ᚐo is used for ᚐe, so commonly found in the ancient written language.

Obs. 2.—The diphthong ᚐo is not found in the English language save in the word GAOL, *a prison ;* in which it is pronounced like *é* in *thére*—agreeing exactly with the sound given this diphthong in Irish by the natives of Munster This analogy, and the fact that words now spelled with ᚐo were, by ancient Irish writers, spelled with ᚐe—which, as we have shown, has the sound of the first *e* in the word *there*—leads us to believe that the sound of this diphthong, as pronounced in Munster, is the correct one.   Add to this, that if ᚐo be pronounced *ee*, it is not easy to distinguish between it and the sound of the triphthong ᚐoᚔ, which is formed from it, nor from that of the diphthong ᚔᚐ.

Obs. 3.—Following the authority of Dr. O'Donovan, eo is placed by us among those diphthongs which are long by nature.   For, as there are only five words in the language in which the sound of eo is found to be short, it is useless to mark it long.   Hence, though hitherto this diphthong has been, by many Irish writers, marked with the accent (´), yet in our Lessons we shall avoid using this notation. It is plainly not only useless, but calculated even to lead astray.

Objection.—In what does the sound of the diphthong eo differ from that of the simple vowel ɔ ?—Answer—e, in the diphthong eo adds to the sound of the simple o in a twofold way: first the sound of e in the diphthong eo is so blended with that of o as to make, as far as possible, only one whole sound—thus differing in their unison from the simple sound of o. Again, the consonant preceding e becomes liquid, so that the same consonant which, before a, o, or u, would be pronounced hard, is pronounced liquid-like when going before e or ı; as, for example, the word bó, *a cow*, is pronounced like the French *beau*, while beo, *alive*, is pronounced as if *be-yo* ; so in ceol, *music*, the eo is pronounced as eo is heard in the Irish proper name *Keogh* (or *Kehoe*, as it is written in some districts), and *Keon* ; while c not followed by e or ı is not pronounced with that slender or liquid strain, but just like *c* in the English word *cow*. So l before e or ı is sounded like *l* in *million*, or *l* in the French word *lieu* ; and r before e or ı is sounded like *sh*, while before a, o, or u it is like *s* in *sound* or *soul*. This slender or liquid sound of the consonants before e and ı should be much attended to; it is the key for getting a proper pronunciation of the Irish language.

Sound the following words according to the pronunciation noted in the commencement of this Lesson:

VOCABULARY.

eu.

beul, mouth.
cneuḋ, what.
teuṗ, grass.
ʒeuʒ, branch.
ʒeuṗ, sharp.
meuṗ, finger, or toe ; finger when speaking of the hand ; toe when speaking of the foot.
ʒeul, cloud.
ṗeulc, star.
ṗeuṅ, happiness.
rʒeul, story.
rpeuṗ, sky, firmament.
cṗeuḋ, herd.
ʒaṅ, without.
lóṅ, a store.
ṅó, or.

ıa.

cıall, sense.
Dıa, God.
ḃıaṗ, blade of corn.
ḟıal, generous.
ʒıall, jaw.
ʒṗıaṅ, sun.
ıarʒ, fish.

mıaṅ, desire.
pıaṅ, pain.
pıarc, worm.
rʒıaṅ, knife.
rıaṅ, westward.
rlıaṗ. a thigh, the loin.
rṗıaṅ, bridle.
ır, (it) is ; (pronounced *is*, and not *ish*. It is the only exception to the rule that r = sh after e or i).

ua.

buaṅ, lasting.
cluaṗ, ear.
cṗuaṗ, hardness.
cuaṅ, harbour.
bual, work, duty ; peculiar to one from some inherent cause.
ḟuaṗ, cold:
ʒṗuaʒ, hair.
rcuaḃ, broom.
ruaṅ, slumber.
ruaṗ, up, erect.
uaṅ, lamb.
lıom, with me ; leac, with thee ; leır, with him ; leıce, with her

Examples formed from the foregoing words :—

EXERCISE VII.

1. ní feur geug. 2. b-fuil feur ort? 3. tá feur orm.
4. b-fuil treud agad? 5. tá treud agam. 6. an reult
an neul? 7. ní reult an neul. 8. an reult an speur?
9. ní reult an speur. 10. creud an sgeul? 11. tá an
speur fuar. 12. tá ciall aige. 13. b-fuil ciall aige?
14. agus tá mian aige. 15. tá fearg aige. 16. tá srian
air. 17. b-fuil pian ort? 18. tá pian orm. 19. tá giall
agam. 21. tá giall air. 21. ní b-fuil srian air. 22. tá
sgian geur. 23. is mian liom srian. 24. b-fuil gruag ort?
25. tá gruag orm. 26. tá gruag air. 27. b-fuil an cuan
fuar nó rian? 28. tá an cuan rian. 29. b-fuil ruan air?
30. tá ruan air. 31. is dual bás. 32. ní dual bás.
33. tá scuab agam. 34. tá cluas air. 35. tá uan óg
aige. 36. tá an lá fuar. 37. tá an im úr.

OBS. 1.—b-fuil, *is*, pronounced *will*, is the third person
singular present indicative of the verb fuilim, *I am*; a form
of the verb "to be," which is always employed instead of
táim, *I am*, after any of the particles of questioning (as
an, *whether*; nac, *whether not*, &c.); of *wishing* (go, *that*);
of *denying* (ní, *not*, nac, *who not*); and of *supposing* (ma, *if*),
and after the relative pronoun a, *who*; nac, *who not*; as ní
b-fuil se, *he is not*; go b-fuil se, *that he is*; an b-fuil se,
is he; nac b-fuil sé, *is he not*; an té a b-fuil, *the person
who is*; an te nac b-fuil, *the person who is not.*

OBS. 2.—The difference between is, *is*, and tá, *is*, is that
the one (is) denotes simply existence; tá denotes existence
in relation to time, state, condition, place.

OBS. 3.—is is omitted in short assertive sentences; as,
fearr mada beo 'na leon marb, *a living dog* (is) *better
than a dead lion*; fearr clú 'na conac, *better fame than
wealth.*

OBS. 4.—is (*is*) is never employed after particles of asking, wishing, denying, supposing, or the like; as, an reult
an grian, *whether* (is) *the sun a star?* nac reult an grian?
is not the sun a star? ní reult an grian, *the sun* (is) *not a
star;* an tu a tá ann? *anne tu qui es illic?* *whether* (is it)

you who are in it? It is left understood, as is done so often
in Latin sentences.

VOCABULARY.

Beginning, cuſ.
Earth, cſe, úſ, calaṁ.
End, beſne, cſíoc.
Foundation, buſ.
Grass, ſeuſ.
It (he), ſe, e ; (she) ſí, í.
In, aſſ, aſſ, (on).
Store, lóſ, ſcóſ.
Top, báſſ.
True, ſíoſ.
This, é ſo : that, é ſiſ.

There is, cá, iſ.
There is not, ſí b-ſuil. The word
there is omitted in translating into Irish.
Thing, ſíċ, (pr. *nhee*) ; ſaċ uile ſíċ
(pr. *gach ooilé nhee*), all things.
White, ſioſſ, (fair, opposed to red,
ſuaḋ ; as, ſeaſ ſioſſ, a fair-
haired man) ; báſ, white ;
ſeal, bright.

Note.—There being in Irish, as in French, only two genders, masculine
and feminine (See Sixteenth Lesson), the pronoun *it*, when referring to
nouns which in Irish are masculine, must be translated ſé ; but ſí
when to nouns which in our language are feminine.

EXERCISE VIII.

1. Is the story true?   2. The story is not true.   3. Is
the grass green?   4. The grass is green.   5. Is prosperity
on the country?   6. Prosperity is not on the country.
7. Prosperity is not lasting.   8. Is fish dear or cheap?
9. Fish is dear.   10. Is that a star or a cloud?   11. It is
neither a star nor a cloud; it is the moon.   12. Is that
a story or a wish?   13. It is a story.   14. Is that a
bridle on the cheek?   15. Is the ear erect?   16. I am
in a slumber.   17. Are you in a slumber?   18. The finger
is cold.   19. The sun is on high.   20. The sun is in the
sky.   21. The sun is in a cloud.   22. Without store,
without friend.   23. A lamb is white.   24. The worm is
on the earth.   25. The clay is cold.   26. There is no
rest on earth.   27. There is rest with God.   28. Is
there a God?   29. There is a God.   30. God is the beginning and the end, the foundation and the top of all
things.

THIRD LESSON.

THE diphthongs long by nature should never be sounded
short; the diphthongs short by nature are, on the contrary,
sometimes sounded long.   This change from short to long

is noted by placing the (′) accent over that vowel of the digraph whose sound is lengthened.

SOUNDS OF THE SEVEN SHORT DIPHTHONGS.

ᴀ́ı, equals the sound of *awi* in the English word *sawing*; as cᴀ́ıl, *fame*; ꜰᴀ́ıl, *fate*.

This sound is nothing more than the united sounds of ᴀ (*aw*), and ı (*i*) or *awi*. It should be carefully noted by the learner, as it is so unlike the sound of the same diphthong in English or French.

ᴀı not accented, = *ai* in the French *taille*, *cut*; as cᴀıll, *loss*; ꜰᴀıll, *a sty*.

The sound of ᴀı short is hard to be learned by an English-speaking student. To pronounce it correctly then, add to the sound of ᴀ that of ı quickly enunciated, yet forming both into one. The consonant following ı receives withal a slender sound, because it is joined to one of the slender vowels.

éᴀ	=	*ea* in *rear, swear*;	...	ðéᴀɲ, *do*.
cᴀ	=	*ea* in *heart*;	...	ɲeᴀꞅ, *respect*.
éı	=	*ei* in *deign, reign*;	...	céꞅ, *wax*.
eı	=	*ei* in *den*;	...	ceıl, *conceal*.
ío	=	*ee* in *green*;	...	ꝼíoɲ, *wine*.

In ío, it·is the sound of the vowel ı (*ee*) that is principally heard, and hence the digraph is noted as having only that leading sound; yet o is not entirely quiescent, for it gives the succeeding consonant a hard and not a liquid sound.

ıo	=	*i* in *grin*;	...	ꝼıoɲ, *white*.
ıú	=	*iew* in *view*;	...	ꞅıúꞅ, *a kinswoman, a sister*.
ıu	=	*oo* in *flood*;	...	ꝼluċ, (pr. *flyuch*), *wet*.
óı	=	*oi* in *toil*; (*o* long)	...	cóıꞅ, *just*.
oı	=	*u* in *shut*;	...	coıꞅ, *a crime*.
úı	=	*ui* in *fruit*;	...	ꞅúıl, *eye*.
uı	=	*ui* in *guilt*;	...	ꝼuıl, *blood*.

Sound the following words according to the pronunciation noted above:—

VOCABULARY.

áı, and aı.

áıl, pleasure, agreeableness.
aıll, a cliff, a rock.
áıc, a place.
áıc, pleasure, fancifulness.
báıl, blessing; happy issue; success.
báıll, members.
cáıl, fame.
cáıll, loss.
cáıṅ, tax, reproach.
caıṅ, chaste, undefiled.

éa, and éa.

beaṅ, a woman; (aṅ beaṅ, an van, the woman).
bṙeac, speckled, and hence it signifies a trout.
céaḋ, a hundred, first.
ceaḋ, leave.
ṙeaṙ, a man; (Lat. vir).
ṙeaṙṙ, better.
ṡeaṅ, affection.

éı, and eı.

béıṁ, a beam, a stroke, a stain.

ıo, and ıo.

cıoṅṅ, esteem, regard.
cṙıoṅ, withered.
cṙıoṡ, a girdle.
ṙıoṅ, wine.
ṙıoṅṅ, fair.
ṙıoṙ, true; (Latin, verum)
ṙıoṡ, knowledge.

ıú, and ıu.

bıul, to suck.
ṙıú, worthy.
ıúl, knowledge
ṙıúṙ, sister, a kinswoman;—as in Hebrew, a female relative is called sister.
ṙcıúṙ, a rudder; an affected appearance of the countenance; an angry look.

ıu is short only in very few words; as,

ṙlıuċ, wet; cṙıuġ, thick; ṙıuċ, boil.

It ought, therefore, to be ranked amongst the long diphthongs.

óı, and oı.

cóıṙ, just.
coıṙ, a crime.
ṙóıl, while.
ṙóıṙ, help.
moıll, delay.
ṙcoıl, school.

úı, and uı.

cṙuıc, a hump, a harp.
cúıġ, five (hence cúıġe, a province, because Ireland was formerly divided into five parts or kingdoms).
ḋṙuıṁ, a back.
muıṙ, the sea; Welsh, môr; Latin. mare; German, meer.

PERSONAL PRONOUNS SINGULAR.

me, I; cu, thou; ṙe, or e, he, (it); ṙí, or ı, she, (it): aıġ, at; le, with; aıṙ, on; ḋo, to.

COMPOUND PRONOUNS.

Aʒam, at me—compounded of aiʒ (at), and mé (I or me); aʒab, at thee, (of aiʒ and cu, thou); aiʒe, to him, (of aiʒ and e); aici, at her, (of aiʒ and i); liom, with me; same as le, with, and me, mo or I; leac, with thee; leir, with him; leice, with her; orm, on me; orc, on thee; air, on him; airri, or, airci, on her; ŏam, to me; ŏuic, to thee; ŏo, to him; ŏi, to her.

POSSESSIVE PRONOUNS.

mo, my; ŏo, thy; a his, its; a, her, its.

EXERCISE IX.

1. b-fuil mear mór orc? 2. cá mear mór orm. 3. b-fuil an lá fliuc? 4. cá an lá fliuc. 5. b-fuil fuil ann ŏo fuil ŏeir? 6. cá fuil ann mo fuil ŏeir. 7. an ail leac a ceacc (pr. *héacht*, to come) liom? 8. ní ail liom a ŏul (to go) leac. 9. b-fuil an cran crion? 10. cá an cran crion. 11. b-fuil fion fionn aʒur rion ŏearʒ aʒaŏ? 12. cá fion fionn, aʒur fion ŏearʒ aʒam. 13. b-fuil an bo (*woe*) fionn, an ʒé bán, an ʒeir ʒeal, an eac ruaŏ, an cu rean, an fean creun, an bean ŏilir? 14. cá: ir fion ʒo b-fuilib. 15. b-fuil fior mór aʒaŏ? 16. ir fion nac b-fuilim ʒan fior. 17. b-fuil fior aʒaŏ ʒur fiú fean maic, cion aʒur cáil aʒur mear?

Obs. 1.—The sound of e or ı is, in Irish, infused into all these diphthongal sounds, even though it cannot be correctly noted in English corresponding vowel marks. All we can do is to give the nearest possible English equivalent. The learner should well note, then, the fact—first, that each of the two vowels is sounded, yet blended into one; and, secondly, that the consonant after ı or e is liquid or slender. This he will observe on reading or speaking the first sentence in Irish.

Irishmen, like the ancients of Athens and Rome, enunciate, in pronouncing a diphthong, the two vowels of which it is composed, more fully and distinctly than English-speaking people are wont to do. The two vowels of the diphthong, though united, should be each distinctly heard.

Obs. 2.—The diphthongs éa (marked long) and eu are

sometimes, in manuscripts and publications, written indif-
ferently one for the other, as—

éaʒ } death; péaṅ } grass; ʒéaṅ } sharp; cṅéaṅ } brave;
euʒ }   peuṅ }   ʒeuṅ }   cṅeuṅ }

ṁéaṅ } a finger; τéaḃ } a string;
meuṅ }   τeuḃ }

Only one form of spelling shall, in words in which this
digraph occurs, be followed in these Lessons. Instead of
éa we shall adopt, for uniformity, the diphthong eu ; as
peuṅ, *grass;* ʒeuṅ, *sharp,* &c. Excepting, however, eaḃ
or eaʒ, *in* or *un* (in composition) : Example, eaḃ-cṅom,
unheavy, that is, *light ;* eaʒ-coṅ, *in-justice ;* ḋéaṅ, *do ;*
ḋéaṅ-paḃ, *I shall say ;* words in which éa is regarded as a
settled form ; or in which this form of spelling has a different
meaning from another of the same sound. This unsettled
spelling is not unlike the yet unsettled form of *ou* in
English ; as, *endeavour, honour, favour, labour,* which Web-
ster has, " for the sake of uniformity," endeavoured to
correct.

Obs. 3.—There are a few words spelled with the digraph
ea short, and only a few, in which a, the second vowel, and
not e, the first, is marked with the accent ; as, peáṅṅ (pronounced *fár*), *better ;* ʒeáṅṅ (*gárr*), *short ;* pcáṅṅ (*fárn*),
the alder-tree; merely to distinguish them from other words
spelled with the same short diphthong ; as, peaṅ (like *far*
in *farthing*), *a man ;* ʒeaṅ (as *gar* in *garden*), *cut ;* peaṅṅ,
a shield.

Obs. 4.—In Tipperary, Waterford, and Kilkenny, the
diphthongs ea, ṅo, and sometimes ṅu, on coming before l, m,
ṅ, are incorrectly pronounced *ow ;* as, ʒleaṅ, *a valley,* is
pronounced *glown ;* so pṅoṅṅ, *fair,* is pronounced *fown.*
Their correct pronunciation is noted in the paradigm, p. 12.

EXERCISE X.

1. Ir aṅl lṅom [It is a pleasure with me], *i.e.,* I am pleased.
2. aṅ aṅl lṅom? 3. τá aṅ aṅll aṅḃ? 4. ḃ-puṅl aṅ aṅll aṅḃ?
5. baṅl ó Oṅa (God) oṅτ. 6. τá cáṅl oṅτ. 7. τá ceaḃ
aʒam. 8. τá aṅ pṅoṅ pṅoṅṅ, aʒur aṅ ʒeṅr báṅ. 9. τá aṅ
τeaṅ cóṅṅ. 10. póṅṅ oṅm. 11. τá mé cṅṅoṅ. 12. τá

beᴀⁿ ᴀⁱʒe. 13. b-ꝼuⁱl beᴀⁿ ᴀⁱʒe? 14. ᴛᴀ ceⁱᴦᴛ ᴀʒᴀm oⁱᴛ
15. b-ꝼuⁱl ceⁱᴦᴛ ᴀʒᴀᴆ oⁱᴍ? 16. ⁱᴦ ꝼlᴀ́ ᴍé. 17. ᴛᴀ cᴦuⁱᴛ
oⁱᴍ, ᴀʒuᴦ ᴛᴀ cᴦuⁱᴛ ᴀʒᴀm. 18. ⁱᴦ ꝼeᴀᴦᴦ lⁱom cᴦuⁱᴛ ᴀʒᴀᴆ
'ⁿᴀ oⁱᴛ. 19. ᴛᴀ ꝼⁱoᴦ ᴀʒᴀm. 20. b-ꝼuⁱl ꝼⁱoᴦ ᴀʒᴀᴆ? 21. ᴛᴀ
cⁱoⁿⁿ oⁱᴍ. 22. b-ꝼuⁱl cⁱoⁿⁿ oⁱᴛ? 23. b-ꝼuⁱl cᴀⁱl oⁱᴛ?
24. ⁿⁱ b-ꝼuⁱl. 25. b-ꝼuⁱl cᴀⁱll oⁱᴛ? 26. ᴛᴀ cᴀⁱll oⁱᴍ.

Obs. 1.—There is a peculiar Irish idiom which should
be noticed by the learner, that the state, condition, or suffering under which a person labours expressed in English
by the verb *to be* and the adjective—is expressed in Irish
by the noun, after the verb ᴛᴀ (b-ꝼuⁱl), *is*, and the prepositional pronoun, *on me*, *on thee*, &c., oⁱᴍ, oⁱᴛ, &c.: as, ᴛᴀ
ᴛᴀᴦᴛ oⁱᴍ, thirst is on me, *i. e.*, I am thirsty: ᴛᴀ ꝼeᴀᴦʒ oⁱᴍ,
anger is on me—I am angry; ᴛᴀ cᴦuⁱᴛ oⁱᴛ, there is a
hump on you—you are hunchbacked; ᴛᴀ ᴦoⁿᴀᴦ oⁱᴛ, prosperity is on you—you are prosperous.

Obs. 2.—The auxiliary verb, 'have," is expressed in Irish
by the third person singular or plural of the verb *to be*, and
the prepositional pronoun ᴀʒᴀm, at me, or to me; ᴀʒᴀᴆ, at
thee; ᴀⁱʒe, at him; ᴀⁱcⁱ, at her; as, ᴛᴀ ᴍᴀc ᴀʒᴀm, I have a
son (literally, a son is to me), ᴛᴀ óᴦ ᴀʒᴀᴆ (gold is to you),
you have gold; ᴛᴀ beᴀⁿ ᴀⁱʒe, he has a wife; ᴛᴀ ꝼeᴀᴦ
ᴀⁱce, she has a husband.

Those two idioms enter much into the spoken and
written Irish language, and therefore deserve the particular attention of the learner. There is not a page written in which they are not found, nor can there be a single
conversation without their use.

Obs. 3. Ownership or exclusive possession is expressed
by the assertive verb ᴆo beⁱᴛ, to be (ⁱᴦ, is; buᴆ, was); with
the prepositions ᴆo, to; le, with; as, ⁱᴦ ᴍᴀc ᴆᴀⁿ ᴀⁿ ꝼeᴀᴦ
óʒ (he is a son to me, the young man), *i. e.*, the young man
is a son of mine; ⁱᴦ lⁱom ᴀⁿ óᴦ, (it is with me the gold).
i. e., the gold is mine; ⁱᴦ leᴀᴛ ᴀⁿ ᴛⁱᴦ, (it is with thee, the
country), *i.e.*, the country is thine :—as Abraham said to
Lot.

Choice, pleasure, taste, distaste, displeasure, and the like,
are expressed by the prepositional pronoun, lⁱom, with me;
leᴀᴛ, with you; leⁱᴦ, with him, after the noun or adjective

with the assertive verb ᵹ; as, ᵹ aⁱl lⁱom, it is a pleasure
with me, *i.e.*, I wish; ᵹ ꝼeáꝑꝑ lⁱom, it is better with
me, *i.e.*, I prefer; ᵹ meaꞃa leaꞇ, it is worse with you—
you think worse of; ᵹ aⁱꞇ leⁱꞃ, it is a pleasure with him.

EXERCISE XI.

1. ꞇá ceaꞃꞇ aᵹam (I have a right). 2. b-ꝼuⁱl ceaꞃꞇ
aᵹam? 3. ꞇá ceaꞃꞇ aᵹam aⁱꞃ (I have a right on it).
4. b-ꝼuⁱl ceaꞃꞇ aᵹam aⁱꞃ? 5. ꞇá ceaꞃꞇ aᵹaꝺ aⁱꞃ. 6. ꞇá
ceaꞃꞇ aⁱcⁱ aⁱꞃ. 7. ꞇá ceⁱꞃꞇ aᵹam. 8. ꞇá ceⁱꞃꞇ aⁱcⁱ.
9. ꞇá ceⁱꞃꞇ aⁱᵹe oꞃꞇ. 10. b-ꝼuⁱl ceⁱꞃꞇ aᵹaꝺ oꞃm? 11. ꞇá
cⁱoꞃn oꞃm. 12. b-ꝼuⁱl cⁱoꞃn oꞃm? 13. ꞇá cⁱoꞃn aᵹam.
14. ꞇá cⁱoꞃn aᵹam oꞃꞇ. 15. b-ꝼuⁱl cⁱoꞃn aᵹaꝺ oꞃm?
16. ꞇá ᵹeaꞃn aⁱᵹe oꞃꞇ. 17. b-ꝼuⁱl ᵹeaꞃ aⁱcⁱ oꞃꞇ? 18. ꞇá
ᵹꞃaⁱn aᵹam oꞃꞇ. 19. b-ꝼuⁱl ᵹꞃaⁱn aᵹaꝺ oꞃm? 20. ꞇá
ꞃeaꞃꞇ aⁱᵹe aⁱꞃ (he has help for it—*i.e.*, can prevent it).
21. b-ꝼuⁱl ꞃeaꞃꞇ aⁱᵹe aⁱꞃ? 22. nⁱ b-ꝼuⁱl ꞃeaꞃꞇ aⁱᵹe aⁱꞃ
(he has no help for it). 23. naċ b-ꝼuⁱl ꞃeaꞃꞇ aᵹaꝺ aⁱꞃ?
24. ꞇá ꞃeaꞃc aⁱᵹe ꝺuⁱꞇ. 25. ꞇá ꞃeaꞃc aᵹam ꝺuⁱꞇ. 26. a
ꞃuⁱn, b-ꝼuⁱl ꞃeaꞃc aᵹaꝺ ꝺam? 27. ꞇá ꞃeaꞃc aᵹam ꝺo
Ꝺⁱa. 28. ꞇá ꞃeaꞃc aⁱᵹ Ꝺⁱa oꞃm. 29. ᵹ ꝺuⁱne le Ꝺⁱa
an ꝼeaꞃ óᵹ. 30. ᵹ mac ꝺuⁱꞇ an ꝼeaꞃ óᵹ. 31. an mac
ꝺuⁱꞇ an ꝼeaꞃ óᵹ? 32. ᵹ ꝼeáꝑꝑ lⁱom clú 'na óꞃ. 33. ᵹ
ꝼeáꝑꝑ cⁱal 'na óꞃ.

NOTE.

It has been recommended to us by many of our readers that we should
give in Roman letters the pronunciation of every Irish word that occurs
in these Lessons, and that such an additional help would greatly facilitate
the study of the language for those who know nothing at all about it.
Our reasons for not complying with this wish are :

First.—From our own experience of the manner in which correct pronunciation of any language is acquired in Seminaries, Colleges, Universi-
ties, we know that dictionaries, in which each word is pronounced, give
little or no additional help to the student above that which is rendered
by other dictionaries furnished with no so such aid. The student prefers
rather to rest on the general principles on which the peculiar pronunciation of the language is founded, than to recur repeatedly to his pronouncing vocabulary for the correct pronunciation of each recurring word.
What student learning French, having once learned the peculiar sounds
of the terminations *am, em, im, an, en, in, ant, ent, int,* or that of the vowel
u, or the diphthong *eu,* would require to refer to a pronouncing dictionary
in order to know how they are sounded in this and that other word? No
one would act thus. Should not then, in a language like ours, in which
invariably the same vowels, and the same combinations of them and of

consonants, are sounded always alike, the general principles of its distinctive pronunciation suffice? Let the student bear always in mind one great principle—that all the vowels and consonants are sounded with a broad, full, clear enunciation; let him refer from time to time to the principles laid down in our First, Second, and Third Lessons.

Secondly.—Neither "The Self-Instructor" nor "Ollendorff" gives any such aid in teaching foreign languages.

Thirdly.—It is very difficult to convey in Roman letters the *precise* sounds of Irish words; for this reason, it is much better to endeavour to pronounce, without any such aid, the words given in the various Lessons, referring from time to time, if necessary, to the examples before each Exercise.

FOURTH LESSON.

Taking the five vowels from the seventeen Irish letters, there remain twelve consonants. Of the consonants, three —viz., l, ɲ, p—never change their primitive or radical sound; the remaining nine do change their radical sound into one of a kindred nature, which is formed by a like opening of the mouth.

This change in the nine mutable consonants is caused either by the natural sound of the word in which any mutable enters, requiring it, by their position in a word or sentence; by their relation, or connection with other words that have an influence on their sound. Thus c at the end of the word cac (a battle), must be aspirated, as the natural sound of the word requires it, in order to distinguish it from the word cac (a cat); b in beaɲ, a woman, a wife, is pronounced with all the native force that the Roman or English b has in the English word *ban*, or the Latin *bannum*; but if any of the possessive pronouns mo, my; ɗo, thy; a, his, and some of the simple prepositions go before it, b immediately assumes the sharper or flatter sound of *v* or *w*; of *v* if b be followed by the vowels e or ı; of *w*, if followed by any of the broad vowels a, o, u : Ex., mo beaɲ, my woman ; pronounced *mo vann* ; mo baɲɗ, my bard, is pronounced *mo wardh*.

Excluding then l, ɲ, p, from the twelve consonants, we have b, c, ɗ, f, ʒ, m, p, ɼ, c, subject to this change in their primitive sound.

This change, arising from an *aspirate* or rough breathing after the vowel sound, is at present correctly called *aspiration*, incorrectly *mortification;* for the change does not destroy, it only modifies the sound of the consonant. Besides, it rests on the same principle, and is regulated precisely by the same rules as those to which *aspiration* in Hebrew, Greek, Latin, Spanish, German, or English is subject.

The consonants p, ꝼ, b, ꝿ, are called *labials* or lip-letters, because one cannot sound them without compressing the lips. If their primitive sounds are cognate, is it not natural that when penetrated by the aspiration, the sounds of these same kindred letters should, on philosophic principles, remain cognate, or of the same organ? This is what exactly takes place.

c and ᵹ, palatals, have their aspirate form perfectly cognate, both partaking, when affected by the rough breathing, of the guttural sound.

From this principle of similarity of sound in letters of the same organ, and of their retaining still a similarity in their aspirated forms, a table of the aspirable consonants, and of their aspirate sounds, as represented by Roman letters, can be formed.

(This Table should be referred to till the aspirate sounds are known by the learner.)

₊ The notation for the aspirate sound is a dot (·) or ħ.

Plain or Primitive Form.		Aspirated or Secondary Form, as Spelled.	Pronunciation or Secondary Form, as Articulated.	
Labials	p	ṗ, or Pħ,	F.	
	b	ḃ, or bħ,	V, or W.	
	ꝿ	ꝿ̇, or ꝿħ,	V, or W.	
	ꝼ	ꝼ̇, or ꝼħ,	H.	
Palatals	c	ċ, or Cħ,	Guttural	KH, or X.
	ᵹ	ᵹ̇, or ᵹħ,		GH, Y.
Dentals	ꝺ	ḋ, or ꝺħ,	DH, Y.	
	ꞇ	ṫ, or ꞇħ,	H.	
Sibilant	s	ṡ, or Sħ,	H.	

A fuller explanation of the Aspirated Consonants.

ṗ (asp.) = *ph* or *f.*

ḃ ... = *v* (before or after e or ı); *w* (before or after ᴀ, o, ıı).

ṁ ... = *v* (before or after e or ı); *w* (before or after ᴀ, o, u); ṁ is slightly nasal, as in cuṁᴀ (pronounced as if cuınɣᴀ), sorrow.

ḟ ... is silent : it has the sound of *h* in some words; as ḟeın, self; ꝺo m' ḟeın, (*dhom* héen) to myself.

ċ ... = *ch* in *och*, oċ; or the Greek χ (chee). It is invariably sounded like the Greek χ (chee) when it goes before e or ı; but before ᴀ, o, or u, it has a thicker sound, as heard in the exclamation oċ! (och,) oċoın! (ochon); or of the German ch.

There is no sound in English like that of ċ (asp.); for when it is said that ċ aspirated sounds like *gh* in *lough*, very few take up that sound, for few in these countries, except Irish-speaking people alone, pronounce that digraph with a guttural tone. To pronounce it correctly add to the sound of *k* (or Irish c) a little rough breathing from the throat; as oċ, (och!)

ʒ (asp.) = *gh*, guttural, in the beginning of a word, if before the vowels ᴀ, o, u : before e or ı, it has the less guttural sound of *y*; as, mo ʒeᴀn, my affection. But in the end and middle of words, it has no other power than that of lengthening the sound of the preceding vowel, and fixing the spelling, just as *gh* in the English words—high, highness, nigh, neighbour, thought, thoughtful, thoughtfulness, tends to lengthen the vowel *i*, or the diphthongs *ei*, *ou*, and to aid in forming a correct orthography.

Example: ρıʒ, a king, pronounced as if written ρı, (*ree*), ρıʒeᴀċꞇ, a kingdom, ρıʒ-ᴀṁᴀıl, kingly;

ροʒ, happiness, prosperity, pronounced *só*, ροʒ-ᴀṁᴀıl, pleasant, prosperous; ροʒ-ᴀṁlᴀċꞇ, pleasantness.

ꝺ has a thick, guttural sound very like that of ʒ. In the beginning of a word, ꝺ before e or ı has exactly the sound of *y*, as mo ꝺıᴀ (*mo Yia*), my God. In the *middle* or *end*

of words ó (asp.) is the same in all respects as ᵹ aspirated—
i.e., it only lengthens the sound of the preceding vowel
or diphthong.

Obs.—There is another sound peculiar to ᵹ and ó when
following the vowels a or o, in the first or second syllable
of a word, which deserves particular attention. The two
letters aᵹ, or aó, sound like *i* in ire; or *ey* in eye, eyre, as
aóaín (*ey-en*,) aspen; aóaіrt, (*ey-arth*,) a bolster; aóarc,
(*eye-ark*,) a horn; aólacaó, (*ey-luck-oo*,) burial; aóraіm,
I adore; aórᴄar, a halter; ealaóan, a science; ᵹaóaіr, a
beagle; raóarc, sight; Ꞇaóᵹ Thaig; laᵹaó, fewness;
aᵹaіó, face, against; laᵹaіr, a unger, toe, prong, fork;
(rleaᵹan, a turf-spade; and Seaᵹan, John, are exceptions)
The exceptions are generally marked with the grave accent,
as aóbar, a cause; aómuó, timber; aó, luck.

ᴄ̇ ... = *h* ⎱ Aspiration so affects these letters that
ŕ* ... = *h* ⎰ their power as consonants is lost,
while the aspirate alone is heard. r final is never aspirated.

VOCABULARY.

a, who.
aᴄᴄ, but.
aó, luck.
aɲ ᴄe, the individual, the person
  who; ᴄe, means any one, a person, like the Greek τις (*tis*), any
  one; ᴄe is sometimes written
  ᴄі, but this is not a fem. form.
baᴄ̇, death, murder.
baᴄ̇, cows.
beaᴄa, life; bᴄ̇, life; Gr. βίος (*bios*);
  Latin, *vita*.
boᴄᴄ, poor.
bŕaᴄ̇, (to spy, *v.*, a design, *n.*) ever;

as, ᵹo bŕaᴄ̇, for ever; literally
  to (the last) judgment.
bŕeáᵹ, fine.
caó, what (Latin, *quid*).
caᴄ̇, a battle.
caіᴄ̇, spend; cáіᴄ̇, chaff.
cіa, who (Italian, *che*).
ᴄ̇o, so, as; co, so; when followed by
  the demonstrative pronoun rіɲ,
  that; as ᴄá aɲ lá ᴄ̇o bŕeáᵹ rіɲ,
  the day is *so* fine, literally, the
  day is so fine that; b-ʄuіl re
  ᴄ̇o ⅿaіᴄ̇ rіɲ? is he *so* good? it
  means *as*, and is followed by

---

* "The sibilant letter had probably its mutation into the aspirate; but
this is lost in Welsh, though preserved, as we shall see, in the Erse."
Prichard's *Eastern Origin of the Celtic Nations*; Edited by R. G. Latham,
M.A., London: Quaritch, p. 163.

  Súіl, an eye; a ʄuіl, his eye; rlaіɲᴄe, health; ᴅo rlaіɲᴄe, your health,
p. 168, *ibid.*

  "In these instances the initial *s*, though converted into an aspirate in
pronunciation, is sometimes retained in orthography, either with a dot
over it, or followed by *h*. But in either case the sibilant is entirely lost."
Note by Dr. Latham.

le (with) when a comparison is made; as, he is *as* gentle *as* a lamb, tá ṡe ċo caoin " le" uaiṅ, literally, he is *so* mild (that he can be compared) *with* a lamb; where no comparison is drawn, but a certain condition pointed out, it is followed by aġuṡ, *and, as*;—Ex. : he is as well as (is) possible, tá ṡe ċo maiṫ " aġuṡ" iṡ ḟeiḋiṅ; we are as fortunate as we can be, támuiḃ ċo roṅa " aġuṡ" ṫiġ liṅṅ.

crioċ, end.
duiṅe, man, a person.
faċ, cause, reason.
ʒaḃ, take, conceive.
ʒaċ, each.
ʒraḋ, love.
laoċ, a hero.
leaṅḃ, a child.
maiṫ, good.

maṅ, as; like; maṅ blaṫ an ṁaiġ, as the flower of th. field.
moċ, early.
niḋ, a thing.
oiġ, virgin.
iṁ, course, a flight.
riṅṅ, we, us.
riḃ, ye, you.
riaḋ, they.
snaṁ, to swim.
roʒ, happiness.
an-roʒ, misery.
talaṁ, earth; as, aiṅ talaṁ, on earth.
teaċ, a house; tiġe, a house's.
tnaḋ, time; an tnaċ, the time; hence means, when.
truaġ, pity.
uċt, bosom; ar, from; thus, ar uċt, from the bosom, i. e., by virtue of, through; ar uċt Ḋé, for God's sake.

EXAMPLES.

tá an lá breaġ, the day is fine; tá an báḋ faḋa, the boat is long; tá an fean maiṫ, the man is good.

bí an teaċ boċt aċt bí roʒ aṅṅ an tnaċ bí fean an tiġe beo, the house was poor, but happiness was there the time (while) the man of the house was alive.

tá ʒaċ niḋ maiṫ aṅṅ fein, everything is in itself good.

bí Dia aṅṅ, ʒaċ aṁ, aġuṡ ni beiḋ crioċ aiṅ, ʒo braṫ. God was in being at all times, and there never will be an end for Him.

EXERCISE XII.

1. cia an niḋ báḋ? 2. b-fuil báḋ maiṫ aʒaḋ? 3. iṡ maiṫ liom snaṁ. 4. an maiṫ leat snaṁ? 5. b-fuil teaċ boċt aʒaḋ? 6. ni b-fuil teaċ boċt aʒaṁ? 7. oċ, iṡ truaġ é do ṫeaċ aċt tá roʒ aṅṅ. 8. ʒo raiḃ roʒ aġuṡ feun aʒaḋ ʒo braṫ. 9. cia leiṡ an leaṅḃ boċt? 10. le fean an tiġ. 11. caḋ faċ b-fuil tu aṅṅ ro ċo moċ? 12. maṅ atá an t-aḋ aiṅ an te a tá moċ. 13. ʒaḃ mo laiṅ an do laṁ. 14. iṡ truaġ aġuṡ iṡ ʒeaṅṅ beaċa an duiṅe aġuṡ lán de anroʒ. 15. iṡ caċ beaċa an duiṅe ċo faḋa a'ṡ tá ṡe aiṅ talaṁ. 16. ar uċt Ḋé caiṫ beaċa naoṁċa. 17. cia ṡe Dia? 18. b-fuil Dia aṅṅ ʒaċ áiṫ? 19. tá Dia aṅṅ ʒaċ áiṫ. 20. tá Dia maiṫ do ʒaċ duiṅe; aṅḋ-niʒ veiṁe a tá, a bí, aġuṡ a beiḋeaṡ ʒo braṫ.

VOCABULARY.

áṫ, a kiln.
áṫ, ford.
balb, dumb; Heb. בָּלַל (balal);
  Latin, balbus.
beaċ, a bee.
buiḋe, yellow.
caoi, crying, wailing.
cliaṫ, a hurdle of wattles, a harrow,
  a shield.
daṫ, colour.
daiṁ, an ox; Latin, dama. daiṁ-
  allta, a buffalo, (allta means
  living among cliffs, wild;)
  fiaḋ-ḋaiṁ, a stag.
deoċ, a drink.
iṫ, eat.
laoġ, a calf; Welsh, lho; laoġ-liġeaċ,
  a cow after calving, a milch

cow, from laoġ, a calf, and
  liġeaċ, licking.
liaṫ, grey.
loċ, a lake.
maġ, a plain, a field.
marb, dead; Latin, mors; French,
  mort.
nuaḋ, red; Latin, rufus.
dearg, a bright red.
taiṁ, pleasant, agreeable; Latin,
  suavis.
sleaġ, a spear.
sleaġán, a turf-spade.
sliaḃ, a mountain.
sruṫ, a stream.
tarb, a bull; Latin, taurus.
tuaiṫ, the country, as opposed to
  the word "city" or "town."

From áṫ, ford, and cliaṫ, a hurdle of wattles, is formed
the compound word áṫ-cliaṫ, the ford of hurdles—Dublin;
from áṫ, and buiḋe, yellow, áṫ-buiḋe—Athboy, the yellow
ford; áṫ and cinn, the plural of ceann, head, áṫ-cinn—
Head-ford; áṫ, and dara, the possessive case of dair, oak
—Adare; from áṫ, and na riġ, possessive plural, "of
kings," áṫ-na-riġ—Athenry; from áṫ, and coille, of a
wood—Woodford; from áṫ, and luan, of warriors—Athlone; from beul, mouth, and áṫ, and leaṫan, wide—Bally-
lahon; from áṫ, and liag, a rock—Ballyleague, on the
Shannon.

EXERCISE XIII.

1. Is the cow red and is the calf black? 2. The cow is
not red, but she is yellow; and the calf is not black, but
grey and white. 3. Is the child dumb? 4. The child is
not dumb. 5. Is there a ford at the mouth of the lake?
6. There is not a ford in it. 7. Is that a plain or a lake?
8. It is neither a plain nor a lake; it is a mountain.
9. What colour do you like (is pleasing with you), yellow,
grey, or red? 10. I like the yellow. 11. What use
(feiḋm) have we of (with) the spear, or of the turf-spade?
12. We have great use (of) with it. 13. Are you cold

(is cold on you)? 14. I am not cold (cold is not on me).
15. Do you like a drink (is drink good with thee)?—an
maiṫ leaṫ beoċ? 16. Is the grass wet with dew? 17. The
grass is wet with dew. 18. Have you an ox and a bull?
19. I have not an ox and a bull, nor a buffalo; but I have
only a cow and a grey calf. 20. What colour is the cow
(is on the cow)? 21. Yellow. 22. Yellow is a good
colour. 23. What is a mountain? 24. A mountain is a
high hill. 25. You are lucky and happy.

FIFTH LESSON.

CONJUGATION OF THE PRESENT TENSES OF THE VERB
to be, ᴅo beiṫ.

The nominative case comes always after the verb.

Present tense.

SINGULAR.	PLURAL.
1. Tá me, I am.	Tá rinn, we are.
2. Tá tu, thou art.	Tá ríb, you are.
3. Tá ré, he (or it) is ; tá rí, she (or it) is.	Tá riaᴅ, they are.

The following is another form, in which the nominative
case is embodied in all the persons except the third person.
This is called the Synthetic form, as the foregoing is called
the Analytic:

Táim, I am.	Támuiᴅ, we are.
Táir, thou art.	Taċaoi, you are.
Tá ré, he (or it) is ; tá rí, she (or it) is.	Tait, they are.

THE INTERROGATIVE FORM.

An b-ḟuil-im, am I ?	An b-ḟuil-muiᴅ, are we ?
An b-ḟuil-ir, art thou ?	An b-ḟuil-ib, are you ?
An b-ḟuil re, is he ?	An b-ḟuil-ib, are they ?

Or, taking the third person singular, b-ḟuil, is, and placing the personal pronoun—me, I ; tu, thou ; re, he, (it) ;
rí, she, (it); rinn, we ; ríb, you ; riaᴅ, they, after it, this
interrogative form is gone through in the simple Analytic way, as—

SINGULAR.	PLURAL.
b-ᵹuɪl me, am I ?	·b-ᵹuɪl rɪnn, are we ?
b-ᵹuɪl cu, art thou ?	b-ᵹuɪl rɪb, are you ?
b-ᵹuɪl re, is he ?	b-ᵹuɪl rɪᴀᴅ, are they ?

When an assertion is made—ɪr, is; with the personal pronouns is the form adopted ; as, ɪr me, it is I ; ɪr cu, it is thou; ɪr é, it is he; ɪr rɪnn, it is we; ɪr rɪb, it is you ; ɪrᴀᴅ, it is they.

This ɪr is omitted, as has been observed (see Second Lesson, Observations 3, 4, page 10), when any of the particles of asking or denying, or the like, are employed , as, who (is) God, cɪᴀ h-é Oɪᴀ? ɪr, after cɪᴀ, is omitted : cᴀᴅ é ᴀn nɪᴏ ᴀn eᴀᴣlᴀɪr, what is the church? ɪr is omitted after cᴀᴅ, what.

The present tense, as it is formed regularly from the root bɪ, be thou; is bɪᴏɪm, which implies a state or continuance in present existence, as—

bɪᴏ-ɪm, I am wont to be.	bɪᴏ-muɪᴅ, we are wont to be.
bɪᴏ-ɪr, thou art wont to be.	bɪᴏ-ɪᴅ, you are wont to be.
bɪᴏ re, he is wont to be.	bɪᴏ-ɪᴅ, they are wont to be.

So, bɪᴏ, the analytic form, with the personal pronouns, me, cu, re, expresses the same. Also, the termination, eᴀnn, denotes habit or continuance; as, bɪᴏ-eᴀnn me, I am wont to be; bɪᴏ-eᴀnn cu, thou art wont to be; bɪᴏ-eᴀnn re, he is wont to be

The endings, such as ɪm, of the first person; ɪr, of the second person singular; muɪᴅ, of the first person plural; ɪᴅ, of the second; ɪᴅ, of the third person plural, express in Irish what the pronouns *I, thou, we, you, they*, in union with the verb, convey in the English language; and also the time or tense which such helps as *do, may, can*, suggest in the conjugation of Saxon verbs. Few languages, indeed. are as limited as English is in its verbal inflections

Observe, therefore, that *do, dost, does, doth*, the emphatic and interrogative forms of the present tense in English, have, in Irish, as in every other language of Europe, no distinct word by which they can be translated. The verbal inflection peculiar to the present tense supplies its place as, I *do* be, bɪᴏɪm; *do* I be? ᴀ m-bɪᴏɪm, (*a mee-yim?*) *dos* thou be? ᴀ m-bɪᴏɪr? *does* he have? ᴀ m-bɪᴏeᴀnn ᴀɪᴣe he *does* have, bɪᴏeᴀnn ᴀɪᴣe.

This observation should be remembered.

VOCABULARY.

Aran, bread.
Ban, white (pale).
Bonb, haughty.
Blaċ, blossom, flower.
Doiġ, opinion, expectation.
Feoil, meat.
Flaiċ, a prince.
Fós, yet.
Geallaċ, the moon; from geal, white (bright).
Leiġ, read (thou).
Liaġ, a physician.
Luċ, a mouse; luċóg, a little mouse.
Lonnraċ, bright, shining.
Luaiċ, ashes; from luaċ, swift.
Luas, swiftness.
Luaċ, swift, *adj.*, swiftness, *n.*
Lus, an herb; some of its compound forms are—slán-lus, (from slán, safe, sound, and lus), all-heal; rib-wort; lus-món (from lus, and món, large), fox-glove; garb-lus (from garb, coarse, and lus) clivers.
Maoċ, soft, mild, tender; as, feoil maoċ, tender flesh.
Mod, manner, form, respect; Lat. *modus.*

Neam, heaven.
Roċa, a wheel; hence Latin *rota,* a wheel.
Riam, ever; up to this time.
Saiċ, plenty; L. *satis.* I have plenty is expressed in Irish, I have my plenty, ta mo saiċ agam.
Sgiam, beauty.
Suiġ, sit (*v*).
Teiċ, hot; also flee (*v*).
Tiuġ, thick, plenty.
Traiġ, the shore at low water; from traiġ, ebb.
Treab, a tribe; Latin, *tribus.*
Treiċ, feeble, ignorant.
Triaċ, a Lord, a high wave, a hill.
Troiġ, a foot: the sole of the foot; a measure of twelve inches.
Uaċ, a will or testament.
Uair, hour, as an uair, and contractedly 'n-uair, the hour; that is, when :—hence it is always translated *when*; but whenever a question is asked, the words an uair, are not contracted into nuair; as cia an uair, when? *i.e.,* what hour?
Uisge, water.

EXERCISE XIV.

1. The day is fine. 2. This month is wont to be fine. 3. My son is young. 4. Is my son young? 5. He is not young. 6. He is usually good. 7. He is not wont to be up early 8. Is every man good? 9. Every cat is not grey nor black. 10. God is good. 11. Who is God? 12. What is heaven? 13. There is happiness in heaven. 14. Are you lucky (is the luck on you)? 15. No, I am not lucky. I am unlucky. 16. *Do* you love me? 17. I *do* not love you. 18. I love God, and God loves me. 19. God loves every person. 20. God is king in heaven and on earth. 21. The field is yellow and white. 22. The virgin is young and mild. 23. Luck attends those that are good; (idiomatic form is—luck is usually on the good). 24. Are you good when you are lucky? 25. I was never

lucky, yet I am of opinion (ır ᴅoıᵹ lıom) that I am good.
26. Is the sun bright (lonnᴜᴀċ)? 27. The sun is bright.
28. Have you got (ᵬ-ᵱuıl ᴀᵹᴀᴅ) white (ᵹeᴀl) bread ?
29. I have plenty, and milk. 30. Have you enough of
everything? 31. I have. 32. You are as generous (ᵮıᴀl)
as (le) a prince.

Obs.—The sentences in the several exercises embrace
only such words, for the greater part, as are given in the
lists at each heading. Sometimes words in former lists or
exercises are again brought into account. The learner
should therefore make himself thoroughly familiar with
the words, their sounds, and their idiomatic turns of expression, to prevent reference to former Lessons.

To translate these English sentences into Irish, and to
write them in the Celtic character, to speak them from time
to time when alone or with others, must at once ensure a
knowledge of the language as it is spoken and written.
Begin forthwith to speak it.

EXERCISE XV.

1. Is bread cheap or dear? 2. It is cheap. 3. Is butter
dear? 4. Yes, it is dear this month. 5. Wine is dear,
meat is usually dear, and water is usually cheap 6. The
virgin is handsome (ᴀluın). 7. The haughty is found
under beauty's dress (ᵮᴀoı rᵹeın). 8. You are not wont
to be early at the house. 9. They are usually at an early
hour at the house. 10. Are you early from home? 11.
You are in happiness. 12. They are usually unhappy.
13. The moon is bright, the cloud is grey; the day is dark,
the month is beautiful. 14. When I am well (ᵲlᴀn) I am
happy. 15. When *do* you be well? 16. The physician *does*
have a secret. 17. The wheel is red. 18. The eye is grey.
19. The cat is black. 20. What hour is it? (cıᴀ ᴀn uᴀır
í). 21. It is early yet (ᵮór). 22. The day is long. 23
Many a day we shall be in the tomb; (ır ıomᴅᴀ lá 'r-ᴀn
ᵹ-cıll onᴀınn.) 24. Man's life is short. 25. It is like the
flower of the field: It is like a vapour (ceo) ; it is a warfare,
as Job says (mᴀr ᴅeır Job). 26. If you wish (mᴀ ır mᴀıċ
leᴀc) to live old, take hot and cold, is an old saying (reᴀn
rᴀᴅ.)

Obs. 1.—The first letter of a word—if it be one of the
nine mutables—suffers aspiration after the possessive pronouns singular—mo, my; ꝺo, thy; a, his.

EXAMPLE.

		Pronounced
beaꞃ, a woman,	mo beaꞃ, my woman;	*mo van.*
báꞃꝺ, a bard,	ꝺo báꞃꝺ, thy bard;	*do wawrdh*
boꞃꝺ, a table,	a boꞃꝺ, his table,	*a wordh.*

b in the words beaꞃ, báꞃꝺ, boꞃꝺ, when not preceded by
the possessive pronoun singular, is not aspirated; put the
possessive pronouns singular before the same words, and
then b immediately assumes the aspirate sound, and is, of
course, pronounced like *v*, if e or ı follow; and like *w*, if
a, or o, or ú follow.

a, her, the possessive pronoun singular, feminine, is an
exception:—it does not cause aspiration, and it is in this
non-aspirating power only that it can be distinguished
from a, his; as a boꞃꝺ, her table; a boꞃꝺ, his table.

Obs. 2.—The vocative case, or as it is called by English
grammarians—the nominative case of address—has the
first letter, if aspirable, invariably aspirated.

EXAMPLE.

cuıꞃle, pulse ; cꞃoıꝺe, heart:
a ċuıꞃle, O pulse; a ċuıꞃle mo ċꞃoıꝺe, pulse of my heart.
Oıa, God; ꝺılıꞃ, dear (from ꝺıl, fond):
a Ꝺé, Oh, God; O a Ꝺé ꝺılıꞃ, O! dear God.
ᵹꞃáꝺ, love:
a ᵹꞃáꝺ, oh Love: ᵹꞃáꝺ m' aꞃama, love of my soul.
ꞃeaꞃc, affection, affectionate one:
a ṛeaꞃc ᵹꞃáꝺ, oh, love of loves.
Ϻuıꞃe, and ⎱ Mary:
Ϻaıꞃe, ⎰
a Ϻuıꞃe ꝺılıꞃ, oh, dear (Virgin) Mary; a Ϻaıꞃe ꞃuıꞃ, oh,
Mary, secret love.

In these exclamations, the c of cuıꞃle; O of Oıa; ᵹ of
ᵹꞃáꝺ; Ϻ of Ϻuıꞃe; ꞃ of ꞃeaꞃc, are aspirated on account
of the vowel sound of a in the nominative case of address
preceding the aspirable consonants, c, ꝺ, ᵹ, m, ꞃ.

SIXTH LESSON.

Obs. 1.—In compound words the first letter of the second part is aspirated should it be aspirable—as claon, inclined, crooked; beapc, an act, an exploit, form the compound claon-beapc, a deceitful act; so feill-beapc, a treacherous act; reapc-ṡpáḃ, dearest love; deáṡ, good; duine, person; deáṡ-duine, a good person, rean, old; rean-ḟear, an old man; rean-bean, an old woman. The b, in beapc; ṡ, in ṡpáḃ; d, in duine; f, in fear; b, in bean, in the foregoing examples are aspirated, because they form the second part of compound words.

Except—Words beginning with any of the dental consonants, d, c, r, when the preceding part of the compound ends in d, l, n, r, c; as and, high; ciṡeapna, Lord; and-ciṡeapna, sovereign Lord; caol, slender; dub, black; caol-dub, slender black; an buacaill caol-dub, the slender-black boy; buan, lasting; raoṡal, life, age; buan-raoṡal, long life; buan-raoṡalaċ, long-lived. The initial letter in the second part of the compound in those words is not aspirated, agreeably to the terms of the exception.

The dentals, d, c, r, do not undergo aspiration, because they are sufficiently clear and musical in their combination with other dentals or linguals, l, n, and do not require, like the gutturals and the palatals, the aid of aspiration, to render them flexible.

Obs. 2.—In general, then, the dentals, d, c, r, following d, c, r, or l, n, (and sometimes r,) final, or otherwise, are never aspirated.

VOCABULARY.

Anoir, now.

Aċair, father; Latin, *pater.* Aċair-món, grandfather.

Buacaill, a boy; derived from bó, a cow, and caill (Latin, *colere*), to attend, to mind.

Capa, a friend; from car, dear (Latin, *chara*, dear); Greek, χαριεσσα.

Cneaċ, destruction.

Cnom, crooked, bent down.

Cupam (Latin, *cura*), care; applied in Irish to all over whom one has charge.

Deáṡ, good; in composition, as deáṡ-duine, a good person; while maiṫ, good, is used out of composition; as, duine maiṫ, a good person.

Deáṡ, good, is opposed to droc, bad; maiṫ, good, is opposed to olc, bad. The former are placed before the noun, the latter after it.

Druim, back (Greek, δερμα, skin; and δérn, the shoulders).

Faiṫeaċ, fretful. Fuaċc, cold.

Ṡan, without (French, *sans*).

Ṡlóir, (Latin, *gloria*), glory.

Glún, knee (Greek, γόνυ).	Míle, a thousand (Latin *mille*).
Gráḋ. love.	Sioc, frost (Latin, *siccus*; Heb. קרח).
Gráḋṁar, loving.	Sláṅ, (Latin *salvus*), safe, healthy
Iuḋ, day (French *hui*.)	sound; sláinte, health; eug-sláṅ,
Luaḋ, motion, freedom of the limb	unwell.
in acting.	Smúiṫ, mist.
Maċair, mother; the dam of a beast;	Sneaċta, snow.
a cause, source; maċair-ṁór,	Teaṡ, heat.
grandmother.	Truaġ, pity.

The Irish of the word, *to-day*, is pronounced *an yuh*, and spelled by some thus: an iuḋ, (O'Brien and O'Reilly); by others, thus: a n-diu. Which is the more correct? For the former we have the authority of O'Brien and O'Reilly, and analogy with the French and Spanish languages; *hui; oi;*—for the latter, usage to some extent, and analogy with the word *day*, old Irish, *dia*; Latin, *die*; Welsh, *dydh*;* and Sanscrit, *dyu*.

EXERCISE XVI.

1. Mo ḃrón! 2. Mo ċreaċ! 3. Mo ṁíle truaġ. 4. Mo ċuisle agus mo rún geal. 5. A ċuisle mo ċroiḋe, mo ċara, mo gráḋ is tú. 6. A ċéile m'anama is tú. 7. Naċ mo ċara ċóir, ḋil, gráḋṁar, tú? 8. Is me do ċara ċóir, ḋil, gráḋṁar. 9. B-ḟuil do ḃean agus do ṁac agus rún geal do ċroiḋe leat ann iuḋ? 10. Tá gráḋ liom ann iuḋ. 11. Ca b-ḟuil do ḟear ann iuḋ? 12. Tá se liom. 13. B-ḟuil a ċos slán, no tinn anois, agus a ḟal agus meur a ċois? 14. Tá a ḟal agus a ċos agus a ṁeur slán; aċt tá a ċeann tinn ó am go am agus pian ann a ċaoḃ. 15. Tá an t-ḟuil ḋeas bog aige. 16. Ca b-ḟuil an ḃean a tá eag-slán? 17. Tá sí ann so. 18. Cia an níḋ tá air sí? (What thing is on her?—*i.e.*, what is it that ails her?) 19. Tá a glún gan luaḋ, a ḋruim crom, a cluas gan clos. 20. Raiḃ liaiġ aici ó 'n am ro a nae, 'n uair bi do ḃuaċaill aig teaċ mo ṁaċair? 21. Bi; agus deir se naċ b-ḟuil fáṫ air biṫ aici a beiṫ faiteaċ air bár. 22. Naċ breaġ an aimsir í so? 23. Is breaġ, glóir do Ḋia. 24. Ní b-ḟuil fuaċt ann, no ceo, no gaoṫ; aċt tá gaċ aon lá, breaġ; an grian air neaṁ gan smuit, gan neul. 25. An fearr leat teas no fuaċt? 26. Is fearr liom fuaċt le rioc agus le sneaċta 'na teas agus grian. 27. B-ḟuil do ċuram agus curam d' aṫair a sláinte? 28. Táid, go raiḃ maiṫ agad agus aig gaċ duine aig a b-ḟuil deaġ-ċroiḋe. 29. B-ḟuil d'aṫair-ṁór sean? 30. Ní b-ḟuil; ní b-ḟuil sean-fear no sean-ḃean air biṫ againn, tamuid uile óg agus slán.

OBSERVATION 1.—When the article ᴀɴ (the) is placed before nouns, it aspirates the first consonant, if aspirable, in the nominative and objective cases singular of nouns feminine; but of nouns masculine the first consonant in the possessive case singular. Example—

beᴀɴ, a woman; ᴀɴ beᴀɴ, the woman.

ḟɪɼ, possessive case of ꝼeᴀɼ, a man; ceᴀċ ᴀɴ ḟɪɼ, the man's house.

EXCEPTION 1.—Nouns whose first letter is ᴅ, or c, do not take the aspirate form: Example—ᴀɴ ᴅuɪl, f., (nom. or obj. case) the wish, the element; ᴀɴ ᴅoṁᴀɪɴ, the world's; Cɪ̇ʒeᴀɼɴᴀ ᴀɴ ᴅoṁᴀɪɴ, the world's Lord.

The reason is, the dental ɴ of the article ᴀɴ (the), and the dentals ᴅ, or c, are quite euphonious without the aid of aspiration, as has been shown in the Exception to Observation 1, at the commencement of this Lesson (p. 29).

EXCEPTION 2.—S, ꞃ, is an unique kind of letter, which in this particular form does not, after the article, bear to be aspirated, but instead takes the letter c before it, in the nominative and objective cases, if the noun be feminine; in the possessive case, if the noun be masculine, as—

ꞃeoᴅ, f., a jewel;	ᴀɴ c-ꞃeoᴅ, the jewel; (nom. or obj. case.)
ꞃlᴀc, f., rod;	ᴀɴ c-ꞃlᴀc, the rod. ...
ꞃɼᴀɪᴅ, f., street;	ᴀɴ c-ꞃɼᴀɪᴅ, the street. ...
ꞃᴀʒᴀɪɼc, priest's;	ᴀɴ c-ꞃᴀʒᴀɪɼc, the priest's (the poss. case).

as; Ꭺɴ c-ꞃeoᴅ ᴅo-ḟᴀʒᴀlᴀ 'ꞃ ɪ ɪꞃ ᴀɪlɴe; the rare jewel is the most beautiful.

Ꭺɴ c-ꞃlᴀc ɴᴀċ ɴ-ʒlᴀcᴀɪɴ ꞃɴɪoṁ; the rod that takes not twisting.

In these instances, when the two consonants, c and ꞃ, come together, c is pronounced and ꞃ is silent; which indeed is always the case whenever two consonants whose sounds cannot unite in one syllable meet—the first is sounded, the second rendered silent.

It is only after the article (ᴀɴ) that S suffers this change; for if ṁo, ᴅo, or ᴀ (his), the possessive pronouns singular precede; or if it be the nominative case of address; or if the noun beginning with S come after the prepositions ᴀɪꞃ, on, &c., as has been pointed out in the foregoing Observations (See Fifth Lesson, Observations 1, 2, p. 28), S, ſ would, in all such cases, be aspirated according to rule; as,

ſlaꞇ, rod ;	mo ḟlaꞇ, my rod.
ſlaꞇ, rod ;	aiſ ḟlaꞇ, on a rod.
ꞇſoċ, bad ;	ꞇſoċ-ḟlaꞇ, a bad rod.
ſlaꞇ, rod ;	" aꞃ" ꞇ-ſlaꞇ, *the* rod.

VOCABULARY.

Blossom, } blaċ ; ſcoċ.
Flower, }
Dead, maꞃb.
Earth, ꞇalaiṁ ; (Latin, *tellus*).
Fairness or whiteness, ſiꞃꞃe.
(Blossom) of all that is fair, blaċ ꞃa ſiꞃꞃe.
Irishman, Ciꞃeaꞃaċ ; from Ciꞃe, Ireland. Add, eaċ, or aċ, to the name of a country, and the gentile name of one from that country is formed; as, Saꞃſaꞃ-aċ, an Englishman ; Fſaꞃc-aċ, a Frenchman; Spaiꞃ-eaċ, a Spaniard. If the name of the country or place form the possessive case in aꞃ; as Ciꞃe, Ireland ; Alba, Scotland ; Saꞃſa, England ; Muma, Munster; the gentile name is formed from the possessive case ; as, Alba, Albaꞃac ; Saꞃſa, Saꞃſaꞃac ; Muma, Muiꞃaꞃac.
Honour, oꞃóꞃ.
Joy, ꞃóꞃ; luaċ-ꞌaiꞃ, rejoicing (from luaċ, frequent, quick, and ꞌaiꞃ, a laugh).
Mind, *n.*, meiꞃ ; (Latin, *mens*).
Shame, ꞃaiſe.
Store, ſꞇóſ.
Treasure, ꞇaiſꞌe, ciſꞇe ; (Latin, *fiscus*, the king's treasury; *cista*, a purse).

EXERCISE XVII.

1. Is the man old? 2. He is not old; but the old man who was here yesterday is now dead. 3. Is the old woman in the house? 4. She is not; but the grandmother is in the house. 5. Have you a grandmother living? 6. I have, and a grandfather. 7. Is the old man who was in the house yesterday your grandfather? 8. He is; and the old woman who is here to-day is my grandmother. 9. Have you a good (beaꞌ) heart? 10. I have a good heart and a well-disposed mind; for every good man has a good heart and a well-disposed mind. 11. The Lord my God is Sovereign (aſꞂ, high, supreme, sovereign,) Lord of (aiſ, on,) heaven and of earth. 12. The Irishman is long-lived. 13. How are all those under your care? 14. Those under my care are well (ſlaꞃ, safe). 15. How are those under your care, and your father's, and your grandfather's? 16. Your fame and your reputation are dear to me.

17. Oh! my sad sorrow that you are not happy. 18. Oh! my treasure and love of loves, how great is my affection for you! 19. Mary, pulse of heart, flower of all that is fair! 20. You are my sorrow and my joy—my honour and my shame, my life and my death.

SEVENTH LESSON.

CONJUGATION OF THE VERB " *to be*," oo beɪċ,—CONTINUED.
(See Fifth Lesson.)
INDICATIVE MOOD.
Imperfect Tense.

This tense is by some called the *habitual past*, because it expresses no particular action, or state of being, but a habit, or action repeated in the one case, and a continued state of existence in the other. We call it by the name *Imperfect*, in order to conform to the established divisions of Tense, and because it agrees very closely with the *Imperfect* in Greek, Latin, and French verbs. The first letter of this tense is aspirated, if it be one of the nine mutable consonants.

SINGULAR.	PLURAL.
1. bɪ̇ó-ɪ̇ηη, *veeyinn*, I was wont to be.	1. bɪ̇ó-mɪr, *veemush*, we were wont to be.
2. bɪ̇ó-ċeá, *eechaw*, thou (you) wast wont to be.	2. bɪ̇ó-ċɪ, *veehee*, you were wont to be.
3. bɪ̇ó-eáó ré, *veeyoo shé*, he was wont to be.	3. bɪ̇ó-óɪr, *veedeesh*, they were wont to be.

This tense, of which the Irish-speaking people make such frequent use, is by them translated, when conversing in English, by the words, " used to be."

The interrogative form is gone through by placing the particle aη, whether, before each of the persons; as, aη bɪ̇ó-ɪ̇ηη, was I wont to be, &c.

The verbal form of the third person singular, bɪ̇óeáó, with the personal pronouns me, I; ċu, thou (you); ré, he, (it); ɪ̇, she, (it); rɪ̇ηη, we; rɪ̇ó, you; rɪ̇aó, they; placed after it, gives the analytic conjugation of this tense.

Obs.—eáó, and áó, final, is, in Connaught, pronounced oo, (English); in Munster, a   As the final syllable of the imperfect tense, it is pronounced incorrectly in Munster, and in some districts in the southern parts of Connaught—like *agh*, guttural. Of the sound of ᴀꝺ final, we shall treat in the Twelfth Lesson.

The word synthetic, as applied to the conjugation of Irish verbs, means that the personal pronouns me, ᴄú, ꞃinn, ꞃib, ꞃiᴀꝺ, are, in each tense, combined with the verb, so as to make one word, thus—ᴄáim, I am, is composed of ᴄá, am, and me, I, and is as much a *synthesis*, that is, a joining together of the two words ᴄá and me, as ᴀɣᴀm, at me; oꞃm, on me; liom, with me, is of ᴀɣ, at, and mé, me; ᴀiꞃ, on; and me, le, with; and me. In some persons of the compound pronouns, equally as of the verbs, this synthetic union is not clearly, at first, perceived; as, in leo, with them, compounded of le and ꞃiᴀꝺ; in biꝺ-inn, I used to be, compounded of biꝺ and mé.

The *Analytic* is, in meaning, opposed to *Synthetic*, and indicates that the pronoun and verb are not combined in one

From the nature therefore of the synthetic form, it is plain the personal pronouns cannot, in the nominative case, be expressed after the verb when conjugated synthetically: and should the personal pronouns be found so expressed, they must be necessarily in the objective case. Thus—

> ᴄáim=ᴄá me, I am.
> ᴄáim me=ᴄá me, me, I, I am;
> buᴀil-im mé=buᴀiliꝺ mé me, I strike (I).

which clearly is very incorrect. Yet the third person plural is excepted, and is often elegantly employed, with this double form of nominative case, to add weight and strength to the ordinary power of language.

The reader cannot fail to perceive, that inflecting the verb synthetically, the third person singular has not the pronoun combined with the verb, as the other persons have, and he will naturally ask the reason. It is, as Doctor O'Donovan remarks, because the third person singular is always absent, and needs therefore to be expressed, that its gender may become known, whereas the first person or speaker, and the person spoken to " being always supposed to be present, there is no necessity of making any distinction of gender in them."

When therefore, in the analytic form, the nominative or
subject is, in the first and second persons singular and in
all the persons of the plural, actually expressed, one uninflected form of the verb suffices for all, since the relation
of its persons is sufficiently marked by the subject, just as
in English; I *loved*, thou *lovest*, he *loved*; we *loved*, you
loved, they *loved*. The verbal form " loved" is the same
in each of five personal endings, yet from the subject, or
nominative, each person of the verb is clearly known.

THE ANALYTIC IMPERFECT OF THE VERB " *to be.*"

	SINGULAR.			PLURAL.	
1	bɪ́ò-eaò, (*veeyoo*),	me.	1.	bɪ́ò-eaò, (*veeyoo*)	rinn.
2.	bɪ́ò-eaò,	,, ɰu.	2.	bɪ́ò-eaò,	,, rɪb.
3.	bɪ́ò-eaò,	,, ré or rɪ.	3.	bɪ́ò-eaò,	,, rɪaò.

I was wont to be; thou wast wont to be; he or she was
wont to be; we were wont to be; you were wont to be;
they were wont to be.

VOCABULARY.

2ɪn, whether, (a, is pronounced
short). It is put before the
perfect tense, just as an, whether, is put before the present tense, when a question
is asked. an, whether, is a
compound form of an, whether,
and ro—which, in the ancient
language, was a mere sign of
past time.

2ɪn, whom, or which; a relative
pronoun compounded of a,
who, which; and ro, the ancient sign of the perfect tense.

2ɪn, our; a possessive pronoun,
plural of mo, my : an in each
of these instances is pronounced *urh* (*u* short). It
takes n before a vowel; as, an
n·ataɪn, our father.

2ɪn, *awr*, slaughter; hence the
Greek name of the god of
Slaughter, Aƿŋ; Welsh, *acr*.

2ɪn, plough (to); Latin, *arare*, to
plough; ploughing; the action
of ploughing, bɪ na baɪm aɪ5
aɪn, the oxen were ploughing—

Job. 1. 14. Ploughed land,
Welsh, *ār;* Germ. *erde;* Gr.
ʾΑρόω.

2ɪn, for aɪn, upon: aɪn for beɪn, says;
as, aɪn, or an ré, says he;
Latin, *ait.*

beɪò, will be, future tense of beɰ,
to be.

béɪl, possessive case of beul, mouth.

beɰ, to be, being; a being by excellence; a lady.

buò, and ba, was; may be.

bɪaò, food; Greek, βɪoɾ, life.

buɪn, (to, or from, &c.) a cow;
the prepositional case—*i e.*,
the objective case governed by
a preposition—of bu, a cow.

Céɪm, a step; grade, dignity; as,
coɪr-céɪm, a foot-step; aɪò-
céɪm, high grade, great dignity.

Dɪneaċ, direct (*adjective*), straight;
Latin, *dirigere.*

Duɪne, a person.

Cɪc, possessive case of eaċ; Latin,
equus, a horse.

Cɪle, (and in old Irish aɪle, and

oile) another; Greek, ἄλλη, another; Latin, *alius.* From eile and tíreaċ, one of any (tír) country, is derived eilcneaċ, and sometimes written oiltneaċ, a stranger.

Feann, better.

Fóill, a while; go fóill, for a while, yet; fan go fóill, wait yet.

Fa, for; as cad fa, for what.

Faoi (pr. *swee*), under, for; as cad faoi, under what? *i.e.,* on what account.

Faoi, in; as, he is in power and respect, ta ré faoi ċéim, agus faoi meaṙ. These extrinsic qualities are, as it were, laid on him; he is therefore justly said to be under them.

Faċ, reason, cause; as, cia an faċ what reason; ta faċ le gaċ nió, there is reason (with) for every thing. fa, for; and faċ, cause, reason, are pronounced nearly alike, faċ=*fawh,* fa= *faw.*

Ganaṡ, scarcity; from gan, without, *prep.,* scarce, *adj.*

Lón, a luncheon, a viatic, a store.

Raiḃ, was; is employed in the perfect tense, exactly like b-fuil, is; in the present tense (See Second Lesson, page 10), after particles of denying, questioning, wishing, or supposing, after the relative pronouns a, who; naċ, who not.

EXERCISE XVIII.

1. Raiḃ a ċeann crom? 2. Ḃí a cean crom. 3. Raiḃ a láṁ caol? 4. Ḃí a láṁ caol agus ḃí a cor cam. 5. Raiḃ a ġruaġ liaċ (grey)? 6. Ḃí a ġruaġ liaċ. 7. Raiḃ an ḃó donn no bán? 8. Ḃí rí donn 9. Raiḃ mo ċarḃ gorm? 10. Ní raiḃ, aċt ḃí re buiḋe. 11. Raiḃ an ḃean óg agus an fear sean? 12. Ḃí an ḃean óg, agus ḃí rí faoi ṁeaṡ agus faoi ġean. 13. Ḃí bo feaṡ sean, agus beiṡó bo ṁac món mar ḃí a aċaiṡ. 14. Ḃ-fuil mac aiġ d'inġean go fóill? 15. Tá mac óg aiġ m' inġean óg ó nae. 16. Ḃí bo ṁaċ faoi clú agus faoi ġlóiṙ. 17. Ḃiḋeann uḃ bán aiġ cearc duḃ. 18. Tá agus baine ġeal aiġ buiṡ donn. 19. Raiḃ cluar an eiċ, beaġ; a cor díreaċ, a ḃruim fada? 20. Ḃí a cluar beaġ, a ḃruim fada, a cor díreaċ; agus naiḃ ré faoi ċarr a nae, dul ruar an cnoic? 21. Ní naiḃ, aċt ḃí ré ann teaċ m' aċaṡ. 22. Bud maiṫ liom ceol do ḃéil; Tá do ġuṫ óo binn agus do ġlón co arú, gur mian liom a beiṫ aiġ clor leiṡ. 23. An te bíḋeaṡ ruar bíḋeann re faoi ċéim agus clú; agus an te bíḋeaṡ rioṡ bíḋeann re faoi caiṡl agus faoi ġanaṡ. 24. Creud é do mian? 25. 'S é mo mian a beiṫ faoi ṁeaṡ, agus tá an mian ro ann mo ċroiḋe féin. 26. Ní naiḃ roġ agam. 27. Bíḋeann a roġ agus a feun a láṁ gaċ duine; óir is roġ a beiṫ go maiṫ le gaċ duine eile. 28. Bud dear do cor clé agus bud ġorm do fuil deir, bud min agus ġeal do láṁ, agus bud

ḟaḃa ḃo ṁeuṗa, buḋ cṁuĝ, ḟaṁneaċ, ḃo ĝnuaĝ aĝuṗ buḋ lon-
ṗaċ, ṗoṁlṗeaċ ṗaḃaṗc (pr. *ryark*: See Fourth Lesson, Observation, p. 21), ḃo ṗoṁĝ ĝoṗm.

EXERCISE XIX.

1. Was the weather rough yesterday when ye were on
the sea? 2. No; the weather was fine, though the wind
was high, and the sea was rough. 3. Were they on the
top of the mountain? 4. They were not on the top of the
mountain, but they were at the foot of it (aiĝ a bun).
5. Had ye a guide? 6. We had no guide, as we were
not on the top of the mountain. 7. It was not cold,
though there was a fog on the hill's side. 8. I do not like
a fog on a hill. 9. The view from off the top, over the
country and over the sea was not far. 10. There were
boats on the sea, and people on the shore, which was very
white, and a ship in the harbour. 11. The sun was red
when going down (aiĝ bul ḟaoi). 12. The moon was full,
and large, and luminous, and the firmament was blue, without a cloud. 13. The fame which this country has is very
great. 14. Do you be early at the sea and along the shore?
15. No; I am not usually well, and I do not like to be at the
sea till the end of summer; (beiṗe an c-ṗaṁṗaiḃ.) 16. You
are lucky to be here on the side of this beautiful valley. 17.
I am lucky; but, as the proverb says, (maṗ beiṗ an ṗeaṁ-
ĝeul) " there is luck with a fool;" (biḃeann aḋ aiṗ aṁa-
ḃan). 18. I like (it is a wish with me) to be in this delightful country. 19. May God's blessing be on you. 20. Farewell (ṗlan leac).

EIGHTH LESSON.

CONJUGATION OF THE VERB " *to be*," ḃo ḃeiċ,—CONTINUED.
INDICATIVE MOOD.

Perfect Tense.

THIS tense, like the first perfect in French, the historic
perfect in Latin, the aorist in Greek, conveys the idea of
time past generally—whether some time ago, or just now

passed—and is translated into English either by the remote perfect, *was;* or by the present perfect, *have been.*

	SINGULAR.		PLURAL.
1.	ḃíḋ-eaṙ, *veeyes,* I was.	1.	ḃí-maṙ, *reemur,* we were.
2.	ḃíḋ-ṡ, *veeyish,* thou wast.	2.	ḃí-ḃaṙ, *veewar,* you were.
3.	ḃí ré, *ree shé,* he (or it) was; ḃí rí, *vee shee,* she (or it) was.	3.	ḃí-ṫaṙ, *veedar,* they were.

The Analytic form of this tense is very simple. (See preceding Lesson; paragraph immediately before VOCABULARY, p. 35).

1.	ḃí mé, I was; or have been.	1.	ḃí ṙinn, we were.
2.	ḃí ṫu, thou wast.	2.	ḃí ṙíḃ, you were.
3.	ḃí ré, he (or it) was; ḃí rí, she (or it) was.	3.	ḃí ṙiaṫ, they were.

Sometimes the particle ꝺo—and in the ancient language ꞃo—is placed before this tense. Its use in this respect, in Irish, is not unlike that of the particle *to* before the infinitive mood in English verbs. Raḃaṙ (and not ḃíḋeaṙ, the direct perfect of the verb ꝺo ḃeiṫ, *to be*), follows those particles into which ꞃo enters, forming the latter part of a compound; as, ꞃuṙ, that (compounded of ꞃo, that, would that; and ꞃo, sign of the perfect tense), *e. g.,* ꞃuṙ ꞃaḃaṙ, that I was; naṙ, that not (negative interrogative), as naṙ ꞃaḃaṙ, was I not; naṙ ṁolaṙ, did I not praise; naṙ, may not, (compounded of the particle na, not, and ꞃo); a negative used when a wish is expressed; as, naṙ ꞃaiḃ ré, may he be not; naṙ ṁolaiḃ ré, may he not praise; níoṙ, not; from ní, not, and ꞃo; naċaṙ, which not. (See in preceding Lesson, page 36,—the word ꞃaiḃ; also Second Lesson, Obs. 1 page 10).

INTERROGATIVE AND NEGATIVE PERFECT.

1.	Aṙ ꞃaḃ-aṙ, *rowas,* was I?	1.	Aṙ ꞃaḃ-maṙ, *rowmar,* were we?
2.	Aṙ ꞃaḃ-aiṙ, *rowish,* wast thou?	2.	Aṙ ꞃaḃ-ḃaṙ, *rowwar,* were you?
3.	Aṙ ꞃaiḃ ré, *rowv shé,* was he?	3.	Aṙ ꞃaḃ-ṫaṙ, *rowdhar,* were they?

Analytic—ꞃaiḃ (was), mé, ṫu, ré ꞃinn, ꞃíḃ, ꞃiaṫ?

ꞃaḃ-aṙ, is compounded of ꞃo; and the perfect ḃíḋeaṙ, which we have conjugated above.

The learner cannot fail to observe that the verbal endings, aṙ, aiṙ, for the first and second persons singular; and maṙ, ḃaṙ, ṫaṙ, for the persons of the plural, are the same

in both forms (bʀᴅeᴀʀ, and pᴏḃᴀʀ) of the perfect indicative.
The same are the endings of the persons of the perfect tense
in every verb regular and irregular in the Irish language.

In some grammars there is a vowel (ᴀ) placed before
the plural terminations, mᴀʀ, bᴀʀ, ᴅᴀʀ, to lend fulness of
sound to the word. We have omitted it in the conjugation
of the substantive verb, as we do intend to omit it in every
other, for the sake of having in all verbs the endings of the
several persons in each tense uniform. Besides, the inser-
tion of a vowel is rarely necessary to lend euphony to the
sound of two consonants in two distinct syllables.

THE PERFECT OF ιʀ, *it is*—THE ASSERTIVE FORM OF THE
VERB, *to be*. (see p. 25).

1. bᴀ or buᴅ me, it was I.	1. bᴀ or buᴅ ʀιɴɴ, it was we.
2 bᴀ ... ᴄu, it was thou.	2. bᴀ ... ʀιb, it was you.
3. bᴀ ... ʀe, it was he.	3. bᴀ ... ʀιᴀᴅ, it was they.

buᴅ is also the subjunctive present; as ᴣo m-buᴅ ʀlᴀɴ ᴀɴ ᴄo ʀιᴀʀʀuιᴣeᴀʀ,
may he who enquires be safe.

bᴀ becomes b' when a vowel follows; as, b' ᴀʀᴅ é ᴀɴ ᴄʀᴀɴ,
the tree was high. The b' or b, becomes united with ᴀ, a
particle which is sometimes placed for emphasis before bᴀ
or buᴅ, and thus forms one word—ᴀb, was. The forms ᴀb;
ʀob (from ʀo and bᴀ); bᴀm (from bᴀ and me); cumᴀᴅ
(from ᴣo, that, and bᴀ) ; and coʀbᴀm (from ᴣo, that ; ʀo,
sign of the perfect tense, and bᴀ); so frequently met with
in the ancient language, are not found in lately-printed
Irish works, and indeed ought not at all to be henceforth
employed.

The initial letter of every adjective—if one of the *four*
labials b,ꝑ,m,ꝑ,coming after buᴅ, is aspirated; as, buᴅ ṁᴀιᴄ ᴀɴ
ʀeᴀʀ Seᴀᴣᴀɴ (*Shawn*), the man John was good ; *i.e.*,
John was a good man.

The personal pronouns coming after bᴀ, or buᴅ, take the
Objective form—which, in this shape, are, properly speaking, only aspirated nominatives ; as, buᴅ ᴄu, and not buᴅ
ᴄu ; buᴅ é or buᴅ ʀe, and not buᴅ ʀe ; buᴅ ʀιᴀᴅ, or ιᴀᴅ, and
not buᴅ ʀιᴀᴅ. It appears to us, therefore, that after buᴅ,
the aspirated nominative, ʀe, ʀι, ʀιɴɴ, ʀιᴀᴅ, ought to be
employed, and not é, ι, ιɴɴ, ιᴀᴅ, the objective forms, in

which ḟ (aspirated) is omitted. The latter spelling, how
ever, is entirely in use in all printed books and manuscripts.

On this Dr. Latham observes: "There seems to be no precise rule of
orthography in this instance." We would recommend the learner to
adopt that spelling which is philosophically the correct one, ṫe, ṫi, rinn,
riað; although usage is quite against us

<h2 style="text-align:center">VOCABULARY.</h2>

Áinde, height; from áno, high.
baoṫ, vain, silly.
beiðṁið, we will be.
Caora, sheep.
Da, two; as, ða ḟeaṟ, two men.
Deáȝ, teen.—the decimal ending;
    from deịc, ten; Greek, δέκα;
      Fr. *dix;* oċṫ-ðeáȝ, eighteen;
      reaċṫ-ðeáȝ, seventeen.
Déan, do; make.
Ȝnáṫ, custom.
Maraċ, to-morrow.
Namaðaċ, inimical, hostile; (from
    naṁað, an enemy.)

Póṫ, marry; as it were—bóṫ, from
    bo, a cow, because in kine the
    dowry was usually paid.
Póṫa, married.
Róṁam, before me; compound pro-
    noun; from roiṁ, before; and
    me, me.
Róṁaṫ, before thee (you).
Roiṁe, before me.
Roiṁṗi, before her.
Spṟé, a dowry given with females.
Suiȝ, sit.

<h2 style="text-align:center">EXERCISE XX.</h2>

1. An ṫé a bị maiṫ léaṫ a nae beið ṟe olc ðuịṫ á maraċ
aȝuṟ an ṫe a bị ðịl leaṫ uaịṟ aṁáịn, beið ṟe namaðaċ leaṫ
uaịṟ eịle, óịṟ ṟo é ȝnáṫ aȝuṟ nóṟ an ṫ-raoȝaịl. 2. Beiðṁið aịṟ aon rȝeul ȝaċ lá 'nuaịṟ beióṁṗð aịṟ ċṟaịȝ, no aịṟ
luịnȝ aịȝ ṟṅaṁ, aịȝ clor leịṟ an ṁuịṟ ṁóṟ ḟaoị ḟeanȝ aịȝ
cuṟ a bịuċ ṟuaṟ ann áịnðe. 3. Ịr álaṁ an nịð luịnȝ aịȝ
ṟnaṁ aịṟ ṁuịṟ. 4. Naċ ðeaṟ ala aịȝ ṟnaṁ aịṟ lịnn? 5.
Ịr ðeaṟ ala aịȝ ṟnaṁ aịṟ lịnn. 6. Ịr ðeaṟ leanb óȝ ann
uċṫ a ṁaċaṟ. 7. Náṟ b' aoịbịn (delightful) an ȝleaṅ bị
ṟoṁam (before me) ṟịnṫe (stretched)? 8. b' aoịbịn an
ȝleaṅ bị ṟoṁaṫ ṟịnṫe. 9. Bịðeann bonb ḟaoị rȝéịṁ. 10.
Naċ maiṫ Oịa ȝo lá? 11. Ịr maiṫ Oịa ȝo lá. 12. Beið
an ṫ-ṟṅáịð bṟeaȝ, aȝuṟ an ṫeaċ móṟ. 13. Ṫá ða ḟuịl aịȝ
ȝaċ ðuịne, aȝuṟ ða coịṟ, aȝuṟ ða láịṁ, aȝuṟ ċeann. 14.
Naċ cóịṟ ðo ȝaċ ðuịne aịṟ an ṫṟáịȝ, bað a beịṫ aịȝe, aȝuṟ
luịnȝ aȝuṟ ȝleuṟ le ịaṟȝ a ȝabaịl (pronounced *gowal,* to
take)? 15. Ịr cóịṟ ðo ȝaċ ðuịne ȝaṟ ðo'n ṁuịṟ bað 'a beịṫ
aịȝe. 16. Cṟeuð é an luaċ a ṫá aịṟ ịaṟȝ anoịṟ? 17. Ṫa
ịaṟȝ raoṟ. 18. B-ḟuịl maṟṫ aȝað? 19. Ṫá maṟṫ áȝam,
aȝuṟ ðaṁ, aȝuṟ caoṟa, aȝuṟ uan? 20. Cịa an luaċ ṫá

air daṁ, agus air ċaora, agus air uan? 21. Tá daṁ daor, agus tá luaċ uain saor. 22. Is áil liom do ċaint. 23. Is saor caint. 24. Naċ dall an gráḋ baoṫ? 25. Is dall an gráḋ baoṫ. 26. Naċ milis fíon; naċ searḃ a íoc? 27. Is milis fíon; is searḃ a íoc. 28. Ma 's maiṫ leat a ḃeiṫ buan, caiṫ fuar agus teiṫ. 29. Is fíor duit, aċt naċ b-fuil fáṫ le gaċ nið? 30. Tá fáṫ le gaċ nið. 31. Suiġ ann so le mo ṫaoḃ agus déan caint liom. 32. An maiṫ leat a ḃeiṫ caint liom? 33. Is maiṫ liom go deiṁin (indeed). 34. B-fuil d' inġean óg pósta? 35. Ní b-fuil, mar naċ b-fuil spré aici. 36. Cia an aois í; seaċt-déag, an eaḋ (*an yah*, is it)? 37. Tá, oċt-déag ó Ṁárt (March). 38. Cia an ainm tá airṫi? 39. Sinéad (Jane). 40. Slán go raiḃ si.

NINTH LESSON.

THE following simple prepositions, de, of; do, to; fa, for; faoi, under; ó, from; tar, over; tre, by, through; and sometimes air, on; ċum, to, towards; gan, without, aspirate the initial aspirable letter of a noun when the article is not expressed.

EXAMPLES.

Briġ, efficacy; de ḃriġ, of, or from efficacy;

hence de ḃriġ comes to signify, *because*; and is now used as an adverbial phrase.

Taoḃ, side; de ṫaoḃ, concerning; *i.e.*, of the side of; Latin, *relate ad.*

Tus, beginning; ó ṫus, from the beginning; Latin, *ab initio.*

Seamus, James;	do Ṡeamus, to James.
Seaġan, John,	ċum Ṡeaġan, to John.
Beaṫa, life;	tar ḃeaṫa, above life.
Biṫ, life, existence;	air ḃiṫ, in life, *i.e.*, at all.
Barr, top;	air ḃarr, on top.
Talaṁ, earth;	air ṫalaṁ, on earth;

as, tá Dia air neaṁ agus "air ṫalaṁ," agus ann gaċ

uile ball de'n doṁan, God is in heaven and *on* earth, and in every place in the world. b, of bpuṫ; c, of caob; b, of beaċa, Ṡ of Ṡeamur, and of Ṡeaġan, ṫ of ṫapp, are aspirated by the prepositions.

> " Seal ain meirȝe, real ain buile,
> 　Reubaḋ ceuḋ 'r aȝ dul ain mine
> an fairiun rin do ċleaċcaman, ní rȝaimfam' leir ȝo beo."
> 　　　—*Hardiman's Irish Minstrelsy,* vol. i. p. 22.

(See following Exercise for the translation of these words).

In the above distich m, in the word meirȝe, and b, in the word buile, and m, in mine, after air, are not aspirated. Again—

> Ȝan circe ir fuar an ċlu;
> Without treasure fame is cold.

C in the word circe, after the preposition ȝan, is not aspirated. Nouns beginning with d, c, f, after air, car, (commonly) ann, ar, or any preposition ending in d, c, f, l, n, (see Obs. 2, page 29), have not the initial letter aspirated.

VOCABULARY.

Ailȝe, for aluine, comparative degree of aluin, beautiful.

Airȝeaḋ, money of all kinds; derived from airȝ, an old Irish word signifying white; and riaeḋ, *res,* a thing; Gr., ἀργος, whence *arguros,* the Greek term for silver; French *argent,* money; Latin, *argentum,* silver.

Beiṁ, a stain.

Benur, Venus; derived from the Irish bean, a woman, as she was by excellence the—bean.

Braṫair, a brother; a friar; Latin, *frater.*

Buile, frenzy; Latin, *bilis.*

Cleaċca, a habit.

Ċleaċcamair, we practised.

Cleib, breast, a basket; possessive case of cliab, breast, because, like a basket, it is set with ribs.

Cliaṁuin (from cliab, breast, and buine, a person), a son-in-law; aṫair-ċliaṁuin, a father-in-law; bean-ċliaṁuin, a daughter-in-law; maṫair-ċliaṁuine, a mother-in-law.

Cnearca, honest.

Dearb-ḃraṫair, a (real) brother, as opposed to braṫair, a friar, *i.e.,* a brother in religion.

Ȝrara, grace, naoṁ, holy, a saint; naoṁ-ȝrara, holy grace.

Lil, lily; Gr. λείριον; Latin, *lilium;* Welsh, *llyren.*

Maiṫear, goodness; from maiṫ, good.

Meirȝe, drunkenness.

Mine, wanton madness, frolic.

Reubaḋ, tearing; from reub, to rend.

Reulcan, diminutive of reulc, a star.

Rór, a rose.

Saoȝal, the world; Latin, *seculum.*

Seal, a turn, a while.

Sȝaimfam', for rȝaimfamuiḋ, we shall cease.

Tiȝearna, and ciarna, Gr. τύραννος, lord, sir; Ger. *Herr;* derived from cir, country, and nae or nai, the ancient Irish for neaċ, a person, a man.

Uile, all.

EXAMPLES.

Iʃ bⱃeaȝa 'na Ƀeṅuʃ ꜩu,
Iʃ aɪlɲe 'na ꞃeulꞓaɲ ꜩu,
Ṁo h-Elen ȝaɲ beɪm ɪꞃ ꜩu,
   A Eɪƀlɪn a ꞃuɪn !

Ṁo ꞃóʃ, mo lɪl, mo ꞔaoꞃ ɪʃ ꜩu,
Ṁo ꞃꜩóꞃ a ƀ-ꝼuɪl 'ʃaɲ ꜩ-ꞃaoȝal ʃo, ꞔu,
Ꞃun ṁɔ ꞔꞃoɪƀe 'ʃ ɪno ꞔleɪƀ ɪʃ ꜩu,
   A Eɪƀlɪn a ꞃuɪn !

More beauteous than Venus, far,
More fair than the midnight star,
My Helen, without stain you are,
   Eibhlin a Ruin !

My red Rose, my Lily white,
My Treasure, unfading bright,
Darling ! my soul's delight !
   Eibhlin a Ruin !

Hardiman's Irish Minstrelsy : Translated for The Nation.

EXERCISE XXI.

1. Ꜩá me ȝaɲ ꞃɪuꞃ, ȝaɲ bꞃaꞔaɪꞃ. 2. Ꜩá ꜩu ȝaɲ óꞃ ȝaɲ aɪꞃȝeaḋ. 3. Ꜩá ꞃí ȝaɲ olc no maɪꞔ. 4. Ƀ-ꝼuɪl ꞷo Ꞟeaꞃƀ-bꞃaꞔaɪꞃ aȝuʃ ꞷo Ꞟeaꞃƀ-ꝼɪúꞃ le ꞷo ṁaꞔaɪꞃ aɲɲ aon ꜩɪȝ? 5. Ꜩá mo ṁaꞔaɪꞃ aȝuʃ mo ꞷeaꞃƀ-ꝼɪuꞃ aɲɲ aon ꜩɪȝ lɪoɲꞃ-ʃa. 6. A Şɪnéaḋ, ƀ-ꝼuɪl ꜩu aɲɲ ꞃɪɲɲ? 7. A Şeamuɪʃ aȝuʃ a Şeaȝaɪɲ ƀ-ꝼuɪl ȝꞃáḋ aȝaɪƀ aɪꞃ mo ṁaꞔaɪꞃ? 8. Ƀ-ꝼuɪl ꞷo ṁac beo, a h-Eɪƀlɪn? 9. Ca ƀ-ꝼuɪl mac an ꝼɪꞃ ꞔꞃeaꞃꜩa a bɪ aɲɲ ʃo a Ꞁae? 10. Ꜩá aɲ bean ṁóꞃ aȝuʃ mac an ꝼɪꞃ ṁóꞃ aɲɲ ó ꞔuʃ aɲ lae a Ꞁae. 11. A Şɪnéaḋ ꜩuȝ ꜩu aɲ ꞔlꞃu leaꜩ. 12. Ꝼaꞷa buaɲ-ʃaoȝalaꞔ ȝo ꞃaɪb ꜩu, a ꞃuɪɲ ȝeal mo ꞔꞃoɪƀe. 13. Ꞷe bꞃɪȝ ȝo ƀ-ꝼuɪl ꜩu ꞃo-maɪꞔ, a ꞒɪȝeaꞃꞀa, ꜩá ꞃún aȝam aʃ ʃo ʃuaʃ a beɪꞔ ꞷɪlɪʃ ꞷuɪꜩ. 14. O a Ꞷé ꞷɪlɪʃ, a ꝼeaꞃc-ȝꞃáḋ mo ꞔꞃoɪƀe, mo ṁɪle ʃꜩóꞃ, m' uɪle ṁaɪꜩeaʃ, beɪꞃꞃm me ꝼéɪɲ ʃuaʃ ꞷuɪꜩ le beɪꞔ ꝼaoɪ ꞷo ʃꜩɪúꞃ ȝo bꞃáꞔ; ꞷe bꞃɪȝ ȝo ƀ-ꝼuɪl ꜩu maɪꞔ aȝuʃ ȝꞃáḋṁaꞃ lɪoɲ, aȝuʃ ȝo ꜩuɪlleaɲɲ (deserve) ꜩu mo ȝꞃáḋ uɪle; aʃ ʃo ʃuaʃ (up, forward, henceforth); beɪḋ ȝꞃáḋ aȝam ó ꞔꞃoɪƀe oꞃꜩ, aȝuʃ Ꞁí beɪḋ cꞃɪoꞔ leɪꞃ ȝo bꞃáꞔ le coɲȝꞀaṁ (help) ꞷo Ꞁaoṁ-ȝꞃáʃa. 15. O, a ʃꜩóꞃ mo ꞔleɪƀ Ꞁaꞔ móꞃ aɲ ȝꞃáḋ bɪ aȝaꞷ aɪꞃ ꞷ' aꞔaɪꞃ cꞁabuɪne, Ꞁuaɪꞃ a ꞷ' ɪoc ꜩu aɲ meuꞷ a bɪ aɪꞃ. 16. Ƀ-ꝼuɪl ꞷo ṁaꞔaɪꞃ cꞁabuɪne 'ʃ aɲ ꜩɪȝ. 17. Ꜩá, ꞷe ꜩaob ȝo ƀ-ꝼuɪl a h-ɪɲȝean ꜩɪɲ: acꜩ beɪḋ bꞃóɪꞷ aɪꞃꞔɪ 'Ꞁuaɪꞃ beɪḋ ꝼɪoʃ aɪcɪ ȝuꞃ ꞃaɪb

feaṙ cneaṙċa maṙ ċu-ṙa aiṡ ḟiaḟṙuṡaḋ (enquiring) aiṙéi.
18. Iṙ móṙ a cáil aṡuṙ a clú ṫṙiḋ an ṫíṙ.   19. Iṙ ḟioṙ ṡo
ḃ-ḟuil.   20. Ṡo ṙaiḃ ṙe maṙ ṙin aṙ ṙo ṙuaṙ.

Obs. 1.—The final vowel of the possessive pronouns mo,
my; ḋo, thy; and of the prepositions ḋe, of; ḋo, to; is
elided, and an apostrophe (') substituted for the elided
letter, when a vowel comes immediately after: as—ḋ'
ainm, thy name, for ḋo ainm; ṡo naoṁṫaṙ ḋ' ainm, hallowed
be thy name: ḃ-ḟuil ḋ' aṫaiṙ aṡuṙ ḋo ṁaṫaiṙ ṙlán, are
your father and mother well?   D'aoiṙ Cṙíoṫ, of the age
of Christ.

Obs. 2.—ḋ, of the possessive pronoun ḋo, thy; should
never, when o is elided, be changed into ṫ—a cognate letter
of a near kindred sound—a process which has, very incorrectly, been often gone through; as, ṫanam, for ḋanam,
which itself is an old stenographic form for ḋ'anam, thy
soul; so again, ṫainm, thy name, for ḋ'ainm; ṫaṫaiṙ, thy
father, for ḋ'aṫaiṙ; ṫeaṡna, thy wisdom, for ḋ'eaṡna;
ṫoṡlaċ, thy man-servant, thy young man, for ḋ' oṡlaċ.
This mutation of the linguals ḋ, ṫ, one for the other, is so
puzzling to mere learners that it should never in future be
practised.

ᴀ, her; takes the aspirate ħ before the vowel immediately following it; as—Is *her* father alive, ḃ-ḟuil a ħ-aṫaiṙ
beo?   Is *her* soul safe, ḃ-ḟuil a ħ-anam ṙlán?   If *his*, and
not *her*—both of which are expressed in Irish by the letter
ᴀ—was meant, the expression should have been written
thus—ᴀ aṫaiṙ, and not ᴀ ħ-aṫaiṙ; ᴀ anam, and not ᴀ ħ-
anam.

This difference is very carefully attended to by Irish-
speaking people.   The sound of ħ before the initial vowel
falling on the ear tells them at once that the subject to
which ᴀ refers is feminine.   Example—

> Iṙ ḟaḋ í ó'n ṡ-cṙiċ, ḃ-ḟuil a " ħ-óṡ laoċ " 'n a luiḋe,
>   'S ṡan aṁ́ḃ aṙ a ṙuiṁṫiḃ 'ṡ a ḃṙeuṡaḋ;
> Aċṫ iompuiṡeaṁ ṡo ṙuaṙ ó ṙuiḃ ṡaċ ṙéoi,
>   Oiṙ ṫá a cṙoiḋe le n-a céile 'ṡ a ḋi-ṡaḋ.

She is far from the land where her young hero sleeps,
   And lovers are round her sighing;
But coldly she turns from their gaze and weeps,
   For her heart in his grave is lying.
                              —*Irish Melodies, by Dr. MacHale.*

Theſe particles take ɦ before the succeeding vowel.

Cᴀ, what, were; as cᴀ ɦ-ᴀoⅰⱤ ʙuⱤⱦ, what age is to you, *i.e*, what age are you; or how old are you?

Ꝝo, that (*conj.*); a particle that renders the *adj*. before which it is put, an *adverb*. ⅰⱬ Ꝝo ɦ-ᴀꞃᴀɰ ʙⅰꝺeᴀꞃꞃ ⱦu ᴀꞃꞃ ꞃo, It is seldom you is be here.

Ꞟᴀ, not (in commanding); as, ꞃᴀ ɦ-oʙ ᴀꝫuⱤ ꞃᴀ ɦ-ⅰᴀꞃꞃ oꞃóⱤꞃ, do not refuse and do not seek honour.

Le, } with,
Ꝛe, }
Ⱦᴀ Ꞃe ⱦⅰꞃɦ le ɦ-eᴀꝫlᴀ, He is sick (with) from fear.

When the possessive pronouns ᴀ, his, her, their; ᴀꞃ, our, follow the simple prepositions that end in a vowel, ꞃ ⅰs, for euphony, inserted *before* the pronoun to prevent hiatus—as, ᴀꝫuⱤ cloc Fᴀoⅰ " ꞃ-ᴀ " ċeᴀꞃꞃ, and a stone under his head; ó " ꞃ-ᴀ " cꞃoⅰꝺe, from her heart; ó " ꞃ-ᴀ " ꝫ-cꞃoⅰꝺe, from their heart. In these Examples ꞃ is inserted before ᴀ, his; ᴀ, her; and ᴀ, their, following Fᴀoⅰ; ó.

TENTH LESSON.

CONJUGATON OF THE VERB " *to be*," ꝺo ʙeⅰⱦ,—CONTINUED.
INDICATIVE MOOD.
Future Tense.

SINGULAR.

1. ʙéⅰꝺ-ⅰꝺ, *beyid*, I will be.
2. ʙéⅰꝺ-ⅰꞃ, *beyirh*, thou wilt be.
3. ʙéⅰꝺ Ꞃé, *bey shé*, he (or, it) will be; ʙeⅰꝺ Ꞃⅰ, *bey shee*, she (or, it) will be.

PLURAL.

1. ʙéⅰꝺ-ɰⅰꝺ, *beymidh*, we will be.
2. ʙeⅰꝺ-ⱦⅰꝺ, *beyhee*, you will be.
3. ʙéⅰꝺⅰꝺ, *beyidh*, they will be.

Like the Present tense, the Future, after the relative pronouns ᴀ, who; ꞃoċ, who; adopts the termination—eᴀꞃ; as, from ʙeⅰꝺ, will be; and ʙⅰꝺ (present tense), is usually; is formed ʙéⅰꝺeᴀꞃ; and ʙⅰꝺeᴀꞃ; as, ᴀꞃ ⱦé ᴀ ʙéⅰꝺeᴀꞃ, he who will be; ᴀꞃ ⱦé ᴀ ʙⅰꝺeᴀꞃ, he who is usually. This ending is assumed after the same relatives (ᴀ, and ꞃoċ) by every other verb, neuter and active, in the language. In the coming Lessons it will not, therefore, be necessary to give,

in other verbs, the relative assertive form of the Present
or Future tenses indicative. The relative form of the
verb for the other tenses—imperfect, perfect, conditional;
or for the relative *negative* of even the present and future,
is that of the third person singular of each respective
tense.

This special ending of the tenses after the relative pronoun, is a peculiarity in Irish.

The future of ιρ, it is; bᴀ or buᴏ, it was; is buρ, it will
be; which is seldom employed except before adjectives in
the superlative degree with a contingent or future meaning; as ᴀη ce ιρ ρeᴀρρ, he who is best; ᴀη ce ᴀ b' ρeᴀρρ,
he who was best; ᴀη cé buρ ρeᴀρρ, he who will be best.

CONDITIONAL.

SINGULAR.	PLURAL.
1. béιᴏ-ιηη, *veyhinn*, I might, or could be.	1. béιᴏ-ɱuρ, *veymush*, we might, or could be.
2. béιᴏ-ċeᴀ, *veyhaw*, thou mightest, or couldst be.	2. béιᴏ-éιᴏ, *veyhee*, ye might, or could be.
3. béιᴏ-eᴀᴏ, *veyhoo*, *shé*, he (or it), might or could be.	3. béιᴏ-ᴏιρ, *veydish*, they might, or could be.

The first letter of the foregoing tense, like that of the
imperfect, is aspirated, if it be one of the nine mutable
consonants.

OPTATIVE MOOD.

1. ᴼo ρᴀᴃ-ᴀᴏ, *go rowadh*, that I may be.	1. ᴼo ρᴀᴃ-ɱuιᴏ, *go rowmudh*, that we may be.
2. ᴼo ρᴀᴃ-ᴀρρ, *go rowirh*, that thou mayest be.	2. ᴼo ρᴀᴃ-ċᴀιᴏ, *go rowhy*, that you may be.
3. ᴼo ρᴀιᴃ ρé, *go rowv shé*, that he (or, it) may be; ᴼo ρᴀιᴃ ρí, *go rowv shee*, that she (or, it) may be.	3. ᴼo ρᴀᴃ-ᴀιᴏ, *go rowidh*, that they may be.

buᴏ, that it may be, is the Optative form of ιρ, it is; buᴏ,
it was; and buρ, will be; as, ᴼo ɱ-buᴏ ρlᴀη ρᴀᴃ-ρᴀoᴣᴀ-
lᴀċ éu, health and long life to you; literally, may you
be healthy and long-lived.

IMPERATIVE.

1 … … …, … …	1. bι-ɱuρρ, *beemush*, let us be.
2. bι, *bee*, be thou.	2. bιᴏ-ιᴏ, *beeyee*, be ye.
3. bιᴏ-eᴀᴏ ρé, *beeyoo shé*, let him be.	3. bι-ᴏιρ, *beedish*, let them be.

The second person plural bíoḃ, is commonly, in the spoken language, pronounced as if written, bígíḃ, *beegee.*

The infinitive mood and participles are formed by putting certain prepositions before the verbal noun—beiṫ, being—as, in English, *to; about to;* in French, *pour;* is placed before the infinitive,

beiṫ, a being; do beiṫ, to be;
le beiṫ, in order to be.

Le, with; placed before the infinitive mood, gives, like *pour*, in French, the idea of intent, purpose, to perform what is expressed by the verb.

Air tí beiṫ (on the point of being), about to be.

Aig beiṫ (at) being; same as the old English form, a-being, a-walking, a-loving; for—being, walking, loving.

Air beiṫ, on being.

Iar m-beiṫ, after being, having been.

VOCABULARY.

Branch, bough, craoḃ, geug.
Bush, sgeaċ.
Bank, border, edge, bruaċ; as air bruaċ na linne, on the border of the pond; air bruac na h-aille, on the verge of the cliff; air bruaċ na h-aiḃne, on the bank of the river.
Comet, reannain, from reann, a star, and air, beautiful, sparkling; reult, also means star; and reultan, a small star, same as reultog; or a star-measuring instrument, an astrolabe. Comet, can well be called also reult gnuagaċ; or reult tinteaċ; Reannain may be considered by many to be only merely the diminutive of reann.
Cut, gearr; from gearr, short; because whatever is cut is shortened.
Deep, doimin.
Dike, fail; Latin, *vallum.*
Ditch, cliaḋ.
Dust, ashes, luaiṫre (from luaṫ, quick, and cré, earth); luaiṫre cnaṁ, bone dust.

For, because, óir; Greek, γαρ; Fr. *car.*
Farm, feilm.
Fertile, saiḋḃir; rich;—saiḋḃir is derived from ro, ease; and aḋḃar, cause.
Fertilize, dean saiḋḃir, (make fertile).
Granary, stall, mainnreaċ, sgiobol; Heb. שׁיבול, *shibol,* an ear of corn.
Harrow, cliaḋ-fuirtea.
Harbinger, tuar; a rainbow is called "the harbinger of a shower," "tuar ceaṫa."
Irrigated, fliuċta; from fliuċ, to irrigate, to wet; fliuċ, *adj.,* wet, moist.
Lake, loċ; Fr. *lac;* Basq. *lac;* Greek, λακκος; Latin, *lacus;* Italian, *lago;* Spanish, *lago;* Welsh, *llwch.*
Manure, aolaċ, from aol, lime.
Marsh, low meadow land, léan.
Moor, riasg; (as if from riṫ, flowing, and uisge, water).
Moory, riasgaċ; moory land, talaṁ riasgaċ.
Nutriment (juice), sug.

Oak, ꝺꝏ; Greek, δρῦς; Sansk., *druh*; Welsh, *derw*. Hence the name Derry, from the grove planted there by Columbkille.

Pile, a heap of stones, cꙗṅ.

Pit, cⅼꙗṙ, a sand-pit, cⅼꙗṙ ᵹꙗṅe.

Philosopher, ꝼꙗoⅼ; Greek, σοφος. In Irish it means also, a man of letters; any man of position in the world; ꙇ Śꙗoⅼ, Sir.

Plough, céꙗċꙇꙇ; to plough, ꙇṅeꙗḃ; ꙇṅeꙗḃꙇꝺ ꙇᵹꙇṙ ꙗᵹ ꝼꙇṙṙꙗꝺ, ploughing and harrowing; cꙗṅ-céꙗċꙇꙇ, the plough; Charles's Wain.

Purpose, ꙇꝺḃꙗṅ; that purpose, ꙇn ꙇ-ꙇꝺḃꙗṅ ṙꙇṅ; for that purpose, therefore, ꙗꙇṙ ꙗn ꙇꝺḃꙗṅ ṙꙇṅ.

Rock, cꙗṙṙꙗⅼc, ꙗⅼⅼ.

Soil, earth, cṅé. úꙗṅ.

Sowing, cꙩṙ; from cꙩṙ, to put, to sow, to set.

Spring (time), eꙗṙṙꙗċ; from eꙗṙⅼᵹ, spring up, arise, when mother earth rises, as it were, from the dormant state in which she lay during winter; Greek, ἔαρ.

Stack, cṙꙩꙗċ; from this word is derived Cṙꙩꙗċ Pꙗꝺṙꙩꙗc, the name of a mountain in Mayo, six miles from Westport; called cṙꙩꙗċ, from its conical, reek-like shape; and Pꙗꝺṙꙩꙗc, Patrick's; because the Saint, like another Moses, spent, while preaching the faith in Connaught, forty days on its summit, in prayer and fasting.

Swamp, ⅼꙗṅṅ, ṙꙗṙċ.

Surround (to), cꙩṙ ꙇꙇꙝ꙯cꙩⅼⅼ.

Uplands, ꙗṅꝺꙗꙝṅ, ṙceꙗⅼꝑ.

Use, ꝼeꙩꙝꙝ; pronounced *feyim*.

Very, ꙗn, ṙꙗn, both employed only in composition, as, ꙗn-ꙝꙗꙗċ, very good; ṙꙗn-ꙝꙗꙗċ, surpassingly good; úṙ, very; as, úṙ-ꙗṙⅼꙩⅼ, very low; úṙ-ᵹṅꙗṅꙗ, very ugly; úṙ-eꙗṙḃꙗ, great want.

EXERCISE XXIL

1. God bless your work (ḃꙗꙇⅼ ó Ḋꙗꙗ ꙗꙗṙ ꝺ' oḃꙗꙗṙ—literally, prosperity from God on thy work). 2. In what state is your sowing? 3. My sowing is exceedingly good. 4. Have you the farm cheap? 5. I have the farm cheap; my father had it cheap; and my grandfather had it cheap; and may it never be dear. 6. Is the soil fertile? 7. It is fertile; for, it is irrigated by the water of the lake, which is at the mearing, or the border of the marsh. 8. Have you got sand from the seashore to put on the moory land? 9. No: for I have a sandpit in my own farm, the sand of which is of great use to me for that purpose. 10. Has the ploughshare overcome the stones and rocks of the craggy uplands which bound (are on the border of) your farm? 11. It has, and even the harrow: there is not a rock nor a stone which I have not put into one pile; and I have surrounded (put around) the whole (with) a high ditch and a deep dike. 12. What manure do you put on the land in the time of spring? 13. I put bone-dust. 14. Is not bone-dust dry,

and without nutriment to the earth? 15. No; it is possessed of a certain property (bríġ) which fertilizes the soil. 16. Is there a large oak tree in your farm? 17. There is not, nor even a bush. I cut every bush from the root. 18. See (féuċ) that field how green it it. 19. Was it not always green? 20. It is good to be here. 21. Have you all your corn in stack, and in granary? 22. I have not. This season was very wet. 23. Philosophers say (deir saoiṫe) that a comet brings hot weather (that there is usually hot weather with a comet), but truly this blazing comet (réultan) which was lately with us* was the harbinger of rain and wet weather. 24. When will it be back again to us? 25. It is not easy to tell—ní ḟorus a ráḋ.

* Written in the end of October, 1858.

ELEVENTH LESSON.

ADJECTIVES have their first letter, if aspirable, affected by aspiration, in the same manner as the nouns with which they agree, and arising from the same causes; Ex. Mo Róis ġeal, ḋuḃ, my fair black (haired) Rose; a leinḃ ḋil mo ċleiḃ, fond child of my bosom; Mo ċara ḃuan, ċóir, ḋain-ġean, ḋílis tu, my constant, true, firm, fond friend thou (art); A ċeann ḋuiḃ, ḋílis, O dear head of dark (hair).

The initial in each adjective in these sentences is aspirated on account of the possessive pronoun mo, which, as has been shown (p. 28), aspirates the initial aspirable of nouns.

The same letters, d, t, s, which in nouns are exempted from aspiration, when they come immediately after the dentals, d, l, n, s, t, (See Sixth Lesson, Obs. 2, page 29,) are exempted also in adjectives.

Every adjective in Irish becomes an adverb by placing the particle go before it. To this rule there is no exception

ADJ.	ADV.
Beaċt, trim, neat, perfect, complete.	Go beaċt, perfectly, completely.
Binn, melodious.	Go binn, melodiously.
Caoċ, blind; Latin, *cæcus*.	Go caoċ, blindly,
Crom, crooked, bent; Ger. *krom*.	Go crom, in a bent manner.
Dian, Greek, *δεινά*, *deinà*, vehement.	Go dian, vehemently.
Nuaḋ, new.	Go nuaḋ, Latin, *de novo*; Spanish, *de nuévo*.

Obs.—Adjectives beginning with a vowel take, on becoming adverbs, ḣ, before them, not only after ʒo, but also
after ıſ, it is; ba, or buḋ, it was; ını, not; as,

> Ba ḣ-aṅb bo labaıṅ (*lowrh*) ŕċ, it was loudly he spoke.
> b' aṅb ċ aṅ ſuaʒṅaḃ o'ŋ c-ſaoıŕaċc bo ʒaıṅ.
> Grand was the warning when liberty spoke.
> *Irish Melodies, by John Archbishop of Tuam.*

The adverb whose initial is a vowel, on coming after ıſ,
it is; ba, it was; nı, not; is distinguished from the adjective whence it is derived by the aspirate, ḣ, which it assumes; as, Jſ olc aŋ ſeaṅ ċ, he is a bad man; Nı olc aŋ
ſeaṅ ċ, he is not a bad man; Jſ ḣ-olc bo ċaıŋc ſe, it is
badly he spoke; Nı ḣ-olc bo ċaıŋc ſe, it is not badly he
spoke; Ba ḣ-olc bo ċaıṅ ſe, it was badly he spoke—in
which sentences to—olc, as an adverb, ḣ is prefixed, as well
for euphony as to distinguish it from the adjective from
which it is derived.

THE ARTICLE.

In Irish, there is but one Article, aŋ, the. In the singular number it is aŋ, the; in all cases and genders,
except the possessive case feminine, in which it becomes
ṅa, of the. In the plural it is ṅa (the) in all cases and
genders; as,

	Singular.		Plural.
	Mas.	Fem.	Mas. & Fem.
Nominative and Objective ...	aŋ, the ;	...	ṅa, the.
Possessive ...	aŋ of the ;	ṅa	ṅa. ...ſ
Prepositional ...	(bo) 'ŋ to the ...		ṅa ...

An ḣ is prefixed to the initial vowel of the noun or word
immediately following the form ṅa of the Article aŋ—the
possessive feminine, and all the cases of the plural. Ex.:—

> Aıṅ baṅ ṅa ḣ-aılle oſ cıoŋŋ aŋ ċuaıṅ.
> Where the cliff hangs high and steep.

Literally:—

> On the cliff's top, above the beach.
> Song—"*By that lake whose gloomy shore.*"

Na ḣ-oıʒe, the virgin's, poss. case of oıʒ, a virgin; derived
from oʒ, young; ṅa ḣ-aċaıṅe, the fathers; plural of aċaıṅ; ṅa
ḣ-óʒaṅaıʒ, the young men; plural of oʒaṅaċ, a young man;
derived from óʒaṅ, a youngster, and that from óʒ, young.

The possessive plural, however, which takes ŋ and not h, is excepted; as, ᵭṗéṫ ŋᴀ ŋ-oᵹᴀŋᴀċ, the contention of the youths.

Masculine nouns take after the article in the nominative and objective singular ᴅ, before the initial vowel; as, ᴀŋ ᴅ-ᴀᴅᴀṗ, the father; ᴀŋ ᴅ-oᵹlᴀċ, the young servant man; ᴀŋ ᴅ-ᴀṗᵭ-ṗᵹ, the sovereign king; ᴀŋ ᴅ-ṗᴀŋ, the lamb.

TRIPHTHONGS.

All the triphthongs—ᴀoṗ, eoṗ, ṗᴀṗ, ṗṗ, ṗᴀṗ,—are pronounced long, and differ very little in their sounds from those of the long diphthongs, ᴀo, eo, ṗᴀ, ṗṗ, ṗᴀ, from which they are formed. The sound of each triphthong differs from that of the diphthong from which it is derived in two points—first, in a slight prolongation of the diphthongal sound; secondly, in imparting to the consonant immediately following, on account of its proximity to the slender vowel ṗ, a liquid or slender sound, which otherwise it would not receive.

Ju, though ranked amongst the diphthongs naturally short, is found long in most words into the spelling of which it enters.

ᴀoṗ is sounded like *uee* in Queen, as ṗᴀoṗ *(fuee)* under; cᴀoṗ, *kuee*, crying; a way. Jᴀṗ, is sounded like the diphthong ṗᴀ *(ee)* except that the final ṗ, influences the succeeding consonant, so as to make it have a slender or liquid sound.

Jṗ, *eeyu*, as cṗṗŋ (pr. *keeyuin*, in one syllable), calm.

As the Triphthongs are naturally long, placing the accent over them is unnecessary.

VOCABULARY.

bᴀoṗṗ, wantonness, foolish mirth; from bᴀoċ, soft, effeminate.

bᴀṗṗéᴀᵭ, a cap or hat—any covering for the head; derived from bᴀṗṗ, top; and éᴀᵭ, for eᴀᵭᴀċ, clothing; the top, or head-dress. Italian, *berretta;* French, *barette*, a cap; such as clerics wear.

ᵭeᴀŋŋᴀċᴅ, a blessing; from beᴀŋ-ŋṗᵹ, bless (thou).

bṗṗᵭeᴀċᴀṗ, thanks, thankfulness; from bṗṗᵭe, or bṗṗᵭeᴀċ, thankful.

Cᴀoṗ, and cᴀoṗŋ, weeping, wailing; which in its wild, plaintive

notes is a kind of mournful melody. Latin, *cano*, to sing, to blow, to proclaim aloud. Hebrew, קָנֶה, *kanna*, a reed,

a pipe; and קִינָה, *kina*, a lamentation. Cᴀoṗ, is in the ancient language, properly written cṗ (O'Brien).

Cᴀṗ, also written cᴀoṗ, a way, a road, manner; as, cṗᴀ ᴀŋ cᴀoṗ, what way? How? Greek, κεῖ, *kiei*, he goes, moves; Latin, *cieo*, I move.

Cᴀoṗŋ, gentle.

ṅór, how? in what way? An adverb, compounded of ċa, what; an, the; nór, way, manner.

naoi, a consumption; phthisic; Gr. *χναεῖ, knaei.*

aoi, a dunce, a low fellow; a wicked man, opposed to raoi, a sage, a gentleman; baoi, *adj.*, wicked; buiṅe baoi, a wicked man.

Ouair, a reward.

Duil, desire, wish.

Foil, a while; go fóil, for a while, yet.

Fuair, he found, got; *perf tense of* faġ, get.

Go, that; a conj., *que*, Fr., go, for, to, towards; a prep. Every adjective before which it is placed becomes an adverb. It is not unlike, in this respect, to *con* Italian; as, *con amore*, lovingly.

Maireaḋ (*musha*), *adv*, well then; from ma, if; ir, is; re, it; is commonly spelled maire It is readily distinguished from maire, *máshé*, beauty, grace, loveliness, from its adverbial or interjectional use.

Naoi, nine; Latin, *novem*. An naoi, nine in the abstract; Gr., *ἐννεα, ennea*.

Noċt, to-night; Latin, *nocte*; Gr. *νυχτι, nukti*.

Onórać, honourable; from onóir, honour.

Poll, a hole; a pit; poll-rṅóṅa, a nostril; poll moiṅe, a bog-hole.

Suairc, pleasant, facetious.

Camall, a while; as if cam, time; and aile, or eile, other; yet other time; or a while.

Uair, opportune time, respite, leisure; turn, change.

EXERCISE XXIII.

1. Cia an ṅór táim, a ċara óilir mo ċroiḋe; ir anaṁ biḋeann tu ann ro, agur air an aḋḃar rin, ir maiċ liom gur táinic (came) tu? 2. Tá me go maiċ, go beiṁin, go raiḃ maiċ agad. Beirim buiḋeaċar do Ḋia, ní raiḃ me ċo maiċ a riaṁ (ever; up to this). 3. Cia an ċaoi ḃ-fuil do ṁac a tá pórta—Seamur? 4. Tá re go maiċ a rlainte; aċt go beiṁin tá baoir na h-oige (of youth) go fóil ann a intin (mind). 5. Ní maiċ liom rin; óir ir aḋḃar caoi agur cnaoi, baoir; agur beanann (makes) rí (she, *i.e.*, it; referring to baoir) baoi de neaċ air biċ, a biḋear raoi n-a rciur. 6. An fuair re áit air biċ ann do feilm? 7. Ní fuair, níor ċug (gave) me áit do, de briġ nan riṅṅe (did make, or perform) re an raeḋ buḋ ṁian liom. 8. Oċ, buḋ cóir (just, fit) duit duair a ċabairt (howyrth) óó, mar bí re cóir, ruairc a riaṁ. 9. Maireaḋ, tá duil agam duair a ċabairt do go fóil. 10. Cia an caoi ḃ-fuil Tomár—an buacaii maiċ é? 11. Tá re go h-an-maiċ: Ir reaṅṅ naoi ṅ-uaiṅe é 'na a ḋearḃḃṅaċaii. 12. Ir maiċ liom rin—an ḃ-fuil re le fada man rin? 13. Tá le camal

 maiċ. 14. Cia an caoi b-ꝼuil o' aċaiṟ-ṁóṟ, aguꞃ oo ṁaċaiṟ ṁóṟ? 15. Tá m' aċaiṟ-ṁóṟ maꞃḃ; aċt tá mo maċaiṟ-ṁóṟ, ꝝo ꝼóil a ꞃláinte ṁaiċ. 16. Cia an uaiꞃ ꞃuaiꞃ o' aċaiṟ-ṁóṟ báꞃ? 17. Ꝼuaiꞃ ꞃe báꞃ (ꝼuaiꞃ báꞃ, got death, i.e., died) mí ó ꞃae. 18. beannaċt Oé le ꞃ-a anam; buo ꝼeaꞃ caoiṇ. maiċ, onóꞃaċ é. 19. Cia an uaiꞃ a béioeaꞃ tu ann ꞃo aꞃíꞃ? 20. Ní béjó uaiꞃ agam, tá ꝼioꞃ agam ꝝo maiċ, ꝝo bliaꝝaiṇ ó 'n ꞃuo. 21. beióꞃ 'ꞃ-an baile noċt. 22. Tabaiꞃ (thowar) oam mo baꞃꞃꝝao. 23. Na bioeao oeiꝼiꞃ ċo móꞃ ꞃiṇ oꞃt; tá aꝝao oo ꝼaiċ aṁa; óiꞃ tá ꞃe moċ ann ꞃ-an lá ꝝo ꝼóil. 24. Tá an ꝝꞃian anoiꞃ aiꝝ oul ꝼaoi; aguꞃ tá ꝼioꞃ aꝝao ꝝo tuiteann (ralls) ꞃóiṇ 'ꞃa b-ꝼoꝝṁaꞃ (an evening in harvest) maꞃ ċuiteaiṇ cloċ a b-ꝼoll móiṇe. 25. Iꞃ ꝼioꞃ ouiꞃ. 26. beannaċt leat.

TWELFTH LESSON.

CONJUGATION OF A REGULAR VERB IN THE IMPERATIVE AND INDICATIVE MOODS.

ACTIVE VOICE.

Mol, praise (thou).

IMPERATIVE MOOD.

THE second person singular, Imperative mood, like the third person singular perfect tense in Hebrew, is the root of all verbs in Irish; because it is the simplest form of the verb, and because from it spring, by certain suffixes, all the other moods and tenses.

Present Tense.

SINGULAR.	PLURAL.
1.	1. Mol-muiꞃ, *molmuish* } let us Mol-muio, *molmuidh* } praise.
2. Mol, praise thou.	2. Mol-aiċ, *mol-lee*, praise ye.
3. Mol-ao, *moloo shé*, let him praise.	3. Mol-oiꞃ, *moldeesh*, let them praise.

The terminations uiꞃ and uio are both in use; uiꞃ, in the Imperative, first person plural, is to be preferred to uio, because it perfectly agrees with oiꞃ, the ending of the third person plural which has a settled form; and because it is quite analogical with the Latin ending of the plural of verbs—*mus;* and besides aids the learner to distinguish it from the first person plural present tense, Indicative. The form ᵯuꝺ, however, for the Imperative, is very usual.

INDICATIVE MOOD.

Present Tense.

SINGULAR.	PLURAL.
1. Ⳳol-ᴀⳜᵯ, *molimh*, I praise.	1. Ⳳol-ᵯuꝺ, *molmuidh*, we praise.
2. Ⳳol-ᴀⳜⱃ, *molirh*, thou praisest.	2. Ⳳol-ᴄᴀⳜꝺ, *molthee*, ye praise.
3. Ⳳol-ᴀⳜꝺ ⱃé, *molee shé*, he (or it) praises; Ⳳol-ᴀⳜꝺ ⱃⳜ (*shee*), she (or it) praises.	3. Ⳳol-ᴀⳜꝺ, *molaidh*, they praise.

The Interrogative is formed by putting ᴀⳞ (whether) before the verb; as, ᴀⳞ molᴀⳜᵯ, do I praise?

The Relative form, by adding ᴀⱃ to the root, mol; as, ᴀⳞ ᴄe ᵯolᴀⱃ, he who praises:—ꝼᴀⱃ, for the Future Indicative, after the relative: the ending, ᴀⱃ, is used in other instances whenever emphasis is employed. (See Tenth Lesson, Observation First, after the Future Tense.)

Imperfect Tense.

1. Ⳳol-ᴀⳜⳞⳞ, *wolinh*, I was wont to praise.	1. Ⳳol-ᵯuⱃⱃ, *wolmuish*, we were wont to bless.
2. Ⳳol-ᴄᴀ, *wolthaw*, thou wast wont to praise.	2. Ⳳol-ᴄᴀⳜꝺ, *wolthee*, you were wont to bless.
3. Ⳳol-ᴀꝺ ⱃe, *woloo shé*, he was wont to praise.	3. Ⳳol-ꝺⳜⱃ, *woldeesh*, they were wont to bless.

We promised (Seventh Lesson, page 34) " to treat in a future Lesson about the sound of ᴀꝺ final."

Obs. 1.—As *a general rule,* ᴀꝺ final, in words of two or more syllables, is pronounced, in Munster, like ᴀ unaccented; in Connaught and Ulster, like *oo* (English), or u (long) Irish. This peculiar pronunciation the learner should remember, as ᴀꝺ final occurs almost in every sentence of Irish, read or spoken.

With regard to words of *one* syllable, and their compound forms, the Munster pronunciation of ᴀꝺ final, is adopted not only in the South, but in the West and North of Ireland. Ex., ᴀꝺ, luck; ᵯⳜ-ᴀꝺ, bad-luck, misfortune; bⳜᴀꝺ, food (pronounced as if bⳜᴀ, *beea*); blᴀꝺ, fame, renown; clⳜᴀꝺ, a ditch (formerly spelled, cluⳜ); cⱃᴀꝺ, anguish; ʒeuⱜ-ċꞃᴀᴆ, piercing anguish; buᴀⱺ-ċꞃᴀᴆ, lasting anguish; ꞃeᴀᴆ (pr. *fah—a* short,) length, duration; ᴀⱤ ꞃeᴀᴆ, for the length, during; ꝼleᴀᴆ (*fleh*), a feast; ʒᴀᴆ, peril; ʒꞃᴀᴆ, love; ᴆꞼᴀⱺ-ʒꞃᴀᴆ, intense love; ᴄꞼⱤ-ʒꞃᴀᴆ, patriotism; ꞃᴀᴆ, speaking (Gr. ῥεο, I speak); coṁ-ꞃᴀᴆ, speaking together, a chat; cuⱺⱺ-ꞃᴀᴆ (from cuⱤⱺʒ, a bond; and ꞃᴀᴆ), a covenant; ꞃoⱤ́ṁ-ꞃᴀᴆ, a preface, a prologue; ꞃeᴀᴆ, *shah* (for ⱤꞼ e), yes; and its compound, mᴀⱤꞃeᴀᴆ, well then.

Obs. 2.—In verbs, participles, and verbal nouns, the ending uʒᴀᴆ, is pronounced *oa, i.e.,* uʒ, as if ᴀᴆ were not in the syllable—ᴀᴆ being like *ent* in French verbs, not sounded. This pronunciation of uʒᴀᴆ is common throughout Ireland It is a termination like "*tion*" in English, peculiar to a vast number of words; as, beᴀⱺⱺuʒᴀᴆ (*bannoo*), a blessing—from beᴀⱺⱺuⱤʒ, bless thou; cꞃuċuʒᴀᴆ (*kruhoo*), creating, creation, proof—from cꞃuċuⱤʒ, create thou, prove thou; ʒꞃᴀᴆuʒᴀᴆ (*grawoo*), loving—from ʒꞃᴀᴆuⱤʒ, love thou; ꞃlᴀⱺuʒᴀᴆ (*slawnoo*), salvation—from ꞃlᴀⱺuⱤʒ, save thou.

In Munster and in the South of Connaught—in parts of the counties of Galway and Roscommon—the ending ᴀᴆ of the third person singular imperative, and of the imperfect tense, indicative, is sometimes vulgarly and incorrectly pronounced with a guttural accent like *agh;* as ʒlᴀⱺᴀᴆ (*glonagh,* instead of *glonoo*) ꞃe, let him cleanse; ʒlᴀⱺᴀᴆ (*ylanagh,* instead of *ylonoo*) ꞃe, he used to cleanse; bⱤᴆeᴀᴆ (*beeyagh,* instead of *beyoo*) ꞃe, let him be. (See Seventh Lesson—Imperfect Tense, p 33.)

The learner is at liberty to adopt, in words of two or more syllables, the Munster or Connaught pronunciation of this ending, ᴀᴆ, or eᴀᴆ; viz., that of ᴀ unaccented, or of *oo* (English). But he should be careful not to entertain the not uncommon erroneous impression, under which those who have only a slight acquaintance with the Irish language labour, of imagining that the written language of Munster differs from that of Connaught, because the Irish-speaking natives of the two provinces differ in their pronunciation of some syllables.

VOCABULARY.

Aoḋ (*eey*), Hugh; Mac-Aoiḋ, Mac-Hugh; from which Irish name have sprung—M'Coy, M'Gee, M'Kay, M'Cuy; Hughson, Ua Aoiḋ (the descendant of Hugh), Hughes.

Aos, age, folk, class; Latin, *aetas*; an t-aos óg, the young folk; an t-aos eata, the old folk; aos ceoil, musicians (literally, the folk of music); aos uasal, nobility.

Art, Arthur.

Binne, *adj.*, plural of binn, melodious.

Biotáille, liquor, whiskey, punch; it is a generic name, like the English word liquor, for all the generous liquids; derived from bioṫ, existence, and ail, to nourish, to sustain.

Braic, malt (undistilled).

Brian. Brian; Ua Briain, O'Brien.

Clár, board, table, chapter; clár-éadain, forehead.

Coirce, oats.

Daiḃiḋ, David.

Daoine, plural of duine, a person; Gr. δεινα, *deina*, a person:

Donnchaḋ (*Dhoncha*), Dionysius, Denis.

Éanlaiḋ, birds, fowl; from éan, a bird.

Eilís, Alice.

Eoġan, Owen, Eugene; Mac-Eoġain, the son of Owen; hence, in English, Mac-Keon, Keon, Coyne, Owens, and Owenson—all from the same name in Irish.

Eoġainín, young Owen, or John; Mac Eoġainín, Jennings.

Eoróip, Europe.

Fraince, France.

Fonn, delight, desire, pleasure; a tune, the air of a song.

Iotáile, Italy; from iot, a region; and aille, or ailne, beauty.

Lán, *adj.*, full; *n.*, fulness, a large number; a gathering; the tide, because when it has flowed, the shallows and strand appear all full, like the sea itself. Spanish, *lléno*, full.

Lorcan, Lorcan, Laurence; Naoṁ Lorcan, St. Lawrence (patron of the archdiocess of Dublin).

Laḃrás, Laurence (the martyr).

Maidne (possessive case of maidin), morning; Latin, *mane*; when bn come together, b, for the sake of euphony, is sounded like n; maidne is, therefore, pronounced *moynné*; (n requiring a liquid sound.)

Mart, a beef; the word feoil, flesh, annexed to the names—beef, sheep, swine, calf, deer, gives the Irish term for the meat which these animals supply; as, mart-ḟeoil (beef-flesh), beef; caor-ḟeoil (sheep-flesh), mutton; muc-ḟeoil (swine-flesh), pork; fiaḋ-ḟeoil, venison.

Nóra, Honora.

Orna, barley.

Peadar, Peter.

Preab, dance (thou).

Risdeard, Richard, Mac Risdeard, Richardson, Richards, Dicson, or Dixon.

Roinn, *n.*, a share, a dividend; *v.*, divide, carve.

Saḋḃ, Sophia.

Siġile, Julia.

Síle, Celia.

Sinéad, Jane, Johanna; as Seaġán, is Johannes, John.

Siuḃán, Judith.

Scriall, to read, to carve (fowl).

Suġ, juice; Latin, *sugo*, I suck; *succus*, juice.

Sult, jollity; sultṁar, jolly; go sultṁar, with jollity.

Suḃa, mirth; go suḃaċ, merrily.

'Sé do ḃeaṫa, hail! (it is your life).

Ua, or O, a grandson, a descendant; Gr. υιος, *uios*, a son.

Ua Connaill, O'Connell, the descendant of Connall.

Ua Néill, O'Neil, the descendant of Niall.

EXERCISE XXIV.

'Sé do beaċa, a Ṡcaẑaiṁ, clayṅoṛ a b-ꝼuiḷ ċu? 2. Ċáiṁ ẑo maiċ, ṛiáṅ ẑo ṗaiḃ aṅ ce ꝼiaṛꝼuiẑeaṛ (enquires). 3. Raiḃ ꝼleaḋ móṛ aẑaiḃ a ṗéiṅ, aiẑ ciẑ o' acaṛ? 4. Ḃí ẑo deiṁiṅ:—bṁaṛ aiẑ iċeaḋ aẑuṛ aiẑ ól ẑo ṛulcṁaṛ, aẑuṛ bṁaṅ uile ẑo ṛubaċ ẑo eiṅiẑe na maioṅe; do ṗneab aṅ c-aóṛ óẑ le ꝼoṅṅ aẑuṛ do ṛeiṅoaṛ ceolca Ḷṁṅe. 5. Ca ṁcuo ouiṅe bí aṅṅ? 6. Ḃí deiċ ꝼiṛ óẑa, aẑuṛ oċc mna óẑa. 7. Buo ṛulcṁaṛ aṅ oáil bí aẑaiḃ: b-ꝼuiḷ ꝼioṛ aẑao aiṛ aiṅṁ ẑaċ ouiṅe oe na ꝼiṛ? 8. Ċa, ẑo deiṁiṅ, ꝼioṛ aẑaṁ oṅċu—bí Aoo, Aṛc, bṛiaṅ, Oaiḃio, Ooṅṅċao, Eoiṅ, Seaṁuṛ, Loṛcáṅ, Peaoaṛ, aẑuṛ Ṛiṛveaṅo aṅṅ, maṛ aoṅ le ṛcaiċ (the choice, the best) aṅ baiḷle. 9. Cia ṛiao na mna óẑa: b-ꝼuiḷ aẑao ꝼioṛ aiṅ aiṅṁ ẑaċ aoṅ oiob? 10. Ċa ꝼioṛ—bṛiẑio, Caiclíṅ, Eilíṛ, Ẇaiṅe, Nóṛa, Róiṛ, Saob, Siṅeao, aẑuṛ Siẑile; ṛiṅ e aṅ meuo a bí aṅṅ. 11. Níoṛ ṁóṛ aṅ láṅ a bí aṅṅ. 12. Ċa ꝼioṛ aẑam ṅaṛ ṁóṛ; aċc buo oaoiṅe ṁuiṅcṛeaċa (relatives) ṛiṅṅ uile. 13. Cia ṛuiẑ aiẑ ceaṅṅ aṅ cláiṛ? 14. Ṡuiẑ m' aċaiṛ aiẑ ceaṅṅ aṅ cláiṛ. 15. Aṅ blaṛ cu oe'ṅ m-biocaille? 16. Oo blaṛaṛ oe biocaille. 17. Aṛ ól cu ꝼioṅ ẑo ṛubaċ? 18. O'ól me ꝼioṅ ẑo ṛubaċ. 19. Aṛ ṛabaiṛ aiṛ meiṛẑe? 20. Iṛ ꝼioṛ ṅaċ ṛaiḃ me aiṛ meiṛẑe. 21. Cia aṅ ṅio ꝼioṅ? 22. 'Sé ṛuẑ na ꝼioṅ-ċṛaṅṅ (vine) e, a ꝼaṛaṛ ṛa b-Ꝼṛaṅc, ṛ-aṅ Iocaile aẑuṛ cṛio aṅ Euṛóiṗ. 23. Ḃ-ꝼuiḷ ꝼioṛ aẑao cia aṅ ṅio uiṛẑe beaċa? 24. Ċa ꝼioṛ; uiṛẑe na biocaille a ċiẑ ó ṛuẑ aṅ oṛṅa, ṅo coiṛce ṅuaiṛ oéaṅcaṛ (is made) oí bṛaiċ aẑuṛ ẑabal (g'wal, barm). 25. Aṅ ṛaiḃ aṅ caoṛ-ꝼeoil aẑuṛ aṅ maṛc-ꝼeoil maiċ, ṛeiṅb? 26. Ḃí ẑo deiṁiṅ ṛaṛ-maiċ aẑuṛ aṅṛeiṅb. 27. Cia ẑeaṛṛ (carved) aṅ ꝼiao-ꝼeoil (venison)? 28. Ẑeaṛṛ Séaṛlaṛ (Charles) ẆacAoio. 29. Cia ṛciall (carved) na h-eaṅlaio aẑuṛ na ẑeaṛṛ-ceaṛca (chickens)? 30. Oo ṛciall ṁe ꝼéiṅ. 31. Cia aṅ uaiṛ ro bṛiṛ ṛuaṛ aṅ oáil? 32. Oo bṛiṛmaṛ ṛuaṛ aiṛ aṅ h-oċc aiṛ maioiṅ, 'ṅuaiṛ bí aṅ ẑṛiaṅ ẑo h-aio ṛ-aṅ ṛṗéiṛ.

The English student will please

OBSERVE—That in Irish the Article is prefixed to certain classes of Nouns which in English do not admit its presence

1.—Before *sirnames*, for the sake of distinction or emphasis; as,

Was Walsh here, Raib " an " bpeaċanaċ ann po ?

Walsh was not, but O'Reilly was, Ní paiḃ " an " bpeaċanaċ, (pr. in two syllables *Bĕrhannach*), aċc bí " an " Raġallaċ (pr. *Rhy-alloch*).

Before *titles* or *qualities* ; as, God Almighty, Oia " an " uile-Ċuṁaċcaċ.

2.—Before the names of *virtues* and *vices* ; as,

What is faith, Cao é an níó " an " cneideaṁ ?

What is hope, Cao é an níó " an " boċċur ?

What is sin, Cao é an níó " an " peacaó ?

Patience is good, Ir maiċ í " an " foiġib.

3.—Before *abstract* nouns; as,

Hunger is good sauce, Ir maiċ" an "c-anlan " an " c-ocpur.

When beauty and brilliancy fade from the gems, 'Nuain éaluiġear ó na peobaiḃ " an " rġiaṁ ġur " an " blaċ.

"And from love's shining circle the gems drop away."

—*Irish Melodies.*

4.—Before *adjectives* taken substantively; as,

There is not much between (*the*) good and (*the*) bad ;

Ir beaġ a cá eibin an c-olc aġur an ṁaiċ.

5.—Under this view it precedes numerals, not influencing nouns; as,

It has struck (*the*) two, Oo buail re " an " oó.

It has struck (*the*) three, Oo buail re " an " crí.

6.—Before a noun accompanied by the *demonstrative* pronouns; as,

This man (Irish form, *the* man this), " an " pean ro.

That woman (*the* woman that) " an " bean rin.

7.—Names of countries; as, (the) Spain, " an " **Spain**; (the) France, " an " **Fnainc**;(the) Scotland, " an " **Albain**; (the) Germany, " an " **Allaṁain**; before the name of " Rome," o'n **Roiṁ**; from (the) Rome; before months, as, (the) April, an **Abpain**: mí na **Saṁna**, the month of (the) November.

8.—Before uile, when it precedes a noun, meaning *every*; as, (the) every man, " an " uile ouine; (the) every house, an uile ceaċ.

<hr>

NOTE.—The few analogies of Irish with the Semitic languages, presented to the reader in the foregoing Vocabularies, are not intended as a proof of cognate origin between them and Keltic, but as striking instances of primeval, radical sameness.

KEY TO EXERCISES—

eoċuir na n-Ġnáṫuiġeaḋ.

FIRST LESSON—an céud léiġeann.

EXERCISE I.—an céud Ġnáṫuġaḋ (pr. *gináhoo*).

1. Time and gold. 2. Slaughter and death. 3. The palm (of the hand) and foot. 4. White and blue. 5. A garment and rod. 6. A son and a beloved one (a secret). 7. Thigh and heel. 8. Honey and gold. 9. Fresh and bad. 10. (The) palm and the clenched hand. 11. Lip and the mouth (closed). 12. A sweet poem. 13. Hunger and sorrow. 14. Butter and honey. 15. A day and a month. 16. A bad month, a white (uncultivated) orchard, heavy gold; fine sweet meal. 17. A blue garment; fresh butter; and a melodious poem. 18. A white board; heavy sorrow, and a bad death. 19. Soul and body. 20. A wand (yard, rod,) and gold; fine (pulverized) earth, and fresh meal.

EXERCISE II.—an dara Ġnáṫuġaḋ.

1. A young brood. 2. A white swan. 3. A large swelling. 4. A large paunch. 5. A black cow. 6. A crooked cause. 7. A green top. 8. A long boat. 9. A blind prince. 10. A fond mamma. 11. A rare stalk. 12. A large ship. 13. A clean track. 14. A blue eye. 15. A young king 16. A near order. 17. A large wave. 18. A soft stalk. 19. A sweet tune. 20. A high wave, and a large swelling. 21. A black pig, and a grey (greenish) cow. 22. A soft eye, and a large paunch. 23. A late swan, and a

scanty brood.   24. A white stalk and a soft top.   25. Full peas, and a crooked stalk.   26. A fresh rose, and heavy gold.

EXERCISE III.—ᴀN CRIᵗhᴀḋ ᵹNᴀᵗuᵹᴀḋ.

1. The limb is ailing.   2. The cat and the badger. 3. The left palm (hand) is sore.   4. The country is white. 5. The print is black.   6. The wave is blue.   7. The cat is brown.   8. The son is young.   9. The day is long. 10. The tower is high.   11. The butter is fresh.   12. The table is high.   13. The goblet is bent (crooked)

EXERCISE IV.—ᴀN CCᴇᴀᵗᴀʀᵐᴀḋ ᵹNᴀᵗuᵹᴀḋ.

1. Mil aguſ im.   2. Barr aguſ bunn.   3. Ḃor aguſ mar.   4. Gorm aguſ ban.   5. Ór aguſ tír.   6. Tá an lá fada.   7. Tá* an tír donn.   8. Tá an ríġ óg.   9. Tá an t-orc ard.   10. An capa aguſ an pún.   11. An lá aguſ an mí.   12. An mac aguſ an clan.   13. Tá an cré úr.   14. Tá an gar glaſ.   15. Tá an corn ard.   16. Tá an porg gorm.   17. Tá an tonn mór (no ard).   18. An mac aguſ an ṁam.   19. Olc aguſ úr.   20. Tá an min mín.   21. Tá an dún ard.   22. Tá an ċor fada.   23. Tá an túr olc.   24. Tá an clar mór aguſ ard; aguſ tá an ċlan óg aguſ dil.   25. Cú donn aguſ cat bán.   26. Tá an im úr; tá pun milir.   27. Tá an ḃór úr.   28. Tá ór gann.   29. Tá an bar mal.   30. Tá capa aguſ ór gann.

SECOND LESSON—ᴀN DᴀRᴀ LEIᵹEᴀN.

EXERCISE V—ᴀN CuIᵹᴇᴀḋ ᵹNᴀᵗuᵹᴀḋ.

1. Is the air high?   2. The air is high.   3. Is the day long?   4. The day is long.   5. Is the son sick since yesterday?   6. The son is sick since yesterday.   7. Is the moon white?   8. The moon is white.   9. Is the top of the arrow rough?   10 The top of the arrow is rough.   11. Bread is cheap.   12. Is lime cheap?   13. Lime is cheap.

* As a general rule, the vowel in words of one syllable is naturally *long*, yet we have marked it so, to aid the young student.   When a little more advanced he will not require such aid.

A vowel followed by a double consonant, ll, nn, rr; aa, bunn, conn, gann, is usually short.

14. Have you a shell?　15. I have a shell.　16. Have you any drop?　17. I have a drop.　18. Is there a fit on you?　19. There is a fit on me.　20. Is the son weak? 21. The son is weak.　22. Is the cow alive?　23. The cow is alive.　24. Is the steward sick?　25. The steward is sick.　26. The paste is dear.　27. There is music with (at) him.　28. Is there a drop with you (have you any drop)?　29. There is a fog (a fog is in it.—See Thirty-fourth Lesson).　30. Have you a key?　31. I have a drink here—literally, in this.

EXERCISE VI.—AN SÉ-ṁaḋ ĠNAṪUĠaḋ.

1. Ḃ-ḟuil an bó (vó) bán? 2. Tá an bó, bán? 3. Ḃ-ḟuil an mac, ard? 4. Tá an mac, ard. 5. Ḃ-ḟuil an lá fada? 6. Ní ḃ-ḟuil an lá fada. 7. Ḃ-ḟuil caor agad? 8. Tá caor agam. 9. Ḃ-ḟuil an maor beo? 10. Ní ḃ-ḟuil an maor beo. 11. Bí an maor beo a ṅae. 12. Ní raiḃ re beo a ṅae. 13. Bí re tinn a ṅae. 14. Ḃ-ḟuil tura tinn? 15. Ní ḃ-ḟuil. 16. Tá an mar ceo. 17. Ḃ-ḟuil ceol binn? 18. Seaḋ, tá ceol binn. 19. Do raob re tenn na cruite. 20. Tá ceol raor. 21. Do raob re an reol le barr an ġae.

EXERCISE VII.—AN SEAĊTṁaḋ ĠNAṪUĠaḋ.

1. A branch is not grass.　2. Is there prosperity on you (are you prosperous)?　3. I am prosperous.　4. Have you a flock?　5. I have a flock.　6. Whether (is) the cloud a star?　7. The cloud (is) not a star.　8. Whether (is) the firmament a star?　9. The firmament (is) not a star.　10. What (is) the story?　11. The firmament is up.　12. He has sense.　13. Has he sense?　14. And he has a wish.　15. He has a fish.　16. There is a bridle on him; (or on it).　17. Is there pain on you (are you in pain)?　18. There is pain on me—I am in pain.　19. I have a jaw.　20. There is a jaw on him.　21. There is not a thigh on him.　22. A knife is sharp.　23. A desire with me (is) a bridle, i.e., I wish for or require a bridle.　24. Is there hair on you?　25. (There) is hair on me.　26. (There) is hair on it.　27. Is the harbour up (southward), or back (westward)?　28. The harbour is westward.　29. Is there

slumber on him (is he in a slumber)? 30. There is a slumber on him (he is in a slumber). 31. Death is natural. 32. Death (is) not natural. 33. I have a broom. 34. There is an ear on him. 35. He has a young lamb. 36. The day is cold. 37. The butter is fresh.

EXERCISE VIII.—An t-Oċtṁaḋ Gnáṫuġaḋ.

1. An fíor an sgeul? 2. Ní fíor an sgeul. 3. B-fuil an feur glas? 4. Tá an feur glas. 5. B-fuil feur air an tir? 6. Ní b-fuil feur air an tir. 7. Ní buan feur. 8. An b-fuil iarg raon no daon? 9. Tá iarg daoir. 10. An reult no neul é rin? 11. Ní reult no neul e, ri an iae í. 12. An sgeul é rin, no mian? 13. Is sgeul e. 14. An rrian o rin air an giall? 15! An b-fuil an cluas ruas? 16. Tá mé a ruan, no tá ruan orm. 17. B-fuil ta a ruan, no, b-fuil ruan ort? 18. Tá an meur ruar. 19. Tá an grian ruar. 20. Tá an grian air an rreur. 21. Tá an grian ann neul. 22. Gan lón, gan cariad. 23. Tá an t-uan bán. 24. Tá an piart air an talam (pr. *thawlawv*). 25. Tá an cré (pr. *chré*) ruar. 26. Ní b-fuil ruan air talam. 27. Tá ruan le Dia. 28. B-fuil Dia ann? 29. Tá Dia ann. 30. Sé Dia túr agur déire, bunn agur bair gac uile nió.

THIRD LESSON—An Treas Léiġeann.

EXERCISE IX.—An Naoiṁaḋ Gnáṫuġaḋ.

1. Is (there) great esteem on you, *i.e.*, are you greatly esteemed? 2. I am greatly esteemed. 3. Is the day wet? 4. The day is wet. 5. Is (there) blood in your right eye? 6. There is blood in my right eye. 7. Is it pleasing with you (are you pleased) to come with me? 8. I am not pleased to go with you. 9. Is the tree withered? 10. Is there white wine, and red wine with you (have you white and red wine)? 11. I have white wine and red wine 12. Is the cow fair, the goose white, the swan white, the horse red, the hound old, the wife fond? 14.

They are; it is true that they are. 15. Have you great knowledge? 16. It is true that I am not without knowledge. 17. Have you knowledge (do you know) that a good man (is) worthy (of) regard, and fame, and esteem?

EXERCISE X.—ᴀɴ ᴅᴇɪᴄᴎᴀᴅ ᴈ́ɴᴀᴄᴜᴈ́ᴀᴅ.

1. I am pleased. 2. Is it a pleasure with me, *i.e.*, am I pleased? 3. The cliff is high. 4. Is the cliff high? 5. A blessing from God on you, *i.e.*, God bless you. 6. There is fame on you, *i.e.*, you are famous. 7. (There) is leave with me, *i.e.*, I have leave. 8. The wine is white, and the swan is white. 9. The man is just. 10. Help me. 11. I am withered. 12. He has a wife. 13. Has he a wife? 14. I have a question on you, *i.e.*, I have a question to put to you. 15. Have you a question (to put) to me? 16. I am worthy. 17. There is a hump on me, and I have a harp. 18. It is better with me, *i.e.*, I wish rather you to have a (cᴩᴜɪᴄ) harp, than a hump. 19. There is knowledge with me. 20. Do you know—literally—is knowledge with you? 21. There is esteem on me, *i.e.*, I am esteemed. 22. Are you esteemed? 23. Are you famed? 24. I am not. 25. Is there want on you, *i.e.*, are you in want? 26. Want is on me, *i.e.*, I am suffering from want.

EXERCISE XI.—ᴀɴ ᴄ-ᴀᴏɴᴎᴀᴅ ᴈ́ɴᴀᴄᴜᴈ́ᴀᴅ ᴅᴇᴜᴈ́.

1. I have a right. 2. Have I a right? 3. I have a right (to) it. 4. Have I a right to it? 5. Thou hast a right to it. 6. He has a right to it. 7. I have a question. 8. She has a question. 9. He has a question on you (to put you). 10. Hast thou a question on me? 11. There is esteem on me. *i.e.*, I am esteemed (by others). 12. Am I esteemed? 13. I have esteem (for some one). 14. I have esteem for you—literally—there is esteem at me on you. 15. Have you esteem for me? 16. He has affection for you. 17. Has she affection for you? 18 I have a dislike for you. 19. Have you a dislike for me? 20. He has help (strength) for it, *i.e.*, against it. 21. Has he help for it? 22. He has no help for it. 23. Have not you help for it? 24. He has affection for you.

25. I have affection for you. 26. My secret (treasure), have you love for me? 27. I have love for God. 28. God has love for me. 29. He is a person with (*i.e.*, devoted to, belonging to) God, the young man. 30. The young man is a son to you. 31. Whether is the young man your son? 32. It is better with me (*i.e.*, I consider it better; I'd rather have) fame than gold. 33. I'd rather have sense than gold.

FOURTH LESSON—
an ceaṫaraṁaḋ leiġeaṅ.

EXERCISE XII.—an dóṁaḋ gnáṫuġaḋ deug.

1. What the thing, a boat. 2. Have you a good boat? 3. I like to swim. 4. Do you like to swim? 5. Have you a poor house? 6. I have not a poor house. 7. Alas, thy house is pitiable, but there is happiness in it. 8. Mayest thou have happiness and prosperity for ever. 9. With whom (*i.e.*, whose is) the poor child? 10. With (*i.e.*, belonging to) the man of the house. 11. What reason art thou in this (place *i.e.*, here), so early? 12. Because (the) luck is on the person who is early. 13. Take my hand in thy hand. 14. Pitiable and short is the life of man and full of misery. 15. The life of man is a warfare as long as he is on earth. 16. For God's sake spend a holy life. 17. Who is he—God? 18. Is God in every place? 19. God is in every place. 20. God is good to every person; the sovereign king of heaven, who is, who was, and who shall be for ever.

EXERCISE XIII.—an tríṁaḋ gnáṫuġaḋ deug.

1. B-ḟuil an bo ruaḋ, agus b-ḟuil an laoġ duḃ? 2. Ní b-ḟuil an bo ruaḋ, aċt tá rí buiḋe; agus ni b-ḟuil an laoġ duḃ, aċt liaċ agus fionn. 3. B-ḟuil an leanḃ balḃ? 4. Ní b-ḟuil an leanḃ balḃ? 5. An b-ḟuil aċ aig beul an loiċ? 6. Ní b-ḟuil aċ ann. 7. An maġ é rin, no loċ? 8. Ní maġ é, ni loċ é, aċt ir rliab é. 9. Cad é an dait

Ir ail leat—buiḋe, liaṫ, ruaḋ (no ḋearg)? 10. Ir ail liom an buiḋe. 11. Caḋ e an feiḋm tá againn leir an pleaġ, no an rleaġan? 12. Tá feiḋm móir againn leir. 13. Ḃ-ḟuil ḟuaċt orт? 14. Ní ḃ-ḟuil ḟuaċt orm. 15. An maiṫ leат beoc? 16. An ḃ-ḟuil an feur fliuċ ó ċeo? 17. Tá an feur fliuc ó ċeo. 18. An ḃ-ḟuil agaḋ ḋaṁ agur тarḃ? 19. Ní ḃ-ḟuil again ḋaṁ agur тarḃ, no ḋaṁ allтa, aċт тá aṁain agam bó agur laoġ liaṫ. 20. Caḋ é an daiт тá air an m-buin? 21. buiḋe. 22. Ir maiṫ an daiṫ, buiḋe. 23. Caḋ e an níḋ rliaḃ? 24. Ir cnoc áрḋ, rliaḃ. 25. Tá reun agur roinar orт.

FIFTH LESSON—AN CUIGṀAḊ LEIᵹEAN.

EXERCISE XIV.—AN CEAṪarṁaḊ ᵹNáṪuᵹaḊ ḋeug.

1. Tá an lá breaġ. 2. Bíḋeann an mí ro breaġ. 3. Tá mo ṁac óg. 4. Ḃ-ḟuil mo ṁac óᵹ? 5. Ní ḃ-ḟuil re óg. 6. Bíḋeann re ruar moċ? 7. Ní ḃíḋeann re ruar moċ. 8. Ḃ-ḟuil ᵹaċ fear, maiṫ? 9. Ní ḃ-ḟuil ᵹaċ caт liaт no dub. 10. Tá Oia maiṫ. 11. Cia ré Oia? 12. Cia an níḋ neaṁ? 13. Tá roᵹ air neaṁ. 14. Ḃ-ḟuil an т-aḋ orт? 15. Ní ḃ-ḟuil an т-aḋ orm. 16. Tá an mí-aḋ orm. 17. Ḃ-ḟuil ᵹraḋ aᵹaḋ orm? 18. Ní ḃ-ḟuil ᵹraḋ agam orт. 19. Tá ᵹraḋ agam air Oia; agur тá ᵹraḋ aiᵹ Oia orm. 20. Tá ᵹraḋ aiᵹ Oia air ᵹaċ duine. 21. Ir miṫ Oia air neaṁ agur air тalaṁ. 22. Tá an ᵹorт buiḋe agur bán. 23. Tá an oiᵹ óᵹ agur maoċ. 24. Bíḋeann aḋ air an ṁuinтir maiṫ. • 25. Ḃ-ḟuilir maiṫ 'nuair a тá an т-aḋ orт? 26. Níorr raiḃ an т-aḋ orm a riaṁ, agur fór, ir doiᵹ liom ᵹo ḃ-ḟuilim maiṫ. 27. Ḃ-ḟuil an ᵹrian lonrac? 28. Tá an ᵹrian lonraċ. 29. Ḃ-ḟuil aᵹaḋ arán ᵹeal? 30. Tá; mo faiṫ; agur bajne. 31. Ḃ-ḟuil aᵹaḋ do faiṫ de ᵹaċ níḋ? 32. Tá. 33. Tá тu co fial le flaiṫ.

EXERCISE XV.—AN CUIᵹṀaḊ ᵹNáṪuᵹaḊ ḋeug.

1. Ḃ-ḟuil arán raor, no daor? 2. Tá re raor. 3. Ḃ-ḟuil in daor? 4. Tá re daor, an mí ro. 5. Tá fíon daor; bíḋeann тeoil daor, agur bíḋeann uirᵹe raor. 6. Tá

an aiġ aluin. 7. biḋeann an borb faoi sġeiṁ. 8. Ní biḋeann tu moċ aiġ an teaċ. 9. biḋeann riaḃ air uair ṁoċ aiġ an teaċ. 10. ḃ-fuil tu moċ ó baile? 11. Tá roġ ort. 12. biḋeann anroġ orrċa. 13. Tá an ġeallaċ lonraċ; tá an neul liaċ; tá an lá duḃ; tá an mí aluin. 14. 'Nuair tá me slán, tá roġ orm. 15. Cia an uair ḃ-fuil tu slán? 16. Tá run aiġ an liaṫ. 17. Tá an roċa dearġ. 18. Tá an t-suil liaċ; (liaċ-ġorm, grey-blue, or purple): 19. Tá an cat duḃ. 20. Cia an uair í? 21. Tá se moċ fós. 22. Tá an lá fada. 23. Is ioṁḋa lá annr an ġ-cill orainn. 24. Is ġeárr beaṫa an duine. 25. Tá se mar blaṫ an ṁaiġ: tá se mar ceo! is caṫ é, mar deir Job. 26. Ṁa 'r maiṫ leat, a beiṫ buan caiṫ fuar aġur teaṫ, deir an sean-ráḋ.

SIXTH LESSON—an seiseaḋ léiġeann.

EXERCISE XVI.—an seiscaḋ ġnatuġaḋ deuġ.

1. My sorrow! 2. My destruction! 3. My thousand (times) pitiable. 4. My pulse, and my fair secret love. 5. O, pulse of my heart, my friend, my love art thou! 6. O, partner of my soul it is thou. 7. My friend, right, fond, loving, (art) thou not? 8. I am thy right, fond, loving friend 9. Is your wife, and your son, and the fair, secret love of your heart, with you to-day? 10. They are with me to-day. 11. Where is your husband to-day? 12. He is with me. 13. Is his foot sound (well), or ill now, and his heel and the toe of his (foot)? 14. His heel, and his foot, and his toe are safe; but his head is ailing from time to time, and a pain (is) in his side. 15. The right eye is soft at (with) him. 16. Where is the woman who is un-well? 17. She is here (literally, in this [place].) 18. What thing is on her (what ails her)? 19. Her knee is without motion (motionless, powerless), her back crooked, her ear without hearing. 20. Was there a physician with her from this time yesterday, when your boy was at the house (of) my mother? 21 There was, and he says there

is no cause at all at (for) her to be fearful on (of) death. 22. (Is) this not beautiful weather? literally, (is) not beautiful weather she this?—weather being feminine gender, is referred to by the pronoun í, she (see Seventeenth Lesson, on the Gender of Nouns in Irish). 23. It is beautiful, glory be to God. 24. There is not cold in it, nor fog, nor wind; but every single day is fine; the sun in the heavens (being) without mist, without cloud. 25. Is it better with you, heat or cold—*i.e.*, do you prefer heat to cold? 26. Better with me (I prefer) cold with frost and with snow, than heat and sun(shine). 27. Are your care (those under your charge) and the care of your father, in health? 28. They are, thank you, (may good be to you), and each person who has a good heart. 29. Is your grandfather old? 30. He is not; (there) is no old man nor old woman at all with us; we are all young and healthy.

EXERCISE XVII.—An Seaċtṁaḋ Ṡaoṫruġaḋ Déaṡ.

1. B-ḟuil an fear sean? 2. Ní b-ḟuil se sean, aċt tá an sean-ḟear a bí ann ro a nae anois marb. 3. B-ḟuil an t-sean-bean anns an teaċ? 4. Ní b-ḟuil, aċt tá an ṁáṫair-ṁór anns an teaċ. 5. B-ḟuil agad ṁáṫair-ṁór beo? 6. Tá, agus aṫair-ṁóir. 7. An sean-ḟear a bí anns an teaċ a nae, an e d' aṫair-ṁór a? 8. Is e; agus an sean-bean a tá an ro an juḃ, sí mo ṁáṫair-ṁór í. 9. B-ḟuil agad deaġ-ċroiḋe? 10. Tá agam deaġ-ċroiḋe agus deaġ-méin; óir tá aig gaċ uile deaġ-ḋuine, deaġ-ċroiḋe agus deaġ-méin. 11. An Tiġeanna mo Dia is an d-Tiġeanna e air neaṁ agus air talaṁ. 12. Tá an t-Éireanaċ buan-ṡaoġalaċ. 13. Ciannór b-ḟuil do ċuram, or, an muintir uile a tá faoi do ċuram? 14. Taid an muintir faoi mo ċuram slán. 15. Ciannór a b-ḟuil an meud a tá faoi do ċuram, agus faoi ċuram d' aṫair, agus faoi ċuram d' aṫair-ṁóir? 16. Is ionṁuin liom do ċlú agus do ċáil. 17. Oċ! mo brón, naċ b-ḟuil sonas ort. 18. Oċ! mo ċairṡe, agus mo ṡearc ġráḋ, naċ mór mo ġean ort! 19. Ṁaire, cuisle mo ċroiḋe, blát na finne. 20. Is tu mo brón, agus mo rós; m' onóir agus mo náire; mo beaṫa agus mo bás.

SEVENTH LESSON—

ᴀɴ seᴀċᴄᴍᴀꝺ ᴌejꝼeᴀɴ.

EXERCISE XVIII.—ᴀɴ ᴄ-oċᴄᴍᴀꝺ ꝼᴍᴀᴄuꝻᴀꝺ ꝺeuꝼ.

1. Was his head bent? 2. His head was bent. 3. Was his hand slender? 4. His hand was slender, and his foot was crooked. 5. Was his hair grey? 6. His hair was grey. 7. Was the cow brown or white? 8. She was brown. 9. Was my bull blue? 10. He was not, but he was yellow. 11. Was the woman young, and the man old? 12. The woman was young, and she was under (held in) esteem, and in affection. 13. Your husband was old; and your son will be tall as was his father. 14. Has your daughter a son yet? 15. My young daughter has a young son since yesterday. 16. Thy son was under (held in) esteem and glory. 17. A black hen lays a white egg; literally, there is wont to be a white egg at a black hen. 18. There is (so); and white milk with a brown cow. 19. Was the ear of the horse small; his foot straight; his back long? 20. His ear was small, his back long, his foot straight, and he was yesterday under car (drafting a car) going up the hill. 21. He was not, but he was in my father's house. 22. The music of thy mouth was sweet with me (to me): your voice is so melodious and your tone so high, that I have a desire to listen to it. 23. The person who is up (in high station) is usually under (in) dignity and reputation; and he who is down (in low station) is usually under (in) loss and in want. 24. What is your wish? 25. It is my wish to be under (held in) esteem; and this wish is in my own heart. 26. I had not happiness. 27. His happiness and prosperity is commonly in the hand of each person; for it is a happiness to be good with (towards) every other person. 28. Thy left foot was pretty, and blue was thy right eye; smooth and white was thy hand, and long were thy fingers; thick and in ringlets (ꝼᴀᴉꞃeᴀċ) was thy hair, and resplendent and sparkling was the sight of your blue eyes.

EXERCISE XIX.—an neoċṫao ṡnaċuṡaḋ ḋeuṡ.

1. Raiḃ an aimriṅ ṡaṅb anṅ naċ ṅuaiṅ bi riḃ aiṅ an ṅuiṅ? 2. Nỉ ṅaiḃ; bi an aimriṅ bṅeaṡ, ṡiḃ ṡuṅ ṅaiḃ an ṡaoċ aṅḃ, aṡuṅ an ṁuiṅ ṡaṅb. 3. Raiḃ riaḃ aiṅ baṅṅ an ċnoiċ? 4. Nỉ ṅaḃaḋaṅ aiṅ baṅṅ an ċnoiċ, aċc biḋaṅ aiṡ a ḃunn. 5. Raiḃ cṅeoṅ aṡaiḃ? 6. Nỉ ṅaiḃ cṅeoṅ aṡainn, maṅ naċ ṅaḃaṅaṅ aiṅ baṅṅ an ċnoiċ. 7. Nỉ ṅaiḃ re ḟuaṅ, ṡiḃ ṡuṅ ṅaiḃ ceo aiṅ caoḃ an ċnoiċ. 8 Nỉ maiċ ḷom ceo aiṅ ċnoc. 9. Aṅ ṫ-aṁaṅc ó baṅṅ, caṅ an ciṅ, aṡuṅ caṅ aṅ ṁuiṅ ṅoṅ b' ḟaḋa é 10. Biḋaṅ baiḋ aiṅ an ṁuiṅ, aṡuṅ ḋuiṅe aiṅ an cṅaiṡ, a bỉ an-ḃan, aṡuṅ lonṡ annṅ aṅ ṡ-cuan. 11. Bi an ṡṅiaṅ ḋeaṅṡ a ḋul ḟaoi. 12. Bi an ṡeallaċ láṅ aṡuṅ móṅ, aṡuṅ loṅṅaċ; aṡuṅ bi an rḟaṅṅ ṡoṅṅ, ṡan neul. 13. Ṫá an clú a ṫá aiṡ an ciṅ ro an-ṁóṅ. 14. Aṅ m-bỉḋeann cu ṁoċ aiṡ an ṁuiṅ aṡuṅ aiṅ an cṅaiṡ? 15. Nỉ bỉóiṅ; nỉ b-ḟuiḷiṅ ṅláṅ, aṡuṅ nỉ maiċ ḷom beiċ aiṡ an b-ḟaiṅiṡe ṡo ḋéiṅe an ṫ-raṁṅaiḃ. 16. Ṫá an ṫ-aḋ oṅc a beiċ anṅ ro aiṅ caoḃ an ṡleinn aluiṅe ro. 17. Ṫá aḋ oṅm; aċc maṅ ḋeiṅ an rean-ṅṡeul " bỉḋeann aḋ aiṅ amaḋaṅ." 18. Iṅ ṁian ḷom a beiċ annṅ aṅ ciṅ aluiṅ ro. 19. Beannaċc Ḋé oṅc 20. Sláṅ leaċ.

EIGHTH LESSON—an ṫ-óċṫṁaḋ ḷeiṡeaṅ.

EXERCISE XX.—an ḟiċeaḋ ṡnaċuṡaḋ

1. He who was (in your opinion) good to you yesterday, will be bad to you to-morrow; and he who was friendly with you one time, will be hostile to you at another time, for that is the custom and manner of the world. 2. We will be of one story (united on the same subject) every day, when we be at the shore, or on board taking a sail, listening to the angry ocean spouting its foam on high (to the clouds). 3. A ship under sail on the sea is a beautiful thing to be seen. 4. Is not a swan, swimming on a lake, a pleasing sight? 5. A swan, swimming on a lake, is a pleasing sight. 6. A young child (nestling) in its mother's

bosom is pleasant. 7. Was not the vale that lay stretched out before me delightful? 8. The vale that lay stretched before me was delightful. 9. The proud are usually under beauty, *i.e.*, arrayed in beautiful dress. 10. Is not God good (from day) to-day? 11. God is good from day to day. 12. The street will be beautiful and the house large. 13. Every person has two eyes, and two feet, and two hands, and a head. 14. Is it not fit for every person along the strand, to have a boat, and a ship, and means by which to catch fish? 15. It is fit for every person (living) near the shore to have a boat? 16. What is the price of fish now? 17. Fish is cheap. 18. Have you a beef? 19. I have a beef, and an ox, and a sheep, and a lamb. 20. What price is for an ox, and a sheep, and a lamb? 21. An ox is dear, but the price of a lamb is cheap. 22. I like your conversation (talk) 23. Talk is cheap. 24. Is not self-love blind? (literally, vain love.) 25. Self-love is blind. 26 Is not wine sweet; is not paying for it sour? 27. Wine is sweet; but paying for it is sour. 28. If you like to live old, use hot and cold. 29. It is true for you, but is there not reason for everything? 30. There is reason for everything. 31. Just sit by my side here, and converse (a while) with me. 32. Do you like to be talking with me? 33. I do like it, indeed. 34. Is your young daughter married? 35. She is not, because she has no dower. 36. What age is she—seventeen is it? 37. Yes; she is eighteen since March. 38. What is her name? 39. Jane. 40. May she be safe.

NINTH LESSON—An naoiṁaḋ leiġeaṅ.

EXERCISE XXI.—An t-aonṁaḋ gnáṫuġaḋ aiṙ féin.

1. I am without sister, without brother—without a relative, male or female. 2. Thou art without gold, without silver. 3. She is without bad, without good, (without any thing either bad or good in itself—having nothing at all). 4. Are your brother and sister with your mother

in one house? 5. My mother and my sister are in one
house with me. 6. O, Jane, are you there? O, James
and John, have you love on (for) my mother? 8. Is your
son alive, Eleanor? 9. Where is the son of the honest man
who was here yesterday? 10. The tall woman and the son of
the tall man, are in it from the beginning of the day—yesterday. 11. O Jane, you have borne the sway with you.
12. O long enduring (lived), mayest thou be, bright, secret
love of my heart. 13. Because thou art, O Lord, very
(infinitely) good, I am resolved, from this forward, to
be faithful to Thee. 14. O loving God, O loveliest love
of my heart, my treasure a thousand times, my universal
goodness, I give myself up to Thee, to be under thy
guidance for ever, because Thou art good to me and loving
in my regard, and that Thou deservest my entire
love; from this forward I will love thee from my heart,
and there will never be an end to it, by the help of Thy
holy grace. 15. O treasure of my bosom, how great was
the love you had for your father-in-law, whereas you paid
all that was on him, (all his debts—See Thirty-second Lesson). 16. Is your mother-in-law in the house? 17. She is,
in consequence of her daughter being ill; but she will be
glad, when she will have learned that an honest man like
you was inquiring for her. 18. Her fame and reputation
through the country is great. 19. It is true they are.
20. May she be so from this onward.

TENTH LESSON—an deiċṁaḋ leiġean.

EXERCISE XXII.—an ḋara ġnáṫuġaḋ air fiċo.

1. baile ó Dia air d' obair. 2. Cia annor b-ḟuil do ċur?
3. Ta mo ċur rár-ṁaiṫ. 4. b-ḟuil an ḟeilm raor aġaḃ?
5. Ta an ḟeilm raor aġam; bi ri (referring to ḟeilm,
which is feminine—See Seventeenth Lesson, on the Gender
of Nouns in Irish), raor aiġ m' aṫair; aġur bi ri raor aiġ
m' aṫair-ṁóir, aġur nar raiḃ ri ḋaor ġo ḋeo. 6. b-ḟuil
an cré raióḃir? 7. Ta re raióḃir; óir ta re ḟliuċta

le uirʒe an loić, noć atá aiʒ an ceopain, no air bruać an leain. 8. B-ḟuil aʒaḋ ʒaine o'n craiʒ le cup air an calaṁ riarʒać? 9. Ní b-ḟuil, oir a tá aʒam clair ʒaine ann mo ḟeilm, aʒur ir mór an ḟeióṁ ḋaṁ i air an aḋḃar rin. 10. Ar ḟuair (perfect tense of the verb ḟaʒ, get) an ceaćta buaiḋ air cloća aʒur carraiɟiḋ na rceilpe, a tá air ceopain ḋ' ḟeilme? 11. Ḟuair aʒur ḟór an cliać-ḟuirta: Ní b-ḟuil carraic no cloć nar ćur mé ann aon ćann aṁain; aʒur do ćuirear timćioll an ionlán cliaḋ aṇḋ aʒur ḟail doiṁin. 12. Caḋ é an t-aolać cuireann tu air an calaṁ ann aimrir an earraiʒ? 13. Cuirim luaitre cnaṁ. 14. Naċ b-ḟuil luaitre-cnaṁ tirim aʒur ʒan ruʒ do 'n calaṁ? 15. Ní b-ḟuil; tá briʒ airiḋe ann a ḋeanar an cré, no an uir, raiḋḃir. 16. Naċ b-ḟuil cran mór daire ann ḋ' ḟeilm? 17. Ní b-ḟuil, no ror rʒeać: do ʒearr me ʒać uile rʒeać ó ḃunn. 18. Ḟeuć an maʒ rin naċ ʒlar é? 19. Naċ raiḃ re a ʒ-coṁnuiʒe ʒlar. 20. Ir mait a beit ann ro. 21. B-ḟuil aʒaḋ ḋ' airḃar uile a ʒ-cruać aʒur ánnr an manrać? 22. Ní b-ḟuil, bi an náite ro an-ḟluić. 23. Dein raoite ʒo m-biḋeann aimrir teit le reultan iarballać : aćt ʒo ḟirinneać buḋ tuar ḟartaine aʒur aimrire ḟluice an reultan lonrać bi aʒainn ʒo deiʒionnać. 24. Cia an t-am beiḋ re air air ćuʒainn airir? 25. Ní ḟorur a raḋ.

———

ELEVENTH LESSON—

ᚐN C-UON₥UḊ LEIɟEᚐN DEUɟ.

EXERCISE XXIII.—ᚐN CRIᚐḊᚐḊ ɟNᚐCUɟᚐḊ ᚐIR ḞCᚊD.

1. In what manner (how) are you, O dear friend of my heart? it is seldom you be here, and for that reason (therefore,) I like well that you have come? 2. I am well, indeed, I am obliged to you (literally, may good be to you). I give thanks to God, I was never so well (in such health). 3. How is your son, James, who is married? 4. He is well in health: but, indeed, the folly of youth is still in his

mind. 5. I do not like that, for youthful folly is the cause of grief and pining, and it makes a very wretch of any individual at all that is under its control. 6. Has he obtained any place at all in your estate? 7. He has not; I did not give him a place, because he did not perform the thing which was pleasing with (to) me. 8. Oh, it was right for you to give him a gift, because he had ever been upright and agreeable. 9. Well, I have a wish to give him a gift yet 10. How is Thomas—is he a good boy? 11. He is very well; he is better nine times than his brother. 12. I like that; is he (le ꝼaꝺa—with, *i.e.*, during long) so? 13. He is with—(during) a good while. 14. How are your grandfather and your grandmother? 15. My grandfather is dead, but my grandmother is yet in health. 16. When (what is the hour) did your grandfather die (get death)? 17. He died a month since yesterday. 18. May the blessing of God be with his soul; he was a gentle, good, honourable man. 19. When will you be here again? 20. I will not have leisure again, I well know, till a year from this day. 21. You will be at the home (village) to-night. 22. Give me your cap. 23. Do not be in such a hurry, you have enough of time; for it is early in the day yet. 24. The sun is now going down, and you know that an evening in harvest (time) falls (as quickly) as falls a stone into a bog-lake. 25. It is true for you. 26. God speed you (a blessing with you).

TWELFTH LESSON—

aN ꝺaRa leigeaN ꝺeug.

EXERCISE XXIV.—aN ceaꝓaRꝝaꝺ ꝺNaꝏuꝝaꝶ aiR ꝼiꝺ

1. You are welcome, John; how are you? 2. I am well; may he also who enquires be well. 3. Had ye a great feast last night at your father's house? 4. We had, indeed; we were eating and drinking with pleasure, and we were all merry to the breaking of the dawn (of morn); the

young people danced with delight, and they sang melodious strains. 5. How many persons were in (it)? 6. There were ten young men, and eight young women. 7. It was an agreeable meeting you had; do you know the names of each of the men? 8. I do, indeed, know them; there was Hugh, Arthur, Brian, David, Denis, Eugene, James, Laurence, Peter, and Richard in it, along with the *élite* (ſcαiṫ) of the town. 9. Who are the young women? do you know the name of each of them? 10. I do know; Bridget, Catherine, Eliza, Mary, Honora, Rose, Sabia, Jane, and Celia; that is all who were in it. 11. There were not many in it. 12. I know there were not; but we were all (of) us relatives. 13. Who sat at the head of the table? 14. My father sat at the head of the table. 15. Did you taste of (the) spirits? 16. I did taste of spirits. 17. Did you drink wine cheerily? 18. I did drink wine cheerily. 19. Were you drunk? 20. It is true that I was not drunk. 21. What is wine? 22. It is the juice of the vines that grow in France, in Italy, and throughout Europe. 23. Do you know what thing is uiſᵹe beαṫα (water of life)? 24. I do; water or spirits, that comes from the juice of the barley or oats, when there is made of it malt or barm. 25. Were the mutton and the beef good, rich? 26. They were, indeed, very good, and very rich. 27. Who carved the venison? 28. Charles M'Hugh carved it. 29. Who carved the fowl and the chickens? 30. I carved them myself. 31. At what hour did the meeting separate? 32. It separated at eight o'clock in the morning, when the sun was high above the horizon.

SYNOPSIS OF Táim, *I am.*

		SINGULAR.	PLURAL.
IMPERATIVE. MOOD.		1. —————— 2. bí. 3. bídeaḋ ꞃe.	1. bímíꞃ. 2. bíoꞅ. 3. bíoꞃ.
INDICATIVE MOOD.	**Present Tense.**	1. táim. 2. táiꞃ. 3. tá ꞃé.	1. támuiḋ. 2. taċaoi. 3. táiḋ.
	Present tense preceded by the particles an, *whether;* go, *that;* ní *not;* naċ *not.*	1. b-ꝼuil-ꞅm. 2. „ -iꞃ. 3. „ ꞃé.	1. b-ꝼuil-miḋ. 2. „ -ċí. 3. „ -iḋ.
	Habitual Present.	1. bíð-im. 2. „ -iꞃ. 3. „ ꞃé. bíð-eaṅ mé, tú, ꞃé.	1. bíðmiḋ. 2. bíðċí. 3. bíðiḋ. bíð-eaṅ ꞅiṅ, ꞅiḃ ꞅiaḋ.
	Assertive Present.	1. iꞅ mé. 2. iꞅ tú. 3. iꞅ ꞃé.	1. iꞅ ꞅiṅ. 2. iꞅ ꞅiḃ. 3. iꞅ ꞅiaḋ.
	Imperfect.	1. bíð-iṅ. 2. „ -ċeá. 3. „ -eaḋ ꞃé.	1. bíðmiꞅ. 2. bíðċí. 3. bíðiꞅ.
	Perfect.	1. bíð-eaꞅ. 2. ḃíð-iꞅ. 3. ḃí ꞃé.	1. ḃiamaꞃ. 2. ḃiaḃaꞃ. 3. ḃiaḋaꞃ.

		SINGULAR.	PLURAL.
INDICATIVE MOOD.	Perfect after the particles an, go, ní, &c.	1. rab-ar. 2. „ -air. 3. „ raib ré.	1. rab-amar, or rab-mar 2. -abar, „ -bar. 3. -adar, „ -dar.
	Assertive Perfect.	1. buḋ, or ba mé. 2. „ „ tú. 3. „ „ ṙé.	1. buḋ, or ba riñ. 2. „ „ riḃ. 3. „ „ ṙiad.
	Future.	1. beiḋ-id. 2. „ -ir. 3. „ ṙé.	1. beiḋ-mid. 2. „ -ti. 3. „ -id.
	Conditional.	1. beiḋ-iñ. 2. „ -ceá. 3. „ -eaḋ ré.	1. beiḋmir. 2. beiḋti. 3. beiḋḋir.
OPTATIVE MOOD.		1. go rab-aḋ. 2. „ rab-air. 3. „ raiḃ ré.	1. rab-muid. 2. „ -taoi. 3. „ -aid.
Assertive form.		1. go m-buḋ mé. 2. „ „ tu. 3. „ „ ṙé.	1. go m-buḋ rinn. 2. „ „ riḃ. 3. „ „ ṙiad.
INFINITIVE MOOD.		Do beiṫ. PARTICIPLES. a13 beiṫ.	

☞ Observe in the foregoing Synopsis, that in every tense—Imperative present, Imperfect indicative, Conditional,—in which the first person plural ends in ir, the third person plural also of the same tense ends in ir; and again, in every tense,—Indicative Present, Future; and Optative,— in which the first person plural ends in id, the third person plural likewise of the same tense ends in id. The learner will find this observation useful in endeavouring to remember the personal endings of the different tenses, as the remark holds true for every verb in the language, regular and irregular, as well as for the verb, *to be*, do beiṫ.

PART II.

THIRTEENTH LESSON.

CONJUGATION OF A REGULAR VERB "ᴅo ṁol," *to praise—*
CONTINUED.

INDICATIVE MOOD.

Perfect Tense.

SINGULAR.

1. Ṁol-ᴀꞅ, *wollas,* I praised.
2. Ṁol-ᴀıꞅ, *wollish,* thou praisedst.
3. Ṁol ꞃé, *wol shé,* he (or it) praised; Ṁol ꞃí, *wol shee,* she (or it) praised.

PLURAL.

1. Ṁol-ṁᴀꞃ, *wolmarh,* we praised.
2. Ṁol-bᴀꞃ, *wolwarh,* you praised.
3. Ṁol-ᴅᴀꞃ, *woldarh,* they praised.

Analytic form, ṁol mé, I praised; Interrogative, ᴀꞃ ṁolᴀꞅ, have I praised? or did I praise? and its Analytic, ᴀꞃ ṁol me, have I praised? (See in Eighth Lesson, the several Observations relating to the Perfect Tense of the verb ᴅo beıċ, pp. 38, 39.)

Future Tense.

1. Ṁol-ꞅᴀᴅ, *molfadh,* I will praise.
2. Ṁol-ꞅᴀıꞃ, *molfirh,* thou wilt praise.
3. Ṁol-ꞅᴀıᴅ ꞃé, *molfy shé,* he will praise.

1. Ṁol-ꞅᴀṁuıᴅ, *molfamuidh,* we will praise.
2. Ṁol-ꞅᴀıᴅ, *molfy,* or *molfwy,* you will praise.
3. Ṁol-ꞅᴀıᴅ, *molfwidh,* they will praise.

CONDITIONAL.

1. Ṁol-ꞅᴀıꞁꞁ, *wolfwinn,* I would praise.
2. Ṁol-ꞅᴀ, *wolfaw,* thou wouldst praise.
3. Ṁol-ꞅᴀᴅ ꞃé, *wolfoo shé,* he would praise.

1. Ṁol-ꞅᴀṁuıꞅ, *wolfamush,* we would praise.
2. Ṁol-ꞅᴀıᴅ, *wolfwy,* you would praise.
3. Ṁol-ꞅᴀıᴅıꞅ, *wolfueedeesh,* they would praise.

The Analytic, or simple form, of each tense in this and in every other mood, is conjugated by placing after the *third person singular* in each the personal pronouns, me, ᴄu, ꞃé, ꞃı, ꞅıꞋꞋ, ꞅıꞃ, ꞅıᴀᴅ. Ex.—

FOR THE PRESENT TENSE INDICATIVE.

SINGULAR.

Ṁolᴀıᴅ (*mollee*) me, I praise.
Ṁolᴀıᴅ ᴄu, thou praisest.
Ṁolᴀıᴅ ꞃé, he praises.

PLURAL.

Ṁolᴀıᴅ ꞅıꞋꞋ, we praise,
Ṁolᴀıᴅ ꞅıꞃ, you praise,
Ṁolᴀıᴅ ꞅıᴀᴅ, they praise.

J

FOR THE IMPERFECT.

Ϻolaḃ (*wulloc*) me ; I used to praise.	Ϻolaḃ rinn ;
... ᴄu ;	... riḃ ;
... re ;	... riaᴅ

FOR THE PERFECT.

Ϻol me ;	Ϻol rinn ;
... ᴄu ;	... riḃ ;
... re ;	... riaᴅ.

In the same manner the Future and Conditional Tenses are conjugated. (See Seventh Lesson, page 35.)

The habitual present ends in—aɲɲ: by annexing aɲɲ, therefore, to the root, the *habitual* present is formed; as, mol, molaɲɲ me, I am wont to praise; molaɲɲ ᴄu, thou art wont to praise; molaɲɲ ʃe, he is wont to praise.

So, too, the relative and emphatic forms of the present and future are formed from the root mol, by annexing for the present tense—aʃ; for the future—faʃ; as,

aɲ ᴄe a ṁolaʃ, he who praises ; aɲ ᴄe a ṁolfaʃ, he who will praise.

The personal inflections of the *imperfect* and *conditional* tenses are alike; so are those of the *present* and *future* tenses— except that the *first* person singular future ends in ḃ.

In the second person plural which ends in aiḃ, the vowel ɪ is pecularly long; as, indeed, it commonly is before ḃ (or ᵹ) aspirated.

Obs.—The first letter, if aspirable, of the imperfect, perfect, and conditional tenses, must be always aspirated. So, in verbs, every initial letter that admits aspiration, should it follow—aʃ, ᴅo, ʃo, ᵹuʃ, ma, maʃ, ɲacaʃ, ɲí, ɲioʃ, or the pronouns, a, ɲoċ, in the nominative case,—suffers aspiration.

VOCABULARY.

A'r, contracted form of aᵹuʃ, and.

Aʃaɲ, bread; Greek, ἄρτος. All nouns of two syllables in Irish are accented on the first, a few, like the present instance, (aʃaɲ) excepted : it is commonly pronounced as if written *raan*, but the first a should be slightly sounded.

baɪle, a town, a village ; Latin *villa*.

baɪle móʃ, a large town, the metropolis ; a market town, as opposed to a village. From this Irish word baɪle, are derived all those topographical names in Ireland beginning with the word *Bally, Ballin* ; as Ballingarry (baɪle-aɲ-ᵹaʃʃḃa), the town of the garden, in Ormond; Ballintober, (baile-an-tobair), the town of the well, in Roscommon, and in Mayo; Ballynahinch (baile-na-h-innre), the town of the island. There are many names of places in Ireland spelled commonly, yet incorrectly, with the prefix *Bally*, *Ballin*, that are not derived from baile, a town; but from the compound word—beul-áċa; from beul, mouth; and áċa, ford's; as Ballina, from beul-anáċa; Ballinasloe (beul áċa na rluaṡ), the mouth of the ford of the hosts; Ballyshannon (beul áċa reanaiṡ), the mouth of the ford of the fox.

Bliaṡan, a year; derived, according to Dr. O'Brien, from bel, the sun—the god of the Chaldeans and of the pagan Irish; and ain, a circle; an apparent revolution of the sun during his annual course in the heavens.

bruiċte, boiled, from bruiċ, to boil.

Ceub, first; ceub, a hundred. Ceub, first, has the article an, always before it; ceub, a hundred, has not; as, ceub rean, a hundred men; an ceub rean, the first man; please remember this.

Cloṡ, a bell, a clock; Welsh, *cloec;* from which Dr. Johnson derives the English word clock.

Conn, a goblet, a drinking cup, a tumbler. So called because in days of old, drinking cups were commonly, amongst the Kelts, made of horn (conn); Latin, *cornu;* Conn-aill, the horny cliff; Cornwall.

Col, a hindrance, a prohibition, a disgust; Gr. κολúω, I hinder; col ṡaoil, a prohibition on account of kindred. Col ceaċán, (from col, and ceaċán, four), a prohibition arising from kindred in the fourth degree. Hence col comes, in a secondary sense, to mean, kin, and kindred; col-ceaċán, at present means cousin german, the fourth from the stem, reckoning according to the *civil*, and not the *canonical*, law; col-cuiṡeán, five a kin; col-reirean, six a kin; second cousins; col-monṫerren, seven a kin; col-oċċán, eight a kin, third cousins.

Fáilte, welcome; Latin, *valete*, you are well. Ceub míle fáilte, a hundred thousand welcomes— our national salutation.

Mónán, a great many, much; from món, great.

Muinċin, a tribe, a family, a society; from mo, an old Irish word signifying person; aon, one; ċín, a country.

Muinċreaċ, of the same people, friendly, sociable.

'Na, for iona, than.

Proinn, anciently written praind— Latin, *prandium*—a meal; ceabproinn, the first meal, breakfast; proinnuiṡ, dine.

Suṡcruaó, sugar; from ruṡ, juice, and cruaió, hard.

Cé, tea, (a Chinese word), Fr. *thé.*

Crianoióe, poss. case of crianoió, Trinity; from crí, three; and aonab, one (state, or) nature.

Uar, above, high (*prep*); Uaral (from uar and aill, to educate), noble. Uairle, the derivative of uaral, nobility. Uairle Cireann, Ireland's nobility.

Uaċbar, what is, (uar) up, on top Hence it signifies cream; because the top part of the milk, as iaċċán (from ior, below), means the milk at the bottom of the pail; also the upper leather of a shoe; iaċċán, the sole; in music soprano; iaċċán, *bass*; on high, victorious; as, Lam laiom ann uaċbar, the strong hand victorious—the motto of the O'Briens.

Uaċbarán, a president, a ruler, one in command.

Ub, (*uv*) an egg; Latin, *ovum;* Gr ὠόν.

EXERCISE XXV.

1. Cia an biað ir maiṫ leaṫ a beiṫ aṣað air maiḋin, air do ċeuð proinn? 2. Ir maiṫ liom apán aṣur im; ṫe aṣur uaċðan, aṣur feoil fuair-ḃruiṫṫe ó ṅae. 3. An leiṣfið ṫu ðam ṫé a lionað ðuiṫ? 4. Leiṣfið a'r fáilṫe, ma 'r ṙé do ċoil é. 5. An ṣlacann ṫu ruṣcruað leir? 6. Ṣlacaim; aṣur leir rin, ir maiṫ liom mónán ruṣcruaið. 7. An feánn leaṫ uaċðair 'na bainne? 8. Ir feánn liom uaċðair. 9. Tabair (thower, give) ðam roinn de 'n ċaor-feoil, ma 'r ṙe do ċoil é. 10. Béarfað (I shall give) aṣur fáilṫe. 11. b' feiðir ṣur maiṫ leaṫ ub (egg)? 12. Ni maiṫ liom; ṫá mo ṙaiṫ annr an feoil. 13. Tabair ðam conn an uaċðair, ma 'r ṙe do ċoil é. 14. So é ðuiṫ, aṣur ceuð mile fáilṫe. 15. Cia an uair iṫeann ṫu do ċeuð proinn ṣaċ lá? 16. Air leaṫ uair n-deir an oċṫ; no air an naoi ó ċloiṣ. 17. Cia an uair iṫeann ṫu do lón? 18. Iṫim é air an ðó, no air an h-aon ó 'cloiṣ. 19. Cia biðear leaṫ aiṣ iṫeað an ceuð proinn? 20. Biðeann muinṫir an ṫiṣ, mar aṫá m' aṫair aṣur mo ṁaṫair, mo ðearbḃraṫair aṣur mo ðeirb-ṙiur, mo ċlaṅ mac, aṣur mo ċlaṅ inṣean. 21. Ca b-fuil do ðearb-braṫair Uilliam, an am ro? 22. Tá ṙé ann Aṫ-ċliaṫ, ano-baile mór (metropolis) Eireann. 23. Raib ṫu-ra a riaṁ ann Aṫ-cliaṫ? 24. Biðear; aṣur ṣo deiṁin leaṫ, ir breaṣ, aṣur ir món an baile é: buð ṁaiṫ liom a beiṫ ann ṣaċ bliaṣain air feað do no ṫri mi. 25. b-fuil ðuine air biṫ ann, ṣaolṁar (related to) ðuiṫ aiṣ coṁnuiðe (residing)? 26. Tá; m' aṫair-món, no aṫair mo ṁaṫar, mar aon (along with) col-ceaṫar, aṣur mónan ðaoine muinṫireaċa eile. 27. An colceaṫar ðuiṫ Seamur MacAoið, a ṫá, ma 'r fion é, mar uaċðaran a ṣ-colairṫe (college) na Triaṅoiðe? 28. Ir col-ceaṫar do mo ṁaṫair é, aṣur cul-cuiṣean ðam fein: ṫá-ṙé ṣo deiṁin an-maiṫ ðam; óir bronann ṙe mónan airṣið orm-ra (on me) ṣaċ am' a ṫeiṣim do'n m-baile móir. 29. Ir maiṫ rin; cia an ṫ-am bi ṫu ann Aṫ-cliaṫ? 30. Ta ṙe anoir ṣo deiṁin ṫri mi; aċṫ ṫá ðuil aṣam ṣo m-beiðið ann roiṁ mi eile. 31. A ṫiocfaið (will come) ṫu liom ann mo ṫiṣ fein a noċṫ? 32. Ni maiṫ liom é; ṫá ṫeaċ m' aṫar móir an-ṣar ðam, aṣur raċfað (will go) ann; ir maiṫ le muinṫir an ṫiṣe

(of the house) ᵹo ᶂaɲᶂaɪɲɲ (that I should tarry) acu. 33.
b-ᶂuɪl ᴛu aɪᵹ ɪɲⲥeaⲥᴛ? 34. Ⲧáɪɱ. 35. beaɲɲaⲥᴛ Ꝺe
leaᴛ. 36. Ꙛo ɲaɪb ɱaɪⲥ aᵹaꝺ; ⱄláɲ ᵹo ɲaɪb ᴛu ᶂeɪɲ aᵹuⱄ
ꝺo ɱuɪɲᴛɪⱃ.

FOURTEENTH LESSON.

The relative pronouns are—a, who, which, what; ɲoⲥ,
who, which; ɲaⲥ, who-not, which-not. These are all indeclinable; and cause, when nominative case, the initial
aspirable consonant of the verb to be affected by aspiration.

The particle ꝺo, sign of the past tense, has the force of
a relative pronoun; as, ꝺaoɪɲe ᴛⱃeuɲa ꝺo ᶂuaɪⱃ ɱóⱃ-ⲥaɪl
aɲɲⱄ aɲ ᴛ-ⱄeaɲ-aɪɱⱄɪⱃ, brave men who obtained renown
in the olden time. In this sentence there is apparently no
relative nominative case to ᶂuaɪⱃ, and accordingly, ꝺo,
which immediately precedes it, is regarded, in this and
such cases, as a relative. But sentences of this form are
really elliptical, and can be filled up, as in the present instance, thus: ꝺaoɪɲe ᴛⱃeuɲa " ɲoⲥ" ꝺo ᶂuaɪⱃ ɱóⱃ-ⲥaɪl aɲɲⱄ
aɲ ᴛ-ⱄeaɲ-aɪɱⱄɪⱃ.

The interrogative pronouns are—cɪa, who; ca, what,
where; caꝺ, what—Latin, *quid;* as, caꝺ é? what (is) it?
cⱃeuꝺ, what, what thing; compounded of caꝺ, what; and
ⱃaeꝺ, thing.

Obs. 1.—Such English sentences as—" who am I? who
is he? what is it? what is the matter? what was the
matter? is it he? is it not he? it is not he;—this is the
man"—are translated into Irish by omitting the verb, is,
are, am, was—cɪa ɱɪⱃe? cɪa ᶂe? caꝺ ᶂé? caꝺ ᶂé aɲ ɲɪꝺ?
aɲ ᶂé? (is it) he? ɲaⲥ ᶂe? ɲɪ ᶂe, (it is) not he? ⱄo ᶂe aɲ
ᶂeaⱃ. (See Note, p. 21, and p. 40).

VOCABULARY.

Ⴀꝺaɱ (*Aw-oo*). Adam.

Alone, only, aɱaɪɲ; (solitary)
 aoɲⲥⱃ; from aoɲ, one, and
 ᶂeaⱃ. a man.

Although, ce, ᵹɪꝺ, and cɪꝺ; (as it
 were. the verb cɪꝺ, seeing
 that).

Angel, aɪɲᵹeal.

Anger, ꝼeᴀᴣ.

Always ꞃíoꞃ, ᴣo ꞃíoꞃ; Latin, *semper*; ᴣo ꞃíoꞃ, perpetually; ᴣo bꞃáċ, ever, till the day of (bꞃáċ) judgment; ᴣo buᴀn, lastingly; ᴣo h-euᴣ, till (euᴣ) death; ever, ᴀ ꞃiᴀn, ever, referring to time past; ᴀ ᴣ-coṁnuiᴣe, (from coṁnuiᴣ, abide thou), always, abidingly; ever; ᴣo beo, till the last (beo) breath, ever; ᴣo beoiᴣ, till the (beoiᴣ) end, always, ever.

Author, uᴣbᴀꞃ.

Beginning, ꞇuꞃ, ꞇuꞃáċ (and ꞇoꞃáċ); ꞇuiꞃeáċ, a leader or duke; ꞇuꞃuiᴣ, begin; ꞇoꞃuᴣᴀb (the act of) commencing.

Covetousness, ꞃᴀinꞇ.

Create, cꞃuꞇuiᴣ, from cꞃuꞇ, shape, form.

Dispraise, bío-ṁol, from bí or bíċ, want of; (*dis*, Latin), and ṁol, praise; cᴀin, to dispraise; bío-ṁol, is to give negative praise; cᴀin, to give actual dispraise. "Nᴀ ṁol ᴀᴣuꞃ nᴀ cᴀin ꞇu ꝼéin," do not praise, and do not dispraise yourself.

Envy, ꞇnuċ.

Eve, Ébᴀ.

Gluttony, cꞃᴀoꞃ; cꞃᴀoꞃáꞃ, cꞃᴀoꞃín, and cꞃᴀoꞃᴀꞃᴀċ, a glutton; cꞃᴀoꞃ-ól, drinking to excess; cꞃᴀoꞃ-ꞃluᴣᴀb, (from cꞃᴀoꞃ, and ꞃluᴣᴀb, to swallow) to eat greedily; cꞃoiꞃeáċ, a spear which, as it were, eats up the flesh.

Illumine, to redden, to blush, to ignite, to light,
} lᴀꞃ; Latin, *lux*, *i.e.*, *lu(k)s*, light, loꞃꞃᴀb, ꞃoiꞃꞃuᴣᴀb; beᴀlꞃᴀb.

Kingdom; ꞃiᴣeᴀċꞇ; from ꞃiᴣ, a king, and eᴀċꞇ, a state, condition, an achievement.

Might, cuṁᴀċꞇ; mighty, cuṁᴀċꞇᴀċ; Almighty, uile-cuṁᴀċꞇᴀċ.

Moralist, oibe; beᴀᴣ-oibe

Parents, ᴀꞇᴀiꞃ, mᴀꞇᴀiꞃ; first parents ceᴀp-ꞃinnꞃioꞃ, from ceᴀp (Latin, *caput*) head, chief; and ꞃinnꞃioꞃ, elder, a progenitor (from ꞃinne, elder, and ꝼeᴀꞃ, man).

Pride, uᴀbᴀꞃ; (as if from uᴀ, issue, and bᴀꞃꞃ, superiority, excellence) ciᴀ ᴀn níb uᴀbᴀꞃ, what is pride?

See, ꝼeuċ! I see, ꝼeicim.

Self, ꝼéin; myself, me-ꝼéin; ꞇu-ꝼéin, thyself.

Seven, ꞃeᴀċꞇ; French, *sept*.

Sin, peᴀcᴀb; Latin, *pecco*.

Sloth, leiꞃᴣ.

Source, pꞃíoṁ-ᴀbbᴀꞃ; buꞃ, ꞇóbᴀꞃ.

Tongue, ꞇeᴀnᴣᴀ; Saxon, ꞇuꞃᴣ; Danish, *tunge*; Belg. *tonge*; Dutch, *tonghe*; Latin, *lingua*; French, *langue*; Spanish, *lengua*; Italian, *lingua*. The analogy is very striking.

Vanity, bícṁᴀoin, and bíoṁᴀoiꞃeᴀꞃ (from bí, wanting, and mᴀoin, substance) bᴀoiꞃe; bᴀoiꞃ, wanton folly.

Walk, ᴀiꞃbiꞃ, ꞃubᴀl (pr. *shoo-al*, because i follows ꞃ; bear in mind Obs. 1, p. 2.)

William, Uilliᴀm, (the first syllable is pronounced short), Ṁᴀc-Uilleᴀm, Fitzwilliam; Williams, Williamson, MacWilliam—the Irish name assumed by the Bourkes of Connaught on the death of their chief, William De Bourg, third Earl of Ulster.

EXERCISE XXVI.

1. This is a very fine day (lá ᴀn-bꞃeaᴣ é ꞃo). 2. It is indeed a very fine day. 3. Have we not had (nᴀċ ꞃᴀib ᴀᴣᴀinn) very beautiful weather now for a long time (past)? 4. We have had, indeed, very good weather, as you ob-

serve (map бeɪp cu), this good while past. 5. Has not God been very good to us? 6. Yes, God has been very good to us. 7. Who is good but God alone? 8. Who is God?—you, who know so much (aɪʒ a b-ꝼuɪl aɲ oɪɲeaб rɪɲ eoluɪr), know this question (ceɪrб) well. 9. He is the author and first source of all that are in (on, aɪɲ) heaven and on earth; He is the beginning and end of all that are, or that will be; it is He who created the sun, the moon, and all these stars that illumine the firmament; He always is and abides for ever: Let every tongue sound his praises (praise him). 10. Who is he who praises the Lord always? 11. It is the just man, who knows who God is—how great, how mighty; and who himself is—how poor and vile. 12. What is this world? (caб é aɲ ɲɪб aɲ raoʒal ro?) 13. It is only a vapour that lasts (is) for a little, and then is no more. 14. What is heaven? 15. It is the kingdom in which God reigns in glory; and in which all the blessed praise for ever His blessed name. 16. Are you holy? 17. No; I am not holy. I do not praise myself (me-ꝼéɪɲ) although I like to be good. 18. You know the saying, or the advice (comaɪrle), of the old man—do not praise, and yet do not dispraise yourself; for much praise is bad. 19. What is pride? 20. Pride is sister to vanity—pride is one of the seven deadly sins. 21. Do you know the seven deadly sins? 22. I do (know them)—they are pride, covetousness, lust (бruɪr), anger, gluttony, envy, and sloth. 23. Pride, I see, is the head and root of all—it was the sin of the angels, and the cause of the sin of our first parents, Adam and Eve. 24. I see you are a moralist 25. Who is this coming (aɪʒ ceaċc)? 26. It is my dear and faithful friend, William. 27. Is it he that comes (aɲ é a cá aɪɲ)? 28. It is he; here he is. You are welcome, my dear friend (ceuб mɪle ꝼaɪlce ɲomac, a ċaɲaб mo ċleɪб); how are you to-day? 29. I am well, thank you (buɪбeaċ buɪc; or beɪrɪm buɪбeaċar buɪc) 30. Let us have a walk.

In the two preceding Lessons we have shown how a verb active in Irish is conjugated. In addition to those tenses already given, which, from the employment of a twofold conjugation—the synthetic and analytic—present to every Irish speaker for selection more than an ordinary variety of terms by which every modification of time can be expressed; there are yet others, formed by the aid of the substantive verb, ᴅo ƀeiċ, "to be;" and of the present participle.

Present Tense	… …	ᴛᴀ ḿé ᴀiᴣ molᴀᴆ, I am (a') praising, &c.
Imperfect	… …	ƀi ḿé ᴀiᴣ ᴖolᴀᴆ, I was (a') praising, &c.
Future	… …	ƀéiᴆ me ᴀiᴣ molᴀᴆ, I will be (a') praising, &c.
Second Future	… …	ƀéiᴆ ḿé iᴀʀ (after) molᴀᴆ, I shall have praised, I shall be after praising, &c.

These compound tenses are quite analogous to the compound tense in French; *J'ai parlé*—or the continuated form in English verbs; I was loving.

OPTATIVE MOOD.

SINGULAR.	PLURAL.
1. ᴣo mol-ᴀᴆ, *moladh*, may I praise.	1. ᴣo mol-muiᴆ, *molmuidh*, may we praise.
2. ᴣo mol-ᴀiʀ, *molirh*, mayest thou praise.	2. ᴣo mol-ᴄᴀiᴆ, *molthee*, may you praise.
3. ᴣo mol-ᴀiᴆ ʀé, *moles shé*, may he praise,	3. ᴣo mol-ᴀiᴆ, *molidh*, may they praise.

INFINITIVE MOOD.

(Verbal noun—Ꝡolᴀᴆ, praise.)

ᴅo ṅolᴀᴆ, to praise.
ʟe molᴀᴆ, in order to praise.
ᴀiʀ ᴄi molᴀᴆ, (on the point of praising) about to praise.

PARTICIPLES.

ᴀiᴣ molᴀᴆ, (at) praising; ᴀiʀ molᴀᴆ, on praising; iᴀʀ (after) molᴀᴆ, having praised. (See Tenth Lesson, Infinitive Mood, page 47.)

The Subjunctive Mood is the same in form as the Indicative, taking, however, for present time, ᴣo (that); for past time ᴣuʀ (that); before its tenses.

FIFTEENTH LESSON.

The demonstrative pronouns are—ɼo, this, these; (French,
ce; Hebrew, *zo, zu*) ; ɼɪn, that those; uᵭ, ɼuᵭ, that yonder,
those yonder, that there, those there, or of whom or which
there may be question. It is true, these pronouns ɼo, ɼɪᵾ,
come after the noun, which they help to point out; yet
their demonstrative character is fully attained by aid of
the article (ᴀn, or nᴀ, the) which must always go before
the noun, whenever the demonstrative is to follow; as,
' this man,' is in Irish expressed thus, ' the man this,' ᴀn
ɼeᴀɼ ɼo; ' these men,' the men these, nᴀ ɼɪɼ ɼo.

The emphatic particles, ɼɪ, ɼe, ɼᴀ, (Latin, *ce;* French,
ci), which are manifestly traceable from ɼo, this; ɼᴀn (and
ɼeᴀn), which appears to be derived from ɼɪn, that; are employed after the pronouns personal and possessive.

1st. After the personal pronouns; as, me, I; ɪne-ɼɪ, and
now commonly spelled ɪnɪɼe, I; ᴄu, thou; ᴄu-ɼᴀ, thou; ɼɪ,
she; ɼɪ-ɼe, she ; ɼe, he; ɼe-ɼᴀn, he; ɼɪᵬ, you; ɼɪᵬ-ɼe, you;
ɼɪᴀᵭ, they; ɼɪᴀᵭ-ɼᴀn, they. The emphatic suffix for the
first person plural is—ne (Latin, *nos;* Heb. *nu*, we) ; as,
ɼɪn, we; ɼɪn-ne, we (as it were, we, we).

2nd. After the possessive pronouns: ɪno, my ; ᵭo, thy ;
ᴀ, his, her, their; ᴀɼ, our; ᵬuɼ, your; as, ɪno ᴄᴀɼᴀ, my
friend; ɪno ᴄᴀɼᴀ-ɼᴀ, my friend ; ᵭo ᴄᴀɼᴀ-ɼᴀ, thy friend ;
ᴀ ᴄᴀɼᴀ-ɼᴀ, her friend; ᴀ ᴄᴀɼᴀ-ɼᴀn, his friend; ᴀ ᵹ-ᴄᴀɼᴀ-
ɼᴀn, their friend; ᵬuɼ ᵹ-ᴄᴀɼᴀ-ɼᴀ, your friend ; ᴀɼ ᵹ-ᴄᴀɼᴀ-
ne, our friend.

These particles are placed last, no matter what number of nouns and
adjectives follow the possessive pronouns ; as, my dear, loving, amiable
friend, ɪno ᴄᴀɼᴀ ᵭɪl, ᵹɼᴀᵭɪnᴀɼ ᵹeᴀnᴀɪnᴀɪl-ɼᴀ. If a possessive pronoun do
not precede the noun and adjective, the particles ɼᴀ, ɼᴀn, ne, will not be
employed; as, this dear, loving, amiable friend, ᴀn ᴄᴀɼᴀ ᵭɪl, ᵹɼᴀᵭɪnᴀɼ
ᵹeᴀnᴀɪnᴀɪl ɼo. In this last instance it is ɼo that is employed ; in the
former ɼᴀ. Another Example :

This beloved man, ᴀn ɼeᴀɼ ᵹɼᴀᵭ ɪnᴀɼ " ɼo."
That beloved man, ᴀn ɼeᴀɼ ᵹɼᴀᵭɪnᴀɼ " ɼɪn."
My beloved man, ɪn' ɼeᴀɼ ᵹɼᴀᵭɪnᴀɼ " ɼᴀ."

In the two first lines, the pronouns ɼo, ɼɪn, are demonstrative ; in the
third, ɼᴀ is merely an emphatic particle.

These particles of emphasis are employed after the persons of the verb, in the same manner as after the pronouns.
Ex. :—

I praise, molaim.	We praise, molmuid.
Thou praisest, molair.	You praise, moltaid.
He praises, molaid re.	They praise, molaid.

EMPHATIC FORM.

Molaim-re.	Molmuid-ne.
Molair-re.	Moltaid-re.
Molaid re-ran.	Molaid-ran.

Obs.—Contrast or opposition requires the employment of
the emphatic particles, as is illustrated in the accompanying
Exercise.

VOCABULARY.

Agaid (pr. *eye-a*), the front, the face ; Greek, εἶδος, the appearance ; Agaid, having ain, on, placed before it, has the meaning of ahead, on straight, over ; as, d'imtig re ain agaid, he went on straight, he prospered ; ain agaid na n-uirzce, on the face (over) of the waters. Like the Hebrew, *hal penei*, on the face. Ann (in) agaid, means against ; d'imtig re ann agaid, he went against, he opposed.

Asraim, I entreat, I beseech ; from an, very ; and gairim, I cry out.

Anoruas, Andrew ; Mac-Anoruas, MacAndrew, Anderson, Andrews.

Aonteact, (*én-yacht*), *adv.*, along with, together ; from aon, one, and feact, a turn.

A steac, *adv.*, in, within ; from a for ann, in ; and teac, house.

Ceacoar, either, as if cac, other, any one ; and cirn, between.

Ceile, an equal, a companion—man or woman ; a spouse, a wife, a husband. Ceile, with the possessive pronoun a, his, her, its, mean each other ; ta fuat acu ain a ceile, they hate each other. le (with) ceile, together ; as, beidmid le ceile a baile, we will be home *together*, is applied only to companionship between two ; a g-cuideact, when the number is either two or more than two. O ceile, (from other) asunder ; ta riad o ceile, they are separated ; ta re o ceile, it is asunder ; trid a ceile, through each other ; in disorder ; in confusion.

Corcaig, Cork ; so called because its early foundations were laid by St. Finbar, near a "corcac," or marsh.

Cruine, the world ; *orbis terrae*, the globe ; from cruin, gathered like a ball, round ; cruinig, gather (thou) ; cruinugad, a gathering, a meeting, ; hoarding up, gains ; cruinigteoir, a gatherer, a collector ; cruine-eoluir, a knowledge of cosmography ; cruine-rgriobad, cosmography.

Cuideact, company, society ; from cuid, a portion ; and feact, an act, turn, change. A g-cuideact, together ; beidmuid a g-cuideact, we shall be together.

Cuimin, mindful ; cuimne, memory, remembrance.

Dearg, red.

Doman, the world, in its moral and physical acceptation.

Dreac, the visage ; from deapc, see, look at ; Gr. δέρκω, I see.

Egin, certain, definite, necessary ;

as duine eigin, a certain person; is eigin a ḋeanaḋ, it is necessary to do it.

Fana, a declivity, a slope; le fana, headlong.

Firinne, truth; from fior, true.

Focail, a word (spoken); Latin, *vocale;* briaṫar, a word written, spoken, or conceived in the mind; in grammar, the *verb.*

Garrḋa (pr. *gorry*), a garden; Welsh, *gardd;* from which Dr. Johnson derives the English word, garden.

Ionnos, *adv.*, in order that; compounded of ann, in; which in composition often assumes the form ion; and nós, manner, order.

Leaca, a cheek; Heb. לחי, *lechi*, a jawbone; Ramath-*lechi*, "the lifting up of the jawbone," where Samson slew the thousand Philistines.

Leacanaċ, having a good cheek; fad-leacanaċ, long-cheeked.

Luaḋraḋ, report, fame, notoriety; from luaḋ, to speak openly and frequently, to impute; raḋ, discourse.

Mála, (*mawla*), a bag, mail.

Mala, (*molla*), eyebrow; the slope of a hill; plural, malaiḋ.

Magaḋ, mocking, jeering, humbugging.

Padruic, Patrick; MacPadruic, Fitzpatrick; MacFadden, and MacPadden.

Scoil, school; Greek, σχωλη; Latin, *schola.*

Seorsa, George.

Sibéal, Isabella.

Tarla, it happened; ó ṫarla, since it has happened; whereas.

Tomas, Thomas; Mac-Tomais, Thompson; Thomas, and MacThomas.

Triur, three men, a trio; from tri, three; and fear, a man.

Uiṁal, humble; Latin, *humilis.*

EXERCISE XXVII.

1. Cia ta ann sin? 2. Me-si. 3. Cia ṫusa? 4. Seamus Ua Briain. 5. Tarr asteaċ a Ṡeaṁuis, sé do ḃeaṫa; suiġ sios agus déan do ċoṁraḋ. Is maiṫ liom go ḟeicim ṫu a slainte. Is fada an lá ó ḃi tu-sa agus me-si roiṁ an lae 'n iuḋ, a g-cuideaċt; agus go deiṁin leat tá ḃróid (gladness) orm anois go ḃ-fuilmid-ne ann so le ċéile —tu-sa aig a ḃ-fuil mór-ċéim agus cáil air fead na cruinne; agus me-si, a tá ann so, ann iaċtar na tíre gan-fios gan luaḋraḋ. 6. Oċ, agraim ort, na tosuiġ ċo luaṫ sin, do mo ṁolaḋ; no, se is cóir dam a ráḋ, a maġaḋ fúim. 7. Go deiṁin ni'l (for ni ḃ-fuil) me-si a magaḋ fúṫ; aċt tá me a ráḋ na firinne; tá fios agam go ḃ-fuil tu an-uiṁal agus ní labaroċtaḋ (I shall not speak) focail eile ann do ṁolta (in your praise). Mar dubairt me (as I have said), is fada ó ḃimar-ne le ceile aig dul (going) ann scoile 'nuair ḃimar-ne a teaċ d' aṫarṁoir; beannaċt Dé le n-a anam. Nar ṡiubail tu-sa go leor de 'n doṁain ó ṡin? 8. Ṡiubalas; tá agam mórán le raḋ air gaċ nið

do ċualas (I heard), agus gaċ níḋ do ċonnarcas (I saw), dá m-beiḋeaḋ faill (opportunity) agam real a ċaiteaḋ (to spend) leat. Aċt beiḋ faill agam am eigin eile. 9. An cuiṁin leat, nuair a bi me-si agus tu-sa lá eigin ag siubal amaċ ó baile Corcaiġ, agus duḃrais go m-buḋ ṁaiṫ leat ruaṁ; a's 'nuair bi sinn-ne 'r an uisge, ċainic (came) tonn mór, a ṫug (brought) air filleaḋ leis tu; agus d'imiġis (you went) le fána leis an t-sruṫ no gur ċuirlig tu air ċarraig; ann sin do snaṁas-se do ḋiaiġ agus ṫug a steaċ do 'n traiġ tu-sa leaṫ-beo mar bióir. 10. Is fíor gur cuiṁin liom-sa go maiṫ an lá ud, agus beiḋ cuiṁne agam air go deo; is air an aḃḃar sin, tá agam-sa a ġ-coṁnuiḋe, gean agus cloinn mór oit-sa, buiḋeaċ fa an meud rinne tu dam. 11. Naċ raiḃ buaċaill óga eile linn-ne an lá sin? 12. Bi go cinte (certainly); aċt níor ṁiau le ceaċdar diob dul ann aġaiḋ na b-tonn faoċṁar (angry billows). 13. Buḋ ṁaiṫ do rinndar-san é. O tarla (whereas) gur ċorṫuiġ tu aig cainт orruċu, cia fiaḋ na fir óga a bi ann aon-ḟeaċt linn ann lá sin? 14. Bi Aindriar MacPaḋraic, Seorra Mac Uilliaim, agus Tomás Mac-Domnaill, triur aig a raiḃ fior le rnaṁ go h-an-ṁaiṫ. 15. B-ḟuiliḋ uile beo go fóil? 16. Ní b-ḟuiliḋ; fuair beirt (couple) diob bás; aċt tá Tomás MacDomnall beo fós; agus tá, ní se aṁain 'un a ḟear maiṫ, aċt oide árd-muinte (highly-learned), agus raoi andceimeaċ. 17. Is maiṫ liom sin; an b-ḟuil se a b-ḟad ó ċuailiḋ (heard) tu uaiḋ? 18. Oċ, tá; níor ċualas uaiḋ le cuig bliaḋna. 19. Cia an corairlaċt (like; appearance) duine a bi ann, ionnas go b-ḟeicim an cuiṁin liom é? 20. Bi se 'nn a ḟear árd timċioll ré troiġte; dearg ann a aġaiḋ; lonnaċ ann a ḟuil, rgiaṁaċ, fad-leiceanaċ, a ṁallaiḋ cruin, agus a ġruag air daiṫ an óir, a ḃreaċ reiṁ (mild), tlaċṁar (handsome). 21. Tá fíor agam go maiṫ anois air; is anṁaiṫ an cuiṁne tá agad-sa. 22. Naċ raiḃ deirbṡiur aige d'a n' b' ainm Siḃéal—an fi-sin a h-ainm? 23. Is Siḃéal bi mar ainm airċi. 24. B-ḟuil tu tuirseaċ (tired) deir d' aisriġe (journey)? 25. Ní'lim. 26. Tig linn-ne (we can; literally, it comes with us) mar sin, siubal tríd an garrḋa; tá an traṫ-nona (evening) co breaġ sin. 27. Is maiṫ liom-se é, ma's maiṫ leat-sa. 28. Cinte is maiṫ liom-ṙa é. Cia leir an ġairnḃa ṙo? 29. Liom-ṙa. 30. Feicim gur mór an raor-talṁan (agriculturist) ṫu. 31. Ní bióim leir zo minic, aċt ó am zo am. 32. Tairr a rteaċ agur feuċ air na bláṫaib. 33. Raċfaò a'r failte.

SIXTEENTH LESSON.

Since we commenced our Easy Lessons in Irish, we have omitted to note the gender of each particular noun, because we intended to devote a special Lesson to this subject, and to render it a matter of no difficulty for any learner to know, at a glance, the particular gender of every noun in the Irish language.

In English Grammar sex and gender are so allied that one betokens the other. Whatever is of the male sex is masculine in gender; whatever is of the female sex is feminine in gender; and whatever is of neither sex is in gender, neuter—that is, of no gender. This is the simple, grand, English rule relative to the gender. Lindley Murray has said, and the philosophic error has been taught in all our schools, "that gender is the distinction of sex."

English-speaking students, on not finding gender as readily distinguishable in foreign languages as in their native tongue, laud the beautiful simplicity of English, and cannot at all understand why the languages of other nations should, on the simple subject of gender, differ so widely from that of the Anglo-Saxons.

Gender, however, is even in English, quite a different thing from "the distinction of sex," the latter regards *things;* the former, not things, but their names. For example, we say a *man,* as a living being, is of the male sex—and not male gender: and a *woman,* as a living being, is of the female sex—not female gender; while the word " man," as a mere part of speech, is said to be, not *male,* but, *masculine ;* and the word " woman," not *female,* but *feminine.*

"In English grammar sex and gender are confounded: yet they differ widely. Sex is a natural distinction; gender a grammatical one. Sex appertains only to living things; gender to the names of all things. Sex is limited in its extent; gender extends to all classes of nouns. Sex is, however, a sure sign by which the gender of certain nouns becomes known."—*College Irish Grammar, p.* 52.

This becomes very plain if we take examples from other languages; *child*, as a human being, admits of sex; yet the Greek word for child βρέφος, is neuter gender; in like manner πάδιον; and in German, *das kind*, the child; *das pserd*, the horse, is each of the neuter gender.

Again, sex regards only things that have life; gender extends to names of all kinds, as well to those that do not convey the idea of life, as to those that do.

In the next Lesson we shall see that nouns have gender, though the things of which they are names have not sex.

In Irish there are only two genders—the masculine and feminine.

Our language is, in this respect, quite like that of our neighbours the French, which has only two genders, preserving, it seems, in this singular feature, a trait of its early Keltic parentage.

Nouns are divided into two great classes—those that convey the idea of life; and those that do not.

RULE.—In those that convey the idea of life, the gender of the noun accords with the sex of the object; if the object is male, the noun is masculine; if female, the noun is feminine.

MASCULINE NOUNS.
Proper Names.

Ἀcuil, Achilles.

Ἀǵuirtín, Augustine.

Ἀlirten, and Ἀlirtenin, Alexander.

MacἈlirten, MacAlister.

Aonǵur (*eny-as*), Angus, Æneas.

    Mac Anǵuir, Mac Guiness.

Caoimǵein (from caoin, gentle; and ǵein, an offspring,) Kevin; Naoim Caom-ǵein, Saint Kevin; Latin, *Coemgenius.* From the prefix, caoin, gentle, is derived the family name of the O'Keefes; as, *Seamur O'Caoin*, James O'Keefe.

Cormaic, Cormack; MacCormaċ, MacCormack.

Names peculiar to men.

1. Aċair, father.
2. buaċall, boy; as, buaċall tiǵe, a servant boy.
3. bodaċ, a grown boy, a clown. Ǵeann-bodaċ, a lad; a boy not fully grown,

FEMININE NOUNS.
Proper Names.

Ἀimil, Amelia.

Ἀinǵcaloǵ, Angelica; from anǵeal, an angel, and óǵ, young.

Anna, Anne.

banba, Barbara.

Cáic, Kate.

Caitlín, Little Kate.

Catrina, Catherine.

Lararinǵiona, Lasarina; from laram, a flame, redness, blushing; and fíona, of wine.

luri, Lucy.

Maible, Mabel.

Seiǵöan, (*Shel-yawn*) Julia.

Suranna, Susanna.

Una, Winefrid.

Names peculiar to women.

1. Maċair, mother.
2. Caile, a woman; a stout country woman.
3. Cailín, a girl; caileaċ, an old woman; a hag. Ǵeann-cailín, a little girl. Ǵionnraċ, a grown up girl

4. Oṡan,
   Oṡanaċ, } a youngster.

5. Deaṛb-bṛaċaṛ, (pr. *dherwrá-her*) a brother.
6. Feaṛ, a man.
7. Flaiṫ, a prince.
8. Ríż, a king.

9. Feaṛ-żaoil a male relative.
10. Mac, a son.

Names of brutes.
11. Baṛball, a drake.
12. Seaṛṛaċ, a young colt; a foal.
    Bṛomaċ, a colt.
13. Capall, a pack horse, a hack;
    Gr. καβάλης; Latin, *caballus.*
    Sċáil, a horse.
    Żeaṛṛan, a horse; from the verb żeaṛṛaḋ.
14. Cóileaċ, a cock (l after i is liquid, like *l* in William); as if from coill, watch, attend; and teaċ, a house; Latin, *gallus.*
15. Collaċ, a boar.
16. Fiaḋ, a stag, a hart.

17. Żanball, a gander.
18. Mart, an ox; ḋaṁ, a steer.
19. Reiċe, a ram.
20. Taṛb, a bull.

Names derived from offices peculiar to men.

Ceannuiḋe, a merchant; Heb., *keneyan,* a merchant.
Clabaṛe, a babbler; from clab, the mouth open.
Cruṫuiżṫoiṛ, creator; from cruṫuiż, create; root, cruṫ, form
Dorṛoiṛ, a porter, a doorkeeper; from doruṛ, a door; Gr., θυρα, *thura,* a door.
File, a poet.
Żaḋaiḋ, a thief; from żoiḋ, steal thou.
Manaċ, a monk.
Maṛcaċ, a rider; from maṛc, an

4. Oiż, a virgin; from óż, young
   ainṫiṛ, a maiden; from ain, suitable for, and feaṛ, a man.
5. Deaṛb-ṡiuṛ, (pr. *dhervhoor*) a sister.
6. Bean, a woman.
7. Bean-flaiṫ, a princess.
8. Bean-ṛiożan, a queen; the wife of a king.
   Ríż-bean, a Sovereign Queen
9. Bean-żaol, a female relative.
10. Inżean, a daughter.

Names of brutes.
11. Laċa, a duck.
12. Seaṛṛaċ-laiṛ, a filly.
    Bṛoṁaċ-laiṛ, a filly.
13. Laiṛ, a mare.

14. Ceaṛc, a hen.

15. Cṛáin, a sow.
16. Eiliṫ, a hind, a roe; Greek, ἔλαφος.
17. Żé, goose.
18. Colpaċ, heifer.
19. Caoṛa, a sheep.
20. Bo, a cow.

Names derived from offices peculiar to women.

Bean-altṛa, a nurse; from bean, a woman; (a prefix which, when put before nouns, denotes an agent of the female sex;) and altṛa, a nurse; which is itself derived from ail, support thou.
Coṁuṛsa, a neighbour, is feminine, because it is derived from com, together, and uṛṛa, *a support, a prop;* which is feminine. Neighbours, according to our Irish notions, ought to lend mutual aid to each other.
Peaṛsa, f, a person, is feminine. As it is a word that can be

old Keltic word, signifying "horse."

applied to either sex, its termination causes it to be classed with those that are feminine. Cᴘᴊᴀɴoᴊᴅ, Trinity, is a feminine noun, like its Latin and French equivalent, *Trinitas*, *Trinité*, on account of the termination of the word.

VOCABULARY.

Aᴣᴀʟʟᴀᴊɲ, a dialogue ; Gr. ἄγγελλω, *aggello*, I narrate. Aᴣᴀʟʟᴀɲ Oᴊᴘᴊɲ ᴀᴣ uꞅ Pᴀᴛᴘuᴊc, the dialogue of Ossian and St. Patrick.

Aᴊɲɲ, a name ; in grammar, the noun ; Latin, *nomen*.

Aᴊᴛ́ɲᴊᴣ̇, know (thou) ; Aᴊᴛ́ɲᴊᴣ̇ᴛ́eᴀᴘ, is known.

Aᴍᴀᴊʟ, like to ; from which is derived ꞅᴀᴍ̇ᴀᴊʟ ; Latin, *similis*.

Aᴍ̇ʟᴀᴊᴅ, *adv.*, so ; in that manner ; from ᴀᴍ̇ᴀᴊʟ ; and uᴊᴅ, way.

ʋeᴀɲᴅᴀ, feminine ; from ʋeᴀɲ, a woman ; ʙᴊ, coming together, are pronounced like ɲɲ.

ʋeᴘᴛ́eᴀᴄ̇, a beast, a brute ; from ʋeᴘᴛ́, existence ; or, ʙeᴀᴛ́uᴊᴣ̇, feed ; (Heb., בָּעִיר, *behir*, a brute, from בָּעַר, *bahar*, to devour.)

ʙeuᴘʟᴀ, (from ʙeuʟ, mouth ; and ᴘᴀᴅ, utter,) a language, speech, dialect ; Fr., *parler* ; Italian, *parlare*, to speak ; ᴣɲᴀᴛ́-ʙeuᴘʟᴀ, the common (Irish) language ; ʙeuᴘʟᴀ ɲᴀ ʙ-ꞅᴊʟʟeᴀᴅ, the language of the poets. In modern Irish, ʙeuᴘʟᴀ, means the English tongue, and in this sense, is used in contradistinction to ᴣᴀoʟᴀᴊᴣ, the Irish tongue, *Gaelic* ; as, ᴣᴀɲ ʙeuᴘʟᴀ, ᴣᴀɲ ᴣᴀoʟᴀᴊᴣ, without English or Irish. Sᴀᴄꞅ, Saxon ; placed before the word ʙeuᴘʟᴀ, defines and strengthens its meaning ; Sᴀᴄꞅ-ʙeuᴘʟᴀ, Saxon-tongue, English ; ᴣꞅeuᴣ-ʙeuᴘʟᴀ, Greek-tongue ; ʟᴀᴊʙᴊɲ, Latin ; Fᴘᴀᴊɲᴄᴊꞅ, French ; Sᴘᴀᴊɲeᴀᴄ̇, Spanish ; ᴊoᴛᴀᴊʟʟeᴀᴄ̇, Italian ;

Aᴊʟʟᴀᴊɲᴀɲɲᴀᴄ̇, German, Éᴀʙꞅᴀᴄ̇, Hebrew ; Cuᴊꞅᴄᴊꞅ, Turkish.

ʋoᴊɲᴊoɲɲ, *adj.*, female ; from ʙeᴀɲ, a woman ; and ᴣᴊɲ, offspring.

Duᴀʟᴣᴀꞅ, duty ; from ᴅuᴀʟ, due, inherent right, law.

Coᴊᴛ́ᴄeᴀɲ, common, public.

Dʟuᴛ́, warp ; from ᴅʟuᴛ́, thick, close.

Eᴀʟᴀᴅᴀ, a science ; from eoʟ, as if eoʟuꞅ, knowledge, and uᴊᴅ, a way.

Feᴀɲᴅᴀ, masculine, from ꞅeᴀɲ, a man.

Fᴊoꞅꞅᴀɲ, a male ; from Feᴀɲ, a man, and ᴣᴊɲ.

Foᴊuꞅ, easy ; Latin, *facile*.

ᴣɲé, appearance, distinction ; sex.

ᴣꞅᴀᴍᴊɲeᴀꞅ, grammar ; which, like its equivalent in English, French, German, and Latin, is derived from the Greek, γϱᴁμμᴁτιϰή.

ᴊɲɲeᴀᴄ̇, woof.

ᴊɲᴊᴣᴊɲ, gender, as if from ᴊɲɲᴊꞅ, tell, and ᴣᴊɲ, offspring, generation ; ꞅeᴀɲ-ᴊɲᴊᴣᴊɲ, masculine gender ; ʙeᴀɲ-ᴊɲᴊᴣᴊɲ, feminine gender.

ʟeᴊᴣ̇, read ; Latin, *legé*.

Meuᴅ, size, bulk, number ; cᴀ ᴍeuᴅ, how many, how much ; cᴀ ᴍeuᴅ ᴊɲᴊᴣᴊɲ ᴀɲɲ ? how many genders are there ?

Mᴊɲuᴣᴀᴅ, explanation, a note, a comment ; from ᴍᴊɲ, fine ; ᴍᴊɲᴊᴣ̇, make fine.

Neᴊᴛ́e, things ; the plural of ɲᴊᴅ.

Pᴘᴊoᴍ-ᴘᴀɲᴛ́ᴀ, principal parts ; from ᴘᴘᴊoᴍ, first, principal ; and ᴘᴀɲᴛ́ᴀ, divisions, parts ; ꞅoᴊɲᴊᴍ, I divide. Rᴀɲɲᴀ, also means divisions.

Sgríob, write; Lat., *scribe*; Welsh,   *sol*, the sun; ruil, the men-
   ysgriveny.   tal eye; expectation.
Suil, the eye; rolur, light; Latin,   Scáb, a state.

EXERCISE XXVIII.

Aġallaṁ cíoin ḋa mac-léiġean.

A DIALOGUE BETWEEN TWO STUDENTS.

1. A Ṁartpín, raiḃ tu aiġ rcoil, an jnḋ? 2. Ḃíḋear; ní maiċ liom a beiċ lá ain biċ ó rcoil. 3. Ní cóin do ḟean óg ain biċ, man táin-re, a beiċ lá ó rcoil aġur é ann a ċumar a beiċ ann. 4. Tá ruil aġam go ḃ-ḟuil tu aiġ leiġeaḋ ealaḋan áirḋ? 5. Ṁaire, ní ḃ-ḟuilim, aċt aṁain iaḋ ro a tá coitċean, man tá rgríobaḋ, leiġeaḋ, cruine-eoluir aġur ġraimméir, a'r neiċe de'n t-raṁail rin, man aon le teanġa Sacr-beupla, Ġréuġ-beupla, Ḟraincir, aġur Laiḋin. 6. Tá eolur aġaḋ, naċ ḃ-ḟuil, ain príoṁ-pantaiḃ ġaċ beupla ḋioḃ ro, re rin, tá ḟior aġaḋ ain a roinneaḋ aġur ain a ṁínuġaḋ? 7. Tá; áin ir ropur iaḋ ro aiċnuġaḋ: tá naoi roinne beupla ann; aġur ḋioḃ ro tá ḋa roinn—an ainm (noun) aġur an briaċain (verb)—man inneaċ aġur ḋluċ, aiġ cur ġ·a coṁraḋ aḋn a ċeile (together); aġur ní 'l annir na roinniḃ eile aċt man beiḋeaḋ ḋaiċ aġur ḟuipim (as it were, colour and form). 8. Ciannor a m-beiḋeaḋ ḟior aġaḋ ain " ainm?" 9. Ir ropur do ḋuine ḟior a beiċ ain; oin ainm ġaċ níḋ ḋ' a ḃ-ḟuil cruċuiġċe; no le 'n b' ḟeiḋin linn cuiṁnuġaḋ ir " ainm" í; man tarbanaḋ (for example)—ainmne (names) ḟean aġur ban; man tá Acuil, Aġuirtin, Alartpin, Aonġur, no Caoṁ-ġein Conmac, Eamon, Aimil, Ainġealoġ, no Ḃanba, Blaċnaiḋ no Cáit; no apir ainmne a ḃainnear (that appertain to) le ḟeanaiḃ no le mnaiḃ, taoḃ a n-ḋualġair no taoḃ a rtaḋ; man tá aċain' aġur maċain; riur aġur braċain; dopróin, ḟile, manaċ; no ainmne beaċeaċ,—capall, láin, reanaċ, tanḃ; ann aon ḟocail, ainm ġaċ níḋ cruċuiġċe no le 'n ḟeiḋin ḋuinn cuiṁnuġaḋ, ir " ainm" í. 10. Ca meuḋ ingin ann? 11. Ní ḃ-ḟuil aċt ḋa ingin, re rin ḟean-ingine aġur bean-ingine; aġur ó ċanla, naċ ḃ-ḟuil ó naḋun aċt ḋa ġné ḋuine, ḟirionn aġur boininn; man an ġ-ceaḋna ní ḃ-ḟuil aiġ ainmniḃ aċt ḋa ingin—ḟeanḋa aġur beanḋa. 12. Oċ, tá ḟior aġam go maiċ naċ ḃ-ḟuil aċt ḋa ingir nuain caintimiḃ ain na h-ainmniḃ ro a ċuirear a ġ-cial

ðuınn neıċe beo ; aċc nuaın cnaċcmuıð (we treat) aın
neıċıb naċ b-ꝼuıl beo, cıa an ċaoı a m-beıð ꝼıor aġaınn
aın ınꞃʒın na h-aınme 'nuaın nı b-ꝼuıl ʒné aıʒ an nıð?
13. béanꝼað eoluꞃ ðuıc aın ꞃın aṁ am eıle, nı b-ꝼuıl ꝼaıll
aʒam an ꞃuð. 14. Ann am eıʒın le cᴣaċc beıðıꞃ-ꞃe aʒuꞃ
me-ꞃe a ʒ-cuıðeaċc, aʒuꞃ béıð aʒaınn coṁꞃað aın an
ꞃʒeul ꞃo. 15. bıðeað ꞃe maꞃ ꞃın (let it be so). 16. Aċc,
ꝼan (stay), nıoꞃ ınnꞃıʒıꞃ ðam ꝼocaıl aın an noꞃ le 'ꞃ ꝼeıðıꞃ
ðo ꝼeaꞃ óʒ eoluꞃ ꝼáʒaıl ʒo ꞃeıð aın ʒaċ bꞃıaċaꞃ a ċaꞃlaꞃ
aıꞃ, ann ʒ-coṁꞃað. 17. Leıꞃ ꞃın (with that, withal) beıð
am aʒaınn aıꞃ, uaıꞃ eıle ; nı'l anoıꞃ ꝼaıll aʒam. Iꞃ eıʒın
ðam-ꞃa ımċeaċc ; cá an cloʒ 'ʒ a bualað.

SEVENTEENTH LESSON.

In ascertaining the gender of nouns which are names
common to males and females, and of those which are names
of inanimate objects, the entire difficulty relative to gender
in Irish rests. Inanimate objects have no sex, and therefore,
their *names* in English have no gender. But in all languages,
except English, the names of inanimate objects have a gender—masculine or feminine—which is known from, and
regulated by, the termination of the noun. The gender,
in Irish nouns, is known by the same universal guide.
These terminations, therefore, which point out one class of
nouns as feminine, and another class as masculine, shall be
shown in the following Rules.

Obs.—The learner should know that the vowels in Irish
are divided into two classes (See First Lesson, Obs. 2, page
3), called *broad* and *slender*. The broad vowels, a, o, u,
are pronounced not only full and open, but they impart to
the consonants near which they are placed a broad sound.
On the other hand the slender vowels, e, ı, pronounced according to the notation shown in Lesson the First, impart
to the consonants in union with which they happen to be
pronounced, a slender, liquid sound. Not only do the
vowels in this way affect the consonants in unison with
which they are sounded, but they carry their assimilating
influence to the beginning of the next syllable, so as to
cause the first vowel in the adjoining syllable to be of the

same class (*broad* or *slender*,) as the final vowel in the pre-ceding syllable.*

This distinction of vowels into *broad* and *slender*—leatan agur caol—has never, though resting on the first principles of melody and euphony been philosophically treated, nay, even noticed by English philologists. Yet its use is not foreign to the Saxon tongue; for, c, and g, before the broad vowels, a, o, u, are pronounced—c, like k; and g, like g hard;

a.   o,   u,

as, c,   *cut;*   *cow;*   *cud;*

„ g,   *garden;*   *gone;*   *gun;*

while before the vowels e, i, called slender, the same consonants are pro-nounced soft:

e,   i,

cent;   *ci*der;

*gin*GER.

Rules for knowing the gender of those Irish nouns, which are names of inanimate objects.

[The exceptions are in the opposite column.]

MASCULINE NOUNS.

Rule 1.—All nouns generally, whether primitive, or derivative, that end in a single or double consonant, immediately preceded by one of the three broad vowels—a, o, u—are masculine; as, rac, a sack; bao, a boat; loc, a lough; lúb, a button; fóo, a sod; nór, a manner; cúr, a tower; carb, a chariot, a coach, a litter, a basket; ronar, happiness, prosperity; donar, ill-luck, misery; derived from the *adj.* rona, happy, prosperous; dona, unhappy, bad, evil.

Rule 2.—All verbal nouns ending in ugao, ao, eao, or with any of the broad vowels immediately preceding the final consonant or consonants; as, beannugao, blessing; graougao, loving; dunao, shutting; rineao, stretching.

FEMININE NOUNS.

Exception 1.—All derivative abstract nouns that end in acc (or aco); as, ceanracc, mildness; from ceanra, mild; danacc, boldness; from bana, bold; milreacc, sweetness; from milir, sweet; (root, mil;) raoiracc, freedom; from raor, free; ru5cacc, a kingdom.

Exception 2.—Diminutives ending in ó5 (young); as, crarnó5, a chafer; orbó5, a thumb.

Exception 3.—Some words of one syllable, a knowledge of which can only by study be acquired; as, 5rian, the sun; cor, a foot; lam, a hand; neam, heaven; pian, pain; rliab, a mountain; rneab, a tribe.

Exception.—Verbal nouns ending with a slender termination; as, ruar5alc, redemption; reicrinc, vision, sight; are feminine.

* The learned reader who wishes to see more on this subject of vowel assimilation, will find it well treated in the Atlantis, Vol. I. p. 77, in an article, *Influence of Physical Causes on Languages, Mythology, &c.*, by W. K. Sullivan

[The exceptions are in the opposite column.]

MASCULINE NOUNS.

Exception 1 to Rule 3.—Nouns ending in óιρ, αιηε, αιό, uιό, αιόε, which, although common to males and females, imply offices peculiar to men (See last Lesson).

Exception 2.—Diminutives ending in ιη are of that gender to which the nouns from which they are formed belong; as, cηοιcιη, *m.*, a little hill; from cηoc, *m.*, and cηocαηιη, a very little hill; from cηocάη, a hillock; leαbαιηιη, *m.* a little book, a pamphlet; from leαbαιρ, *m.* a book.

Exception to Rule 4.—Nouns derived from adjectives in the *nominative* case, are masculine or feminine, according to the termination; if the ending is broad, the noun is masculine; if slender, it is feminine; as, αη c-olc, *m.* evil; αη c-ρuαιηc, *f.*, the sweet; ιρ beαʒ eιόιρ αη c-olc α'ρ αη ιηαιc, little (difference) exists between the good and bad; ιηαιc is *fem.* according to Rule 3.

FEMININE NOUNS.

Rule 3.—All nouns generally, whether primitive or derivative, that end in a single or double consonant, preceded immediately by one of the two slender vowels e or ι, are feminine; as, cιρ, a country; oηóιρ, honour: uαιρ, an hour; uαιll, howling; lαραιρ, a flame; from lαρ, ignite; coιρ-céιη, a footstep.

Rule 4.—Abstract nouns formed from the possessive case singular *feminine* of adjectives, are, like the stock from which they spring, of the feminine gender; as, αιlηe, beauty; from αιlηe, for αluιηe, more beautiful; poss. case, sing. fem., of αluιη, beautiful; αιρόe, height; from αιρόe, more high, poss. case, sing fem., of αρό, high; bιηηe, melody, sweetness of sound; from bιηη, melodious; ηιoρ bιηηe, more melodious; ριηηe, fairness; from ριoη, fair; ʒιle, whiteness, from ʒeαl, white: uαιρle, nobility; from uαραl noble.

VOCABULARY.

Attached (fond of), cuιηαηαc; attachment, affection, cuιηαη; from coιη, co, together; Latin, *cum*, with; and ιηeιη, mind.

Architect, αιρό-clocαιηe; ραoιρ-ceαc; from ραoιρ and ceαc, a house; Sαoιρ, free, cheap; one following the liberal arts, as opposed to (bαoιρ) the state of a bond-man. Its secondary meaning implies, one following any trade or profession; and in that sense it is much used as a prefix. Example: Sαoιρ-αιηuιό, a joiner; ραoιρ-cloιce, a mason; ραoιρ-cραη, a carpenter; ραoιρ-cαlιηαη, a husbandman; ραoιρ-ρeoιl, a shipwright. From ραoιρ, is derived a great number of words of which it may be well to instance a few: ραoιρe, a holiday—a day when one is free from servile work; ραoιρρe, *f.*, freedom, cheapness, immunity; ραoιρραcc, *f.*, the state of being free, cheap, &c.; ραoιρρ, a handicraft; ραoιρραc, a freeman; ραoιρρeαcc, *f.*, the act of working at any trade, particularly that of carpenter; ραoιρcuʒαó, *m.*, labouring; ραoιρcuιόe, a labourer; ραoιρcαcαó, *m.*, toil, tillage.

Barry, bᴀᵲᵲᴀ̇ó ; Castlebar, Cuᵲ-leᴀᵹ ᴀ Vᴀᵲᵲᴀ̇ó.

Charity, cᴀᵲᴀᵹċᴀ̇ċ, f.; from cᴀᵲᴀ, a friend ; they are on very friendly relations with each other, cᴀᴊó ᴀᵹċᴀᵲċᴀᵹᴀċ le ceᵲle.

Communion, cṁᵲᵹᴊᵹ, f.; from coᵹ, and ᴀoᵹ, one ; united in one ; the Holy Communion, ᴀᵹ Ɲᴀoᵯ Coᵯᴀoᵯᵹeᴀċ, (the Blessed Sacrament).

City, cᴀċᴀᵲᵲ, f.; metropolis, ᴀᵲó-cᵲċᴀᵲᵲ, f.; the metropolis of Ireland, ᴀᵲó-cᴀċᴀᵲ ᵹᴀ h-Eᵲᵲeᴀᵹ.

Christmas, Ɲoóᴧᴀ̇ċ, m.; from Latin, *natalis*, birth ; French, *noel ;* ' t' is changed into ' ó,' a letter of the same organ ; ' is,' into ' ᴀċ,' the ending peculiar to such nouns.

Estate, inheritance, óᵤċcᴀᵲó ; native land, cᵲᵲ óᵤċcᴀᵲᵲ, *i.e.,* the land of one's inheritance.

Foreign, coᵲᵹcᵲᵲóċ, from coᵲᵹ ; as if coᵹᴀó, war ; and cᵲᵲóċ country—a stranger ; one of a hostile country. Others may be inclined to derive it from cuᵲᵹe, a province, as one of the five divisions of ancient Ireland ; and cᵲᵲc. The former appears the truer, and therefore better.

Fetid, bᵲeuᵹ.

Go, *Irr. verb*, ceᵲᵹ (go thou) ; óᵤl, to go ; ᴀᵲᵹ óᵤl, going ; ċᵤᴀᵲó, went ; ᵲᴀċᵲᴀó, I shall go.

Holy Land, cᴀlᴀᵯ ᵹᴀoᵯċᴀ, pos. case, cᴀlᵯᴀᵹ ; Lat. *tellus.*

Horseback, ᴀᵹ ᵯᴀᵲcuᵲᵹeᴀċċ ; from ᵯᴀᵲc, an old Irish word for horse.

I intend ; I purpose ; I am resolved ; cᴀ ᵲᵤᵹ ᴀᵹᴀᵯ ; or cᴀ óᵤᵲl ᴀᵹᴀᵯ ; ᵲᵤᵹ, a resolution, a mystery ; óᵤᵲl, wish, desire.

Kent, Ceᴀᵹcᵲᵲ, f.; from ceᴀᵹ, head, and cᵲᵲ ; Latin, *Cantium.*

London, loᵹᵹóᵲoᵹ, m.; from loᵹᵹ, a ship ; and óᵲoᵹ, a harbour ; a place of shelter.—Dr. O'B.

Manchester, Ɱᴀᵹᵹᴀconᵹ, the plain of heroes. Its Latin name is *Mancunium ;* formed from ᵯᴀᵹ ᵹᴀ ᵹ-coᵹᵹ ; or from ᵯᴀ, ᴀᵹ cuᵲᵹᵹ, the field of bondage ; Whittaker says its British name is Mancenium ; which favours the former derivation, " the plain of heroes ;" or the following, ᵯᴀᵹ ᴀᵹ ċᴀoᵲᵹe, " the plain of mourning," He calls it " the place of tents," which is incorrect ; for, firstly, ᵯᴀᵹ is not a *place*, but a *plain ;* and *scené*, a tent, is Greek, and not British nor Keltic.

NOTE.—In modern Irish it would be better to adopt the names by which this and other English towns are familiarly known, than endeavour to revive those that are now obsolete. Hence Ɱᴀᵹċeᵲceᵲ, (from the British ᵯᴀᵹ, a plain, and the Saxon, *Caester*, of camps), would not be incorrect Irish.

Mansion, ᴀᵲᴀᵲ, m., a place; Welsh, *aros ;* ᴀᵲᴀᵲᴀċ, full of dwellings, habitable.

Probable, óoᵲᵹċeᴀċ ; from óoᵲᵹ, fancy ; hope ; óoᵲᵹċeᴀċ, hopeful ; ᵲ óoᵲᵹċᵲᵹ, most probable.

Parliament, ᵲeᵲᵲ, f..(pr. *fesh*), as the Parliament of Tara, every third year, ᵲeᵲᵲ Ceᴀᵲᵲᵲᴀċ ᵹᴀċ cᵲᵲeᴀᵲ blᵲᴀᵹᴀᵹ ;—ᵲeᵲᵲ Sᴀcᵲᴀᵹ, the Parliament of England.

Promised, ᵹeᴀllcᴀ.

River, ᴀᵯᵤᵲᵹ, *f.,* (pr. *awan*) ; a word that is found compounded in the names of many places, as well on the Continent, as in England, Scotland, and Ireland. Example—Rhine, ᵲᵲᵹ-ᴀᵯᴀᵹ, the king of rivers ; Rhone, ᵲo-ᴀᵯᴀᵹ, the rapid river ; Garonne, ᵹᴀᵲó-ᴀᵯᴀᵹ, the rough river ; Seine, ᵲeᴀc-ᴀᵯᴀᵹ, the separating river ; the four *Avons*, in England, are derived from ᴀᵯᴀᵹ, river ; the Shannon in Ireland, from ᵲeᴀᵹ, old, and ᴀᵯᴀᵹ, river ; Latin, *amnis ;* Welsh *avon ;* Armorie, *aun.*

Sir. ᴄ⁊ᵹeáⱥⱥ; Ɽáoⱼ; ᴐⱥⱼⱦe ⱥⱥⱤⱥⱡ; and as a title of honour, Ɽⁱⱦⱼⱷe (knight). Ⲧⁱᵹeáⱥⱥⱥ literally means "Lord," same as the Greek term Κύϱιος, *Kurios*, the Latin *Dominus*, or the German *Herr*. Hern : now *Kurios*, or *Dominus*, are the only words, one in Greek and the other in Latin, for the term *Sir*, and though they signify " Lord," as fully as does the Irish word ᴄ⁊ᵹeáⱥⱥⱥ, yet by usage they answer quite naturally the purposes of the English word " Sir." So does " Herr" in German. And in truth what is " Sir," but another name for Sire or Lord ? Why, then, should there be any difficulty in adopting the word, ᴄ⁊ᵹeáⱥⱥⱥ, in Irish, for the same polite use for which the word " Sir," in English, is very naturally employed. The word Ɽáⱼ, or Ɽáoⱼ, a man of letters, is also sometimes used in Irish to answer the purposes of the English term " Sir." So is the word ᴐⱥⱼⱦe ⱥⱥⱤⱥⱡ,

gentleman. Let the learner, then, select whichever he pleases. Ⱥáoⱼ is short and simple, and, if generally adopted, would answer very well all the ends of modern etiquette. Ⲧⁱᵹeáⱥⱥⱥ is, perhaps, the fittest word, as it has analogy in the learned languages to support its use in ours ; and if our tongue became common, this would appear very soon a natural and a very correct form of address

Stephen, Ⱥᴄeⱥⱥⱥ ; Ⲙⱥc-Ⱥᴄeⱥⱥⱼⱥ, Fitzstephens ; Stephenson; Ⱨⱥoⱥ Ⱥᴄeⱥⱥⱥ, St. Stephen.

Thames, Ⲧⱥⱥ-ⱥⱼⱤᵹ, f., from ᴄⱥⱥ, still, sluggish, placid ; and ⱥⱼⱤᵹe, water. From this latter are derived the word *whiskey;* and those names of English, Welsh, and Scotch rivers and towns that have the prefix *esk, axe, exe, ox, ush, ax* ; as Hexham, the town or hamlet on the water; Oxford is ȺⱼᵹⱤⱥⱼᴐ, *i.e.,— Waterford,—*O'Brien.

<h3 style="text-align:center">EXERCISE XXIX.</h3>

1. You are welcome, Charles, (ceⱥᴐ ⱥⱼⱡe Ɽáⱼⱡce ⱥⱥⱥⱥ, ⱥ ShⱥⱥⱡⱥⱼⱤ,) how are you? 2. I am well, thank you. 3. I am glad, really, to see you in good health, (ᴄⱥ ⱷⱤⱥⱼᴐ oⱥⱥ ᵹo ᴐeⱼⱥⱼⱥ ᵹo ⱷ-Ɽⱥⱼⱡ ᴄⱥ ⱥ Ɽⱡáⱼⱥce ⱥⱥⱼᴄ). 4. How have you travelled (Ɽⱼⱥⱥe ᴄⱥ ⱥⱼⱤᴐⱼⱥ) to-day—was it on horseback (ⱥⱼᵹ ⱥⱥⱥcⱥⱼᵹeáᴄᴄ), or on foot (ⱥo, ⱥⱼⱤ ᴄoⱼⱤ)? 5. I travelled in the old style (ⱥⱼⱤ ⱥⱥ ᴄ-Ɽeⱥⱥ ᵹⱥáⱤ), on foot. 6. How are all your friends at home, your father and mother, your brother John, and your sister Julia, and your cousin James Johnson (Ⲙⱥcⱥeⱥᵹⱥⱼⱥ)? 7. They are all well, thanks to God (ᴄáⱼᴐ ⱥⱼⱡe ⱥ Ɽⱡáⱼⱥce ⱥⱥⱼᴄ, ⱥⱥⱼᴐeⱥᴄⱥⱤ ᴐo Ⱥⱥⱼⱥ). 8. How is your brother Andrew, is he well? 9. I do not know how he is at present (ⱥⱼ 'l ⱤⱼoⱤ ⱥᵹⱥⱥ cⱼⱥⱥⱥoⱤ ⱥ ⱷ-Ɽⱥⱼⱡ Ɽe ⱥⱥoⱼⱤ), for I have not heard from him these three months (le [with, during] ᴄⱤⱼ ⱥⱼ). 10. I wonder at that (ᴄⱥ 'oⱥᵹⱥⱥ [*eenna*] oⱥⱥ Ɽⱥoⱼ Ɽⱼⱥ), because

he was so fond of you, and so much attached (cumaṅaċ) to his relatives, that I thought (ᵹuṅ ḟaoıl me) he would not allow one month even (ṅaċ leıᵹḟaḃ ṙe aoṅ ṁı aṁaıṅ) to pass by (ċapṫ) without writing to you, or to your father or mother. 11. It is true he was always kind and affectionate, and very good to me: I cannot account for this silence (aᵹuṙ ṅı ċıᵹ lıom-ṙa aoṅ ḟaċ a ċaḃaıṅṫ aıṅ aṅ ṙoṙḃ ṙo), any other way, than by supposing what is truly said of many others, is true of him also, (aċṫ aṁaıṅ ᵹo ḃ-ḟuıl aṅ ṅıḃ a ḃuḃṙaḃ aıṅ moṅáṅ eıle, ḟıoṅ aıṅ-ṙaṅ maṙ aṅ ᵹ-ceaḃṅa); "out of sight out of mind" (aṙ aṁaṅc aṙ cuıṁṅe). 12. Where was he when you heard from him on the last occasion? (Ca aṅ áıṫ a ṙaıḃ ṙe, 'ṅ uaıṙ ḃo ċualaıṙ uaıḃe (ooy-a) aṅ am ḃeıᵹıoṅoċ?) 13. He was in London ; and he said that he intended to go to France, thence along to the Rhine ; to cross the Alps, (ṅa ḣ-Aılṗ) and visit Italy. 14. Oh! I see; It is very probable ('ṙe ıṙ ḃoıᵹċıᵹ) that he is at present taking his intended tour (aıᵹ ḃċaṅaḃ aṅ aıṙ-ḃıṅ aıṅ a laḃaıṅ ṙé) through Europe; he may go to the Holy Land, for one is not learned till he go to foreign lands (ıṅ muıṅce ᵹo coıᵹcṙıoċ). 15. No, he does not, for he promised to be home at Christmas, (ḃo ᵹeall ṙe 'ḃeıċ ṙ-aṅ m-baıle aıᵹ aṅ Noḃlac). 16. Have *you* (ṫuṙa) ever travelled far beyond your native country? 17. I never went (ṅıoṙ ċuaıḃ mé a ṙıaṁ ċaṙ) further than London and Kent. I left London, and the banks of that sluggish, fetid river, the Thames, a year ago. 18. Have you been at the new Parliament House (ṫeaċ ṅuaḃ ṅa ḟeıṙe)? 19. Yes; I have been at the Parliament House—as well in the House of Lords as the House of Commons (a ṫeaċ ṅa ḃ-Tıᵹeaṙṅaıḃ aᵹuṙ a ṫeaċ ṅa ᵹ-coıṫċeaṅ). 20. Is not the new House a grand building, well worthy of Sir Charles Barry the architect, and of the age in which we live? (Naċ maıṙeaċ aṅ caṙṅ oıḃṙe ṫeaċ ṅuaḃ ṅa Feıṙe,—obaıṅ ḟıuṅṫaċ ṅı ṙe aṁaıṅ ḃo 'ṅ Rıoıṙe Séaṙlaṙ a ḃṙaṙṙaıḃ a cuṁ e, aċṫ ḃo 'ṅ aoıṙ aṅṅ a ḃ-ḟuılmıḃ?) 21. Were you in St. Stephen's Hall? 22. I was; it is superb. 23. By what route did you return from London? 24. I made Manchester my way; for I intended to see some friends of mine who resided there, and who have always been friendly-disposed towards my father's family (a bí a ʒ-comnuió an-ċapanċac le muinċip m' aċap). 25. I suppose you are quite well acquainted with the topography of every leading town in England ? 26. Indeed, no ; I assuré you I have never left my own country save once; I am fond of (ca ʒpaó aʒam aip) her fields (a ʒoinċib), and plains (maʒaib), her glens (a ʒleanċaib), her lakes, and her mountains (a ṙiabċaib); give me a vale in the sunny south, with a neat mansion, and I care not for the gold and wealth of London (cabaip bam cumap a Ḋumáin ċeiċ aʒur bíl bionn aʒam aip óp aʒur maon Loinʒóin).

EIGHTEENTH LESSON.

For the learner's sake we endeavoured, and have done so with some success, to write all the Exercises hitherto given in our Lessons without introducing an element which, like aspiration, is so peculiar to Irish, that it may well be deemed essential to it.

This element, though, in its present form, peculiar to Gaelic alone, is not foreign to other languages. The learned who write of the Sanscrit 'tongue, say that Gaelic, in the phonetic laws that regulate its consonantal changes, is analogous to those of *Shandi*, or conjunction, by which consonants at the end, and sometimes at the beginning, of words in that language, have their sounds suppressed for those of cognate letters. In Greek, Latin, German, this change of consonants is chiefly confined to words united by composition, and is seldom observed in words that remain distinct, or form the constituent parts of sentences.

This quality of which we are treating, so peculiar to Irish, is called ECLIPSIS ; and consists in the suppression, under certain circumstances, of the sound of the initial mute consonant for that of another cognate, or homorganic letter, which, in the written language, is inserted immediately before the initial whose sound is to be passed over.

The circumstances under which this suppression of the

sound of the initial letter takes place, shall, in coming Lessons, be pointed out.

It will aid the learner considerably to see at one view those consonants that are homorganic, or pronounced by the same organ; and it will afterwards be seen, if a mute consonant is eclipsed by no other than by an homorganic letter of a more mellow sound, that eclipsis in Gaelic is founded on those laws by which euphony, or the facility of utterance, is regulated.

The organs which chiefly aid in producing articulate sounds, are the lips, tongue, teeth, palate, and in those languages that require a strong guttural enunciation, as Hebrew, German, Spanish, Irish—the throat. Those letters are homorganic that are articulated by the same organ; as, b, ꝼ, m, p; ḃ or bh, (*i.e.*, v, or w,) ṁ, or mh, (*i.e.*, v, or w,) ph, or ṗ, (*i.e.*, f), which are called *labial* or lip-letters;—c, (*i.e.*, k), ᵹ, ċ or ch, ġ or ᵹh, are *palatal* in English; in Irish *guttural*, or *glottal*. See the annexed Table.

		Labial.	Dental.	Palatal.
Sibilants ...			ꞅ	...
Aspirants ...		ꝼ, ḟ (h)	ṡ (h)	...
Liquids	*oral*	...	l	ꞃ
	nasal	m ṁ	n	nᵹ
				Guttural
Mutes	*soft,*	b	ꝺ	ᵹ
	hard,	p	ꞇ	c
	soft.	ḃ (*i.e.* v or w)	ḋ (*y*)	ġ (*gh* En. or *y*)
	hard,	ṗ (*ph* or *f*)	ṫ (*h*)	ċ (χ *chi* Gr. or ċ in oċ.)

"The letters in the same horizontal line are homogeneous; those in a perpendicular line homorganic."—*Atlantis,* Vol. I. p. 64.

The *homorganic* are those pronounced by the same organ of articulation, as, the lips, the teeth, the palate; the *homogeneous* are those formed by the same kind of action, or which spring from a kindred agency.

TABLE OF ECLIPSES IN IRISH.

		Is eclipsed by	As,	Pronounced as if written.
Labials	b (a soft mute)	m (a liquid, nasal)	an m-bord, our table.	an mord.
	f (asp. hard)	b (an asp. mute, soft)	an b-fíon, our wine	an bíon.
	p (hard)	b (soft)	an b-pian, our pain	an bian.
Gutturals	c (hard)	g (soft)	an g-cara, our friend.	an gara.
	g (soft)	n (liquid, nasal)	an ngul, our crying	an ngul.
Dentals	d (soft)	n (liquid, nasal)	an n-Dia, our God	an nia.
	t (hard)	d (soft)	an d-tír, our country.	an dír.
	s (sibilant)	t (a mute)	an t-slat, the rod.	an tlat.

From the examples in the third column the learner perceives that the sound of the initial consonant is suppressed, and that of the prefixed cognate sounded instead.

Initial g, however, when eclipsed by n, has its sound not suppressed, but blending with that of n, forms one new sound —viz., ng, nasal; and for this reason there is no hyphen mark denoting eclipsis placed between n and g. "It is a well-known fact," says a distinguished modern scholar, "that certain articulate sounds are found in one language, or group of languages, which may be wanting in another." The sound of ng, nasal, is not found in the beginning of a word in the English language; it is found, however, in the middle and end of words of Saxon origin; as, "mingling," "bungling," "wrangling," or of *im, in, en, em,* in French.

The sound ng should be distinguished from that of gn —the latter is pronounced by introducing between the sounds of g and n a slight vowel-sound; as, gne, appearance, sex; as if *gĭné* (*i,* very short); so gníom, an act; as if *gĭníom.* In like manner cn; as, cnoc—pronounced as *kĭnock,* a hill.

VOCABULARY.

Аmаċ, out; as тeiġ аmаċ, go out.

Аmuiġ, without, outside; as тá mе аmuiġ, I am without.

Boċ, *m.*, a tabernacle, a tent, a cot. Hebrew, בּ, *beth*, a house; as, *Beth-el*, the house of God; the name Jacob called Luz, after the vision in which the Lord appeared to him, on his going to and returning from Padan Aram. *Beth*-lehem, the *house* of bread.

Boṫаn, *m.*, a cot, a cabin.

Сiúnаs, *m.*, calmness; from сiun, calm.

Cluаn, *m.*, a retreat, a sequestered spot; a plain or lawn between two woods. To quiet retreats of this kind the early Irish Saints, like St. Finian at Clonard, (from cluаn, and áрd, high); St. Brendan, at Clonfert, (from cluаn, and feаrт, a wonderful act, a miracle); St. Jarlath, at Cluanfoish, (from cluаn, and foiṡ, the possessive case of fos, rest, a settled abode); retired to devote themselves to prayer, contemplation, and study. On this account we meet with many names of places in Ireland commencing with Cluan or Clon.

Сnoc, *m.*, a hill, Anglicised, *knock*, in Irish topographical names.

Cuimin, *f.*, a valley, a flat between elevated ridges or continuous heights. Cuimin nа тri n-uiṡġe, the valley of the three waters, where the Suir, Nore, and Barrow meet. Hence the names of the early inhabitants of *Cumber*land and Wales, the *Cameri*, *Cumbri*, or *Cimbri*.

Déаn, do; act; *v. ir.*; *perf.* rinneаr; *fut.* déаnfаd; *Inf.* déаnаḋ.

Fаġ, get; *v. ir.*, *perf.* fuаrаr; *fut.* ġeаbfаd; *Inf.* fáġаil.

Féin, self; as mе-féin, myself; own; as, аr d-тir féin, our own country.

Fonn, *m.*, desire, delight, pleasure; the air of a song; a tune.

Geаll, *m.*, a promise, a pledge; mаr, as; placed before, gives the word an adverbial meaning; as, mаr ġeаll, on account of; because of.

Geаll, *v.*, to promise.

Gleаn, *m.*, a glen, a vale.

Mаon, *m.*, (pr. as if *mween*) wealth, substance; díomаoin, *f.*, (from dí, wanting, and mаoin), vanity; idleness.

Miаn, *m.*, (pr. *meean*) desire; аinmiаn, inordinate desire; fаoi аinmiаn, under the influence of inordinate desire.

Mullаċ, *m.*, the summit; the top part; as, mullаċ cnoic, the top of a hill; mullаċ do ċinn, the top of your head.

Reiḋ, ready; reiḋeаċт, *f.*, readiness.

Reileаġ, *m.*, a churchyard.

Seаċт-mаin, *f.*, a week; from seаċт, seven, and mаin, a day, morning; Latin, *mane*, morning.

Siubаloid, *f.*, the act of walking.

Sruċ, *f.*, (See Exception 3 to Rule 1, Lesson Seventeen,) a stream.

Sтаir, *f.*, history; story; fable.

Тiġ, the *prepos. case* of теаċ, *m.*, a house; аrd-тiġ, a big house.

Тiġ liom, it comes with me: I can.

Tobаr, *m.*, a well; a fountain;—a word which enters into the composition of names of many places in this country.

NOTE.—Apply Rules I. 3, for ascertaining the gender of nouns (See Seventeenth Lesson, p. 93,) to those which have the gender marked in the foregoing Vocabulary.

EXERCISE XXX.

1. Ꝝo m-beannuiɠe Ꝺia ꝺuiꞇ, (God save you: literally—May God give you a blessing) a Sheamuir ꝺil, ċanaꝺ mo ċroiꝺe. 2. Ꝝo m-beannuiɠe Ꝺia aɣur Ꝡuine ꝺuiꞇ-re a Peaꝺain, blaċ na h-uairle (flower of nobility); naċ moċ air maiꝺin ꞇair air ꝺo ċoir? 3. Ir moċ ɣo ꝺeiṁin, man ɣeall ɣo b-ꝼuil an maiꝺin ċo breaɣ rin, aɣur ꝺuil aɣam airꝺir mór a ꝺéanaꝺ an ꞃuꝺ ann aonꝼeaċꞇ leaꞇ-ra. 4. Ir mór an ꝼean ꞃiubaloiꝺe ꞇu, ɣo cinꞇe (certainly); ni b-ꝼuil lá maiꞇ air biꞇ, naċ b-ꝼuil, ꞇu aiɣ imċeaċꞇ (going), ó cnoic ɣo cnoc; ó ɣlean ɣo ɣlean; ó ċluan ɣo cluan, aɣur ó ċuman ɣo cuman ꞇriꝺ an ꞇir. 5. Ꝡaire, ir ꝼior ꝺuiꞇ; ɣo cinꞇe ir aoibin liom a beiꞇ, ann air ꝺ-꞉ir ꝺuꞇċair ꝼéin amuiɣ ɣaċ uair aꝺ-ꞇiɣ liom, air ṁullaċ na rliaꝺ, air bann na ɣ-cnóc, aɣur a ɣ-ciunar na nɣlean; no air aiɣ riubal air bꞃuaċ na loċ (on the border of lakes) no le h-air na ɣ-cuan. 6. Ni maiꞇ liom-ra ꝺul amaċ an ꞃuꝺ, ꞇá aɣam ɣo leon le ꝺéanaꝺ. 7. Oċ, ꝺubꞃair an lá ċeanna, aɣur ɣeall ꞇu, ɣo m-beiꝺċeá ꞃeiꝺ an ꞃuꝺ, aɣur ɣo m-beiꝺeaꝺ ꝼail aɣaꝺ imċeaċꞇ liom ꞇriꝺ an ꞇir; óir ɣo ꝺeiṁin leaꞇ nior maiꞇ liom aon ꝺuine eile aċꞇ ꞇu, oir ꞇáir-re ċo colɣaċ rin air ɣaċ ꞇiɣ aɣur air ɣaċ áiꞇ, air ɣaċ boꞇ, aɣur air ɣaċ anꝺ-ꞇiɣ; air ɣaċ ċluan aɣur ɣaċ ċomair, rleib, ɣlean, ꞇobair, rnuċ, (steam) aṁuin (river) cairn, neiliɣ, cill, aɣur ni ꝼe rin aṁain, aċꞇ ꞇá ꝼior aɣaꝺ air rꞇáir ɣaċ niꝺ air buꝺ ṁaiꞇ liom cairꞇ, no air buꝺ ṁaiꞇ liom eolur ꝼaɣail. 8. Ꞇá me buiꝺeaċ ꝺuiꞇ, ꝼaoi an ṁear (esteem) mór ꞇá aɣaꝺ onm;—mear naċ ꝼiú me, aɣur ɣo h-airiꝺe (especially) ó ꝼean aiɣ a b-ꝼuil an oiꞃeaꝺ (so much) ꝼóɣlaim (of learning) a'r ꞇá aɣaꝺ-ra. Ni maiꞇ liom, mair rin, naċ ꝺ-ꞇiɣ liom ꝺul leaꞇ an ꞃuꝺ; aċꞇ beiꝺ lá eile aɣainn. 9. Nan ɣeall ꞇu ꝺam, ɣo m-beiċeá ꞃeiꝺ an ꞃuꝺ? 10. Ꝺo ɣeallar; aċꞇ naċ b-ꝼuil ꝼior aɣaꝺ ɣo b-ꝼuil aɣam ɣo leon le ꝺéanaꝺ; aɣur naċ ꝺ-ꞇiɣ liom ꝼail ꝼaɣail (pr. *áw-il*) an ꞃuꝺ? 11. Ir ꝼior ɣur ċóir ꝺo ɣaċ uile ꝺuine na neiċe a ꝺéanaꝺ, a ꞇá ꝼaoi n-a rꞇiur, aɣur air an aꝺbar rin, ni maiꞇ liom ɣo n-ꝺeanꝼa niꝺ air biꞇ naċ m-beiꝺeaꝺ ceanꞇ ꝺuiꞇ a ꝺéanaꝺ. 12. Ꝼeicim, ɣo b-ꝼuil cial (sense) aɣaꝺ, aɣur naċ b-ꝼuil ꞇu man ɣo leon ꝺaoine óɣa ꝼaoi anṁan aiɣ ɣaċ uile ꝺioṁaoin. 13. Ꞇá me buiꝺeaċ ꝺuiꞇ; ir ceanra (meekly)

cınealca (kindly), labaṁaıṁ cu (you speak) aıṙ ʒaċ ṅıб.
14. Cıa aṅ lá aṅoıṙ (now) a m-beıб ċu ṙeıб, le ċeaċc
lıom; abaıṙ e (name it). 15. Lá ṙaoıṙe aıṙ bıċ; ṅo aṅ
ceuб lá бe'ṅ c-ṙeaċcṁaṅ, ṁa bıбeaṅṅ ṙe maıċ. 16. Iṙ
ṙaбa, b' ḟeıбıṙ (perhaps ; literally, it may be possible) ʒo
m-beıб la eıle aʒaıṅṅ maṙ aṅ lá ṙo; cá aṅ c-aeṙ áṙб,
aṅ ṙpéıṙ ʒoṙm, ʒaṅ ṅeul, ṅo ṙmuб; aṅ ʒṙıaṅ aıʒ eıṙı-
ʒeaб ʒo ṙoıllṙeaċ (radiantly) ; na h-eıṅ (the birds) aıʒ
ceolṅaб aıṙ ʒaċ ċṙaṅ ; aʒuṙ aṅ cṙuıṅe ʒo leıṙ (the world
entirely) ṙaoı ṙʒeıṁ, maṙ aṅ ceuб lá aṅṅ a б-caıṅıc ṙe
amaċ ó laıṁ aṅ Cıʒeaṙṅa. 17. Cá ṙoıṅṅ ṁóṙ oṙm a бul
leac. 18. Na caṙṙ; beıб la eıle aʒaıṅṅ ċo maıċ. 19. So
ı mo ṁaċaıṙ, aıʒ ceaċc ; ca aṙ ʒ-ceuб ṗṙoıṅ ṙeıб.
20. U ṁaċaıṙ ṙo é Peaбaṙ O'Caoıṁ aıṙ a labaıṙ me ʒo
mıṅıc leac, caṙaб óʒ aıṙ a b-ṙuıl aʒam meaṙ ṁóṙ.
21. 'S é a beaċa; ceuб mıle ṙaılce ṙoṁac. 22. Iṙ maıбıṅ
bṙeaʒ ı ṙo, a beaṅ uaṙaıl. 23. Seaб ʒo беıṁıṅ; ṙo e aṅ
ceuб lá bṙeaʒ bı aʒaıṅṅ, le ṁı (for the month past—
literally, with month). 24. U Seamuıṙ, cá бo ċeuб-
ṗṙoıṅ ṙeıб; aʒuṙ cá б'aċaıṙ aʒuṙ бo беaṙb-ṙıuṙ aıʒ бuıl
leac; b' ḟeıбıṙ ṅaṙ ıċ aṅ бuıṅe-uaṙal óʒ ṙo a ċeuб-ṗṙoıṅ
ʒo ṙóıll. 25. Cabaıṙ бuıṅṅ, a Peaбaıṙ, oṅóıṙ бo coṁlua-
бaıṙ aıʒ boṅб? 26. Le ṙaılce, ʒo беıṁıṅ; aċc ċıʒ lıom
a ṙaб ʒo ṙıoṙ ʒuṙ oṙṅ-ṙa беaṅcaṙ aṅ oṅoıṙ (on me the
honour is done—bestowed) a beıċ aıṅṅ buṙ ʒ-coṁluaбaṙ-
ṙa. 27. Ceıʒ ṙoṁam (before me), ṁa 'ṙ ṙe бo ċoıl é; ṙo
é aṅ beallaċ (this is the way).

NINETEENTH LESSON.

In which is shown when Eclipses in Gaelic occurs.

RULE 1.—Eclipsis is caused by the *possessive pronouns
plural*, aṙ, our; buṙ, your; a, their; as, ʒṙaбuıʒċeoıṙ eaб-
ṁaṙ, aṙ б-Cıʒeaṙṅa, aṙ ṅ-Oıa, aʒuṙ aṙ b-ḟuaṙʒalcoıṙ, a
jealous lover is our Lord, our God, and our Redeemer.

C, the initial mute of Cıʒeaṙṅa, is eclipsed by б; O,
in Oıa, by ṅ ; and ṙ, by b (b aspirated, sounds as *v*).

If mo, mine, or any of the possessive pronouns *singular*

(except ᴀ, her;) precede Ꞓⁱ5eᴀпⁿᴀ, Oⁱᴀ, or ꝼuᴀⁱ5ᴀlꞇoⁱⁿ, the initial letters would be only aspirated. (See Fifth Lesson, Obs. 1, page 28.)

The Lord, and *the* God; ᴀⁿ Ꞓⁱ5eᴀпⁿᴀ, ᴀ5uⁱ ᴀⁿ Oⁱᴀ.

My Lord, and *my* God; mo Ꞓⁱ5eᴀпⁿᴀ, ᴀ5uⁱ mo Oⁱᴀ.

Our Lord, and *our* God; " ᴀⁿ" ᴅ-Ꞓⁱ5eᴀпⁿᴀ, ᴀ5uⁱ " ᴀⁿ" ⁿ-Oⁱᴀ.

His Lord, and *his* God; ᴀ Ꞓⁱ5eᴀпⁿᴀ, ᴀ5uⁱ ᴀ Oⁱᴀ.

Their Lord, and *their* God; " ᴀ" ᴅ-Ꞓⁱ5eᴀпⁿᴀ, ᴀ5uⁱ " ᴀ" ⁿ-Oⁱᴀ.

Her Lord, and *her* God; ᴀ Ꞓⁱ5eᴀпⁿᴀ, ᴀ5uⁱ ᴀ Oⁱᴀ.

Its, referring to the name of an inanimate object, is, in Irish—as all names are, either masculine or feminine—expressed by the words *his* or *her* (ᴀ).

Thus, eclipsis follows the *plural* possessive pronouns; aspiration, the *singular* possessive pronouns.

The letter S, ⁱ, is not affected by ᴀⁿ, buⁿ, or ᴀ; as, ᴀⁿ Slᴀⁿuⁱ5ꞇeoⁱⁿ, our Saviour; ᴀⁿ Sᴀ5ᴀⁿꞇ, our priest.

Rule 2.—The *possessive* case plural of nouns declined with the article (ᴀⁿ, the); as—

> Oꞓ, ᴀ Fⁱⁿⁿ " ⁿᴀ b-Fⁱᴀⁿⁿ" ᴀ'ⁱ ⁿᴀ ⁱluᴀ5 !
> Alas, O Fionn of the Fenians and of the Hosts.
>
>   —*Ossian's Lament.*

> O, Oⁱ5ᴀⁱⁿ " ⁿᴀ ⁿ5leo," mo mᴀc !
> O Oscar of the lights, my son,
> Cⁱⁱ5, ᴀ Oⁱⁱⁱⁿ, ᴀ ᴅeⁱⁿ Pᴀᴅⁱuⁱc " ⁿᴀ ⁿ-bᴀcᴀll."
> Arise, O Oisin, says Patrick of the Croziers.

Rⁱ5 ⁿᴀ ⁿ-ᴅul, King of the Elements, *i.e.*, the Elements' King; possessive case—

> ᴅ'. Fⁱeᴀ5ᴀⁱⁿ Ꞓcuⁱl " ⁿᴀ 5-coⁱ" luᴀꞓ,
> Replied Achilles of the fleet feet.
>
>   —*Irish Homer.*

In English the possessive case is seldom employed; in its stead the objective case governed by the preposition *of* is quite common. The mere English student should learn that whenever *of* denotes possession, it is translated into Irish—as it is into Latin or into Greek—by merely causing the noun before which, in English, it is placed, to be put into the possessive; as—

The house *of* the Lord—*i.e.*, the house *belonging to* the Lord—is translated, ꞇeᴀꞓ ᴀⁿ Ꞓⁱ5eᴀпⁿᴀ ; *Domus Domini.*

The word " Lord," the possessor, is in Irish, in the possessive case, while in English it is governed by the preposition
of. We shall advert to this again.

Initial S, ſ, is excepted from this Second Rule also; as,
ceaſc ṅa Saʒaſc, the Priest's right. Coṁaiſle " ṅa Saoi,"
a counsel of the Sages.

VOCABULARY.

Allſoṅ, *m.*, Alphonsus.

Aoḋʒaṅ (the descendent (ʒaṅ or
ʒiṅṅ) of Aoḋ, Hugh), Egan.
Ṁac Aoḋʒaiṅ, Mac Egan ;
O'Aoḋʒaṅ, O'Hegan ; Claṅ Aoḋʒaṅ, MacEgans (the clan or
family of the MacEgan.)

ball, *m.*, spot, member (of the
body); aſſ ball, on the spot,
presently.

beallaċ, *m.*, way, passage ; Persian,
balak ; ſaʒ aṅ beallaċ, leave
the way.

beaſſ, *v.* to cut, to prune, to shave,
Inf. ; ꝺo beaſſſaḋ, to shave, to
prune, to clip.

Caṁ, *adj.*, Gr., καμπη, *kampe,* a
bending ; crooked, bent,
curved ; obliquely directed,
awry ; blind of one eye ; *noun,*
a bending ; *v.* to bend ; Welsh
and Bret., *camm.* Its indirect meaning is deceit, deceitful ; as in the words of Juno
to Jove—

  " Aċc leaṅ ꝺo ċoṁaiſle, a'ſ
    cioſſſ aṅṅſ aṅ aṁ
    Naċ m-beiꝺ ṅa ꝺeiċe leaċ
    'ſaṅ ʒ-coṁaiſle " ċaṁ."
        —*Homer*, B. 4, l. 45.

Caṁaṅ, *m* , diminutive of preceding, a hurl ; a stick curved at
the end ; (Gr., καμαξ, a stake,)
aʒ iṁiſc caṁaṅ, playing at
hurley ; (Scotch—shinty playing.) From caṁ, is derived the
word *comma,* which is a little
crooked turn ; Irish, caṁoʒ ;
also caṁ-al, a humped animal, a camel. Liaċſoiꝺ, the
ball used at hurley.

Ceaċaſ, four ; Latin, *quatuor.*

Cloʒ, *m* , a bell ; a clock, because,
like a bell, it sounds. Welsh,
cloch ; Fr. *cloche.* From the
Keltic cloʒ, Dr. Johnson derives the English word *clock.*

Cloiʒiṅ, *m..* a little bell ; a bunch of
berries ; a cluster ; a pendant.

Cloiʒeaṅ, *m.*, the head ; the skull
(from cloʒ and ceaṅṅ, the
head,) because the shell of the
head or skull is not unlike a
bell.

Cloʒaꝺ, *m.*, (from cloʒ. and éaꝺ,
dress, covering,) a helmet ; so
called because of old it was
made like a bell.

Craṅṅ, *m.*, a tree ; a mast ; a frame
for network or woof ; a beam,
a block ; craṅṅ ubal, an apple tree ; craṅṅ peiſe, a pear
tree ; craṅṅ róſa, a rose tree ;
craṅṅ criċeaċ, an aspen tree ;
craṅṅ ola, an olive tree ; craṅṅ
ſeoil, a mast (of sailing); craṅṅ
ceaṅṅca, a press (literally, a
block or frame of pressing) ;
craṅṅ ꝺeilbċe, a frame or bars
for warping.

Cuaiſc, *f.*, a circle, a round ; ſa
ċuaiſc, in a circle, round about;
a visit, a visitation ; aſſ cuaiſc,
on a visit ; aʒ ꝺeaṅaḋ cuaiſce,
making his visitation ; cuaiſc.
a court; iſ feaſſ caſa 'ſ aṅ
ʒ-cuaiſc 'ṅa boṅṅ ſa ſpoſaṅ, a
friend at court is better than
a groat in the purse.

Cuaſcuʒ, go about ; search, inquire diligently.

Cuaſcuʒaḋ, investigation.

Faiſſʒe, *m.*, (from faiṅſʒaḋ, to destroy, to wreck,) the ocean,
the deep; muiſ, also means sea

Fán, *m.*, stray; stroll; aɼ ɼán, astray; as, tá na caoɼaiġ aɼ ɼán, the sheep are astray.

Fánaċ, strolling, wandering; aiɼoiɼ fánaċ, a strolling walk.

Feaḃaɼ, *m.*, goodness; in good plight, comeliness; the best possible state of anything. Tá ɼe aɼ feaḃaɼ, it (or he) is in the best possible way.

Foiɼġneaṁ, *m.*, (from foiɼneaḋ, suit; fit; and ġníḋ, perform, make) a building; offices, appurtenances.

Gaɼ, near; gaɼne, *adj.*, nearer; *n. f.*, nearness.

Comġaɼ, } (com and gaɼ,) con-
Comġaɼaċ, } venient.

Gíḋ, although; quasi, ġo bíḋ, that it be.

Luimneaċ (from luime, or loime, bareness; and neaċ, for na eaċ, of the horses), *Limerick*, which was built on a peninsula made bare by the number of horses sent thither to graze.

Meacán, *m.*, a tap-rooted plant, such as a parsnip, carrot, radish; as, meacán buiḋe, a carrot; meacán ɼuġ, a parsnip.

Ponɼa, *m.*, beans.

Potaiḋ, *m.*, (for potataiḋ, plural of potato, a potato; a word of Indian origin), potatoes; in Munster commonly pronounced pɼátaiḋ.

Suḃ, *m.*, sap, juice; ɼuḃtalṁan, (the sap of earth) strawberries; ɼuḃ cɼaoḃ, a raspberry.

Spíne, *f.*, a thorn; Latin, *spina*.

Spionán, *m.*, (from ɼpíne, a thorn) a gooseberry; the shrub that produces that fruit.

Taɼ, *prepos.*, over, above, beyond; taɼt, passed over, gone by, undone; round about; tá an t-am taɼt, the time is gone by; cuɼ taɼt an cuaċ, send round the bowl; tá me taɼt, I am undone.

Tuiɼle, the hinge of a door.

Tuiɼliġ, *v.*, turn as on hinges; to stumble; bann-tuiɼluġaḋ, to stumble headforemost.

EXERCISE XXXI.

1. A h-Éinɼi iɼ tu ɼgaiċ (the chief, the best) na b-feaɼ, a beiċ ann ɼo co luaċ a'ɼ táiɼ—ca b-fuil do ḋeaɼḃ-ḃɼátaiɼ? 2. Beiḋ ɼe ann ɼo aɼ ball; níoɼ b' feioɼ leiɼ teaċt liom-ɼa an uaiɼ bi me ɼeiḋ, maɼ ġeall ġuɼ ɼaiḃ aɼ g-colceataɼ Alɼoin O'Aoḋgain aɼ cuaiɼt aġainn, aġuɼ b' eiġin do fannaċt (because our cousin-german, Alphonsus O'Hegan, was on a visit with us, and it was necessary for him to stay) le beiċ ann aonfeaċt leiɼ (to be along with him). 3. Oċ, feicim; iɼ ceaɼt ɼin. 4. Ca ṁeiḋ de cloig é anoiɼ? 5. Ní'l (for ní b-fuil) ɼe aċt an ceataɼ de clog. 6. Tá ɼe moċ ɼ-an tɼáċnóna (evening) maɼ ɼin. 7. Taɼɼ liom amaċ aġuɼ tiġ linn ɼiubut (pr. *shool*) no aiɼoiɼ fanaċ a ḋeanaḋ taɼt, aġuɼ caiɼt aġuɼ com-ɼaḋ a ḋeanaḋ eaḋɼainn fein (among ourselves, *i.e.*, with each other). 8. Tiġ linn; aġuɼ iɼ maiċ liom-ɼa e, óiɼ ní maiċ liom a beiċ a ɼtiġ aċt co beaġ a'ɼ tiġ liom.

9. So é an beallaċ le ṫaoḃ an ṫiġ. 11. Go raiḃ maiṫ agaḋ; is fonur tuirluġaḋ (to stumble) ann beálaċ cam, sleaṁain (slippery), mar uḋ ċall (like that yonder). 12. Caḋ é do ṁear air an ḃ-teaċ agus air an n-áit, air an ḃ-talaṁ, agus an ḃ-foirġneaṁ? 13. Is e mo ṁear go ḃ-fuil bur ḃ-teaċ maiṫ, bur ḃ-talaṁ an-ṁaiṫ, bur n-áit áluin, agus bur ḃ-foirġneaṁ air feaḃar. 14. Cia acu is fearr, bur ḃ-teaċ-ra, no air ḃ-teaċ-ne,—which is the better, your house or our house? 15. Is fearr bur ḃ-teaċ, na air ḃ-teaċ-ne. 16. Tamuiḋ ann ro, comġarraċ do'n t-sruiṫ, do'n baile ṁóir, do'n ḃ-fairrġe,—neiċe (things) a beirear (that give) luaċ mór do ċeaċ tuaiḋe (enhance the value—give a great price to—a country house). 17. An fe ro bur nġarraḋ? 18. Is e an nġarraḋ é, tarr arteaċ agus amarc air. 19. Ca an niḋ ta ann? 20. Go leor; —ta potaiḋ (potatoes) agus gabáirḋe (cabbage), pir (pease), agus ponairne (beans), meacon buiḋ, meacan bán, meacan raidiġ (radish), meacan garḃ no turnap, ruba-craoḃ, ruba-talṁan, oirnuin, crain póra, crain ubal, crain peire, srionán agus a leiṫiḋiḋ. 21. Feicim gur an-ṁaiṫ a amarcann re anoir. 22. Caḋ re do ṁear air an ċaoi ta na crain (the trees), agus air gaċ far eile a ta 'r an ġarraḋ? 23. Mearaim go ḃ-fuil bur g-crain ubal ro-árḋ, agus bur ruba-craoḃ rġarta amaċ gan bearraḋ. 24. Cia leir (with whom, i.e., to whom belong) an garraḋ uḋ ċall, agus an gort ro gar ḋam? 25. Le mo ṁuintir féin, mo ċuiḋ gaol, Paḋruic agus Seamur O'Ḋalaiġ. 26. Is fearr a nġort na do ġort-ra. 27. Ni fearr go deiṁin. 28. Is fearr a g-crain ubail, a g-crain peire agus a g-crain nór, agus gaċ lur no planḋa a ta 'far ann a nġort, no bur g-crain agus bur ḃ-far-re. 29. b' feiḋir rin (perhaps so; literally, that may be possible) aċt is fearr liom-ra mo ċuiḋ féin 'na a g-cuiḋ-ran, giḋ go ḃ-fuil ri ċo maiṫ rin. Ta fior agam, air ċaoi air biṫ, gur b' fearr an g-coince agus an g-croineaċt 'na a g-coince, a g-croineaċt agus a u-arḃar-ran. 30. Naċ an-eolgac táir-re de ċaoḃ talṁan?......31. Ta re am proinne, tarr a rteaċ, ta an comluaḋar aig cruinuġaḋ. 32. Beiḋ fleaḋ rubġaċ againn, ta ruil agam. 33. Beiḋ, ma ta an fion agus an feoil is fearr a Luimneaċ ann, daoine (people) óga a ḋeanaḋ rub

ʒac.   34. Naċ m-beiġ ṗịnc no ḃaṁṗa aʒaịnn? Shall we
not have dancing?—literally, will there not be dance or
merriment (at) for us.   35. beiġ, (there will be) ma 'ṛ
coịl lịb (if there is will with ye, *i.e*, if you wish) ʒo
ḃ-cị éịṗịʒ an lae.

Obs.—" Have," in the English language is called an Auxiliary, though
it is not always such, but an independent verb, signifying to possess : it
is a sign of the perfect tense.   In the former sense, as a word denoting possession, it has, in Irish, no verb corresponding to *avoir*, in French ;
or *avere*, in Italian.   Instead of it, the verb *to be*, ḃo beịċ, with the compound pronouns, aʒam, at me, or to me; aʒaḃ, to you (thee) ; aịʒe, to
him ; aịcị, to her ; aʒaịnn, to us ; aʒaịb, to you (ye) ; acu, to them, is
employed.   (See Obs. 2, in Third Lesson, p. 16.)
    " Have," as a sign of the perfect tense expresses the idea of time just
now passed.   In Irish, as in every learned or ancient language, the idea
of past time is conveyed by the ending of the perfect tense of the verb,
or by the past participle and the verb *to be*, ḃo be ċ ; as, I *have* come, ḃo
ṫaịnịceaṛ ; John *has* come, ḃo ċaịnịc Seaʒan ; the day *has* been ended,
ċa an lá caịċce. (See Fifth Lesson, on the verbal endings, p. 25.)

TWENTIETH LESSON.

Obs. 1.—Eclipsis affects only the *initial* mute consonant.
It is never, like aspiration, found in the middle or end of
a word.

As a general rule, when any noun in the *singular*
number, preceded by the article an (the) is governed by
any of the simple, or non-compound prepositions (except
ḃe, ḃo, ʒan, eịḋịṗ—see Exception 2, p. 110,) eclipsis is produced, if the initial consonant (that is, the consonant with
which the word *begins*,) be of that class that undergoes
this suppression ; as,   -

My father was *through the* garden.	ḃị m'aċaịṗ " ċṗịḃ an" nʒaṗḃa (pr. *ngárrhy*).
John has the land at (*under*) *the* highest rent.	Ċa an calam aịʒ Seaʒan " ṗaoị n" ʒ-cịoṛ ịr aịnḃe.
James is *at the* market town.	Ċa Seamuṛ " aịʒ an" m baịle ṁóịṛ.

What is little is sweet (there is taste *on the* scanty meal).	Tá blas "air an" m-beagán

G, of garrḋa, is eclipsed by n; c of cíos, by g; b, of baile, by m; b, of beagan by m, according to the terms of the rule.

Exception 1—To this rule nouns singular, whose first letter is d or t, are exceptions, because the letter "n" of the article an, which precedes them, is itself of cognate origin with t, or d ; as,

Thy will be done on earth as it is in heaven.	Go n-déantar do ṫoil "air an talaṁ" mar gniḋtear air neaṁ.
Everything *on* (in) *the world* passes away like a vapour.	Imiġeann gaċ niḋ ta "air an doṁan," mar an g-ceo.

It would be well to except also from this rule nouns beginning with g, for as its eclipsing letter is n, the n of the article an, answers the purpose fully as well; Ex.—

Ḃi an long air "an ġaineaṁ" agus an tuile d'éis traġaḋ, The bark was still there but the waters were gone ; literally —the bark was *on the sand* and the tide after ebbing. The g of gaineaṁ, is here not eclipsed, because n of the article an, dispenses with its use.

Initial S, s, followed by a vowel, or any of the liquids l, n, r, is eclipsed in accordance with *this* rule, though excepted from the others; as,

Now Jacob had pitched his tent *on* the mountain.	Anois do ḃi aig Jacob a ḃoṫ suiġte "air an t-sléiḃ."

Or, in the words of the angels to Lot—

No, but we shall remain *on the street* during the night.	Ni seaḋ, aċt fanfamuid "air an t-sráid" feaḋ na h-oiḋċe.
Who created and placed you *in the world.*	Cia ċruṫuiġ agus ċuir air "an t-saoġal" ṫu?

If any of the consonants b, c, ð, ʒ, m, p, c; and not l,
n, ɼ, or a vowel follow ɼ, at the beginning of a word, no
change, either *eclipsis* or *aspiration* ensues, because, nor c,
nor aspirated ɼ (h), could unite with any of these letters;
as, ꝼaoɪ "ꞃʒac" aɲ cꞃaɪɲ, under the shade of the tree; ɪꞃ
ꝼeaɼɼ caꞃað 'ꞃaɲ ʒ-cuaɼꞃc 'ɲa boɲɲ 'ꞃ aɲ "ꞃpaꞃáɲ," a
friend at court is better than a groat (taken in a wide
sense for money) in the purse; ɼ, in ꞃʒac, is not aspirated
by ꝼaoɪ; nor ɼ, in ꞃpaꞃaɲ eclipsed, because neither a vowel
nor liquid consonant immediately follows initial ɼ.

S, ɼ, is never eclipsed except in the two instances pointed out—firstly,
as in the foregoing examples, when with the article (aɲ, the) going before, it
is governed by one of the simple prepositions; and secondly, in those cases
in which other consonants suffer aspiration—for instance, in the nominative
and objective cases of feminine nouns singular, and in the possessive case
of nouns masculine preceded by the article. (See Sixth Lesson, Exception 2, p. 31, PART I.)

On this account some Irish grammarians consider that *S*, ɼ, should not
be ranked among those consonants which suffer eclipsis, since it is not
influenced by those eclipsing causes which affect the mutes. (See Table
of Eclipsis.)

Exception 2.—The simple prepositions ðe, of; ðo, to;
ʒaɲ, without; and ɪðɪꞃ, or eɪðɪꞃ, between, do not always,
on being followed by the article aɲ (the), produce eclipsis;
many instances are found in which aspiration alone occurs
in its stead; as, he went to town, ðo cuaɪð ꞃe ðo'ɲ ɓaɪle
moɪꞃ. ð of ɓaɪle is aspirated, and not eclipsed, although
according to rule, the article and governing preposition
precede it.

It appears right, on general principles, that there should be no such
exception as this just noticed, and that it would be better to conform to
the general rule. The prevailing usage among our people, however, lends
great weight to this second exception. (See Dr. O'Donovan's *Irish Grammar*, pp. 393, 394.)

In the Ninth Lesson we showed that when the article
(aɲ, the) is not expressed, the noun suffers aspiration, and
not eclipsis, after the preposition. Yet there are four prepositions—a, in; ðaꞃ, by (in swearing); ɪaꞃ, after; ꞃɪa,
before—which *eclipse* the noun they govern, although the
article be *not* expressed; as,

At Tara to-day, I call on the mighty power of the Holy Trinity.	"A d-Ceaṁraiġ" an ȷuḃ aċċuȷȷȝȷȷ neaṗc cṗeuȷ ȷa Cṗȷaȷoȷḃe.
By (the) hope, he is there.	Oaṗ ȷ-ḋoȷȝ, cá ṗe aȷȷ ṗȷȷ
He is in Dublin; in Cork.	Cá ṗé a ȷȷ-baȷle Aċacȷaċ; a ȝ-Coȷcaȷȝ.
After Easter.	ȷaṗ ȝ-Caȷṗȝ.

Obs. 2.—The prepositions, aȷȷ, in; ȝo, to; ȷaṗ, after; le, with; cṗe, through, going before the article aȷ, take ṗ annexed for sound's sake, on account of the vowel of the article; as, *in the* town, aȷȷ 'aȷ ȷȷ-baȷle; is written, "aȷȷṗ" aȷ ȷȷ-baȷle; and contractedly, 'ṗ aȷ ȷȷ-báȷle, or 'ṗa ȷȷ-báȷle; *in the* place, aȷṗ aȷ aȷc; he came *across the* country, caȷȷȷc ṗe "cṗeaṗ" aȷ cȷṗ; to Dublin, ȝo baȷle Aċc-cȷȷac; but *to the* town (with the article) ȝuṗ aȷ ȷȷ-baȷle.

When aȷȷ is employed the euphonic ṗ is, by some, put before the vowel a of the article, in this following the ear chiefly as their guide; but ṗ, as Dr. O'Donovan remarks, "belongs to the preposition, not to the article."

This is certain, as well from the authority just quoted, as from analogy; for le, with, becomes leȷṗ; cṗe, cṗeaṗ; therefore aȷȷ, should be aȷȷṗ. In Latin and Greek too, *à*, *ab*, becomes *abs*; and *é*, *eks*, i.e., *ex*, before a vowel.

VOCABULARY.

Aċ-luaȷȷ, *m.*, Athlone; (the ford of warriors); luaȷ means also 'moon," as, Oȷa-luaȷȷ. Monday; *dies lunae.* The former derivation is preferable.

Boċaṗ, *m.*, a road; way; street; aȷṗ aȷ ȷȷ-boċaȷṗ, on the road; boċaṁ ȷaṗȷȷaȷȷ, a railroad, a road of iron; like the French *chemin de fer;* Italian, *camino di ferro.*

Cóṁ, *adj.*, just; courteous; *n. f.*, justice.

Cóṗaċ, equitable; upright.

Coȷċubaṗ, pronounced as if written Cȷoċubaṗ, (derived from coȷ, possessive plural, *of heroes;* and cubaṗ, careful of, fond of,) the Irish of O'Connor; also of the Christian name—Cornelius.

Coȷȷaċc, *f.*, the province of Connaught; from coȷȷ, of heroes;

and aċc, a termination, like *tas* in Latin, or *tion* in French or English, peculiar to very many derivative words. Others derive it from the proper name —Coȷ (of the Hundred Battles); but the province was called Connaught long before the time of that monarch.

Coṗaȷȷ, *v.*, defend; inf. cȷṗaȷȷc.

Coṗaȷ, *m.*, (from coṗ, a foot,) a way, a pathway.

Ouḃ, black; *n. m.*, ink; buṗaȷ, *m.* blackness; buḃaȷ, a kidney; a hook; a snare; buḃaȷ ȷaṗȝaȷṗcaċca, a fish hook; buḃaċ, *m.*, ink; any black liquid; *adj.*, melancholy, sad-looking, dismal; buḃaċaṗ, sadness, melancholy; buḃabaȷ, *m.*, an ink-horn, or ink-bottle; buḃaȷȝeȷȷ, *f.*, the deep; the dark ocean; (from buḃ and aȷȝeȷȷ, ocean).

Ḋuiḃe, *adj.*, more black; *n. f.*, blackness, darkness.

Ġall, *m.*, a Gaul; a foreigner; an Englishman. From this root is derived Ġailliṁ, Galway, "the town of the strangers;" and Ḋun-na-ġall, Donegal, "the fort of the strangers." To this day the terms Ġael, Gael, and Ġall, stranger, are in common use amongst the peasantry, to denote Catholic and Protestant, the latter—for the greater part—being to the natives Ġaill, *i.e.*, aliens, in race, in country, and creed.

Ġallḋa, foreign in dress, in language, or tone.

Innir, *v.* tell; *Inf.*, inḣreaċt, and inḣireaḋ; (from in, in; and ḟior, knowledge;) to make a thing known to another.

Loċ, *m.*, a lake; Latin, *lacus*; Italian, *lago*; Greek, λακκος. Loċ-na-ṅiaċ, Loughrea.

Loṅg, *f.* (See Exception 3 to Rule 1.), a ship. Loṅg reoil, a sailing vessel; loṅg ġaille, a steamer; ġail, means steam; ġaille, (poss. case) belonging to steam; like the French, *bateau à vapeur*.

Oilean, *m.*, island.

Oilean ún, the new island; Newfoundland; sometimes applied to the whole continent of America.

Or cionn, at the head; above; or cionn ġaċ niḋ, above every thing.

Ṗraṫṅeaċ, solicitous, earnest; devoted to with enthusiasm.

Sil, (spelled also raoil) think; *inf.* ṙileaḋ.

Saoċar, *m.*, labour; raoċaraċ, laborious.

Soiṁ, prosperous, happy.

Soiṁḃiġim, I prosper; ó roṁḃiġ an Tiġearna ṫu, Since the Lord has prospered you.

Ġo róṁḃiġe Ḋia ḋuit, God speed you; the parting farewell of the Irish peasantry.

Traill, *f.*, a slave; a servant; a dastard. Sax. *thrael*; Eng. *thrall.*

Trailleaċ, slavish; trailleaċt, *f.*, slavishness.

Treaḃ, *m.*, a tribe; a family. Caḃ e an treaḃ an leir e? What is the tribe to which he belongs? Latin, *tribus*.

Treaḃaċ, *m.*, one of a tribe. Also a farmer.

Coṁ-treaḃaċ, *m.*, one of the same tribe. Welsh, *kiddtrevaug*.

Di-ṫreaḃaċ, *m.*; a hermit: one separated from his kith and kin.

Di-treaḃ, *m.*, a wilderness, an hermitage. Welsh, *didreṡwar*: a wilderness.

Treaḃaḋ, *m.*, ploughing.

Treaḃaire, *m.*, a ploughman.

Triall, *v.* repair, devise; go, march, travel.

Tlaċt, a superficies; the earth, or a portion of it; a region; a market town, a churchyard or green; vesture, covering; its secondary meaning is, beauty, loveliness; again, pleasure, satisfaction arising from the enjoyment of what is agreeable; delight, endearment, delectation.

Tlaċtṁar, pleasant, handsome, fine, agreeable.

Tlaċtṁaraċt, *f.*, agreeableness, delightfulness.

Tlaċt-ġraraċt, topography; from tlaċt, and ġraraḋ, an old Irish verb, signifying to write. Gr. γραφὼ, *grapho*.

EXERCISE XXXII.

1. So lá breaġ, a Sheamuir? 2. Ir lá breaġ é, buiḋeaċar do Ḋia.* 3. Naċ moċ tá tu, aṁail liom féin,

NOTE—In Irish ḣ, and the (˙) are mere marks of Aspiration. Whenever, therefore, it happens, as it sometimes must, that an ḣ is placed aft

ᴀɪɼ ᴀn m-boċᴀɼɼ? 4. Jɼ moċ ʒo beɼṁɪn, ċᴀ me ᴀɼɼ ᴀn m-
boċᴀɼɼ. 5. b-ꝼuɪl ɼʒeul nuᴀó (new story—news) ᴀɼɼ bɼċ
ᴀʒᴀó óᴀm? 6. Ⱳᴀɼɼe, nɪ b-ꝼuɪl ɼʒeul nuᴀó ᴀɼɼ bɼċ ᴀʒᴀm
óuɪċ. 7. b' ꝼeɪoɪɼ ʒo b-ꝼuɪl; nɪ ɼᴀɪb ċu ᴀ ɼɪᴀṁ ʒᴀn ɼʒeul
eɪʒɪn bo óuɪne, óɼɼ ċᴀ ċu ꝼᴀoɪ 'n ʒ-cᴀɪl (under the repute)
—ᴀ beɪċ ʒɼeᴀnṁᴀɼ, (entertaining, funny) meɼɼeᴀċ (merry);
ᴀʒuɼ nᴀċ m-beɪóeᴀó ċuɼɼɼe (weariness) ᴀɼɼ ᴀon óuɪne ᴀ
beɪóeᴀó ᴀɼɼ ᴀn m-boċᴀɼ, no ᴀɼɼ ᴀn nʒoɼċ ᴀnn ᴀonꝼeᴀċċ
leᴀċ. 8. ʒo ɼᴀɪb mᴀɪċ ᴀʒᴀó ᴀ Conċubᴀɼɼ, bɪ ċu ᴀ ʒ-com-
nuɪóe cóɪɼ, ċlᴀċċṁᴀɼ, ɼɪᴀmɼᴀċ (mirthful). 9. N'ɪl me ᴀɪʒ
ɼᴀó ᴀ Seᴀmuɪɼ, ᴀċċ ᴀṁᴀɪn (but only) ᴀn nɪó ċᴀ ʒᴀċ óuɪne
ᴀ ɼᴀó oɼċ. 10. Jɼ ꝼᴀóᴀ ᴀn ċ-ᴀm ó bɪ ᴀʒᴀm ꝼᴀɪl (pronounced quickly in one syllable *fah-yil*) cᴀɼɼċ ᴀ óeᴀnᴀó
leᴀċ—ċᴀ m-bɪóeᴀnn ċu ᴀnoɪɼ ᴀɪʒ coṁnuɪʒ? 11. Ċᴀ ᴀɼᴀɼ
(a dwelling) ᴀʒᴀm 'nn ʒᴀɼ ʒo ʒᴀɪllɪṁ—bᴀɪle ᴀ ʒ-Connᴀċċ,
ɼuɪʒċe (situated) ᴀɼɼ ᴀn ʒ-cuᴀn. 12. Ó; ċᴀ ꝼɪoɼ ᴀʒᴀm;
bᴀɪle é ɼɪn ċᴀ ᴀɪʒ eɪɼɪʒ ʒo móɼ; bᴀɪle ᴀ ċᴀ ᴀnoɪɼ ᴀɼɼ ᴀn
ʒ-coɼᴀn óɼɼeᴀċ bo 'n oɪleᴀn úɼ, ᴀʒuɼ bᴀɪle ᴀɪʒ ᴀ b-ꝼuɪl ʒo
leoɼ ᴀɪʒ ċeᴀċċ ʒᴀċ lᴀ ó ʒᴀċ cᴀɼɼóe (quarter, direction);
ᴀʒuɼ ꝼóɼ oɼ cɪonn ʒᴀċ nɪó bᴀɪle ᴀnn ᴀ b-ꝼuɪl ᴀɼ ó-ċeᴀnʒᴀ
óuċċᴀɪɼ ꝼᴀoɪ ṁeᴀɼ. 13. bɪ ċɼeɪb nᴀ ʒᴀɪllɪṁe ᴀ ʒ-coṁnuɪʒe
pɼᴀɪóɪneᴀċ ᴀɼɼ ċeᴀnʒᴀ ᴀ n-ᴀċᴀɼᴀċ, the tribes of Galway
were always studiously fond of the language of their fathers. 14. Ⱥċċ nᴀɼ ċᴀɪnɪc bo óeᴀɼbɼᴀċᴀɼɼ Cᴀmon ᴀɼɼ
ᴀɼɼ? 15. Ċᴀɪnɪc; ꝼᴀoɪl me (I thought) ʒuɼ ɼᴀɪb mé ᴀɪʒ
ɪnɼeᴀċċ óuɪċ ᴀɼɼ. 16. Nɪ ɼᴀbᴀɪɼ. 17. Ⱳᴀɼɼe ċᴀɪnɪc ɼe
ᴀ bᴀɪle. 18. Ⱥn 'ɼ ᴀn Oɪleᴀn úɼ ᴀ bɪ ɼé? 19. Seᴀó.
20. b-ꝼuɪl ʒo leoɼ ᴀɪɼʒɪó ᴀɪʒe ᴀɪʒ ċeᴀċċ bo? 21. Nɪ
b-ꝼuɪl ᴀɪʒe ʒo leoɼ ᴀɪɼʒɪó, óɼɼ nɪ b-ꝼuɪl ɼe ᴀnn ᴀċċ óᴀ blɪ-
ᴀʒᴀn, ᴀʒuɼ bɪ ᴀn ċ-ᴀm olc le ɼᴀoɼċuʒᴀó ó'ꝼᴀʒᴀɪl; nɪ b-ꝼuɪl,
ᴀɼɼ ᴀn ᴀóbᴀɼ ɼɪn, móɼᴀn ᴀɪɼʒɪó ᴀɪʒe. 22. Ⱥn n-óeɼɼ ɼe
nɪó ᴀɼɼ bɼċ mᴀɪċ ᴀɼɼ ᴀn ċɪɼ ᴀʒuɼ ᴀɼɼ nᴀ óᴀoɪnɪb? 23
Oeɼɼ ɼe ʒuɼ mᴀɪċ ᴀn ᴀɪċ í; ʒo b-ꝼuɪl nᴀ óᴀoɪne ʒᴀn ċɼᴀɪl-

one of the nine aspirable consonants, it has, it should be remembered, no
other effect on that consonant than what the (·) dot, had it been placed
over the said consonant, would have produced.

bh, therefore, is the same as ḃ.
ch, ... ċ.
gh, ... ġ.
ph. ... ... ṗ.
bh, ... ·– ḃ, &c. See page 19.

leaċt, ʀaoʀ, cóʀaċ, ʀaoċaʀac, onóʀaċ. 24. Raıb aımʀıʀ
bʀeaʒ aıʒe aıʀ an b-ꝼaıʀʀʒe? 25. Nı ʀaıu aımʀıʀ bʀeaʒ
aıʒe aıʀ an b-ꝼaıʀʀʒe—bı an ʒaoċ áʀo, an ʀpéıʀ ꝼaoı ou-
ban aʒuʀ ʀımuo no neul aıʀ an nʒʀéın aıʀ ꝼeaó óa lá. 26.
An aıʀ loınʒ ʀeoıl oo ċaınıc ʀe?—was it in a sailing vessel he came? 27. Nı ꝼeaó; aċc aıʀ loınʒ ʒaılle (pronounced in two syllables, gahyil-le; gaɫyil, as one syllable;
no, but in a steamer). 28. Cıa an aınm cá aıʀ an loınʒ
ʒaılle aıʀ o-caınıc ʀe? 29. Pʀıonʀa Albeʀc. 30. An
ann ʒaıllım oo ċuıʀ ʀıaó ʀceaċ a ʒ-cuan?—was it at Galway they put into harbour?. 31. Iʀ ʀeaó. 32. Oaʀ
m'ꝼoċaıl camuıo a nʒaʀ ʒo Loċ-na-ʀaċ (Loughrea); ʀo
e oeıʀe m'aıʀcıʀe-ʀe, an ıuó. 33. b-ꝼuıl cuʀa aıʒ oul a
b-ꝼaó? 34. Cá me oul ʒo Aċ-luan. 35. ꝼan lıom-ʀa ann
ʀo a noċc aʒuʀ beıóıʀ ann, am ʒo leoʀ a máʀaċ. 36. ʒo
ʀaıb maıċ aʒao, nı ꝼanꝼaó. 37. Maıʀe, cá ꝼaılce ʀomac,
ma ꝼanaıʀ. 38. Nı ꝼanꝼaó; cʀıallꝼaó lıom. 39. ʒo ʀeıʀ
bıʒe Oıa ouıc.

TWENTY-FIRST LESSON.

Obs. 1.—All verbs beginning with one of the seven
mute consonants (b, ꝼ, p, c, ʒ, o, c,) are eclipsed after
particles of interrogation—an, whether; a (for an), whether; naċ, whether not; ca, where;—also after ʒo, that,
would that; oa, if, suppose if ; (sign of the conditional
mood); muna, if not; and after naċ (relative pronoun),
who not; which not; as,

" An b-ꝼuıl" cu ʒo maıċ?	Are you well?
" A ʒ-cluın" cu me?	Do you hear me?
" Naċ o-cuıʒeann" ʀe ċu?	Does he not understand you?
" Ca b-ꝼuıl" Oıa?	Where is God?
" Ca b-ꝼuıl" cu Aóaım?	Where art thou, Adam?
" Oa m-beıċea" ann ʀo nı ʒabꝼaó mo óeaʀb-bʀacaıʀ baʀ.	Hadst Thou been here my brother had not died.

" Ⲙⲩⲛⲁ ⲟ-ⲧⲓⲟⴜⲫⲁⲓⲟ" ⲣⲓⲁⲟ ⲁⲓⲣ   If they will not come at
ⲁⲛ ⲧⲣⲓ, ⲃⲉⲓⲟⲓⲟ ⲙⲁ̀ll.   three, they shall be late.

" Ꙅⲟ ⲙ-ⲃⲉⲁⲛⲛⲩⲓⵣ" Ⲟⲓⲁ ⲟⲩⲓⲧ.   May God save you.

OBS. 2.—ⲁ, *who, which*; when nominative case, causes aspiration; (See Fourteenth Lesson, first paragraph, p. 79), but when objective case, governed by a preposition expressed or suppressed, causes eclipsis; as,

Ⲁⲛ ⲧⲉ " ⲁⲓⲣ ⲁ" ⲙ-ⲃⲣⲟⲛ ⲧⲩ   He *on whom* thou hast be-
ⵣⲣⲁⲟ.   stowed love.

Ⲫⲁⲛ, ⲁ'ⲣ ⲛⲁ ⲫⲓll 'ⲣ ⲁⲛ ⲛⵣleo   Stay, and do not return to
" ⲟ'ⲁ" ⲟ-ⲧⲩⵣⲁⲓⲣ ⲥⲩl.—*Ho-*   the fight *to which* thou
mer, l. 524, *B.* I.   hast given (turned) thy
                    back.

Ⲁⲛ ⲧ-ⲁⲙ " ⲁ" ⲟ-ⲧⲁⲓⲛⲓⲥ Ⲡⲁ-   The time (in) *which* (when)
ⲟⲣⲩⲓⲥ ⵣⲟ ɧ-Ꭼⲓⲣⲓⲛⲛ.   Patrick came to Ireland.

It may be well to see at a glance, the instances in which ⲁ, in its several acceptations, affects, and when it does *not* affect with aspiration or eclipsis, the initial mute of the noun or verb immediately following it :—

Eclipsis is **produced** **by**	ⲁ, when it signifies *all who, all that*; as, ⲁ ⲃ-ⲫⲩⲓⲗ ⲟⲉ ⲙⲛⲁⲓⲃ ⲁⲓⲣ ⲁⲛ ⲃⲟⲙⲁⲛ, *all that* are of women on earth. ⲁ, when it signifies *whom, which*, governed by a *preposition* (See preceding Examples, under Obs. 2.) ⲁ (for ⲁⲛ) ... ... *whether?* as, Ⲁ ⲟ-ⲧⲓⲟⲥⲫⲁⲓⲟ ⲧⲩ, ⲛⲟ ⲁ ⲃ-ⲫⲁɧⲫⲁⲓⲟ ⲧⲩ, Ꭼⲓⲗⲓⲛ ⲁ Ꮢⲩⲓⲛ? Wilt thou come or stay, Eileen a Rún? ⲁ, ... *their*; as, ⲁ ⵣ-ⲥⲁⲛⲁ, their friend. ⲁ, (for ⲁⲛⲛ) ... ... *in*; as, Ⲁ ⵣ-Ⲥⲁⲓⲣⲓⲗ ⲛⲁ Ꮢⲓⵣ, in Cashel of the Kings.
Aspiration **is produced** **by**	ⲁ, when it signifies *his*; as " ⲁ" ⲥⲁⲛⲁ, his friend. ⲁ, ... *who, which*; as, ⲁⲛ ⲧⲉ " ⲁ" ⲙⲟⲗⲁⲣ, he *who* praises. ⲁ is a sign of the Inf. mood; as, " ⲁ" ⲙⲟⲗⲁⲟ, to praise. ⲁ ... a sign of the nom. case of address; as, " ⲁ" ⲥⲁⲛⲁ ⲙⲟ ⲥⲣⲟⲓⲟⲉ, oh, friend of my heart.
No change **is produced** **when**	ⲁ signifies *her*; as, " ⲁ" ⲥⲁⲛⲁ, her friend. ⲁ strengthens an affirmation; ⲁ ⲟⲉⲓⲣⲓⲙ, I say.

OBS. 3.—In every situation in which an initial consonant is eclipsed, an initial vowel takes ⲛ; as, ⲁⲣ " ⲛ-ⲁⲧⲁⲓⲣ" ⲁ ⲧⲁ ⲁⲓⲣ ⲛⲉⲓⲙ, Our Father who art in heaven; ⲧⲁⲃⲁⲓⲣ ⲟⲩⲓⲛⲛ ⲁⲛ

ᴛᴜḃ oṗ " ṅ-aṗáṅ" laċċaṁaḃ, give us this day our daily bread.

Aᵹuṗ ᴅo ṁeall ᴛuṗ " ṅ-aċaṗṗ" me aᵹuṗ ᴅo ṁallaṗc mo ċuaṗaṗaì ᴅeìċ ṅ-ṇaṗṗe.	And "your father" cheated me, and changed my hire ten times.—*Words of Jacob to Rachel and Lia.*

When, however, the article an (the), governed by a preposition, precedes the initial vowel, n is not, in that case, prefixed; because n of the article (an) answers the requirements of euphony quite as well; as, aṗ an aóḃaṗ ṛiṅ, on that account.

There is not, as should be, according to Obs. 3, an h placed before a in aóḃaṗ, since the final n of the article produces the required euphony.

Noᴛᴇ.—By means of Eclipsis and Aspiration in Irish, the varying sounds of the mutable consonants are clearly noted, while, at the same time, the radical *unvarying* spelling of each word is preserved. From the non-use of this system of notation for the variable consonants, the Welsh have, in changing the consonant with every successive mutation of sound, sadly destroyed the orthography of their language, and rendered Etymology a puzzle.

The difference in the manner of notation is best seen from the following example :—

Irish.	Welsh.	English.
Caṗ ṗoᵹuṗ.	Câr agos.	A near kinsman or friend.
A ċaṗ.	Ei gûr.	His friend.
A caṗ.	Ei châr.	Her friend.
Mo ċaṗ.	Vy nghâr.	My friend.
Aṗ ᵹ-caṗ.	...	Our friend.

The radical initial is four times changed in Welsh; in Irish it is preserved *unchanged*; its various permutations in sound being noted by means of Aspiration and Eclipsis.

VOCABULARY.

Aólacaḃ,, (pr. *eyelakoo*), was buried; from aóìac, (aó, the first syl. sounds like *eys*. See Fourth Lesson. p. 21).

Aṗreol, Apostle : from the Greek, Ἀπόστολε

bṛeìċ, to held ; to hold in the mind; form a judgment ; bṛeìċ bṛeìċe, to judge, judgment.

bṛu, *f.*, a womb ; poss. case, bṛuṅ, or bṛoṅ, of the womb.

Caċ, *f.*, a battle ; ceuḋċaċaḃ, of the hundred battles.

Catuṡaḋ; *m.*, fighting, temptation.

Ceur, *m.*, a cross; a crucifix; *v.*, to crucify.

Cṙeiḋim, I believe; cṙciḋ, believe thou; Latin, *crede.*

Cuaiḋ, went; per. tense of teiḋ; *ir. v.*, go thou.

D'ainm, for do ainm, thy name.

Déancaṙ, pass. voice, present tense of the verb déan, do; is done; ṡo n-déancaṙ, subj. pres., that may be done; ṡniḋċeaṙ, is done; is another form of the pass. voice of the verb "to do;" coming from a different radix—ṡniḋ, act, do, perform. Three of the irregular verbs—(which in Irish, amount in all only to ten)—are found in the Lord's Prayer. They are—tiṡiḋ. may come; déancaṙ and ṡniḋċeaṙ, is done; tabaiṙ (pr. *thóir*), give.

Eaṡlaiṙ, *f.*, church; resembling the French *eglise,* is, like it, derived from the same root, *ekklesia*, Gr.

Fiaċa, *m.*, debts; trespasses.

Fiaċaṁ, *m.*, a debtor; Latin, *debitor,* or, as the English paraphrase has it, "those who trespass against us;" aṙ b-ḟiaċaṁṅaiḃ, (to) our debtors.

Fuaiṙ, pres. tense of faṡ, get; fuaiṙ baṡ, got, or suffered, death.

Ṡaḃ, take, receive, capture, conceive, to act upon; to perform; ṡaḃaiḋ aiṙm, take (ye) up arms; ṡaḃaiḋ ṡeiḃ, take possession; aṙ ṡaḃaḋ é, was he captured? a ṡaḃaḋ, who was conceived of or by; do ṡaḃaḋaṙ cṙaṅ, they cast anchor; ṡaḃaiḋ aḃṙaiṅ, sing songs.

Ṡein, to beget; to be born of; Gr. γίνου, *ginou;* a ṡeiṅeaḋ, who was born of; begotten of; Welsh, *geni;* Lat. *gigno;* Sans. *janih.*

Fulanṡ, suffer, endure; a ḋ' fulanṡ páiṙ; who endured the passion.

Irṅion, *m.*, Hell; Lat. *infernum.*

Laeċaṁail, daily; derived from lae, poss. case of lá, day; and amail, like, *i.e.*, day-like; as daily in English has come from the Saxon *day-lic*, day-like.

Leiṡ, let, allow, permit; ṅa leiṡ ṙinṅ, do not permit us, lead us not.

Maṙḃ (pr. *márw*). dead; Lat. *mors,* death, and *mortuus*, dead; ó maṙbaiḃ, from *the* dead. Welsh, *marw*, to die; Heb. מת, *meth.*

Naoṁ, *m.*, a saint; *adj.* holy; naoṁaḋ, to make holy; naoṁċa, made holy, blessed, sanctified; naoṁ-ċaṙ, pass. voice, is made holy; ṡo naoṁċaṙ, *subj. mood,* that may be made holy.

Neaṁ. f., Heaven; *poss. case,* neiṁe; *prep. case,* néiṁ.

Paiḋiṙ, *m., Pater;* from which the former is derived by changing *t* into ḋ.

Peacaḋ, *m.*, a sin; Latin, *peccatum.*

Peacaċ, a sinner; peacaċaiḃ, (to) sinners.

Spioṙaḋ, *m.*, Spirit, Ghost; aṅ Spioṙaḋ Naoṁ, the Holy Ghost.

Talṁaṅ, f., poss. case of talaṁ, earth.

Tiṡiḋ, comes; Ir. verb; ṡo d-tiṡiḋ, subj. mood, may come; root—taṙṙ, come.

Uile, all; as, uile-ċuṁaċtaċ, Allpowerful, Almighty.

EXERCISE XXXIII.

[There are many of our readers, we feel certain, anxious to see the *Pater noster* in Irish. In this Lesson we relieve this anxious feeling, and give, too, the *Ave Maria* and *Creed.* There is no way for learning a language better

than to commit to memory as many words as one possibly
can from that language.

Aṅ Paiḋiṛ, the "Pater."

Aṛ n-aṫaiṛ, a ṫá aiṛ néiṁ: ᵹo naoṁṫaṛ ḋ'aiṇm; ᵹo
ḃ-ṫiᵹiḋ ḋo ṛiᵹeaċṫ; ᵹo n-ḋéanṫaṛ ḋo ṫoil aiṛ aṇ ṫalaṁ,
maṛ ᵹníḋṫeaṛ aiṛ néiṁ.　Taḃaiṛ ḋuiṇn aṇ ṛuḋ aṇ n-
aṛáṇ laeṫeaṁail; aᵹuṛ maiṫ ḋúiṇn aṛ ḃ-ḟiaċa, maṛ ṁaiṫ-
muiḋ-ṇe ḋ'aṛ ḃ-ḟiacaṁnaiḃ ḟéiṇ; aᵹuṛ ná léiᵹ ṛiṇn a
ᵹ-caṫaᵹaḋ; aċṫ ṛaoṛ ṛiṇn ó olc.　Aṁéṇ.

Aṇ ṫ-Aue-Ṁaṛia; nó, ḟáilṫe aṇ Aiṇᵹil.

'S é ḋo ḃeaṫa, a Ṁuiṛe, a ṫá láṇ ḋe ᵹṛáṛa, ṫá aṇ Ṫiᵹ-
ṫeaṛna leaṫ; iṛ beaṇnuiᵹṫe ṫu ṫaṛ na mnáiḃ, aᵹuṛ iṛ
beaṇnuiᵹṫe ṫoṛaḋ ḋo ḃṛoṇn, Joṛa.　A naoṁ Ṁuiṛe, a
ṁáṫaiṛ Ḋé, ᵹuiḋ oṛaiṇn-ne na peacaċaiḃ, anoiṛ, aᵹuṛ
aiṛ uaiṛ aṛ m-báiṛ.　Aṁéṇ.

Cṛé na n-Apṛtol.

Cṛeiḋim aṇn Ḋia, aṇ Aṫaiṛ uile-ċuṁaċṫaċ, cṛuṫuiᵹ-
ṫeoiṛ neiṁe aᵹuṛ ṫalṁaṇ: aᵹuṛ aṇn Joṛa Cṛíoṛṫ, a aoṇ-
ṁac-ṛaṇ, aṛ ḃ-Ṫiᵹeaṛna; a ᵹabaḋ ó 'n Spioṛaḋ Naoṁ,
a ᵹeiṇeaḋ ó Ṁuiṛe óiᵹ, a ḋ'ḟulaṇᵹ paiṛ ṛaoi Poiṇṫ Pio-
laiḋ; a céaṛaḋ, a ḟuaiṛ báṛ aᵹuṛ a h-aḋlacaḋ; a ċuaiḋ
ṛíóṛ ᵹo h-iḟṛioṇn; a ḋ' eiṛiᵹ aṇ ṫṛeaṛ lá ó ṁaṛbaiḃ; a
ċuaiḋ ṛuaṛ aiṛ néiṁ: a ṫá 'ṇn a ṛuiḋe aiṛ ḋeiṛ Ḋé, aṇ
Aṫaṛ uile-ċuṁaċṫaiᵹ: aṛ ṛiṇ ṫiocṛaṛ le bṛeiṫaṁnaṛ ṫa-
baiṛṫ aiṛ beoḋaiḃ aᵹuṛ aiṛ ṁaṛbaiḃ.　Cṛéiḋim 'ṛ aṇ
Spioṛaḋ Naoṁ, 'ṛ aṇ naoṁ Eaᵹlaiṛ Caṫoiliceaċ, a ᵹ-
cumaoiṇ na naoṁ; a ṁaiṫeaḋ na b-peacaḋ; aṇn eiṛeiṛiᵹe
na ᵹ-coṛp aᵹuṛ 'ṛ aṇ m-beaṫa ṛuṫaiṇ.　Aṁéṇ.

TWENTY-SECOND LESSON.

Some of the numeral adjectives have already, from time to time, appeared in our Lessons. A full list of both *Ordinal* and *Cardinal* is here subjoined:

CARDINALS.

1. Aon, or aen, (pr. in one syllable *ee-un*.)

2. Do, two in the abstract —as, it has struck (the) two; buail re an dó.
Do, never precedes a noun.
Dá, two, accompanies the noun, and qualifies it.

3. Trí.

4. Ceatar, four in the abstract; as, five is better than four, ir reann cuig na ceatair; it struck four, do buail re an ceatair.
Ceitre, four; as, four feet, ceitre cor.

5. Cuig.
6. Sé.

7. Seact.
8. Oct.
9. Naoi
10. Deic.
11. Aon-déag.
12. Dó-déag.

ORDINALS.

1st. Ceud, aonmad (pr. *ee-unwoo*): the ending mad (*woo*) suffixed to any cardinal adjective, gives its corresponding ordinal.

2nd. Do-mad.

2nd Dara.

3rd. Treas; trimad (pr. *threewoo*.)

4th. Ceatarmad, *keharwoo*, signifies also a quarter, because it is the fourth part; the thigh; a stanza, or quartan; a quadrant; a ploughland, pasturing.

5th. Cuigead.
6th. Sé-mad, and read, (*sheshoo*).

7th. Seact-mad.
8th. Oct-mad.
9th. Naoi-mad.
10th. Deicmad.
11th. Aonmad déag.
12th. Domad déag.

13. Trí déaġ.	13th. Tríṁaḋ déaġ, or treas déaġ.
14. Ceaṫair-déaġ.	14th. Ceaṫarṁaḋ déaġ.
15. Cúiġ-déaġ.	15th. Cuiġṁaḋ déaġ.
16. Sé-déaġ.	16th. Seṁaḋ déaġ.
17. Seaċt-déaġ.	17th. Seaċtṁaḋ déaġ.
18. Oċt-déaġ.	18th. Oċtṁaḋ déaġ.
19. Naoi-déaġ.	19th. Naoṁaḋ déaġ.
20. Fice.	20th. Ficeaḋ.
21. Aon a'r fice, or aon air ficiḋ.	21st. Aonṁaḋ air ficiḋ, one (*on*) twentieth.
22. Dó a'r fice, or dó air ficiḋ.	22nd. Dóṁaḋ air ficiḋ.

Numerals from ten to twenty are formed by annexing the suffix "déaġ," "teen," (from deiċ, ten) to the simple numerals aon, do, trí, ceaṫar, cuiġ, &c.

Adjectives come *after* the nouns with which they agree; numeral adjectives, however, go *before* them.

When a number greater than ten—composed, of course, of the simple numeral and the decimal ending déaġ—is joined to a noun, the latter is placed neither before nor after the compound numeral, but *between* the decimal ending (déaġ) and the digit; as,

Anois buḋ dá "fear"-déaġ, claṅn Iacoib.

Now the sons of Jacob were twelve.

—*Irish Translation of the Book of Genesis, by John Archbishop of Tuam. Dublin—Duffy.*

Of the first ten numerals or digits, some aspirate; others eclipse; the rest cause no change.

Aspiration is produced by	Aon, one,
	Dá, two; except the expression, dá d-trian, two thirds; as,
	    Dá d-trian sneaċta le sleiḃtiḃ,
	    Two-thirds snoẇ in mountains.

Eclipsis by	Seaċt, seven, Oċt, eight, Naoi, nine, Deiċ, ten,	and the compound forms of 7, 8, 9—seaċt-déaġ, 17; oċt-déaġ, 18; naoi-déaġ, 19.

No
change
occurs
after
{
Τ{ιe, three.
Ceιτ{ιe, four.
Cuιჳ, five.
Sé, six.
Fιċe, twenty.
Τ{ιocα, thirty, &c.
}

Obs.—In English, to a question in which the verb is
.ally expressed, the mere *sign* of the tense suffices for
answer—the rest being clearly understood from the question put; as, in the following, *Have* you *gone* to town to-
day? I *have*. *Do* you *play* on the harp? I *do*. *Will*
your friend be always remembered by you? He *shall*.
To the reply, "I have," the word "gone," is understood;
to the phrase, "I do," the word "play" is understood; and
"be remembered," is clearly supposed to come after the
answer, "he shall," in the foregoing sentences.

In Irish, however, no such suppression as this pointed
out does or can occur, for the idea of *time* is expressed
by the verbal *ending*, which accordingly necessites the
enunciation of the entire verb; as, αn ჳ{ιαბuιჳeαnn τu mé?
Do you love me? Ჳ{ιαბuιჳιm, I do (love). Ἁ ბ-τιoc"{ιαιბ"
τu ბo'n ჳ-cα{ι{ιαιჳ? Will you come to the rock? Τιoc-
"{ιαბ," I shall (come); see page 108.

Do, did, may, can, might, could, shall, will, when mere
signs of grammatical time, are translated into Irish by the
inflection or ending peculiar to each tense, and consequently the verb must be, even in answering to a question,
expressed fully.

VOCABULARY.

Accompany (go with), bul le; please
accompany us, ταnn lιnn, mα
'r re bo τoιl é.
Azure, ჳo{ιm, ჳ{αċ-ჳo{ιm.
Clear, ჳlαn.
Cloudless, ჳαn neul; adjectives ending in *less*, are translated by
the preposition ჳαn, without
(Fr. *sans*), governing the noun
which forms the forepart of the
adjectives; as *spotless*, (without
spot), *reproachless*, (without reproach), ჳαn rmαl, ჳαn cαιh,
sans tache, sans reproche.
Constellation, coιm{ιeulτ, *m*,
Contemplate, b{ιeατnuჳαბ, derived
from b{ιeιτ, to conceive, to
hold, to judge.
Delia (Bridget), b{ιჳιბ.
Dionysius, } boncαბ.
Denis, }
Footstool, coιr-τċöl, *m*.
Freezing, αιჳ rιoc; Latin, *siccus*.
... neo (freezing bard),

L

Welsh, *rheu*; ɼeolaċ, ice; ɼe-olacaó, to become icy.

Happiness, ɼonaɼ, *m.* (from ɼona, happy), ɼeuṅ, *m.*

Horn, aóaɼc, *m.* (aó in the beginning or middle of words sounds like *ey*) ɼaoi aóaɼncib, under horns, horned.

Aóaɼcaċ, horny.

  ,,   beṅn, a horn, a pinnacle, gable, peak, mountain. Hence the names of so many cliffs or mountains in Scotland, *Ben-wyvis*; *Ben-Lomond*; *Ben-Nevis*;—as well as in Ireland Ben-Burb; Ben-bulban; Ben-Edair (Howth). In Welsh, *pen* means peak, or headland; as, Penkillan. The name *Twelve Pens*, by which the twelve cliffs in Connemara are called, is manifestly for "*twelve benns.*"

beṅnaċ, horned, curled, peaked, nimbus-like, pointed, forked. An ᵹeallaċ beṅnaċ, the horned moon. Heb. בָּנָה, *bana*, to build; בֵּן, *Ben*, a son, because the *prop* of the family.

Ignatius, Naɼᵹúɼ; Naoṁ Naɼᵹúɼ aɼ Loᵹola, St. Ignatius of Loyola.

Lawn, cluan, *m.*; macaiɼe, *m.*, maᵹ, *f.*

Light, (lustre, effulgence), leuɼ, *m.*
... (a blaze), laɼaṁ, *f.*
... (brightness), ɼoluɼ, *m.*
... (to ignite), laɼ, *v.*
... (not heavy), eaó-cɼoṁ.

Mercury, aiɼᵹeaó beo (*i.e.*, quicksilver).

Moon, ᵹeallaċ, *f*

Miles, Ṁaolṁuine (pr. as ṁaolne), from maol, bald, shaven, devoted to; as clerics were; and Ṁuine, Mary.

Night, oióċe, *f.*, (pr. *ee-ché*), as opposed to lá, day; nóċt, to-night, opposed to an iuó, to-day.

Opinion, baɼaṁail, *f.*

Orio (Mount), remarkable for being the hill on which SS. Peter and Paul suffered, is called by the author of the "Roman Vision" óiɼcɼoc-Ċepaiɼ, the golden hill of Cephas, or Peter.

Promenading, ɼpaiɼóinċáċt, *f.*; derived from ɼpáɼ, a space, *m.*, a little time; and aiɼoṁ, *f.*, a journey; *i.e.*, walking about for a time.

Reflect, ɼmuaineaó, leuɼrmuaineaó.

O'Reilly, Ua Raᵹallaċ. The O'Reillys were Princes of East Brefny, or Cavan; the Ruaɼcaᵹ, O'Rourkes, Princes of East Brefny, or Leitrim. Raᵹalac, from whom the family took its name, lived in the tenth century.

Terrace, aɼbán.

Threshold, caiɼreaċ, (as if caiɼɼ rceaċ, come in); bonuɼ.

Throne, a royal chair, caċaoiɼ nioᵹóa, *f.*

Vatican Hill, cnoc ɼaióican: *Vates*, in old Latin *fates*, is from the Irish ɼaió, a prophet; and not, as Scalinger derives it, from the Greek φατης, *phates*, a talker.

Vestibule, fóɼbonuɼ, *m.*

Weather, aiṁɼiɼ, *f.*; frosty weather is fine, iɼ bɼeaᵹ aiṁɼiɼ ɼioca.

EXERCISE XXXIV.

1. Denis, are you after tea? A Óoncaó, an ól tu no cuió (thy portion of) té? 2. I am; (ó' olaɼ—I have drunk it). 3. Well, as the night is fine, let us go out and have a short stroll on the terrace, and enjoy an agreeable conversation—maiɼe ó cáula ᵹo b-ɼuil an oióċe bɼeaᵹ

ceigmuiṙ amaċ aזuṙ ḃeaɲṁuiṙ ṙpaiṙóiṙeaċc aip aɲ aṙbaɲ, aזuṙ biḃeaḃ aזaiɲɲ coṁṙaḃ caiċɲeaṁaċ. 4. I am pleased; but my sister Dela is most anxious that I should remain with her for an hour, aċc cá mo ḃeaṙb-ṙiuṙ biṙiᴣiḃ ṙaoi buil ṁoiṙ ᴣo b-ṙaɲṙaiɲɲ aice aiṙ ṙeaḃ uaiṙe. 5. Well, ask her to accompany us. 6. Yes, I shall (iaṙṙaḃ). 7. Delia, will you be pleased (aṙ ṁaiċ leac) to accompany Miles O'Reilly and. myself while taking a promenade on the terrace? 8. I shall (iṙ maiċ liom); I am just so glad to be able to gain something from your wisdom. Well, what a beautiful night! 9. (Miles)—It is a very beautiful night, indeed. 10. (Delia)—It is freezing hard—is it not? (Cá ṙe aiᴣ ṙioc ᴣo ᴣeuṙ—ɲaċ b-ṙuil?) 11. It is freezing hard, for all the signs (coṁaṙċaiḃ ṙioca) of frost are apparent (ṙoluṙ); the sky is cloudless and azure; the wind is blowing from the north (cá ɲa ᴣaoċ o'ɲ cuaiḃ); the stars sparkle very brilliantly (cá ɲa ṙeulca aiᴣ ḃealṙaḃ ᴣo h-aɲloɲɲaċ); the atmosphere (aɲ c-aeṙ) is intensely cold, and my brother James told me the mercury was very low (ṙioṙ ᴣo ṁóṙ). 12. (Denis)—Delia, do you like frosty weather? 13. Yes, very much. 14. I like to walk out at night when all is still—not a sound to be heard; when earth is, as it were, going to slumber ('ɲuaiṙ a cá aɲ calaṁ, maṙ m-beiḃeaḃ, bul aɲɲ ṙuaiɲ), the moon in her horns (ᴣo beaɲɲaċ ɲo, ṙaoi aḃaiṙciḃ), shining, as she is to night, in a clear sky, while the stars, like sentinels (maṙ luċc ṙaiṙe) before the threshold of Heaven (oṙ coṁaiṙ ḃoṙuiṙ ɲeiṁe), hold out their lights (leuṙa) pointing to that home above where light (ṙoluṙ) eternal dwells. 15. (Miles)—It is sweet, indeed, to ponder on these things, and raise ourselves above earth; saying, if the vestibule is so luminous, how glorious must the dwelling of the Great King be!—if the footstool is so beautiful, what must His throne be! 16. (Delia)— Oh, in that land of eternal brightness, there is no sun, no moon—God himself is the light, and glory, and happiness of the citizens of heaven. 17. (Denis)—You put me in mind of what is told of St. Philip Neri (aɲ ṙcáiṙ a ḃeiɲceaṙ caob Naoiṁ Ṗilip Néṙi) and of the great Saint Ignatius Loyola, who, when gazing from Mount Orio, near the Vatican Hill, in Rome (ṙ aɲ Ṙoiṁ) on the sparkling threshold of Heaven (aṗ ʒeaṫa ḃealṗaċ ṇa b-ḟlaiṫeaṗ) yearned for that home beyond the stars where our dear Lord dwells in glory. 18. (Delia)—Indeed such thoughts are natural; for on contemplating (aiʒ bṗeaċnúʒaḃ) the heavens (aṗ ṇeiṁ) I often call to mind (ir miṇic cuiṁnuiʒim aṗ) what faith tells us of " that place which God has prepared for those who love him," and say, in our country's adage, " there is no glory to be compared with the glory of heaven"—ṇíl ʒlóiṗ maṗ ʒlóiṗ ṇeiṁe. 19. (Miles)—Although such thoughts are natural, and ought to strike any one, how few there are who make such reflections—ʒiḃ ʒo b-ḟuil ṡmuaiṇċe maṗ ṡo ṇaḃuṗḃa, ɩ ʒuṗ buḃ cóiṗ a ṫeaċṫ aṇṇ iṇṇċiṇ ʒaċ ḋuiṇe, ṇaċ beaʒ a ḋeaṇaṗ ṡmuaiṇċe maṗ ṡaḃ? 20. (Denis)—That is true; all arises (eiṗiʒeaṇṇ aṇ meuḃ ṡo) from not thinking. 21. (Delia)—I feel chilly (ṫá ḟuaċṫ oṗm-ṡa); it is time to go in. 22. (Miles)—I thought we were to say something about the constellations. 23. (Denis)—It is too late now ; besides my dear sister feels chilly. 24. (Delia)—The clock strikes. 25. (Miles)—What hour is it? 26. (Denis)—It is only nine o'clock, I suppose. 27. (Delia)—One, two, three, four, five, six, seven, eight, nine, ten—I have counted ten (ḋo ċoṁaiṗ me aṇ ḋeiċ) 28. (Denis)—It is ten o'clock, but you must remain with us till eleven at least—aċṫ caiṫṗiḃ ṫu ḟaṇṇaċṫ ʒo ḃ-ṫí aṇ aoṇ-ḋéaʒ aiṗ aṇ laʒaḃ (pr. *lly-adh*). 29. (Miles)—I am sorry I cannot wait so long; yet I shall go in to see your father and mother, your brother, and sister Jane.

TWENTY-THIRD LESSON.

In this Lesson is shown the manner in which the plural of nouns in Irish is formed.

The student who is acquainted with no other language but English, thinks the way in which the plural of nouns is formed in the language he speaks is very simple ; yet actually the inflections which characterize, in English nouns, the formation of the plural, are very varied, as may be perceived even from the few following examples—man, men ; foot, feet ;

cow, kine; child, children; box, boxes; ox, oxen; arch, arches; elf, elves; ruff, ruffs; fly, flies, echo, echoes; tyro, tyroes; money, monies; penny, pence; deer, deer; alms, alms.

In Hebrew and in the Romance languages, the formation of the plural is not difficult.

But in Latin and in Greek, the manner in which nouns form the plural is much more complex. The student must, in order to be able to tell with ease and fluency the plurals of all kinds of nouns in these ancient languages, devote much time to their study, and be familiar with their several forms of declension.

The formation of the plural of Irish nouns has been considered very difficult, yet we shall endeavour to make it as simple as possible.

In classifying Irish nouns we have observed, in the formation of their plural, a feature common to nouns in the Latin and Greek vocabularies—a feature, too, not foreign to English,—that one class takes an *additional* syllable in forming the plural; another class merely *inflects* the *final* syllable. The latter are called parisyllabic, or equal in the number of syllables; the former, imparisyllabic, or unequal in the number of syllables.

The plural of Irish nouns is, therefore, formed from the singular chiefly in both these ways:

First—*by a change in the final syllable.*

Secondly—*by annexing an additional syllable.*

The question arises, what class of nouns forms the plural by a mere change in the final syllable; and what class by annexing to it an additional syllable?

RULE I.—All *masculine* nouns (See Seventeenth Lesson, Rule 1, for knowing the Gender, page 93,) "ending in a single or double consonant, preceded immediately by one of the broad vowels ᴀ, ᴏ, ᴜ," form the plural from the singular by inserting the slender vowel—ı, after ᴀ, or ᴏ, or u; as—

SINGULAR.	PLURAL.
Aḃꞃᴀn, a song.	Aḃꞃᴀın, songs.
Aoḃᴀꞃ, a reason; cause, material.	Aoḃᴀıꞃ, reasons, causes.
Anꞃóᵹ, misery (from ᴀn, not; and ꞃóᵹ, ease, prosperity).	Anꞃóıᵹ, miseries

SINGULAR.	PLURAL.
baoġal, danger.	baoġail, dangers.
boċaṗ, a road, a highway.	boċaṗ, roads, highways.
Doṁan, the world.	Doṁaṗ, worlds.
Ȝaḃaṗ (Latin, *caper*) a goat.	Ȝaḃaṗ, goats.
Ȝaḃaṗ, a beagle.	Ȝaḃaṗ, beagles.
Ionṁuṗ, a treasure.	Ionṁuṗ, treasures.
Leiȝaṗ, a cure.	Leiȝaṗ, cures.
Peacaḋ, a sin.	Peacaiḋ, sins.
Sȝiobol, a barn.	Sȝioboil, barns.
Ceampoll (Latin, *templum*), a church.	Ceampoill, churches.

Nouns masculine ending in aċ, not only have the vowel ı inserted, but change the aspirated (ċ) into ȝ; as—

bacaċ, a cripple.	bacaiȝ, cripples.
beallaċ, a passage, a way.	beallaiȝ, ways.
Ⅿaṗcaċ, rider.	Ⅿaṗcaiȝ, riders.
Ⅿullaċ, a summit.	Ⅿullaiȝ, summits.
Sionnaċ, a fox.	Sionnaiȝ, foxes.
Uallaċ, a load, obligation.	Uallaiȝ, loads, obligations.

OBS.—This change in the final syllable, by inserting ı before the last consonant or consonants, is called by grammarians *Attenuation*, or making *slender*, because the syllable in which ı is inserted is no longer pronounced broadly, but rather with a slender, fine-drawn enunciation; for example, aḃṗan, in the singular number, is pronounced *aw-rawn;* in the plural it is aḃṗaın, (*awraw-in,*—the last two syllables being pronounced, as much as possible, in one)—so, aḃḃaṗ, *aw-war;* and in the plural, aḃḃaṗ, *áw-whir;* ionṁaṗ, a treasure, *ienwus;* in the plural, ionṁaṗ, *ienwish.*

EXCEPTION 1.—Some nouns of this class have a double form in the plural.

Ⅱinȝeal, an angel,	Ⅱinȝil, ainȝliḋ, angels.
biolaṗ, water-cresses.	biolaṗ, biolṗa, water-cresses.
Leabaṗ, a book.	Leabaṗ, leabṗa, books.
Leanḃ, a child.	Leinḃ, leanba, children.

SINGULAR.	PLURAL.
Meacan, a carrot or parsnip.	Meacain, meacna, carrots.
Uan, a lamb.	Uain, uana, lambs.

Exception 2.—Some words of one syllable insert ı, but drop the broad vowel; as—

Mac, a son.	Mıc, sons.
breac, a trout.	brıc, trouts.
Ceann, a head.	Cınn, heads.
Mulceann, pole (of the earth).	Mulcınn, poles.
Fear, a man.	Fır, men.
Peann, a pen.	Pınn, and peanna, pens.
Sınrear, progenitor.	Sınrır, progenitors.

Rule 2.—Some words of two syllables ending in a vowel remain parisyllabic, but change the final syllable by inserting c (smooth) or ċ (aspirated) before the final vowel; as,

baıle, a town.	baılce, towns.
Leıne, a shirt.	Leınce, shirts
Cuılle, a stake, a baton.	Cuaıllce, and cuaıllceaċa.
Cuaıne, a corner.	Cuaınce, corners.
Cúma, a form, a way, a manner.	Cumaıð, forms, ways; also cumċa, is a form of its plural.
Múılle, a mule.	Múıllce, and muıllıð, mules.
Ceıne, a fire.	Ceınce, fires.
Ceanȝa, a tongue.	Ceanȝċa, tongues.

Other few nouns form the plural in different ways; as,

Clabaıre, a blab.	Clabaırıð, blabs.
Duıne, a person.	Daoıne, persons, people.
Caora, a sheep.	Caoraıȝ, sheep.
Fıle, a poet.	Fılıð, poets.
Cıȝearna, a lord.	Cıȝearnaıð, lords.

VOCABULARY.

Calaṁ, f., the earth, land.	Annaccaċ, Harriet.
Aıl, pleasure, will.	Ceanra, meek, mild.
Aıc, (pr. aith short), pleasure, fancy, agreeableness.	Cle, left; laṁ cle, left hand.
	Deacaır, difficult.

Ɗiaɼmuid (from Ɗia, God, and aɼm-muid, of arms; poss. plural of aɼm; Latin, *arma*), Dermot, Darby. ᵯacƊiaɼmuid, Mac-Diarmod, or, as it is now spelled, MacDermott, a family name of the highest antiquity and of princely origin. The royal house of O'Connor, the MacDermotts, O'Rorkes, and O'Reillys, are descended from Eoca, supreme King of Connaught, Ulster, and Meath, in the fourth century.

Ɗeaɼ, *adj.,* ƀeiɼc, *poss. case fem.,* right; as, an ƀeaɼ laiṁ, the right hand; handsome; as, cailin ƀeaɼ, a handsome girl. It means also south; because the Druids of old, turning to the rising sun, for the purpose of adoring—as did the Jewish priests and Hebrew people to the East in worshipping God —had the *right* hand (ƀeaɼ) towards what we call the south; and to which accordingly they gave the same name as that by which they denominated the hand turned in that direction.

For the same reason they called the North tuaċ, or the country to the *left* hand—from tuaċ, the left hand; and the west, iaɼ, behind, hinder, rear-ward, because it was to them, on this occasion, the land to which the back was turned.

The East is called "oiɼ," from "oiɼ," *over, in front;* or from an old word of the same orthography signifying *light,* allied in meaning with the Hebrew word אוֹר, *ôr,* light; with which the modern Irish term for gold, óɼ, is identified —a metal with whose kindred brilliancy the beams of the rising sun light up the eastern sky. O'n ƀeaɼ, from the south, southerly; as, ʒaoċ ó'n ƀeaɼ,

south wind; o'n tuaċ, from the north, northerly; as, ʒaoċ o'n tuaċ, north wind; ó'n iaɼ, 'in the west, westerly; as, ʒaoċ ó'n iaɼ, west wind; ó'n oiɼ, in the east, easterly; as, ʒaoċ ó'n oiɼ, east wind. From these four words are formed many derivatives, some of which we shall, in the coming Lessons, present to our readers.

Ɗoṁan, *m.,* aiṅ, *pl.,* the world, in its physical and moral acceptation; as, ta an ƀoṁan ƀul ċaɼċ, the world is going round; ta an ƀoṁan aiʒ ƀul ƀo'n ƀonaɼ, the world is going to misfortune.

Saoʒal, *m.,* ail, *pl.,* the world; the life of man—like the Latin *sæculum;* as, ta an ɼaoʒal ɼo man ceo, this world passes away like a shadow.

Cɼuiṅne, *f.,* the physical world; the earth; the globe.

Uiɼ, the earth, soil; mould; aʒuɼ bɼeaƀ an uiɼ tiniṁ le ƒeicint, and let the dry land appear. —*Irish Genesis,* c. i. v. 9.

Cɼé, *m.,* clay; as, ta ɼe ɼinte ɼ'an ʒ-cɼé, he is laid in the clay.

Iṫiɼ, *f.,* the clay, or soil dug up; arable land, land producing corn.

Ɗuil, *f.,* ƀuille, *pl.,* expectation, desire, wish; as, ta ƀuil aʒaṁ leiɼ, I expect him; ta ƀuil aʒaṁ ƀul aṅn, I wish to go to it.

Ɗuil, *f.* element, creature; as, Cɼu-ċuiʒċeoiɼ na ṅ-ƀul, the Creator of the elements.

Ʒlaoiƀ, call; (Greek, καλίω, *kaleo.*)

Leaċt, *m.,* a lesson, written or imparted.

Leiʒean, *m.,* a lesson; also learning; from leiʒ, read thou. Leaċt is also a mound, a grave, a pile of stones heaped together in memory of the dead. Taṁleaċt, from taṁ, sleep, plague, death, and leaċt; Tallaght, near

Dublin, commemorative of the death of Partholan's followers. Leáċɖ, flattened.

Ⅿⅰꞃ, *adj.*, fine, thin; ⅿⅰꞃⅰꞡ. *v.*, make fine, explain; ⅿⅰꞃꞃⅰꞡⅾⅾ, *v.*, making fine, mincing, explaining; *n. m.*, explanation.

Ⅿⅰⅼ, *m.*, axletree, the beam or axle turned by the wheel in a mill, and which sets the whole machinery in motion; the axis of the earth: a mound, a knoll. Ⅿⅰⅼⅾ ꞃⅾ ꞃoċⅾ, the axle of the wheels; ceⅾꞃ ⅾꞃ ⅿⅰⅼ, the head of the axle; ⅿⅰⅼ-ċeⅾꞃ, the pole of the axle; ⅿⅰⅼ-ċⅰꞃꞃ ꞃⅾ cꞃⅰⅰꞃe, the poles of the world. This word ⅿⅰⅼ, is the root of the Greek μυλη, and Latin *molare*, and all their derivatives.

Ⅿⅰꞃꞃeⅰⅼ, f., neck; Latin, *monile*, a necklace.

Oⅰⅼⅾꞃ, *m.*—ⅾⅰꞃ, *plu.* an island; ⅰꞃⅰꞃ, f., plu. ⅰꞃꞃe, an island; ⅰ, an island; as, Ⅰ Coⅼⅰⅿ Cⅰⅼⅼe, the

Island of Columb Kille. Heb. ʼꞃ, *ai*, an island: ⅰ and ⅰꞃⅰ are contracted forms of ⅰhⅰꞃ, as, isle in English, for island. From ⅰꞃⅰ are derived names of many places in Ireland; as, ⅰꞃⅰꞃ, *Inch*; an island in Lough Swilly; Ⅰꞃⅰꞃ-eoꞡⅾⅰꞃ, *Innishowen*, (Eugene's Island), in the county Donegal; Ⅰꞃⅰꞃ-Cⅾċⅾⅰꞡ, *Innishcathy*, in the Shannon; Ⅰꞃⅰꞃ-Cⅾⅰċⅼeⅾꞃꞃ, *Enniskillen*; Ⅰꞃⅰꞃ, Ennis, chief town of Clare; Leⅾċ-ⅰꞃꞃe, *Lehinch* (half-island).

Oⅰⅾe, *m.*, oⅰⅾⅰ, *pl.*, a teacher, a professor; oⅰⅾe ꞗⅾoⅰꞃⅰⅾⅰꞃe, a confessor; from oⅰⅾe, and ꞗⅾoⅰꞃⅰⅾⅰꞃ, confession; oⅰⅾe ⅾⅰꞃꞏⅰⅾ, a godfather; oⅰⅾe ⅾⅰċꞃoⅿⅾ, a foster-father.

Pꞃⅰoⅿ, first, principal. Latin, *primum*. Pꞃⅰoⅿⅾⅾⅾⅾꞃ, first cause; Pꞃⅰoⅿ-ꞃoⅰꞃ, principal divisions.

Séoⅿꞃⅾ, *m.*, ⅾⅰċe, *pl.* a chamber; Welsh, *siambr*.

<h2 align="center">EXERCISE XXXV.</h2>

1. Ⅾ ⅾċⅾⅰꞃ, ꞗ-ꞗⅰⅼ ⅰⅾⅰꞃ (leisure) ⅾꞡⅾⅾ ⅾꞃoⅰꞃ? 2. Cⅾ, ⅾ ⅿⅰc, cⅰⅾ ⅾꞃ ꞃⅰⅾ ⅰꞃ ⅾⅰⅼ leⅾⅾ? (What thing is desired by thee?) 3. Cⅾ ⅾⅰⅼ (desire) ⅾꞡⅾⅿ ꞡo ⅾꞃⅾċⅾꞃⅾⅰꞃ (that you will treat) ⅾⅰꞃ ċꞃⅰċ-eoⅼⅰꞃ ꞃⅾ ⅾⅾⅼⅿⅾꞃ (geography). 4. Ⅿⅾⅰꞃe ⅿⅾꞃ ⅾⅰꞗⅾⅰꞃⅾ ⅿe, ⅰꞃ ⅾⅰⅾ ⅼⅰoⅿ ⅾꞃⅾċⅾⅾ ⅾⅰꞃ leⅾⅾ ⅾꞃoⅰꞃ. Cⅰⅾ eⅰⅼe ⅾ ꞗeⅰⅾeⅾꞃ ⅾꞃꞃ ⅾoꞃꞗeⅾċⅾ leⅾⅾ (who else will be along with you)? 5. ꞗeⅰⅾ ⅿo ċoⅼ-ċeⅾⅾⅾꞃ Pⅾⅾꞃⅾⅰc ⅾꞡⅰꞃ ⅿo ⅾeⅾꞃꞗ-ꞗⅰⅰꞃ Ⅾꞃꞃⅾⅾⅾⅾ;—ⅾⅾⅰⅾ ⅾⅰꞡ ꞗⅰⅰꞃeⅾċⅾ ⅼⅰꞃꞃ ⅾꞃꞃꞃ ⅾꞃ ꞃeoⅿꞃⅾ ꞃⅾⅰⅾeⅰꞃ (they are waiting for us in the study-room). 6. Ⅾꞗⅾⅰꞃ (say) leo ⅾeⅾċⅾ ⅾⅰⅾeⅾċ ⅾꞃꞃ ꞃo (into this place); ꞃⅰ ꞗeⅰⅾⅰꞃ ⅼⅰoⅿ-ꞃⅾ ⅾⅰⅼ ċⅰⅰⅰ (to go to them). Ⅾꞡⅰꞃ ⅾꞃoⅰꞃ, ꞃⅾċ ꞗ-ꞗⅰⅼ ꞃé ꞃⅰoꞃ ꞗeⅾⅰꞃ ⅾⅾoⅰꞗ (to you) eoⅼⅰꞃ ꞗⅾꞡⅾⅰⅼ ⅾⅰꞃ ⅾꞃ eⅾⅼⅾⅾⅾꞃ (*all-ee-yan*) ꞃo oʼꞃ oⅰⅾe ʼꞃⅾ ⅰⅾⅰⅿ-ꞃe? And now is it not easier for you to obtain knowledge of this science from your professor than from me? 7. Ⅾ ⅾċⅾⅰꞃ ꞡⅰⅼⅰꞃ, ⅰꞃ ꞗeⅾⅰꞃ ⅼⅰꞃꞃ ⅰⅾⅰⅾ-ꞃe (from you), ⅿⅾꞃ ꞡeⅾⅼⅼ (because) ꞡo ꞗ-ꞗⅰⅼ ⅾⅰ ċo ceⅾꞃꞃⅾ, ⅾꞡⅰꞃ ċo ꞡꞃⅾⅾⅾċ ꞃⅰꞃ ⅾꞃꞃ ⅾo ċⅾⅰꞃⅾ ⅼⅰꞃꞃ, ⅾꞡⅰꞃ ⅿⅰꞃⅰꞡeⅾꞃꞃ ⅾⅰ ꞡⅾċ ꞃⅰⅾ ⅾ ⅾⅾ ⅾeⅾⅾⅾⅰꞃ ċo ꞃoⅰⅼⅼeⅰꞃ ꞃⅰꞃ ⅾⅰⅰꞃꞃ (to us), ꞡo ⅾⅰⅰꞡⅿⅰⅾ ꞡⅾċ ꞗoⅾⅾⅰⅼ ⅾ ⅾeⅰⅰⅰꞃ, ⅾꞡⅰꞃ ⅰꞃ ⅾⅰⅾ

linn do briaṫra (thy words are a pleasure to us). 8.
Creidim, mar sin, ʒur éiʒin dam leaċt a ṫabairt daoib ó
ċarla (whereas) ʒo b-ḟuiliḋ ċo duilṁar ann eolur faʒáil:
ʒlaoiḋ air Apaċtaċ aʒur air do ċoi-ċeaċar Padraic. 9.
Ʒlaoiḋfeaḋ, I shall [call]. Cá riaḃ ċuʒainn (they are towards us): camuiḃ ollṁuiʒċe. 10. A Ḋiarmuiḃ a ṁic,
cia an niḃ an ċruinne, no cia b-ḟuil rí (she; referring to
cruinne, which is feminine)coraṁail leir? 11. Déir an
t-uʒḃar a caim-re leiʒeaḋ ʒur coraṁail í le liaċroiḃ, no
le ubal leaċta aiʒ na mulċinn (flattened at the poles). A
Apaċtaiċ ciannor a b-ḟuil fior aʒainn ʒo b-ḟuil an doṁan ro cruin? 12. Ir fior a ráḃ ʒo b-ḟuil re cruin ó
ċarla ʒur rnaṁ luinʒe ċant air aiʒ dul a ʒ-cóṁnuiʒe
caob ó n-iar. 13. Ir maiċ ċu: cia aċu line air ir faiḃe,
an line lár ó ḋear ʒo cuaċ, no an line lár ó n-oir, ʒo n-
iar? 14. Ir faiḃe an line lár ó n-oir ʒo n-iar le cuiʒ
inile air fíciḃ. 15. Ir an-maiċ ċu:—a Padraic ciannor
a roinncear an cruinne? 16. An ḋa priompoin—calaṁ
aʒur uirʒe. 17. Ciannor a ainmniʒċear roinn an uirʒe
(how are the divisions of water named)? 18. Fairʒiḃ
(oceans), mara (seas), dubaiʒin (gulfs), cuain (bays) loċa
(lakes), caoil fairnʒe (straits), aṁana. 19. Caḋ iaḃ roinn
na calṁan? 20. Cinċe (continents); niʒeaċta, oilain,
rainn (promontories), cinn (headlands or capes), muineil-
ċire. 21. An eol duic ceiċre-airc (points or quarters) na
cruinne? 22. Ir eol dam:—cuaċ (north), dear (south),
oir (east), iar (west). 23. A Ḋiarmuiḃ, b-ḟuil aʒaḋ-ra
fior caḋ fa a nʒlaoiḋcear "cuaċ," aʒur "dear," "oir" aʒur
"iar," air ceiċre airc an doṁain? 24. Níl fior, a aċair.
25. Wairc ir ionʒancaċ liom rin, ċo minic aʒur ċulaiḋ
cu (you heard) mé aiʒ innreaċt daoib. 26. (Apaċtaċ)
O! cá fior aʒam-re an t-aḋḃar, aċair. 27. Innir anoir
do do ḋearbraċair é. 28. Nuair bi na draoiċe (druids)
annr an t-rean-aimrir aiʒ aḋruʒaḋ (adoring) na ʒréine aiʒ
eiriʒ ḋi (on its rising) d' iompuiʒ riaḃ a n-aʒaiḋ airċi,
aʒur ʒlaoḃar mar rin air an cir or a ʒ-coṁair "oir;"
aʒur air caob a ʒ-cul "iar;" caob a n-dear laiṁe "dear;"
aʒur air an cir air a' laṁ cuaċ no cle, "cuaċ." 29. Ir
maiċ ċu, a Apaċtaiċ ʒo deiṁin. 30. (Diarmuiḃ) an "oir"
ʒlaoḃfaiḋ me air barr (top) na cir-ċairce ro (map)? 31.

Ní feaḋ aċt " ċuaċ," aġuſ " ḃeaſ" aiſ an m-bunn (foot or bottom); " oiſ" aiſ an caoḃ na ḃeaſ-laiṁe, aġuſ " iaſ" aiſ caoḃ na laiṁe clé: 32. Ní ċuiġim é. 33. Iſ fonuſ (it is easy) a aiċnuġaḋ, a ṁic: aġuſ anoiſ ſo é miṅuġaḋ. Ann aimſiſ apſaiġe (ancient) ḋ'iompuiġ na ḋſoiċe, maſ ḋuḃaiſc ḋo ḋeaſb-fiuſ aiſ an ġſian aiġ eiſiġ; ġlaoḋḋaſ maſ ſin, " ċuaċ," aiſ an ġ-caiſḃe a ḃi caoḃ na laiṁe ċuaiċe; aċc anoiſ 'nuaiſ ſġſioḃann luċc cſiċ-eoluiſ, iompuiġeaḃ ſiaḋ a n-aġaiḋ aiſ an ċuaċ, aġuſ cuiſeann ſiaḋ í aiſ baſſ na ċiſ-ċaiſce, aġuſ iſ eiſin maſ ſin ḋo'n caoḃ ċa ó ḋeaſ ḃeiċ aiġ bunn; an " oiſ," caoḃ na laiṁe ḋeiſe, aġuſ an " iaſ" caoḃ na laiṁe cle. 34. Ċuiġim, ċuiġim, anoiſ é. 35. Ċá ḋuine eiġin aiġ bualaḋ aiġ an ḋoſuſ (some one is knocking at the door). 36. Feuċ cia ċa ann? 37. Iſ ſe aſ n-oiḋe a ċá ann (it is our professor that is come). 38. Ċeiġiḃ, maſ ſin ċuiġe; ċá leiċiſiḃ aġam-ſa le ſġſioḃaḋ (go then to him; I have letters to write).

TWENTY-FOURTH LESSON.

The *imparisyllabic* class—or those which take in forming the plural an additional syllable, are comprised under the following Rules:—

RULE 1.—Nouns *feminine* (See Exceptions 1, 2, 3, to Rule 1, for formation of Gender, p. 93) ending in one or more consonants immediately preceded by a *broad* vowel (a, o, u); as:

SINGULAR.	PLURAL.
Ceaſc, a hen.	Ceaſca, hens.
Ciaſ, a comb.	Ciaſa, combs.
Coſ, a foot.	Coſa, feet.
Fuineoġ, a window.	Fuineoġa, windows.
Ġeallaċ, the moon.	Ġeallaċa, moons.
Inġeau, a daughter.	Inġeana, daughters.
Láṁ, a hand.	Láṁa, hands.
Lioſ, a fort.	Lioſa, forts.
Peacóġ, a pea-hen.	Peacóġa, pea-hens.

SINGULAR,	PLURAL.
Ríżeaċτ, a kingdom.	Ríżeaċτa, kingdoms.
Scιaċ, a buckler, a shield.	Scιaċa, bucklers, shields.
Slaτ, a rod.	Slaτa, rods.

Again, all nouns *feminine* in which the vowel preceding the final consonant is *slender;* as,

bρuιδ, captivity.	bρuιδe, captivities.
Ɔuιl, desire, an element.	Ɔuιlle, desires, elements.
Feιċ, a sinew.	Feιċe, sinews.
Peιρτ, a worm.	Peιρτe, worms.
Pιżιn, a penny.	Pιżιne, pence.

From these examples it is seen that, generally, when the vowel in the last syllable is broad (a, o, u,) the vowel in the annexed syllable is broad (a); and when slender (ι), the vowel in the annexed syllable is slender (e), according to rule.

Yet many nouns of this class, masculine as well as feminine, form the plural in a, omitting the final slender vowel; as,

Abaιn, a river.	Abana, contractedly, aιbne, rivers.
Aċaιρ, father, *m.*	Aċaρa, ... aιċρe.
bρaċaιρ, a brother, a friar.	bρaċaρa and bρaιċρe, brothers, friars.
Caċaιρ, a city, *f.*	Caċaρa, and caιċρe, cities.
Ɯuιρ, the sea, *f.*	Ɯaρa, seas.
Ɯaċaιρ, mother, *f.*	Ɯaċaρa, mothers.

Some nouns form the nominative plural from the nominative singular by taking τ before the additional vowel; as,

Ʒριan, the sun, *f.*	Ʒριanτa, suns.
Coιll, a wood, *f.*	Coιllτe, woods.
Pιan, pain, *f.*	Pιanτa, pains.
blιażaιn, a year.	blιażana, and blιażanτa, years.

Feminine nouns terminating in a *vowel* in the nominative singular form the plural from it by adding na; as,

Coṁuρρa, a neighbour.	Coṁuρρana, neighbours.

SINGULAR.	PLURAL.
Laŋaṁa, a married couple.	Laŋaṁna, married couples.
Ʒuala, a shoulder.	Ʒualaŋa, shoulders.
Peaṗṗa, a person.	Peaṗṗaŋa, persons.
Uŋʒa, a nail.	Uŋʒaŋa, nails.

RULE 2.—*Masculine* nouns (See Exception 1, to Rule 3, p. 94,) ending in óɲ, and masculiues and feminines in ɲn, (pr. *een,*) form the plural from the nominative singular by adding ɲó; as,

Slánuɩʒċeoɲɲ, Saviour.	Slánuɩʒċeoɲɲó, Saviours.
Doṗṗoɲɲ, a door-keeper.	Doṗṗoɲɲó, door-keepers.
Ʒaɲróɲŋ (from ʒaṗṗóa), a garden.	Ʒaɲróɲŋó, gardeus.
Caɩlɲŋ, a girl.	Caɩlɲŋó, girls.

NOTE.—" e," in the plural ending of this class of nouns, appears redundant (though quite in accordance with the usage of the written language), since the letters " ɲó" alone represent equally as well the sound, and the plural infléction. The final syllable in the plural of Latin and Italian nouns terminating in *i*, sounds exactly like the Irish plural ending ɲó. We have, therefore, analogy to some extent in favour of this slight change.

Others by adding ċe ; as,

Saoɲ, a sage.	Saoɲċe, sages.
Daoɲ, a dunce, a simple person.	Daoɲċe, dunces.
Dṗaoɲ, a druid.	Dṗaoɲċe, druids.
Céaŋŋuɩʒe, a merchant.	Ceaŋŋuɩʒċe, merchants.
Sŋaṁuɩóe, a swimmer.	Sŋaṁuɩóċe, swimmers.
Nɲó, a thing.	Neɲċe, things.

RULE 3.—Verbal nouns, *i.e.*, nouns derived from the infinitive mood, or present participle of transitive verbs, form the plural from the singular by changing the ending of the active participle into that of the passive participle; as,

Molaó, praise (from mol).	Molca, praises.
buaɩleaó, beating.	buaɩlce, beatings.
Alcuʒaó, thanksgiving (from alcuɩʒ, exalt, extol ; Latin, *altus*, high).	Alcuɩʒċe, thanksgivings
Fulaŋʒ, suffering.	Fulaŋʒca, sufferings.

VOCABULARY.

Aır, back; as, táınıc re aın aır, he came back; also, *again*, in composition, *re*; as, aır-eırıġ, rising again, resurrection.

Vaŕ, *m.*, death; baċ, destruction, slaughter; baŕ, to destroy by drowning; baıċeaḋ, *past tense pass.* was drowned; báċaḋ, *part.* drowning.

Caırġ, *f.*, Easter; from the Heb. pws, *pasak.* This is an instance in which the *labial p* is transmuted—not into a cognate letter, but into a palatine, *c.* The Irish, like the Æolic Greeks, prefer the use of *c* (*k*) to the softer vocable *p.*

Caṗbaḋ. *m.,* áıḋ, plu., a coach, waggon.

Caṗbaḋ, and } the gums, the palate, the jaws; nı'l
Caṗbal,   } fıacal ann a ċaṗbaḋ, there is not a tooth in his jaw.

Oıa, day; *dies* (Latin) at present found only in compound Irish words; as Oıa-luaın, Monday; Oıa-maırc, *dies martis*, Tuesday; Oıa-ceḋın, or (ʒeḋeın) Wednesday. The German god Woden, from which name Wednesday is derived, is the Irish Ceḋen, or Mercury. Oıa-ċoṗbaın, Thursday. (Coṗḋan. the Thunderer, from coṗ, coṗan and coṗṗaċ, noise—thunder; being the Keltic name of Jove; (Oıa-

beıṗe, now Oıa aoıṗe, Friday; (beıṗe, from bean, a woman. *Venus*, as *frau*, a woman, is the radix of Friday); Oıa-Sáċuıṗın, Saturday: Ooṁṗaċ, Sunday, from the Latin, *Dominica.* In pagan times Sunday was called Oıa-ruıl, the Sun's day.

Ooṁṗaċ is also the name of great churches built by our early Irish Saints; as, Ooṁṗaċ Ṗaḃṗaıc, Donaghpatrick, in Meath; Ooṁṗaċ-Sheaċnaıll, Dunshaughlin.

Oıabaıl, the devil; from oıa, god, and aḃaıl, fearful, terrible; Gr. διάβολος, *diabolos*; Latin, *diabolus*; Welsh, *diavol*; Italian, *diavola*; the Greek derivation from διάβαλλω, *didballo*, is more than doubtful.

Eaḃṗaċ, a Hebrew.

Féıle, *f.,* a festival.

Ʒaın, *f.,* an outcry, a rejoicing, laughing. Luaċʒaın, from luaċ, free, quick; and ʒaın, rejoicing, gladness, merriment.

Uıl-ʒaınḃeaṙ, *m.,* gladness; (from uıle, all; and ʒaınḃeaṙ, gladness).

Iora (*Eesa*), Jesus.

Maıṗe Maʒḋaléne, Mary Magdalen.

Maoıre, Moses.

EXERCISE XXXVI.

Páḋṗaıc aʒur Seoṗra (Patrick and George).

1. B-ḟuıl cu-ra, a Sheoṗra, aıʒ ḟoʒlam ʒaoḋaılʒe (are you, George, learning Irish)? 2. Cáım. 3. Innır ḋam anoır, ma 'r re ḋo ċoıl é, ca ṁeuḋ lá 'r an c-reaċc-ṁaın? 4. Seaċc lá. 5. Abaıṗ ıaḋ ann ʒaoḋaılʒe (say them in Irish). 6. Oıa-luaın, oıa-maırc, oıa-ceḋeın, oıa-ċoṗḋaın, oıa-beıṗe, oıa-Saċuıṗın, oıa-ḋoṁṗaıʒ. 7. Ir maıċ cu: cıa an c-reaċc-ṁaın ı ro? 8. So ı reaċc-ṁaın na caırʒe. 9. Caḋ é brıʒ no mınuʒaḋ an ḟocaıl,—caırʒ? 10. Focaıl é cá aʒaınn ḋ'n ceanʒa Eaḃṗaıʒ—aʒur cıalluıʒeann re (it

signifies) " ᴠul ᴄᴘıᴠ" ᴠe bᴘıᴈ ᴈuᴘ ᴄuᴀıᴠ (pr. *choo-y*, went) ᴀıᴠᴈeᴀl Oe ᴄᴘıᴠ ᴀᴠ Eᴈıᴘᴄ ᴀᴈuᴘ ᴠo ᴍᴀᴘbuıᴈ ᴀᴠ ᴍᴀc buᴠ ᴘıᴠᴠe (the eldest son) ᴀᴠᴠ ᴈᴀᴄ ᴄıᴈ ᴠe ᴄıᴈᴄıb ᴍuıᴠᴄıᴘe ᴠᴀ ᴄıᴘe, ᴍᴀᴘ ᴈeᴀll ᴠᴀᴘ leıᴈ Ᵽᴀᴘᴀo ᴠᴀ h-Cᴀbᴘᴀıᴈ ᴠul le ᴍᴀoıᴘe le ᴀᴠᴘuᴈᴀᴠ ᴄᴀbᴀıᴘᴄ ᴠo Oıᴀ ᴠᴀ ᴄᴘuıᴠᴠe. 11. Cᴀ ꜰıoꞃ ᴀᴈᴀᴍ ᴀıᴘ ᴀᴠ ꞃᴄᴀıᴘ ᴄᴀ ꞃᴈᴘıobᴄᴀ ᴀᴠᴠꞃ ᴀᴠ leᴀbᴀıᴘ ᴠo ꞃᴈᴘıob ᴍᴀoıᴘe ᴄᴀob ᴠᴀ ᴠ-Cᴀbᴘᴀᴄ ᴀ ᴄuᴀıᴠ ᴀᴍᴀᴄ ꜰᴀoı ᴠ-ᴀ ꞃᴄıúᴘ o'ᴠ Cᴈıᴘᴄ, ᴀᴈuꞃ ᴀıᴘ ᴀᴠ ᴄᴀoı ᴀ bᴀıᴄᴄᴀᴠ ᴠᴀ ᴍᴀᴘcᴀıᴈ ᴀᴈuꞃ ᴠᴀ cᴀᴘᴀıl, ᴠᴀ cᴀᴘbᴀıᴠ ᴀᴈuꞃ ꜰıᴘ ᴄoᴈᴀıᴠ (fighting men), ᴀᴠ ᴘıᴈ ē ꜰeıᴠ ᴀᴈuꞃ ᴠᴀ ceᴀᴠꜰᴀıᴘᴄ (the king himself and the chieftains), ᴠᴀ lᴀoᴄᴘᴀ (the warriors), ᴀᴈuꞃ ᴠᴀ ꞃluᴀᴈᴄᴀ (and the hosts); ᴍᴀᴘ ᴠo ꞃluᴈᴀᴠ ꞃuᴀꞃ ıᴀᴠ (how they were swallowed up) ᴄᴘe ᴄuᴍᴀᴄᴄ Oe, ᴀᴠᴠ uıꞃᴈᴄıb ᴠᴀ ꜰᴀıᴘᴘᴈe. 12. Cᴀ ꜰıoꞃ ᴀᴈᴀᴍ ᴀıᴘ ᴀᴠ ᴍeuᴠ ꞃo, ᴀᴄᴄ ᴠı b-ꜰuıl ꜰıoꞃ ᴀᴈᴀᴍ cᴀᴠ ꜰᴀᴄ ᴠo ᴈlᴀoıᴠ ᴠᴀ Cᴘıoꞃᴠᴀıᴈᴄe cᴀıꞃᴈ ᴀıᴘ ᴀıᴍꞃıᴘ ᴀıꞃ-eıᴘıᴈe ᴀᴘ Slᴀᴠuıᴈᴄeoᴘᴀ? 13. ᴈlᴀoıᴠᴀᴘ cᴀıꞃᴈ ᴀıᴘ, ᴍᴀᴘ ᴈeᴀll ᴈuᴘ ᴄᴀᴘluıᴈ ꞃe (because it happened) ᴀ ᴠ-ᴄuꞃ, ᴀıᴘ ᴀᴠ ᴀıᴍ ceᴀᴠᴀ ᴀᴘ ᴄᴀᴘluıᴈ ꜰeıle ᴀıᴘ ᴀᴘ ᴈlᴀoıᴠ ᴠᴀ h-ᴊuᴠᴀıᴈᴄe—cᴀıꞃᴈ. 14. Nᴀᴄ ᴍóᴘ ᴀᴠ ꜰeıle, ꜰeıle ᴠᴀ cᴀıꞃᴈe? 15. ᴊꞃ móᴘ ᴈo ᴠeıᴍıᴠ; ꜰeıle ᴀıᴘ ᴀᴘ eıᴘıᴈ Slᴀᴠuıᴈᴄeoıᴘ ᴀᴠ ᴠoᴍᴀıᴠ o'ᴠ uᴀıᴈ ᴀıᴈ bᴘeıᴄ buᴀıᴠ (getting victory over) ᴀıᴘ ᴀᴠ ᴍ-bᴀꞃ, ᴀᴠ b-peᴀcᴀᴠ, ᴀᴈuꞃ ᴀᴠ ᴠıᴀbᴀl (devil). 16. Nᴀᴄ cóıᴘ ᴍᴀᴘ ꞃıᴠ, ᴈo ᴍ-beıᴠeᴀᴠ luᴀᴄ-ᴈᴀıᴘ cᴘoıᴠe (joy of heart) ᴀıᴘ ᴈᴀᴄ ᴄᴘıoᴘᴠuıᴈe ᴀıᴘ ᴀᴠ lᴀ ꞃo, ᴀᴈuꞃ ᴈo ᴍ-beıᴠeᴀᴠ ᴠᴀ ᴠuılle ꜰeıᴠ (and that the elements themselves should be) lıoᴠᴄᴀ le ulᴈᴀıᴘᴠeᴀꞃ, ᴠe bᴘıᴈ ᴈuᴘ eıᴘıᴈ ᴀᴘ ᴈ-Ceᴀᴠᴠ ᴈo buᴀıᴠeᴀᴄ (victoriously) o'ᴠ uᴀıᴈ ᴀıᴈ buᴀlᴀᴠ ᴀᴠ bᴀꞃ ᴀᴈuꞃ ᴀᴠ ᴠıᴀbᴀl ᴈo ᴠeo ꜰᴀoı ᴄoıꞃ? 17. Aıᴈ ᴄᴘᴀᴄᴄ ᴀıᴘ ᴠᴀ ᴠuıllıb beıᴄ ꜰᴀoı ulᴈᴀıᴘᴠeᴀꞃ;—ᴠo ꜰıl ᴍe-ꞃe ᴀ ᴈ-coᴍᴠuıᴈe ᴈo ᴍ-buᴠ ᴠeᴀꞃ ᴀᴠ ꞃᴈeul ē ꞃıᴠ ᴄᴀ ᴠe ᴈuᴀᴄ ᴀıᴘ beul ᴠᴀ ᴍ-boᴄᴄ, ᴈo ᴍ-bıᴠeᴀᴠᴠ ᴀᴠ ᴈᴘıᴀᴠ ᴀıᴘ ᴍᴀıᴠıᴠ ᴠoᴍᴠᴀᴄcᴀıꞃᴈe ᴀıᴈ ᴘıᴠc le luᴀᴄ-ᴈᴀıᴘ, ᴍᴀᴘ ᴈeᴀll ᴀıᴘ eıᴘuᴈᴀᴠ ᴀᴠ ᴄ-Soluıᴘ ᴠıᴀᴠᴀ. 18. Aᴘ ᴄoᴠᴠᴀıᴘc ᴄu-ꜰeıᴠ ᴀᴘıᴀᴍ ᵻ ᴀıᴈ ᴠᴀᴍᴘᴀᴠ? 19. Nıoᴘ ᴄoᴠᴠᴀıᴘc, ᴀᴄᴄ ᴠúbᴀıᴘᴄ ᴍ'ᴀᴄᴀıᴘ lıoᴍ ᴈuᴘ ᴄoᴠᴠᴀıᴘc ꞃe ꜰeıᴠ ᵻ ᴀıᴘ ᴍᴀıᴠıᴠ bᴘeᴀᴈ ᴠoᴍᴠᴀıᴈ ᴀıᴘ eıᴘuᴈᴀᴠ ᴠo ᴈo ᴍoᴄ. 20. b' ꜰeıᴠıᴘ ᴠᴀ ᴍ-beıᴠeᴀᴠ ᴀᴘ ᴈ-cᴘeıᴠeᴀᴍ ᴀᴈuꞃ ᴀᴘ ᴠ-ᴈᴘᴀᴠ ᴄo ᴠıᴀᴠ ᴀᴈuꞃ ᴄo ᴄeıᴄ ᴀ'ꞃ bı cᴘeıᴠeᴀᴍ Nᴀoᴍ Ᵽeᴀᴠᴀıᴘ ᴀᴈuꞃ ᴍᴀᴈᴠᴀleᴠe ᴠᴀᴄ ᴍ-beıᴠeᴀᴠ ıoᴠᴈᴀᴠ (*een-yoo*) ᴀıᴘ bıᴄ oᴘᴀıᴠᴠ ꜰᴀoı. 21. ᴊꞃ cıᴠᴠᴄe ᴠᴀᴄ ᴍ-beıᴠeᴀᴠ. 22. A ᴍ-beıᴠıᴘ 'ꞃᴀᴠ ᴍ-bᴀıle ᴍóıᴘ ᴀᴠ ıuᴠ? 23.

beiḋiḋ.   24. Taṙṙ ċuġam-ṡa, má'ṡ ṙe do ṫoil é, a ṁaṙac.
25. Tiocfaḋ aġuṡ fáilte; óiṙ beiḋ uaiṙ no faill aġam.
26. beannaċt leat.   27. Ṡo ṡoiṙbiġ Dia ḋuit.

VOCABULARY.

Annaṙ, *m.*, sense, feeling.
Caṫ-aḃna, battle of rivers.
Comġaṙ, *m.* whispering.
Cṙionfaṙ, shall wither; *fut. tense* of cṙion, to wither.
Cṙioṙtal, *m.*, crystal.
Daṁ, *f.*, assent, free will.

Ealuiġṫe, *past part.*, from ealuġaḋ, to separate, go away, divide.
Euġ-ċeol, death song.
Loinneaṙ, *m.*, brightness.
Meuḋuiġeaṅ, *pres. tense* of the verb meuḋuiġ, increase; root—meuḋ, size.

EXERCISE XXXVII.

THE MEETING OF THE WATERS.

[Taken from the Irish Version of the " Melodies," by his Grace the Archbishop of Tuam.]

Fonn—" *The old head of Denis.*"

I.

Ní b-fuil annṙ an ġ-cṙuinne aon ċumaṙ, no ġleann,
Maṙ an laġ a b-fuil có-ṙṙuṫ na dír aḃan ann;
Iṙ luaiṫe béiḋeaṙ ealuiġṫe uaim, m' annaṙ, 'ṙ mo ḃṙíġ,
'Ná ċṙionfaṙ an ġleann ġlaṙ úḋ úṙ aṙ mo ċṙoiḋe.

II.

Ní ṙé an t-aṁaṙc bṙeaġ, aoiḃinn bí ṙġaṙṫa aiṙ ġaċ taoḃ,
Ní ṙé loinneaṙ an ċṙioṙtaiḷ, no úṙ-ḃláṫ na ġ-cṙaoḃ,
Ní ṙé comġaṙ na ṙṙuṫa maṙ euġ-ċeol mná-ṙíġe,
Aċt níḋ éiġin níoṙ ḋíḷṙe, tá ann doiṁneaċt an ċṙoiḋe.

III.

'S iaḋ mo ċáiṙṙe, do ċeanġail mo ċumann 'ṙ mo ċlaon,
Do ṙcap aiṙ ġaċ níḋ ann, ṙġéiṁ ṙaṙta na mian;
Óiṙ ni'l aon níḋ ḋ'a aiḷle naċ meuḋuiġeann a ḃláṫ,
Ḋ'a ḟeicṙin tṙe ṙúiḷiḃ`aiṙ a m-bíḋeann aġainn ġṙáḋ.

IV.

A ġleann aoiḃinn Caṫ-aḃna,* buḋ ṙuaiṁneaċ mo ṙuan
Faoi ḟaṙġaḋ do ċaḃaiṙ le mo ċaṙa fíoṙ-buan;
'Ṅ áit a m-béiḋmuiḋ ó na ṙíoṅtaiḃ faoi ḋíḋean ġo ṙáiṁ
S an ġ-cṙoiḋṫe maṙ do ċiúṅ-ṙṙuṫa cóṁeaṙġṫa le daiṁ

* Avoca.

I.

There is not in the wide world a valley so sweet
As that vale in whose bosom the bright waters meet;[*]
Oh! the last ray of feeling and life must depart,
Ere the bloom of that valley shall fade from my heart.

II.

Yet, it was not that Nature had shed o'er the scene
Her purest of crystal and brightest of green;
'Twas not the soft magic of streamlet or rill,
Oh! no—it was something more exquisite still.

III.

'Twas that friends, the beloved of my bosom, were near,
Who made every dear scene of enchantment more dear,
And who felt how the best charms of nature improve,
When we see them reflected from looks that we love.

IV.

Sweet Vale of Avoca! how calm could I rest
In thy bosom of shade with the friends I love best,
Where the storms that we feel in this cold world should
    cease,
And our hearts, like thy waters, be mingled in peace!

"The Meeting of the Waters" forms a part of that beautiful scenery which lies between Rathdrum and Arklow, in the county of Wicklow, and these lines were suggested by a visit to this romantic spot, in the summer of the year 1807.—*Note by* Mr. Moore.

[*] The rivers Avon and Avoca.

VOCABULARY.

Ⰰⁱⱃⱥⰶⰼ, *adj.*, *gen. fem.* of ⰰⱀⱃⰰⰵ, ancient, old, sage.

bⱃⱆⰹⰼ, f., captivity; bⱃⱆⰹⰼⰼ, poss. case.

Clⰰⱀⱃⰶ, *prep. case* of clⰰⱀⱃⰼⰰⰵ, a harp.

Cⱆⱀⰶ, *f.*, a chain, a fetter.

Oⰰoⱃⰰⰼ, condemning, enslaving; while ⱃⰰⱆⱃⰰⰼ, is acquitting, freeing.

Eⰰⰶlⰰⰵ, fearful; ⱒⰼⰰⱀⰼ-eⰰⰶlⰰⰵ, fearless.

Feⰰⰵ, music, melody, science, skill.

Lⰰⱀⱀ, a sword; a knife; a sword-blade.

Óⰶ-lⰰoⰵ, young warrior.

Lⰰoⰵ-ceoⱳl, warrior of song.

… ⱃⰰⱀⱀ, of verses, of song; oⰶ-lⰰoⰵ ⱀⰰ ⱃⰰⱀⱀ, the young hero of song.

(Oo) ⱃcⱆⰰⰼ, he swept; ⱃcⱆⰰⰼ, *v.*, to sweep; *n.*, a broom.

EXERCISE XXXVIII.

THE MINSTREL BOY.

Fonn—Móṙín.

I.

Do ċrrall ċum caṫa óᵹ-laoċ na rann,
  Lár naṁaḋ Eireann árraiᵹe;
Lann aṫar fáirᵹṫe air ᵹo ṫeann,
  Ann aoinḟeaċṫ le n-a ċláirriᵹ.
A ṫír na n-ḋan! ar an laoċ-ċeoil ᵹrinn,
  Da m-beiḋeaḋ an raoᵹal do d' ḋaoraḋ,
Ṫá aon ċruiṫ aṁáin le do ṁolaḋ ᵹo binn,
  'S aon lann aṁáin le do ḟaoraḋ.

II.

Do ċuiṫ an bárd, aċṫ má ċuiṫ, ᵹo fóill
  bí a ċroiḋe neaṁ-eaᵹlaċ, ṫreunṁar;
A'r raob re ṫeuda cláirriᵹe an ċeoil,
  Do rcuab ré, an ṫrá bí reunṁar:
A'r dúbairṫ; ní ṁillfiḋ cuinᵹ do ᵹuṫ,
  A ċruiṫ ċaoin na b-feaċ raora;
Ir ní cluinḟear ᵹo h-euᵹ do lán binn-rruṫ,
  Lár bruiḋe a'r broin na ṫíre.

I.

The Minstrel Boy to the war is gone,
  In the ranks of death you'll find him;
His father's sword he has girded on,
  And his wild harp slung behind him.
" Land of Song !" said the warrior-bard,
  " Tho' all the world betrays thee,
" *One* sword, at least, thy rights shall guard,
  " *One* faithful harp shall praise thee !"

II.

The Minstrel fell !—but the foeman's chain
  Could not bring his proud soul under;
The harp he loved ne'er spoke again,
  For he tore its chords asunder;
And said, " No chains shall sully thee,
  " Thou soul of love and bravery,
" Thy songs were made for the pure and free,
  " They shall never sound in slavery !"

KEY TO EXERCISES—

eοċᴧɹɳ ᴎᴀ ɲ-ȝᴎᴀċᴜȝᴎὁ.

THIRTEENTH LESSON—

ᴀᴎ ᴄɲᴇᴀs ʟᴇɟᵶᴇᴀᴎ ᴏᴇᴜȝ.

EXERCISE XXV.—ᴀᴎ ᴄᴜɟȝᴓɟᴡὁ ȝᴎᴀċᴜȝᴀὁ ᴀɪʀ ḟɪċɪὁ.

1. What (kind of) food do you like to have in the morning, for (your) breakfast? 2. I like bread and butter, tea
and cream, and cold meat prepared since yesterday (the
day before). 3. Will you allow me to fill tea for you?
4. I shall, and welcome (*i.e.*, with pleasure), if you please
(if it is your will). 5. Do you use sugar with it? 6. I
do so; and besides, I like much sugar. 7. Do you prefer
cream to milk (literally, is cream better with you than
milk)? 8. I prefer cream. 9. Give me a portion of the
mutton, if you please. 10. I shall (give it) and welcome.
11. Perhaps you like an egg? 12. I do not; I have
plenty (my sufficient share is) in the meat. 13. Give me
the cream-ewer, if you please. 14. Here it is to you and
a hundred thousand welcomes. 15. At what hour do you
breakfast each day? 16. At half hour after (at half-past)
(the) eight, or at (the) nine o'clock. 17. What hour do
take (eat) luncheon? 18. I eat it at (the) two, or at (the)
one o'clock. 19. Who is usually with you eating breakfast? 20. The family of the house, as are my father,
and my mother, my brother and my sister, my children
(of) sons, and my children (of) daughters, (*i.e.*, my children male and female). 21. Where is thy brother Wil-

liam this (present) time? 22. He is in Dublin, the capital city of Ireland. 23. Were you ever in Dublin? 24. I was; and in truth to you a beautiful and extensive city it is: I would like to be in it each year for two or three months. 25. Is there any person at all residing in it related to you? 26. There is; my grandfather, or the father of my mother, along with a cousin-german, and many other persons—relatives. 27. Is James M'Hugh a cousin-german of yours—he who is, if it be true, as president or chancellor in Trinity College? 28. He is a cousin-german of my mother, and he is related to myself, in the fifth degree: he is indeed very generous to me, for he bestows much money on me every time (whenever) I go to the city. 29. That is good; what time were you in Dublin? 33. It is now indeed three months; but I expect that I shall be in it before another month. 31. Will you come with me to my own house to-night? 32. I do not wish it; the house of my grandfather is very near to me; and I will go to it; the people of the house wish that I should tarry with them. 33. Are you going? 34. I am. 35. God's blessing be with. 36. Thank you (may good be to you); safe mayest thou be, and thy kindred.

FOURTEENTH LESSON—
An ceaċaraṁaḋ leiġean deuġ.

EXERCISE XXVI.— An seiseaḋ ġnaċuġaḋ air ficiḋ.

1. Lá anḃreaġ é ro? 2. Ir lá ḃreaġ é ġo deiṁin. 3. Naċ raiḃ aġainn aimriṗ anḃreaġ anoir le raḋa? 4. Ḃi aġainn, ġo deiṁin, aimriṗ anḃreaġ, maṗ deiṗ cu, le camal maiċ. 5. Naċ an-ṁaiċ Oia duinn? 6. Seaḋ, ir an-ṁaiċ Oia duinn. 7. Cia cá maiċ aċc Oia aṁain? 8. Cia re Oia? Aġaḋ-ra aiġ a ḃ-ḟuil an oineaḋ rin eoluir, cá ḟior an ċeirḋ ro ġo maiċ. 9. 'Se uġḋar aġur prioṁ-aḋḃar é ġaċ niḋ a cá air neaṁ aġur air calaṁ; Se cur aġur crioċ é ġaċ niḋ a cá, no a beiḋear; ir re a ċruċuiġ an ġrian aġur an ġeallaċ, aġur na reulca ro uile a ḟolruiġeann an

ṙeun: ca Se ann ġaċ am aġur beiḋ ġo bṙaċ: molaḋ ġaċ
ceanġa é. 10. Cia ṙe a ṁolar ġo ṙíoṙ an Tiġeanna?
11. Se an ṙean cóiṙ aiġ a b-ṙuil eolur cia ṙe Oia, ġo b-
ṙuil Se móṙ; ġo b-ṙuil Se ċuṁaċtaċ; aġur eolur cia ṙe
ṙéin, ġo b-ṙuil ṙe boċt, cáiṙ. 12. Caḋ é an níḋ an ṙaoġal
ro? 13. Ní b-ṙuil ann aċt cec, a cá ṙeal ġeáṙṙ aġur ann
riṙ imiġear. 14. Caḋ é an níḋ neaṁ? 15. Si an ṙíġeaċt
ann b-ṙuil Oia aiġ ṙiaġail ṙaoi ġlóiṙ, aġur ann a b-ṙuil
na (h-anama) beannuiġte aiġ cabaiṙc molta ḋ' a ainm
naoṁta. 16. B-ṙuil cu-ṙa naoṁta? 17. Ní b-ṙuilim naoṁta, ní molaim me ṙein, ġíḋ ġo b-ṙuil mian aġam a beiċ
maiċ. 18. Cá ṙíor aġaḋ ṙaḋ no coṁaiṙle an t-ṙeanḋuine:
" na mol aġur na cáin ċu-ṙéin;" óiṙ iṙ olc an níḋ móṙṁolaḋ.
19. Caḋ ṙe an níḋ uabaṙ. 20. Iṙ ṙiuṙ bo baoṙṙa uabaṙ
—iṙ ceaṅ be na ṙeaċt b-peacaiḋ ṁaṙbċa—uabaṙ. 21. B-
ṙuil ṙíor aġaḋ na ṙeaċt b-peacaiḋ ṁaṙbċa? 22. Ca ṙíor
—uabaṙ, ṙaiṅc ḋṙuiṙ, cnuċ (envy), cṙaor, ṙeaṅġ (anger),
aġur leiṙġe. 23. Ṙeicim ġuṙ b' e an t-uabaṙ, bun-ṙṙuċ aġuṙ
ṗṙeuṁ na peacaiḋ eile—buḋ é peacaḋ na ṅ-beaṁaṅ e,
aġuṙ aḋḋaṙ ṗeacaiḋ aṙ ġ-ceuḋ ceapṙiṅṙiṙ Aḋaiṁ aġuṙ
Eaba. 24. Ṙeicim ġuṙ oiḋe ċu. 25. Cia ṙe an ṙeaṙ ro
aiġ ceaċt? 26. Iṙ ṙe, Uilliam mo ċaṙaḋ óiliṙ, buaṅ.
27. Aṅ ṙé a cá ann? 28. Iṙ ṙe; ṙó ṙe. 29. Ceuḋ míle
ṙáilte ṙoṁac, a ċaṙaiḋ mo ċléiḃ; ciaṅṅoṙ a b-ṙuiliṙ aṅṅ
ṙuḋ? 30. Cá me ġo maiċ, ca me buiḋeaċ ḋuic. 31. Biḋeaḋ aġaiṅṅ aiṙbeaṙ beaġ, or beaṅamuiḋ aiṙḃiṙ ṙaṅaċ le
ceile.

FIFTEENTH LESSON—

AN CUIGAṁaḋ LEIġeaN DEUġ.

EXERCISE XXVII.—AN SCAċtaṁaḋ ġNaċuġaḋ aiṙ ṙiċro.

1. Who is there? 2. I. 3. Who (are) you? 4. James
O'Brian. 5. Come in, James; you are welcome; sit down
and converse; I am glad that I see you in health. It is a
long time (day) since thou and I were together before this

day; and assuredly to you, I am glad now that we are here with each other—you who have a high estate, and a reputation throughout the globe; and I who am here in the extremity of the country, without knowledge and without notoriety. 6. Oh, I implore of you do not commence so soon to praise me; or I should rather say, quizzing me. 7. Certainly I am not quizzing you; but I am telling the truth. I know that you are very humble, and I shall not speak another word in your praise. As I said, it is long since we were with each other going to school, when we were in your grandfather's, God's blessing be with his soul. Have you not travelled much of the world since then? 8. I have. I have much to tell of everything which I heard, and every thing I saw, if I had an opportunity to spend a while with you. But I will have an opportunity at another special time. 9. Do you recollect when I and you on a certain day were walking out from the town of Cork, and you said that you would like to swim, and when we were in the water, there came a large wave, which brought, on its returning, you with it, and you went along with the stream, until you alighted on a rock; then I swam after you, and brought you to shore half alive as you were? 10. It is true that I recollect well that day, and I shall have a recollection of it for ever; it is for that reason I have (entertain) affection and great esteem always for you, thankful for all you did for me. 11. Were there not other young men with us that day? 12. There were certainly; but neither of them wished to go against the angry billows, 13. It was well they acted so. Since you have commenced to speak of them, who were the young men who were along with us on that day? 14. There were Andrew Fitzpatrick, George Williamson, and Thomas MacDonnell, three who knew how to swim extremely well. 15. Are they all alive yet? 16. They are not all; two of them (got death) died; but Thomas MacDonnell is yet alive; and he is not only a good man, but a highly learned doctor, and a renowned sage. 17. I am well pleased at that; is it long since you heard from him? 18. Oh, it is; I have not heard from him these five years. 19. A person of what likeness was he, in order that I may see, do I re-

collect him? 20. He was a tall man, about six feet; red
in his complexion; beaming in his eye, handsome, long-
cheeked; his brows compact, round, and his hair the colour
of gold; his visage mild, handsome. 21. I know him well
now; you have great memory. 22. Had he not a sister
whose name was Isabella—is that her name? 23· Isabella
was her name. 24. Are you tired after your journey? 35.
I am not. 25. We can therefore walk through the garden,
the evening is so fine. 27. I like it, if you like it. 28. Certainly, I like it. To whom does the garden belong? 29.
To me. 30. I perceive you are a great agriculturist.
31. I do not be often (employed) at it, but from time to
time. 32. Come in and view the flowers. 33. I shall and
welcome.

SIXTEENTH LESSON.

an seiseaḋ leiġeaṅn deuġ.

EXERCISE XXVIII.—an t-oċtaḋ ġnaċuġaḋ air fiċid

A DIALOGUE BETWEEN TWO STUDENTS.

1. Alexander, have you been at school to-day? 2. I
have been; I do not wish to be a day at all from school.
3. It is not right for any young man, such as you are, to
be a day from school, whilst it is in his power to be at it
(to attend). 4. I trust you are reading the high sciences?
5. Well, I am not (reading), but those only that are ordinary, such as writing and reading, a knowledge of the
globe and grammar, and things of that kind, along with
the languages—English, Greek, French and Latin. 6:
You have a knowledge, have you not, of the principal parts
of each language of these—that is, you know their division and their explanations? 7. I have: for it is easy to
know these. There are nine divisions of language; and
of these are two parts, the noun and the verb, like woof
and warp, framing every discourse together, and there is
not in the other parts, but as it were, colour and form.

8. How could you know a *noun?* 9. It is easy for a person to know it; for the *name* of every thing that is created, or of which we can form a notion (it) is a *noun;* for example, the names of men and women, as Achilles, Augustine, Alexander, Æneas, or Kevin, Cormac, Edmund, Amilia, Angelica, or Barbara, Blathny, or Kate; or again the names that appertain to men or to women, in relation to their duty or in relation to their state,—such as father, mother, sister and brother, porter, poet, monk; or the names of brutes —horse, mare, filly, bull; in one word, the name of every thing created, or of which we can form a notion (it) is a *noun.* 10. How many genders in it (are there)? 11. There are only two genders, that is, the masculine and feminine : and since from nature there are only two sexes (amongst) mankind, male and female, in like manner, nouns have only two genders, masculine and feminine; 12. Oh, I know well that there are only two genders when we speak of those names which present to our minds (ideas of) things living; but when we treat of the names of things that are not living, in what manner will we have a knowledge of the gender of the noun, when the object is devoid of sex? 13. I shall give you a knowledge of that at another time, I have not leisure to-day. 14. At a certain time to come, you and I shall be together, and we shall have a conversation on this subject. 15. Let it be so. 16. But stay: you have not told me a word of the manner in which a young man can obtain readily a knowledge (of the grammatical meaning) of every word that occurs to him in discourse. 17. Withal we shall have an opportunity for that on another occasion; I have not leisure just now. I am obliged to depart, the bell is tolling.

SEVENTEENTH LESSON—

an seaċtṁaḋ leiġeaḋ ḋeuġ.

EXERCISE XXIX.—an naoṁaḋ ġnáċuġaḋ air fiċiḋ.

1. Ceuḋ míle ḟáilte roṁat a Ṡeaplair; cianṅor a ḃ-fuil tu? 2. Tá me rlán; buiḋeaċar ḋuit. 3. Tá bróiḋ orm

ʒo ⲇⲉⲓṁⲓⲛ, ʒo ḃ-ꝼⲩⲓl ⲧⲩ a ꞃlaⲓⲛⲧⲉ ṁaⲓⲧ. 4. Cⲓaⲛⲛoꞃ a ꞃⲓⲛⲛⲉ ⲧⲩ aⲓꞃⲇⲓⲛ aⲛ ⳟⲩⲇ—aⲛ aⲓʒ maꞃⲕⲩⲓʒⲉaⲕⲧ, ⲛo aⲓꞃ ⲕoⲓꞃ? 5. Ⲇo ꞃⲓⲛⲛⲉaꞃ aⲓꞃⲇⲓⲛ aⲓꞃ aⲛ ⲧ-ꞃⲉaⲛ-ʒⲛaꞃ, aⲓꞃ ⲕoⲓꞃ. 6. Cⲓaⲛⲛoꞃ a ḃ-ꝼⲩⲓlⲓⲇ ⲇo ⲕaⲓꞃⲇⲉ aⲛⲛꞃ aⲛ m-baⲓlⲉ, ⲇ' aⲧaⲓꞃ aʒⲩꞃ ⲇo ṁaⲧaⲓꞃ, ⲇo ⲇⲉaꞃḃ-ḃꞃaⲧaⲓꞃ Ⲉⲉaʒaⲛ, aʒⲩꞃ ⲇo ⲇⲉaꞃḃ-ꝼⲓⲩꞃ Ⲉⲉⲓlⲓⲇaⲛ, aʒⲩꞃ ⲇo ⲕol-ⲕⲉaⲧaꞃ Ⲉⲉamⲩꞃ ⲘaⲕⲈⲉaʒaⲓⲛ. 7. Ⲧaⲓⲇ ⲩⲓlⲉ a ꞃlaⲓⲛⲧⲉ ṁaⲓⲧ, bⲩⲓⲇⲉaⲕaꞃ ⲇo Ⲇ̇ⲓa. 8. Cⲓaⲛⲛoꞃ ḃ-ꝼⲩⲓl ⲇo ⲇⲉaꞃḃ-ḃꞃaⲧaⲓꞃ Ⲁⲛⲇꞃⲉaꞃ; ḃ-ꝼⲩⲓl ꞃⲉ ꞃlaⲛ? 9. Ⲛⲓ'l ꝼⲓoꞃ aʒam ⲕⲓaⲛⲛoꞃ a ḃ-ꝼⲩⲓl ꞃⲉ aⲛoⲓꞃ, oⲓꞃ ⲛⲓ ⲕⲩalaⲓⲇ mⲉ ⲩaⲓⲇⲉ lⲉ ⲧꞃⲓ mⲓoꞃa. 10. Ⲧa ⲓoⲛʒa oꞃm ꝼaoⲓ ꞃⲓⲛ, maꞃ ʒⲉall ʒⲩꞃ ꞃaⲓḃ ꞃⲉ ⲕo ⲕⲉaⲛaṁaⲓl oꞃⲧ, aʒⲩꞃ ⲕo ⲕⲩmaⲛaⲕ lⲉ ⲛ-a ⲕaⲓꞃⲇⲓḃ, ʒⲩꞃ ꝼaoⲓl mⲉ ⲛaⲕ lⲉⲓʒꝼaⲇ ꞃⲉ aoⲛ ṁⲓ aṁaⲓⲛ ⲇⲩl ⲧaꞃⲧ ʒaⲛ ꞃʒꞃⲓoḃaⲇ ⲕⲩʒaⲇ-ꞃa ⲛo ⲕⲩm ⲇ' aⲧaꞃ ⲛo ⲇo ṁaⲧaꞃ. 11. Ⲓꞃ ꝼⲓoꞃ ʒⲩꞃ ꞃaⲓḃ ꞃⲉ a ʒ-ⲕoṁⲛⲩⲓⲇⲉ ⲕⲓⲛⲉalⲧa aʒⲩꞃ ⲕⲩmaⲛaⲕ, aʒⲩꞃ aⲛṁaⲓⲧ ⲇam-ꞃa; ⲛⲓ ⲧⲓʒ lⲓom-ꞃa aoⲛ ꝼaⲧ a ⲧaḃaⲓꞃⲧ aⲓꞃ aⲛ ⲧ-ꞃoꞃⲇ ꞃo, aⲓꞃ ⲕaoⲓ aⲓꞃ bⲓⲧ ⲉⲓlⲉ aⲕⲧ aṁaⲓⲛ aⲓʒ ⲕⲩⲓṁⲛⲩʒaⲇ ʒo ḃ-ꝼⲩⲓl aⲛ ⲛⲓⲇ a ⲇⲩbꞃaⲇ ʒo ꝼⲓoꞃ ⲧaoḃ ṁoꞃaⲛ ⲉⲓlⲉ, ꝼⲓoꞃ aⲓꞃ-ꞃaⲛ maꞃ aⲛ ʒ-ⲕⲉaⲇⲛa : " aꞃ aṁaꞃⲕ, aꞃ ⲕⲩⲓṁⲛⲉ." 12. Ca aⲛ aⲓⲧ a ꞃaⲓḃ ꞃⲉ 'ⲛⲩaⲓꞃ ⲇo ⲕⲩalaⲓꞃ ⲩaⲓⲇⲉ aⲓꞃ aⲛ ⲇⲕaⲓⲇ ⲇⲉⲓʒⲓoⲛaⲕ? 13. Ḃⲓ ꞃⲉ a Loⲓⲛʒⲇⲓoⲛ; aʒⲩꞃ ⲇⲩbaⲓꞃⲧ ꞃⲉ ʒⲩꞃ ꞃaⲓḃ ⲇⲩⲓl aⲓʒⲉ ⲇⲩl ʒo Ꝼꞃaⲓⲛⲕ; aꞃ ꞃⲓⲛ lⲉ ⲏ-aⲓꞃ ⲛa Rⲓʒaṁⲩⲓⲛⲉ;* ⲛa ⲏ-Ⲁⲓlⲡ a ⲧꞃⲉaꞃⲛⲩʒaⲇ, aʒⲩꞃ ⲕⲩaⲓꞃⲧ a ⲧaḃaⲓꞃⲧ aⲓꞃ Ⲓoⲧaⲓllⲉ. 14. Oⲕ, ꝼⲉⲓⲕⲓm; 'ꞃⲉ ⲓꞃ ⲇoⲓʒⲧⲓʒⲉ ʒo ḃ-ꝼⲩⲓl ꞃⲉ aⲛoⲓꞃ aⲓʒ ⲇⲉaⲛaⲇ ⲛa ⲏ-aⲓꞃⲇⲓⲛⲉ aⲓꞃ a labaⲓꞃ ꞃⲉ, ⲧꞃⲉaꞃ aⲛ Ⲉⲩꞃoⲓꞃ; ꞃaⲕꝼaⲓⲇ ꞃⲉ b' ꝼⲉⲓⲇⲓꞃ, ʒo ⲇ-ⲧⲓ aⲛ ⲧalṁaⲛ ⲛaoⲙⲧa oⲓꞃ " ⲛⲓ mⲩⲓⲛⲧⲉ ʒo ⲕoⲓʒⲕꞃⲓoⲕ." 15. Ⲛⲓ ḃ-ꝼⲩⲓl, oⲓꞃ ⲇo ʒⲉall ꞃⲉ a bⲉⲓⲧ 'ꞃ aⲛ m-baⲓlⲉ aⲓʒ aⲛ ⲛoⲇlaⲕ 16. Ⲁⲓꞃ ꞃⲓⲩbaⲓl ⲧⲩ-ꞃa a ḃ-ꝼaⲇ ⲧaꞃ ⲇo ⲧⲓꞃ ⲇⲩⲧⲕaⲓꞃ. 17. Ⲛⲓoꞃ ⲕⲩaⲓⲇ mⲉ a ꞃⲓaṁ ⲛⲓoꞃ ꝼaⲓⲇⲉ ⲛa Loⲓⲛʒⲇⲓoⲛ aʒⲩꞃ Cⲉaⲛⲧⲓⲛ, ⲇ'ꝼaʒ mⲉ Loⲓⲛʒⲇⲓoⲛ aʒⲩꞃ bꞃⲩaⲕa ⲛa ⲏ-aṁⲩⲓⲛⲉ Ⲧaṁⲩⲓꞃʒⲉ bꞃⲩaⲓʒⲉ ꞃⲓⲛ, blⲓaʒaⲛ o ꞃⲓⲛ. 18. Ⲛaⲓḃ ⲧⲩ aⲓʒ ⲧⲉaⲕ ⲛⲩaⲇ ⲛa ꝼⲉⲓꞃⲉ? 19. Ⲉⲉaⲇ; ḃⲓⲇⲉaꞃ aⲓʒ ⲧⲉaⲕ ⲛa ꝼⲉⲓꞃⲉ, a ḃ-ⲧⲉaⲕ ⲛa ḃ-Ⲧⲓʒⲉaꞃⲛaⲓⲇ ⲕo maⲓⲧ a'ꞃ a ḃ-ⲧⲉaⲕ ⲛa ʒ-ⲕoⲓꞃⲕⲉaⲛ. 20. Ⲛaⲕ maⲓꞃⲉaⲕ aⲛ ꝼoⲓꞃⲛⲉ ⲧⲉaⲕ ⲛⲩaⲇ ⲛa ꝼⲉⲓꞃⲉ —obaⲓꞃ ꝼⲓⲩⲛⲧaⲕ ⲛⲓ ꞃⲉ aṁaⲓⲛ ⲇo 'ⲛ Rⲓoⲓꞃⲛⲉ Ⲉⲉaꞃlaꞃ a Ḃaꞃⲛaⲓⲇ a ⲕⲩm ⲉ, aⲕⲧ ⲇo 'ⲛ aoⲓꞃ aⲛⲛ a ḃ-ꝼⲩⲓlmⲓⲇ? 21. Ⲛaⲓḃ ⲧⲩ a ⲧalla ⲛaoⲓṁ Ⲉⲧⲉⲡaⲓⲛ? 22. Ḃⲓⲇⲉaꞃ, ⲓꞃ alⲩⲓⲛ ⲉ. 23. Caⲇ ꞃⲉ aⲛ bⲉallaⲕ aⲓꞃ ꝼⲓll ⲧⲩ o Loⲓⲛʒⲇⲓoⲛ? 24. Ⲇo ꞃⲓⲛ-

---

* The Rhine, from ꞃⲓʒ, and aṁⲩⲓⲛ ; others derive it from ꞃⲉⲓⲇ aṁⲩⲓⲛ, *the smooth river.*

ⴖeaⱃ Ɯaᵹⓝċaeⱃⲧeⱃ, mo ƀeallaċ; óⱼⱼ, buⱸ ṁⱼaⱳ lⱼom ⱃeⱼⲟⱃⱼⱳ caⱼⱃⱸe-ᵹaoⱼl aⱼⱃⱼⱸe a ƀⱼ 'ⱳⱼ a ᵹ-coṁⱳuⱼᵹe aⱳⱳ, aᵹuⱃ a ƀⱼ a ᵹ-coṁⱳuⱼⱸ aⱳċaⱃⲧaⱳaċ le muⱼⱬⲧⱼⱃ m'aⲧaⱃ. 25. Cⱃeⱼⱸⱼm ᵹo ƀ-ⱪuⱼl ⲧu eolᵹaċ aⱼⱃ-ⲧláċⲧ-ⱃᵹⱃⱼoƀaⱸ ᵹaċ uⱼle baⱼle ṁoⱼⱃ a Sacⱃaⱳⱼaċ? 26. Ꝺo ⲧeⱼⱬⱼⱳ ⱳⱼ ƀ-ⱪuⱼlⱼⱳ; ⱸeaⱃƀaⱼm ⱸuⱼⲧ ⱳáⱃ ⱪaᵹ me mo ċⱼⱃ ⱸuċċaⱼⱃ ⱪéⱼⱳ a ⱳⱼaṁ aċⲧ aoⱳ uaⱼⱃ aṁaⱼⱳ; ⲧá ᵹⱃaⱸ aᵹam aⱼⱃ a ᵹoⱃⲧaⱼƀ, aᵹuⱃ maᵹaⱼƀ, a ᵹleaⱳⲧaⱼƀ, a loċaⱼƀ aᵹuⱃ a ⱃⱼaƀⲧaⱼƀ: ⲧaƀaⱼⱃ ⱸam-ⱃa cumaⱃ a Ɯuṁaⱼⱳ ⲧeⱼċ, aᵹuⱃ ⱳⱼ 'l bⱼoⱳⱳ aᵹam aⱼⱃ óⱼⱃ aᵹuⱃ aⱼⱃ ṁaoⱳ Loⱼⱳᵹⱸⱼⱳ.

EIGHTEENTH LESSON—
ⱭN ⲦⓄⱭⲦ40Ɑⱷ LEⱼⱤEⱭN ꝺEUᵹ.

EXERCISE XXX.—ⱭN ⲦⱤⱼoċⱭꝺⱭⱸ ᵹNⱭⲧUᵹⱭⱸ; or, ⱭN ꝺEⱼⱥ2Ɑⱸ ᵹNⱭⲧUᵹⱭⱸ ⱭⱤ ⱧⱾⱬ.

1. God save you, James, dear friend of my heart! 2. May God and (the blessed) Mary save you, Peter, flower of nobility! is it not early you are this morning on foot? 3. It is early, indeed; because the morning is so fine, and I feel inclined to have a walk along with you. 4. You are a great walker certainly: there is not a good day at all that you are not rambling from hill to hill, from glen to glen, from plain to plain , from glade to glade, through the land. 5. Well, it is true for you: certainly, I am delighted, in our native land, to be out every time I can, on the summit of the mountains, on the tops of the hills, and in the retired recesses of the valleys; or again walking on the border of lakes, or along the coast. 6. I do not like to go out to-day; I have much (business) to perform. 7. Oh, you said the other day, and you promised that you would be ready to-day, and that you would have an opportunity to drive with me through the country; for, in truth to you, I would not like to be with any other but yourself—for you are so acquainted with every house, and with every place, with every cabin, and every chateau (big house); with every glade and every valley, mountain, glen, well, stream, river, mound, cemetery, churchyard; and not only that, but you know the history of everything of which I wish

to speak, or of which I should like to get information.
8. I am thankful to you for the great appreciation in which
you hold me, an appreciation of which I am not worthy,
and especially from a man who is possessed himself of so
much learning as you have. I do not therefore feel satisfied
(from the fact) that I cannot accompany you to-day; but
we shall have another day. 9. Did you not promise that
you would be prepared to-day? 10. I did (promise); but
do you not know that I have much (business) to do, and
that I cannot have (obtain) leisure to-day. 11. It is true
that each person ought to perform the things that are under
his (charge) direction, and on that account I do not wish that
you should do anything that would not be right for you to
do. 12. I see that you have sense, and that you are not
like a great many young people (filled) with an over desire
for every vain pursuit. 13. I am thankful to you; it is
meekly and kindly you speak on every matter. 14. What
day now will you be ready to come with me? name it.
15. Any day of leisure (holy-day); or the first day of the
week, if it be fine. 16. It is long, perhaps, until we have
another (fine) day like the present—the air is high; the
firmament azure; without a cloud (cloudless); without a
mist; the sun rising radiant; the birds warbling on every
tree; and all creation lightsome with beauty as on the first
day it issued forth from the hand of the Lord. 17. I am
greatly disposed (there is an inclination or desire on me)
to go with you. 18. Do not come; we will have another
day equally as fine. 19. This is my mother coming; our
breakfast is ready. 20. Mother, this is Peter O'Keefe, of
whom I often made mention (spoke) to (with) you;—a
young friend for whom I entertain great respect. 21. He
is welcome: ten thousand welcomes to you. 22. This is a
beautiful morning, madam. 23. Yes indeed; this is the
first beautiful morning we have had (for the) last month.
24. James, your breakfast is ready, and your father and
sister are awaiting your presence; perhaps this young gentleman has not yet breakfasted. 25. Peter, give us the
honour of your company at table. 26. With pleasure, indeed; but I can with truth say that (it is) on me the honour is conferred, to be in your society. 27. Please just
go before me; this is the way.

NINETEENTH LESSON—
AN NAOIDHEADH LÉIGHEANN DEUG.

EXERCISE XXXI.—AN T-AONMHADH GNÁTHUGHADH AIR TRÍOCHAD; or AN T-AONMHADH GNÁTHUGHADH DEUG AIR FICHID,

1. Henry, you are the best of men to be here so soon as you are—where is your brother? 2. He will be here immediately (on the spot, air ball); it was not possible for him to come with me when I had been ready, because our cousin-german Alphonsus O'Hegan was on a visit with us, and he was obliged to stay in order to be along with him. 3. Oh, I see; that is right. 4. What o'clock is it now? 5. It is only four o'clock. 6. It is early so, in the evening. 7. Just accompany me, and we can have a walk; or a sauntering stroll around here, and have a *conversazione* with each other. 8. We can so; and I like it, for I do not wish to be inside doors but as short as I possibly can. 9. This is the way by the side of the house. 11. Thank you (may good be to you); it is easy to stumble in a crooked, slippery road like that yonder. 12. What is your opinion of our own residence and position here, of our land and of our appurtenances? 13. I am of opinion that your residence is good; your land very good; your position delightful; and your appurtenances of the best. 14. Which is the better—your house, or our house? 15. Your house is better than our house. 16. We are convenient to the running water; to the large town (market-town); to the sea—things that enhance the value of a country-house. 17. Is this your garden? 18. It is our garden; come in and view it. 19. What the thing in it? *i.e.*, what does it contain? 20. Much—there are potatoes and cabbages, peas and beans, carrots, parsnips, radishes, turnips, raspberries, strawberries, onions, rose-trees, apple-trees, pear-trees, gooseberries, and such like. 21. I perceive that it looks well just now. 22. What is your notion of the manner in which the trees are, and of every growth (growing plant) which is in the garden? 23. I am of opinion that your apple-trees are too high, and your raspberry (trees)

scattered without pruning. 24. To whom belongs that garden yonder, and this orchard which is near me? 25. To my own people—my relatives, Patrick and James O'Daly. 26. Their orchard is superior to yours. 27. It is not indeed. 28. Their apple-trees are superior; their pear-trees, their rose-trees, and every herb or plant which is growing in their orchard is superior to your trees and your growing (plants). 29. Perhaps so, but I rather have my own than their share, though it be so good (as you assert). I know, at all events, that our oats and our wheat is better than their oats, their wheat, and their corn. 30. Are you not very well informed in regard to land—*i.e.*, how well informed you are in regard to land......31. It is dinner-time; come in; the company are assembling. 32. We shall have a merry feast, I expect. 33. We shall, if the best wine and the best meat to be had in Limerick can make young people feel merry. 34. Shall we not have dancing? 35. You will, if you wish, to the dawn of day.

TWENTIETH LESSON—

An Fiċeaḋ Léiġeann.

EXERCISE XXXII.—An doṁianaḋ gnáċuġaḋ deug air ḟiċiḋ.

1. This is a beautiful day, James? 2. It is a beautiful day, thanks be to God. 3. Is it not early, that you as well as myself are on the road? 4. It is early indeed I am on the road. 5. Have you any news at all for me? 6. Well, I have no news at all for you. 7. Perhaps you have; you were never without some new story for an individual, for you are under the repute of being entertaining, facetious, and that weariness would not be on (could not come near) any one that would be with you on the road or in the field. 8. Thanks to you, Connor (or, Cornelius); you were always agreeable, pleasant, mirthful. 9. I am only expressing, James, what each person is saying of (on) you. 10. It is a long time since I had an opportunity of having

a conversation with you—where do you now reside? 11 I have a dwelling near Galway—a town in Connaught, situated on the coast. 12. O, I know; that is a town that is progressing greatly—a town that is now on the straight course (*i.e.*, necessarily the shortest) to New-foundland, and a town to which each many are coming from every quarter, and besides a town in which above all things our native language is held in esteem. 13. The tribes of Galway were always studiously fond of the language of their fathers. 14. But has not your brother Edmund come back? 15. He has; I thought that I was telling you of it. 16. You were not. 17. Well, he came home. 18. Is it in America he was? 19. Yes. 20. Has he much money on his return, literally—on coming to him? 21. He has not much money, for he has been in it only two years, and the time was unfavourable for obtaining employ-ment; he has not therefore much money. 22. Does he say anything good of (on) the country and of (on) the peo-ple? 23. He says it is a good place; that the people are without slavishness, free, just, laborious, honourable. 24. Had he fine weather on (the) sea? 25. He had not fine weather on sea, the wind was high, the firmament (covered) with darkness, and a mist or cloud on the sun for two days. 26. Was it in (on) a sailing vessel he came? 27. No; but in a steamer. 28. What is the name of (which is on) the steamer in which he came? 29. Prince Albert. 30. Was it at Galway they put into harbour? 31. It is. 32. By my word, we are near Loughrea; this is the term of my journey to-day. 33. Are you going far? 34. I am going to Athlone. 35. Remain with me here to-night, and you will be in (it) in time enough to-morrow. 36. Thanks to you; I shall not wait. 37. Well, there is welcome for you, if you remain. 38. I will not wait; I shall repair onward. 39. God speed you.

NOTE.—The learner should not avail himself of the aid of a *Key* or *translation* but as seldom as possible, and never until after he has first done his best to translate the exercise proposed.

He should also write out the translation oftener than once.

TWENTY-FIRST LESSON—

an ꞇ-aonꝫaꝺ leiꞃean aiꞃ ꝼiꝺio.

EXERCISE XXXIII.—an ꞇꞃiꞃaꝺ ꝝnaꞇuꝫaꝺ ꝺeuꞃ aiꞃ ꝼiꝺio.

The Lord's Prayer.

Our Father who art in heaven, hallowed be thy name; thy kingdom come; thy will be done on earth, as it is in heaven. Give us this day our daily bread; and forgive us our trespasses, as we forgive them who trespass against us; and lead us not into temptation; but deliver us from evil. Amen.

The Angelical Salutation.

Hail Mary, full of grace, the Lord is with thee, blessed art thou among women, and blessed is the fruit of thy womb, Jesus. Holy Mary, Mother of God, pray for us sinners, now, and at the hour of our death. Amen.

The Apostles' Creed.

I believe in God the Father Almighty, Creator of heaven and earth; and in Jesus Christ, his only Son, our. Lord; who was conceived by the Holy Ghost; born of the Virgin Mary; suffered under Pontius Pilate, was crucified; dead and buried, he descended into hell; the third day he rose again from the dead; he ascended into heaven; and sitteth on the right hand of God the Father Almighty; from thence he will come to judge the living and the dead. I believe in the Holy Ghost; the holy Catholic Church; the communion of saints; the forgiveness of sins; the resurrection of the body, and the life everlasting. Amen.

Above all, he must, if he wish to learn the language, repeat the sentences presented in these exercises, and form new ones. There is no learning a language thoroughly without assaying to *speak* it.

TWENTY-SECOND LESSON—
AN DÓṀAḊ LEIĠĊEAN AIR ḞIĊID.

EXERCISE XXXIV.—AN CEAṪRAṀAḊ ĠNÁṪUĠAḊ DEUG AIR ḞIĊIT

1. A Ḋonċaḋ, an ól tu do ċuid té? 2. D'ólar. 3. Ṁaire, ó ṫarla go b-fuil an oiḋċe breaġ, téiġmuir amaċ agur ḋéanmuir rpairḋineaċ air an árdán, agur biḋeaḋ againn comḃraḋ taitneaṁaċ. 4. Ir mait liom é; aċt tá mo ḋearb-ṡiur briġid faoi ḋuil móir go b-fanfainn aice air feaḋ uaire. 5. Ṁaire iarr airṫí ṫeaċt ann aonḟeaċt linn. 6. Seaḋ: Iarrfaḋ. 7. A Ḃriġid an mait leat ṫeaċt ann aonḟeaċt le Ṁaolṁuire O'Raġallaċ agur liom féin coṗraḋ a'r beiḋmuiḋ aig rpairḋineaċ air an árdán? 8. Ir mait liom; tá bród mór orm é beiṫ ann mo ċuṁaċt eiriolloġ eoluir ḟaġail ó bur n-eaġna—maire naċ áluin (or riġṁeudaċ) an oiḋċe í! 9. (Ṁaolṁuire) ir oiḋċe anriġṁeudaċ í go cinte. 10. Tá re aig rioc go ġeur—naċ b-fuil? 11. Tá re aig rioc go ġeur, óir taid comarṫaiḋ uile rioca rolur; tá an rpeur gan neul, agur gorm; tá an ġaoṫ ó'n tuaiḋ, tá na reulta aig dealraḋ go h-anlonraċ; tá an t-aer an-ḟuar, agur dubairt mo ḋearb-ḃraċair Seamur liom go b-fuil an t-airgead beo rior go mór. 12. (Ḋonċaḋ)—a Ḃriġid an áil leat aimrir rioca? 13. Ir áil liom go h-anṁór. 14. Ir áil liom riubal amaċ annr an oiḋċe 'nuair ata ġaċ niḋ ciun,—gan fuam le clor; 'nuair a tá an talaṁ, mar m-beiḋeaḋ, dul ann ruain, an ġeallaċ go beannaċ a dealruġaḋ mar tá a noċt ann rpeur ġlinn, agur na reulta mar luċt faire or comair doruir neiṁe aig rceiċeaḋ a leura, tairbanaḋ duinn an arar no fuar ann a b-fuil an Solur rioṗraiḋe 'ó a ċomnuiġe. 15. (Ṁaolṁuire) ir ruairc go deiṁin rmuaineaḋ air an neiċiḃ ro agur rinn féin arduġaḋ or cionn na talṁan; aig raḋ, ma tá an fordorur ċo lonraċ ro, naċ ġlormar lann no dún an ard-riġ!—ma tá an coir-rtól ċo áluin, naċ áluin go mór an caṫaoir rioġḋa. 16. Oċ, aynr an tir rin na lonra rioṗruiḋe, ní'l grian, no ġeallaċ,—re Dia Eféin rolur agur glóir agur roġ luċt ċómnuiġe na b-flaiṫear. 17. (Ḋonċaḋ) cuineann tu o ġ-cuiṁne dam an rtáir a

ḃeirtear a b-taoḃ Naoiṁ Pilip Náiri, aᵹur a b-taoḃ an
Naoiṁ ṁorr—San Naríúr Loḋola, ᵹur ᵹáir, air breaċnuᵹaḋ o óir-ċnoc na Roiṁe ann ᵹar do'n b-Faiḋican, air
ᵹeata ḋealrac na b-flaiċear, anḋuil a ᵹ-croiḋe a beiċ annr
an árar uḋ or cionn na reulta ann a b-fuil ar b-Tiᵹearna
na ᵹ-cuman a rᵹeiċeaḋ na ᵹlóire. 18. (Briᵹiḋ) Cinte
tá rmuainte mar iaḋ ruḋ naḋurḋa; óir aiᵹ breaċnuᵹaḋ
air neiṁ ir minic cuiṁniᵹim air an niḋ ṁuirear an creiḋeaṁ
ḋuinn b-taoḃ na h-aite uḋ a ḋearuiᵹ Dia do'n ṁuintir a brio-
nar a n-ᵹráḋ air, aᵹur ḋeirim a b-foclaiḃ reannraiḋ ar ḃ-
tíre, " ni b-fuil ᵹlóir mar ᵹlóir néiṁe." 19. Ꝺiḋ ᵹo b-fuil
rmuainte ṁar iaḋ ruḋ naḋurḋa aᵹur buḋ cóir ᵹo b-tiocfaiḋ
ann inntin ᵹaċ ḋuinne, naċ beaᵹ a ḋeanar leuirrmuainte mar
iaḋ? 20. (Doncaḋ), ir fíor rin; eiriᵹeann an meuḋ ro ḋ
euᵹṁair rmuainte. 21. (Briᵹiḋ)—Tá fuaċt oirm-ra; tá re
ann am ḋul a rteaċ. 22. (Maolmuire) Saoil me ᵹur
raḃamar le coṁraḋ a ḋeanaḋ air na coṁreulcaiḃ? 23.
(Donċaḋ) Tá re anoir mall. 24. (Briᵹiḋ) Tá an cloᵹ
'ᵹ a ḃualaḋ. 25. (Maolmuire)—Ca ṁeuḋ be ċloiᵹ é?
26. (Donċaḋ)—Nı'l re aċt an naoi be ċloiᵹ, mearaim
27. (Briᵹiḋ) Aon, do, trí, ceaċar, cuiᵹ, ré, reaċt, oċt, naoi,
ḋeiċ. 28. (Donċaḋ) Tá re an ḋeiċ be ċloiᵹ, aċt caiċfiḋ
tu fannaċt ᵹo b-ti an aon-ḋeuᵹ air an laᵹaḋ. 29. Ni
ṁaiċ liom, naċ b-tiᵹ liom fannaċt an fáḋ rin; aċt raċfaḋ a rteaċ le aṁarc faᵹail air b' aċairr aᵹur bo ṁaċair,
bo ḋearḃḃraċair, aᵹur bo ḋearḃ-fiur Sinéiḋ.

TWENTY-THIRD LESSON.

ᴀn Triᵹṁaḋ Leiᵹeann air Fíciḋ.

EXERCISE XXXV.—ᴀn Cuiᵹṁaḋ Ꝺnacuᵹaḋ ḋeuᵹ air Fíciḋ.

1. Father, have you leisure at ₍resent? 2. I have,
my son; what thing is desired by thee? 3. I wish that
you will treat of geography. 4. Well, as I said, I just
wish to treat of it now with you; who else will be along
with you? 5. My cousin Patrick and my sister Harriet;
they are awaiting (with) us in the study-room. 6. Say

(with) to them to come in; I cannot go to them. And now, is it not better for you to get knowledge on this branch (of science) from the teacher than from me? 7. Dear father, we prefer it (it is better with us) from you, because you are so gentle, and so loving in your speaking with us, and you explain every thing that is difficult, so plainly to us, that we understand every word you say, and your words are a pleasure to us. 8. I believe so, that it is necessary for me to give you a lesson, since you are so desirous to get knowledge; call in Harriet and your cousin Patrick. 9. I shall (call): They are towards us (*i.e.*, they are coming); we are ready. 10. Dermot, my son, what is the world; or, (with) what is it like? 11. The author whom I am reading says it is like to a ball, or to an apple; being flattened at the poles. 12. Harriet, how (is it shown) do you know, that the world is round? 13. It is true to say that it is round, since ships have sailed around it, always steering a westward course. 14. You are good: which line is the longer—the (meridian) line from north to south, or the equator, (which is) the middle line from east to west? 15. The equator or middle line from east to west is longer by twenty-five miles. 16. You are very good: Patrick, how is the world divided? 17. Into two principal divisions—land and water. 18. How are the divisions of water named? 19. Oceans, seas, gulfs, bays, lakes, straits, rivers. 20. What are the divisions of (the) land? 21. Continents, kingdoms, islands, promontories, headlands or capes, isthmuses. 22. Do you know (how to name) the four cardinal points? 22. I do (know):— north, south, east, west. 24. Dermot, do you know the reason why the four cardinal points were called ꞇuaꞇ, ꝺeaꞃ, oiꞃ, and iaꞃ? 25. I do not know the reason, father. 26. Well, it is surprising to me, (after) so often as you have heard me tell to you. 27. (Harriet) Oh, I know the reason, father. 28. Tell it now to your brother. 29. When the Druids were wont, in the olden time, to adore the sun on its rising, they turned their faces to it, and they called therefore the country before them oiꞃ, and that to their back iaꞃ (behind); that to which the right (ꝺeaꞃ) hand was turned, ꝺeaꞃ (or right), and to the country on their left (tuaṫ) hand, tuaṫ, north. 29. Indeed, Harriet, you are good. 30. Dermot, is it east I shall call the top of this map? 31. It is not, but *north;* and *south* to the bottom, *east* to the side on (of) the right hand, and *west* to the side on (of) the left hand. 32. I do not understand it. 33. It is, easy to know it, my son; and now this is the explanation (of it). In ancient times the Druids turned, as your sister has remarked, towards the rising sun; they called therefore left-hand side, or tuaṫ, to that direction which was on the side of the left hand; but now-a-days, those who write about geography or a knowledge of the countries (of the earth) make the north the point to which they turn, and therefore they place it (north) at the top of the map, and hence the country to the *south* must be at the bottom; the *east* to the right hand, and the *west* to the left hand side. 34. I understand it, I understand it now. ......35. Some one is knocking at the door. 36. See who is in it. 37. It is our professor that is come. 38. Go to him; I have letters to write.

TWENTY-FOURTH LESSON.

AN CEAṪRAṀAD LEIĠEAN AIR FIĊID.

EXERCISE XXXVI.—AN SEISEAḋ ĠNAṪUĠAḋ DEUG AIR FIĊID.

PATRICK AND GEORGE.

1. Are you, George, learning Irish? 2. I am. 3. Tell me now, if you please, how many days in the week? 4. Seven days. 5. Say them in Irish. 6. Dia-luain, Monday; Dia-mairt, Tuesday; Dia-cedin, Wednesday; Dia-tordain, Thursday; Dia-ḃeine, Friday; Dia-Saṫuirn, Saturday; Dia-doṁnaiġ, Sunday. 7. You are good; what week is this? 8. This is the week of Easter. 9. What is the meaning, or interpretation of the word Caisg (Easter)? 10. It is a word which has come to us from the Hebrew, and it signifies *passing through,* for the angel of the Lord passed through Egypt, and killed the eldest son in

every mansion of the habitations of the people of that country, because Pharaoh did not allow the Hebrews to go with Moses, to give adoration to the God of the universe 11. I am acquainted with the story that is written in the book which Moses penned in regard to the Hebrews, who went out under his guidance from (the) Egypt, and of the way in which the horsemen and the horses, the chariots and the fighting men, the king himself and the chieftains, the warriors and the hosts (how they) were swallowed up by the power of God in the waters of the sea. 12. I am acquainted with all this; but I know not what reason the Christians called (Cáirg) Pasch to the time of our Lord's resurrection? 13. They called it (Cáirg) Easter, because it happened at first on the same time on which happened the feast to which the Jews applied the name (Cáirg) *Pasch.* 14. Is it not a great festival, the festival of the (Christian) Pasch? 15. It is a great festival indeed—the festival on which arose from the grave the Saviour of the world, gaining victory over death and sin and the devil. 16. Is it not right therefore that there should be joy of heart over every Christian on this day, and that the elements themselves should be filled with great joyousness, because our head arose victorious from the grave, striking (the) death and the devil for ever under foot? 17. Speaking of the elements being filled with great joyousness; I always thought that was a pretty story which is usually in the mouths of the poor, that the sun bounds with joy on account of the rising of the divine Light. 18. Did yourself ever see him (her, grian, is *fem.*) dancing? 19. I did not (see); but my father told me that he saw it on a delightful (Easter) Sunday morning, on rising very early. 20. Perhaps if our faith and our love were as strong and as ardent as was that of St. Peter, and that of St. Mary Magdalene, we should not be at all surprised at it. 21. Certainly we would not. 22. Will you be in the city to-day? 23. I shall (be). 24. Come to me, if you please, to-morrow. 25. I shall, with pleasure, for I will have occasion, or an opportunity. 26. Adieu: (blessing [be] with you). 27. God prosper you.

PART III.

TWENTY-FIFTH LESSON.

The personal pronouns me, I, me; τu, thou; re, é, he, him; rinn, we, us; rib, you; riad, iad, they, them; are usually incorporated with the simple prepositions, whenever, in collocation, they fall under their governing influence.

Of the twenty simple prepositions, the following seventeen thus incorporate; and to the union of both is correctly given the name "*prepositional pronouns:*"— aɪʒ, at; aɪr, on; ann, in; ar, out of; cuɪʒe, unto; be, from, of; bo, to; eɪbɪr, or ɪbɪr, between; raoɪ, under, for; le, with; roɪme, before; reac, beside; car, beyond, over; crɪb, or cré, through, or by means of; ua, or ó, from; uɪm, about—as clothes about the body; uar, above.

From them have sprung the following :

1st Person.	2nd Person.	3rd Person.	
		Mas.	Fem.
S. aʒam, at (or in the possession of) me,	aʒab,	aɪʒe,	aɪcɪ.
P. aʒaɪnn, at us,	aʒaɪb,	aca,	
S. orm, on me,	orc,	aɪr,	aɪrrɪ.
P. orraɪnn, on us,	orraɪb,	orra, or orcu,	
S. aram, out of me,	arab,	ar,	aɪrcɪ.
P. araɪnn, out of us,	araɪb,	arcu.	
S. cuʒam, unto me,	cuʒac,	cuɪʒe,	cuɪcɪ.
P. cuʒaɪnn, unto us,	cuʒaɪb	cúca.	
S. bɪom, of me,	bɪoc,	bé	bɪ.
P. bɪnn, of us,	bɪb,	bɪob, or bɪobéa.	
S. bam, to me,	buɪc,	bo,	bɪ.
P. búɪnn, to us,	baoɪb,	bóɪb.	
S. eabram, between me,	eabrab, or eɪbɪrcu,	eɪbɪr é	eɪbɪr í.
P. eabraɪnn, between us,	eabraɪb,	eacra.	
S. fúɪm, under me,	fúc,	faoɪ,	fúɪce.
P. fúɪnn, under us,	fúɪb,	fúca,	
S. ɪonnam, in me,	ɪonnab,	ann,	anncɪ.
P. ɪonnaɪnn, in us,	ɪonnaɪb	ɪonnca.	

Thus it is seen from the foregoing that ᴀзᴀᵯ is the compound form of ᴀɪз ᵯᴇ, at or to me; ᴀзᴀᴆ, of ᴀɪз ᴄu, to thee; ᴀɪзᴏ, of ᴀɪз ʀᴇ, to him; ᴀзᴀɪɲɲ, of ᴀɪз ʀɪɲɲ, to us; ᴀзᴀɪᴆ, of ᴀɪз ʀɪᴆ, to you; ᴀcᴀ, of ᴀɪз ɪᴀᴆ, to them.

The suffix ɪᴀᴆ, they, has become, by time, almost effaced in the compound form of the third person plural.

The verb ᴆo ᴆᴇɪᴄ, to be, with the prepositional pronoun ᴀзᴀᵯ, to me, ᴀзᴀᴆ, to thee, &c., denotes possession; as ᴄᴀ ᴀɪɲзɪoᴆ ᴀзᴀᵯ, there is money to me, *i.e.*, I have money. The verb "have," therefore, when in English it expresses the idea of possession, is translated into Irish by means of the verb ᴆo ᴆᴇɪᴄ with the prepositional pronoun ᴀзᴀᵯ, and its inflections. (See Obs. 1, 2, in Third Lesson; p. 16, also p. 108.)

<h2 style="text-align:center">VOCABULARY.</h2>

Austria, 2ɫuʀᴄʀɪᴀ.

Country (a large territory), ᴄɪʀ, *f.*

— (a rural district), ᴄuᴀɪᴅ, *f*; (pr. *thoo-ay*). Ꞇuᴀɪᴄᴇᴀᴄ, *m*, a countryman, a clown; also a layman, as opposed to cɫᴇɪʀᴇᴀᴄ, a cleric. Ꞇuᴀᴄᴀ (same); *plur.* ᴄuᴀᴄᴀɪᴅ, boors. Ꞇuᴀᴄᴀᴄ, *adj.*, rustic. Ꞇuᴀᴄᴀ, a people, a race; as ᴄuᴀᴄᴀ Ꞓɪʀᴇᴀɲɲ, the people of Ireland; ᴄuᴀᴄᴀ ᴆᴇ Ꝺᴀɲᴀɲ, the Danaan race.

Echo, ᵯᴀc-ᴀɫɫᴀ, literally, the son of the cliff. The word ᵯᴀc, a son, is applied also to the young of brutes, and, in a figurative sense, to that which springs from any source or cause, as, ᵯᴀc-ᴄɪʀᴇ, a wolf (the son of the wild country); ᵯᴀc-ɫᴇᴀᴆᴀɪʀ, copy of a book; ᵯᴀc-ᴀɫɫᴀ, echo; ᵯᴀc-ɫᴇɪзᴇᴀɲ, a student, *i.e.*, a son of learning, from ɫᴇɪз, read; ᵯᴀc-ʀᴀᵯᴀɪɫ, the like, or equal; as, ᴆo ᵯᴀc-ʀᴀᵯᴀɪɫ, your like.

Fear (apprehension, dread of consequences), ᴨᴀɪᴄᴄɪoʀ, *m* (pr. *fátchees*); dread, terror, ᴇᴀзɫᴀ; ɪʀ ᵯᴀɪᴄ ᴇ ᴀɲ ᴨᴀɪᴄᴄɪoʀ, fear is salutary.

Germany, 2ɫɫᴀᵯᴀɪɲ, *f.*, Зᴀɲᴆᵯᴀɪɲ, *f.* A German-Keltic word, derived from ᴀɫ, powerful, prodigious, large, and ᵯᴀɲɲ, man, German (old Irish ᵯoɲ, persons). The usual derivation of *Allemagne* is *alles* (Ger.), all, and *mannes*, men; a name which, in strict propriety, cannot with this radical meaning, be applied—as it was at first—to the few who, with their neighbours the *Marcomanni* (Irish ᵯᴀʀc, a horse; ᵯᴀʀcᴀᴄ, a rider), lived between the Rhine and the Danube. Зᴀɲᴆᵯᴀɪɲ, Germany; from зᴀɲᴆ, rough, fierce, and ᵯᴀɪɲ, men.

Power (command, headship), cᴇᴀɲɲᴀʀ, *m* (from cᴇᴀɲɲ, head), ᴀɲᴆ-ᴄᴇᴀɲɲᴀʀ, *m*, sovereignty.

— influence, control, ᴀʀʀᴀᴄ, *m*, as, ɲɪ'ɫ ᴀʀʀᴀᴄ ᴀзᴀᵯ ᴀɪʀ, I cannot help it (there is no controlling influence to me in its regard).

— ability, force, strength, ɲᴇᴀʀᴄ, *m*, ᴄʀᴇuɲᴀʀ, *m*, ɪʀ ᴨᴇᴀʀʀ ʀᴄuᴀɪᵯ 'ɲᴀ ɲᴇᴀʀᴄ, ingenuity is better than strength.

— moving force, ᴆɪᴀɲᴀᴄ, *f* (vehemence, boldness).

— sway, ʀᴇɪᵯ, *f*; high station, ᴀɲᴆ-ʀᴇɪᵯ, *f.*

— martial greatness, cᴀɪᴄ-ʀᴇɪᵯ, *f.*

— animal strength, ᴆʀɪз, *m*, luᴄ, ɫᴀɪᴆɪʀᴇᴀᴄ, *f.*

— capability, efficacy, ᴆʀɪз; as ʀᴀᴇᴆ зᴀɲ ᴆʀɪз, a thing without efficacy.

— mightiness, government, cuᵯᴀᴄ, cuᵯᵯᴀʀ.

Powers (qualities), cᴀɪɫɪᴆᴇᴀᴄ; as, the powers of the soul, cᴀɪɫɪᴆᴇᴀᴄᴀ ᴀɲ ᴀɲᴀᵯᴀ.

— governments, ᴀɲᴆ-ᴄuᵯᴀᴄᴀ, or ᴀɲᴆ-ᴨɫᴀɪᴄᴇᴀʀᴀ; as, the powers of Europe, ᴀɲᴆ-ᴄuᵯᴀᴄᴀ ɲᴀ ʜ-Ꞓuʀoɪᴘᴇ; ᴀɲᴆ-ᴨɫᴀɪᴄᴇᴀʀᴀ ɲᴀ ʜ-Ꞓuʀoɪᴘᴇ.

— an army, ʀɫuᴀз.

— many, ᵯóʀᴀɲ, зo ɫᴇoʀ, ɪoᵯᴀᴆ;

as, a power of people, ¡omⷂo ⷂⷂoⱵne.
Shake, v, cⱧⱭⱼⱬ-eⱭⷁ, inf.
Spread, v, leⱭⱬ⷏Ⱨ⏤, -nⱨⷂⷁ, inf.
Terrible, uⱭⱬ⷏ⱭⱧ, adj. (from uⱭⱬ, loneliness, solitariness); uⱭⱬⱠⱭⱧⱭⱬ, adj., from uⱭⱬⱠⱭⱧ, desolateness, wildness, terribleness; cⱧⱷⷁⱭ, hard-fought, valiant, terrible; as, cⱭⱬ

cⱧⱷⷁⱭ, a terrible battle; ⷁ¡Ɑn, vehement; m¡lⱬⱷⱭⱬ, destructive; from m¡ll, destroy.
Tuscany, ⱮⱨⱧcⱭ¡n, f.
War, coⱠⱭⷁ. m, cⱭⱬ (battle), m, ¡m⷏ⱧⱭⱧ (strife), m, co¡⷏ⱧⱭc, m, (contention, struggle, in which the contending parties meet).

EXERCISE XXXIX.

1. Have you any news (nuⱭⷁⱭⱬⱬ, pr. *nooyacht*)? 2. I have no news. 3. Has your father any news? 4. My father has no news; we who live in the country, have no news (idiomatic form—there is no news at, or for us who live in the country); you who live in the town ought to have the news of the day (¡⷏ cⷅ¡Ⱨ ⷁⱭo¡Ⱡ Ɑ ⱬⱭ 'Ⱨ-Ɑn m-bⱭ¡le ⷇ⷅ¡Ⱨ, ⷠo m be¡ⷁeⱭⷁ nuⱭⷁⱭⱬⱬ ⷠⱭⱬ Ɑon lⱭe ⱭⷅⷅⱭ¡Ⱡ)? 5. Have you heard of this terrible war which is about to shake Europe?* 6. Of course I have (ⷅo c¡nⱬe ⱬuⱭlⱭⱧ): its roar has been heard not alone throughout the land (ⷁo clu¡ⱧeⱭⷁ Ɑ ⷅⷅ¡m ⱠⱠ h-e ⱭⷠⱭⱧⱠ ⱬⱧⱠⷁ Ɑn ⱬ¡Ⱨ), but has echoed in every valley, and glen, and dell, from Howth to Urrus Head (Ɑⱬⱬ ⷁo ⷅⱭ¡Ⱨ Ɑ mⱭc-Ɑ¡lle Ɑnn ⷅⱭⱬ lⱭⷅ ⱭⷅuⱧ ⷅleⱭnn, ⱭⷅuⱧ cluⱭn ⷅ B¡nn-ƎⷁⱭ¡Ⱨ, ⷅo ceⱭnn ¡ⱭⱧⱧu¡Ⱨ). 7. Is it likely that its flame will spread towards us (ⱬuⷅⱭ¡nn-ne)? 8. I am under no apprehension that it will (Irish idiom—there is no fear on me that it will). 9. My brothers James and William are under the apprehension that it will (a fear is on my brothers James and William, &c.) 10. Indeed there should be no apprehension *on them*. 11. I said so (ⷁuⱠⱭ¡Ⱨⱬ m¡Ⱨe Ⱨ¡n), and that they should be possessed of courage (Irish idiom—and that it is right for them that courage should be *in them*). 12. Are you afraid (is there fear on you)? 13. I am not afraid—I never was, and never shall be (there is not fear *on me*—there never was, and never shall be). 14. Are your father and cousins afraid? 15. They are not afraid: they are possessed of that bravery which the race of the Fitz-Geralds are wont to exhibit (ⱬⱭ ¡onnⱬu Ɑn ⱬⱧeunⱭⱧ Ⱡⷁ, ¡Ⱨ ⷁuⱭl ⷁo clⱭn ⷅeⱭⱧⱭ¡lⱬ Ɑ ⱬⱭ¡ⱧbⱭnⱭⷁ). 16. What Powers

* Written during the week in which the war between France and Austria commenced, April, 1859.

are engaged in this war? 17. France (an Ḟⱃⱥⁱnc), and Sardinia (Sⱥⱃⱛⁱⱀⁱⱥ), and the north of Italy, on the one side—Austria on the other? 18. What is the cause of war *between them* (cⱥⱒ é an ⱺ-aḃḃaⱃ coⱛaⱛ ⱜá eⱥⱼⱃⱥ)? 19. A desire on the one side to obtain liberty; on the other to retain power (ⱺⱥⁱl aⁱⱃ aon ⱜaoḃ le ⱃaoⱼⱃⱥⱜ ⱝⱥⱛaⁱl, aⱛⱦⱃ le ceⱥnnⱥⱼ a ⱛoⱼⱛⱳaⁱl aⁱⱃ an ⱜaoḃ eⁱle). 20. Is not war a great scourge to mankind (naⱛ móⱃ an ⱃⱼⱦⱃⱃⱥ, coⱛaⱛ aⁱⱃ an cⁱnne ⱛaonⱥ [human race])? 21. It is indeed. 22. What a lovely thing peace is. 23. Oh! yes, it is very lovely; we do not know its value till we see what evil war has done. 24. I like peace very much (ⁱⱼ áⁱl lⁱom ⱃⁱoⱜ-ⱛáⁱⱼ ⱛo h-an-móⱃ). 25. Do not be afraid of this war (Irish form—let not fear be on you with regard to this war). 26. I am not afraid; for I put my hope in the God of battles (cⱦⁱⱃⁱm mo ⱛoⱜⱛaⱼ ann ⱛⁱa na ⱛ-caⱜ) and in the God of peace, and take from His hands (aⱛⱦⱃ ⱛlacaⁱm ó n-a láⱦⱼaⁱḃ) war or peace, as He wishes (ⱃⁱoⱜ-cáⁱⱼ no coⱛaⱛ ⱃéⱼⱃ maⱼⱃ ⁱⱼ ⱜoⁱl leⁱⱃ). 27. You are very wise I see—as well in matters of this world as in matters relating to the next (a neⁱⱜⁱḃ an ⱜ-ⱃaoⱛaⁱl ⱃo aⱛⱦⱃ a neⁱⱜⁱḃ an ⱜ-ⱃaoⱛaⁱl eⁱle). 28. Do not praise me if you please. 29. I shall not; I only tell the truth (nⁱ ⱦolⱃaⱛ; ⱼⁱ ⱛeⁱⱃⁱm aⱛⱜ an ⱃⁱⱃⁱne). 30. Good-by (beⱥnnⱥⱛⱜ leⱥⱜ). 31. Good-by kindly (ⱛo ⱃaⁱḃ maⱼⱜ aⱛaⱛ).

TWENTY-SIXTH LESSON.

The preposition le, leⁱⱃ, with, conveys the idea expressed by the words "belonging to," "on the side of," "under the dominion of;" as,

Iⱼ leⁱⱃ an Ⱅⁱⱛeaⱃnⱥ, an cⱃⱦⁱnne aⱛⱦⱃ an meⱦⱛ a ⱜá aⱼn. The earth, and all that is in it, belong to the Lord.

Aⱼn le ⱛ' aⱜaⱼⱃ an ⱃeaⱃḃⱃoⱛanⱜaⱼⱛ ⱃo? Does this servant belong to your father?

Aⱼn le mⱦⱼnⱜⁱⱃ an ⱜⁱⱃ-ⱛⱃaⱛa ⱛⱦⱃa? Do you belong to the patriotic party?

When le, or leⁱⱃ, refers to the *subject* of a proposition, it

means literally " with one's self," or " with themselves," and,
therefore, *alone*, or *away*—as,

Τá ρe leιρ ρéιη. He is alone (literally, with himself).

> Nι ραζραδ leαc ρéιη cu, le ɱeαδαδ,
> Αιɲ αη ζeuζ.
>
> I'll not leave thee, thou lone one,
> To pine on the stem.
> —*Irish Melodies.*

Ceιc leαc, α ρeαη-ριη, ηα δéαη ɱoιll ηα ɼζιc.
Flee *with thyself* (*i.e.*, away !) old man, do not make delay, nor rest.
> —*Irish Homer*, book 1.

> Ɗ' ιɱιζ leιρ ζο ɼoɼcαċ.
> He went *away* silently. —*Ibid.*

Literally :—

> He went with " himself " silently.

Leιρ, as we see from last lesson, is the *prepositional* pronoun, for le, ρe.

The English phrase, " he is alone," or " they are alone,"
is, therefore, rendered—cá ρe leιρ ρéιη ; cá ɼιαδ leo ρéιη.

These various meanings the preposition le retains in its compound form :

Lιoɱ,   leαc,   leιρ,   leιċe,   lιηη,
With me;   with thee;   with him;   with her,   with us;

lιδ,   leo,
with you;   with them.

leo, with them, is pronounced as if spelled " leov," and vulgarly " leofa."

> Cá " lιηη-ηe " ceαɼc, Eιɼe, 'ɼ αη ζ-cαιɲδe.
> On *our side* is virtue and Erin.

Literally :—

> Are with us justice, Eire, and our friends.
> —*Irish Melodies*, p. 39.

Observe how the verb (cá) goes before ceαɼc, Eιɼe, &c.

bιδeαηη ηα coηηα, αιɲ αη ɲιηceαδ δ' αη δ-cɲéιζɼιη ceαċc αoιɼe,
'S δ'αη b-ραζáιl cɲáċ-ηóηα αιɲ αη cɲáιζ báη " lιηη ρeιη."
And the wave that we danced on, at morning, ebbs from us,
And leaves us at eve on the bleak shore, *alone.*

Oʙs. 1.—When le, leιρ, conveys the idea of " possession,"
" dominion," it follows the assertive form of the verb δo
beιċ, to be—viz., ιρ, it is; buδ, bα, it was; buδ, that it may
be (but it has only its primary meaning, that of *with, along
with*, after the other forms, cá, is; bι, was; beιδ, will be;
and their inflections) ; as in the following axiom on justice
from the Irish code—the Brehon Laws :

"Iſ le fear" an bó an gabán.
To the owner of the cow the calf belongs.

Literally :—

It is *with the man* of the cow the calf—*partus sequitur ventrem.*

In this sense Irish peasants ask children, Cia leir tú?—
Whose child are you? (Literally, whom with, you.) Cia
leir tú, a buacail?—Whose son are you, boy? Cia leir
tú, a cailín?—Whose daughter are you, girl? Cia an
treib ar leir tú?—To what tribe do you belong?

Obs. 2.—The possessive pronouns mine, thine, his,
her, our, your, their; and the form, my own, our own,
&c., are translated into Irish by means of the prepositional
pronouns, liom, leat, leir, leite, linn, lib, leo (see next
Exercise).

VOCABULARY.

About (around), timcioll; for a d-timcioll (a preposition compounded of a, in, and timcioll, border), in the borders, surrounding.

Ass, aral.

Cow, bo; *plur.* ba.

Dowry, tpné, *m.* This Irish word originally meant *cattle*, because the marriage portion in olden times given to daughters consisted in cattle — a custom existing still among the peasantry.

May (month of), bealteine. The month of May is called mi na beal-teine, or "the month of Bel's fire," because on the first of this month the pagan Irish lighted, on the tops of the highest hills, purificatory fires in honour of their god Bel—the *Belus* of the Persians—i.e., the Sun, to which deity they paid divine honours. bliaġan, a year, more correctly spelled belain, is derived from bel, the sun, and ain, a circle.

Mill, muillin, *m* (Welsh, *melin;* Fr., *moulin;* Dut., *molen;* Gr., μŭλη, *mulé;* Lat., *mola*), from the Irish term mol, the axle, on which it turns; *plur.* muillinib.

Mule, muille, *m, plur.* muillte. Lat., *mula.*

Ox, daih, *m,* maic, *m; plur.* daim; maic.

Pagan, Paganác, *plur.* aiġ, from the Latin, *Pagus.*

Poet, band, file, *plur.* bainn, filib.

Poultry, éanlait, a generic plural term, meaning birds of all kinds.

Pound, punta; as, a pound weight, punta meabacain; a pound sterling, punta airgib; from *pondus,* Latin.

Robes, culaib (dress), from cut, or col, from which comes colan, the body; and ead, dress.

Stock, airneir, *f.*

Turkey (the country of), Tuircir, *f.*
— a bird of that name, francac.

Woo, ruiriġ, *imp. m;* ruiruġad, *inj.;* breuġ, *imp. m;* breuġad, *inf.;* from breuġ, a lie, for those who woo, flatter, and in doing so, over-colour the truth; ruirġteac, a lover, a suitor; also, in a secondary sense, a trifler. The u is pronounced short; the syllable ruir in the foregoing is pronounced like the English word *ser.*

EXERCISE XL.

Robert and Michael—Riobapð aʒuf Ⱥꞃicael.

1. Is this mine or yours?—Ⱥn liom-ꞅa é ꞅo, ꞃo leaꞇ-ꞅa?
2. It is not mine nor yours; it is my father's. 3. It is
therefore, yours, for what belongs to your father belongs to
you (aꞁ an aðbaꞁ ꞅin, iꞅ leaꞇ-ꞅa é, óiꞁ iꞅ leaꞇ-ꞅa an
meuð a baꞁneaꞅ le ð' aꞇaiꞁ). 4. Are not you his own
especial son (Naċ mac leiꞅ ꞅeiꞃ ꞇu-ꞅa)? 5. I am his own
especial son. 6. You appear to have been all alone (Irish
idiom—*with yourself*) this evening. 7. Indeed-I have been
all alone till you came (ꞃo ʒuꞁ ċaiꞃic ꞇu-ꞅa), thanks for
your friendly attention (buiðeaċaꞅ ðuiꞇ ꞅaoi ðo ċaꞃaðaꞅ).
8. I am sorry I had not been able to come yesterday
evening to meet your friends (ꞃi maiċ liom ꞃaꞁ b' ꞅeiðiꞁ
liom ꞇeaċꞇ ꞇꞃaꞇ-ꞃóꞃa a ꞃae aiʒ báiꞁ ðo ċaiꞃðe). 9. I
was sorry too, for all our friends were *with us*—you alone
(aꞃáiꞃ) of all were not with us. 10. When did the meeting (báiꞁ) separate (bꞁiꞅ ꞅuaꞅ)? 11. It did not separate
till four o'clock this morning. 12. Is this house your
father's own? 13. No, it is mine; for my grandmother
(maċaiꞁꞁmóꞁ), to whom it belonged, left it to me; it is now
mine. 14. Has she left the houses, the mill (muiliꞃ), the
farm (ꞅeiꞁm), and stock (aiꞁnéiꞅ) to you? 15. No, she has
not; these are not mine, they are James O'Brien's, my cousin. 16. But to whom do the cows (ba), and the horses
(See Sixteenth Lesson, p. 89), and all the sheep on the
other farm belong? 17. They are all the property of my
brother Stephen—the cows are his; the horses are his; the
oxen (baiꞁ) are his; the mules and asses, the sheep and
goats, the poultry even, such as geese, ducks, turkeys, hens,
cocks (See Twenty-third and Twenty-fourth Lessons), all
belong to him. 18. Has he a thousand oxen? 19. Indeed
he has, perhaps more. 20. "Whose child" is this boy
yonder? "Cia leiꞅ" an buaċaill óʒ ꞅo ċall? 21. He is
my brother's child—a fine boy, and very like (" coꞅaꞃaiꞁ
le") his father. 22. Who has all the money your grandfather had amassed? 23. It has been all, only about a thousand pounds, bequeathed to my sister Anne—ꞅaʒað ꞁomlaꞃ
an aiꞁʒeið, ꞇimċioll miꞁe puꞃꞇa, aiʒ mo ðeaꞁb-ꞅiuꞁ Ⱥnna.

24. It will make a handsome dowry for her—ბéaɲꝼaɼö ɼe ɼɼɲé ბeaɼ ɒɲ? 25. It will, indeed. 26. Is she not going to get married this month—the lovely month of May? 2l ɲaċ mɼaɲ leɼċe ɼoɼaö a ბeaɲaö, aɲ mɼ ɼo—mɼ áluɼɲ ɲa Beal-ceɼɲe? 27. She is not; it is in her own power (ɼɼ ꝼeɼɒɼɼ leɼċe), but she has deferred the marriage till the beginning of the coming month (ჳo coɼɼeaċ aɲ mɼ ɼo ċuჳaɼɲɲ), from the old pagan notion which still exists among some people, that it is not lucky to marry (ɲaċ ɓ-ꝼuɼl ɼe ɼoɲa ɼoɼaö) in May. 28. Is it in that month of which poets love to sing—that month which appears to be the most delightful month of all the months in the year (ɒe mɼoɼaɼɓ ɲa ɓlɼaჳaɲa); when earth and sky, wooing us to the transient things of life, put on their newest robes, and look charming and joyous, as if telling all Adam's race "Be happy." It is the month, too, of Mary; a month full of benedictions to every child who loves so good a mother—2lɲ mɼ aɼɼ a ɓ-ꝼuɼl ɲa ꝼɼlɼö ჳo ɼɼoɼ aɼჳ ბeaɲaö ɼaɲɲ—aɲ mɼ ɼɼ ɼulcmaɼɲe ɒe mɼoɼaɼɓ ɲa ɓlɼaჳaɲa, 'ɲuaɼɼ a cuɼɼeaɲɲ aɲ cɼuɼɲɲe aჳuɼ aɲ ɼɼeuɼ, le ɲ-aɼ m-ɓɼeuჳaö aɼჳ ɲeɼċe cáɼɲe aɲ c-ɼaoჳaɼl ɼo, a ჳ-collaɼö ɼɼ úɼa oɼɼċu, aჳuɼ aɱaɼcaɲɲ ჳo ɼჳɼaɱaċ, ɼeuɲɱaɼ aɱaɼl a'ɼ aɼჳ ɼaö le ɼɼol 2löaɼɱ—"Bɼöɼö ɼuɓaċ." Iɼ ɼe mɼ 2ɦaɼɼe e—mɼ a cá láɲ ɒe ɓeaɲɲaċcaɼɓ ɒo ჳaċ uɼle leaɲɓ aɼჳ a ɓ-ꝼuɼl ჳɼaö aɼɼ ɱaċaɼɼ ċo ceaɲaɱaɼl. 29. Does your sister know all this? ɓ-ꝼuɼl ꝼɼoɼ aɼჳ ɒo ბeaɼɓ-ꝼɼuɼ aɼɼ aɲ meuö ɼo? 30. She does (cá ꝼɼoɼ); but, like many in matters of this kind (aċc maɼ ჳo leoɼ a ɲeɼċɼɓ ɒe'ɲ c-ɼaɱaɼl ɼo), she follows the words of foolish women, and sets common sense and reason aside. Leaɲaɲɲ ɼɼ caɼɲc ɼaoɓ-ɓaɲ aჳuɼ cuɼɼeaɲɲ aɼɼ leɼċ cɼall aჳuɼ cuɼჳɼɼɲc. 31. Please tell her what I have been remarking. 32. I shall, but it is no use (ბéaɲꝼaö; aċc ɲɼ'l aoɲ ჳaɼ aɲɲ). 33. Good-by (ɼlaɲ leac).

TWENTY-SEVENTH LESSON.

Obs.—The English verbs, I choose; I desire; I disregard; I care not; I like; I pity; I prefer; I love rather; I wish; I wish rather; I am fond of; I remember;

I wonder; I am surprised, I am wont; it seems right; poor; just; bad; hard; pleasant; wonderful; and others of kindred meaning, are rendered into Irish in a peculiarly idiomatic way—viz., by the assertive verb ιγ, is; bα, was; followed by an adjective or noun, with the noun or pronoun which in the English is the subject or nominative, governed in Irish by the preposition le, with; as,

I choose, ιγ γοζα ιοιη; literally, it is choice *with me*.

I desire, or intend, ιγ ηιαη ιοιη; literally, there is desire with me.

Ταιηιc me le τειηe α γcαγαδ αιη αη ταιαη αζυγ cγα ιηδ eιle ιγ ηιαη ιοιη αcτ ι βειτ αιη ιαγαδ—I came to cast fire on the earth, and what will I but that it be enkindled.

> Ιγ ηιαη ιοιη γeαγδα ζιυαγαcτ
> Ζο cυαη ceαηc ηα γιοηα δι.
>
> **I desire henceforth to repair**
> **To the real haven of wine-drinking.**
> —*Carolan's Song, " Lord Mayo."*

I care not, ιγ cυηα ιοιη; literally, it is equal with me.

> Cυηα ιοιη' cαc υιη τοηη.
> **I care not for all, about esteem.**
> —*O'Daly Fionn.*

Thou likest, ιγ ηαιτ leατ; literally, it is good with you.

21α 'γ ηαιτ leατ α βειτ βυαη, cαιτ γυαγ αζυγ τειτ—If you like to live long use hot and cold.

You like, { Ιγ δeαγ leατ; literally, it is proper with you.
{ Ιγ βγeαζ leατ; „ it is elegant with you.
He pities, { Ιγ cγυαζ leιγ; „ it is pitiful with him.
{ Ιγ cγυαιδ leιγ; „ it is hard with him.
She prefers, ιγ γeαγγ leιτe; „ it is better with her.
She loves rather, ιγ αηγα leιτe; „ it is more loving with her.

> Ιγ αηγα leo coιηζιoll α'γ cαιδe ζο ηοη.
> **They love honour and virtue more.**
> —*Irish Melodies*, p. 10.

We wish, { Ιγ αιl ιιηη; literally, it is pleasing with us.
{ Ιγ τοιl ιιηη; „ it is will with us.
We wish rather, { Ιγ γeαγγ ιιηη.
{ Ιγ γοζα ιιηη.

You remember, ır cuıṁne lıḃ.

> A cuıṁne leac Eıḃlín, reoıḃ a'r rġaıċ oıġe.
>
> You remember Ellen, our hamlet's pride.
>
> —*Moore's Melodies*, p. 41.

They are wont, ır ġnáċ leo; literally, it is usual with them.

John thinks it hard, and wonders that you have his money—Ir cruaıḃ le Seaġan é, aġur ır ıonġa leır ġa b-ḟuıl a aırġeaḃ aġaḃ.

OBS. 2.—The verbs can; could; may; might (denoting ability, power, opportunity, and not a mere sign of tense); am able; am capable; have the power to; and the like, are translated by the expression ır ḟeıdır, it is possible, followed by the preposition le, with; as, ır ḟeıdır lıoṁ a ḋeanaḃ, I can do it; ır ḟeıdır leır ċeaċc, he can come; or by the third person singular of the irregular verb cıġım, I come; cıġ, it comes; as cıġ lıoṁ, I can—*i.e.*, it comes with me; nı cıġ leac, it comes not:—nı cıġ leac ḃ' aran a ḃeıċ aġaḃ aġur a ıċe, you cannot have your bread, and have eaten it.

Cıġeaḃ (imperfect), it used to come; cıġeaḃ lıoṁ, I used to be able.

Caınıc, it came; caınıc leır, he could, he was able.

Cıocḟaıḃ, it will come; cıocḟaıḃ leır, he will be able.

Cıocḟaḃ, it would come; cıocḟaḃ leır, he would be able.

Ġo b-cıġıḃ, that it may come; ġo b-cıġıḃ leıċe, may she be able; ġo b-cıġıḃ ḃo rıġeaċc, thy kingdom come.

VOCABULARY.

Daisy, noınean, *m*; from nóın, day, noon; like the Saxon term daisy, derived from day.

Field, paırc, *f*; as, paırc breaġ, bán, a fine white (*i.e.*, uncultivated) field; a plain, a level country, maġ (pr. *mawh*). From maġ are derived the names of many localities in Ireland beginning with the syllable *Moy*, *May*, or *Mo*, as Moyglass, Maynooth, Movilla.

Meadow, *m*, macaıre; derived from maġ, and ġıonna, smaller, denotes a smaller portion of level country than that indicated by the term maġ. It is a name applied by our tenant farmers to sheep-walks, meadows, paddocks.

Flower, blaċ, *m*, blaċa, *plur.*; a rose, rór, *m*, *plur.* róra; a flower in bloom, rcoċ, *plur.* rcoċa; blaċa bána, blossoms; as, cá blaċa bána aır na ġaır, there are blossoms on the (potato) stalks—the Irish idiom for "the stalks are in blossom."

Garland, ḟlearġ, *m*, ḟlearġ blaċ.

Harvest, autumn, roġar, *m*, from roġ, produce, reward, booty, spoil; and ár, tilling. For the same reason roġmaıre means a pirate, one living on the spoils taken from the deep, from ꝼoɜ, booty, spoil, and mꜽꞃꜳ, of the sea. From ꝼoɜmꜽꞃe is derived the name of the Femorians, the second colony that took possession of Ireland. |ꝼoɜꜽl, ꝼ, booty; from ꝼoɜ, and ɜꜳbꜽl, taking; ꝼoɜꜳlꜳċ, *adj.*, predatory.

ꝼoɜnꜳṁ (from ꝼoɜ, and ɜníṁ, to do), *m*, means service, ceremony; ꞃeꜳꞃb-ꝼoɜꜳꞃcꜳíṁ, a servant; one who renders service, yet feels the bitterness (ꞃeꜳꞃb) of servitude.

November, Sꜳṁuꝼn, *f*; mí nꜳ Sꜳṁnꜳ, the month of November. Hallow-Eve, oꝼ-ꞁe-Sꜳṁnꜳ. Sꜳṁuꝼn is derived from ꞃꜳ, calm, serene, and ꝼuꝼn, end, because the serene seasons end at November.

Ripe, *adj.*, ꜳꞃuꝼṁ, ripeness, ꜳꞃuꝼ-ꜳċ, *f*.

Sports, ꞃuɜnꜳṁ ꜳɜuꞃ ɜꞃeꜳn.

Summer, ꞃꜳṁꞃꜳṁ, derived from ꞃꜳṁ, and cꞃꜳ, time, season; or ꞃꜽꞇe, a quarter of a year, as it is, by excellence, the serene season of the year; cꝼocꝼꜳíṁ ꜳn ꞃꜳṁꞃꜳṁ ꜳɜuꞃ ꝼꜳꞃꝼꜳíṁ ꜳn ꝼeuꞃ, the summer will come, and the grass will spring up.

Strand, cꞃꜳíɜ; hence cꞃꜳíɜ-ṁóꞃ, Tramore, the great strand (from cꞃꜳíɜ, and móꞃ, great, large), a fashionable watering-place near Waterford; ꝼꞁonn-cꞃꜳíɜ, Ventry.

Thyme, cꝼme.

EXERCISE XLI.

Margaret, Elizabeth, and sister.—Ⱳꜳꞃɜꜽꞃeꜳṁ, Eꞁꝼꞃꜳbec, ꜳɜuꞃ ꜳ ꞁeꜳꞃbꞃꝼuꞃ.

1. Do you like to walk, my dear, ꜳn mꜽċ leꜳc ꞃꝼubꜳl, ꜳ ċꜳꞃꜳ mo ċꞃoꝼꞁe? 2. I *do like* to walk; but, tell me (ꜳċc ꝼnnꝼꞃ ꞁꜳm), *can* we walk through the fields; for to tell you the truth, I will not walk on the road (óꞃ leꝼꞃ ꜳn ꝼꝼꞃꝼne ꜳ ꞃꜳꞁ leꜳc, ní ꞃꝼubꜳlꝼꜳꞁ ꜳꝼꞃ ꜳn m-bocꜳꞃ ṁóꞃ)? 3. Yes, we *can* (ꞃeꜳꞁ, "cꝼɜ lꝼnn"), for there is neither dew (ꞁꞃucc) nor rain (ꝼeꜳꞃċꜽn) on the grass. 4. I think it pleasant (ꝼꞃ ꞁeꜳꞃ lꝼom) to walk through the fields. 5. Do you prefer the fields to the road? (Irish idiom—are the fields better with you than the road?) 6. I do (ꝼꞃ ꝼeꜳꞃꞃ lꝼom). 7. Do you think it pleasant to walk out in the morning? 8. No; I love rather to walk out in the evening. 9. Perhaps your sister *would like* to come with us, and to pull flowers? 10. She *cannot* come. 11. Try (ꝼeuċ), perhaps she *can* (b' ꝼeꝼꞁꝼꞃ ɜo b-cꝼɜ). 12. Certainly, *I do not like* to leave her *alone;* she is such a charming girl. 13. She says (ꞁeꝼꞃ ꞃꝼ) that she *likes* to come, but that it is not possible for her unless you get leave (ꜳċc ní ꝼeꝼꞁꝼꞃ leꝼċe, munꜳ b-ꝼꜳɜꜽꞁ cuꞃꜳ ceꜳꞁ). 14. I *can* myself give her leave. 15. Very well; I am sure she is more willing to come than to remain. 16. I too would *prefer* that she would come. 17. *Is* she *wont* to remain at home? 18. No; she is not wont; in fact

it is usual with her to be out with her sisters.   19. Oh!
how beautiful the meadows look; how beautiful (oċ ŋaċ
áluıŋ aṁaɼcaŋŋ ŋa macaıɼıȯ, ŋaċ áluıŋ) ; see the daisies,
the wild thyme, the honeysuckles (ŋa ɼeıċleoȝa), and all
the wild flowers (ŋa blaċa ɼıaȯaŋa uıle) ; what a nice garland I shall make for mother. 20. That child wonders
(there is wonder [ıoŋȝŋa] on) at everything new she sees.
21. Sister, will you *please* pluck flowers, and we will make
a garland (aŋ áıl leaċ ṗóɼa ɼıaȯaŋa ċɼuıŋŋuȝaȯ aȝuɼ
ȯeaŋɼamuıȯ ɼleaɼȝ ȯıoḃ). 22. Pluck flowers yourself, my
girl, just as you *please*. 23. Margaret, *do* you like the
summer quarter better than any of the other seasons of the
year (Ⱥ Ṁaɼȝaıɼéaȯ, aŋ ɼeaɼıɼ leaċ-ɼa aŋ ɼaṁɼaȯ ŋo
ɼaıċe aıɼ bıċ eıle ȯe'ŋ ṁ-blıaȝaıŋ)?   24. I *do ;* for not
only *can* one walk out through the fields more readily then
than at other times, but the meadows and everything around
you look gay. 25. That is true : yet what do you think
of harvest time, the lovely harvest time, when all fruits are
ripe?   26. I know it is a joyful season ; but then the
thought that the fine days are past, and all the exciting,
healthful sports of the year coming to a close, is not agreeable.   27. Well, my dear girl, do you not know that such
is life—at one time sunshine, at another storm ; at one time
summer, again winter ; but every one to his choice (ȝaċ
ȯuıŋe ȯo ɼéıɼ a ṁıaıŋ). 28. *Do* you *remember* the sports
we had last summer at the sea-side at Tramore (Ⱥŋ cuıṁŋe
leaċ aŋ ɼuȝɼaȯ aȝuɼ aŋ ȝɼeaŋ bı aȝaıŋŋ. aŋ ɼaṁɼaȯ ɼo
ċuaıȯ ċaɼċ ċaoḃ aŋ ɼaıɼɼȝe aıɼ aŋ Ⱦɼaıȝ-ṁóıɼ)?   29. I
do, well (ıɼ cuıṁŋe łıom ȝo maıċ). 30. I assure you we are
just at my cousin's house ; will you come in (aŋ áıl leaċ
ċeaċċ a ɼċeaċ)?   31. I shall, with pleasure.

TWENTY-EIGHTH LESSON.

Oʙs. 1.—Between the idiom "ıɼ łıom"—it is with me, I
possess (ıɼ leaċ, thou possessest ; ıɼ leıɼ, he possesses) ; and
"ċá aȝam"—it is at or with me, *i.e.*, I have (ċá áȝaȯ, thou
hast ; ċá aıȝe, he has ; ċá aıcı, she has), &c., the difference

in the meaning is, that the latter expresses the presence or use of the thing named; the former indicates a right to its possession; as, "τά αιηзιοδ αзαϻ" αċτ "ɲι ljoϻ" ϝέιɲ έ, "I have" money, but it is not my own. "Τά αзαϻ," shows the money is in hand; "ɲι ljoϻ," (not with me) indicates the person's right to it.

EXERCISE XLII.

1. You have money, but is it your own? 2. I have money, but it is not my own. 3. My father has land, but it is not his own. 4. My mother has a house, but it is not her own. 5. My brother usually has (bjδeαɲɲ αiз) money, but it is not his own. 6. Has your sister a book which is not her own? 7. My sister has not a book which is not her own. 8. The landlord (αiз τiзeαρɲα ɲα ταlϻαɲ) has herds (τρeυδα), cows, horses, sheep, and goats, but they are not his own. 9. This land (ταlαϻ) is good, but it is not our own. 10. To speak the truth (leiɼ αɲ ϝiριɲe α ράδ), there is nothing our own.

Obs.—Leiɼ, with, is formed from le, by adding to it the euphonic sibilant ɼ, a letter which, in every cultivated language, is annexed to certain vocables, to prevent hiatus. Its correct spelling, therefore, is leɼ, but usage has adopted the spelling leiɼ.

Le, with, assumes the form leiɼ (pr. *lesh*) before the article αɲ, the; after the interrogative pronoun ciα, who; and the relative pronoun α, who; as, "Ciα leiɼ" αɲ δoϻαɲ ɼo?—To whom does this world belong? Leiɼ αɲ Τiзeαρɲα (with), *to the* Lord. Ciα ɼe α b-ϝυιl ɼe coɼαϻαιl leiɼ? Who is it whom he is like to (with)?

Leiɼ is also the third person singular masculine of the prepositional pronoun, ljoϻ, with me; leατ, with thee; leiɼ, with him, or with it; as, 2ιɲ le Séαρlαɼ αɲ leαbαɼ ɼo? (Is it with Charles this book) Does this book belong to Charles? Iɼ "leiɼ" (it is *with him*), it does.

EXERCISE XLIII.

1. Ciα leiɼ αɲ bαιle ɼo? 2. Iɼ leiɼ αɲ Τiзeαρɲα έ? 3. Ciα leiɼ αɲ τιɼ ɼo? 4. Iɼ le ϻυιɲτιɼ ɲα h-Θιɼeαɲ i. 5. Ciα leiɼ αɲ ταlαϻ ɼo? 6. Iɼ ljoϻ-ɼα i. 7. Nαċ le δ' αċαιɼ i? 8. Ni leiɼ. 9. Ciα leiɼ ɲα bα αзυɼ ɲα cαο-

ṁaiġ, an talaṁ aġur an tpaiġ? 10. Ir le tiġeaṁṁa na talṁan iað. 11. Cia leir an ʒaban ro? 12. Ir le ꝼeaṁ an bó é, maṁ beiṁ an ꝼean-ṁáð. 13. ʒo ṁaib maiċ aʒáð, tá ꝼior aʒam ṁin, ʒuṁ le ꝼeaṁ an bo, an ʒaban. 14. Aċt cia aṁ leir an bo; an le ðo ðeaṁb-bṁaċaiṁ í? 15. Ir leir. 16. Cia leir an t-óʒanaċ ro? 17. Aṁ leir an ʒaiṁðinea. é, no le ꝼeaṁ an tiʒ móiṁ. 18. Ir leir an ʒaiṁðineaċ (gardener) é. 19. Ir maiċ an ꝼeaṁ oʒ é.

Obs.—The interrogative possessive pronoun *whose* is translated into Irish in the form *whom with*, cia leir; as, "whose is this book" (Irish idiom—whom with the book this)? cia leir an leabaṁ ro? liom-ṁa (with myself) *mine.* (See Obs. 2, in Twenty-sixth Lesson, p. 162.) For examples, see the foregoing and following Exercises.

"Whose," meaning " of whom," " of which," " on whom," as being a part of, the likeness of, is translated, not by leir, but the preposition ðe, of; or aiṁ, on; and cia; as, *whose* image and likeness is this? cia ðe an ioṁaiġ aʒur an ċoṁaṁlaċt ro? ðe Caeraṁ (of Cæsar), Cæsar's.

VOCABULARY.

From the following few generic names, cú, a hound, a greyhound, any dog (maðað, a dog), coṁṁ, a crane, ṁíol, any animal, is derived—by adding to each a word expressive of the peculiar quality of each species—a great number of specific terms by which the various kinds contained under these *genera*, and other animals of kindred characteristic features, are denominated:

Dog, hound, cú, m; *plur.* coiṁ; Gr. κυων; Lat. *canis.*

Wolf, cú allaið; maðað allaið, from cú, or maðað, and allaið, wild; mac-tíṁe is another name for wolf; and ꝼaol-ċú, from ꝼaol, wild, cruel.

Pointer, } Cú, or maðað eunaċ, (from
Spaniel, } the same, and eunaċ, of birds); maðað uiṁʒe, a water-dog, a spaniel.

Moth, cú ꝼionna, the mildew worm, fur insect.

A ranger, a slow-hound, cú-luiṁʒé, from loṁʒ, to seek, to trace.

Greyhound, ṁíol-ċu.

Otter, maðað uiṁʒe; cú ðonn; cú ṁaṁa.

Rabbit, coiṁín, the diminutive of coiṁ; Latin, *cuniculus.*

Falcon, large hawk, ꝼaolċon.

Bandog, aṁ-ċu, from áṁ, a chain, and ċu; naṁc-ċu, same, from naṁc, a collar, and ċu.

Fox, ꝼionaċ, maðað ṁuað.

Crane, coṁṁ, coṁṁ móna.

Bittern, coṁṁ ʒṁeiṁe. This bird is commonly called buṁan leuṁa.

Cheslip, coṁṁ-ċoṁaċ.

Earwig, coṁṁ-ʒoblaċ.

Grasshopper, coṁṁ caol.

Heron, coṁṁ ʒlar.

Salamander, coṁṁ-caʒaiṁte.

Screech-owl, coṁṁ-ṁʒṁiaċóʒ.

Stork, coṁṁ bán.

An animal, a beast, large or small, ṁíol; as, ṁíol-móṁ, a whale; ṁíoltoʒ (as if ṁíol-óʒ, a diminutive animal), a fly, μῆλον, *mélon* (Gr.) a sheep; míl, Welsh.

Bat, mjolcóg leaċajne (leaċajn, leather).

Crab, mjol ṫpaᵹáċ (from ṫpaᵹ, a claw); a frog or toad, mjol máᵹan (from maᵹ), a small paw.

A gut-worm, mjol ᵹojle.

A moth, mjol cojlle.

A hare, mjol bujóe, from mjol, and bujóe, yellow. The common name for hare is ᵹjoṫṫfjaó, from ᵹjoṫṫ, short, and fjaó, a deer, any wild animal.

EXERCISE XLIV.

1. Whose hat is this? Cja lejṫ aŋ baṫṫéaó ṫo? 2. Mine (ljom-ṫa). 3. Whose house is this? 4. It is John's. 5. Whose knife is this? 6. Jane's. 7. Whose pen (peaŋŋ) is this? 8. Whose paper (papéjṫ) is this? 9. Whose ink (óubaċ) is this? 10. Whose ink-bottle (óubaóaŋ) is this? 11. Whose slate (ṫláca) is this? 12. Whose quill (clejce) is that? 13. Whose is this horse (capal, eaċ) James has? 14. Whose likeness is this? 15. Whose image is this? 16. Whose history is this (on whom is this a history)? 17. Whose history (ṫcájṫ) is this (with whom, i.e., to whom belongs this book of history—leabaṫ ṫcájṫo)? 18. Whose bread is this? 19. Whose meat is that? 20. Whose is that hound—Cja lejṫ aŋ ċu ṫjŋ? 21. It is my father's—jṫ le m'aċajṫ j. 22. Whose is that dog, and this greyhound, and that spaniel which you have? 23. They are not yours. 24. Will you, if you please, walk with me along the bank of this river?—Aŋ ṫjubalfajó cu ljom, má 'ṫ ṫé óo ċojl e ajṫ bṫuaċ ŋa h-abajŋe ṫo? 25. I will—ṫjubalfaó. 26. Do you see the crane yonder (ċall) on the brink of the pond—ajṫ bṫuaċ ŋa ljŋŋe? 27. I do—fejcjm. 28. I see hares, and rabbits, and herons, and storks, all here; it is an amusing spot (jṫ ṫjamṫaċ aŋ ájc e), whose is it—cja lejṫ e? 29. It belongs to the Duke of Leinster—le ceaŋṫaṫc ŋa Lajᵹeaŋ é. 30. I am obliged to you for your attention, but I must go to Dublin to-night—Jṫ ejᵹjŋ óam óul ᵹo Bajle Aċa-cljaċ a ŋoċc. 31. It is time to go—cá ṫé ajŋ am jmċeaċc.

TWENTY-NINTH LESSON.

OBS. I.—Adjectives signify fitness, unfitness, profit, disprofit, pleasure, pain, convenience, inconvenience, indifference, agreeableness, are followed by the prepositions óo, to; ajṫ, on; aŋŋ, in; le, lejṫ, with; faoj, under. The four former, do, air, ann, faoi, impart to the noun the usual prepositional meaning of relation; le, however, betokening an affection of the mind, adds to its prepositional force the idea of opinion, judgment; as,

Is buntáirteac "do" Seagán an obair ro—This work is profitable to John (expressing merely that, in relation to John, the work is profitable, without specifying whether or not he considers it such).

Is buntáirteac "le" Seagán an obair ro—This work "is considered" profitable by John.

Is "olc leo" é—"They consider" it evil.

Is olc "doib" é—It is "bad for them."

Má'r olc "orraib" é—If it be bad on you (a form of expression used by those who do a thing to grudge or vex).

Má'r olc ort é, déanfaib me é—If it be evil for you (just to spite you) I shall do it.

Bub geanamail "orm" é—He was friendly "towards" me.

Bub geanamail "dam" é—He was friendly "to" me.

Bub geanamail "ann" a teac féin é—He was friendly "in" his own house.

Bub geanamail "liom" é—I "considered" him friendly.

Is "mait dam" act "ni mait liom"—It is *good for me*, but I *do not consider it good.*

VOCABULARY.

Cean, *m*, fondness, regard; of a kindred meaning with cionn (*kynn*), affection.

Ceanamail, friendly; from cean, and amail, like. Just as from gean, affection, love, is derived geanamail, amiable, lovely; from grád, love, grádamail, loveable; and, in general, adjectives with a passive signification are derived from primitive nouns by annexing to them the suffix amail, like; as, flait, a prince; flaiteamail, princely, munificent; fear, a man; feanamail, manly; meas, respect; measamail, respectable; mod, esteem; modamail, estimable.

Daidbir, poor; opposed to saidbir, rich.

Deacair, difficult, impossible (from do, like *dus*, in Greek, a particle betokening difficulty, and cuir, put, settle); its second meaning is, strange, mournful—derived from do, and car, friendly.

Dianar, *m*, violence, vehemence, force; from dian, vehement.

Flaitear, *m*, a kingdom, heaven; from flait, a prince. It is at present applied to that kingdom of which our Lord Jesus Christ is King, "flaitear na naoim," the kingdom of the saints.

EXERCISE XLV,

1. Is maiṫ "duiṫ" a ḃeiṫ boċt giḋ ní maiṫ "leaṫ" é. 2. Is maiṫ "liom" a ḃeiṫ ann so, giḋ naċ maiṫ "dam" é. 3. An maiṫ "leaṫ" teaċt liom? 4. Ní maiṫ "liom" dul leaṫ, giḋ b' ḟeidir go m-buḋ maiṫ dam é. 5. An maiṫ "le d' aṫair," bás ḟáġail? 6. Níor maiṫ "leir," no "linn-ne," giḋ go m-buḋ maiṫ do mórán da ḃ-ḟuigeaḋ se bás (if he should get death, *i.e.*, die). 7, Is deacair "le gaċ duine" an saoġal dona do ḟáġail. 8. Is deacair "leir an daiḋḃir" (poor) e, agus is deacair "leir an saiḋḃir" é. 9. Is deacair "do'n ḃ-ḟear saiḋḃir" dul go flaiṫeas, giḋ ní deacair "leir." 10. An olc "leaṫ" go ḃ-ḟuil do ċomursa saiḋḃir? 11. Ní h-olc liom; aċt go cinte, is olc dam, óir déanḟaiḋ se (he will make [commit]) dianas orm ḟein agus air mo ċeallaċ (hearth, household). 12. Is olc "le Seorsa" go ḃ-ḟuair a namad bás, giḋ ní ḃ-ḟuil aon maiṫ dó ann. 13. Le h-olc orm rinne mo ḃuaċail ġoid (committed theft) mar ġeall gur olc "liom" gur raiḋ se ann aonḟeaċt (along) linn (with us). 14. Déan caint leir (speak to him). 15. Is maiṫ "liom" laḃairṫ leir, aċt ní maiṫ "dam" laḃairṫ leir. 16. Ḃ-ḟuil tu ceanamail "air?" 17. Tá me ceanamail "air," giḋ ní ḃ-ḟuil me ceanamail "leir." 18. Na bí mar sin. 19. Ní ḃeiḋiḋ.

Obs. 2.—"Le, with," following adjectives of the class specified in the foregoing observation, imparts to the infinitive mood active of some transitive verbs depending on them a passive meaning, such as is peculiar to the *second* supine or the participle ending in *dus* of Latin verbs; as,

Eve was fair "to be seen"—B' aluin Éḃa "le ḟeicsin."

It is a wonderful story "to be told"—Is iongantaċ an sgeul é "le innsin."

It is hard "to be got"—Is deacair e "le ḟáġail."

It is joyous "to be told"—Is luaṫ-ġairdeaċ é, "le rad."

The goods were profitable "to be sold"—Buḋ buntairteaċ na h-earraiḋ iad "le diol."

Obs. 3.—The English *infinitive present*, expressive of purpose, intention, or the *future*, known in English Grammar by the words "about to," must, when translated into Irish, be preceded by "le," for; as, le rad, to speak; *pour parler*; le ბeaṅaḃ, to do; she stooped to conquer—ბo ċroṁ ſi le buaiḋ ḟáżail; they came to see, táinic riaḋ le feicſin; he is about to come, tá ſé le teact; Jane is about to go, tá Sიnéiḃ le imteact.

VOCABULARY.

Evening, nóin, *f*; even-tide, trát-nóna, the time of the evening, or after-noon; nóna, the poss. case of nóin.

Opinion, baſnaṁail, from baſn, the top, produce, happy issue, success; and aṁail, like—*i.e.*, what is likely to follow from given premises—opinion, conjecture.

Saddle, ბiallait (from ბiall, the breech, and áit, place), ბiall-atóiſ, a saddler.

Sail (to), swim, rnáṁ.

Sign (omen), tuaſ, *m*; as, tuaſ ceata, a *shower-omen*, the Irish term for rainbow. Tuaſ żonta żailſon ażuſ żanbſſon, the forerunner of famine is tempest and storm.

— (a demonstration, an example), taiſbeanaḃ.

— (a token, a mark), comaſta.

— (a miracle), mionbuille.

EXERCISE XLVI.

1. Look to the west (aṁaiſc aiſ an iaſ). 2. I do look (aṁaſcaim). 3. See how red (naċ ბeaſż) the sun is now, when he is going to rest (anoiſ 'nuaiſ tá ſí le ბul faoi). 4. Oh! he is to be seen in great splendour and glory this evening—Oċ tá ſí le feicſin faoi loiſſaḃ ażuſ faoi żloiſ móiſ an tſát-nóna ſo. 5. Really the sea appears on fire—2ṁaſcann an ṁuiſ a beiċ aiſ teine. 6. Indeed it does. 7. Is your friend the saddler (about) to go to America? 8. He is (about) to sail this week. 9. Indeed (żo beiṁiṅ). 10. "Wonderful to be told," I thought (faoil me) he would never go (in it), naċ nacſaḃ ſe a coიḋċe ann. 11. Earning is "hard to *be* obtained" these days—tá ſaotſużaḃ "ბeacaiſ le fáżail" 'nna laetიḃ ſo. 12. Is his business (obaiſ, ceiſბ) not good (ბona). 13. It is not good for making a quick fortune—ní maiċ ſ "le taiſce a ſaotſużaḃ" żo tapaიḃ. 14. Are you "to go" (*i.e.* intending to go, about to go) home to-night. 15. Yes, I am—tá me le ბul. 16. Is it not late to go? 17. No, it is not; for I am wont (See Lesson Twenty-sixth) to travel at night—aiſბiſ a ბeaნaḃ 'ſ an oიḋċe; besides the moon is (about) to rise—tá an żeallaċ le eiſიżaḃ. 18. I advise you (beiſim comaიſle ბuit) not to go (żan a ბul); for it is my opinion (ſ mo baſiaṁail) that we will have a storm—żo m-beიḃ ſtoſſიn ażaიnn. 19. It is my opinion that we

will not.   20. Do you not perceive (naċ peiceann tú) how
red the sky is—ċo beaṙʒ a'r tá an rpeur?   21. Is redness
in the sky at this time a sign of a coming storm (of a storm
to come—le teaċt)?   22. It is.   23. Well (Ⓐaire), I do
not care about these signs—ir cuma liom (See Lesson
Twenty-sixth) taoḃ na tuar ro; I like the proverb (rean-
raḋ) that tells us not to heed omens—ʒan mear a ḃeiċ
aʒainn air tuaraiḃ.   24. Have your own way then—
Bíoċaḋ do ċoil féin aʒaḋ.

THIRTIETH LESSON.

In the Twenty-fifth Lesson we showed that the *personal
pronouns* and simple prepositions unite. Of the *prepositional*
pronouns formed by this union we gave a partial list. We
now subjoin those not yet presented to the learner :

	1st Person.	2nd Person	3rd Person. Mas.	Fem.
S.	rómam, before me,	rómat,	roime,	roinpi.
P.	rómainn, before us,	rómaiḃ,	rómpa.	
S.	ċarm, over me, by me.	ċarat,	ċairir,	ċairrti.
P.	ċarainn, over us, by us,	ċaraiḃ,	ċarrta.	
S.	tríom, through me,	tríot,	tríḋ,	tríċi.
P.	trínn, through us,	tríḃ,	tríoċa.	
S.	uaim, from me,	uait,	uaiḋe,	uaiḋċe.
P.	uainn, from us,	uaiḃ,	uaċa.	
S.	uaram, above me,	uaraḋ,	uara,	uairti,
P.	uarainn, above us,	uaraiḃ,	uarta.	
S.	umam, about me,	umaḋ,	uime,	uimpi.
P.	umainn, about us,	umaiḃ,	umpa.	

VOCABULARY.

Before, roiṁ, *prep.* It expresses priority of time and precedence in place; as, ċainic re rómam, he came before me; fear re rómam, he stood before me; tá an bár rómainn, death is before us.

Courageous, *adj.*, mirneaṁail; from mirneaċ, *m*, courage.

Dead, maṙḃ (Welsh, *marw*, to die; Latin, *mori*). Tá an rean maṙḃ, the man is dead; maṙbaḋ, to kill.

Death, bár; baruʒaḋ, to put to

death, to perish. Heb., *bas*, death, rottenness.

Eternal, ríoṁ (always, perpetual) ríoṁṅuiḋe; eternity, ríoṁṅuiḋeaċt, *f.* (See the word *always*, p. 80.)

Fortune, luck, áḋ; as, ʒo ṁaiṫ an t-áḋ oṛt, may good luck attend you; ʒo ʒ-cuiniḋ Dia an t-áḋ oṛt, may God prosper you.

— prosperity, ṛeun, biṛeaċ, ṛonaṛ.

— plight, event, state, ṗaḋ; as, ḃeaʒ-ṗaḋ; ḃroċ-ṗaḋ.

— dowry of a man, cṛoḋ (cattle); as, Sichem said to Jacob and his sons, "Raise the dowry and ask gifts, méaḃuiʒiḋ an cṛoḋ, aʒuṛ

toṛuiʒiḋ tioḃlacaiḋ."—*Genesis*, xxxiv. 12.

— dowry of a woman, ṛpṅé.

Hope, ḃuṫċuṛ, *m*; ḃoiʒ, *f.*

— ṛuil, *f* (expectation).

Keep, retain, conʒḃail' (pr. *congáil*); from coṅ, together, and ʒaḃail, to take.

Whither, where, cá, for cá an áit, what place? Like the Latin *quo*, for *quo in loco*. Cá ḃ-ḟuil tu aiʒ ḃul, *whither* art thou going? Cá ḃ-ḟuil Dia, *where* is God?

Wish (I), iṛ ṁaiṫ liom; iṛ ṁian liom, (See Twenty-Seventh Lesson, Obs. 1.)

EXERCISE XLVII.

1. Well, John, whither art thou going?—maiṛe, a Seaʒáin, cá ḃ-ḟuil tu aiʒ ḃul? 2. I am going home. 3. And who is this walking *before you?* 4. It is my servant man, William—m' oʒlaċ, Uilleaṁ. 5. When, *before this* (ṛoiṁe ṛo), were you at home? 6. I have not been, *before this*, at home for (le) years! 7. Who is *before you* now at home? 8. There is none of my friends *before me* to greet me (le ḟailte ċuḃaiṛt ḃaṁ); all are now dead—my father and my mother, my brothers and my sisters, all are gone. 9. It is sad, indeed, to think of this—iṛ ḃṛónaċ ʒo ḃeiṁin cuiṁṅiuʒaḋ aiṛ ṛo. 10. Yet we should not grieve at the death of friends, for death is *before us* all—ní cóiṛ ḃuinn ḃeiṫ ḟaoi ḃṛoin aiṛ ḃáṛ an ʒ-caṛaḋ óiṛ tá an ḃáṛ "ṛoṁainn" uile. 11. You are a great philosopher—iṛ ḟaoi ṁóṛ tu. 12. Thank you—tá me ḃuiḋeaċ ḃuit; here I am, the world is *before me*—fortune, good or ill, *before me*—death and eternity *before me*—yet I have a heart hopeful and courageous, because I keep always *before me* God's law and his holy (naoṁċa) love. 13. I wish every man would keep these ends *before him.* 14. The saints, like the Jews of old (maṛ na h-Juḃaiḋċe 'r-an t-ṛean-ṗeaċt) always kept God's law (ḃliʒe Dé) *before them.* 15. Ought not we (naċ cóiṛṛ ḃuinn), in like manner (maṛ an ʒ-ceaḃna), keep it before us? 16. I think you are right (ṛaoilim ʒo ḃ-ḟuil tu ceaṛt).

Nᴏᴛᴇ.—"Re, or its combinations with the personal pronouns, though found in modern printed books and manuscripts, is not used in the spoken language in any part of Ireland, le being invariably used in its place."—*O'Donovan's Irish Grammar.*

"Re, with, is used in manuscripts and printed books for le : its compound form is—

S.	ɼᴊᴀᴍ, with me,	ɼᴊoᴄ,	ɼᴊᴦ,	ɼᴊᴀ.
P:	ɼᴊɴɴ, with us,	ɼᴊḃ,	ɼᴊu."	

—*College Irish Grammar.*

" Le is the only form of this preposition now used in Ireland in the spoken language, though ɼe is found in most modern books and manuscripts."— *O'Donovan's Irish Grammar,* p. 285.

Seaċ, beside (Latin, *secus*), is at present seldom found in the compound form :

ɼeaċaᴍ;	ɼeaċaᴄ,	ɼeaċ é,	ɼeaċ í,
beside me ;	beside thee ;	beside him ;	beside her ;
ɼeaċaᴊɴɴ,	ɼeaċaᴊḃ,	ɼeaċa,	
beside us ;	beside you ;	beside them.	

Neither is uaɼaᴍ (above me) now in use; in its stead, oɼ cᴊoɴɴ (above) is employed; nor are these combinations— ᴊoɼaᴍ (under me), ḃeaɼaᴍ (at my right hand), ᴄuaċaᴍ (at my left hand)—which are found in St. Patrick's Hymn, in *Liber Hymnorum :*

Cɼᴊoɼᴄ ᴊoɼaᴍ ! Cɼᴊoɼᴄ uaɼaᴍ !
Cɼᴊoɼᴄ ḃeaɼaᴍ ! Cɼᴊoɼᴄ ᴄuaċaᴍ !
Christ be *under me !* Christ be *over me !*
Christ be beside me,
On *left hand* and right.

VOCABULARY.

Aɼɼa, *adj.*, written also aɴɼaᴊḃ, old, ancient, stricken in years; aɴɴ aᴊᴍɼᴊɼ äɴɼa, in times of old ; ḃuᴊɴe aɴɼa, an aged person.

Fallaᴊɴ, a hood or mantle, a cloak; Latin, *pallium.*

Faɼaoɴ ! alas ! *interj.*, as if from ɼa (or ɼaċ), cause; aɼ, our ; áɼ, calamity.

Foᴊɼɼé, old, perfect, grown to maturity ; from ɼoᴊɼ, very (*per*), and ɼé, mature, perfect.

O, *prep.*, from, proceeding from ; as, ᴄaᴊɴᴊc ᴍe aᴍaċ ó Ḋᴊa; I came out from God ; ó Loɴḃuᴊɴ ᴣo Paᴊɼᴊ ꜱ, from London to Paris ; "ó" ᴣaċ uᴊle oᴊlc ɼaoɴ ɼᴊɴɴ, a Ċᴊᵹeaɼɴa, from all evil, O Lord, deliver us.

ó, same as the Latin *de,* of, from ; as, ɼeaɼ ó Alḃaᴊɴ, a man from Scotland.

— absence; as, ᴄá aɼ ḃ-ᴄáca "uaᴊɴɴ," we have lost our support, our strength.

ó, *adverb, conj.*, for ó a, from *which* (either time or cause understood) ; if of time, then it means *since ;* as, ó ᴄaᴊɴᴊc ᴍe aᴊɼ aɴ ᴄ-ɼaoᵹal ɼo, *since* I came on this world ; if of cause, then it means *because, seeing that, whereas* (*conj.*) ; ó ᴄáᴊᴍ lo ḃáɼ ɼáᵹaᴊl, ɼlaɴ leᴊɼ aɴ ḃoᴍau ᴍóɼ, whereas I am to die, farewell to the whole world. From the idea of "proceeding from" conveyed in ó (or ua, which is the same), is obtained the word ua, a grandson, a descendant, which, with the family prefix mac, is so peculiar to Irish names.

Táin, *f*, a herd or drove of cattle; as, táin bo Cuailgne, the cattle spoil of Cooley (in Louth). Táinte, the plural of táin, means herds, stock, wealth, affluence.

Táin, *f*, a region or country, territory. This *Keltic* root forms the suffix to the names of many countries in both Europe and Africa; as, brutáin, Britain, the táin or country of the *Brith*, *i.e.*, painted, speckled—for the ancient Britons, as Cambden says, painted their bodies (from brut comes brjotnac, and breatnac, a Welshman, the family name Walsh; as, Tomás breatnaig, Thomas Walsh; also brjccjnnear, the measles or *speckled sickness*); Mauritania, Aquitania, Lusitania. From tan, or táin, is derived tanairte, the airte, or *Seigneur* of the country (táin); tanairteact, *f*, tanistry, the ancient law which in Ireland regulated the right of succession to the throne, and by virtue of which the eldest and most experienced of the family was entitled to succeed on the death of the reigning prince.

Tré, *through*; as, tré n-a croiõe, through his heart. It denotes the cause or means; as, tré bo croir agur bo pair, raon rinn, a Tigeanna, through thy cross and passion, deliver us, O Lord.

— *on;* as tré larað, on flame; tré teine, on fire.

Tar, over, beyond, by, above, in its twofold relation to time and place; as, támuib 'cur na aimrijte "tarainn," we are putting the time *over us* (passing the time); cuaiõ Caerar "tar" an Rubicon, Cæsar went over the Rubicon; tá an rgeul rin "tar" cuimne, that story is *beyond* recollection; cuir "tarm" an folac ro, put this garment *over* me; cuaiõ re tar an bórur, he passed *by* the door; ir beannuigte tu "tar" na mnaib, blessed art thou *amongst* (beyond, above) women; gnáõuigim tu, a Tigeanna "tar" gac niõ, I love you, O Lord, *above* all things. Tar following the verb béan, do, make, means *without* (Fr. *sans*); as, béan tar an niõ rin, do *without* that thing; an mait leat airgead? do you like money? Ir mait, I do; béan tairir, do *without it.* Tairir is the third person singular masculine of the prepositional pronoun tarm.

Uaim, from me, is in meaning opposed to agam, at me; as, tá agam, I have, *habeo;* tá uaim, I have not, I want, *careo.* Uaim is pronounced *wem.*

Uim, *prep.*, about, around; it is written also im and uim; Greek, αμφι, *amphi.* From uim or im, and ball, a part, member, portion, is derived imeall, a border or edge, and foin-imeall, a circumference; also uimpuigim, I turn round; as if iomcuigim, from uim, and cáoi, way.

— concerning; as, uime rin, concerning that, because of that, therefore.

EXERCISE XLVIII.

Comráõ eioir comarra agur fear boct, tinn.—A conversation between a neighbour and a poor sick man.

1. Fáilte romat, ceuõ mile fáilte romat, a caraõ

mo ċɾoıḋe. 2. Ʒo ɾaıḃ maıċ aʒaḋ a ḋuıne ċóıɾ: Ƒeıcım
ʒo b-ḟuıl cu ann ɾo leac ḟéın—that you are here *alone*
(See Lesson Twenty-sixth, p. 161). 3. Ʒo beıɾṁın cáım
ann ɾo lıom ḟéın ċo boċc aʒuɾ ċo lom (bare) le Job, ʒan
nıḋ aıɾ bıċ le cuɾ "ḟuım" no "ċaım." 4. Caḋ uıme,
b-ḟuıl cu ċo boċc aʒuɾ ċo lom; ca b-ḟuıl na caıɾbe a bı
aʒaḋ, ca b-ḟuıl bo ṁuıncıɾ a bı ʒeanaṁaıl oɾc, aʒuɾ bo
ḟeaɾ ʒaol Daıbıḋ (*Dávee*, and commonly pronounced *Dáh-
yé*) Bɾun? 5. Da m-beıḋeaḋ Daıbıḋ anoıɾ aʒam, nı beıḋınn
maɾ cáım; aċc nı'l aɾɾaċ aıɾ (See Lesson Twenty-fifth,
Vocabulary, under the word *Power*, p. 158) b'ımıʒ ɾe "uaım,"
ċaɾ an ṁuıɾ ṁóɾ ʒo cıɾ a cá ɾaoɾ, aʒuɾ b' ḟáʒ ɾe mıɾe
maɾ Oıɾın ann ḋıaıʒ na b-Ƒıan, "'mo ḟeanóıɾ aɾɾaıḋ,
ɾoıɾɾe, lıaċ——ʒan bıaḋ, ʒan eaḋaċ, ʒan ceol." 6. Iɾ
cɾuaʒ é bo ċáɾ, aʒuɾ ıɾ boċc a cáıɾ: Aċc ḟóɾ naċ
b-ḟuıl calaṁ aʒaḋ, aʒuɾ cáınce, nó maɾ b-ḟuıl—cá aıɾʒeaḋ aʒaḋ, óıɾ bı cu ɾaıḋbıɾ ameaɾʒ (among) bo ʒaolca.
7. Iɾ ḟıoɾ ʒo ɾaıḃ am, 'n uaıɾ bı me ɾaıḋbıɾ, ḟaoı ṁeaɾ,
aʒuɾ ḟaoı ċlıu ṁóıɾ, aċc cá an c-am ɾın anoıɾ "ċaım,"
b'ımıʒ na cáınce "uaım," ċaıl me an c-aıɾʒeaḋ bı aʒam;
ċoʒ an Aḋaıɾcıɾ mo ċalaṁ "uaım," ċuıc me a b-cınneaɾ,
aʒuɾ cá me anoıɾ laʒ, boċc, ḟaon, ḟalaṁ, ɾoıɾɾe. 8. A
b-cıʒ lıom-ɾa (See Obs. 2, Lesson Twenty-seven), nıḋ aıɾ
bıċ a ḋeanaḋ, a beıḋeaḋ maɾ ɾoʒ (comfort) ḋuıc. 9. Iɾ
ɾoʒ ḋam ʒuɾ ċaınıc cu (that you came) ċuʒam, óıɾ nı
ʒaċ buıne a cıʒeaɾ le coṁɾaḋ a ḋeanaḋ le buıne cá
boċc; óıɾ maɾ beıɾ an ɾean-ɾaḋ:

An ce cá ɾuaɾ olcaɾ beoċ aıɾ;
An ce cá ɾıoɾ buaılceaɾ coɾ aıɾ.

He who is up is·toasted;
He who is down is trampled upon.

10. Nı b-ḟuıl cu-ɾa ɾıoɾ ḟóɾ, oıɾ ma ċaıll (did lose) cu
b' aıɾʒeaḋ, aʒuɾ ma b' ımċıʒ bo ṁuıncıɾ uaıc nıoɾ ċaıll
cu ṁeaɾ, aʒuɾ nıoɾ ımċıʒ bo ċlıu uaıc. 11. Iɾ ḟıoɾ ɾın,
aʒuɾ cá mo ḟlaınce ceaċc ċuʒam aɾıɾ; aʒuɾ maɾ bu-
baıɾc cu ḟéın (as you yourself said) ʒo mınıc (often) ıɾ
ḟeaɾɾ an ɾlaınce 'na na cáınce (health is better than
wealth); aʒuɾ caoḃ m' aıɾʒıḋ, ıɾ cuma lıom "aʒam" no
"uaım" é (and, with regard to my money, I care not [ıɾ

cuma ljom] whether I possess it or not).   12. Táiṁ maṁ
iṙ cóiṙ do ᴣaċ duiṅe a beiṫ—céilḃ (having sense), aᴣuṙ
'ᴣlacaḃ ᴣaċ nḃ ó laiṁ Dó.   13. Beiṙ do comṙaḃ rolaṙ
móṙ "dam."   14. Aiṙ m' focail duiṫ 'nuaiṙ ċuaileaṙ—
(upon my word to you, when I heard) ᴣaṙ ṙaiḃ tu faoi
leiṅ (under affliction) ċuaiḃ an rᴣeul ᴣo móṙ "triom."
15. Ni h-ioṅᴣa (eenyoo) ljom—it is not a wonder with me,
i.e., I do not wonder.   16. Ta aᴣam anoiṙ duiṫ culaiḃ
úṙ, cuiṙ an cóta ro d' "uiṁe," cuiṙ an fallaiṙ ro aiṙ
do ᴣualaṅaiḃ (on your shoulders); aᴣuṙ taṙṙ ljom.   17.
Beiṙim buiḃeacaṙ ó mo ċṙoiḃe duiṫ; aᴣuṙ ᴣo m-buḃ
roaċt feaṙṙ beiḃeaṙ tu bljaᴣaṅ ó 'n ṙuḃ.

NOTE—One of our readers inquired why ṁ in dam (to me) was not, in
accordance with written authorities, aspirated in our Lessons.   We gave
the following reply :

Our reasons for not aspirating ṁ in the prepositional pronoun dam (to
me—compounded of do, to ; and ṁe, I, or me) are :

First, because in the spoken language the word has not been, by any whom
we have heard speak Irish, pronounced with ṁ aspirate. Dr. O'Donovan
says ("Irish Grammar," p. 140), "that in the South of Ireland dam is generally pronounced dam, and sometimes even um ; as, tabaiṙ dam do lam,
pronounced as if written, tabaiṙ um do lam."   Besides, if ṅ be aspirated,
the pronoun dam, *to me*, cannot be distinguished from dam, *an ox*.

Secondly, because it is opposed to a principle of analogy clearly deducible
from the body of prepositional pronouns—that the initial consonant of the
personal pronoun does not, when combined with the preposition, suffer aspiration ; as, oṙm, on me ; oṙt, on thee ; diom, of me ; diot, of thee ; fuim,
under me, for me, about me ; fuit, under thee ; ljom, with me ; taṙm, over
me ; triom, through me, &c.   Now, in these and all other instances, the
initial of the personal pronoun ṁ or t is not aspirated when compounded
with those prepositions which usually cause aspiration.   Why, then, in this
particular instance, should ṁ be aspirated when compounded with do, to, and
not when compounded with the other prepositions ?   It is clear that there is
no reason for it ; if, however, there were, should not t of tu (*thou*), compounded with do (*to*), be also, for that same reason, aspirated in duit, thus,
duiṫ ?   But it is not, and never has been ; therefore ṁ, in the pronoun dam,
should not.   Taking both reasons together, you see that, contrary to your
own inference, the form dam, (having ṁ aspirated) is not "strictly and clas-
sically correct."

"But," you will say, "are all the authorities—Vallancey, O'Reilly, Book of
Common Prayer, Grammar of the Gælic language by E. O'C., Rev. Paul
O'Brien, &c., whom I quoted in support of the spelling dam, to go for
naught ?"   Yes.   "And why ?"   Because authorities quoted to sustain an
argument, or settle a point in dispute, have weight only in proportion to the
strength of the reasons by which they uphold their views.   If a writer give
no valid reason, and can give no valid reason, for an opinion, of course his
authority is worth nothing on that particular point.   The best authority on
any subject is he who gives the best reasons in support of his views.   These

principles applied to your authorities show them to be of very little weight on settling a point in philology or etymology.

The translators of the Protestant Bible, and of the other Protestant works in Irish—Drs. Donnelan, Bedel, O'Donnell, and their associates—do not seem to have much appreciated correct orthography. Any one who reads a page or two of their " authorised" versions, will find the *same* word spelled differently in different places. ᴅᴀṁ (*dhow*) is an incorrect pronunciation, heard (especially in the emphatic from ᴅᴀṁ-ᵴᴀ *dhow-so*—to me) in Thomond and in other parts of the south of Ireland—in Connaught too, but not generally. Vallancey, although a philologist, never made *special* etymology his particular study ; and when writing his treatise on Grammar, had not the advantage, which a native who speaks Irish has, of being able to compare the spoken with the written forms of our language. He, as well as O'Reilly, whom you quote, followed the forms of spelling which they found in use by those who went before them, without investigating whether such forms were or were not philologically correct. Their authority is therefore worth nothing on this point, nor is the authority of any succeeding Irish writer, till Dr. O'Donovan's time. He is the first who has treated, as a master and as a philosopher, the subject of Irish Grammar. His authority alone is, therefore, speaking generally, of greater weight than all whom you quoted. He has been followed by other labourers in the same field, who are endeavouring to settle disputed points of Irish orthography. Among these few is to be ranked pre-eminently the Archbishop of Tuam, in whose works you will find, for the prepositional pronoun, the spelling ᴅᴀṁ invariably adopted. The spelling of this particular word Dr. O'Donovan does not settle. The weight of authorities against the correct spelling was so great that, perhaps, he did not wish to set them aside, and adopt that spelling which reason and analogy show to be right. Besides, his admirable Grammar treats of the language as it was in times past, and as it is found in works such as those you consulted, and such as are commonly found in the hands of Irish scholars.

This explanation pleased our correspondent, for he wrote in reply :

"Manchester, 23rd August, 1859.

" I am obliged to you for the full and satisfactory information contained in your present number, concerning the pronoun ᴅᴀṁ. I am glad to find that this spelling is correct, and that I may make use of it without hesitation, disregarding the other form (ᴅᴀṁ), notwithstanding the apparent authorities in its favour.

" Some of your arguments, especially the second—the analogy deducible from the other prepositional pronouns—have been very often before my mind, and, after much perplexity, I came to the conclusion that the form ᴅᴀṁ was an irregularity, and that ᴅᴀṁ would be more rational, but I had no Irish scholar to give me a clear opinion on the matter, until I took the step, which I now rejoice at, of applying to you. . . .

" Ever since I became aware that there was an Irish language distinct from the language I was taught to speak, I have burned to acquire it ; and I have pursued this desire through difficulties which residents in Ireland can scarcely imagine. But for want of a teacher with whom I could regularly converse, and whose knowledge would help me over my difficulties, I have failed as yet to acquire conversational fluency. Nevertheless I have not given it up. I will speak Irish yet, I trust, and speak it well. In fact, although I have lived all my life in England, I am an enthusiast with regard to the Irish language, and would like to have every Irishman, high or low, well acquainted with it."

o

THIRTY-FIRST LESSON.

Aiṙ, *preposition*, means, in its literal and figurative sense, firstly, on, upon; as,

"Aiṙ" baṙṙ na conn—*On* the surface of the waves

"Aiṙ" mullaċ an tiġe—*On* the summit of the house.

"Aiṙ" bruaċ na linne—*On* the border of the pond,

"Aiṙ" tonntaiḃ na mara—*Upon* the waves of the sea.

Bí an long "aiṙ" an gaineaṁ—The ship was (still there) *on* the sand.

"Aiṙ" an t-sráid—*On* the street.

"Aiṙ" aon ċos—*On* one foot.

"Aiṙ" leaṫ-láiṁ—*On* (with) one hand; literally, *on* half hand.

Maireann sé "aiṙ" arán agus uisge—He lives *on* bread and water.

On this day—"Aiṙ" an lá 'n diú.

On to-morrow—"Aiṙ" an lá márac.

He plays *on* the violin—Imrigeann sé "aiṙ" an b-fídil.

She plays on the harp and *on* the piano—Imrigeann sí aiṙ an g-cláirsiġ agus "aiṙ" an piano.

Have mercy *on* us, O Lord!—Déan trocaire "orainn," a Ṫiġearna.

On the board—"Aiṙ" an g-clár.

He treats *on* that subject—traċtann sé "aiṙ" an sgeul sin.

He speaks *of* him (*i.e.*, on him as on a subject)—Labrann sé aiṙ.

He speaks of us—Labrann sé orainn.

Obs. 1.—Whenever aiṙ (on) refers to feelings which affect the body or mind, it points them out as being *on* the patient or sufferer. From this use of aiṙ, there exists in our language an idiom which we pointed out in the Third Lesson; as, he is affected with sickness—he is sick, tá tinneas aiṙ (sickness is *on* him); I am affected with sorrow, I am sorry—tá doilġios orm, tá brón orm (sorrow is on me); she fears, is afraid, is affected with fear—tá eagla aiṙti (fear is on her); we are glad, joyful—tá bíod orainn (there is joy on us).

Obs. 2.—Therefore the English expression "*what ails*

you," is rendered into Irish by the words, cᴀᴅ é cᴀ " oᴘc"— what is it that is *on* you? Cᴀ cɪɴɴeᴀʄ oᴘm—sickness is *on* me (I am sick). Cᴀᴅ e ᴀɴ ɴɪᴅ cᴀ " ᴀɪᴘ" ᴅo ṁᴀc—what is the thing that is *on* your son (what ails your son)? Nɪ b-ᶠuɪl ɴɪᴅ ᴀɪᴘ bɪc " ᴀɪᴘ"—there is nothing *on* him (nothing ails him). And again—

Obs. 3.—Applied to money it betokens debt; as, cᴀ ᴀɪᴘᵹeᴀᴅ oᴘm—money is *on* me, *i.e.*, I owe money; cᴀ ceᴅ puɴcᴀ ᴀɪᵹ Seᴀᵹᴀɴ oᴘm, I owe John an hundred pounds, *i.e.*, literally, according to the idiomatic use of the preposition ᴀɪᴘ, an hundred pounds is for John *on* me.

VOCABULARY—OF DISEASES.

Aɪcɪᴅ, *f, plur.* ᴀɪcɪᴅɪᴅ, accident, sickness, distemper, epidemic.

Aɪᴘeᴀᵹ, *v.* (from ᴀɪᴘ, back, and cɪᵹ, comes), to ferry; *n.*, a ferry, a return, a vomit; ᶠeᴀᴘ ᴀɪᴘɪᵹ, a ferryman; bᴀᴅ-ᴀɪᴘɪᵹ, a ferry boat.

Aɪᴘ-ɪoc, repayment, from ᴀɪᴘ, back, and ɪoc, payment.

Aɴᴘᴀɪɴᵹ, *f, plur.* ᴀɴᴘᴀɴᵹᴀ, a pang, a stitch, convulsions—ᴀɴᴘᴀɴᵹᴀ ᴀɴ bᴀɪᴘ, the pangs of death.

bᴀc, *m, plur.* bᴀɪc, an hindrance, an impediment; as, ɴᴀ cuɪᴘ bᴀc ᴀɪᴘ, do not prevent him.

— *v,* to hinder, to prevent; as, bᴀc é, hinder him; bᴀc leɪᴘ, to threaten, or attempt to impede : ɴᴀ bᴀc lɪom, do not attempt to impede me, do not mind me; ɴᴀ bᴀc leɪᴘ, do no mind it; also, you will regret it—a secondary or idiomatic meaning.

bᴀcᴀc, *plur.* bᴀcᴀɪᵹ, a lame person, a cripple, one who is *impeded* from walking; ɴɪ ɪoɴᴀɴɴ coᴘᴀ ᴀɴ bᴀcᴀɪᵹ, the legs of the lame are not equal.

bᴀlbᴀᴘ, *m,* and bᴀɪlbe, *f,* dumbness, stammering.

bᴀlbᴀɴ, *m, plur.* ᴀɪɴ, a mute; also applied to one who speaks without meaning; Latin, *balbutio.*

boᴅᴀᴘ (pr. *bower*), *adj.,* deaf; Welsh, *byddar;* boᴅᴀᴘᴀɴ, a deaf person.

boᴅᴀᴘᴀcc, *f,* deafness.

bᴘeoɪce, sick, ailing, delicate; cᴀ ᴘɪ bᴘeoɪce, she is ailing.

Clᴀɪbe, *m,* scurvy, manginess; Welsh, *clav,* a sick person.

Clᴀoɪᴅ, to feel sick, to waste, to destroy.

Clᴀoɪᴅeᴀcc, *f,* sickness of any kind, languor; hence, clᴀɪᴅeᴀṁ, (*plur.* ᴀ), a sword; Latin, *gladium.* Clᴀɪᴅeᴀṁ is not commonly pronounced *cly-av,* but by metathesis, *cláiva,* thus changing the syllables. In like manner, Irish-speaking natives pronounce ᴀᴅbuɪᵹɪm, *I confess,* as if written ᴀbᴅuɪᵹɪm.

Cɴᴀoɪᴅ, pining, wasting; cɴᴀoɪᴅeᴀcc, *f,* the state of pining.

Cᴘɪc, *v,* shake; ᴀɪᵹ cᴘɪc, shaking; Welsh, *kryd;* cᴘɪc-cᴀlṁᴀɴ, an earthquake.

Cᴘɪc, *n, f,* the ague, the palsy.

Dɪuᴅᴀɴ, *m,* giddiness.

Doᴘuɪɴᵹ, *f,* pain, agony; cᴀ ᴘe ᴀɴɴ boᴘuɪɴᵹ ṁoᴘ, he is in great agony; boᴘuɪɴᵹeᴀc, very sick, agonizing; cᴀ ᴘe ᵹo boᴘuɪɴᵹeᴀc cɪɴɴ, he is very sick.

Ecɪɴɴ, consumption; from eᴀᵹ, death, and cɪɴɴ, sick.

Fɪᴀbᴘᴀᴘ, *m,* fever; Latin, *febris;* ᶠɪᴀbᴘᴀᴘ ceɪɴcɪᵹe, a burning fever.

ᵹᴀlᴀᴘ, *m,* a disease (from ᵹᴀl, a blast,

strange, and ản, calamity), *plur.* ȝalana—a generic word, from which the names of many special distempers are, by the addition of certain suffixes, formed.

Ȝalan na n-aran, disease of the reins or loins.

Ȝalan buiḋe, jaundice (buiḋe, yellow).

Ȝalan cneaċa, palsy.

Ȝalan dub, cholera (the black disease).

Ȝalan breac, the small-pox (breac, speckled).

Ȝalan teiṫ, scarlatina.

Ȝalan uirȝamail, dropsy.

Ȝéarb, *m*, scab; ȝearbar, scabbiness.

Ȝiorra anala (shortness of breath), asthma.

Ȝuta, *m*, gout.

Laȝan, *m*, weakness.

Otan, sick, wounded, weak; oṫarċa, an hospital.

Pian, *m* (*plur.* pianta), pain; il-ṗian (from il, many, varied, and pian, torments); áit ḣa n-ilṗian, the place of torments.

Seilȝ ar aeḋaib, liver complaint.

Sȝoilteaċ, *m*, rheumatism; from tȝoilt, split, rend, tear.

Slaiȝbeán, *m*, cough, a severe cold, bronchitis; from rlaiȝ, to slay.

Taom, *plur.* a, a fit; taom tinoir, a fit of sickness.

Taċtuȝaḋ, quinsey, smothering.

Teme, weakness, sickness, death.

Tinn, *adj.*, sick; tinnear, *m*, sickness, *plur.* tinnir. This word is the parent of many names of particular diseases; as,

Tinnear cinn, headache, sickness of head.

Tinnear croiḋe, disease of the heart.

Tinnear boilȝ, bowel complaint; rȝaoileaḋ (from rȝaol, loose), diarrhœa—*coup de ventre*.

Bniċ-tinnear, measles.

Tinnear fiacal, toothache.

Tinnear na rul, ophthalmia.

Tinnear clainne, or tinnear leinb, travail in childbirth.

Tinnear coiȝċriċeaċ (the strange sickness), epilepsy.

Tinnear rcamóȝ, bronchitis, disease of the lungs.

Tinimear, *m* (dryness), dyspepsia.

Tocar, *m*, itch; ȝalan ȝan náinne an toċar, itch is a disease of no shame.

Treoċ, *m*, hooping-cough.

EXERCISE XLIX.

1. Ȝo m-beannuiȝe Dia duit a Ṡaoi (God save you, Sir). 2. Ȝo m-beannuiȝe Dia aȝur Muinne duit (God save you kindly; or, literally, God and Mary bless you). 3. Aimrin breaȝ i ro, buiḋeaċar do Dia. 4. Ir aimrin breaȝ i ȝo deimin, mile altuȝaḋ (a thousand acts of grace—thanks) le Dia. 5. Cad é an caoi a b-ḟuil do maċain an iuḋ? 6. Maire, ni 'l ri rlán. 7. B-ḟuil niḋ air bit airċi (is there anything on her, *i.e.*, is she ailing in any way)? 8. Maire, ni'l mórán (well, there is not much—she is not much ailing). 9. Cad é tá airċi? 10. Ni 'l raeḋ air bit aċt rlaiȝbeán (pr. *slydawn*). 11. Raib tu aiȝ an liaȝ (were you with the physician)? 12. Ni rabar aċt tá me dul anoir ċuiȝe. 13. Ir maiċ rin, ni beiḋ ceo (a mist, a mere trifle); airċi a maraċ (there

will be nothing on her—*i.e.*, amiss with her—to-morrow).
14. Ḃ-ꝼuil bꝛiċ-ṫinneaꞋ aiꞃ do leanḃ? 15. Tá ꝣo deiꞃṁin; aꝣuꞋ iꞋ boċc a tá ꞃe leiꞋ. 16. Raiḃ an ꝣalaꞃ-
ḃꞃeac aiꞃ a ꞃiaṁ? 17. Ḃi, aꝣuꞋ, mo ċꞃáḋ (and my
sorrow)! ꝣaċ uile ꝣalaꞋ iꞋ ꝼeiḋiꞋ leac ainmniuꝣaḋ. 18.
IꞋ iomḋa (pr. *umhee*—many, various) ꝣalaꞋ ṫiꝣeaꞋ aiꞃ
paiꞃḋiḃ (many a disease comes on children). 19. IꞋ iomḋa;
tiꝣeaꞋ oꞃċu (there comes on them) tinneaꞋ na ꞃul, tinneaꞋ na b-ꝼiacal, tinneaꞋ boilꝣ, bꝛiċ-tinneaꞋ, an ꝣalaꞃ
bꞃeac, aꝣuꞋ aiꞃ amaiḃ (and at times) an ꝣalaꞃ buiḋe,
ꝼiabꝛaꞋ na b-peiꞃc (worm-fever) tinneaꞋ cinn, aiꞃeaꝣ,
laꝣaꞋ, ꞃlaiꝣḋeaꞋ, taċtuꝣaḋ, aꝣuꞋ tꞃeoċ. 20. IꞋ maiċ
an t-eoluꞋ tá aꝣaḋ-ꞃa aiꞃ ꝣaċ uile tinneaꞋ. 21. Ni
h-ionꝣa (pr. *eenyoo*) ꝣo m-beiḋeaḋ eoluꞋ maiċ aꝣam aiꞃ
ꝣaċ uile aiciḋ, ꝣalaꞋ no tinneaꞋ, óiꞃ bi me aimꞃiꞃ ꝼaḋa
ann teaċ na n-oċaꞃ (in the house of the infirm or sick,
i.e., infirmary). 22. Ḃ-ꝼuil eoluꞋ aiꞃ biċ aꝣaḋ aꞋ lea-
ḃaꞃaiḃ? 23. Tá; óiꞃ leiꝣ nꞋe ꝣo leoꞃ aiꞃ liaꝣaꞋ (on
medicine, or medical art) ċo móꞃ ꞃin ꝣo b-ꝼuil duil aꝣam
ceaḋ (permission) ꝼáꝣail ó ciꝣꞃiḃ (from the doctors) an
ealaḋaiꞋ (*al-y-an*—of the faculty), ꝼeiḋin a ḋeanaḋ de
m' eoluꞋ. 24. Ca meud cineal (how many kinds—pr.
kynawl) tinneaꞋ ann? 25. IꞋ iomḋa cineal tinneaꞋ
ann, ꞋꞋ ꝼeiḋiꞋ ainm a ċuꞃ oꞃċu (there are many kinds—
it is not possible to give each a name), tá aꝣaḋ ꝼéin
eoluꞋ aiꞃ ꞃoin,—maꞃ tá na tinniꞋ coitċeana—tinneaꞋ
cinn; tinneaꞋ cꞃoiḋe; tinneaꞋ ꝼiacal; tinneaꞋ na ꞃul;
tinneaꞋ coiꞃp no boilꝣ; an tinneaꞋ coiꝣċꞃiċeac; bꝛiċ-
tinneaꞋ; aꝣuꞋ iꞋ iomḋa ꝣalaꞋ, aꝣuꞋ plaiꝣ (plague) a
ṫiꝣeaꞋ aiꞃ an duiꞋe ó 'n am a ṫiꝣeann ꞃe ó 'n m-bꞃoiꞋ
(from the time he comes from the womb) ꝣuꞋ an am a
ċeiꝣ ꞃe do 'n uaiṁ; ꞃo ꞃoiꞋn diob—ꝣalaꞋ bꞃeac; ꝣalaꞋ
teiċ; ꝣalaꞋ buiḋe; ꝣalaꞋ duḃ; ꝣalaꞋ uiꞃꝣeaꞋaiꞃl; ꝣalaꞋ
cꞃeaċa; aꝣuꞋ leiꞋ an meud ꞃo, tá aiciḋ ꝣo leoꞃ de
ꝣnaċ (usually) aiꞃ claiꞋn an duiꞋe (on the children of
man.) 26. Tá ꝣo deiꞃṁin—ꞃeiciꞋ ꝣo b-ꝼuil an beaċa
ꞃo lán de ꝣalaꞋ aꝣuꞋ de ċꞃáḋ, d' aiciḋ, aꝣuꞋ de plaiꝣ,
ó ċuꞋ na h-oiꝣe no ꝣo d-tiꝣ uaiꞃ aiꞃ m-baiꞃ; aċt buiꞋ-
ḋeaċaꞋ do Ḋia, tá beaċa eile ann, aꞋn a m-beiḋꞋmiḃ
ꝣan aiciḋ, ꝣan ꝣalaꞋ, ꝣan tinneaꞋ, ꝣan plaiꝣ, ꝣan báꞋ

ꞇ ꞃeꞇ Ꞁꞇ ꞃꞇ (during eternity). 27. Iꞇ
ꞇ ꞇ ꞇꞇ (thought) é. 28. Iꞇ ꞇꞇ ꞇꞇ
b'ꞇꞇ ꞇꞇ-ꞇ ꞇ ꞇꞇ ꞇ ꞇꞇ ꞇꞇ ꞇꞇ. 29. ꞇꞇ
ꞇꞇ ꞃꞇ ꞇ ꞇ ꞇ ꞇ ꞇ ꞇ ꞇ. 30. ꞇꞇ-
ꞇ ꞇ ꞇ ꞇ ꞇꞇ—ꞇꞇ ꞇꞇ ꞃꞇ ꞇ ꞇꞇ ꞇ ꞇꞇ
ꞇꞇ ꞃꞇ.

VOCABULARY.

bapaille, *m*, *plur.* aió, a barrel;
Welsh, *baril*; French, *baril*.

Cáin, *f*, dispraise; *v*, to dispraise;
buine a cáineaó, to dispraise
one; Welsh, *kuyn*, complaint.

— rent, tax, fine; tá cáin opm,
there is a fine on me; tá me
ꞇan cáin, I am without fine.

— *adj.*, dear, beloved, cherished.

— undefiled, chaste; a máṫaiꞃ
cáin, undefiled mother.

Cluiꞃ-iꞃ, I hear, *v. irr*; cualaꞃ, per.
tense, I heard; cualaió ꞃe, he
heard; cluiꞃ-ꞇaó, I shall hear;
aiꞃ ꞇꞇoꞃ, hearing; Greek, κλύει,
klúei, he hears, *v*; κλυτὸς, *klutos*,
adj.; Welsh, *clyw*; *clust*, an ear;
Irish, cluaꞃ, an ear; clú. fame;
Sancrit, *srutah*; Russ, *sluch*; the

guttural letters ċ, *k*, are changed
into the sibilant, ꞃ.

ꞇꞇaoió, *v*, call; ꞇꞇaoió-aiꞃ, call him;
ꞇꞇaoióear, I called.

ioc, *v*, pay; iocaꞃ, I paid; iocꞇaó, I
shall pay.

Maiꞇiꞃꞇiꞃ (pr. *máishther*), master.

Maiꞇiꞇꞃeaꞃ, *f*, mistress.

Mioꞃuꞃ, *m*, a measure.

Mioꞃúiꞃeaꞇꞇ, *f*, measurement.

Ola, *f*, oil; Latin, *oleum*.

Scóꞃ, *m*, much, plenty, score, twenty;
plur. ꞃcóiꞃ; as, ꞇꞃi ꞃcóiꞃ, three
score.

Soꞃꞇeul, *m*, gospel, good story, from
ꞃo, happy, and ꞃꞇeul, story,
news; Greek, ευ-άγγελλιον, *ev-
angellion*, good news.

EXERCISE L.

1. Ca meuó tá opm, a maiꞇiꞃꞇiꞃ; óiꞃ iꞃ miaꞃ liom
m' ꞇiaca ó'ioc. 2. Tá ceuó puꞃꞇa opꞇ. 3. Ni móꞃaꞃ
é. 4. Aꞃ maiꞇ leaꞇ ꞇiaca buine aiꞃ biꞇ eile, ó'ioc? 5.
Iꞃ maiꞇ liom. 6. Ca meuó tá aiꞃ m'aꞇaiꞃ? 7. Tá bá
ceuó puꞃꞇa. 8. Caó é tá aiꞃ mo óeaꞃbꞃaꞇaiꞃ? 9.
Tá ꞇioꞃ bliaꞇaꞃa, aꞇuꞃ luaċ cuiꞇ ꞃcóiꞃ caoꞃaċ. 10.
Ca meuó ꞃiꞃ? 11 Tiꞃċioll cuiꞇ ceuó puꞃꞇa. 12. Má
iocꞇaió me ꞃa ꞇiaca uile a tá opaiꞃꞃ, beió ꞇapꞃ ꞇo
mile puꞃꞇa aꞇaó le ꞇaꞇail (to get). 13. Beió ꞇo beiꞃ-
iꞃꞃ. 14. Iꞃ cóiꞃ buiꞇ a óeaꞃaó maꞃ ꞃiꞃꞃe aꞃ maoꞃ
aiꞃ a leiꞇmuió aꞃꞃꞃ aꞃ ꞇ-ꞃoiꞃꞇeul? 15. Caó é ꞃiꞃ?
16. Naċ b-ꞇuil ꞇioꞃ aꞇaó; ꞃaꞃ leiꞇ ꞇu ꞇo miꞃic é? 17.
ꞇió ꞇuꞃ cualaꞃ (although I did hear it), iꞃ maiꞇ liom a
ꞇꞀoꞃ aꞃiꞃ. 18. Do bi ꞇeaꞃ ꞃaióbiꞃ aꞃꞃ (there was a
rich man) aiꞃ a ꞃaió maoꞃ, aꞇuꞃ ꞇaiꞃic cáin aiꞃ, ꞇuꞃ
ꞃcaꞃ ꞃe a ṁaoiꞃ. Aꞇuꞃ bo ꞇꞇaoió a Tiꞇeaꞃꞃa aiꞃ,

aᵹur oubaịᚱᴛ leịᚱ; cao e ᚱo a cluịnịm oᚱᴛ; ᴛabaịᚱ
oam conoaᚱ aịᚱ oo ṁaoᚱaċᴛ. 19. Aċᴛ cao é ᚱịnne an
maoᚱ? 20. Ꝣlaoịo ᚱe aịᚱ an ṁuịnᴛịᚱ aịᚱ a ᚱaịb
ᚠịaċa, aᵹuᚱ oubaịᚱᴛ ᚱe leịᚱ an ceuo ouịne, "Cao e ᴛa
aịᵹ mo Ꞇịᵹeaᚱna oᚱᴛ-ᚱa." Aᵹuᚱ o'ᚠᚱeaᵹaịᚱ an ᚠeaᚱ;
ceuo baᚱᚱaịle ola; oubaịᚱᴛ ᚱe, ᵹlac oo peann aᵹuᚱ
ᚱᵹᚱịob oeịċ baᚱᚱaịle ᚠịċịo. Aᵹuᚱ oubaịᚱᴛ ᚱe leịᚱ an
oaᚱa ᚠeaᚱ, aᵹuᚱ ᴛuᚱa, "Ca ṁeuo ᴛa oᚱᴛ?" A oeịᚱ,
ceuo mịoᚱúịᚱ cᚱuịċneaċᴛa (wheat). Dean ceịᴛᚱe ᚱcóịᚱ
oe, aịᚱ ᚱe. Ṁolann an Ꞇịᵹeaᚱna an ᚱeaᚱbᚠoᵹanᴛaịo
ᚱo—an oeanᚠaịo ᴛuᚱa ḽom-ᚱa maᚱ ᚱịnne ᚱe-ᚱan leịᚱ
an ṁuịnᴛịᚱ aịᚱ a ᚱaịb na ᚠịaċa? 21. Buịoeacar ᚱaoị
an ᚱᴛịᚱᴛịúᚱ; aċᴛ nị oeanᚠao ᚠéịᚱ o' ịaᚱᚱaᴛaịᚱ. 22.
Iocaịm, maᚱ ᚱịn, an meuo a ᴛa oᚱm ᚠéịn aᵹuᚱ aịᚱ mo
ᵹaolᴛa.

THIRTY-SECOND LESSON.

OBS. 1.—Aịᚱ, *on*; and the prepositional pronouns, oᚱm,
on me; oᚱᴛ, on thee; aịᚱ, on him; aịᚱᴛị, on her; óᚱaịnn,
on us, &c., follow verbs of asking, entreating, imposing an
obligation on one, and the like; as, ịaᚱᚱ ᴛᚱocaịᚱe "aịᚱ"
Dịa, ask mercy (*on*) of God; ịmpịᵹịm oᚱᴛ a Dịa, I entreat
(*on*) thee, O Lord; ᚱuo oᚱᴛ, there is (a toast) *on* you—
your health—a short form of address used by the peasantry
in drinking healths.

Secondly, aịᚱ means *for*. In this sense it is put before
the noun of price, and also the thing priced; as, what ex-
change shall man give *for* his soul, cao é an ᴛ-aċᚱuᵹao
beaᚱᚠaịo an ouịne "aịᚱ" a anam? He shall not give it
for silver or gold, nị ᴛabaᚱᚠaịo ᚱe é "aịᚱ" aịᚱᵹịoo no
"aịᚱ" óᚱ. I shall not do so *for* love, *for* fear, or *for*
hatred, nị oeanᚠao é "aịᚱ" ᵹᚱao, "aịᚱ" uaṁan, no "aịᚱ"
ᚠuaċ. *For* the love of God, "aịᚱ" ᵹᚱao De; *for* mercy's
sake, "aịᚱ" ᚱon na ᴛᚱocaịᚱe; do it not *for* all you ever
saw, na oean é "aịᚱ" a b-ᚠaċaịo ᴛu ᚱịaṁ.

OBS. 2.—In buying or selling, therefore, when the preposition "for," in English, governs the noun of price, or
the thing priced, it is translated into Irish by "aịᚱ;" as,

how do you sell (how much is *for*) this?—Ca meuḃ tá aiṙ ṙo? How do you sell the cloth?—Irish form: How much have you *for* (on) the cloth?—Ca meuḃ tá aᵹaḃ "aiṙ" an euḋaċ? It is seven shillings "per" yard, tá ṙeaċt ṙcill[iᵹ "aiṙ" an t-ṙlat. Sometimes the preposition is left understood; as, tá ṙe ṙeaċt ṙcill[iᵹ an t-ṙlat, it is seven shillings the yard.

Thirdly, aiṙ means *in*; as, aṙ n-aċaiṙ a tá "aiṙ" Néiṁ, Our Father who art *in* heaven; "aiṙ" ḟaḃ, *in* length; "aiṙ" leiċeaḃ, *in* breadth.

Fourthly, aiṙ means *against*; as, ᵹo ṙabalaiḃ Dia ṙinn, "aiṙ" ᵹaċ aiciḋ, "aiṙ" tinneaṙ, aᵹuṙ "aiṙ" ᵹaċ anaċan na bliaᵹna, may God preserve us *against* every distemper, sickness, and harm of the year.

Cṙioṙt ḃo mo ċoiminceaḃ ann iuḃ "aiṙ" niṁ; "aiṙ" loṙcaḃ; aiṙ baċaḃ; "aiṙ" ᵹuin—May Christ, I pray, protect me to-day, *against* poison and fire, *against* drowning and wounding.—*St. Patrick's Hymn.*

VOCABULARY.

Buiḃéal, *m, plur.* eil, a bottle, a cask, a silly person; French, *bouteille;* Spanish, *botella;* Italian, *budello.*

Buiḃéalaiṙ, *m,* a butler (as it were bottler), from buiḃéal and ḟeaṙ.

Coċal, *m* (from cuaċ, hollow, concave, and ḟal [hence ḟalaċ], a cover, a garment), a hood, a cowl, a mantle, a vestment; coċal an t-ṙaᵹaiṙt, the priest's vestment; coċal an manaiᵹ, the monk's cowl.

— a husk, a shell, a circular covering; coċal a ċṙoiḃe, the heart sac, the pericardium; Welsh, *cochl;* British, *cucal;* hence Latin, *cuculus* (Camden); German, *kugel;* English, *cowl,* ancient spelling, *cowel.* Secondary meaning is, cuckold; one *hoodwinked.*

Coċail, *v,* to roll up, to coil, to gather into a heap; Greek, κυκλέω, *kukleo,* to turn, to whirl, to roll up, to coil; κυκλος, *kuklos,* a circle.

Cuaċ, *adj.,* hollow, empty, concave.

Cuaċ, *m, plur.* cuaċa, a cup, a bowl, a bumper; so called on account of its concavity—

"Cuiṙ ťaṙt an cuaċ,"
"Send round the bowl;'.

"An cuaċ maṙ iṙ cóiṙ ṙuaṙ lion,"
"Fill the bumper fair."

— a fold, a plait, a curl;

"A ṙioᵹain ṙuaiṙc na ᵹ-cuaċa n-óiṙ,"
"O charming queen of the golden curls."

Laoiḃ Oiṙin aiṙ tṙi na n-Oᵹ.

Cuaċ, the cuckoo; perhaps so called on account of the hollow tone in which it sounds its own name.

Cuaċoᵹ, *f,* a little bowl or cup, a young cuckoo, a young little girl.

Cuaċan, *m,* a small cup.

Cuaċaċ, *adj.* abounding in cups, plaited, folded.

Cuaṛ (as if cuaċaṛ), *m*, a cave, a hollow, a cavity such as is found at the core in fruit.

Cuaṛaċ, *adj.*, hollow, concave, unsound, porous.

Cuḃaṛ, *m* (pr. *koo-ar*, in one syl.), froth, foam; ṁaṛ aṅ ṡ-cuḃaṛ aiṛ aṅ ṫ-ṛṅue, like the froth on the stream; Greek, κύμα, *kuma*.

Cuḃaṛaċ, *adj.*, frothy, foamy, spumy; ḟion cuḃaṛaċ, champagne.

Cuiṛ (written also coiṛ), *f*, foam; as, ṁaṛ ċuiṛ cuḃaiṛ a lá ċeo, like the foam of froth during a hazy day.

Cupaċ, and copaċ, *adj.*, foamy, hollow, unsubstantial.

leaṫ (spelled also leṫ), *n. m*, a half; as, ḃeaṅ ḃa leaṫ ḃé, make (two) halves of it; a side; as, aiṛ ṡaċ leṫ, on each side. leaṫ. in composition, means *one of two* (Lat., *alter*); as, ṫá ṛe a luiḃe aiṛ a leaṫ-ṫaoḃ, he is lying on *one* side; aiṛ leaṫ-ċoiṛ, on *one* foot; aiṛ leaṫ-láṁ, with *one* hand; a leaṫ-ṛuil, his *single* eye; leaṫ-ċluaṛ, a *single* ear; leṫċiṅṅ (half a head), a cheek; leaṫṁaṛ, one thigh; leaṫ-ċṛuiṅṅe, a hemisphere; leaṫ-ċṛoiṅ, a half-crown; leaṫ-ṗiṡiṅ, a half-penny; leaṫ-ṗuṅṫa, a half-pound; leaṫ-uṅṛa, a half-ounce; leaṫ-ċuaiṛṫ,

a half-round, a semicircle; leṫ-iṅṛe (a half-island), a peninsula; leaṫ-ḟocail, a by-word, a proverb; cuiṛeaṅṅ ṛeaṅ leiṡeaṅ leaṫ-ḟocail, *verbum sapientibus sat*, a man of learning understands a half-word; leaṫ-ċeaṅcail, a semicircle. It forms the prefix of those Irish topographical names that begin with *La*; as, Lara, *i.e.*, leaṫ-ṛaṫ, the half fort; Lahinch, *i.e.*, leaṫ-iṅṛe; Lahardaun, leaṫ-áṛḃaiṅ, half-a hillock; Lecale (in Down), leaṫ-Ċaṫail, Cahal's half. Ṡo leiṫ, literally, to or with half, *i.e.*, one-half more of any specified measure; as, ḃa ṛlaṫ ṡo leiṫ, two yards and a half; ṫṛi ṁile ṡo leiṫ, three miles and a half; a leiṫ, a part; ṫaṅṛ a leiṫ, come apart; aṅṅ a leiṫ, in behalf of; ṛá leiṫ, severally, each, one by one.

Ṡioḃa, *m*, silk; as, colaiṫ ṛoḃa, a silk dress.

Ṡṛol, *m*, satin; as, coċal ṛṛoil, a satin vestment.

Caḃaiṛ (*thow-ar*), give; *v. irr*; ṫuṡaṛ, *perf.*, I gave; ṫaḃ'ṛṛaḃ, I shall give; ḃeaṅṛaḃ, affected future; as, ṅi ḃeaṅṛaḃ, I shall not give; aṅ m-ḃeaṅṛaḃ, shall I give.

EXERCISE LI.

1. Aṅ éaḃaċ é ṛo? 2. Seaḃ. 3. Ca meuḃ ṫá aṡaḃ "aiṛ." 4. Ceiṫṛe ṛcilliṅṡ ḃeuṡ "aiṛ" aṅ ṫ-ṛlaṫ. 5. Iṛ ḃaoṛ é; ṅi ḟiú ṛiṅ é. 6. Ṡo ḃeiṁiṅ iṛ ḟiú; 'aṡuṛ ṫá ṛé ṛaoṛ "aiṛ" aṅ luaċ uḃ. 7. Ḃ-ṛuiḃ éaḃaċ ṛṅoil, ṅo ṛioḃa aṡaḃ? 8. Ṫá. 9. Ca meuḃ ṫá aṡaḃ "aiṛ?" 10. Ḃá ṗuṅṫa aiṛ aṅ ṫ-ṛlaṫ. 11. Iṛ ṛaoṛ e "aiṛ" ṛiṅ. 12. Aṅ miaṅ leaṫ a ċeaṅṅuṡaḃ? 13. Iṛ miaṅ; ṡeaṅṛi ḃé ḃa ṛlaiṫ ṡo leaṫ. 14. Ḃ-ṛuiḃ eaṅṅaiḃ (wares) eile aṡaḃ? 15. Ṫá aṅṅṛ aṅ ṫaoḃ uḃ ṫall ḃe 'ṅ ṫ-ṛiopa (shop). 16. Iṛ maiṫ liom ṫé aṡuṛ ṛuṡċṛuaiḃ ṛáṡail; ca meuḃ ṫá aṡaḃ "aiṛ" aṅ ṛuṡċṛuaiḃ? 17. Ṫá cuiṛ ṛcilliṅṡ aṅ puṅṫa "aiṛ" ṫé, aṡuṛ ṛé ṗiṡiṅe aṅ puṅṫa "aiṛ" ṛuṡ-

cṙuaıḋ. 18. Ꞇá ṙın ḋaoṙ, nı béaṙṗaıḋ me an oıṙeaḋ ṙın "aıṙ" an ꞇé; ꞇá an ṙuġcṙuaıḋ ṙaoṙ ʒo leoṙ; ʒlac ceıꞇṙe ṙʒıllınʒ aʒuṙ ṙé ṗıʒıne an punꞇ "aıṙ" an ꞇé. 19. Ⱥꞁaıṙe, ó ꞇaṗla (whereas) ʒuṙ ʒnáꞇaċ leaꞇ (that it is customary with you) ꞇéaċꞇ ċuʒam, bıḋeaḋ ṙe aʒaḋ "aıṙ" ṙın; aċꞇ aıṙ m' ḟocaıl ḋuıꞇ ꞇá ṙe ṙaoṙ; aʒuṙ muna ʒuṙ ꞇu-ḟéın a ꞇá ann, nı béaṙṙaınn (I would not give) ḋuıꞇ é aıṙ an luaċ ṙın. 20. Ʒo ṙaıḃ maıꞇ aʒaḋ, aʒuṙ ꞇá me buıḋeaċ ḋuıꞇ. 21. Caḋ e ṙo ꞇa aʒaḋ annṙ an m-baṙṙaıle? 22. Ꞇá, ḟıon. 23. Caḋ e an ꞇ-ṙaṁaıl ḟıona é—ḟıon Spáıneaċ, no ḟıon Ḟṙaınceaċ, ḟıon ḟıonn (white wine), no ḟıon ḋeaṙʒ (red wine), ḟıon cubaṙaċ, no ḟıon ʒan cubaṙ? 24. Nı'l (for nı b-ḟuıl) ann aċꞇ ḟıon coıꞇċean (common), ḋeaṙʒ; aʒuṙ ꞇá ṙé ꞇṙı ṙʒıllınʒ an buıḋéal. 25. Nı beıḋ me leıṙ (I shall not be with it, i.e., I shall not have it, nor buy it); ꞇa ḟıon ḋaoṙ 'ṙ-an ꞇıṙ ṙo; buḋ maıꞇ lıom a beıꞇ a b-Ḟṙaınc. 26. B' ḟeıḋıṙ ʒuṙ ṙeaṙṙ ḋuıꞇ a beıꞇ ṙ-an m-baıle. 27. Ḃ-ḟuıl ṙoʒaṙ maıꞇ aʒaınn an blıaʒan ṙo? 28. Ꞇá. 29. Ḃ-ḟuıl coıṙce ḋaoṙ aʒuṙ cṙuıꞇneaċꞇ? 30. Ꞇáıḋ. 31. Caḋ é ꞇá aıṙ óṙna (barley), aıṙ ṙeaʒaıl (rye)? 32. Ꞇáıḋ ṙaoṙ. 33. An m-beıḋ beoċ aʒaḋ, ó ꞇaṗlá ʒo b-ḟuılmuıḋ a ʒ-ceann a ċeıle (since we have met together—literally, since we are at the head one of the other). 34. Beıḋ. 35. Caḋ é ıṙ maıꞇ leaꞇ? coṙn ḟıona, an ḟeaḋ (is it?), no cuaċ puınṙ? 36. Beıḋ an coṙn ḟıona aʒam. 37. Naċ ṙeaṙṙ ḋuıꞇ cuaċ puınṙ, óıṙ ıṙ maıꞇ lıom an cuaċ ḋul ꞇaṙꞇ (go round)? 38. Iṙ ṙeaṙṙ lıom-ṙa an ḟıon. 39. Bıḋeaḋ aʒaḋ:—beaċa ḋuıne a ꞇoıl.

Obs.—In such sentences as, "which of us" (of you, of them); "how many of us;" "some of us," the words *of us, of you, of them*, are translated, not ḋınn (of us); ḋıḃ (of you); ꞇıoḃ; but aʒaınn (at us); aʒaıḃ (at you); aca (at them)—which is peculiar to the plural form alone of this prepositional pronoun, aʒam; as, every one *of us* is good—ꞇá ʒaċ ḋuıne "aʒaınn" maıꞇ; which *of them* do you like best?—cıa "aca" ıṙ ṙeaṙṙ leaꞇ? I do not like either *of them*—nı maıꞇ lıom ceaċꞇaṙ "aca;" many *of you* are rich—ꞇá moṙán "aʒaıḃ" ṙaıḋḃıṙ; bṙıṙḟıḋ cıuʒeaṙ "aʒaıḃ-ṙe" ceuḋ, aʒuṙ cuıṙḟıḋ ceuḋ aʒa ḃ-ṙe ḋeıċ mıle ċum

ceιċe.—five *of yours* shall pursue a hundred others, and a
hundred *of you* ten thousand.—*Leviticus,* xxvi. 8.

Sometimes both pronouns, ᴀcᴀ (to them), and ᴅιοḃ (of them), are employed to render this distributive meaning stronger; as, Which of them is the best?—cιᴀ " ᴀcᴀ ᴅιοḃ" ιr ꝼeᴀrr? Which of your relatives is dearest to you?—cιᴀ !" ᴀcᴀ ᴅe" ᴅo ṁuιnnιr ᷎ᴀᴏl ιr ᴀnrᴀ leᴀc? Which of the two is the better?—cιᴀ "ᴀcᴀ ᴅe" 'n ṁ-beιnc (couple) ιr ꝼeᴀrr?

VOCABULARY.

Hostile, nᴀṁᴀᴅᴀċ.

Madam, beᴀnᴀlcrᴀ, . beᴀn cóιr, rcᴀιοḃeᴀn.

Lady, heᴀn-cιᷤeᴀrnᴀ (wife of a lord).

— beᴀn-ꝼlᴀιċ (wife of a prince).

— beᴀn uᴀrᴀl (a noble or gentlewoman).

— beιċ, a being by excellence, an elegant person, a lady.

Please, rιᴀrᴀḃ, *v*; rᴀruᷤᴀḃ; if you please, mᴀ 'r ré ᴅo coιl é (if it is your will); mᴀ ιr mᴀιċ leᴀc (if it is good with you); mᴀ ιr mιᴀn leᴀc; mᴀ ιr ᴀιl leᴀc; mᴀ 'r cᴀιċneᴀṁ leᴀc. Whatever you please, cιᴀ ᴀιr bιċ nιᴅ ċoᷤnᴀr cu.

Pleasant, cᴀιċneᴀṁᴀċ, cᴀιοḃeᴀc, roᴌᴀrᴀc, nιᷤṁeuḃᴀċ.

Pleasure (delight, gratification of mind or body), ꝼonn; cᴀιċneᴀṁ; rᴀruᷤᴀḃ, rolᴀr, roᷤ, clᴀr.

— choice, roᷤᴀ, coιl, coᷤruᷤᴀḃ.

— ease, rᴀιmeᴀr, roᷤᴀṁlᴀċc, nιᷤṁeuᴅ.

— kindly feeling, cιneᴀlcᴀr, ꝼᴀιlce, ꝼonn.

— what the will dictates, coιl, roᷤᴀ, mιᴀn.

— gratification, cᴀᴅᴀιl, clᴀr.

With pleasure, le ꝼonn, le ꝼᴀιlce, or ᷎o ꝼonmᴀr.

You ought, ιr cóιr ᴅuιc (it is right for you).

Visit, cuᴀιrc, *f;* come on a visit, cᴀrr ᴀιr ċuᴀιrc; cuᴀιrc means, literally, a circle, circumference, circulation; as, ꝼᴀ ċuᴀιrc, round about; cuᴀιrc nᴀ ꝼolᴀ, circulation of the blood; hence, a visit, ᴀιr ċuᴀιrc, on a visit; cuᴀιrceᴀċᴀr and cuᴀιrcιοḃeᴀċc, visiting, gossiping.

EXERCISE LII.

1. Sir (ᴀ ṡᴀoι), do me the honour of taking wine (onóιr ꝼιon ól lιom). 2. With pleasure, Sir (le ꝼonn, ᴀ Ṡhᴀoι). 3. Which (*of them*—cιᴀ ᴀcᴀ) do you prefer (like the better—ιr ꝼeᴀrr leᴀc), the red or the white wine? 4. I like the white better than the red. 5. The pleasure of wine with you, Madam (ᴅeᴀn ᴅᴀm cιneᴀlcᴀr ꝼιon ól lιom, ᴀ beᴀn uᴀrᴀιl); please, Sir, help the lady to wine—lιon ᴅo 'n mnᴀoι uᴀrᴀιl ꝼιon mᴀ 'r é ᴅo coιl é. 6. With pleasure, Sir. 7. Which dish do you prefer, Madam— lamb, fowl, or mutton (cιᴀ "ᴀcᴀ" ꝼeoιl ιr ꝼeᴀrr leᴀc— uᴀn-ꝼeoιl, eᴀnlᴀιċ, no cᴀoιr-ꝼeoιl)? 8. I prefer lamb. 9. Sir, *which* (*of them*) will you have? 10. I will have mutton, Sir, if you please. 11. Very well (cᴀ ᷎o mᴀιċ); your friend, Mr. Blake, will do me the honour of wine.

12. With pleasure, Sir. 13. Which do you prefer—port or sherry? 14. I prefer port. 15. The wines are excellent—ir bɼeaᵹ aɲ ꝼíoɲ e ꞃo. 16. England appears to be much afraid of France at present. 17. She is very much afraid (ca eaᵹla móɼ aɼꞃč). 18. Which *of the two* do you like the better—England or France? 19. *Some of us* prefer England; many *of us* like France better: if England treated us more kindly, and not have us slaves, I should prefer England (ᴅa m-beɼðeað Sacꞃaɲaɼð ɲ’oꞃ ceaɲaṁla lɪɲɲ, aᵹuꞃ ᵹaɲ ꞃclabaɼð a ðeaɲað ðɪɲɲ, b’ ꝼeaꞃꞃ lɪom Saꞃaɲɪač). 20. Of the three last parliaments, which was the best for this country?—"Cɪa aca" ᴅe ɲa cꞃɪ ꝼeɪꞃɪð ᴅeɪᵹɪoɲača, a b’ ꝼeaꞃꞃ ᴅo ’ɲ cɪꞃ ꞃo? 21. It is hard to say, indeed; they are all unfriendly to this country, so I do not like any *of them.* 22. James, tell me, how is your rich friend the Seigneur O'Neil. 23. He is well. 24. Is he well liked; do *many of you* like him well? 25. Indeed, *some of us* do, and *some of us* do not. 26. Which *of you* like him best? 27. I like him very well myself? 28. Sir, you ought to visit us this autumn; *many of us* at home like to see you amongst us. 29. I think I shall. 30. We shall be so happy to see you.

THIRTY-THIRD LESSON.

Prepositions in Irish do not, generally, as in Latin, in Greek, and in the Romance languages, combine with verbs and nouns to express new relations of cause, effect, time, place. In this simple trait, our language bears a strong grammatical affinity to the primitive Saxon tongue. Ex. :

He *descended* into hell; the third day He arose again from the dead, and *ascended* into heaven.—*Apostles' Creed.*	ᴀ "čuaɪð ꞃíoꞃ" (went down) ᵹo h-Jꝼꞃɪoɲɲ, a ð’eꞃꞃɪᵹ aɲ cꞃeaꞃ la ó ṁaꞃbaɪð, a "čuaɪð ꞃuaꞃ" (went up) aɼꞃ ɲeaṁ.—Cꞃé ɲa ɲ-ᴀpꞃcol.

We have said " generally," because the preposition is sometimes, but very rarely, incorporated with a noun or verb; as, ꞃoɼɾ̇-ꞃað, a preface (from ꞃoɼɼ̇, before, and ꞃað, saying, a discourse); eꞃoɼɼ-ᵹuɼðe, intercession (from eіⱃ, between, and ᵹuіðe, praying); just as in English we sometimes meet such prepositional compound words as *fore*-thought, *after*-thought, *in*-lay, *out*-strip, *under*-take. -

From this use of the preposition, and the different relative meanings, primary and secondary, which arise from it and the verb, have sprung many idioms, most of which we have already noticed, and others we shall, as we advance, put before our readers.

Obs. 1.—In familiar discourse, prepositions are, in Irish, as in English, separated from the relative pronouns, and from the interrogative pronouns; as, ⱦaіⱃіc aⱀ ⱁeaⱃ " a" b-ⱁuіl mіⱃe coⱃaṁaіl leіⱃ, the man *whom* I am like *to* came; cіa b-ⱁuіl ⱅu coⱃaṁaіl leіⱃ?—whom are you like to? The former could be, perhaps, more grammatically written thus:— ⱦaіⱃіc aⱀ ⱁeaⱃ le a b-ⱁuіl mіⱃe coⱃaṁaіl; and the latter, cіa leіⱃ a b-ⱁuіl ⱅu coⱃaṁaіl?

Dr. O'Donovan does not approve of thus separating the relative pronoun from the governing preposition, and of placing the latter at the end of the sentence. Lindley Murray condemns the same practice in the English language; yet the best English writers, from Lord Macaulay to Dr. Faber, obstinately continue to practise it, judging the point to be, it seems, in English as it is in Irish, rather a propriety of idiom than an error of grammar.

Note.—"In the English, as in all other languages, a great number of expressions, scarcely warrantable in strict syntax, become part and parcel of the language. To condemn these at once is unphilosophical. The better method is to account for them."—*The English Language, by Dr. Latham.*

Obs. 2.—The prepositions come immediately after the interrogative pronouns; as, cіa " aіⱃ" ⱅuіⱅ aⱀ cⱃaⱀⱀ?— whom *on* did the lot fall? Caⱐ " ⱁaoі" aіⱃ ⱅaⱀіc ⱅu?— what *for* have you come? Cіa "leіⱃ" aⱀ ⱃᵹіaⱀ ⱃo?—whom *with* the knife this? (See Twenty-eighth Lesson, Exercise XLIII., p. 169).

VOCABULARY.

Cheek, leaca, *f;* ᵹⱀuaіð, *f,* complexion, the blush on the cheek;

   " Iⱅ ⱐo ⱅіl ⱀa ⱐeoⱃa 'ⱀuaⱃ le m' ᵹⱀuaіð,"

   " And the tears trickled down by my cheeks."—Laoіð Oіⱃіⱀ.

   " Do ⱐ' ða ᵹⱀuaⱐ ⱐeaⱀᵹ maⱀ ⱦaoⱀⱁoⱀ,"

   " Thy cheek, like rowen-fruits' lustre."—*Irish Songs, by Edward Walsh.*

Create, cⱃuⱦuіᵹ, *v,* from cⱃuⱅ, form, shape, external appearance.

Creator, cⱃuⱦuіᵹⱦeoіⱃ, from cⱃuⱦuіᵹ. The ending, ⱦoіⱃ, ⱦⱁoіⱃ, or oіⱃ, corresponds with the noun-ending *or* in Latin; *er* in English; as, ᵹⱃaⱐuіᵹⱦeoіⱃ, amator, lover.

Christ, Cⱃіoⱃⱐ, our Lord.

Christian, Cⱃіoⱃⱐaіᵹe; as, ⱅeaᵹaⱃᵹ Cⱃіoⱃⱐaіᵹe, Christian doctrine, catechism.

— cⱃіoⱃⱐaṁaіl, from cⱃіoⱃⱐ, and aṁaіl, like.

Doctrine, ⱅeaᵹaⱃᵹ, *m,* teaching, instruction, direction.

Doctor, oіⱐe; ⱅeaᵹaⱃᵹⱦoіⱃ, *m,* a

teacher; doctor of canon law, ceaʒaɼʒċóiɲ be 'ɲ ɗliʒe cá-ɲoɲba; a doctor of theology, ceaʒaɼʒċoiɲ, or oɪbe ɗe 'ɲ ɗia-ɓaċc.

Face, aʒaɪɓ (eye-ye), *f*, face, front, surface. Aʒuɼ ɗo labaiɼ aɲ Ciʒeaɼɲa le Ɱaoɪɼe "aʒaɪɓ aiɲ aʒaɪɓ," And the Lord spoke to Moses *face to face.*

Aɲɲ aʒaɪɓ, in face of, *i.e.*, against; he went *against* his enemy, ċuaɪɓ ɼe aɲɲ aʒaɪɓ a ɲaɱaɪb. A Ciʒeaɼɲa, caɗ ɼa laɼaɲɲ ɗ'ɼeaɲʒ "aɲɲ aʒaɪɓ" ɗo ɗobaɪl? Why, O Lord, is thy indignation enkindled *against* thy people? cried Moses to God. Aiɼ aʒaɪɓ, forward, on front; ceɪʒ aɪɼ ɗ' aʒaɪɓ, go forward (literally, go on your face); fronting, opposing; as, ċuʒ ɼe aʒaɪɓ oɼɱ, he turned (sharply) on me.

Face, euɗaɲ, *m.*

— ɗɼeaċ, *m*, aspect, image, mien; Welsh, *drych.*

— ʒɲuɪɼ, *f*, countenance, mien, visage.

— ʒɲaoɪ, *m*, physiognomy, complexion of features.

— ʒɲe, *m*, form, external appearance, gender, kind.

— ɼɲo, *m*, fashion, appearance of a person or thing, shape.

Human, baoɲɲa, from buiɲe, a person.

Interrogate, ɪaɼɼ, ask; ɼɪaɼɼuɪʒ, inquire; ceɪɼcɲuɪʒ, *v,* question.

Midst, middle, centre, ɱeaɗoɲ; as, a ɱeaɗoɲ a ċaɪɲɗe, in the midst of his friends; ɱeaɗoɲ lae, mid-day, *meridiés;* ɱeaɗoɲ oɪɗċe, midnight; Latin, *medium, medio noctis.* Ɱeaɗoɲ also signifies means; as, leɪɼ aɲ ɱeaɗoɲ ɼo, by this means; Welsh, *moddion,* middle; Fr., *moyen;* Arm., *moyen.*

Ɱeaɗoɲcoɪɼ, mediator; from ɱeaɗoɲ, middle.

Picture, ɪoɱaɪʒ; Latin, *imago;* ɪoɱaɪʒ Cɼɪoɼɗ aʒuɼ ɲa ɲaoɱ, the image or picture of Christ and the Saints. Aɲɲ aoɲ ɼocal, ɲɪ b-ɼuɪl caoɓ ɗ' a b-cɪoɲcoċaɱuɪc ɲaċ b-ɼuɪl ɪoɱaɪʒ aɲ baɪɼ oɼ aɲ ʒ-coɱaɲ: in a word, there is not a side to which we can turn where the image of death does not meet us.—*Dr. Gallagher's Sermon on Death.*

EXERCISE LIII.

A Mother teaching her children:

Ɱaċaɪɼ aɪʒ ɱuɲaɓ a claɪɲɲe:

Richard, Rɪɼcaɪb; George, Seoɼɼa; Eliza, Elɪɼ.

1. (Richard)—See that picture (ɪoɱaɪʒ); whom is it like? 2. (George)—It is like the priest. 3. It is not; but I know whom it is like. 4. Whom now? 5. My father. 6. Indeed it is not; just look at it again—look at his brow and at his cheek. 7. I do (look), at his brow, and at his cheek, and at the chin. 8. But do you look at the eye; the eye is very like the eye of Father John. 9. (Mother)—My children, are you ready? 10. (Richard)—Yes, mamma, we are all ready (ɼeaɓ, a ɱaċaɪɼ caɱuɪɓ uɪle ɼeɪɓ). 11. Do you know your lessons (b-ɼuɪl eoluɼ aʒaɪɓ aɪɼ buɼ leɪʒeaɲ)? 12. (Richard)—I know I have mine. 13.

(George)—So have I mine (lessons). 14. (Eliza)—I have every word in all my lessons, except geography—I have not that. 15. (Mother)—I shall interrogate only in cate-chism ('r·an ceaġarg Criorḃaiġ aṁaiṅ); Richard, who is God (Risċaird, cia ṫe Dia)? 16. (Richard)—The Crea-tor of heaven and earth (cruċuiġċeoir neiṁe aġur calṁan), and Sovereign (aro) Lord of all things (ġaċ uile niḋ). 17. Good boy (maiṫ an buaċaill). How many persons in God? 18. (Richard)—Three persons, the Father, the Son, and the Holy Ghost. 19. Very good boy; which of the three persons, George, assumed (took—ġlaċ) a human body—colan baonna? 20. The Son of God, the second person of the Blessed Trinity—an bara pearra be 'n Trianóid ro naoṁċa. 21. On what day was He born? 22. On Christmas Day, about midnight—lá noolac air uair an meaḋoin oiḋċe. 23. (Richard)—I am tired, mamma—ca me cuir-reaċ a ṁaċair. 24. Well, my boy, you were saying you were like some one. 25. No; but George said that this likeness resembled the priest, Father John—beir Seoirra ġo ḃ-fuil an iomaiġ ro coraṁail leir an t-raġare—an t-aċair Seaġan. 26. And what do you say? 27. I say it is like papa. 28. And whom are you like yourself, with your big cheeks? 29. I am like father. 30. Can you say the "Our Father?" 31. I can, to be sure. 32. What Father is meant there? 33. God—our Father who is in heaven, as St. Francis said: I remember the story you told us. 34. And are you like God, George, tell me? 35. Oh, yes, I am like Him—my soul is like Him. 36. Oh! do you think so? 37. I am sure of it. 38. Take care, then, never to make yourself unlike (neaṁ-coraṁail) Him by staining so lovely an image—cabair aiṫe mar rin ġan ċu féin a ḋeanaḋ neaṁ-coraṁail leir, aiġ milleaḋ iomaiġe ċo aluin.

THIRTY-FOURTH LESSON.

The most peculiar idiom, because the strangest, yet noticed, is that which arises from the use in Irish of the preposition aṅn, *in*, with the possessive pronouns, after the verb cá, is (ḃi, was; beiḋ, will be), and its inflections, to express what is predicated or declared of the nominative case; as, I am a good man, is translated into Irish, τά me "aṅṅ mo" ḟeaṙ ṁaiṫ, I am *in my* good man; the man is a king, τá aṅ ḟeaṙ "aṅṅ a" ṙiġ, literally, the man is *in* his king, *i.e.*, in the state of a king; she is a virgin, τá ṙi "aṅṅ a" h-oiġ; Joseph was steward over all Egypt, bi Joſeṗ "aṅṅ a" ṁaoṙ oṙ cioṅṅ ṅa h-Eġipτe uile; we are Christians, τámuiḋ-ne "aṅṅ aṙ" g-Cṙioṙḋaiġṫiḃ; the Romans were brave wariors, bi ṅa Romáṅaiġ "aṅṅ a" ṅġaiṙġiḋiḃ τṙeuṅa.

NOTE.—The preposition aṅṅ does not follow the *emphatic* form of the verb *to be*, iṙ, is (or buḋ, was), which is a mere copula, expressing simply existence, and not like τá, which expresses existence in a certain state, time, condition.

The preposition aṅṅ is commonly omitted whenever the possessive pronouns of the first and second persons, as well plural as singular, follow; as, *I* am a good man, τá me ' mo ḟeaṙ ṁaiṫ; you are a prince, τá τuṙa 'ḋo ḟlaiṫ: aṅṅ is omitted before mo and ḋo.

In published works the preposition and the possessive pronouns are contracted—aṅṅ mo, *in my*, into a' m' or am; aṅṅ ḋo, *in thy*, to a' ḋ', or aḋ; as,

Reulτaṅ mo ḃóṫaiṙ.

I.

A ḃe! ġaṅ me "am" aḃaillíṅ,
No "am" ṅóiṅiṅ beaġ éiġiṅ,
No "am" ṅóṙ aṅṅṙ aṅ ġáiṅḋíṅ,
Maṙ a ṅ-ġṅáṫuiġeaṅṅ τú "aḋ" aoṅaṙ.

II.

Maṙ ḟáil 'ṙ ġo m-buaiṅṙeaḋ liṅṅ,
Ġeuġáiṅíṅ éiġiṅ,
Do beiḋeaḋ aġaḋ "aḋ" ḃéaṙ láiṁ,
No a m-bṙollaċ ġeal ḋo léiṙe!

STAR OF MY PATH.

I.
Would that I were the apple,
Or the wee daisy only,
Or the rose in that garden
Where thou walkest lonely!

II.

Of my leaflets or flow'rets
I'd hope thou wouldst choose some,
To bear in thy bright hand
Or wear on thy bosom!

—The Poets and Poetry of Munster, Second Series, p. xxii.
ERIONNACH.

Má tá sé-san a stáid na n-grás, agus tu-sa a b-peacaḋ, is feárr e-san míle uair na thusa, cuir a g-cás go b-fuil tú "a'd" ríg no "ad" phrionnsa.

Oir 'r Ṁire an Tiġearna a ċug amaċ ribh ar talaṁ na h-Egipte le beiṫ a'm' Dia agaiḃ.

If he be in a state of grace, and you in sin, he is a thousand times better than you, although you be a king or a prince. — *Dr. Gallagher.*

For I am the Lord, who brought you out of the land of Egypt, that I might be a God to you.—*Lev.* xi. 45.

Before possessive pronouns of the third person, a, his, her, their, ann is written 'nn a, or 'na; as John is a good man, tá Seaġan 'nn a fear maiṫ; Judith is a handsome girl, tá Siuban 'nn a cailín áluin; James was a great scholar, bí Seamur 'nn a scoláire mór; the men are princes, táid na fir 'nn a b-flaiṫiḃ; "If his offering be *a holocaust,* and of the herd," Má bḋeann a ṫabartar 'nn a ioḃairt loirgṫe agus be'n ṫreud.

VOCABULARY.

Bishop, Easpog, *m*, from the Greek, ἐπίσκοπος, *episkopos;* by changing *k* into *g,* and by metathesis alternating the consonants.

Class, cuideaċt, *f,* from cuid, some, a share; comploċt, *f,* a company, a party; compáinc, *f*: ord, *m,* order.

Egyptian, Egipteaċ.

Gaul (a), Gall.

Jacob, Iacob (pr. *Yacob*), Seacob, from the Hebrew, *yacob,* to supplant—because he twice supplanted his brother Esau.

Joseph, Iosep (pr. *Yoseph*), or Seosep (*Shoseph*).

NOTE.—English or foreign names beginning with *J,* or *Ge,* are translated into Irish by *S,* followed by *é* (*Se*), which digraph conveys in Irish the sibilant sound of the English *J, Ge,* as, *James,* Seamur; *John,* Seaġan; *Judith,* Siuban; *Julia,* Seilḃan; *George,* Seonra; *Geoffry,* Sefre. In this respect the Irish translation of names is not unlike the Italian, which follows sound rather than etymology; as, *Joseph, Giuseppe; John, Giovanni.* The Irish forms, Iosep and Iacob, rather than

Seoreṗ and *Seacoḃ*, are more in comformity with the radices of the words, and with the written Irish language.

Julius Cæsar, Iulıur Caeraṅ (*Yulus Kesar*).

Saviour, *Slanuıġṫeoıṙ*, from ṙlan, safe; ṙlanuıġ, save thou.

EXERCISE LIV.

1. Are you *a good boy*, James? 2. I am, Sir, *a good* boy; I *am* always a good *boy*. 3. *Is* your sister Alice *a* good *girl?* 4. She *is a* good girl; and my father says that she will *be a* very good woman. 5. Are your brothers and cousins here? 6. They are. 7. *Are* they *good* scholars? 8. They are, in proportion to (ṫo ṙeıṙ) their years. 9. Is this your cousin Joseph, who is such a great scholar. 10. It is. 11. Well, Joseph, do you know the history of the Bible well? 12. Yes, I know a little of it. 13. Do you know who was Joseph, the son of Jacob? 14. He *was steward* over all the land of Egypt, and *the saviour* of his people. 15. Whether *was* he *an* Hebrew or *an* Egyptian? 16. He *was an* Hebrew. 17. Do you know Roman history? 18. Not much. 19. Can you tell who was Julius Cæsar—whether *was* he *a* Roman or *a* Gaul? 20. He was a Roman, and is famed (aġur ta caıl aıṙ) for having conquered the Gauls; and the first (aġur ġuṙ buḋ e an ceuḋ ṫaoraċ Romanaċ) Roman General who landed in Britain. 21. Who was St. Patrick? 22. He was a holy bishop, and the apostle of our nation. 23. Very well—you are very good in history. 24. Does Master William know history? 25. He does, as well as I (ċo ṁaıṫ lıom-ra); we are both (le ceıle) in the same class. 26. Does he know his catechism also? 27. He does. 28. Who created you, and placed you in this world? 29. It is in the Irish language—the language of fatherland (ır annr an ṫeanġa ġaoıḋılġe—ṫeanġa mo ṫıṙ ḋuṫċaır)—I have learned the catechism (ḋ' ḟoġlam me an ṫeaġarġ cṙıorḋaıġ). 30. Oh, very well; so much the better (ır amlaıḋ ır ḟeaṙṙ); I am delighted at it (ta luaṫġaıṙ oṙm ḟaoı).

VOCABULARY.

Aoıbnear, *m*, gladness, joy, delight; from aoıḃ (pr. *ee-iv*), a courteous look.

Cıġ, sees; present tense of the irreg. verb ḟeıcım, I see.

Com-ıonan, co-equal; from com, and ıonan, equal, same, like.

Cṙe, *f*, creed, the symbol of faith, earth.

Dṙonġ, *f*, a tribe, a people, a number of persons of the same class.

Eidir-ḋealḃṫa, distinct, of different personality; from eidir, between, separate, and dealḃṫa, participle of dealḃaḋ, to frame, to fashion; dealḃ, form, figure, personality.

Ioncolnuiġṫe, poss. case of ioncolnuġaḋ, incarnation; a verbal noun, from ion, a form of aon, in, and -colnuġaḋ (from colan, a living body), to give a body to, to incarnate.

Naḋúr, m, nature, constitution of the material world, or of anything in existence; frame of mind. Welsh, natur; Latin, natura.

Smuaineaḋ, m, thinking, a thought; plur. smuainte, thoughts.

EXERCISE LV.

1. Cia ċruṫuiġ agus cuir air an t-saoġal tu? 2. Dia. 3. Cad é an ceud niḋ, is cóir do ġaċ uile ċriosdaiġe a ċreideaḋ? 4. Ġo ḃ-fuil aon Dia aṁáin ann: is é so an ceud airteaġal (article) de'n ċré. 5. Cia é Dia? 6. Cruṫuiġṫeoir neiṁe agus talṁan, agus árd-Tiġearna ġaċ uile niḋ. 7. An raiḃ Dia ann, ġaċ uile am? 8. Ḃi, agus roiṁ ġaċ uile am; de ḃriġ ġo ḃ-fuil sé ġan tús, ġan deire. 9. Ca ḃ-fuil Dia? 10. Tá sé air neaṁ agus air ċalaṁ, agus ann ġaċ uile ball de'n doṁan. 11. An ḃ-feiceann sé ġaċ uile niḋ? 12. Ciġ sé ġaċ uile niḋ, ġo fiú na smuainte is uaiġniġe a ġ-croiḋe an duine. 13. Ca ṁéiḋ Dia ann? 14. Ni ḃ-fuil aċt aon Dia aṁáin a ḃeirṫear aoiḃneas siorruiḋe do na deaġ-ḋaoiniḃ, agus slanta siorruiḋe do'n dronġ loċtaċ. 15. Ca ṁéiḋ pearsa ann Dia? 16. Tri pearsanna, eidirḋealḃṫa agus coiṁionann, ann ġaċ uile niḋ, mar tá, an t-Aṫair, agus an Ṁac, agus an Spioraḋ Naoṁ. 17. An Dia an t-Aṫair? 18. Is seaḋ ġo deiṁin. 19. An Dia an Ṁac? 20. Is seaḋ ġo deiṁin. 21. An Dia an Spioraḋ Naoṁ? 22. Is seaḋ ġo deiṁin. 23. An tri Déiṫe iaḋ? 24. Ni seaḋ, aċt aon Dia aṁáin a d-tri ḃ-pearsannaiḃ; de ḃriġ naċ ḃ-fuil acu aċt aon naḋúir agus aon t-suḃstaint aṁáin ḋiaḋa. 25. Cad is ainm do na tri pearsannaiḃ ann aoinḟeaċt? 26. An Trionóiḋ ro Naoṁṫa, no aon Dia aṁáin a d-tri ḃ-pearsannaiḃ. 27. Cia "aca" is sine, nó is óiġe, no is cuṁaċtaiġe? 28. Is ionann aois, uaisle agus cuṁaċt ḋóiḃ araon. 29. An Dia Iosa Criosḋ? 30. Tá sé "'nn a" Dia agus "'nn a" duine ann aoinḟeaċt. 31. An raiḃ sé a ġ-coṁnuiġe "'nn a"

Ḋia?" 32. Ḃí. 33. An raiḃ ré a ʒ-coṁnuiġe "'nn a
ḋuine?" 34. Ní raiḃ, aċt ó aimrir a joncoluiġṫe. 35.
Ca méid naḋúir ann Jora Criort? 36. Ta ḋá naḋúir;
re rin, naḋúir ḋiaḋa aʒur naḋúir ḋaonna, óir ta ré 'nn
a Ḋia aʒur 'nn a ḋuine. 37. Ca méid pearra ann Jora
Criort? 38. Ní ḃ-fuil aċt aon pearra aṁáin; re rin,
pearra Ṁic Ḋe aṁáin. 39. Ir maiṫ an buaċail ṫu, a
Uilléim; ta eolur aʒaḋ air Ḋia; tabair mar rin, ʒraḋ
ḋo ċroiḋe ʒo h-iomlán ḋo, aʒur beiḋir fór 'ʒ a railḃeaḋ
a ḃ-flaiṫear.

THIRTY-FIFTH LESSON.

Our readers have already learned, from the first of the " Easy Lessons,"
that in Irish the vowels are divided into two classes, the one *broad*, or *deep*,
leaṫan; the other, *slender*, caol. We then remarked that in a subsequent
Lesson should " be shown the reason of this division, and its utility." In the
" Seventeenth Lesson," 1st Obs., this classification of vowels into broad and
slender has been somewhat explained, and some of the effects resulting from
it are pointed out. In this Lesson, however, we intend to perform fully the
promise made in our First.

The reason of such a division is quite philosophic, for every vowel sound
is produced " by the passage of the air through the opening of the glottis ;"
and thus all intonated vowel sounds " partake somewhat of the character of
musical notes, while, at the same time, they constitute the elements of
speech." In the musical octave each successive note, from the highest to
the lowest, is sounded with a volume of voice deeper than that of the note
preceding ; and conversely the preceding is sounded with a higher, that is, a
more *slender* (we shall so call it) volume of voice than its succeeding note.
The two highest are, therefore, the two which may properly be called *slender*,
when compared to those which, lower in the scale, are pronounced deep, or
broad. In this manner intonated vowel sounds, as far as they partake of this
musical character, are some slender, some broad. Let us arrange them then
in the philosophic order (See *Atlant's*, vol. i., pp. 60, 65), " from the highest
to the deepest ; thus, ɪ, e, a, o, u." And in this arrangement, which is that
made by philologists and philosophers, native and foreign, we find ɪ, e, to
rank highest, that is, to constitute the class called caol, or *slender ;* an'
a, o, u, lowest, that is, to constitute the class called leaṫan, *broad*, or deep.
Thus we see that the classification of vowels made by Irish grammarians
accords exactly with that which the investigations of philosophy point out as
correct. There are in Gaelic, therefore, two classes of vowels clearly and
philosophically distinguishable. Do they differ in their influence and in their
effects ? We shall see :

Vowels and consonants constitute the one grand, universal family of
letters. Consonants derive their name from being *sounded along with*, or by
the aid of, the vowels. When articulated, they partake, therefore, of the
sound of that vowel by the aid of which they are enunciated. Irish vowel
sounds are, as we have seen, of a twofold character, *broad* or *slender ;* each

consonant must, accordingly, partake of a twofold articulation, *broad* or *slender*, according to the broad or slender intonation of the vowel by the aid of which it is sounded. This twofold articulation can, in some measure, be applied with truth to consonants in any language; but, with the exception of the Keltic dialects, and particularly Irish, we know of none in which this phonetic distinction in the articulation of consonants has retained its radically distinctive, philosophic character.

The influence of a twofold sound of the vowels thus acting on the consonants, and causing them to participate in it, is so fused into our national language that it has stamped its pronunciation and orthography with a complexion and individuality quite different from everything English. To Irish-speaking natives this individuality appears quite easy and natural, and, like accent, with which it is essentially blended, is naturally acquired and practised by them without knowing or adverting to the existence of the principle from which it springs; yet, to those who do not speak the language, it appears at once strange and difficult.

As the language is spoken and written, the effects of the influence exercised by the twofold division of vowel sounds, extend to both departments—the written and spoken Gælic. These effects may well, therefore, be called *articulate*, or phonetic, and *orthographic*.

The *articulate* regards the sound of each consonant when it is intonated with a broad or a slender vowel. The *orthographic* regards the laws of spelling.

We shall treat, firstly, in a few sentences, of the *articulate*, or phonetic, and next of the *orthographic* effect.

1. The reader will please bear in mind that the sound of the consonants partakes of the sound of that class of vowels in union with which they happen to be sounded. Now, as the sound of the latter is broad or slender, so must that of the former, according as its articulation is aided by a broad or a slender vowel. Is this true of all the consonants? It is, generally.

In the first of the EASY LESSONS; OR, SELF-INSTRUCTION IN IRISH, we have clearly showed how the consonant S, ſ, is affected by the contiguity of e and ı; and how, by that also of ᴀ, o, or u. In the former case, the queen of consonants, as Irish poets love to call it, is invariably sounded like *sh* English; in the latter, simply like the English *s*, as heard in the word *soon*.

Again, in the "Fourth Lesson," the plain and liquid sounds of ḃ, ṁ, ċ, ᵹ̇, ḋ—*i.e.*, the sounds these consonants have when sounded in company with ᴀ, o, u, and when with e, ı, are shown.

In the "First Lesson," the two sounds of l are pointed out.

ŋ, also, when sounded with e, ı, is more nasal than when articulated by the aid of ᴀ, o, u; as, ceᴀŋŋ, the head; ꞓıŋŋ, of the head; beᴀŋ, a woman; bıŋŋ, melodious; cᴀſᴀŋ, a path; cᴀſᴀıŋ, of a path; ŋ after ı, in those instances, sounds nearly like *ng*, or *n* prolonged.

ʀ broad is like *r* in English.
ʀ slender   „   *rh; rr*   „   or *r* in German, *i.e.*, rough, through the throat.

τ broad   „   *th;* as ατ (*awth*).

τ slender   „   *th;* ἀιτ (*aw-ith,* in one syllable); *th* slender is longer and more sibilant than *th* broad.

In the consonants, ꝼ, ḟ, or ᵽ, this peculiar distinction of sound is not noticeable in any great degree.

Consult Dr. O'Donovan's Irish Grammar on the sounds of the consonants.

VOCABULARY.

Grain, ᵹʀáⁿ, *m.* ᵹʀáıⁿe, *f;* Latin, *granum;* ᵹʀáⁿa, ugly.

Scratch (to), *v,* ʀᵹʀıobaᵭ.

Search, τοıʀıᵹ; τοıʀıᵹeaċτ, *part;* τοıʀıᵹeaċτ, looking for in order to procure; loⁿᵹ, *v,* is to pursue, to track; ʀaⁿʀuıᵹ, search, toss, ransack; cuaʀτuıᵹ, go about looking for.

Straw, cocáⁿ, *m;* coⁿⁿlaċ, stubble; τuıḃe, *m;* ꝼuıp, *f.*

Understand, τuıᵹım (*thigim*), I understand. It differs a little in sound from τıᵹım, I come, and from τuᵹaım, I give, I impart.

EXERCISE LVI.

Fable (ꝼcáıp)—The Cock and the Jewel.

As a cock (Sixteenth Lesson) was scratching up the straw on the dunghill (caʀⁿ aollıᵹ), in search of food for the hens, he hit upon a jewel (Sixth Lesson) that by chance had been there. "Ho!" said he, "you are a very fine (áluıⁿ) thing (ⁿıᵭ) no doubt (ᵹaⁿ aṁʀaꝼ), to those who prize you; but to me a grain of barley (Twelfth Lesson) is more beautiful than all the pearls in the world."

The cock was a sensible (cıalṁaʀ) cock; but there are many silly (oıτ-cıallaıᵭ) people who despise (a cuıⁿeaꝼ ⁿeaṁ-ꝼuıⁿ) what is precious only because they cannot understand it.

VOCABULARY.

Began, τoꝼuıᵹ; from cuʀ, a beginning.

Coward, cⁿaıll, *m,* claᵭaıʀe, pr. *cly-ar-rhe.* (See Fourth Lesson on the sound of ᵭ, asp., in the middle of a word.)

Kid, ⁿıoⁿⁿaⁿ, *m;* from ⁿıoⁿ, little (ᵹaḃaʀ, a goat, is understood), kid being the diminutive of *goat.* —"The English Language," by Robt. G. Latham, ed. iii., p. 284.

Reply, ꝼꝼeaᵹⁿaᵭ, *v.*

Revile, maꝼluᵹaᵭ, *v;* reviling, aıᵹ maꝼluᵹaᵭ.

Roof, mullaċ, *m,* ḃáʀʀ, *m,* oꝼuıⁿ, *f;* on the roof of a lofty house, aʀ mullaċ τıᵹe áıⁿo.

Standing (you are), τáꝼ aıᵹ ꝼeaꝼaᵭ; ꝼeaꝼ, stand; Latin, *sto;* Greek, στaω; Irish, ꝼτaᵭ, stop, stand.

Wolf, mᴀċꞃᴀ ᴀᴌᴌᴀ, a wild dog. A wolf is called, also, mᴀc ꞇꞀꞃo (the son of the country), and ꝼᴀoᴌċu (a wild hound).

EXERCISE LVII.

Fable—The Kid and the Wolf.

A kid was mounted on the roof of a lofty house, and seeing (ᴀꞁᵹ ꝼeꞁcꞀꞁꝩꞇ) a wolf pass below, began to revile him. The wolf stopped but to reply, "Coward! it is not you who revile me, but the place you are standing."

2. The *orthographic* effect is explained in our Seventeenth Lesson : "Not only do the vowels in this way affect the consonants in unison with which they are sounded, but they carry their assimilating influence to the beginning of the next syllable, so as to cause the first vowel in the adjoining syllable to be of the same class (*broad* or *slender*) as the final vowel in the preceding syllable."

Observe in the spelling of the following words how widely and unmistakeably the influence of the broad and slender vowel-sounds has extended :

bꞃeuᵹ-ᴀ-ḃóꞁꞃ, a liar.
Cꞃuċ-uꞁᵹ-ꞇeoꞁꞃ, creator.
Cuꞁṁ-nꞁᵹ-ꞇeoꞁꞃ, a man who remembers.
FuᴀꞱ-ᵹᴀᴌ-ꞇoꞁꞃ, redeemer.
Ꞡꞃᴀḃ-uꞁᵹ-ꞇeoꞁꞃ,
Mᴀꞃḃ-ᴀ-ḃóꞁꞃ, a murderer, an executioner.
Meᴀᴌᴌ-ꞇóꞁꞃ, a deceiver.
Sꞃᴀᴌ-ᴀ-ḃóꞁꞃ, a snuffers.
Smuċ-ᴀ-ḃóꞁꞃ, an extinguisher.

In this list of words the learner cannot but notice that the final syllable is spelled eoꞁꞃ, or óꞁꞃ, according as the preceding syllable ends in a slender or in a broad vowel—óꞁꞃ, if broad, eoꞁꞃ, if slender.

Deoꞃ-ᴀꞁḃe, a mourner, an exile : from beoꞃ, a tear.
Deoꞃ-ᴀꞁḃe-ᴀċꞇ, *f*, banishment.
buᴀn-ᴀꞅ, *m*, durability, perseverance; from buᴀn, lasting, durable.
bꞁnn-eᴀꞅ, *m*, harmony; from bꞁnn. In the spelling of this word, e, in the last syllable, is inserted before ᴀꞅ, because the vowel before nn is slender; so in the following :

Fᴌᴀꞁꞇ-eᴀꞅ, *m*, a kingdom, the kingdom of heaven; from ꝼᴌᴀꞁꞇ, a prince.
Mᴀꞁꞇ-eᴀꞅ, *m*, goodness; from mᴀꞁꞇ, good.
Feᴀꞃ-ᴀṁ-ᴀꞁᴌ, manly.
Fᴌᴀꞁꞇ-eᴀṁᴀꞁᴌ, princely, hospitable; from ꝼᴌᴀꞁꞇ, but e is inserted after ꞇ, on account of the final vowel in the preceding syllable being slender.
Ꞃꞁᵹ-eᴀċꞇ, a kingdom (from ꞃꞁᵹ, a king), is spelled also ꞃꞁoᵹ-ᴀċꞇ. This latter spelling conforms to the common Gaelic usage of vowel-assimilation, having a broad vowel, o, inserted before ᵹ, the last consonant in the first syllable, because the suffix ᴀċꞇ commences with a broad vowel. It is more correct, however, always to preserve the root unchanged—ꞃꞁᵹ is the root, and not ꞃꞁoᵹ. The word should, therefore, be spelled ꞃꞁᵹeᴀċꞇ, or, without urging the assimilating process too far. ꞃꞁ eᴀċꞇ. The root of the word must not be touched.

VOCABULARY.

beart, m, an exploit, an action, a deed good or bad; an engine, machine, frame; rigging, a bundle, a truss.

beart coirce, a stook of corn, clothes, a bundle; a trick, a game; a threatening.

beartaċ, adj., clever, active, up to business, cunning, rich.

beartuiġ, v, adjust, harness, to make ready for action, yoke, brandish, play.

beartnaċ, m, a chess-board.

bróḋ, m, pride, arrogance, gladness, joyousness, a feeling of pleasure; a goad, a sting, a swarm, a blemish, a spot.

Coṁórtas, m, comparison, emulation; from co, and mórtas (mór, great), greatness; comparing the greatness of one with that of another.

Droċ-beart, a bad action, &c.

Droċ-beura, bad habits.

Doṁan, m, the world; doṁan mór, the wide world, is the same as *tout le monde* in French, i.e.. everybody.

Glioġar, m, a tinkling, ringing noise; from glioġ, a clink, a tinkling.

Prais, f, brass.

Praisceaċ, m, a brazen vessel, malt, pottage, a mixture, a slut.

Seaċain and reaċnuiġ, from reaċ. apart, aside; therefore, avoid, shun.

Tugaḋ, perf. pass., was given.

Tugṫa, given; from tabair, give, v. irr.

Tuarasdal, m, wages.

Uṁa, m, copper, brass.

EXERCISE LVIII.

Madaḋ a bí tugṫa do ġearraḋ.

Bí fear tiġe airiḋe a ṫug orduġaḋ cloġ-uṁa a ċur air ṁuinéal madaiḋ a bí tugṫa do daoine a ġearraḋ air ċor go reaċnoċtaḋ gaċ neaċ é. 'Nuair do cuireaḋ air é, agus do ċualaiḋ sé glioġar binn an uṁa, ṫáinic bróḋ mór air, agus do ṁeas gur tugaḋ dó an cloġ mar luaċ tuarasdail, a beiṫ ċo maiṫ. Uime sin ṫosuiġ sé ag caṫaḋ droċṁeasa air gaċ madaḋ eile a g-coṁórtas leis féin. Aċt bí sean-ċu ann, a dubairt leis: "a duine gan céill, naċ b-fuil fios agaḋ go b-fuil an glioġar binn so aċt ag foillriuġaḋ do gaċ duine do droċ-beura."

Ní cóir do aon duine bróḋ a ġlacaḋ as beart a foilruiġear a ṫarcuirne do'n doṁan mór.

THIRTY-SIXTH LESSON.

Spelling in Irish.

The difficulty which presents itself to a Gælic student in the spelling of Irish is only apparent. It arises from not knowing the principle according to which Irish orthography is regulated. It is hard to unlock a door if the proper key be not had; it is difficult to know a foreign language without understanding its vocabulary.

Our last lesson points out the existence of vowel assimilation in Gælic, and how widely, yet minutely, its influence pervades our language. The principle of vowel assimilation is the key by means of which the door of Gælic spelling is unlocked—the lamp by the light of which everything that to the learner appeared obscure becomes lightsome—the solution by which what was so difficult begins to appear, like the secret of a riddle when known, simple and interesting.

Words are of two kinds, *simple* and *compound*.

Obs. 1.—Simple words are generally of one syllable—sometimes, but very rarely, of two. They are the roots from which the *compound* words spring.

Our readers will find in the First, Second, Third, and Fourth of these Lessons numerous examples of *simple* words. Can there be anything easier than the spelling of such monosyllables as ᴀᴍ, time; ᴀᴘ, slaughter; ᴃᴀʀ, death; ʙɪɴɴ, harmonious; ᴍɪʟ, honey; ᴛᴘoᴍ, heavy.—*Easy Lessons, or Self-Instruction in Irish*, p. 3.

Take a few other examples, which, in their spelling, may appear to a young learner a little more difficult than the foregoing, because the final consonant is aspirated—oɪᵹ (*ó-ee*), a virgin; ʀɪᵹ (*ree*), a king; ʀoᵹ (*só*), happiness; ᴍᴀᵹ, a plain, a field; ʟᴀoᵹ (*lhuee*), a calf. Yet are those not as easily spelled as the Saxon words *high, sigh, sought, rough, cough*, and the like, which end in *g* aspirated—*i.e.*, *gh*, a consonant which, though not necessary for the sound, is nevertheless required to fix the identity of these syllables.

Obs. 2.—Compound words are made up of parts. Spell the parts correctly, unite them, and you have the compound word spelled correctly. These parts are—first, either simple words, each of which is very easily spelled; as, ʙeᴀɴ, a woman; and ᵹᴀoʟ, a relative, from which, by composition, is formed ʙeᴀɴ-ᵹᴀoʟ, a woman-relative; ᴀᴘᴅ, high; céɪᴍ, grade; ᴀᴘᴅ-céɪᴍ, high estate; coɪʀ-céɪᴍ, foot-step; oɪᵹ-ʙeᴀɴ, a virgin-woman;—or, secondly, simple words and particles, *i.e.*, parts of simple words, which impart form and completeness to the whole term, springing from the simple root. Of this class are ʀᴀoᴘʀᴀᴄᴛ, freedom, cheapness; from ʀᴀoᴘ, free, cheap; ᴛᴘoᴍ-ᴀʀ, heaviness; eᴀᴅ-ᴛᴘoᴍ-ᴀʀ, lightness, non-heaviness; from eᴀᴅ-ᴛᴘoᴍ, light, not heavy; cᴀᴘᴀᴅ-ᴀʀ, friendship; eᴀᵹ-cᴀᴘᴀᴅ, a foe; eᴀᵹ-cᴀᴘᴀᴅᴀʀ, unfriendliness, hostility; from capad, a friend. Such, too, are zeanamail, amiable; from zean, affection, and amail, like; anzeanamail, *very* amiable; pap-zeanamail, *extremely* amiable; neam-zeanamail, *unamiable*; anzeanamalact, great amiableness; pap-zeanamalact, amiableness in an extreme degree; neam-zeanamalact, unamiableness.

In such compound terms we see that the roots (such as paop, tpom, capad, zean) have before and after them certain particles. Those going before are called *prefixes*— those following, *suffixes* or terminations. If, therefore, the spelling of the simple word or the root, which is not difficult, and the spelling of the prefixes and suffixes also, be known to the learner, what difficulty can there be about the spelling of any derivative or compound word formed from the union of such parts? None whatever.

Take, for instance, one of the foregoing examples, "zeanamail," amiable. You find it is composed of the root zean, and of the suffix amail, like; unite these two, of each of which you know the spelling, and the new yet common word, zeanamail, is properly spelled. Thus from these simple

<table>
<tr><td rowspan="10">Nouns,</td><td>Capad, a friend,</td><td rowspan="10">are formed, by annexing the suffix amail, like,</td></tr>
<tr><td>Feap, a man,</td></tr>
<tr><td>Flait, a prince,</td></tr>
<tr><td>Zean, affection,</td></tr>
<tr><td>Zpad, love,</td></tr>
<tr><td>Meap, esteem,</td></tr>
<tr><td>Mod, respect, manner,</td></tr>
<tr><td>Tip, country,</td></tr>
<tr><td>La, a day,</td></tr>
<tr><td>Mipneac, courage,</td></tr>
</table>

Capadamail, friendly; flaitamail, princely, generous, bounteous; zeanamail, amiable; zpadamail, loveable; meapamail, estimable; modamail, mannerly; tipamail, country-like, homely, social, not foreign in manner or conversation; from la, and mipneac, are formed, not la-amail, but laetamail, by annexing the suffix amail to the possessive case, lae, and inserting t, for euphony; and mipneamail, from the possessive case singular, mipnei3, by omitting 3, and changing] into ᴀ, to correspond with the broad vowel ᴀ in the annexed syllable.

Take another example, ᴠeᴀṁ-ᵹeᴀᴨᴀᴍᴀ]ᴌ, *unamiable.* You find that the root, ᵹeᴀᴨ, has here a particle, ᴠeᴀṁ, *un, not,* going before it. In order to learn the spelling of the word thus enlarged, see how ᴠeᴀṁ is spelled, and the rest of the word is the same as that treated in the foregoing paragraph. Thus, then, is acquired a knowledge of the spelling of such words as ᴠeᴀṁ-ᵹeᴀᴨᴀᴍᴀ]ᴌ; ᴠeᴀṁ-ċᴀᴩᴀᴅᴀᴍᴀ]ᴌ, *unfriendly;* ᴠeᴀṁ-ᵮᴌᴀ]ċᴀᴍᴀ]ᴌ, *unbounteous,* 'not princely; ᴠeᴀṁ-ᴍeᴀᴩ-ᴀᴍᴀ]ᴌ, *not estimable;* ᴠeᴀṁ-ᴍoᴅᴀᴍᴀ]ᴌ, *not respectful,* &c.

If, instead of ᴠeᴀṁ, *un,* the prefix should be ᴀᴠ, ᴅo, eᴀᴩ, ᴍ], ᴩᴀᴩ, or any other, learn its spelling and that of the root, and unite both, and the word is spelled properly, as is seen by the foregoing examples.

From the adjectives ᵹeᴀᴨᴀᴍᴀ]ᴌ, ᴄᴀᴩᴀᴅᴀᴍᴀ]ᴌ, ᵮᴌᴀ]ċᴀᴍᴀ]ᴌ, ċ]ᴩᴀᴍᴀ]ᴌ, ᵮeᴀᴩᴀᴍᴀ]ᴌ, derivative abstract nouns are formed by adding ᴀċᴛ. In suffixing the substantive termination ᴀċᴛ, the final slender vowel] of the adjective is omitted to conform to the rule " cᴀoᴌ ᴌe cᴀoᴌ," &c., which expresses the principle of vowel assimilation. Thus, then, ᵹeᴀᴨᴀᴍ-ᴀᴌᴀċᴛ, and contractedly, ᵹeᴀᴨᴀᴍᴌᴀċᴛ, *amiableness;* ᴄᴀᴩᴀᴅ-ᴀᴍᴌᴀċᴛ, *friendliness;* ᵮᴌᴀ]ċᴀᴍᴌᴀċᴛ, *bountifulness, princely, generosity;* ċ]ᴩᴀᴍᴌᴀċᴛ, *sociableness;* ᵮeᴀᴩᴀᴍᴌᴀċᴛ, *manliness;* are formed.

NOTE.—When we come to the declension of adjectives, we shall find that this class, ending in ᴀᴍᴀ]ᴌ, make the possessive case ᴀᴍᴌᴀ, to which annex ᴀċᴛ, and the noun is formed.

And, again, ᴩ]ᵹ-eᴀċᴛ, a kingdom; from ᴩ]ᵹ, a king (e is inserted before ᴀċᴛ, to conform to the assimilating process).

In this manner are spelled the abstract nouns terminating in ᴀᴩ or eᴀᴩ; as, ᴃ]ᴨᴨeᴀᴩ, melody, from the adjective ᴃ]ᴨᴨ, melodious; ᴍᴀ]ċeᴀᴩ, goodness, from ᴍᴀ]ċ, good; oᴌcᴀᴩ, badness, from oᴌċ, bad; ᴄ]ᴜᴨᴀᴩ, quietness, calmness, from ᴄ]ᴜᴨ, calm, quiet.

The termination ᴀᴩ is annexed to the primitive adjective when its final vowel is broad; that of eᴀᴩ when the final vowel is slender. In this way are formed also personal nouns ending in ó]ᴩ, ᴀ]ᴅe, ᴜ]ᴅe, ᴀċ; others ending in ᴀᴠ,]ᴠ, óᵹ, and the like.

Adjectives, as we have shown, are formed from the simple

roots from which they spring, by annexing amail, mar, ac, aið, ða, ða, or ca, to the primitive noun. Verbs, in like manner, have annexed to the root certain endings which must be determined according to the tense and person in which one wishes to express them; and their spelling is to be regulated by the standard of verbal conjugation.

From the various "Vocabularies" furnished in the Lessons preceding the present one, our readers have become acquainted with a great number of simple words or roots. In a few of the coming Lessons we shall, in order to make Gaelic spelling a matter of no difficulty, treat of the prefixes and suffixes of Irish compound words.

VOCABULARY.

Amaċ, out.

bpeaċnuiġ, v, think, ponder, view, consider, judge; from bpeaċ, a judgment, a conception of the mind.

A b-fað, long (time).

Féaroż, f, beard.

Fiafnuiġ, v, ask, inquire.

Fuiġeað, conditional tense of the verb faġ, get, procure.

Iomanca, m, too much, abundance.

Liomwan, plentiful, abundant, copious; from lión, fill (lán, full), and man, a suffix.

Sionnaċ, a fox. plur. rionnaiġ.

Canla, chanced, happened; also written canluiġ, to conform to the forms of conjugation.

Cuic, fell; per tense.

Uain, f, occasion, favourable juncture, opportunity, turn; fan le ð'uain, wait for your turn.

EXERCISE LIX.

An rionnaċ ażur an żaðan.

Do ċuic rionnaċ a b-cobain uirże: do bpeaċnuiġ re ċanc a b-fað cia an nór a b-fuiġeað re amaċ, 'nuain żo canluiġ fa ðeine żaðan aiż an áic, a ðuil le ðeoċ, ażur ð' fiafnuiġ ðe 'n c-rionnaċ, naib an c-uirże maiċ ażur an naib żo leor ða ann. Cuż ann rionnaċ, cun fa rżáċ an żáð món ann a naib re, an fneażnað ro, "cann a nuar, a ċanaið mo ċnoiðe; cá an c-uirże ċo maiċ riu naċ feiðin iomanca ól ðé, ażur ċo liomwan naċ feiðin a ċaorżað." Żan focail eile a ċlor, do léim an żaðan rior, ażur aiż żlacað uaine ðo léim an rionnaċ żo luaċman ruar, faġail anðuiżċe món ó aðancaib a ċanaið, ażur ann rin ðubainc leir an amaðan żaðan: "ða m-beiðeað ażað leaċ an oineað céile a'r cá féaroż ðo ðeanfá bpeaċnażað noim an leim ðo ċabainc."

Ní cóin bnjaċna żaċ cluanaið a ċneircinc.

VOCABULARY.

Anál, *m*, breath (from **anam**, the soul, and **ail**, to feed; for while there is breath there is life); Welsh, *anadl*; Latin, *anhela*; which a linguist readily perceives is derived from the Keltic **anal**, and not from *am* and *halo*.

An-ṁaiṫ, very good; from **an**, very, and **maiṫ**; ṁ of **maiṫ** becomes aspirated in composition.

Cosaint, *v*, to defend.

Duḃairt, said; perfect tense of the *irr. v.* **beir**, say.

Faiteaċ, *adj.*, fretful, fearful, timorous.

Smigeaḋ, *m*, a smile, *plur.* **smigeaḋ**, from **smig**, the chin—the expression of the lips and chin.

Sciopṫa, *adj.*, speedy; **go sciopṫa**, speedily; from **sciop**, *v*, to carry off with celerity; *n*, swift motion, skipping.

Tafaint, *m, f*, yelping, barking; supposed by Dr. O'Brien to be derived from the sound of the yelping—**haf**, or **taf**, and **caint**.

EXERCISE LX.

An Eilit óg agus a máṫair.

Duḃairt Eilit óg lá ann le n-a máṫair: "A ṁáṫair, táir níos airde 'ná madaḋ, agus níos eargaiḋ agus níos análaiġe, agus tá agaḋ aḋarca le ṫu féin do ċosaint, caḋ uime, mar sin, b-ḟuil tu ċo faiteaċ roiṁ na cuin." Do rinne sí smigeaḋ agus duḃairt. Tá fios agam ro a leanḃ, go h-anṁaiṫ, aċt ní cuirse cluinim madaḋ aig tafaint 'ná imiġeann mo ċosa leo co sciopṫa a's feiḋir é.

Ní'l aon ṁaiṫ aig caint le cladaire air ṁisneaċ a ġlacaḋ.

EXERCISE LXI.

1. Who is there (**cia tá ann sin**)? 2. It is I ('**mire**). 3. Art thou John? 4. I am not John, but George. 5. Where does John happen to be? 6. He is at home. 7. Were you at home? 8. I was not at home, but my servant, Cormack, was at home to defend the house. 9. How is your father; is he manly, courageous, friendly, amiable, lovable, and princely, as people say he is? 10. He is; but my brother, of whom you heard, is unmanly, unamiable—yet he is princely and friendly; he has a smile for all his friends, but he abominates (**tá gráin aige air**) his foes. 11. Think well on what you say. 12. I am not afraid (fretful) to say what I think to be true. 13. That is right.

THIRTY-SEVENTH LESSON.

The principal compound words are *nouns, adjectives, verbs.*

Observe that in a *compound* term resulting from the union of *two* simple nouns in the *nominative* case, or from that of a simple and derivative noun, the *second* part is the leading element, and that the first merely qualifies or defines the meaning of the second.

The declension and inflections of the compound term are, therefore, those peculiar to the second part; so is the gender also, unless the prefixed noun (as beaṅ, a woman, a female) be such as to point out a change.

Substantives compounded with other substantives in the nominative case:

Báṙṙ-tobaṙ, head fountain.

Bo-ṡuil cow-eye; from bo, a cow; and ṡuil, an eye.

Breuġ-ḟáiḋ, a false prophet.

Breuġ-ṙiġ, a pseudo-king; from breuġ, a lie, a false thing; and ṙiġ, a king.

Buṅ-ṡṙuṫ, a fountain, from buṅ, but, source, origin, root; and ṡṙuṫ, a stream.

Caṫ-báṙṙ, a helmet; from caṫ, a battle; and báṙṙ, the top, the head.

Ceaṙt-ṁeoḋaṅ, middle
Ceaṙt-láṙ, the very centre.

Claṗ-ṡoluṡ, twilight.

Cloġ-ṫeaċ, a belfry, a round tower; from cloġ, a bell; and ṫeaċ, a house.

Craoḃ-ḟleaṡġ, a garland; from craoḃ, a branch, a sprout; and ḟleaṡġ, a wreath, fillet.

Cul-ċaiṅt, back-biting; from cul, back; and caiṅt.

Feall-ḃeaṙt, an act of treachery.

Feaṙ-ioṅaḋ, a lieutenant, or vice-gerent; from feaṙ, a man; and ioṅaḋ, a place, a position—one who holds the place of another.

Fioṡ-ḟeaṙ, a messenger, an informant; from fioṡ, knowledge; and feaṙ, a man.

Caoiṙ-ḟeoil, mutton,	} Words compounded of ḟeoil,
Laoiġ-ḟeoil, veil,	and caoṙa, a sheep; laoġ,
Muic-ḟeoil, pork,	a calf; ṁuc, a pig; and
Maiṙt-ḟeoil, beef.	maṙt, a beef.

Láṁ-Ḋía, a household god, } From láṁ, a hand; and Ḋía,
Láṁ-euḃaċ, a handkerchief, a }   a god; euḃaċ, cloth; and
  napkin, }   oṁḃ, a sledge.
Láṁ-oṁḃ, a hand-sledge. }

Leaċ-ċoịr, one foot, } From leaċ, half, or one of
Leaċ-ṛʒeul, a half-story, an }   two; and coṛ, a foot; ṛʒeul,
  excuse, }   a story; ṛuịl, an eye: ċaoḃ,
Leaċ-ṛuịl, one eye, }   a side.
Leaċ-ċaoḃ, one side, }

  Oịʒ-ḃeaɲ, a maiden; from oịʒ, a virgin, and beaɲ, a
woman.

  Oịʒ-ḟeaṛ, a virginal youth.

  Óṛ-ṛlaċ, a sceptre; from óṛ, gold; and ṛlaċ, a rod, a wand.

  Ríʒ-ḟeaṛ, a very good man, a king in his way, from ríʒ
a king, and ḟeaṛ.

  Ċuaċ-ʒaoċ, north wind.

  Seaṛc-ʒṛaḃ, affection, love.

  Sịċ-ḟulaɲʒ, good temper, peaceful endurance; from ríċ,
peace; and ḟulaɲʒ, suffering.

  Ċeaṛ ʒṛaḃ, heat-love, zeal.

  Ċịṛ-ʒṛaḃ, patriotism, country-love.

  The prefix beaɲ, changes the gender, as,

Beaɲ-Ḋea, a goddess.

Beaɲ-Ḋeacuɲ, a deaconess.

Beaɲ-ɲaṁaḃ, a female foe.

Beaɲ-ɲaoṁ, a female saint.

Beaɲ-oʒlaċ, a female attendant.

Beaɲ-ṛịʒe, a witch; a fairy woman, a *bean-shighe*; from
beaɲ, and ṛịʒe, a sprite; root, ríʒ, a happy state.

  Beaɲ-ṛʒlaḃa, a female-slave.

  Beaɲ-ċịʒeaṛɲa, a lady; a woman-lord.

NOTE.—From combinations like the foregoing, for which the Keltic has,
from the earliest period, been remarkable, are derived some proper names
found in Cæsar; as, *Dumnorix*, world-king; from ḃoṁaịɲ, the world; and
ríʒ, king; and *Bituriges*, life-king; from bịċ, life, the world; and ríʒ, king;
Caturiges, battle-king.

  OBS. 1.—The following is a class of words which are by
many regarded as compounds, because their corresponding
terms in English are compound, but in our language are
simple words followed by the genitive case of a second
noun, which qualifies the meaning of the first; as,

Bρατ-ταιρe, a winding-sheet; from bρατ, and ταιρe, of death; poss. or gen. case.

Coρρ-móηαιḃ, a crane.

Deoᵹ, end, final issue; as, ϝα ḃeoᵹ, at last; τάιηιc ρe ϝα ḃeoᵹ, he came at last; ϝα ḃeιρe, αᵹuρ ϝα ḃeoᵹ, at length and at last. This word is compounded with lαe, the genitive case of lά; as, ḃeoᵹlαe (pr. *dyo-lae*), the decline or close of the day, the evening; τάιηιc ρe α ḃeoᵹlαe αηη ηαe, he came in the decline of (the day) yesterday; ḃeoᵹ-ϝlαιτ, the last prince: this word is misspelled τιuᵹ; as, τιuᵹ-ϝlαιτ, the last prince. Deoᵹ is not heard in the spoken language, except in the adverb, ϝα ḃeoᵹ, and in connexion with the word lαe, of a day; and oιḃċe, of a night; ḃeoᵹ-oιḃċe, far in the night, end of the night. The word ḃeιρe, end, is, at present, commonly employed in its stead.

Ϝeαρ-ceoιl, a man-of-music, a musician.

Ϝeαρ-ϝeαρα, a man-of-knowledge, a seer; ϝeαρα being the gen. case of ϝιoρ.

Ϝeαρ-τιᵹe, man-of-a-house, a householder.

Lαoċ-ceoιl, warrior-of-music.

Mαc-αllα, an echo (son-of-the-cliff).

Mαc-τιρe, a wolf (son-of-the-country).

Cu-mαρα, an otter (dog-of-the-sea).

Lαoᵹ-mαρα, a seal (calf-of-the-sea).

Teαċ-óρτα, a house of entertainment, an inn.

Now this latter class of compound words differs widely from the former: in these the principal part is the first; in those the principal part is the second: in these the second noun in the genitive case qualifies the meaning of the first. in those the first part qualifies the meaning of the second.

Other names of Keltic origin—as, *Orgetorix*, uρρα ᵹαċ-τοηuιρ, the stay-of-every-journey (and not, as some derive the word, " King of a Hundred Hills," *Cæsar*, edited by Anthon, p. 6); *Cingetorix*, Cιηη ᵹαċ-τοηuιρ, the head-of-every-journey; *Vergobret*, ϝeαρ-ᵹo-bρeατ, the man-for-judgment—are formed much after the same manner.

Adjectives with a Noun prefixed.

Bιċ-buαη, everlasting; from bιċ, life; and buαη, lasting.

Bιċ-ḃeo, sempiternal, everlasting.

Blαċ-ċumρα, blossom-sweet.

Ceaɲɲ-bàɲ, head-white (white-headed).
Ceaɲɲ-bàɲa, headstrong.
Ceaɲɲ-ṁoɲ, head-big, (large-headed).
Cor-luaċ, foot-swift, (swift-footed).
Coɲɲ-bàɲ, ⎫
Coɲɲ-ᵹlaɲ, ⎬ a stork; coɲɲ-ċoɲaċ, a cheslip

Verbs with Nouns prefixed.

Coɲ-ċeaɲᵹaɲl, to tie in a knot; from coɲ, a knot, a twist; and ceaɲᵹaɲl, to bind.

Cɲaob-ɲᵹaol, reveal; from cɲaob, a branch; and ɲᵹaol, to loose, to draw away; because when a branch is torn off a tree, the inner part is revealed.

Cɲaoɲb-bɲɲɲeaᵹ, to heart-break.

Cul-caɲɲaɲᵹ, to retract; from cul, the rear, the hinder part of anything; and caɲɲaɲᵹ, to draw to.

Sɲol-ċuɲ, to sow seed.

Ceaɲ-ᵹɲaᵹuɲᵹ, to be zealously loving of.

Compound words in which Adjectives are prefixed.

Aɲb, high, chief, supreme; as, aɲb-ɲɲᵹ, chief-king; aɲb-cɲᵹeaɲɲa, sovereign lord; aɲb-ɲéɲɱ, high power.

Buaɲ, enduring, lasting; as, buaɲ-ɲaoᵹalaċ, long-lived; buaɲ-ɲeaɲṁaċ, persevering.

Caoɲɲ, gentle; as, caoɲɲ-buċɲaċc, gentle sincerity.

Caoṁ, mild, tender; as, caoṁ-ᵹɲaᵹ, tender love; caoṁ-ċɲuċ, a slender, gentle form.

Claoɲ, inclined, partial; as, claoɲ-bɲeɲċ, partiality; from claoɲ, and bɲeɲċ, a judgment.

Cɲoɱ, crooked, bent; as, cɲoɱ-leaċ, *cromleac*, the druidical altar; from cɲoɱ, crooked, bent as it were in adoration; and leaċ, a flag, or rock.

Daoɲ, dear, condemned; as, baoɲ-bɲeaċ, condemnation.

Daoɲ-oᵹlàċ, a bond slave.

Deaᵹ, good; as, beaᵹ-buɲɲe, a good person.

Deaɲb, real, true; as, beaɲb-bɲaċaɲɲ, a (real) brother, one of the same father and mother; beaɲb-ɲɲuɲ, a sister; beaɲb is now commonly pronounced as if written beɲ, and to write it so is quite conformable to the practice of our ancient writers; as, beaɲċaoɲɲeaᵹ, sadness, lamentation;

from beaʄ, and caoıneaḋ, crying; beaʄṁóʄ, enormous; from beaʄ, and ṁóʄ, large.

Dıaŋ, vehement; as, dıaŋ-ʒʄaḋ, vehement love.

Dluċ, close, thick; as, dluċ-ʈaʄʄaıŋʒ, attract.

Dʄoċ, bad; as, dʄoċ-beuʄa, bad manners; dʄoċ-aıŋm, a bad name.

Fıoŋŋ, fair; as, ʄıoŋŋ-báʄʄ, fair-head; ʄıoŋŋ-ʄʒoċ, a white-flower; ʄıoŋŋ-ʄuaʄ, cool, cold, fresh; ʄıoŋŋ-báŋ, whitish.

Fıoʄ, true, pure; as, ʄıoʄ-uıʒe, spring-water, living water.

Ʒaʄḃ, rough; as, ʒaʄḃ-ʄıoŋ, a tempest.

Ʒeaʄʄ, short; as, ʒeaʄʄ-ʄıaḋ, a hare (a short wild animal).

Ʒlaŋ, clean; as, ʒlaŋ-cʄoıḋe, pure-heart.

Ʒlıŋŋ, clear; as, ʒlıŋŋ-ʄaḋaʄc, clear-sight.

Ṁaoċ, soft; as, maoċ-ʄeoıl, tender meat.

Ṁıoŋ, small, little; as, mıoŋ-áıʄŋeıʄ, small cattle; Ṁıoŋ ċaıʄʒ, small-Easter; low-Sunday; (Latin, *minus*; Greek μειῶν, less).

Ṁóʄ, great; as, móʄ-ċaıl, great fame.

Naoṁ, holy; as, naoṁ-aċaıʄ, holy father.

Nuaḋ, new; as, nuaḋ-duıŋe, an upstart.

Óʒ, young; as, óʒ-ʄeaʄ, a young man; óʒ-ṁaʄʈ, a young ox.

Pʄıoṁ, first, primal; as, pʄıoṁ-aḋḃaʄ, the first cause.

Saoḃ, silly, false; as, ʄaoḃ-ʄaıḋ, a false prophet; ʄaoḃ-apʈol, a false apostle; ʄaoḃ-ċıal, folly, silliness; from ʄaoḃ and cıal, sense.

Saoʄ, free; as, ʄaoʄ-ʄeılḃ, a free-hold; ʄaoʄ-ċoıl, free-will.

Seaŋ, old; as, ʄeaŋ-ʄeaʄ, an old man; ʄeaŋ-aoıʄ, old age; ʄeaŋ-ʄeaċʈ, old law.

Tʄeuŋ, bold, strong, mighty; as, ʈʄeuŋ-ʄeaʄ, a brave man; ʈʄeuŋ-laoċ, a hero.

Tʄom, heavy; as, ʈʄom-ċʄoıḋe, heavy-heart; ʈʄom ʄaıʒ, drink to the dregs (from ʈʄom and ʄaıʒ, squeeze); ʈʄom-luıḋe, the nightmare (from ʈʄom and luıḋe, lying).

Uaʄal, noble (uaʄ, high; aıl, educate); as, uaʄal-aċaıʄ, a patriarch.

Uıle, all; as, uıle-ċuṁaċʈaċ, Almighty; uıle-colʒaċ, all-knowing.

Compound words with Verbs prefixed are only few ; as,
Jċ-ɼompaᵭ, back-biting, slander.

Ꞇapɼanᵹ-aɼꞇ, a magnet , from ꞇapɼanᵹ, drawing ; and aɼꞇ, a mineral, a hard stone.

<h2 style="text-align:center">VOCABULARY.</h2>

2lɪɼ, for ᵭeɪɼ, says.
Caᵭ, what ?
Caᵭ aɼ, from what; wherefore.
Céaᵭna, same ; pronounced *céanna.*
Cɼɪċ, trembling (ꝼaoɪ, under).
Ceɪɼꞇ, the gen. case of ceaɼꞇ, justice.
Eᵹ-ceaɼꞇ, *m,* injustice; from e, and ceaɼꞇ; e causes c to be eclipsed by ᵹ; ɪ is sometimes inserted before ᵹ, and then the word is spelled eɪᵹceaɼꞇ.

Ꝺɼéɪm, *v,* to contend, to wrestle, to attempt.
Ꝺ' ꝼɼeaᵹaɪɼ, *v,* answered.
Ꝣlaoɪᵭ, *v,* called.
Ꞃaᵭaɪᵭ, a thief; from ᵹoɪᵭ, to steal.
Ꞅaluᵹaᵭ, to soil, to muddle; from ɼal, and ɼalaċ, dirty.

<h2 style="text-align:center">EXERCISE LXII.</h2>

<h3 style="text-align:center">THE WOLF AND THE LAMB.</h3>

2ɲ 2ḋaᵭaᵭ-alla aᵹuɼ aɲ ꞇ-Ꝇaɲ.

2ɲ ᵭo bɪ maᵭaᵭ-alla aɪᵹ ól ꝼɪoɼ-uɪɼᵹe aɪᵹ ceaɲɲ-ɼɼuꞇ, ᵭo ċoɲɲaɪɼc ɼe (he saw) uaɲ ɲɪoɼ ꝼaɪᵭe ɼɪoɼ aɪᵹ ól ᵭe 'ɲ ꞇ-ɼɼuꞇ ceaᵭɲa (of the same stream). Ꝺo ɼɪɲɲe ɼe ɼuɲ (he formed a resolution) ᵭɼeɪċ (to seize) aɪɼ aɲ uaɲ, aċꞇ buᵭ ṁaɪċ leɪɼ coɼaṁalaċꞇ céɪɼꞇ a ċuɼ aɪɼ a eᵹ-coɪɼ. Uɪme ɼɪɲ (therefore) ɼɪċ ɼe ɼɪoɼ aɪᵹ aɲ uaɲ aᵹuɼ ᵭubaɪɼꞇ: " 2 ᵹaᵭaɪᵭ, caᵭ aɼ a b-ꝼuɪlɪɼ a ɼaluᵹaᵭ aɲ uɪɼᵹe ꞇaɪm-ɼe aɪᵹ ól?" "Ꞃo ᵭeɪṁɪɲ," aɪɼ (says) aɲ ꞇ-uaɲ ᵹo h-uṁal. "Nɪ ꝼeɪcɪm cɼaɲɲoɼ a ᵭ-ꞇɪᵹ lɪom-ɼe aɲ ꞇ-uɪɼᵹe a ɼaluᵹaᵭ, a ꞇá aɪᵹ ɼɪċ uaɪꞇ-ɼe cuᵹaɲɲ-ɼe." "Ꞃɪᵭ ᵹo b-ꝼuɪl ɼe aṁlaɪᵭ," ᵭ' ꝼɼeaᵹaɪɼ aɲ maᵭaᵭ-alla. "Nɪ 'l ɼe aċꞇ blɪaᵹaɲ ó ᵹlaoɪᵭ ꞇu ᵭɼoċ-aɪɲɲe oɼm." "Oċ, a ᵭuɪɲe ċóɪɼ," ᵭubaɪɼꞇ aɲ ꞇ-uaɲ ꝼaoɪ ċɼɪċ. "Blɪaᵹaɲ ó ɼɪɲ ɲɪoɼ ɼuᵹaᵭ me." "2ḋaɪɼeaᵭ muɲa ɼaɪᵭ ꞇu-ɼa aɲɲ" ᵭ' ꝼɼeaᵹaɪɼ aɲ maᵭaᵭ-alla, "ɼe ᵭ' aċaɪɼ, a ᵹlaoɪᵭ oɼm ɼaᵭ, aᵹuɼ ɼe aɲ cáɼ ceaᵭɲa: aċꞇ nɪ'l aoɲ ᵹaɼ a ᵭɼéɪm mo lóɲ a buaɪɼꞇ ᵭɪom:" aᵹuɼ ᵹaɲ ꝼocaɪl eɪle ċuɪꞇ ɼe aɪɼ aɲ uaɲ bóċꞇ a bɪ ᵹaɲ cabaɪɼ (help) aᵹuɼ ɼꞇeul ɼe e ó ċeɪle.

Nɪ'l ꞇɪoɼaɲ (tyrant) ᵹaɲ leaċ-ɼᵹeul.

2ᵹuɼ nɪ b-ꝼuɪl aoɲ ᵹaɼ ᵭo ᵭuɪɲe ꝼɲɪopɼɪᵭ, ᵭeaᵹ-ċɼoɪᵭeaċ, a beɪċ aɪᵹ ᵭɼéɪm leɪɼ aɲ muɪɲꞇɪɼ eᵹcóɼɪeaċ a ꞇá aɲɲ aɲᵭ-ċeɪɲ.

KEY TO EXERCISES—

Eoċair na n-Ġnáṫuġaḋ.

TWENTY-FIFTH LESSON—

An Cuiġṁaḋ Leiġean air Fiċiḋ.

EXERCISE XXXIX.—An Naoiṁaḋ Ġnáṫuġaḋ deuġ air Fiċiḋ.

1. b-Ḟuil nuaḋaċt air biṫ "aġaḋ?"* 2. Ní b-ḟuil nuaḋaċt air biṫ "aġam." 3. b-Ḟuil nuaḋaċt "aiġ" d' aċain? 4. Ní'l (for ní b-ḟuil) nuaḋaċt "aiġ" m' aċain; ní'l nuaḋaċt air biṫ "aġainn-ne" a tá 'nn an ġ-coṁnuiḋe 'r an tuaiṫ; ir cóir "daoiḃ"† a tá 'r an m-baile móir, ʒo m-beiḋeaḋ nuaḋaċt ʒaċ aon lae "aġaiḃ?" 5. An ċualair air an ʒ-coʒaḋ ṁilteaċ ro atá dul aiʒ cur na h-Eunoipe faoi creaċaḋ? 6. ʒo cinte ċualar: do cluinʒeaḋ a ġéim ní ḟe amain triḃ an tir, aċt do ġáin a ṁac-alla ann ʒaċ laʒ aʒur ʒlean, aʒur cluan ó Binn-Eḋair, ʒo ceann Iarruir. 7. An doiʒ ʒo b-tiocḟaiḋ a

* The words within inverted commas are those which form the special subject of the *Lesson*. The learner should, for that reason, pay particular attention to them. Each Exercise is fashioned chiefly with the view of exhibiting, in a practical way, the leading features of all that has been explained in the Lesson to which it is annexed.

† Observe the difference in sound and meaning between the prepositional pronouns daoiḃ (*dhuee-iv*, pr. in one syllable), *to you*; díḃ (*dheev*), *of you*; dóiḃ (*dhō-iv*), *to them*; díoḃ (*dhee-iv*, pr. in one syllable), *of them*; sometimes written díoḃta. The first, daoiḃ, *to you*, is second person plural, compounded of the preposition do, and riḃ, or iḃ (old form), you. The learner will notice that the broad vowels, a, o, come after d, because o in do, the preposition with which it is compounded, is broad—thus, at first, do-iḃ, and then subsequently it assumed the present spelling, daoiḃ. The second, díḃ, *of you*, is compounded of de, of, and iḃ; e of de is a slender vowel; hence díḃ, í being pronounced long, like *ee*. dóiḃ = "do" iad, to them. díoḃ = "de" iad, of them.

laṗaiṁ "cuᵹaɲɲ-ɲe?" 8. Ní b-ꝥuil imṁiḋe aṁ biṫ "oꝥm" ᵹo b-ꞇiocꝥaiḋ. 9. Ꞇá imṁiḋe "aꞃ" ɲo ḋeaꞃb-bꞃáṫaiꞃiḃ, Seamuꞃ aᵹuꞃ Uilléam, ᵹo b-ꞇiocꝥaiḋ. 10. ᵹo ɖeiṁiɲ ɲi cóiꞃ ᵹo m-beiḋeaḋ imṁiḋe aꞃ biṫ "oꞃꞃa." 11. Ɖubaiꞃꞇ miꞃe ꞃiɲ, aᵹuꞃ ᵹuꞃ cóiꞃ ɖoiḃ, ᵹo m-beiḋeaḋ cꞃoḋaċꞇ "ioɲɲꞇa." 12. Ḃ-ꝥuil ꝥaiꞇċioꞃ "oꞃꞇ-ꞃa?" 13. Ní b-ꝥuil ꝥaiꞇċioꞃ "oꞃm;" ɲi ꞃaiḃ a ꞃiaṁ, aᵹuꞃ ɲi beiḋ a coiḋċe. 14. Ḃ-ꝥuil ꝥaiꞇċioꞃ "aꞃ" ɖ' aṫaiꞃ aᵹuꞃ "aꞃ" ɖo ċol-ceaṫaꞃaiḃ? 15. Ní b-ꝥuil; ꞇá ioɲɲꞇa aɲ ꞇꞃeuɲaꞃ uɖ iꞃ ɖual ɖo ċlaɲ Ᵹeaꞃailꞇ a ṫaiꞃbeaɲaḋ. 16. Cia ꝥiaḋ ɲa h-aɲɖċuꞃaċꞇa a ꞇá aiᵹ coṁꞃaċ 'ꞃ aɲ coᵹaḋ ꞃo? 17. Aɲ Ꝥꞃaiɲc; aᵹuꞃ aɲ Saɲɖiɲia aᵹuꞃ Joꞇaille ó ꞇuaiḋ, aꞃ aoɲ ꞇaob; Auꞃꞇꞃia aꞃ aɲ ꞇaoḃ eile. 18. Caɖ é aɲ ꞇ-aḋbaꞃ coᵹaiḋ ꞇá "eaꞇꞃa?" 19. Ɖuil aꞃ aoɲ ꞇaoḃ le ꞃaoꞃꞃaċꞇ ꝥáᵹail, aᵹuꞃ le ceaɲɲaꞃ a ċoɲᵹbail aꞃ aɲ ꞇaoḃ eile. 20. Naċ móꞃ aɲ ꞃciuꞃꞃa aꞃ aɲ ciɲɲe ɖaoɲa, coᵹaḋ? 21. Iꞃ móꞃ ᵹo ɖeiṁiɲ. 22. Naċ áluiɲ aɲ ɲiḋ ꞃioꞇċaiɲ! 23. Oċ, ꞃeaḋ, ᵹo ɖeiṁiɲ iꞃ aɲ-áluiɲ í; ɲi'l ꝥioꞃ "aᵹaiɲɲ" aꞃ a luaċ, ɲo ᵹo b-ꝥeiꞃꞇuiḃ aɲ ꞇ-áꞃ a ṫaᵹaꞃ le coᵹaḋ. 24. Iꞃ miaɲ liom ꞃioꞇ-ċaiɲ ᵹo h-aɲṁóꞃ. 25. Na biḋeaḋ ꝥaiꞇċioꞃ oꞃꞇ ꝥaoi 'ɲ ᵹ-coᵹaḋ ꞃo. 26. Ní'l ꝥaiꞇċioꞃ oꞃm, óiꞃ cuiꞃim mo ḋoċċuꞃ aɲɲ Ɖia ɲa ᵹ-caꞇ, aᵹuꞃ aɲɲ Ɖia ɲa ꞃiꞇ, aᵹuꞃ ᵹlacaim ó ɲ-a láṁaiḃ ꞃioꞇċaiɲ, ɲo coᵹaḋ ꞃeiꞃ maꞃ iꞃ ꞇoil leiꞃ. 27. Ꝥeicim ᵹuꞃ ɖuiɲe ꝥioꞃ-eaᵹɲaċ ꞇu a ɲeiꞇiḃ aɲ ꞇ-ꞃaoᵹail ꞃo aᵹuꞃ aɲɲ ɲeiꞇiḃ aɲ ꞇ-ꞃaoᵹail eile. 28. Na mol mé ma 'ꞃ ꞃo ɖo ċoil é. 29. Ní ṁolꝥaḋ; ɲi ɖeiꞃim aċꞇ aɲ ꝥiꞃiɲe. 30. Beaɲɲaċꞇ leaꞇ. 31. ᵹo ꞃaiḃ maiṫ aᵹaɖ.

TWENTY-SIXTH LESSON—
AN SEISEAḊ IÉIᵹEAN AIR ꝤIĊIƉ.

EXERCISE XL.—AN CCAṪꞃAĊAɖAḊ ᵹNAṪUᵹAḊ.

Ꞃiobaꞃɖ aᵹuꞃ Aiċael.

1. Aɲ "liom-ꞃa" é ꞃo, ɲo "leaꞇ-ꞃa?" 2. Ní "liom-ꞃe" é, ɲo "leaꞇ-ꞃá;" iꞃ "le" m' aṫaiꞃ é. 3. Aꞃ aɲ aḋbaꞃ ꞃiɲ, iꞃ "leaꞇ-ꞃa" é, óiꞃ iꞃ "leaꞇ-ꞃa" aɲ meuɖ a

bαιηεαρ le ϑ' αċαιρ. 4. Naċ mαc "leιρ" ϝéιη τu-ρα?
5. Ιρ mαc "leιρ ϝéιϑ" miρε. 6. Sαṁluιξεαηη τu ξuρ
ραbαιρ "leατ ϝειη" αη τρáċ-ηóηα ρο. 7. Ϛο ϑειṁιη
biϑċαρ liom ϝειη ηo ξuρ ċαιηιc τuρα, buιϑεαċαρ buιτ
ϝαoι ϑo ċαραϑαρ. 8. Nι mαιċ liom ηαρ b' ϝειϑιρ liom
τεαċτ, τραċ-ηóηα α ηαε αιξ ϑáιl ϑo ċαιρϑε. 9. Nιoρ
mαιċ liom-ρε ϝρε ριη (ϝρε is an old preposition, the same
as ρε or le, *with;* ϝρε ριη means *along with that, besides,
moreover*), óιρ bι αη ξ-cαιρϑε uιle "liηη," τuρα αṁαιη
ϑε'η ιomláη ηαċ ραιb liηη. 10. Cα uαιρ αη bριρ αη ϑáιl
ρuαρ? 11. Nιoρ bριρ ρι ρuαρ ξo b-τι αη cεαċαιρ ϑε
ċloξ αιρ mαιϑιη αηη ιuϑ. 12. 2ιη le ϑ' αċαιρ αη τεαċ
ρο? 13. Nι "leιρ;" αċτ "liom-ρα" óιρ ϑ' ϝáξ mo mα-
ċαιρ-ṁóρ αη buϑ leιċε ε, αξαm-ρα é, ιρ liom-ρα αηoιρ e.
14. 2ιρ ϝáξ ρι ηα τιξċε, αη muιliη, αη ϝειlm, αξuρ αη
αιρηéιρ αξαϑ-ρα? 15. Nιoρ ϝáξ; ηι "liom-ρα" ιαϑ ρo,
ιρ le Sεαmuρ O'Bριαιη mo ċol-ċεαċαιρ ιαϑ. 16. 2ċτ cια
αρ leιρ ηα bα, αξuρ ηα cαραιl, αξuρ ηα cαoραιξ uιle αιρ
αη b-ϝειlm eιle? 17. Ιρ le mo ϑεαρbρáċαιρ Sτεϝαη ιαϑ
uιle: ιρ leιρ ηα bα; ιρ leιρ ηα cαραιl, ιρ leιρ ηα ϑαιṁ;
ηα muιliϑ αξuρ ηα h-αραιl, ηα cαoραξ αξuρ ηα ξαbαιρ,
ηα h-εuηlαιċ mαρ ατá ξεαϑα, lαċαη, Fραηcαιξε, cεαρcα,
coιliξ: ιρ leιρ αη τ-ιomlαη. 18. b-Fuιl mιle ϑαṁ αιξε?
19. Ϛo ϑειṁιη, α τá αξuρ b' ϝειϑιρ τuιle. 20. "Cια
leιρ" αη buαċαιll óξ ρο ċαll? 21. Ιρ le mo ϑεαρbρáċαιρ
é, buαċαιll mαιċ, αξuρ αηcoραṁαιl le η-α αċαιρ. 22.
"Cια αιξ" α b-ϝuιl αη ṁéιϑ αιιξιϑ ϑo ċρuιηηιξ ϑ' αċαιρ-
ṁóρ? 23. Fαξαϑ ιomlαη αη αιιξειϑ, τιmċιoll mιle ρuητα,
αιξ mo ϑεαρb-ϝιuρ 2ηηα. 24. Dεαηϝαιϑ ρε ρρηé ϑεαρ
ϑι. 25. Dεαηϝαιϑ ξo ϑειṁιη. 26. Naċ b-ϝuιl ρι ϑul α
ρoραϑ, αη ṁι ρo—mι áluιη ηα Bεαl-τειηε? 27. Nι'l; ιρ
ϝειϑιρ leιċε, αċτ ċuιρ ρι αη ρoραϑ αιρ ċul ξo τoιρεαċ
αη ṁι ρo ċuξαιηη, o'η τ-ρεαη-bαραṁαιl ραξαηαιξ ατα
ϝóρ αmεαρξ ηα η-ϑαoιηε ηαċ b-ϝuιl ρε ρoηα ρoραϑ α ṁι
ηα Bεál-τειηε. 28. 2η ṁι αιρ α b-ϝuιl ηα ϝιλιϑ ξo ριoη
αιξ ϑεαηαϑ ραηη—αη ṁι ιρ ρulṁαιρε ϑε ṁιoραιϑ ηα
bliαξαηα, 'ηuαιρ α cuιρεαηη αη cρuιηηε αξuρ αη ρρειη,
le η-αρ m-bριεηξαϑ αιξ ηειċε τáιρε αη τ-ραoξαιl ρo, α
ξ-collαιϑ ιρ úρα oρρτα, αξuρ αmαρcαηρ ξo ρξιαṁαċ, ρεuη-
mαρ αṁαιl α'ρ αιξ ραϑ le ριol 2ϑαιṁ—"Bιoιϑ ρubαċ."

Ir rí mí Ṁáirne ī—mí a tá lán be beaṅṅaċtaiḃ do ʒaċ
uile leaṅḃ aiʒ a ḃ-ḟuil ʒráḋ aiṟ ṁáċaiṟ ċo ceaṅaṁail.
28. Ḃ-Ḟuil ḟíor aiʒ do ḋearḃ-ḟiuṟ aiṟ an ṁéiḋ ro?
29. Tá ḟíor; aċt maṟ ʒo leor a ṅeiċiḃ de'ṅ t-raṁail
ro, leaṅaṅṅ rí taiṅt raob-ḃaṅ aʒur cuiṟeaṅṅ aiṟ leiċ ciall
aʒur tuiʒriṅt. 31. Aḃaiṟ, ma 'r re do ċoil é, aṅ ṁéiḋ
a duḃaiṟt miṟe. 32. Ḋéaṅḟaḋ; aċt ṅí'l aoṅ ʒaṅ aṅṅ.
33. Slaṅ leat.

TWENTY-SEVENTH LESSON—
aN SeaċTṁaḋ LeiʒeaN aiR ḞiċiḊ.

EXERCISE XLI.—aN T-aoNṁaḋ ʒNaTuʒaḋ aiR ḋa Ḟiċeaḋ.

Ṁarʒaṁéaḋ, Eliraḃet, aʒur a (her) dearḃṟiuṟ.

1. Aṅ "maiċ leat" riuḃal, a ċara mo ċroiḋe? 2. Ir
"maiċ liom" riuḃal; aċt iṅṅir dam a "ḋ-tiʒ-liṅṅ" riuḃal
ċríḋ na macaiṟiḃ; óiṟ leir aṅ ḟiṟiṅe a ráḋ leat, ṅí
riuḃalḟaḋ aiṟ aṅ m-boċaṟ ṁóṟ? 3. Seaḋ, "tiʒ liṅṅ,"
óiṟ ṅí'l druċt, ṅo ḟeaṟtaiṅ aiṟ aṅ ḃ-ḟeuṟ. 4. "Ir dear
liom" riuḃal ċríḋ na macaiṟiḃ. 5. Aṅ "ḟeaṟṟ leat-ra"
na paiṟtce na aṅ boċaṟ? 6. Ir "ḟeaṟṟ liom." 7. Aṅ
dear leat riuḃal amaċ aiṟ tṟáċ na maidne (pr. *maynh-
ne*—ḋn = double ṅ in sound). 8. Ṅí "dear liom," ir "deiṟe
liom" riuḃal amaċ aṅ tṟáċ-ṅona. 9. B' ḟeidiṟ ʒuṟ "ṁaiċ
le" do dearḃ-ḟiuṟ ċéaċt liṅṅ aʒur blaċa ṅo rcoċa a
buaiṅt. 10. Ṅí "tiʒ leiċe" ċéaċt. 11. Ḟeuċ, b'ḟeidiṟ
ʒo "ḋ-tiʒ." 12. ʒo ciṅte ṅí "maiċ liom" í ḟáʒail "leiċe
ḟéiṅ," cailíṅ ċo áluiṅ a'r tá rí. 13. Ḋeiṟ rí ʒuṟ "maiċ
leiċe" ċéaċt, aċt naċ "ḟeidiṟ leiċe," muṅa ḃ-ḟáʒaiḋ tura ceaḋ. 14. "Tiʒ liom" ḟéiṅ ceaḋ a ċaḃaiṟt ḋi. 15.
Tá ʒo maiċ, ta me ciṅte ʒuṟ "ḟeaṟṟ leiċe" ċeaċt 'na
ḟaṅaċt. 16. "B' ḟeaṟṟ liom-ra" ḟéiṅ ʒo ḋ-tiocḟaḋ rí.
17. Aṅ dual ḋí ḟaṅaċt 'r aṅ m-baile? 18. Ṅí dual,
leir aṅ ḟiṟiṅe 'ráḋ; ir "ʒṅaċaċ leiċe" beiċ a ʒ-cuideaċt
a dearḃṟiuṟ. 19. Oċ naċ áluiṅ amaṟcaṅṅ na macaiṟiḃ,
naċ áluiṅ; ḟeuċ na ṅoiṅíṅiḃ, aṅ ċíme ḟiaḋaiṅ, na ḟeiċ-
leoʒa, aʒur na blaċa ḟiaḋaṅa uile; naċ dear aṅ ḟleaṟʒ-

craoḃ fiġfiḋ (I shall weave) do mo ṁaċair. 20. Tá
ionġa air an leinḃ ud faoi ġaċ niḋ nuaḋ feiceann sí. 21.
A ḋearḃ-ṡiúir ḋil, "an áil leat" rósa fiaḋana ċruinnuġaḋ;
agus deanfamuiḋ fleasg ḋioḃ? 22. Buain scoṫa agus
rósa tu féin, a ċailín, mar is "áil leat." 23. a
Ṁarġairéaḋ, an "fearr leat-sa" an samraḋ, na raiṫe
air biṫ eile de'n m-bliaġain? 24. Is "fearr liom;"
óir ní ṫe amain go d-tiġ le neaċ dul ċriḋ na maċairiḋ
níos fusa annis an am sin, 'na air feaḋamsair biṫ eile,
aċt amarcann na goirt agus gaċ niḋ fa ċuairt go sgia-
maċ. 25. Is fíor sin; aċt cad é do ṁear air traṫ an
foġṁair, an foġṁair aoibin 'nuair táiḋ na torṫa uile
apuiḋe? 26. Tá fíor agam gur aimsir aoibin i; aċt
ní taiṫneaṁaċ an smuaineaḋ, go b-fuiliḋ na laeṫe breaġa
ṫart, agus go b-fuiliḋ grean agus sugraḋ na bliaġna
ann gar a beiṫ caiṫte. 27. Ṁaireaḋ, ċailin mo ċleiḃe,
naċ b-fuil fíor agad gur amlaiḋ ta an saoġal—uair
faoi ġnéin agus uair faoi síon; anois an samraḋ, arís
an geamraḋ; aċt gaċ duine do réir a ṁiain. 28. An
"cuimne leat" an sugraḋ agus an grean bi againn an
samraḋ ro ċuaiḋ ṫart, taoḃ an fairrge air an Traiġ-
móir? 29. Is "cuimne liom" go maiṫ. 30. Ḋearḃaim
duit go b-fuilmiḋ aig teaċ mo ċol-ceaṫair; an "áil
leat" a teaċt arteaċ? 31. Raċfaḋ agus failte.

TWENTY-EIGHTH LESSON—
AN T-OCTṀAḊ LEIĠEAN AIR FIĊID.

EXERCISE XLII.—AN DÓṀAḊ ĠNAṪUĠAḊ AIR DA FIĊID.

1. Tá airgead agad, aċt an leat féin é? 2. Tá
airgead agan, aċt ní liom féin é. 3. Tá talaṁ aig
m' aṫair aċt ní leir féin í. 4. Tá teaċ aig mo ṁaṫair
aċt ní leiṫe féin é. 5. Bídeann airgead aig mo ḋearḃ-
braṫair, aċt ní leir féin é. 6. B-fuil leabar aig do
ḋearḃ-ṡiur naċ leiṫe féin? 7. Níl aig mo ḋearḃ-ṡiur
leabar naċ leiṫe féin. 8. Táid aig tiġearna na talṁan
treuda—ba, capaill, caoraiġ agus gaḃair, aċt ní leir

féin iad. 9. Tá an talaṁ so maiṫ, aċt ní linn féin í.
10. Leis an fírinne a ráḋ, ní linn féin niḋ air biṫ.

EXERCISE XLIII.—an tríṁaḋ gnáṫuġaḋ air dá fiċead.

1. Whose is this town? 2. It belongs to the lord. 3. Whose is this country? 4. It belongs to the people of Ireland. 5. Whose is this land? 6. It is mine. 7. Is it not your father's? 8. It is not. 9. Whose are the cows and the sheep, the land and the beach? 10. They belong to the lord of the soil. 11. Whose is this calf? 12. It belongs to the owner of the cow, as the adáge says. 13. Thanks to you, I know that to the owner of the cow the calf belongs. 14. But whose is the cow; does she belong to your brother? 15. She does. 16. Whose is this stripling? 17. Is he the son of the gardener, or of the *man of the big house?* 18. He is the son of the gardener. 19. He is a good young man.

EXERCISE XLIV.—an ceaṫaraṁaḋ gnáṫuġaḋ air dá fiċead.

1. Cia leis an bairréad so? 2. Liom-sa. 3. Cia leis an teaċ so? 4. Le Seáġan. 5. Cia leis an sgian so? 6. Le Sinéad. 7. Cia leis an peann so? 8. Cia leis an paipéir so? 9. Cia leis an duḃaċ so? 10. Cia leis an dubaḋan so? 11. Cia leis an sláta so? 12. Cia leis an cleite sin? 13. Cia leis an capal so tá aig Seamus? 14. Cia leis an ċosaṁlaċt so? 15. Cia be an iomaiġ so? 16. Cia "air" b-fuil an stáir so? 17. Cia "leis" an leabar stáire so? 18. Cia leis an arán so? 19. Cia leis an feoil so? 20. Cia leis an cú sin? 21. Is le m'aṫair í. 22. Cia leis an madaḋ uḋ aġus an ṁiol-ċu sin, aġus an madaḋ uisge uḋ tá aġaḋ-sa? 23. Ní leat-sa iad. 24. An siubalfaiḋ tu liom, má 's re do ṫoil é, air bruaċ na h-aḃaine so? 25. Siubalfaḋ. 26. An b-feiceann tu an conn tall air bruaċ na linne? 27. Feicim. 28. Feicim gioirrfiaiḋ, aġus coinínió, aġus coinn glasa, aġus coinn bána go h-uile ann so; is siamraċ an áit í; cia leis í? 29. Is le ceanfairt na Laiġean í. 30. Tá me buiḋeaċ duit faoi do ḋeaġ-ḟreastal, aċt is eigin dam dul go baile Áṫa-cliaṫ a nóċt. 31. Tá se ann am imṫeaċta.

TWENTY-NINTH LESSON—
an naoṁaḋ ʒnáṫuʒaḋ air ḟíċiḋ.

EXERCISE XLV.—an cuʒaḋ ʒnáṫuʒaḋ air ba ḟċċaḋ.

1. It is good *for you* to be poor, though you do not think it good (literally, though it is not good *with you*). 2. It is good *with me* (I consider it good) to be here, though it is not good *for me*. 3. Is it good *with you* (do you like) to come *with me?* 4. It is not good *with me* (I do not like) to go *with you*, although perhaps it were good *for me*. 5. Was it good *with your father* (did your father like) to die? 6. It was not good *with him*, nor *with us* (neither he nor we liked it), though it would be good *for many* if he should die. 7. Every person *considers* it *hard* to leave this miserable world. 8. It is *hard with* the poor (the poor think it a hard thing), and it is hard with the rich. 9. It is hard *for* the rich man to go to heaven, though it is not hard *with him* (does not consider it hard). 10. Is it ill *with you* (*i.e.*, do you bear ill the fact) that your neighbour is rich? 11. It is not ill with me (I do not bear it ill), but certainly it is ill *for me*, for he will exercise violence on myself and on my household. 12. It is ill with George (George bears it ill) that his enemy has died, although there is no good for him in it. 13. For ill *on me* (to spite me) my boy (servant man) committed theft, because I considered it ill that he had been along with us. 14. Speak to him (make conversation with him). 15. I wish to speak with him, but it is not good *for* me to speak *with* him. 16. Are you friendly (disposed) towards him? 17. I am friendly disposed towards him, although I am not friendly *with* him. 18. Do not be so. 19. I shall not (be).

EXERCISE XLVI.—an seisċaḋ ʒnáṫuʒaḋ air ba ḟċċaḋ.

1. Amarc air an iar. 2. Amarcaim. 3. Naċ bearʒ tá an ʒrian anoir 'nuair tá rí le bal faoi. 4. Oċ, tá rí (ʒrian, the sun, is fem. gen. in Irish) le féicrin faoi lonnaḋ aʒur faoi ʒlóir móir an traċ-nóna ro. 5. Amarcann an ṁuir a beiċ air teine. 6. ʒo beiṁir aṁar-

cann. 7. B-ḟuil do ċarad an ḋiallacóir le dul go America? 8. Tá sé le dul an t-seaċt-ṁain so. 9. Go deiṁin. 10. Iongantaċ "le ráḋ," saoil me naċ raċaḋ sé a coióċe ann. 11. Tá saoṫruġaḋ "beagán le faġail" 'na laeṫiḃ so. 12. B-ḟuil a ċeird dona? 13. Ní maiċ i le cairce a saoṫruġaḋ go tapaiḋ. 14. B-ḟuil tu-sa le dul a m-baile a noċt? 15. Tá me le dul. 16. Naċ mal e le dul? 17. Ní'l; ni b-ḟuil se mal, óir is dual ḋam-sa airoir a ḋeanaḋ 'san oióċe ċar sin tá an geallaċ le eirġaḋ. 18. Béirim coṁairle duit gan a dul, óir is mo baraṁail i go m-beiḋ scoirm againn. 19. Si mo baraṁail-se naċ m-beiḋ. 20. Naċ ḟeiceann tu ċo dearg a's tá an speur? 21. B-ḟuil deargar 'san speur tuar scoirme le téaċt. 22. Tá. 23. Ṁaire, is cuma liom taob na tuar so; is mian liom an seanraḋ a deirsear linn, gan meas a beiċ againn air tuaraiḋ. 24. Bioeaḋ do ċoil ḟéin agaḋ.

THIRTIETH LESSON—
AN TRIOĊADAḊ LÉIGEAN.

EXERCISE XLVII.—AN SEAĊTṀAḊ GNÁĊUGAḊ AIR DA ḞIĊEAD.

1. Ṁaire, a Ṡeáġain ca b-ḟuil tu aig dul? 2. Tá me aig dul ċum an báile. 3. Agus cia sé so aig siubal "romat?" 4. M' oglaċ Uilleam. 5. Cia an uair "roime so" páib tu aig an m-báile? 6. Níor raib me "roime so" aig baile le bliaġanta. 7. Cia tá "romat" anoir 'san m-báile? 8. Ní'l aon de mo ċaradaiḃ "romam" le failte ċabairt dam; táib uile marb, m' aċair agus mo ṁaċair, mo braċair, agus mo dearbṡiura, uile imiġte. 9. Is brónaċ go deiṁin cuiṁnuġaḋ air so. 10. Ní cóir duinn beiċ faoi brón air bár an g-carad, óir tá an bár "romainn" uile. 11. Is saoi mór tu. 12. Tá me buiḋeaċ duit; feuċ me ann so, agus an doman mór "romam" sonar, no donar "romam," an bár agus an t-sioṛruiḋeaċt "romam;" tá agam fór croiḋe lán de doċur agus de ṁirneaċ, mar geall go b-ḟuil go ríon or mo ċomair (continually in my view) dliġe Dé agus a

ġráḋ naoṁṫa. 13. Buḋ maiṫ liom ḃa m-beiḋeaḋ aig ġaċ ḋuine iaḃ rin "or a ċomair." 14. Bí aig na naoiṁ, mar na h-Juḃaiḋṫe 'r an t-reannaċt, ḋliġe Dé or a ġ-comair. 15. Naċ cóir ḋuinn, mar an ġ-ceaḋna é a beiṫ or an ġ-comair. 16. Saoilim ġo b-fuil tu ceart.

EXERCISE XLVIII.—AN T-OĊTṁAḊ ȝNÁĊUȝAḊ. AIR DÁ-FIĊEAḊ.

A conversation between a neighbour and a poor sick man.

1. You are welcome (welcome *before* you), a hundred thousand welcomes *before* you, friend of my heart. 2. May good be to you (thanks to you), my good Sir: I see that you are here *alone*. 3. Indeed I am here *alone*, as poor and as bare as Job, without anything to put *under me* or *over me*. 4. Why are you so poor and so bare; where are the friends you had, where are your own people, who were fond of you, and where is your relative, David Brown? 5. If David were with me now, I should not be as I am, but there is no help for it; he went *from me*, across the great sea, to a land that is free, and he has left me, like Ossian, after the Fenians: "An old man, stricken in years, decrepid, grey, without food, without clothing, without music." 6. Sad is your case, and poor are you: but still have you not land and herds; or, if you have not, you have money, for you amongst your relatives were wealthy. 7. It is true there was a time when I was wealthy, held in esteem, and in great repute, but that time is now *over* (*me*); the herds have gone *from me*; I lost the money I had; my master took my land *from me*; I fell into sickness, and now I am weak, poor, feeble, forlorn, far in years advanced. 8. Can I do anything at all that would be a comfort to you? 9. It is a comfort to me that you have come to me, for it is not everybody that comes to hold a conversation with a person who is poor, for as the proverb says: "He who is up is toasted; he who is down is trampled upon." 10. You are not down yet, for if you lost your money, and if your people have gone *from you* (forsaken you), you have not lost reputation, and your fame has not passed away. 11. That is true; my health too is returning, and as you yourself often said, "health is better than wealth;" and with regard to my money, I care

not whether it is *with me* or *from me.* 12. You are as every person ought to be, possessed of sense, and accepting everything (as coming) from the hand of God. 13. Your discourse gives (*to*) *me* great solace. 14. Upon my word to you, when I heard that you were under affliction, the intelligence went *through me* (affected me) greatly. 15. I do not wonder. 16. I have for you now a new suit; put this coat *about* you; put this cloak on your shoulders, and come *with me.* 17. I return you thanks from my heart, and that you may be a year from this day (this time twelve months) seven (fold) better.

THIRTY-FIRST LESSON—
An t-Aonṁaḋ Leiġeaṅ Ḋeuġ air Fiċiḋ.

The Forty-ninth Exercise is already sufficiently explained, for many passages are translated in the body of the text.

EXERCISE L.—An Cloẋaḋaḋ Ġnáċuġaḋ; OR, An Deiċeaḋ Ġnáċuġaḋ air Dá Fiċeaḋ.

1. How much do I owe, master (literally, how much is *on me*), for I wish to pay my debts? 2. You owe a hundred pounds (a hundred pounds is on you). 3. It is not much. 4. Do you like to pay the debts of any other person? 5. I do like. 6. How much does my father owe? 7. Two hundred pounds. 8. How much does my brother owe? 9. A year's rent, and the price of five score sheep. 10. How much is that? 11. About five hundred pounds. 12. If I (shall) pay all the debts that are *on us*, there will be for you near (to) a thousand pounds to get. 13. There will indeed. 14. You ought to act as the steward acted, of whom we read in the Gospel. 15. What (how) is that? 16. Do you not know? have you not read it often? 17. Although I even heard it, I like to hear it again. 18. There was a rich man who had a steward, and there came a charge against him (a charge was brought against him) that he squandered his (master's) substance. And his lord summoned him, and said with (to) him: What is this I hear of you? give an account of your stewardship. 19. But what did the steward do? 20. He called together the parties

that were in debt, and he said to the first person, "How much do you owe my lord?" (literally, how much has my lord on you). And the man replied, "A hundred barrels of oil." He said, "Take thy pen and write fifty barrels." And he said to the second man, "And you, how much do *you* owe? Who says, "A hundred measures of wheat." "Make (of) it four score," says he. The Lord praises this steward: now will you act towards me as he acted towards those who owed the debt? 21. Thanks for your Scripture (information), yet I will not act according to your request. 22. I pay then all that is on myself and on my friends (all that I and my friends owe).

THIRTY-SECOND LESSON—
an ḋara leiġean aiṙ triocaḋ.

EXERCISE LI.—an t-aonṁaḋ ṡnátuġaḋ aiṙ ċaoġaḋ.

1. Is this cloth? (literally, whether cloth it, this?—the verb iṡ being omitted before the pronoun e, as is usual in short assertive or interrogative sentences). 2. Yes. 3. How much have you *on it*—*i.e.*, what price have you set on it? what is its price? how is it sold? 4. Fourteen shillings per yard. 5. It is dear; it is not worth that. 6. Indeed it is worth that, and it is even cheap at that price. 7. Have you (cloth of) satin or (of) silk? 8. I have—literally, (it) is; *to me* being understood. 9. How much do you sell it at? 10. Two pounds for the yard (per yard). 11. It is cheap for that. 12. Do you wish to buy it? 13. I do; cut of it two yards and a half. 14. Have you other wares? 15. I have, in that side yonder of the shop. 16. I intend to procure (make a purchase of) tea and sugar; for how much do you sell the sugar. 17. There are five shillings the pound for tea, and six pence the pound for sugar. 18. That is dear; I shall not give that much (price) for the tea; the sugar is sufficiently cheap; take then four shillings and six pence for the tea. 12. Well, whereas it is customary with you to come to me, have it (let it be to you) for that;

but, upon my word to you, it is cheap; and were it not that it is yourself who are there, I would not give it you at that price. 20. May good be (I am much obliged) to you, and I am thankful to you. 21. What is this you have (got) in the barrel? 22. Wine. 23. What kind of wine is it— Spanish wine or French wine, white wine or red wine, Champagne or the contrary? 24. It is only ordinary red wine, and it is three shillings a bottle. 25. I shall not buy it; wine is dear in this country; I wish I were in France. 26. Perhaps it is better for you to be here at home. 27. Have we a good harvest this year? 28. We have. 29. Is oats dear, and is wheat? 30. They are. 31. How much is for barley; (how much) for rye? 32. They are cheap. 33. Shall we have a drink since we are together? 34. We will. 35. What do you like—a goblet of wine or a bowl of punch? 36. I shall have the goblet of wine. 37. Is not a bowl (glass or tumbler) of punch better, for I like to "send round the bowl." 38. I prefer the wine. 39. Have it so; a man's support (is) his will.

EXERCISE LII.—An bóiḋeaḋ ġnáṫuġaḋ air ċuoṫaḋ.

1 A Ṡaoi an ónóir fíon ól liom (the phrase ḃéan, or ḃron orm, is understood). 2. Le fonn, a Ṡaoi. 3. Cia aca is fearr leat, an fíon bearg no an fíon fíonn? 4. Is fearr liom an fíon fíonn 'na an fíon bearg. 5. Ḋéan dam cineáltas fíon ól liom, a ḃean uarail: líon, a Ṡaoi, fíon do 'n ṁnaoi uarail, ṁa 'r é do ċoil é. 6. Go fonṁar, a ḋuine ċóir. 7. Cia "aca" feoil is fearr leat— uan-feoil, eunlaiċ, no caor-feoil? 8. Is fearr liom uan-feoil. 9. A Ṡaoi, cia aca is mian leat-sa? 10. Beiḋ caor-feoil agam, ṁa 'r re do ċoil é. 11. Tá go maiṫ; béarfaiḋ do ċarad an Blacaċ an mear dam fíon ól liom. 12. Go fonṁar, a Ṡaoi. 13. Cia "aca" is fearr leat, an 'pórt no an searraiḋ? 14. Is fearr liom an 'pórt. 15. Is breag an fíon é-so. 16. Tá faitċios mór air Sacsanaiġ anois, faoi 'n b-Ḟrainc; saoilim. 17. Tá eagla mór airṫi. 18. Cia "aca" is fearr leat, Sacsanaiġ no Ḟrainc? 19. Is fearr le roinn "againn" Sacsanaiġ; is fearr le mórán "againn," an Ḟrainc: da m-beiḋeaḋ Sacsanaiġ níor ceanaṁla linn, agus gan sclabaiḋ a ḋea-

naċ binn b' ḟearr liom Sacraniaċ. 20. Cia "aca" de na trí ḟeisiḃ deiġionaċa a b' ḟearr do 'n tír so? 21. Is deacair a ráḋ, go deiṁin; táid uile namadaċ leis an tír so, mar sin ni maiṫ liom ceaċdar "aca." 22. Ṡeamuis, innis dam, cianós b-ḟuil do ċarad toicaṁail an tiġearna Ua Néill. 23. Tá sé go maiṫ. 24. B-ḟuil sé faoi ṁeas mór; b-ḟuil meas mór aig móran "agaiḃ" air? 25. Aig roinn againn, tá; aig roinn eile, ni'l. 26. Cia "agaiḃ" b-ḟuil an cionn is mo air-san? 27. Tá cionn an-mór agam-féin air. 28. A Ṡaoi, is cóir duit cuairt a ṫaḃairt orainn an foġar so; is maiṫ le móran "againn" ṫu ḟeicsint ann ar measg. 29. Saoilim go bearrad. 30. Beiḋ bród mór orainn d' ḟeicsint.

THIRTY-THIRD LESSON—
AN TRIṀAḊ LEIĠEAN AIR TRIOĊAD.

EXERCISE LIII.—AN TRIṀAḊ GNAṪUĠAḊ AIR ĊAOGAD.
Máṫair aig Múnaḋ a Clainne.

Ristard, Seorsa, Eilis.

1. (Ristard)—Feuċ an iomaiġ sin; cia b-ḟuil rí cosaṁail "leis?" 2. (Seorsa)—Tá rí cosaṁail le an t-sagart. 3. Ni'l; aċt tá fíor agam-sa cia tá rí cosaṁail leis. 4. Cia "leis" anois? 5. Le m' aṫair. 6. Go deiṁin ni b-ḟuil; go bíneaċ feuċ airṫi arís. 7. Amarcaim air a ṁalaiḋ, air a ġial, agus air an smig. 8. Aċt amarc ṫusa air an t-suil; tá an t-suil an-ċosaṁail le suil an aṫar Seáġain. 9. (Máṫair)—A leanḃa b-ḟuil siḃ réiḋ? 10. (Ristard)—Seaḋ, a Ṁáṫair, tamuid uile réiḋ. 11. B-ḟuil eolus agaiḃ air bun leiġean? 12. (Ristard)—Tá fíor agam, go d-tuigim-se mo ċuid leiġean. 13. (Seorsa)—Tá mo ċuid féin agam-sa. 14. (Eilis)—Tá agam-sa gaċ focail ann mo léiġeanaiḃ uile aċt aṁain cruinne-eolus—ni'l se sin agam. 15. (Máṫair)—Ni ceirdeoċaiḋ me aċt anns an teagasg Criosdaiġ aṁain; Ristard, cia ḟe Dia? 16. Cruṫuiġ-teoir neiṁe agus talṁan agus ard-tiġearna gaċ uile

bíoḋ. 17. Maiṫ an buaċaill: cia ṁéiḋ pearsa ann Dia?
18. (Risteard)—Trí pearsanna, an t-aṫair, an mac, agus an Spioraḋ Naoṁ. 19. Anṁaiṫ an buaċaill: cia "aca" de na trí pearsannaiḃ, a Ṡeorra, ġlac colan daonna? 20. Mac Dé an dara pearsa de 'n Trianóiḋ ro-naoṁṫa. 21. Cia an lá air a rugaḋ é? 22. Lá Nodlac air uair an ṁeaḋoin oiḋċe. 23. (Risteard)—Tá me tuirseaċ, a ṁaṫair. 24. Tá go maiṫ, a leinḃ, biḋ tu aig raḋ gur naiḃ tu cosaṁail le duine eigin. 25. Ní feaḋ, aċt duḃairt Seorra go ḃ-ḟuil an iomaiḋ ro cosaṁail "leis" an t-sagairt an aṫair Seaġan. 26. Agus cad é deir tusa? 27. Deirim gur cosaṁail le m' aṫair í. 28. Agus cia ḃ-ḟuil tusa cosaṁail "leis" le do ṗluca ṁóra? 29. Tá me cosaṁail le n' aṫair. 30. A ḃ-tiġ leat "ar n-aṫair" a raḋ? 31. Tiġ, go cinte. 32. Cia an t-aṫair air a traċtar? 33. Dia—ar n-aṫair atá air neaṁ, mar duḃairt naoṁ Próinsias: cuimniġim an sgeul a d' innis tu ḋuinn. 34. A Ṡeorra, ḃ-ḟuil tusa cosaṁail le Dia, innis dam. 35. Cinte, tá me cosaṁail "leis;" is cosaṁail m' anam leis. 36. Oċ, a saoileann tu sin? 37. Tá me cinnte dé. 38. Taḃair aire, mar sin, gan tu féin a ḋéanaḋ neaṁ-cosaṁail leis, aig milleaḋ iomaiġe co aluin.

THIRTY-FOURTH LESSON—
AN CEAṪARṀAḊ LÉIĠEAN AIR TRIOĊAḊ.

EXERCISE LIV.—AN CEAṪARṀAḊ ĠNAṪUĠAḊ AIR ĊAOĠAḊ.

1. Ḃ-ḟuil tusa 'do ḃuaċail ṁaiṫ, a Ṡeamuis? 2. Táim, a Ṡaoi, 'mo ḃuaċail ṁaiṫ; táim a g-coṁnaiḋe 'mo ḃuaċaill ṁaiṫ. 3. Ḃ-ḟuil do ḋearḃ-ṡiur Eilis 'nn a cailín ṁaiṫ. 4. Tá sí 'nn a cailín ṁaiṫ; agus deir m' aṫair go m-beiḋ sí 'nn a mnaoi anṁaiṫ. 5. Ḃ-ḟuilid do ḋearḃráiṫre agus do ċol-ceaṫara ann so? 6. Táid. 7. Ḃ-ḟuilid 'nn a sgolairiḋ ṁaiṫe? 8. Táid, a réir a m-ḃliaġan. 9. An é so do ċoilceaṫar Seoirse, a tá 'nn a sgolaire ṁóir? 10. Is é. 11. Tá go maiṫ, a Ṡeoirse, ḃ-ḟuil fios agad sgeulaiḋeaċt an Ḃíobla go maiṫ? 12.

Seaḋ, tá agam eolus air beagán dí. 13. Ḃ-Ḟuil fíos agad cia sé Seoseṗ mac Jacoib? 14. Ḃí sé 'nn a ṁaor air talaṁ uile na h-Egipte, agus 'nn a ḟlanuiġṫeoir aig a ṗobal. 15. An Eabraċ bí ann, no Egipteaċ? 16 Eabraċ bí ann. 17. Ḃ-fuil fíos agad stáir na Roiṁe? 18. Níl mórán fíos. 19. A ḃ-tig leat innsin cia sé Julius Caesar; an Romanaċ a bí ann, no Ġall? 20. Ḃí sé 'nn a Romanaċ, agus tá cáil air, gur fuair sé buaiḋe air na Ġaill, agus gur buḋ é an ceuḋ taoraċ Romanaċ a ṫáinic air talaṁ na Ḃritaine. 21. Cia sé naoṁ Patruic? 22. Ḃí sé 'nn a Easpog naoiṁṫa agus bí sé 'nn a apstol cum an g-criċe. 23. Tá go maiṫ: táir eolgaċ air stáir? 24. Ḃ-fuil eolus aig maġairtir Uilleam air stáir? 25. Tá, ċo maiṫ liom-sa; támuiḋ le ceile anns an g-cuideaċt ceaḋna. 26. Ḃ-fuil eolus aige air a ṫeagasg Críordaiġ mar an g-ceaḋna? 27. Tá. 28. Cia ċruṫuiġ agus ċuir air an t-saoġal ro tu? 29. Is anns an teanga ġaoiḋilge—teanga mo ṫír ḋutċair, ḋ'foġlam me an teagasg Críordaiġ. 30. Ó! tá go maiṫ; is amlaiḋ is fearr; tá luaṫ-gair orm faoi.

EXERCISE LV.—AN CUIGEAḊ GNÁṪUĠAḊ AIR ĊUOGAḊ.

1. Who created and placed you on (in) the world? 2. God. 3 What is the first thing that every Christian ought to believe? 4. That there is only one God. This is the first article of the creed. 5. Who is God? 6. The Creator of heaven and earth, and Sovereign Lord of all things. 7. Was God existing at all times? 8. Yes, and before all time, for he is without beginning and without end. 9. Where is God? 10. He is in heaven and on earth, and in every place in the world. 11. Does he see all things? 12. He sees all things, even to the most silent thoughts of the heart. 13. How many Gods are there? 14. There is but one God, who will reward the good with everlasting happiness, and punish the wicked with everlasting torments. 15. How many persons in God? 16. Three persons, really distinct and equal in all things, the Father, and the Son, and the Holy Ghost. 17. Is the Father God? 18. Yes, truly. 19. Is the Son God? 20. Yes, truly. 21. Is the Holy Ghost God? 22. Yes, truly. 23. Are they then

three Gods? 24. No, but one God in three persons, because they have but one divine substance and nature. 25. What is the name of the three persons together? 26. The Holy Trinity, or one God in three persons. 27 Is any of the three persons more ancient, more wise, or more mighty than the others? 28. Their age, their power, and their glory is the same. 29. Is Jesus Christ God? 30. He is both God and man. 31. Was he always God? 32. He was. 33. Was he always man? 34. No, but from the time of his incarnation. 35. How many natures in Christ? 36. There are two natures, to wit, the divine and human nature, for he is both God and man. 37. How many persons in Jesus Christ? 38. There is but one person, to wit, the person of the Son of God only. 39. You are a good boy, William; you have a knowledge of God: render to him, therefore, the love of your heart entirely, and you shall yet enjoy Him in the kingdom of heaven.

THIRTY-FIFTH LESSON—
AN CUIGṀAḊ LEIGEAN AIR ṪRIOĊAḊ.

EXERCISE LVI.—AN SEISEAḊ GNÁṪUGAḊ AIR ĊAOGAḊ.

Stáir—an Coilleaċ agus an t-seoḋ.

Am do ḃi coilleaċ aig sgriobaḋ cocain air ċarn aol-laiġ aig toirrġeaċt biḋ do na cearcaiḃ, do ċarluiġ leis seoḋ a ḃi go fanaċ ann. "Oċ," air se, "is niḋ áluin ċu gan aṁrus, do'n ṁuinntir air áil leo ċu, aċt is aille liom-sa gráine órna 'na seoḋa na cruinne."

Buḋ cialṁar an coilleaċ é: aċt táid mórán daoine diċċeillḋ ann, a ċuireas neaṁsuim ann niḋ ionṁearca mar ġeall naċ leur dóiḃ a luaċ.

EXERCISE LVII.—AN SEAĊTṀAḊ GNÁṪUGAḊ AIR ĊAOGAḊ.

An Mionán agus an Maḋaḋ Alla.

Bi mionán air ṁullaċ tiġe áird, agus aig feicsint maḋaiḋ alla a dul ċairt do ċoruig se b' a ṁarluġaḋ: do fear an maḋaḋ alla leis an freagraḋ so amain ċabairt dó: "a ċráil, ni ċu a ṁarluiġear me, aċt an áit ann a ḃ-fuilir."

EXERCISE LVIII.—ᴀɴ ᴄ-ocᴜᴀ̇ᴀ̇ 5ɴᴀᴄuᴣᴀ̇ ᴀıʀ ᴄᴀoᴣᴀ̇.

There was a certain householder who gave orders to put
a brass bell on the neck of a dog that was addicted to bite
people, so that everybody might avoid him. When it
had been put on him, and he had heard the tinkling of
the brass, he became very much elated, and he considered
that the bell had been given him as a reward of services, as
he had been so good. Therefore he began to disparage (to
cast disparagement upon) every other dog in comparison to
himself. But there was an old hound, that said to him:
" You foolish fellow, are you not aware that this jingling
ringing is only proclaiming thy bad habits aloud to everybody."

It is not right for any one to become elated at a transac-
tion that reveals to the entire world his own degradation.

THIRTY-SIXTH LESSON—
ᴀɴ seıseᴀ̇ ᴌe̋ıᴣeᴀɴ ᴀıʀ ᴄʀıoᴄᴀ̇.

EXERCISE LIX.—ᴀɴ ɴᴀoıᴀ̇ᴀ̇ 5ɴᴀᴄuᴣᴀ̇ ᴀıʀ ᴄᴀoᴣᴀ̇.

THE FOX AND THE GOAT.

A fox had fallen into a well, and had been casting about
for a long time how he should get out again, when at length
a goat came to the place, and wanting to drink, asked Rey-
nard whether the water was good, and if there was plenty of
it. The fox, dissembling the real danger of his case, replied,
" come down, friend of my heart, the water is so good that
one cannot drink too much of it, and so abundant that it
cannot be exhausted." Upon this the goat, without hearing
another word, leaped down, when the fox, availing himself
of the opportunity, as nimbly leaped up, receiving a great
lift from the horns of his friend, and then coolly remarked
to the poor deluded goat : "If you had half as much brains
as you have beard, you would have looked before giving the
leap."

It is not proper to credit the words of every wily
trickster.

EXERCISE LX.—An Seasgaḋaḋ Ġnáċuġaḋ.
Common form: An Tri-fiċeaḋaḋ Ġnáċuġaḋ.

THE YOUNG HIND AND HER MOTHER.

A young hind said one day to her mother: "Mother, you are taller than a dog, and fleeter, and more long-winded, and you have horns wherewith to defend yourself; why, therefore, are you so timorous before the hounds?" She smiled, and said, "I know this, my child, very well, but no sooner do I hear a dog barking, than my feet run away as speedily as (is) possible."

There is no use speaking to a coward about assuming courage.

EXERCISE LXI.—An t-Aonṁaḋ Ġnáċuġaḋ, air Tri-fiċid.

1. Cia tá ann rin? 2. Mire. 3. An tu Seaġan? 4. Ní mé Seaġan aċt Seorra. 5. Cia an áit ċapluiġeann re ġo b-fuil Seaġan? 6. Tá re 'ran m-baile. 7. Raib tura 'r an m-baile? 8. Ní raib me 'ran m-baile aċt bi mo ṙeaṙbṙoġantaiḋ Cormac 'ran m-baile leiṙ an teaċ a ċoraint. 9. Ciannor b-fuil ḋ' aċaiṙ; b-fuil re feaṙaṁail, mirneaṁail, caṙaḋaṁail, ġeanaṁail, ġraḋaṁail aġur ṗlaiċeaṁail, maṙ deiṙ daoine ġo b-fuil re? 10. Tá; aċt tá mo ḋeaṙbṙaċaiṙ, aṙ a ċuaiḋ tu, neaṁ-feaṙaṁail, neaṁ-ġeanaṁail, ġiḋ ġo b-fuil re ṗlaiċeaṁail aġur caṙaḋaṁail; tá mion-ġáine aiġe do ġaċ ċaraiḋ aċt tá ġráin aiġe aṙ a naiṁaiḋ. 11. Meaṁruiġ ġo maiċ aṙ an ṅeiḋ ta tu ráḋ. 12. Níl me faiṙteaċ a ráḋ an meuḋ meaṙaiṙ a beiċ fíoṙ. 13. Tá rin ceaṙt.

THIRTY-SEVENTH LESSON—
An Seaċtṁaḋ Leiġean air Trioċad.

EXERCISE LXII.—An Dara Ġnáċuġaḋ air Tri-fiċid.

THE WOLF AND THE LAMB.

A time there was a wolf lapping at the head of a running brook, he spied a stray lamb paddling farther down the same stream. Having made up his mind to seize her, he bethought himself how he might give the appearance of justice to his injustice. " Villain !" said he, running up to the lamb, " how dare you muddle the water that I am drinking ?" " Indeed," said the lamb, humbly, " I do not see how I can disturb the water, since it runs from you to me." "Although it is so," replied the wolf, "it was but a year ago that you called me many ill names." "Oh! Sir," said the lamb, trembling, " a year ago I was not born." "Well," replied the wolf, "if it was not you, it was your father, and that is all the same; but it is no use trying to argue me out of my fare ;" and without another word he fell upon the poor helpless lamb and tore her to pieces.

A tyrant never wants a plea.

And there is no use for simple, good-hearted people, to contend with the unjust class who are in authority.

END OF PART III.

PART IV.

THIRTY-EIGHTH LESSON.

The second class of compounds are those formed from simple words and particles. The particles going before the root are called *prefixes*.

The prefixes in Irish orthography are about twenty-four in number. Without a correct knowledge of their import, the proper force of words into which, by composition, they enter, cannot be well understood. We shall, therefore, briefly explain the meaning of each:

Aṅ has two meanings, one *negative* or *privative*, that is, denying or reversing what is implied by the simple root; the other *intensive*, or one which increases the natural force of the word.

Aṅ, *negative*, has the meaning of *un* (English), *in* (Latin); as, eolaċ, knowing, having a knowledge of; skilled in; aṅ-eolaċ, ignorant, illiterate, having no knowledge of; unskilled in.

Aġur ġo ṅaıḃ re-ran aıṅeolaċ aṅnıṫ, and that he (Stanihurst) was unskilled in it (the Irish language).— *Keating's Ireland*, p. 50.

Eolar, learning; aıṅeolar, ignorance, want of learning.

[In published works and MSS., aṅ is spelled aıṅ when the first vowel in the annexed syllable is e or ı.]

Deıre, comfortableness (from ḃear, right); aıṅḃeıre, affliction.

Fıor, knowledge; aıṅḃfıor, ignorance; aṅḃfıoraċ, ignorant. (In this compound, f is eclipsed by ḃ).

Aır m-beıṫ ḃo féıṅ aṅḃfıoraċ 'r aṅ ġaoıḋılġe, on his being (to) himself ignorant of (in) the Irish.— *Ibid.*

Aṅ, *intensive*, means *very*; as, fuar, cold; aṅfuar, very cold; maıṫ, good; aṅṁaıṫ, very good; ċear, heat; aṅ-ċear, excessive heat.

Aıṁ = *dis* or *mis* (English); as, lear, luck, fortune, advantage to one's self; aıṁlear, ill-luck, misfortune, disadvantage to one's self. Ṁa ḃeaṅann ċu ro, ḃeaṅfaıḃ ċu ḋ'aiṁleaſ, if you do this you will do your disadvàntage, *i.e.,* you will do what to yourself will be a disadvantage.

Deoin, according to will; aiṁḋeoin, in spite of; as, ḋ'aiṁḋeoin na Romanaċ, in spite of the Romans.

Aiſ = *again, backwards* (English); car aiſ "aiſ," come back: it enters into composition, and is, as a component particle, incorrectly spelled eiſ.

Aiſ = *re* (Latin); as, ıoc, pay; aiſıoc (with the accent on the second syllable), *re*payment, paying back; eiriġ, arise; aiſeiriġ,, *re*surrection, rising *again;* written eiſeiriġe very commonly.

Aċ has a *reiterative* meaning, or going back again on what is already done. It expresses, therefore, two effects— first, that of cancelling what is conyeyed by the root; and, secondly, that of doing anew what the uncompounded word indicates. Its meaning is sometimes confined to the former, and then it becomes a *negative* particle; sometimes, however, it extends to both, and then it is a *reiterative.*

Aċ, as a *negative,* is not common—aċ-riġeaḋ, to dethrone; from aċ, and riġeaḋ (theme riġ, a king), to enthrone; aċ-cleir:eaċ, a superannuated clergyman; aċ-laoċ, a superannuated warrior.

Aċ, as a *reiterative,* is very common; deanaḋ, to do, to make; aċ-ḋeanaḋ, to *re*make; ſaſ, growth; aċ-ſaſ, a new growth, a second crop; aċ-cuinġe, a petition, an entreaty; from aċ and cuinġe, a bond, a tie or chain—a word implying that, by our prayers, we, as it were, chain Him whom we petition to grant our request.

Dı a *negative* particle; from bıċ, want, like *di, dis* (Latin); as, creideaṁ, faith, belief; dı-ċreideaṁ, *un*belief; cean, a head; dı-ċean, one who lost the head; dı-ċeannaım, I behead; dı-laċca, an orphan; from dı, want; and laċ (gen. case, laċta,) milk.

When compounded with words beginning with b or ſ, it causes eclipsis; as, buıḋeaċ, thankful, grateful; dımbuıḋeaċ, unthankful, ungrateful, grumbling; dımbuan, unlasting.

VOCABULARY:

Certain, aıriṫe; as, ſeaſ aıriṫe, a certain man.

— Aon (one); as, ſeaſ aon, a man, a certain man; and dı

ſeaſ ann, literally, there was a man in being:

This use of the preposition ann is very common; as, là n-ann, a certain day (literally, there was a day in it); bí feaſ aɲɲ, there was a certain man.

Egg, ub, m.; plu. uba; eggs, Latin, *ova*; Ir. ub is, in sense and sound, identical with the French *œuf*.

Gold, ōſ, m. Eng.; *ore*, Latin.

Income, ceact-a-ſceać.

Slow, ſſōɲ, adj.; pronounced *ryan*; mall, slow, late; mal-cſaćać, unreasonable, dilatory.

Treasure, ſoɲṁuſ, m.; caſſ5e.

Whole, ſomlāɲ, *i.e.*, the full, entire, whole; from ſoɱ and lāɲ, full.

EXERCISE LXIII.

THE GOOSE THAT LAID GOLDEN EGGS.

Aɲ 5é a ſu5 uba oſba.

A certain man had a goose that laid him (ſu5 bō) a golden egg every day. But he was not satisfied (ſaſca) with so slow an income; he wished, therefore, to seize the whole treasure at once. So he killed the goose, and, cutting her open, he found (ſuaſſ ſe) that she was—just what any other goose would be.

Through a desire of over-much (ſoɱaſca) we lose (caſl-ɱuſb) the whole.

Saſɲc 5aɲ ſoɲaſ eſſſ5eaɲɲ aɲ boɲaſ bé, hapless greed will not succeed.

Ɖo implies difficulty (Gr. δυς) when compounded with *past participles*; as, béaɲca, done; bo-béaɲca, hard to be done; ōl, drink; ōlca, drunk; bo-ōlca, hard to be drunk; ſc, eat; bo-ſce, hard to be eaten; feſc, see; feſcſſɲce, seen; bo-feſcſſɲce, hard-to-be-seen, invisible; bo-cſſoć-ɲuſ5ce, infinite; from bo and cſſoćɲuſ5ce, ended—root, cſſoć, end; bo-cuſɱſſ5ce, incomprehensible; from bo and cuſɱſſu5ab, to comprehend; from cuɱaſ, power.

Ɖo, before *nouns* and *adjectives*, has the meaning of *ill*, English; as, bo beuſa, ill-manners; bo-cāſl, ill-fame; bo-co5bāſl, ill-education; bo-beuſać, ill-mannered; bo-cāſ-leać, ill-famed.

Ɖo and ſo are opposed in Gaelic: the one means the contrary of that indicated by the other. From this opposition a great number of words antagonistic in meaning, nouns as well as adjectives and participles, exists in the language.

NOUNS.

Saiḃṙeaṡ, riches; from raiḃiṙ, rich; raiḃṙeaṡ a'ṡ baiḃṙeaṡ, riches and poverty.

Saoi, a gentleman, Sir, a hero.

Siṫ, peace, plenty.

Soċaṙ, n. emolument, convenience. Ex.: ṡoċaṙ aġuṡ boċaṙ aṇ ċeiṙde, the profit and loss of the trade; a proverb, like the Latin, *qui sentit commoda et incommoda sentire debetur.*

So-ḋuiṇe, a good man.

Soiṇṡionn, fair weather; from ṡo (or ṡon) and ṡíoṇ.

Solaṡ, solace.

Sonaṡ, happiness, bliss.

So-ċlaoṇaḋ, towardness.

Socul, ease, rest (properly ṡocaṁail); from ṡoġ or ṡoċ, and aṁail, like.

Soṡġeul, the Gospel; from ṡo, happy, and ṡġeul, news.

Suaiṙceaṡ, sweetness.

Subailce, virtue.

Daiḃṙeaṡ, want of riches, penury; from baiḃiṙ, poor, pennyless.

Daoi, a worthless person, a dunce, a poltroon.

Diṫ, want, misery.

Doċaṙ, loss, inconvenience; from bo and caṙ, friendly kind.

Do-ḋuiṇe, a bad man, a rogue.

Doiṇṡionn, foul weather; a storm.

Dolaṡ, sorrow, grief.

Donaṡ, infelicity, misery.

Do-ċlaoṇaḋ, repulsiveness.

Do-cul, difficulty.

Doṡġeul, bad news.

Duaiṙceaṡ, sourness.

Dubailce, vice.

ADJECTIVES.

Saiḃiṙ, rich.

Saoṙ, adj., free, cheap; v., save, redeem; ṡaoṙaḋ, freeing.

Soiṙb, affable, quiet, easy; ṡoiṙbe, affability; ṡoiṙbeaċt, affableness.

Daiḃiṙ, poor.

Daoṙ, in slavery, dear; baoṙaḋ, condemning; baoṙ, v., to condemn.

Doiṙb, peevish, ill-humor, grievous; boiṙbeaċt, peevishness.

Socaiṁ, easy, at leisure, tranquil.

Socaṁaċ, steady, established, immovable; from ṙo and cuiṗ, put, place.

Soċaṁaċ, profitable, easy; from ṙo and caṗ, friendly.

So-ċṙeiṁeaċ, credulous.

Soċṙoiḋeac, kind-hearted, giving ease; from ṙo and cṙoiḋe, heart.

Soṡṙáḋaċ, very loving, affable.

Soléiṗ, clear, bright, lucid; ṣo ṙoléiṗ, clearly, lucidly; from ṙo and leuṗ, seeing.

Soṅa, lucky, happy, prosperous; from ṙo and áḋ, luck.

Suaiṗc, sweet, pleasant.

Docaiṗ, uneasy, difficult.

Docaṁaċ, unsteady.

Doċaṁaċ, hurtful, wrong, injurious.

Do-ċṙeiṁeaċ, incredulous.

Do-ċṙoiḋeaċ, sorrowful; affecting the heart with pain. Do cṙioḋ.

Do-ṡṙáḋaċ, unloving, repulsive.

Doléiṗ, dark, obscure.

Doṅa, unlucky, unhappy, unprosperous.

Duaiṗc, sour, sharp.

PARTICIPLES.

So-ḋoiṗċe, easy or apt to be poured out.

So-ċṙioċnuiṣċe, finite, easily ended, root—cṙioċ, end.

So-ċuiṁṙiṣċe, comprehensible.

So-ḟeicṙinċe, visible, easily seen; root, ḟeic, see.

So-ṣlacuiṣċe, acceptable.

So-ṣluaiṙċe, movable.

So-ċuiṣṙioṅa, intelligible.

Do-ḋoiṗċe, difficult to be poured out.

Do-ċṙioċnuiṣċe, infinite.

Do-ċuiṁṙiṣċe, incomprehensible.

Do-ḟeicṙinċe, invisible, and bo-ḟeicṙioṅa, same.

Do-ṣlacuiṣċe, unacceptable.

Do-ṣluaiṙċe, immovable.

Do-ċuiṣṙioṅa, unintelligible.

VOCABULARY.

Assures, beaṙḃann.
  "That you are a rogue," ṣuṙ ṣaḋaiḋ ċá annac.
Away with you; imiṣ leac; ċeiḋ leac; aṙ m'aṁaṙc leac.

Before (prep.) ṙoiṁe; before this, ṙoiṁe ṙo; adv., ċeaṅa (already).
Betrays, caiṙbeaṅaṅn, bṙaiċeaṅn.
Bribe, bṙiḃ.
Civility, ṙiṫéalcaṙ, m.; from ṙiċ.

gentlemanly bearing; and ᴀɪʟ-
ᴄᴇᴀʀ, education; root, ᴀɪʟ, to
nourish.

Mischief, ᴍᴇᴀбᴀl, ꝼᴄᴀlᴄᴀɴᴀꞅ; from
ꞅᴇᴀl, deceit, treachery; ᴍɪoꞃ-
ᴄᴀꞅꞅ, from ᴍɪ and ᴄᴀꞅ, friendship.

Rob (to), бo ꝼlᴀб; бo ᴄꞃᴇᴀᴄᴀб;
ᴀɪꞃꞃᴇᴀб, from ᴀɪꞃꞃ, plunder.

Sops, ᴀɪꞃ bɪᴇ̆; ꞃꞃᴇᴀᴍᴀ boꞃᴀ.

Stop (to), v., ᴄoꞃꞃ.

Suspicion, ᴀᴍꞃᴀꞅ, m.

Therefore, ᴀɪꞃ ᴀɴ ᴀббᴀꞃ ꞃɪɴ; бᴇ
bꞃɪꞃ ꞃɪɴ; uɪᴍᴇ ꞃɪɴ,—usually
found written and pronounced
thus: б'ᴀ bꞃɪꞃ ꞃɪɴ, composed
of бᴇ (б'), of; ᴀ, its; bꞃɪꞃ, reason, force; ꞃɪɴ, that.

EXERCISE LXIV.

THE THIEF AND THE DOG.

Aɴ ꞃᴀбᴀɪб ᴀꞃuꞅ ᴀɴ ᴍᴀбᴀб.

A thief on coming (ᴀɪꞃ ᴄᴇᴀᴄᴄ) to a house with the intention (lᴇ ꝼoɴɴ) to rob it, would have stopped the barking
(ᴄᴀꝼᴀɪɴᴄ), and therefore threw the dog sops: "Away with
you," said the dog; "I had my suspicions of you before
(ᴄᴇᴀɴᴀ), but this excess of civility assures me that you are
a rogue."

A bribe in hand betrays mischief at heart.

THIRTY-NINTH LESSON.

EXPLANATION OF PREFIXES—*continued.*

Ꜩ, a negative particle, like the Latin *é, ek, eks,* or *ex ;*
as, бᴇɪᴍɪɴ, indeed, certain; ᴇбᴇɪᴍɪɴ, uncertain.

Ꜩ, before a syllable beginning with a broad vowel, takes
ᴀ after it, to conform to the laws of vowel assimilation; as,
бoɪᴍɪɴ, deep, not shallow; ᴇᴀ-бoɪᴍɪɴ, not deep, shallow.

Ꜩᴀ, before the consonants ᴄ and ᴄ, causes eclipses, or
assumes, for the sake of euphony in the enunciation of the
compound term, a letter of the same organ; as, ᴄɪᴀllбᴀ,
intelligent; ᴇᴀꞃ-ᴄɪᴀllбᴀ, devoid of intelligence; ᴄꞃᴀɪbᴄᴇᴀᴄ,
pious; ᴇᴀꞃ-ᴄꞃᴀɪbᴄᴇᴀᴄ, impious, devoid of piety; ᴄꞃoᴄᴀɪꞃᴇ,
mercy; ᴇᴀб-ᴄꞃoᴄᴀɪꞃᴇ, without mercy; ᴇᴀб-ᴄꞃoᴄᴀɪꞃᴇᴀᴄ,
merciless. Ꜩᴀꞃ is the prefix which precedes words beginning with ꞅ; as, ꞅᴀᴍᴀɪl, like, similar; ᴇᴀꞃ-ꞅᴀᴍᴀɪl, dis-
similar, unlike, unusual, matchless. The Scotch Gael do
not admit the use of the eclipsing consonant after ᴇᴀ; as,

eaceaпc, injustice ; eacпocaⴑпeaċ, merciless ; eaⰂoċaⴑ, despair.

In this they are right ; for the eclipsing consonants are, in such instances, useless ; nay, in a small way, they help to puzzle the learner.

Єaⴑ, extreme, *n.* top, end, is an intensitive particle ; as, eaⴑ-ⰃaⰂ, arrest ; eaⴑ-ⴃlaⵑċ, an autocrat ; from eaⴑ, and ⴃlaⵑċ, a prince, a chieftain ; eaⴑⅿall, very slow ; eaⴑ-ċoⴑaⅿaⵑl,' very similar.

Єaⴑ is found only in a few words. It appears to be of kindred meaning with ⵑaⴑ, after, meaning, final, ending, crowning ; as, eaⴑⰂall, a tail, from eaⴑ, and ⰂaⴑⰂ, a member, by metathesis ⴑeaⰂal.

Єaⴑ, not, devoid of ; from aⴑ, out of ; as, eaⴑ-ċaⴑaⰂ, an enemy, from eaⴑ, and caⴑaⰂ, a friend ; eaⴑ-uⅿlaċc, dis-obedience ; from eaⴑ, and uⅿlaċc, obedience ; which comes from uⅿal, humble ; Latin, *humilis ;* eaⴑ-uⴑⴑaⅿ, disre-spect, want of reverence ; from eaⴑ, and uⴑⴑaⅿ, reverence, respect ; eaⴑlaⵑ, sick, infirm ; from eaⴑ, and ⴃlaⵑ, sound in health ; eaⰃ-ⴑlaⵑ, means the same, infirm ; from e, or, as above, eaⰃ ; and ⴑlaⵑ. Єaⴑ is pronounced short.

Ⴔóⵑⴑ, before, in front ; therefore it means advanced ; very. Hence its presence imparts to the meaning of all words with which it is compounded, the idea of fulness or completeness, perfection, intensity ; as, ⴔóⵑⴑ-ⰁⴑeaċⵑuⵑⰃ, fore-think, prophesy ; conjecture, divine ; from ⴔóⵑⴑ, and ⰁⴑeaċⵑuⵑⰃ, meditate on, speculate.

Ⴔóⵑⴑ-Ⰱⴑⵑaċaⴑ, an *adverb ;* from ⴔóⵑⴑ, and Ⰱⴑⵑaċaⴑ, a word.

Ⴔóⵑⴑ-Ⰱⴑuaċ, the edge of a precipice ; from ⴔóⵑⴑ, and Ⰱⴑuaċ, edge, border, brink.

Ⴔóⵑⴑ-ċeaⴖ, the extreme end ; root, ceaⴖ, head, limit.

Ⴔóⵑⴑ-ⵑⅿeal, frontier, limit, furthest, extremity, circum-ference ; from ⵑⅿeal, a border, a hem ; as, ⵑⅿeal a ⴃallaⵑⴖe, the hem of His cloak ; ⵑⅿeal ⴖa calⅿaⴖ, the ends of the earth.

Ⴔóⵑⴑ-ⴖeaⴑc, violence ; ⴖeaⴑc, strength.

Ⴔóⵑⴑ-eⵑⰃeaⴖ, oppression ; root, eⵑⰃeaⴖ, or eⵑⰃⵑⴖ, force, violence, compulsion.

Ⴔⴑⵑċ, back, quick succession ; as, ⴔⴑⵑċ-ċeac, coming and going ; ⴔⴑⵑċ-ⰂualaⰂ, repercussion, a palpitation.

Ɉol, and sometimes written ⵑl, akin in meaning with uⵑle,

all, signifies plenty, variety, diversity—like πολυς, *polús* in Greek; as, ιomaḋ, (adj.), many, numerous; (n.), a multitude; ιol-ιomaḋ, a great multitude; ιol-ċaιnteaċ, many-tongued, a polyglot; ιol-ṗιan, torment; from ιol, and ṗιan, pain; ιol-beuρaċ, arch, sly, versatile; from ιol, and beuρaċ, mannerly; root, beuρ, manners, behaviour; ιolbaċaċ, parti-coloured.

Ιom, around, about; of the same meaning with the preposition uιme, around, about; it is therefore an intensitive particle; as, ӡaoċ, wind; ιomӡaoċ, a whirlwind; làn, full; ιomlàn, entire, complete; ḋρuιḋ, shut, close; ιom-ḋρuιḋ, surround, shut up all around; ƒulanӡ, endure, suffer; ιomƒulanӡ, endure; ιomċρom, very heavy. In two instances it reverses the meaning of the word with which it is compounded; as, ιomċeaċt, to depart; from ιom, and ċeaċt, to come; and ιomρρuċ, a counter-tide; from ιom, and ρρuċ, a current.

Ιon, a particle that expresses fitness, suitableness; as, ιonƒιρ, marriageable (from ιon, fit for, and ƒιρ, gen. case of ƒeaρ, a man), as applied to a maid; ιonmna, as applied to a young man (from ιon, and mna, the gen. case of bean, a woman); ιonaρm, fit to bear arms. Before past participles it can be used at pleasure. It imparts to such participles the same meaning that the suffix "able," "ible" (Latin, *bilis*), gives to English words; as, ιċ, eat; ιċte, eaten; ιon-ιċte, eatable (fit to be eaten); òl, drink; òlta, drunk; ιon-òlta, drinkable (fit to be drunk); mol, praise; molta, praised; ιonmolta, praiseable (fit to be praised); ӡρaḋ (n.), love; ӡρaḋuιӡ (v.), love thou; ӡρaḋuιӡte, loved; ιonӡρaḋuιӡte, loveable (fit to be loved), deserving of love; much like the Latin *amandus;* and, in this sense (as far as the Latin participle ending *dus* betokens suitableness) what O'Molloy says of this prefix is true, that it has the force of the Latin participle of the future in *dus.*

Whenever, therefore, a person translating English into Irish meets with a word ending in *able,* he need only observe its root, learn its Irish equivalent, form the past participle, and prefix ιon.

Ιon differs from the prefix ρo; for ρo implies ease, feasibility; ιon, fitness; as in the annexed example in which ρo-ḋeanta (easily done); ιon-ḋeanta (fit to be done), are contrasted; ní'l ʒać ċá ro-ḋéanca, ion-ḋéanca, everything that is feasible, is not suitable.

Iη and ioη, as found in some compound words, is a form of the preposition aηη, in; as, ioηċolηuʒaḋ, incarnation; from ioη (or aηη), in; and colηuʒaḋ, to give a (colaη) body to; to make flesh; ioη-ṁeoḋaηaċ (adj.), interior, from within; derived from ioη, in, and meoḋaη, middle; Latin, *medium;* English, *mean;* ioηʒaηtar (pr. *ee-yan-thas*), a wonder; from ioη, and ʒaηtar (root, ʒáη, rare, scarce), a thing that seldom happens; iηlaoiʒ, in calf; as, bó iηlaoiʒ, a cow in calf; ioηṁar, a treasure, a valuable thing, in which mear (estimation, value) is placed; iηċiηη, the brain; from iη, and ceaηη, head.

Ioη intensifies; as, ioηʒreim, persecution; from ioη, and ʒreim, a grasp.

The prefixes iol, iom, ioη, are written in published works and MSS. il, im, iη, when preceding a slender vowel.

Anxious to make Irish orthography fixed, we shall write these prefixes in every instance with the broad vowel iol, and not il; iom, and not im; ioη, and not iη, except the prep. i and iη, in. It is desirable to adopt this form for the reason just assigned. Besides iol is preferable to il, for it is synonymous with uile, in which the broad vowel is a leading feature, and because the spelling iol prevails more than il; and lastly, the spelling iol accords with the usual pronunciation better than that of il. These reasons hold for ioη and ioη.

VOCABULARY.

Caiḋreaṁ, n, m, familiarity; from co, together, and aitreaṁ, a dwelling. Welsh, *caidreav.*

Caraḋ (leir), was met; the perf. tense passive of car, to twist, to turn, to twine, to meet by chance, to brandish; n, a twist, turn, a winding, a wile.

Faitċíor, m, fear; faitċeaċ, timid, shy.

Ʒeit, v, to tremble, to show signs of fear.

Leon, a lion; Lat. *leo;* Gr. *león;* Welch, *llan;* Spanish, *leon.*

Oireaḋ, m, a quantity; so much, as much; oireaḋ eaʒla, so much fear; cá meuḋ cá ain, how much for it? Aη oireaḋ ro, this much. Oireaḋ is followed by aʒur, or its contracted form a'r, and then signifies as much as, "oireaḋ a'r" feiḋir liom a ḋeanaḋ, as much as I can do,

Ruċt, m, stead, room, state; as, a ruċt báir, in the state of death, almost dead; cia aη ruċt a b-fuil tu, in what state are you?

Seaηnaċ, a fox; Heb. *shuhul;* from reaηʒ, slender, slim, agile, wily. Following the spelling of its root, it is written reaηnaċ; according to sound, rioηnaċ, the common form.

Tarla, happened, befel, met; a verb def.

Tarlaḋ, a load, a loading in of corn or hay; as much as one can carry.

Tairbeaη, v, show; tairbeaηaḋ, a demonstration, a showing, a vision.

Taire, a dead body; braṫ taire, a winding-sheet; "ḋo ċairiḃ na naoṁ," to the relics of the saints.

Taiḃre (commonly pronounced *thow-she*) a ghost, an apparition.

EXERCISE LXV.— an sionnaċ aɠus an leon.

THE FOX AND THE LION.

Bi ɼionnaċ ann naɼ ċonnaɼc (that did not see) leon
a ɼiaṁ: do ċaɼla lá n-aon ɠuɼ caɼaḋ leiɼ é, aɠuɼ do
ċainic an oiɼeaḋ ɼin eaɠla aiɼ, an ċeuḋ uaiɼ, ɠuɼ ɼaiḃ
ɼe a ɼuċc báiɼ. 'Nuaiɼ caɼaḋ leiɼ é an daɼa uaiɼ,
ċainic ɼaiccioɼ aiɼ, aċc nioɼ ɠeic ɼé. Aiɼ ċaɼluɠaḋ
leiɼ an cɼiɼaḋ uaiɼ, ċuaiḋ ɼe ɼuaɼ leiɼ aɠuɼ duḃaiɼc:
"ciannoɼ a ḃ-ɼuil cu."

Ɠʉɼeann caiḋɼeaṁ, dɼoċṁeaɼ.

Miɼ, ill, amiss; of the same meaning as the Saxon "mis;"
is a negative prefix of frequent use; as, áḋ, fortune, luck;
mi-áḋ, misfortune, ill luck; ɼaċ, success, a prosperous
issue; mi-ɼaċ, calamity, ill success; ɠnioṁ, an act; mi-
ɠnioṁ, an act done amiss; mi-ċlu, ill fame.

Neaṁ, a privative (spelled neḟ in ancient writings, but
in Scotch Gaelic at present, invariably, neo); as, aiɼeaċ,
attentive; neaṁ-aiɼeaċ, inattentive; coɼaṁail, like, similar;
neaṁ-ċoɼaṁail, unlike; leiɼɠ, sloth; neaṁ-leiɼɠ, courage,
spunk; ɼuim, regard; neaṁ-ɼuim, disregard; niḋ, a thing;
neaṁ-niḋ, non-entity, nothing, vanity, a thing without substance or effect; as, iɼ neaṁ-niḋ an uile aċc aṁáin Dia
a ɼiaɼaḋ aɠuɼ a ɠɼáḋuɠaḋ, all is vanity (a useless thing)
but alone to serve and love God.

Oll, great; of kindred meaning with uile, all; or with
áll, prodigious, vast, mighty; as, oll-ɠuċ, a loud voice;
oll-ɠnioṁaċ, of daring deeds; oll-ɠlóɼ, bombast, big sound.
Áll is found as a prefix in a few words; as, áll-ḃuaiḋeaċ,
mighty, all-victorious; "áll-neaɼc," (of) mighty strength.

"Do buaiḋ ó 'n naṁ 'bi uailleaċ 'ɼ áll-neaɼc."

"Which he won from the foe (who) was haughty and (of) mighty strength.'

"Which he won from the proud invader."

Song—"*Let Erin remember the days of old.*"

Ro, large, very, too much; as, ɼo-ċuɼam, very great
caɼe; ɼo-ċɼan, a large tree; ɼo-ṁian, a great wish; ɼo
baɼċa, the influx of the tide. Ro, when fixed to adjectives,
imparts to them the same meaning that the adverb "very"
in English, does to adjectives before which it is placed; as,

ṗo-áṗḋ, very high; ṗo-ṁóṗ, over large. The word ṗiġ, a
king, is employed as a prefix; as, ṗiġ-ṁaiṫ, supremely
good; ṗiġ differs in meaning from ṗo, the latter denotes
excess, the former excellence, superiority, perfection; as,
cá an níḋ ṗo ṗiġ-ṁaiṫ, this thing is very good; cá an níḋ
ṗo ṗo-ṁaiṫ, this is over good, too good.

Saṗ, an augmentative, denoting excellence, superiority,
and gives therefore to adjectives with which it enters into
composition the meaning attached to absolute superlatives;
as, ṗáṗ-ṁaiṫ, exceedingly good; ṗáṗ-ṁaiṗeaċ, exceedingly
handsome; ṗáṗ-aṗuiḋ, quite ripe; ṗáṗ-ḃuine, an excellent
person; ṗáṗ-laoċ, a great hero. Saṗ, as a noun, means a
worthy, a hero, a leading man, compounded, as it were, of
ṗo, worthy; and ṗeaṗ, a man. In this sense we can easily
see the meaning of the Saxon word "Sir," and of the
Russian "tsar" (or "zar"), and "zarina," to be a superior or
distinguished person.

The prepositions eiḋiṗ, or iḋiṗ, between; ṗo, under;
ṗoiṁe, before; cimċioll, around; ċaṗ, over; cṗíḋ, through;
are sometimes employed as prefixes. (See Twenty-ninth
Lesson.) So are iaṗ and ṗeaċ, either as adverb or preposition.

Jaṗ, after, behind, western; as, iaṗ-ḃṗeiṫ, the after-birth;
iaṗ-ḃuille, a blow from behind; iaṗ-ḋeaṗ, the south-west
(west-south); iaṗ-ċuaċ, the north-west; iaṗ-ṁuiṗ, the
Atlantic; iaṗ-ḋoṗṗ, brownish, after-brown; from ḋoṗṗ,
brown; and iaṗ, after, left, remaining; iaṗ-ġuiṗ, grief,
pain; from iaṗ, and ġuiṗ, a sting, a wound; iaṗġculca,
wild, remote, deserted, western; from iaṗ, and cul, a
corner; Jaṗ-Coṗṗaċc, West Connaught.

Jaṗla, an earl; as it were iaṗ, after, inferior; and ṗlaiċ,
a prince, a chief, one in rank next to a chieftain or prince.
Jaṗṗlaiċ, feudatory prince, is the Irish of Jarlath, the Saint
who is patron of the diocese of Tuam.

Seaċ, anciently ṗeċ (Latin, secus), beside, apart, out of
the way; as, ṗeaċ piana, out of the way of pain, not having
to endure pain; ṗeaċaiṗ, avoid, shun; from ṗeaċ and ṗaṗ,
stay, keep—i.e., keep aside, avoid; ṗeaċ-ġaiṗiṁ, I call
aside; ṗeaċ-laḃṗaḋ, an allegory, a discourse having a
meaning beside or apart from that which the plain words

present to the mind. Seaċ is the root of the English words sex, sect; and of the Latin *seco*, I cut, separate, sunder, divide, I rend, and of all its derivatives.

'Seaċ, *n*, means a turn, a bout; ⲧⲁⲃⲁⲓⲃ ⲟⲁⲙ ⲣⲉⲁċ, give me a bout, or turn; ⲣⲁ ⲣⲉⲁċ, by turns.

The term ⲣⲉⲁċ, a turn, a twist, is still in common use amongst those of the country people who indulge in smoking; as, ⲧⲁⲃⲁⲓⲃ ⲟⲁⲙ ⲣⲉⲁċ, give me a smoke.

VOCABULARY.

Ⲁⲛⲁⲟⲁⲛ, a fool.

Ⲁⲓⲣⲁⳑ, *m*, an ass; Latin, *asellus*, a young ass.

Ⲥⲟⲣⲣⲩⳝ, *v*, stir, move; secondary meaning, excite, arouse; endeavour; ⲟⲟ ċⲟⲣⲣⲩⳝ ⲁⲛ ⲧⲁⳑⲁⲙ, the earth shook; ⲥⲟⲣⲣⲟċⲁⲟ, would stir.

Ⲟ'ⲁ ⲃⲣⲓⳝ ⲣⲓⲛ, therefore; ⲃ' for ⲃⲉ, of; ⲁ, its poss. pronoun; ⲃⲣⲓⳝ, virtue, force, power; ⲣⲓⲛ, that; literally, by reason of the force of that; see, "therefore," p. 240.

Ⲓⲟⲙċⲩⲣ, *v*, to carry; to carry oneself, therefore signifies deport, behave.

— *n*, carriage, deportment.

Ⲟⲓⲣⳝⲉ, *f*. office, post, situation (*Armoric*, ⲟⲓⲣⲣⲓⲥ).

Ⲟⲓⲣⳝⲉⲁċ, an officer, one holding an office.

Ⲥⲟⲧⲁⳑ, *m*, arrogance, overbearing impudence. Ⲥⲟⲧⲁⳑⲁċ, *adj.*, proud, saucy, impudent; ⲛⲁċ ⲣⲟⲧⲁⳑⲁċ ċⲩ, how impudent you are.

Ⲥⳑⲉⲁċⲧ, *v*, to bow down, bend, prostrate, adore; ⲛⲁⲣ ⲣⳑⲉⲁċⲧ ⲟⲟ ⲃⲉⲁⳑ, that did not bend the knee to Baal; ⲙⲁ ⲣⳑⲉⲁċⲟⲁⲛⲛ, ⲧⲩ ⲟⲁⲙ, if thou fall down (and adore) me.

Ⲥⲁⲓⲣⲃⲉⲁⲛ, *v*, show; prove manifest; reveal. Ⲁⲣⲁⲛ ⲧⲁⲓⲣⲃⲉⲁⲛⲧⲁ, shewbread. Ⲥⲁⲓⲣⲃⲉⲁⲛⲁⲟ, shewing; ⲧⲁⲓⲣⲃⲉⲁⲛⲟⲁⲣ, perf. tense third person plural; ⲧⲁⲓⲣⲃⲉⲁⲛⲟⲁⲣ ⲛⲁ ⲟⲁⲟⲓⲛⲉ, the people shewed.

Ⲥⲓⲟⲙⲁⲓⲛ, *v*, to drive, to chase; ⲁⳝ ⲧⲓⲟⲙⲁⲓⲛⲧ (participle), driving; ⲣⲉⲁⲣ-ⲧⲟⲙⲁⲛⲧⲁ (a man-of-driving), a driver.

EXERCISE LXVI.

Ⲁⲛ ⲧ-Ⲁⲓⲣⲁⳑ ⲁⳝⲩⲣ ⲁ Ⲟⲓⲣⳝⲉ.

Ⲟⲟ ⲃⲓ ⲁⲓⲣⲁⳑ ⲁⳝ ⲓⲟⲙċⲩⲣ ⲓⲟⲙⲁⳝ ⲧⲣⲓⲟ ⲃⲁⳑⲉ ⲁⲓⲣⲓⲟⲉ ⲁⳝⲩⲣ ⲟⲟ ⲧⲁⲓⲣⲃⲉⲁⲛⲟⲁⲣ ⲛⲁ ⲟⲁⲟⲓⲛⲉ ⲁ ⲙⲟⲟ ⲁⳝ ⲣⳑⲉⲁċⲧⲁⲟ ⲟⲟ. Ⲋⲁⲟⲓⳑ ⲁⲛ ⲧ-ⲁⲓⲣⲁⳑ ⳝⲩⲣ ⲟⲟ-ⲣⲉⲓⲛ ⲧⲩⳝⲁⲟ (was given) ⲁⲛ ⲟⲛⲟⲓⲣ. Ⲟ'ⲁ ⲃⲣⲓⳝ ⲣⲓⲛ, ⳑⲁⲛ ⲟⲉ ⲣⲟⲧⲁⳑ ⲛⲓ ⲥⲟⲣⲣⲟċⲁⲟ ⲣⲉ (he would not stir) ⲥⲟⲣ. Ⲁċⲧ ⲟⲟ ⳑⲉⲁⳝ ⲁⲛ ⲣⲉⲁⲣ-ⲧⲓⲟⲙⲁⲛⲧⲁ ⲁⲓⲣ ⳑⲉ ⲙⲁⲓⲟⲉ, ⲁ ⲣⲁⲟ: Ⲁ ⲁⲙⲁⲟⲁⲓⲛ ⲃⲉⲁⲧⲁⳝ, ⲛⲓ ⲟⲩⲓⲧ-ⲣⲉ ⲁċⲧ ⲟⲟ 'ⲛ ⲓⲟⲙⲁⳝ ⲧⲁ ⲧⲩ ⲁⳝ ⲓⲟⲙċⲩⲣ ⲧⲁⲓⲟ ⲁⳝ ⲧⲁⲓⲣⲃⲉⲁⲛⲁⲟ ⲙⲟⲟ.

Ⲁⲙⲉⲁⲣⲁⲛⲛ ⲟⲁⲟⲓⲛⲉ ⲣⲁⲟⲃ-ċⲉⲓⳑⲟ ⳝⲩⲣ ⲟⲟⲓⲃ-ⲣⲉⲓⲛ ⲧⲁⲓⲣⲃⲉⲁⲛⲧⲁⲣ ⲁⲛ ⲙⲟⲟ ⲓⲣ ⳝⲛⲁċ ⲁ ċⲁⲃⲁⲓⲣⲧ ⲟ'ⲁ ⲛ-ⲟⲓⲣⳝⲉ.

FORTIETH LESSON.

In the two foregoing Lessons have been shown the meaning and use of Irish prefixes, or those particles that go before
the root—in this we shall treat of the particles that come
after the root—suffixes or affixes.

The suffixes are, like the prefixes, of two kinds: either
simple words or fragments of simple words, mere letter-
endings, as they are called, or terminations. When a prefix
or suffix is combined with a word, the term arising from the
union is called derivative, the word from which it has sprung
primitive. Derivative is, in relation, opposed to primitive;
compound, to simple. For instance, ḟeaṙaṁail, manly, is
a primitive, in relation to ḟeaṙaṁlaċt, manliness, which
comes from it; while it is, at the same time, itself a derivative from ḟeaṙ, a man, the stem from which, by adding
aṁail, it has been formed.

Of derivatives, as we observed in treating of compounds
(37th Lesson, p. 210), Nouns, Adjectives, and Verbs are
the leading families. These spring from nouns as roots, or
adjectives, rarely from verbs; for it is from things and their
qualities that mankind first formed notions or ideas, and
therefore the names of such things and of their qualities
were the earliest germs of human speech, in the genealogy
of which history and philology point out Keltic as one of
the earliest offshoots.

From nouns are formed adjectives. These end in aṁail,
maṙ, aċ, iḋ, ḋa, or ḋa, ta:

Aṁail, like.

Nouns.	*Adjectives*
Faílte, welcome.	Faílteaṁail,
Seaṅ, affection, fondness.	Seaṅaṁail, friend-like, amia- ble.
Spáṙa, grace, favor.	Spáṙaṁail, graceful.
Meaṙ, respect.	Meaṙaṁail, respectable.
Moḋ, esteem.	Moḋaṁail, estimable.
Tiġeaṙṅa, a lord.	Tiġeaṙṅaṁail, lordly.
Tṙaċ, occasion, fit time.	Tṙaċaṁail, opportunely.

This suffix aṁail is written in Scotch Gaelic ail, eil, a form which has,
in some instances, been imitated by Irish writers—Furlong, for instance, in

his Irish Prayer-book. In Irish poetry, aṁaıl becomes a'ıl whenever its monosyllabic sound *uil* is required to meet the requirements of poetic measure. Philologists cannot fail to perceive that aṁaıl is the root of the Latin ending *alis, ale,* and its derived forms in the Romance and English languages.

Ⅿaṗ, which some suppose to be the particle maṗ (conjunction) as; while others derive it, as in Erse, from móṗ, great.

Nouns.	*Adjectives.*
Aḋ, luck.	Aḋṁaṗ, lucky; in Scotch Gaelic, aḋṁoṗ.
Bṗıġ, virtue, vigour, force.	Bṗıġṁaṗ, vigorous, solid, substantial, forcible, efficacious.
Ceol, music.	Ceolṁaṗ, musical.
Éaḋ, jealousy.	Éaḋṁaṗ, jealous.
Feoıl, flesh.	Feolṁaṗ, fleshy.
Fuaċ, hatred.	Fuaċṁaṗ, hateful.
Ġṗaḋ, love.	Ġṗaḋṁaṗ, loving, fond.
Luġ, power of motion, strength.	Luġṁaṗ, vigorous, powerful, muscular.

Iḋ, as:

Eaġna, wisdom.	Eaġnaıḋ, wise.
Cıall, sense; genitive case, ceılle.	Céıļıḋ, sensible, wise.

Da (asp. ḋa) or ta.

Aımṗıṗ, weather, time, portion of; hire, aıṗ aımṗıṗ, at service, *i.e.,* "on time," performing service for a limited period.	Aımṗıṗḋa, temporal, ending with time, opposed to ṗıoṗṗaıḋe, eternal.
Coṗp, a body.	Coṗpoṗḋa, bodily, corporal.
Dıa, God.	Dıaḋa, divine.
Neaṁ, heaven.	Neaṁḋa, heavenly; oıġ neaṁḋa, heavenly muse (maid)—*Homer, Iliad* 1.
Fıṗeuŋ, one of the faithful.	Fıṗeuŋta, righteous.
Óṗ, gold.	Óṗḋa, golden.

Aċ (eaċ, after a slender vowel).

Beaṗt, an action, exploit (good or bad).	Beaṗtaċ, tricky, wily.

<table>
<tr><td align="center">*Nouns.*</td><td align="center">*Adjectives.*</td></tr>
<tr><td>Bɼeuʒ, a lie.</td><td>Bɼeuʒaċ, given to lies.</td></tr>
<tr><td>Buaɪ̇ð, victory.</td><td>Buaɪ̇ðeaċ, victorious.</td></tr>
<tr><td>Feaɼʒ, anger.</td><td>Feaɼʒaċ, angry.</td></tr>
<tr><td>Fɪɼɪne, truth.</td><td>Fɪɼɪneaċ, faithful.</td></tr>
<tr><td>Suɪɲ̇ð, glee.</td><td>Suɪɲ̇ðaċ, cheerful.</td></tr>
</table>

From the active signification peculiar to the ending aċ, and from the meaning of the term ɲeaċ, an individual, an agent (a word of which apparently aċ is a mere fragment), adjectives with this suffix become personal nouns, expressive of office, action, or individuality; as—

Aċaċ, a man of terror, a giant; from aċað, fear.

Bacaċ, a lame man; from bac, a hindrance, an impediment; *v*, to hinder.

Cɼuɪ̇ceaċ, hunch-backed; from cɼuɪ̇c, a hump.

Cacoɪ̇lɪceaċ, a Catholic; from the Gr. Καθολικος.

Cɼɪ̇ċeaċ, a Quaker; from cɼɪ̇ċ, to shake.

Ⱶaɲaċ, a monk; from ɱo (old Irish), a person; and aoɲaċ, alone; root, aoɲ, one.

Ⱶaɼcaċ, a rider; from ɱaɼc (old Irish) a horse.

Adjectives ending in aċ are derived from the past participles of verbs, by affixing ċ (asp.) or aċ to the final vowel; as,

Caɪll, lose, perish, destroy; caɪllce, lost; caɪlceaċ, *adj.*, perishing; as, lá caɪlceaċ, a famishing day; caɪlceaċ, *n*, a loser, one that lost; a gelding, an eunuch.

Ⱶɪl, destroy; ɱɪlce, destroyed; ɱɪlceaċ, destructive.

Ⱶol, praise; ɱolca, praised; ɱolcaċ, praising, causing praise.

Obs. 1.—That from the past participle, an adj. having an active or passive meaning is readily formed by suffixing ċ for the active, or prefixing ɪoɲ for the passive; as, ɱolca, praised; ɪoɲɱolca, to-be-praised; ɱolcaċ, causing praise; ɼo-ɱolca, easily-praised; ðo-ɱolca, hard-to-be-praised.

Obs. 2.—Patronymics, sir-names, nick-names, or titles of honor or dishonor, end in aċ; as, Albaɲaċ, a Scotchman; Bɼeacaɲaċ, and, contractedly, bɼeacɲaċ, a Welshman;

Éireannaċ, an Irishman; Spáinneaċ, a Spaniard. Briánaċ, an individual of the family of O'Brien; Blacaċ, Blake; Breatnaċ, Walsh; Brunaċ, Browne; Búrcaċ, Bourke; Domnalaċ, a man of the name MacDonald; Ruarcaċ, O'Rorke; Seoḋac, Joyce; Seabac, Hawkins—from reabac, a hawk. Again, as above, bacaċ, lame—cromaċ, crooked; cruiteaċ, hunch-backed, gibbous; crcraċ, marked with traces of the small-pox—streaked from crois, a cross. Some other nouns of no certain classification end in aċ; as, ʒeallaċ, the moon; fiaḋaċ (*fee-yach*), hunting; venison. But a few end in laċ (which, perhaps, is a broken form of luċt, folk, people [Gr. λαος]); as, teaʒ-laċ, a house, a family, the hearth—from tiʒe and luċt; oʒ-laċ, a young lad; crionlaċ, stubbles—from crion, withered, and laċ; another form of this word is conlaċ; as, in the words of the song: "Conlaċ ʒlas an foʒmair."

MONTHS OF THE YEAR—miora na bliaʒna.

January, Ʒionḃar.

February, Feaḃra.

March, Máirt.

April, Aḃraon (*quasi*); from a, water; or aḋ, prosperous, braon, dropping, distilling.

May, Bealteine.

June, mi meaḋon an t-ram-raḋ.

July, Juil, an mi deiʒionaċ ḋe'n t-ramraḋ.

August, Lúnar, mi na Lúna-'ra, the month of Lammas.

Luanar is derived from Luan (Latin, *Luna*), the moon, and feirḋ, a festival; because that month in which the corn ripens was sacred to Luan, as Bealteine, May, was to Beal, the sun.

September, Seaċt-mi.

October, Oċt-mi.

November, Samain, or mi na ramna.

December, Deiċ-mi.

January is called also an ceuḋ mi ḋe'n m-bliaʒan, the first month of the year.

February, Feaḃra, is called also mi na b-faoilliḋ, the month of winds and storms; and "mi na féile Briʒḋe—the month of the feast of Bridget."

"In all Ireland to this day the month of February is called in Irish 'the month of Bridget's festival,' the festival being on the first day of that month."—*Calendar of Irish Saints*, p. 66, edited by Rev. Matthew Kelly, D.D., Maynooth College.

The middle months of the four seasons, March, June, September, December, are called *the middle months*, March, of Spring; June, of Summer; September, of Autumn; and December, of Winter, thus:

June, mí ṁeaḋan an t-ṡam-ṙaiḋ.

December, mí ṁeaḋan an ᵹeiṁṙe.

September, mí ṁeaḋan an ḟoᵹṁaiṙ.

March, mí ṁeaḋan an earṙaiᵹ.

Spring is called earṙaċ; Autumn, foᵹṁaṙ, and sometimes luanaſ; Summer, ſaṁṙaḋ; Winter, ᵹeiḃṙa. The Irish terms have been already explained in the foregoing Lessons.

VOCABULARY.

Auſtralia, Australia; for Australasia, *i.e.*, Southern Asia. For the meaning of ᵹa, see note, Lesson 41.

Ciun-Ḟaiṙṙᵹe, the Pacific; from ciun, calm, quiet; and faiṙṙᵹe, a sea.

Cuiṁniᵹim, *v*, I remember, recollect; from the root, cuiṁne, *m*, memory, remembrance. Naċ cuiṁne leat? Don't you remember? Iſ cuiṁne liom, I do remember. Cuiṁneaċ, *adj.*, mindful; cuiṁneaṁail, liable to be kept in mind. Cuiṁneaċóiṙ, a recorder; a remembrancer. Cuiṁneaċán, *m*, a keepsake, a remembrance, a memorial. Cuiṁne is a contracted form of coṁeiṙe, a compound formed from co, together;

and méin, mind, *i.e.*, keeping in the mind, remembering.

Ᵹliṙṙ, *adj.*, clear, transparent, pellucid; *n*, the bright heavens, brightness; also a fortress or fort. Ᵹlan, clean; and ᵹle, pure, transparent, are adjectives of kindred meaning.

Muiṙṙneaċ, *adj.*, fond, beloved, affectionate; from muiṙṙn, fondness, joy, natural love.

Muiṙṙnín, fond one; fond love; "Caitlín mo ṁuiṙṙnín—Kathlin, my fond love"—*Song*, by Mrs. Crawford.

Uaiᵹneaċ, *adj.*, lonely, lonesome, solitary; from uaċ, fear, dread; and ᵹineaċ, begetting, producing.

EXERCISE LXVII.

[In this Exercise we give a letter written in very simple language, from a son in London to his father—an Irish peasant.]

Lonḋon,* an ſeṁaḋ la ḋe ṁṡ
An Auᵹuiſt, 1860.

A Aṫaiṙ ḋiliſ—Ta ſe ann am ſᵹṙioḃan a ċuṙ ċuᵹaḋ; ta me anoiſ le ḋa ṁí ann ſo. Iſ móṙ, an-ṁóṙ an baile é. Ní b-ḟuil baile aiṙ biċ ann aṙ ḃ-tíṙ ḟein coṙ-

___

* In page 95 (Part II.) of "Easy Lessons," we give the Irish spelling and derivation of the word "London." In the same page we observe in a note, under the word "Manchester," that "in modern Irish it would be better to adopt the names by which this and other English towns are familiarly known,

aṁail leir. Tá re oċt mile air faḋ agur ré ṁile air
leiċeaḋ ńo mar rin. Giḋ go b-fuil re ċo mor a'r innir-
rim ḋuit, tá mé-re uaigneaċ ann, mar ġeall naċ b-fuil
agam aon ḋuine ḋe mo ṁuintir- féin le feicrint (to see).
Táiḋ ḋaoine ann ro ar gaċ tir faoi 'n ġréin: Feicim
gaċ lá an t-Eireannaċ agur an t-Albanaċ, an Francaċ,
agur an Spaineaċ, an t-Americanaċ, agur muintir ar
`Aurtralia, agur ó h-oileain (islands) an ċiun-ḟairrge
(Pacific).

Cuimniġim go minic air mo ċairoiḃ 'r an m-baile;
ort féin, a aċair ḋilir, air mo ṁaċair, air mo ḋearb-
bráċair Seorra agur air Patruic, air mo ḋearb-ṡuir
Una (Winefrid), agur air mo ċol-ceaċaraċa. Tá ḋuil
agam go b-fuilio uile rlán. Tá mé féin a rláinte maiċ,

<hr>

than endeavour to revive those that are now obsolete." For this reason we
now write London, Lonvon; Australia, Aurtralia; August, Auguſt. For
if foreign words, or those of technical import, and names of special localities,
have been without the slightest hesitation adopted into the vocabulary of the
Teutonic nations, what is to prevent Irishmen from using the same liberty in
adopting, as their own, words designating places and things which, in days
of old, were not known, or if known, not so fully as at present, to our Irish
ancestors, and for which, consequently, they have left us no nomenclature.
The writer of these Lessons has, therefore, no hesitation in introducing, when
necessary, into Gaelic, words like the following:—Electricity, telegraph, tele-
gram, Algebra.

These terms are so familiar to English speakers that we are not surprised
to hear occasionally persons apparently educated, but who cannot certainly
lay claims to scholarship, speak of them as pure English, and with ignorant
simplicity ask those conversant with Keltic, what is the Gaelic or Irish of
technical names of foreign origin, not considering that they are quite as Irish
as they are English or French.

The introduction of words of this class into the Gaelic vocabulary does
not by any means prove that it is wanting in copiousness or richness. On the
contrary there is no tongue, not even Greek or German, that can compete with
Gaelic in its feasibility of forming compounds, and its ever-productive fecun-
dity in yielding, in the hands of any competent linguistic artist, new terms
by which every shade of meaning can be fully and fitly expressed; yet it is
true that, no matter how rich or copious soever or how fecund in giving
birth to terms a language may be, instances will occur in which no combination of primitives or derivatives will convey the exactly identical idea which
a particular name, known from common usage, will convey. This is well
exemplified in the French language. No enemy of the French people can
deny that their language is rich and copious in the highest degree; yet
Frenchmen cannot, it seems, find in their language equivalents for "beef-
steak," "meetings," "tenant-right," "eviction," "poor-house," "my lord,"
"steamer," "Whig," "Tory." No literal translation will convey, in the
French language, the idea attached to these words in English.

buıdeaċar do Ḋhıa, ȝıd nı b-ꝼuıl an ṫpeuṗ ann ṗo ċo ȝoṗṁ aȝuṗ ċo ȝlınn, no an t-aeṗ ċo ṗlaınteaṁaıl a'ṗ caıd aȝaıd-ṗe.

Nı ꝼuaıṗ me ṗaoṗċuȝad aıṗ bıċ ꝼóṗ; aċt tá duıl aȝam leıṗ a ȝ-cıonn ṗeaċtṁaıne (at the end of a week) le conȝ-nad Ḋé. Beıd aȝam aıṗȝead le cuṗ ċuȝad 'nuaıṗ ṗȝṗı-obꝼaıd me anıṗ.

Ȝo b-tı ṗın, aȝuṗ ȝo bṗaċ ıṗ mıṗe, a aċaıṗ óılıṗ, do ṁaċ ṁuıṗṗeaċ,

Coȝaṅ.

FORTY-FIRST LESSON.

Derivative Nouns in Irish are personal or abstract:

Personal Nouns end in óıṗ, aıṗe, aı, aıd, and are formed from primitive nouns or from past participles.

Ḋoṗuṗ, a door; doṗuṗoıṗ, and, contractedly, doṗṗóıṗ.

Saoċ, labour, punishment; ṗaoċóıṗ, a punisher, a torturer.

Ⱳolċa, praised, *past part.* ; molċóıṗ, a praiser.

Ȝṗáduıȝċe, loved; ȝṗáduıȝċeoıṗ.

Saṗuıȝċe, overccme, rescued, surpassed, exceeded, violated; ṗaṗuıȝċeoıṗ, one who by persevering overcomes another; a rescuer, a conqueror, a violater; root, ṗáṗ, very, over-much.

Personal Nouns in aıṗe.

Cealȝ, deceit; cealȝaıṗe, a deceitful, tricky fellow.

Cṗuıt, a harp; cṗuıtıṗe, a harper.

Sealȝ, hunting; ṗealȝaıṗe, a hunter.

The endings óıṗ, aıṗe, are supposed to be broken forms of the word ꝼeaṗ, a man; if so, ꝼeaṗ is also the root of the Latin ending *or;* as, amat*or*, ȝṗáduıȝċeoıṗ; and of the English ending *er;* as, lov*er*.

Personal Nouns in aı, aıd,*-uıd (we omit the usual final e).

Caċ, a battle, a battalion; caċaıd, a warrior.

Ⱳuc, a pig, swine; ṁucaıd, a swine-herd.

---

*In presenting to the student the meaning of the termination aıd, aı, or aoı, we must ascend to the very cradle of Keltic syllabling. In tracing thence

Scaṗ, a story, a history; ſcaṗṗaıṗ, an historian.
Cṗeuṗ, a flock; cṗeuṗaıṗ, a shepherd.

Abstract Nouns terminate in aſ (or eaſ), *m.*; aċc, *fem.*;
or in the gen. case sing. feminine of adjectives.

ᲛᎯ or eaſ, *m.*

Adjs., maıċ, good; maıċeaſ, *m*, goodness.
Olc, bad; olcaſ, badness.
Caṗaṗ, a friend; caṗaṗaſ, friendship.

---

to the present the several meanings of the word, we see an illustration of the
way in which human speech has grown.

Aı, ᲐᎧı, or ᲐᎧıṗ is a primative—the root of many families of words.

In its very earliest acceptation it means (1) element, and, therefore,
(2) fire, air, water. Aı, fire, is still preserved in its derivative, ᲐᎧıṗeal, a
coal; and its diminutive form, ᲐᎧıṗealóꝃ, or ᲐᎧıṗlóꝃ, a spark. Aı, air, in
ᲐᎧeṗaſ or ᲐᎧeſ; aı, water, in aṗ, fluid, the root of aṗaıſ, a river; (3) a first
principle, therefore, or cause; (4) a being, a human being, a person, as we
see in the words ſaoı, a sage (from ſo, good; and ᲐᎧı, being); ṗaoı, a bad
man (from ṗo, bad; and ᲐᎧı); ṗſaoı, a druid (from ṗaıſ, oak; and ᲐᎧı);
ſaıṗ, a prophet (from ſa, a cause; and aıṗ); Latin, *vates;* one of the order
of priests, to whom, among the Celts, the office of offering sacrifice and
explaining natural causes was assigned, O'B. 345; (5) the liver, which so
well aids in supporting life, in this sense it is written ᲐᎧe, and ᲐᎧeṗ—plural
ᲐᎧeṗa. In its signification of person, applied specially, it means (6) stranger,
a guest—in which sense it is commonly written ᲐᎧıṗ. (Hence ᲐᎧıṗeaċ,
hospitable, courteous; ᲐᎧıṗeaċc, hospitality, courteousness.) Also (7) a respectable, skilful, learned person; and, in the abstract, (8) skill, knowledge,
honor, respect, learning, discipline, elegance, stateliness; (9) a swan.

It not only signifies a being, but the abode of beings; therefore, territory,
land, island; as, ı Columḃ Cılle, the Island of Columbkille; (Hebrew, *ai*, an
island); also the substance, or wealth, which any territory must contain.
Hence it signifies cattle, a herd—particularly sheep; from ᲐᎧıṗ, a herd, is
derived ᲐᎧıṗaıſe, a keeper of flocks, and, in a special sense, a shepherd.

From ᲐᎧı, a being, is formed ṅaoı (i. e., aṅ ᲐᎧı), a creature; and its diminutive form, which, to this day, is in common use, ṅaoıṗaṅ, or, by changing ṗ into ṅ, ṅaoıṅaṅ, an infant. Also ṅı, or ṅıꝃ, a girl, a female descendant;
which is employed before the family names of females, as Ua, or O, is before
those of males; as, maıſe "Nı" Coṅṅaıll ıṅꝃeaṅ Ꝺoṁṅaıll Uı Coṅṅaıll,
Mary O'Connell; the daughter of Daniel O'Connell. "Nı," and not "Ua,"
or O, is placed before the family name when women are spoken of.

Oıṗe, a forefather, an educator, a professor, a teacher, is derived from
ᲐᎧı, and ṗe, of; i. e., a man of learning, knowledge, skill, discipline; or from
ᲐᎧı, a being; and Ꝺé, of God; one holding God's place in the guidance of
youth. Aoıṗe, youth, springs from this root, and its derivative ᲐᎧıṗeaṗaċ,
well-behaved: so do many others which apparently are simple words.
Those we have given will suffice.

Oᵹlac, a young man, a bondman; oᵹlacár, bondage, a kind
of metre.

Act, *f.*

Aonᵦa, *adj.*, single; from aon, one; aonᵦact, unity
Daona, *adj.*, human; ᵦaonact, humanity.
Tᵱaill, *n*, a slave; tᵱailleact, slavery.
Sᵹeul, a story; ᵱᵹeulaiᵦ, a story-teller; ᵱᵹeulaiᵦeact, story-
telling.
Sealᵹaiᵱe, a hunter; ᵱealᵹaiᵱeact, hunting.
Meallcóiᵱ, a deceiver; meallcóiᵱeact, the act of deceiving.

e, the gen. case sing. fem. of adjectives.

Aᵱᵦ, high; aiᵱᵦe, height.
Tᵱom, heavy, deep, pensive, pregnant; tᵱoime, heaviness,
pensiveness, pregnancy.
Ȝeal, white, bright; ȝile, brightness, whiteness.
From ᵱlán comes ᵱlainte, and not ᵱlaine; and from ᵱaoᵱ,
ᵱaoiᵱᵱe, and not ᵱaoiᵱe; ᵦaoᵱ, ᵦaoiᵱᵱe; ᵱaoᵱᵱact and
ᵦaoᵱᵱact, freedom and slavery.

Diminutives in aᵱ, *m.;* in iᵱ, *mas.* or *fem.;* in óᵹ, *fem.;* as,

Aᵱᵦ, high.

Aᵱᵦaᵱ, an elevation, a terrace.

Boct, poor.

Boccaᵱ, a poor person.

Cᵱoc, *m*, a hill.

Cᵱocaᵱ, *m*, a hillock; cᵱo-
caiᵱᵱ, a very small hill.

Loc, a lake.

Locaᵱ, a small lake.

Dall, blind.

Dallóᵹ, *f*, play called blind-
man's buff; a bandage co-
vering the eyes; a buffet,
a leech, a mole, a dor-
mouse, blind-fish, or king-
fish.
Dallaᵱ, *m*, a great heap; a
cairn, an Ogham monu-
ment; also for ᵦallaᵱaᵱ,
m, a blind fellow; one who
is purblind.

Cɪaṅ, dusky, grey, dark. From cɪaṅ is derived (St.) Cɪaṅaɲ's name, and that of *Kirwin*, which, in Irish, is Cɪaṅôubaɲ, meaning a swarthy, black haired person.—*Transactions of the Ossianic Society*. (Note by Standish Hayes, vol. iii., p. 50.)

Cɪaṅô5, *f*, a black insect with many claws; a kind of beetle, a chafer; cɪaṅaɲ, *m*, a small black sod; a clod of turf.

Stewart is justly of opinion that the termination ṅaɪ̇ḃ or ṅɪḃ, added to nouns, has a collective (not a plural) import, like the termination *rie* in the French words, *cavalerie, infanterie*, and *ry* in the English words, *cavalry, infantry, yeomanry*; as, laocṅaɪ̇ḃ, a band of heroes.—*O'Donovan*, p. 333.

Of this class are :

Eacṅaɪ̇ḃ, cavalry; from eac, a steed.
Euɲlaɪ̇ḃ, birds; from euɲ, a bird.
Ṁacṅaɪ̇ḃ, youths; from ṁac, a son.

Many words that are not diminutives end in aɲ; as, lub, a bend; lubaɲ, *m*, a bow; môṅaɲ, many, a large number; from môṅ, large; caṅaɲ (from caṅ, turn, or coṅ, foot), a path; oɪlleaɲ, an island; from ol, above, over (as in the word ol-aɪlpeac, cis-alpine), and láɲ, the tide, *i.e.*, land above the waves; or from oɪle, other, apart; and laɲ, land, *i.e.*, land apart from the main land.

Other words ending in aɲ, from caɲ, time; or from caɪṅ, possessions; are of this class; as, ṅucaɪṅ, eternal, ever-lasting, as found in the last part of the Apostles' creed (aɲɲṙ aɲ m-beaca ṙuacaɪṅ, and [in] life everlasting), is derived from ṙo, bliss, blissful, and caɲ, time; meaning the blissful continuity of eternal life. From the termination caɪṅ, or cáɲ, land, a region, riches, possessions in land or in stock, are formed the words ᵹɪoɲcaɪṅ, a vineyard; from ᵹɪoɲ, wine, and caɲ; ṅoṙcaɲ, a rose-garden; muɪṙṙɪcaɲ, a garden of myrtles; Bṙɪcaɪṅ, Britain—the land of the Brits, or speckled people; Ṁaɪṙɪcaɪṅ, Mauritania—the caɲ of the Mauri; Ḣɪɲḃuṙcaɲ, the caɲ or region along the river Indus or Sindus, as it was originally called.

Ɪac, a region, a territory, is in its broken form ṙa, the termination of almost all the Latin topographical names that have that ending. Ex.: Assyria, Αιρυριαċ, from Αιρυρι and ιαċ. It is, however, found as a prefix in the word Jaċαιlle, the region of beauty.

A few words end in bαρ, top, produce; as, ceolαbαρ, melody, warbling; ceolαbαρ, na n-euρ, the warbling of birds; from ceol, song; buιllebαρ, foliage, leaves (Scotch, bιleaċ).

Fαοι Ċοιllτe Ƶlaρ.

We believe the following ' Chansonnette' to be the production of a Connaught poet. His poetry has outlived his name :—

Foρρ :—" *One morning very early, one morning in the Spring.*"

I.

Naċ αοιbιρ bo na h-éιρíριb
  D'eιρíƶean ƶo h-αρb,
'S a bιbeaρρ a ceιleαbαρ le ρ-a ċéιle
  Αιρ αοη ċραοιb amαιρ!
Nι mαρ ρρ bαm féιρ, a'r
  Dom' ċeub mιle ƶραb—
Ir fαbα ó na ċéιle οραιρρ
  D'eιρíƶeαρρ ƶaċ lá.

II.

Ir bαιρe í ιοnα an lιle,
  Ir beιρe í 'na 'n rƶéιṁ
Ir bιρρe í 'n an beιblιρρ,
  'S ιr rοιllιƶe í ná n'ƶρéιρ—
Ir feαρρ ιοná rιρ uιle
  Αι uαιρleaċτ 'r a meιρρ,
'S a Dιa! τá ιr na flαιéιr
  Fuαρƶαιl bo m' péιρρ.

———

(*Translation.*)

UNDER THE GREENWOOD.

I.

How pleasant, O little warblers!
  Smiles Morn upon your bow'rs,
Where each sings to his love, beside him
  In the gladness of sunny hours.
Not thus—ah, not thus—shines morning
  On me and my darling queen;
It may break over both as brightly,
  But far is the way between!

II.

She's whiter than the white lily,
Oh lovelier to gaze upon!
She's sweeter than violin singing—
More radiant than the Sun.
But, than all her beauty, more beauteous
Is her mind's nobility—
O Lord! make short this absence—
This bitter woe to me!

Translated by ERIONNACH.

Verbs end, for the first person singular, in ɪm.

In order to know the verbal endings it is necessary to learn thoroughly the conjugation of a regular active verb, which has been already furnished in the "Easy Lessons;" *see* Lessons 49, 50.

VOCABULARY.

Aṁʒaɲ, *m*, privation, tribulation, affliction; from aṁ (a privative particle), and ʒaɲ, aid, help.

Aɲɲó, m, more correctly, aɲɲá, or aɲɲaċ, from aɲ, not, and ɲaċ, prosperity, misery, hardship, distress, misfortune, great poverty. Ⲧá me aɲɲ aɲɲo, I am in great poverty. Aɲɲóċaċ and aɲɲoḃaċ, afflicted, poor, miserable.

Ḃuaɲ-ɼeaɼṁaċ, *adjec.*, persevering; from buaɲ, lasting; and ɼeaɼṁaċ.

Ⲥeaɲɲ Ⲙaɲá, Kenmare; from ceaɲɲ, head; and ṁaɲa, gen. case of muɪɼ, of the sea.

Ⲫɪoḃáɪl, *f.* (from bɪ, wanting; and báɪl, a blessing, a prosperous issue, success;) loss, defeat, destruction.

Ⲫoġlaṁ, *m*, learning.

Iɲⲧleaċⲧ, *f*, understanding, intellect, ingenuity, device; ɪɲⲧleaċⲧ, for ɪɲɲleaċⲧ; from ɪɲɲ, or ɪɲⲧɪɲ, and leaċⲧ, a lesson.

Ⲓoɲaɲɲ (from ɪoɲ, or aɲɲ, in; and aoɲ, one), the same; ɪoɲaɲɲ aʒuɼ, the same as; b'ɪoɲɲaɲ leɪⲧe aʒuɼ, it was the same with her—*i.e.*, she considered it the same as.

Ⲓoɲɲɼuɪḃ, *m*, an attempt, an attack; ċuʒ ɼe ɪoɲɲɼuɪḃ oɼm, he made an attack on me; *v*, to attack; *prep.*, to, towards; it is derived from ɪoɲɲ, or aɲɲ, in; and ɼuɪḃe, sit.

Laⲧaɪɼ, *n*, *f*, presence, company; laⲧaɪɼeaċⲧ, presence; a laⲧaɪɼ (*adv*), (at) present; as, bɪ me a laⲧaɪɼ, I was present.

Ⲟɪḃeaɼ, *m*, education; from oɪḃe, a teacher, a professor. (*See Note* p. 254)

Sɪl, *v*, to shed, part; aɪʒ ɼɪⲧ ɲa ɲḃeoɲ, shedding tears.

EXERCISE LXVIII.

Ⲥeaɲɲmaɲa,
Aɲ Ⲫɪċċeaḃ lá ḃe ṁɪ ṁeoḃaɪɲ
Aɲ Ⲫoġṁaɪɼ, 1861.

A ṁɪc ṁuɪɼɲɪʒ—Aɲ leɪⲧɪɼ ḃo ɼʒɼɪoḃ ⲧu ó Loɲḃoɲ aɲ ḃoṁaḃ-la-ḃeuʒ ḃe 'ɲ ṁɪ a ⲧá ċaɼⲧ, ḃo ⲫuaɼamaɼ (we received) aɪɼ maɪḃɪɲ (in [the] morning) aɲɲ ɪuḃ. Ḃɪ

bríoḋ mór orainn 'g a leiġeaḋ. Do ḟil do ṁaċaiṗ beorḃa
aig cuiṁnuġaḋ ort, 'nuair conairc (saw) rí do rgrioḃan.
B' ionnan leiċe é aguf ċu beiċ a laċair. Bí luaċġair
mór air Ⅿaire aguf air Ċáit, aguf air Ⅿaible. Na
bí co faḋa airír gan leitir a ċur cuġainn.

Tá tu mar bí Ⅾearalt (Gerald) Ⅾriffin a Lonḋon
éimċioll beiċ m-bliaġna ficċiḋ ó rín, faoi amġar aguf
anró. So é an ċaoi tá re le gaċ uile fear óg, mór-
intineaċ (high-minded), tuigrionaċ (intelligent). Na caill
do ṁirneaċ: Bí buan-rearmaċ; táiḋ laeċe maiċe romat
(good days are before you). Táir óg; táiḋ neart aguf
luḋ do ċnaṁ aġaḋ; táiḋ cial aguf intleaċt aġaḋ, oiḋear
aguf foġlam, rubailciḋ aguf tuigre aġaḋ. Ní beiḋ caill,
no anro ort níor faiḋe, óir cuirim cuġaḋ 'ran leitir ro,
nóta cuig punta: glac leiġean cuġaḋ féin, o'n caill
aguf o'n biċ-braġail ann a raḋ tu. B' feiḋir gur b' é an
nuḋ ir fearr a ċarla leat, an méiḋ rin ḋ' fulang. Ní
forur ḋul air aġaiḋ air fairrge an t-raoġail ro gan
tonta borḃa ionnruiḋe. Cuirim annti ro, leitir cuġaḋ
o'n maiġirtín* aig anḋ-ċeannaiḋ a Lonḋon le a b-fuil aige
caiḋreaḋ. 'Se a banamail, aguf ir ré mo banamail féin
é, naċ b-fuil aig Eirionnaċ aguf go mór-mór aig Ca-
toiliceaċ, maiċ air biċ le faġail mar buḋ cóir a Sac-
ranra: aċt ḋeanfaiḋ an fear caraḋaċ mór ro, nuḋ maiċ
ḋuit. Bí rlán: cuiriḋ do ṁaċair aguf do ḋearḃṗiura a
nġraḋ aguf a m-beann aċt cuġat.

Go raiḋ tu faoi ċuṁḋaċ Ⅾé, re guiḋe

D' aċar ancuṁanaiġ,

Séarun Ⅿac Seaḃaiġ.

EXERCISE LXIX.

Dear Sir—Ⅿ Ṡaoi óil—The young man who will give
you this letter is the son of an honest farmer on my estate.
Ir mac féilmaire cnearta tá air mo ḋuċaiḋ-re an fear

---

* Ⅿ (initial) after the preposition and article is not aspirated in the
spoken language; as, o'n maiġirtín; o 'n meuḋ. To aspirate it, however,
is conformable to principle, and accords with the practice observed in the
written language by the best Irish scholars.

óg a beaṅṗaṫ buiṫ an leiṫiṫ ṫo. He is (judging), from all I have heard, a worthy man. Tá ṫe o'n méiḃ ḃo cualaiḃ me, 'nna ḃuine ṫiuṫṫaċ. The youth has gone to London to carve his own fortune. Do cuaiḃ an ṫ-óganaċ ḃo Lonḃon le n-a ṫoṫṫun a ġeaṫṫaḃ amaċ ḃo ṫéin. I have learned (heard) that he is a person of (in whom there is) promise (aṅḃ-ḃoiġ), learning (ṫoġlaṁ), and virtue (ḃeaġ-ḃeuṫa). See if you can do something for him. I know you possess (ġo b-ṫuil aġaḃ) great influence (cuṁaċṫ). Any thing you do for him I shall consider (ḃo ṁeaṫṫaiḃ me) as having been done for (ġuṫ ṫinneaḃ é aiṫ ṫon).

Dear Sir, your very obedient servant,

Do ṫeiṫḃiṫaiġ ṫo-úṫṫamaiġ,

Seaġan O'Duiḃiṫ.

2l m-ḃaile Coṫcaiġ, an ḃeiċṁaḃ lá ḃe ṁi nẹoṫan an Ṫoġṁaiṫ, 1861.

FORTY-SECOND LESSON.

From words of one syllable, with which our first Lesson commenced, the learner has steadily advanced in knowledge of special etymology to be able now to understand at first sight the meaning of a polysyllable or compound word of any length. Along with special etymology, with which the art of spelling is so combined, he must have acquired, what has been considered a great difficulty in Gaelic learning, a knowledge of spelling with facility and correctness, and become familiar with the idiomatic turns of Keltic speech. We need not, therefore, exclude, as we have hitherto done, "words of learned length" in Gaelic, from our coming Exercises, should their use be required.

The grammatical qualities appertaining to nouns are gender, number, case, person.

Of gender we have already treated fully (See Sixteenth and Seventeenth Lessons, pp. 87-98).

To learn how Irish nouns form the plural, consult Lessons Twenty-third and Twenty-fourth.—*Ibid.*

Person, in grammar, derives its order and relation from the speaker, and is *first*, when it refers to the great *I* (the speaker); *second*, when to the being spoken to; *third*, when to the name of that spoken of.

Case remains yet to be treated. We define it, then, to

be a change or increase in the final syllable of nouns significative of a relative change in meaning.

Gaelic nouns undergo four such changes in their terminations, and consequently there must be four cases. These we call

1st. { Nominative.
{ Accusative.
2nd. Genitive.
3rd. Dative.
4th. Vocative, answering to the nominative case of address in English grammar.

Modern Irish grammarians, who have investigated this subject, seem agreed that the lowest number of cases peculiar to nouns in our language is four. (See *Irish Grammar*, by Dr. Donovan, and the *College Irish Gammar, second edition, p.* 55); from which we quote the following:—

" In regard to the cases, their names and their number, it may be well to propose here a few questions, and to answer them, for the satisfaction of the learned and enlightened student.

" Why are the nominative and accusative ranked as one case? Because according to the definition of case, they have only one or the same inflection. Why then retain the term accusative? Because it expresses an idea different, either in fact, in mode, or in grammatical relation, from those conveyed by the direct or nominative case.

" Dative alone is a name given, in this edition, to the third case, just (1) to lessen the numbers of cases, and (2) because this practice—of calling the third case by the term dative—has the sanction of Greek grammarians in the grammars they have written of that ancient tongue.

" Why is the term *possessive*, as in English grammar, not employed instead of *genitive?* Because less suitable and less truthful to express the meaning of the first oblique case. Let us see what the words possessive and genitive mean, and how far that meaning is applicable to this case.

" The term genitive conveys the idea of *generation, origin, birth, source, first cause,* and indirectly, that of *possession, control, relation;* as, the father's son (generation, birth); this boy is Patrick's son (birth, possession); that is George's gun (possession); father's land (possession); James's arm (connexion, source, origin); the ship's side (same, by analogy). The term possessive conveys only the secondary meaning of the first oblique case—namely, possession, and does not express that of generation, origin, birth, source, while the term genitive does fully convey those ideas along with that of possession. Which term, then, is to be preferred? Certainly that of genitive.

" Again, in English there are two kinds of possessive cases—the real and the false, or the Anglo-Saxon and the Norman:

The Real—Anglo-Saxon.	False—Norman.
Peter's side.	The side of Peter.
The hill's foot.	The foot of the hill.

"We cannot say, the hill's foot; because the possessive, *hill's*, would denote a possessor, and a hill cannot possess. The false possessive (*of*) then must be used in those instances where no real possession is implied. The real and the false English possessives have only one *real* corresponding case in Gaelic, the genitive. It expresses, as in Latin and in Greek, real or analogical origin, cause, connexion, procession, possession. It is better to employ the term genitive, which, as in Latin and Greek, embraces both kinds.

"The vocative singular and plural has in many instances inflections different from the nominative, and is on this account properly called by another name than that of ' nominative case of address.' "

DECLENSION.

Taking the definition of case to be a change or increase in the final syllable of a noun significative of a correlative change in meaning, there are nouns of a certain ending in the nominative that have a class of changes which other nouns of a different ending in the nominative or uninflected form have not. Declension then is the formation of case-endings. In Gaelic there are *five classes* of case-endings, a point on which grammarians seem at present to have agreed. There are, therefore, five declensions.

The key of the series of case-endings of a noun of the first or second declension, is the final vowel of the last syllable of the undeclined noun. This vowel has been called the " characteristic," because by it the character of the declension becomes known. It can, with equal propriety, be called the key-vowel.

Our readers already know that the gender of a noun which is the name of an inanimate object is regulated by this key-vowel. (Nay, the formation of the plural of an immense class of nouns—the parasyllabic class—is directed entirely by it.) It is no wonder then that Dr. O'Donovan says: "the gender has more influence on the formation of the cases than any ending of the nominative."—*Irish Grammar*, p. 78.

The key-vowel is our *principal* guide in the formation of the three first declensions; gender a *necessary* help.

Whenever a noun ends in a consonant it is plain that the vowel immediately preceding it must be broad or slender.

THE FIRST DECLENSION

embraces nouns ending in a consonant which is just preceded in the same syllable by a *broad* vowel, provided the noun is of the masculine gender.

We say: " provided the noun is of the masculine gender," for if it be feminine, it is then not of the first declension; as, cluaṙ, an ear; coṙ, a foot; láṁ, a hand; . rlac. a rod; which are feminine (*see* Part II., p. 93).

All nouns, therefore, specified in "Rule I., for knowing the gender of those Irish nouns which are names of inanimate objects" (*Ibid.*, p. 93), are of the first declension; but all the exceptions to Rule I. are of the second or third. Similarly, names of men, for the greater part, which end in a consonant preceded by a broad vowel, belong to this declension.

EXAMPLES.

Báṗd, *mas.*, a poet, a bard.

Primary, or unaspirated, form :

	Singular.	Plural.
Nom. } Acc. }	Báṗd	Báịṗd
Gen.	Báịṗd	Báṗd
Dat.	Báṗd	Báṗdaịb
Voc.	Báịṗd	Báṗda.

2.

Caṗaṇ, *m.*, a path.

Nom. } Acc. }	Caṗaṇ	Caṗaịṇ
Gen.	Caṗaịṇ	Caṗaṇ
Dat.	Caṗaṇ	Caṗaṇaịb
Voc.	Caṗaịṇ	Caṗaṇa.

3.

Ⅿaṗcaċ, *m.*, a rider.

Nom. } Acc. }	Ⅿaṗcaċ	Ⅿaṗcaịḡ
Gen.	Ⅿaṗcaịḡ	Ⅿaṗcaċ
Dat.	Ⅿaṗcaċ	Ⅿaṗcaịḡịb
Acc.	Ⅿaṗcaịḡ	Ⅿaṗcaċa.

The changes which the initial or first consonant of the word assumes, are regulated by the rules that direct the phonetic use of aspiration and eclipsis of which we have already treated at considerable length (*see* Lessons 18, 19; and Lessons 4, 5, 6, 9, 11). We shall give an example or two of the articulated form.

SECOND DECLENSION.

The key-vowel of the second declension is slender (ị); nouns, therefore, that end in a consonant preceded in the same syllable by the vowel ị, are of this declension.

And these are all feminine (*see* Rule 3, p. 94). Nay, so far does the influence of gender prevail, that nouns having the key-vowel broad (which is the characteristic of the first) are, nevertheless, of the second declension, if they are feminine.

This declension is distinguished from the first by its taking an additional syllable (e) in the genitive case. Nouns belonging to it are then of the *im*parasyllabic class.

EXAMPLE.

Ꝺuıl, *f.*, a wish, a desire, an element.

	Singular.	Plural.
Nom. } Acc. }	ꝺuıl	ꝺuıle
Gen.	ꝺuıle (*dooil-e*)	ꝺuıl
Dat.	ꝺuıl	ꝺuılıḃ
Voc.	ḋuıl	ḋuıle

*** Ꝺuıl, an element, is pronounced short, nearly like ꝺıl; ꝺúıl, a wish—long.

In like manner are declined all nouns of this class which end in a single or double consonant preceded by ı; as, cıll, *f.*, a church; cláır, a sand-pit, a hollow; cáın, *f.*, reproach, a fine; ꝺꞃuım, *f.*, the back; ʒlóıꞃ, glory; mın, *f.*, meal; nıṁ, *f.*, poison; páır, *f.*, passion; ꞅꞃáıꝺ, *f.*, street; ꞅꞇáıꞃ, *f.*, history; ꞅuıl, *f.*, an eye; uaıꞃ, hour.

Example of a noun feminine of which the key-vowel is broad: coꞅ, *f.*, a foot.

2.

Nom. } Acc. }	coꞅ (*kos*)	coꞅa (*kosa*)
Gen.	coıꞅe (*koshe*)	coꞅ
Dat.	coıꞅ (*kosh*)	coꞅaıḃ
Voc.	ċoıꞅ (*chosh*)	ċoꞅa

Observe—In the genitive case singular how a slender vowel ı is inserted before ꞅ, because the increase é in the next syllable is slender. This is caused by the principle of vowel assimilation—slender with slender and broad with broad, caol le caol aʒuꞅ leaṫan le leaṫan—so often explained for the learner.

The entire class of feminine nouns ending in a consonant preceded by a broad vowel are declined like the above:

cloċ, *f.*, a stone,	laṁ, a hand,
cloʒ, *f.*, a bell,	ꞅeoꝺ, a jewel,
cluaꞅ, *f.*, an ear,	ꞅlaꞇ, *f.*, a rod,
cꞃoꞅ, } *f.*, cross,	ꞅꞃon, the nose,
cꞃoċ, } *f.*, cross,	ꞇuaʒ, *f.*, an axe.

And all feminine nouns in ó5 (diminutives and derivatives); as, cιαρό5, a chafer; ϝυιρεό5, f., a lark; ϝυιϝεό5,
f., a window; ρ̇εαcό5, a pea-hen.

THIRD DECLENSION.

The third declension comprises those nouns, as well feminine as masculine, which end in a consonant preceded by a
single or broad vowel.

Though no key-vowel serves to distinguish as a group the class that
belongs to this declension from those of the first and second, yet nouns of a
certain termination and order are classified as belonging to it; for example:
names of offices peculiar to men; as, meαllcóιρ, cϝυ̇cυιϳ̇εeoιρ; abstract
nouns (*fem.*) in αċc; as, ϝαoιϝαċc, freedom; verbal nouns that have a broad
vowel in the final syllable.

The peculiar feature of this declension, by which it is distinguished from
the second as well as from the first, is that the genitive singular takes an
increase not of e but of α.

EXAMPLES.

(1) ℳeαllcóιρ, *m.*, a deceiver; (2) αιϝϝαċc, *f.*, love, fondness; (3) ꝺαιρ, *f.*, oak.

	Singular.	Plural.
(1) Nom. Acc.	meαllcóιρ	meαllcóιϝιꝺ
Gen.	meαllcóϝα	meαllcóιρ
Dat.	meαllcóιρ	meαllcóιϝιꝺ
Voc.	ṁeαlcóιρ	ṁeαllcóιϝιꝺ
(2) Nom. Acc.	αιϝϝαċc	αιϝϝαċcα
Gen.	αιϝϝαċcα	αιϝϝαċc
Dat.	αιϝϝαċc	αιϝϝαċcαιꝺ
Voc.	αιϝϝαċc	αιϝϝαċcα

All derivatives in αċc are declined after the above form.

	Singular.	Plural.
(3) Nom. Acc.	ꝺαιρ	ꝺαϝα
Gen.	ꝺαϝα	ꝺαιρ
Dat.	ꝺαιρ	ꝺαϝαιꝺ
Voc.	ꝺαιρ	ꝺαϝα

So are declined cóιρ, *f.*, justice—gen. cóϝα; cυιꝺ, *f.*, a
portion—gen. coꝺα; mil, *f.*, honey—gen. meαlα; as, mι
ια meαlα; muιρ, *f.*, sea—gen. mαϝα, of the sea. ℳċαιρ,
father—gen. αċαρ; mαċαιρ, mother—gen. mαċαρ; bϝαċαιρ,
brother—gen. bϝαċαρ, are of this declension, though they

form the gen. case commonly by omitting the slender vowel ı before the final consonant; as, aṫaṙ, maṫaṙ, braṫaṙ; caṫaıṙ, *f.*, a city, makes the gen. caṫaṙaċ, and con tractedly, caṫṙaċ.

To the third declension belong — (1) personal nouns ending in óıṙ; (2) abstract nouns, in aċt; (3) verbal nouns that terminate in uġaḋ, aḋ, aıl, aċt; (4) all primitive nouns that form the genitive by taking an additional syllable (a). This last class can be learned only by experience.

In regard to them, the words of Dr. O'Donovan can be appropriately and with truth applied, " the learner will discover that, as in Latin, Greek, and other languages, so in Irish, he must learn the gender and genitive case singular of most nouns, by reading or the help of a dictionary."

FOURTH DECLENSION.

It is a fact, that the final syllable of a noun terminates either in a vowel or a consonant.

Nouns, the final syllable of which end in a vowel, belong to the fourth and fifth declensions. Of these personal nouns, mas. ending in aıṙe, in aıḋe, uıḋe; and other nouns, in e, mas. or fem., are of the fourth declension. Also those that terminate in consonants, viz., ıġ, ıḋ, and diminutives in ın, are of this declension.

It is characterised by having no inflection in the singular. The plural form ends in te, ċe, or ıḋ, as can be learned from Twenty-Fourth Lesson.

EXAMPLES.

Tıġeaṙna, a lord; faınne, a ring.

	Singular.		Plural.
Nom. Acc.	} Tıġeaṙna	Nom. Acc. V.	tıġeaṙnaıḋ
Gen.		Gen.	tıġeaṙnaḋ
Dat.		Dat.	tıġeaṙnaıḋıḃ
Voc.			
Nom. Acc.	} Faınne	Nom. Acc. V.	faınnıḋ
Gen.		Gen.	faınneaḋ
Dat.		Dat.	faınnıḋıḃ
Voc.*			

---

* T, ʀ, and p in the examples, tıġeaṙna, faıne, peaṙṙa, are aspirated in the vocative case.

FIFTH DECLENSION.

The nouns belonging to this declension are very limited in number. Most of them terminate in a vowel, and are of the fem. gender; some few, however, are masculine. Their distinguishing mark is, that in the gen. case they end in ŋ.

See Forty-Fourth Lesson, in which is presented a full list of all the nouns of this declension, pp. 270, 271, 272, &c.

EXAMPLE.

Peaṗṙa, a person.

Singular.		Plural.	
Nom. Acc. V.	peaṗṙa	Nom. Acc. V.	peaṗṙaŋa
Gen.	peaṗṙaŋ	Gen.	peaṗṙaŋ
Dat.	peaṗṙaıŋ	Dat.	peaṗṙaŋaıḃ

VOCABULARY.

Aıḃéıṙ, *f.* 2d dec. (pr. *áyveish*), from aı, element, baıṙ, of death, [abyss, sea, ocean; Welsh, *affwys*; it is like the Greek, ἄβυσσος.

Aıḃéıṙeaċ, vast, immense, prodigious, exaggerating.

Coṗṗuᵹaḋ, stirring, moving; from coṗ, a motion; ŋa ḃéaŋ coṗ, do not move, coṗ aıṙ ċoṗ, rolling over and over; roll on roll.

Ḋoṗċaḃaṙ, *m.* 1st dec., darkness; from ḃoṗċa, dark, black.

Falaṁ, *adj.* empty, void, unoccupied. English " fallow," is not unlike it in sound or sense.

Faoŋ, *adj.* void, empty, vain, devoid of shape, feeble, *wan;* Latin, *vanum,* changing v into f, *faonum.*

Ꝺoıṗ, *v.* to call, to name, to cry, to crow.

Roıŋŋ, *v.* divide, cut into shares; *n.* a share, a part, a sect; (2) a point, nib, a promontary; Greek, ῥιν, a nose, a promontary.

Soluṙ, *m.* light (from ṙol, a word not now in use, but retained in Latin).

Cúṙ, *m.* gen. cuıṙ; beginning, aıṙ ḃ-cuṙ, in the beginning; written also coṙ. From coṙ is derived coṙaċ, beginning, and coıṙeaċ, *thoish-each,* beginning, commencement, origin, precedence, first place; coıṙıᵹ, *v.* begin thou; coıṙıᵹ oṗc, begin, set too.

Uıṙᵹe, water; *plu.* uıṙᵹċe, waters; ŋa ŋ-uıṙᵹe, of the waters; the more modern and the simpler form of the genitive: ŋa ŋ-uıṙᵹeaḋ, also is used.

An easy Exercise, taken from the Bible.

1. Aıṙ ḃ-cuṙ ḃo ċṙuċuıᵹ Ḋıa ŋeaṁ aᵹuṙ calaṁ. Aᵹuṙ ḃo ḃı aŋ calaṁ faoŋ aᵹuṙ falaṁ; aᵹuṙ ḃo ḃı ḃoṗċaḃaṙ aıṙ aᵹaıḃ ŋa h-aıḃeıṙe aᵹuṙ ḃo ḃı Spıoṗaḋ Ḋé 'ᵹ a ċoṗṗuᵹaḋ oṙ cıoıŋŋ ŋa ŋ-uıṙᵹe. 3. Aᵹuṙ ḃuḃaıṙc Ḋıa; bıḋeaḋ ṙoluṙ aŋŋ, aᵹuṙ ḃo ḃı aŋ ṙoluṙ aŋŋ. 4. Aᵹuṙ ḃo ċoŋŋaıṙc Ḋıa ᵹuṙ buḋ ṁaıċ aŋ ṙoluṙ; aᵹuṙ ṙoıŋŋ ṙe ıḋıṙ aŋ ṙoluṙ aᵹuṙ aŋ ḃoṗċaḃaṙ. 5. Aᵹuṙ ḃo

ġoin Dia be'n t-rolur, lá, agur be'n bonċabar bo ġoir
re Oiḋċe: agur bo rinne an nóin agur an maibin an
ceub lá. 6. Agur bubairt Dia: bioeaḋ rreur a meaḋon na n-uirge, agur roinneaḋ na h-uirġċe ó na h-uirġċib. 7. Agur bo rinne Dia an rreur, agur bo roinn
na h-uirġċe raoi an rréir ó na h-uirġċib or cionn na
rréire; agur bi mar rin. 8. Agur bo ġoir Dia be'n
rreur, neaṁ. Agur bo rinne an nóin agur an maibin
ann bara lá.—*Irish Bible, by Dr. MacHale.*

FORTY-THIRD LESSON.

NOUNS DECLINED WITH THE ARTICLE.

An example or two of the articulated form are, according
to promise, here presented :—

Singular.

Nom. and Acc. an bárb, the bard.
Gen.   an báirb, the bard's.
Dat.   ó 'n m-báirb, from the bard.

Plural.

Nom. and Acc. na báirb, the bards.
Gen.   na m-bárb, the bard's.
Dat.   ó an bárbaib, from the bards.

Coṁrac an engagement, a hand-to-hand fight, (from co
or coṁ, together; and brac, old Irish; *brachium*, Latin,
an arm).

	Singular.	Plural.
N. and Ac.	an coṁrac	na coṁraic
Gen.	an ċoṁraic	na ᵹ-coṁrac
Dat.	ó' n-ᵹ-coṁrac	ó na coṁracaib

Cruaċ, a stack; eaċ, a horse; loċ, a lake; luaċ, a price,
&c., are declined like coṁrac.

Obs.—In words of two or more syllables ċ final (aspirated)
is changed in modern Irish into ᵹ (asp.) in the genitive singular. See example, marcaċ, p. 263.

In Erse or Scotch Gaelic, nouns ending in ċ (asp.) follow the general
analogy of inflection, like the unaspirated c in the foregoing example, coṁrac; or aspirated ċ in words of one syllable.

When the noun báꞃꞃ is declined, as in foregoing lesson, *without* the article, initial b in the genitive case singular is not affected in any way; but declined *with* the article, as in p. 268, it becomes aspirated, thus altering its sound from *b* to *w*. (The rules for, and reasons of this change are found in " *Easy Lessons,*" Part I., observation i., p. 31, second edition.) Again, in the dative or prepositional case singular (not the plural) b in báꞃꞃ, and c in coṁꞃac, are eclipsed each by a cognate letter, b by ṁ; c by ᵹ, because the noun in the singular number affected by the article and governed by a preposition suffers eclipsis in its initial or first consonant when it is not either l, ṁ, ꞃ, or ꞃ. (*See Twentieth Lesson*, Part II. *general rule*, p. 108.)

In the genitive plural also, eclipsis takes place when nouns are affected by the article. (*See Twenty-first Lesson*, Obs. iii., p. 115.)

The declension of a noun with the article is the same as that without the article. Attention to aspiration and eclipsis supplies the *initial* changes.

EXERCISE LXXI.

The several cases of nouns of each declension are here exemplified ; the figures indicate the declension.

Toꞃac (1) loꞃꞃᵹe (2) cláꞃ (1)
Toꞃac (1) áꞃce (2) clocaḃ (1)
Toꞃac (1) ꞃlaca (3) ꞃáꞃlce (4)
Toꞃac (1) ꞃlaꞃꞃce (4) oꞃꞃa (4)

Toꞃac, *n, mas.* commencement, beginning ; from coꞃ, first principle, beginning. Toꞃac in each line is nom. case to " ꞃꞃ" understood :—thus, toꞃac loꞃꞃᵹe (ꞃꞃ) cláꞃ; cláꞃ, a board ; clocaḃ, paving, flagging ; from cloc, a stone ; ꞃáꞃlce, welcome, rejoicing ; oꞃꞃa, a sigh ; are in their respective verses, each nom. case after (ꞃꞃ); loꞃꞃᵹe, *of a ship*; áꞃce, *of a kiln*; ꞃlaca, *of a prince* ; ꞃlaꞃꞃce, *of* health ; are gen. case, governed by toꞃac, by the rule common to all languages that when two nouns signifying different things come together, that denoting possessor, originator, cause or source, of that indicated by the other noun, is put in the gen. case.

Again :

Deꞃꞃe loꞃꞃᵹe a bacaḃ
Deꞃꞃe áꞃc' a loꞃᵹaḃ
Deꞃꞃe ꞃlaca a cáꞃꞃeaḃ
Deꞃꞃe ꞃlaꞃꞃce oꞃꞃa.

Deiṛe, end; báṫaḋ, to drown; loṛgaḋ, to burn; cáineaḋ, to disparage; oṛna, sigh.

Nominatives of the first declension.

Iṛ ḟeaṛṛ imṗeaṛ 'na uaiṛ̃ṗeaṛ.

"Strife is better than being alone."

Ní luiġeann ṛonaṛ aiṛ amaḋán (dat. case).

"Prosperity does not befit a fool."

Imṗeaṛ, contention; uaiṛ̃ṗeaṛ, the state of being alone, loneliness.

Nominatives of first and third.

Ní uabaṛ (1) uaiṛleaċt (3).

"Nobility is not pride."

Gen. of first, iṛ ḟaḋa cuiṁne (4) ṛean-leinḃ, (1) gen.

"The recollection of an old child is long."

Ceaṇ móṛ na céille biġe, large head of (the) little sense; ceille is gen. case of ciall, *f.* biġe, is gen. case *f.* of beaᵹ, small.

Gen. of second, 'Sé iṫe na póiṗe (2) ᵹlaiṛe é.

"It is the eating of green grain," (said in regard to something consumed before it has become matured.)

Póiṗe ᵹlaiṛe, is gen. case of póṛ ᵹlaṛ.

Sioṇnaċ a ᵹ-cṛeacan an uaiṇ (2).

"The fox in sheep's clothing."

Sioṇnaċ, is nom., uaiṇ, gen. of uan, ᵹ-cṛeacan, dative or prepositional case, c is eclipsed by ᵹ, on account of the preposition a: all are of the first declension.

Nom. plur., Se a luaċ a loċta ċuᵹaḋ.

"Its faults are its only cost to you," (said to a person who despises a thing given gratis.)

Luaċ, 1st declen.; loċta, nom. plur. 3rd declen., from loċt, ċuᵹaḋ, prep. pron.

FORTY-FOURTH LESSON.
NOUNS OF THE SEVERAL DECLENSIONS.
FIRST DECLENSION.

Абac, *gen*, абaιc, a dwarf, a sprite.

Абaηcuη, *m*, success, good luck; ʒо ηaιb aη c-aδ aʒuη aη c-абaηcuη оηc, "may prosperity and good luck attend you," is a prayer by which the poor express their gratitude to those who do them a kindness.

Абaη, *m*, a marshy portion of land, a swamp; δ'ƒaʒ ηe 'η aη абaη ιηe, "he left me in the lurch," is a common saying.

Абlaη, *m*, from aб, an element, a fluid, water; and lоη, food, provision—the Host, or altar-bread; абlaη cоιηηιʒċe, a consecrated Host; a wafer; paste made thin and baked.

Аηlaη, *m*, from aιη, fine, agreeable, pleasant; and lоη food, provision. For this there is no equivalent in English. The common people supply its want by the generic term 'kitchen;' others employ the word 'condiment.' This latter does not fully express the meaning of the Irish aηlaη. The Latin *obsonium* comes near it in meaning. The Irish word means whatever is eaten with bread, or with the common food of the people. Jη ιηaιċ aη 'c-aηlaη' aη c-оcηuη, "hunger is good sauce."

Аʒallaιη, *m*. dialogue, arguing, speaking or conferring together; from aʒall, speech, conversation, which is, perhaps, from aʒ, at; aιle, another; *i. e.*, interchange of thought in a social way.

Аιƒηιоη, *m*, *gen*, aιƒηιη, Mass; ηaιb cu aιʒ aιƒηιоη, were you at Mass; δ'eιηc ιηe aιƒηιоη, I heard Mass; aιƒηιоη δ'eιηceaċc aιη ʒaċ δоιηηaċ aʒuη lá ηaоιηe, to hear Mass on every Sunday and holyday. The derivation is aιƒιη, or оιƒιη, an offering; and ιоη, worthy, befitting, *i.e.*, an offering befitting or worthy of the Deity. In the opinion of man in every state of society, barbarous as well as civilized, *sacrifice* was considered the befitting offering worthy above all others of being presented to the Supreme Being. Amongst the Pagan Irish, aιƒηιоη meant sacrifice. St. Patrick retained the word as fitly expressing to the minds of his converts the high sacrificial character of the Mass. The Irish after their conversion, retained, as Dr. O'Brien (Bishop of Cloyne) remarks, the words cɼeiḋeaṁ, ḋoċuɼ, ʒɼáḋ, to express (Christian) faith, hope, charity; aḋɼaḋ, for adoration of the true God; and póɼaḋ, (bóɼaḋ, the giving of cows—bo), to express the sacrament of marriage.

Aṫaċ *m.* gen. aṫaiʒ, a man of terror, a gigantic figure, from aṫaḋ, fear; root, aṫ, to fear, to shrink from, to dread; written also faṫaċ, faiṫ, the same as aṫ (hence faiṫċioɼ, fear).

Baċal, *m.* (Latin, *bacul-um*, Cornish, *bagl*), a staff, a shepherd's crook, a crosier; from ba, cows, and cuaille, a staff, *i.e.*, a herd's staff or crook, with which cattle are defended by their keeper; root, col, to protect, to hinder from; *vide*, col.

Baʒaɼ, *m.* a threat; from ba or baṫ, death, and ʒaiɼ, to bawl, to cry out.

Bailteaċaɼ, founding of a town; a derivative from bailte, towns.

Baiɼneaċ, *m.* a limpet; from báɼɼ, because found on tops (báɼɼ) of rocks when the tide has ebbed.

Bɼaḋán, *m.* a salmon.

Bɼaṫaiɼeaċaɼ, *m.* brotherhood; derived from bɼaṫaiɼ, a brother.

Caoiḋean (p. *ky-an*) a pelican; from caoiḋ, lamentation, and eun, a bird; tá` me naɼ caoiḋean aonɼaċ, I am like a solitary pelican.

Colluɼ, *m.* a pigeon; colum (written also colm), a dove, a pigeon.

Columan, and colman, diminutive of colum, a dove, a pigeon—the proper name Colman.

Cɼeaṁaɼ, *m.* a woodcock; the horse-fly; from cɼeiṁ, to gnaw, to nibble.

Caṫal Cahal; from caṫ, battle, al, support.

Ciaɼan, Kiran; from ciaɼ, black.

Coɼmac, Cormack.   Eaḋḋaɼḋ, Edward.
Eamon, Edmund.   Ʒeaɼalt, Gerald.
Lucaɼ, Luke.   Maɼtan, Martin.

Miċeál, Michael, gen. Miċil; as, feile Miċil (the Feast of St. Michael), Michaelmas.

Muiɼeaɼ, Maurice; Mac Muiɼiɼ, Fitz Maurice.

Nicolár, Nicholas.　Rolán, Rowland, Orlando.
Raðmonð, Raymond.　Riobard, Robert.
Seamuʃ, James.　Senom, Jerome.
Simón, Simon.　Uilliam, William.
MacShimóin, Fitzsimon.　Uillioʒ = Uilliam óʒ, Ulick

Dun, m. a hill, a mound, a stronghold, a castle, fortress, or tower. Latin, *dunum*; Welsh, *dyn*. From the word dún are derived the names of many places not only in Ireland and Scotland, but in France, or old Gaul; as, Dun, Down; Dun-aille (the fort of the cliff); Dun an óir (the fort of the gold), Dunamore; Dun-barton, for Dun-bretan (the stronghold of the Britons), Dunbarton; Dun-caillin, Dunkellin; Dundroma (the fort of the back or ridge); Dun-ʒarbain, Dungarvan; Dunʒeanain, Dungannon; Dunmóir, Dunmore; Dunbeaʒ, Dunbeg; Dun-ceallain, Dunkeld, in Scotland; Ebro-*dunum*, *Ambrun*, Augusto*dunum*, *Autun*; Melo*dunum*, Melun, Cæsaro*dunum*, Tours.

Ʒealban (pr. as if ʒeallún), m. a sparrow.

Ʒealban-cuillion, a bullfinch.

Ʒeallan, a linnet.

Ʒliomac, m. a lobster; a loosely-built fellow.

Iarran, m. iron; iarran ʒeal, tin.

Priacán, m. a crow.

Pratán, m. a crab.

Salan, m. salt.

Scaðan, a herring.

Smolac, m. a thrush.

Stán, m. tin; Latin, *stannum*; canna stáin, a tin can.

Tiʒeacar, m. dwelling in a house; aon-tiʒeacar, being in one house; ni eoluʃ ʒan aon-tiʒeacar, no knowledge (of one's character can be gained) unless by dwelling in the same house.

Torc, m. a cod-fish.

SECOND DECLENSION.

Ailp, f. a lump, a height; plu. alpa, hills, mountains; sliab Alpa, the Alps:

Do faið tar Alpa uile,
He traversed all the hills.
—*St. Fiach's Hymn in honor of St. Patrick*, stanza v.

Bríġit or Bríġiḋ, Bridget; from breo, fiery, and raiġit, a dart, an arrow; feile Bríġiḋe, the feast of St. Bridget; mí na feile Bríġiḋe, the month of February.

Bainir, *f.* a wedding; from bean, a woman, and feir, an assembly.

Beoir, *f.* a kind of beer known to the ancient Irish.

Inġean, *f.* gen. inġine, a daughter; from ion, fit, capable; and ʒein, *v.* to beget; or from in, becoming, and ʒein, *n.* an offspring; ʒein is allied to the old English, *quean,* a woman, now *Queen,* a woman of the highest grade.

Feminine Nouns in óʒ.

Anʒealóʒ (a proper noun), Angelica.

Baċlóʒ, *f.* (diminutive of bacal, a staff or crook), a ring-let, curl; the sprouts or buds of potatoes; so called because crook-like at top.

Caonóʒ, *f.* a chafer.

Crupóʒ, *f.* a wrinkle; from crup, a contraction, a shri-velling.

Duilleóʒ, *f.* a leaf; from duille, the same.

Fainleóʒ, *f.* a swallow.

Feadóʒ, a plover.

Féaróʒ, *f.* beard; from far, growth, and óʒ.

Franʒóʒ, Frances.

Fionóʒ, *f.* a scarecrow; from fion, whitish.

Fuinreóʒ, *f.* ash; from fuinre, fountain.

Fuireóʒ, *f.* a lark.

Ʒairleóʒ, *f.* garlic.

Leaċóʒ, *f.* a place, a flounder; from leaċ, half; because it appears as if cut into two parts. Leaċóʒ mara, a turbot. Leaċóʒ fion-uirʒe, a fluke, *i.e.,* a flat fish found in fresh water.

Leitir, *f.* lettuce.

Miadóʒ, *f.* a short knife, a bayonet.

Neanntóʒ, *f.* a nettle.

[Note.—Nouns that end in óʒ in Irish, in Scotch Gaelic end in *ag.*]

Maiġdean, *f,* a virgin; an Maiġdean Muire, the Virgin Mary. Maiġdean is derived from mo or moḋ (old Irish), a person, man or woman; and ʒean, natural affection, love, chastity (for its derivative, ʒeanamnaiḋ, means chaste; and ζεаηαmηаιδελċτ, chastity.) Its proper spelling is, therefore, mаòζελη, but by changing the consonants the word becomes mαζδελη; German, *mädchen*, Saxon, *maeden*; English, maiden.

Scαηρόζ, *f*, shamrock, derived from ρελη̇αιρι, which is itself formed from ρειη̇, sweet, pleasant; and ρειρι, grass, trefoil; ρελη̇αιρόζ, and contractedly ρελη̇ρόζ, the short trefoil or shamrock.

NOUNS OF THE THIRD DECLENSION.

2lb, *gen.* αbα, a father, an abbot, a lord.

Proper Names.

2lοηζυρ, Ængus or Æneas.
Cριορτοιρι, Christopher.
Dιαρmοιδ, Dermott; from Dια, God; and αιρmοιδ, of arms.
Fελριζυρ, Fergus.

ζεαρροιδ, Garrett.
Lυζαιδ, gen. Lυζδαċ, Lewis.
2)υιρċελδ, Mortimer, Murphy.
2)υριρλċ, Murrogh.
Τιοbόιδ, Toby.

Nouns ending in όιρι, *mas.*

Bαδόιρι, from bαδ, a boat, a boatsw*ain.*
Bραċαδόιρι, *m*, a malst*er*; from bραċ, malt.
Cυρρόιρι, *m*, a cours*er*; from cυρρα, a course.
Cυαηζτόιρι, *m*, a help*er*; from cοηζηαm, help, which is itself from cοη, together, and ζηιδ, do.
Cυιδυιζτεοιρι, *m*. an assist*er*, a help*er*, a protect*or*.
Cρυιηηιζτεοιρι, *m*. a gatherer; from cρυιηιζ, gather; root, cρυιη, assembled, round, plump, full.
Cριαδαδόιρι, *m*. a clayman, a worker, a tiller or digger; from cριαδ, earth.
Fόζαητοιρι, *m*. a reliever, a helper, an auxiliat*or*, an assistant; one who aids a person in distress, and lends relief by procuring it; from ρόζηαm, assistance, help, service, goodness.

2lbρταλċτ, *f*. apostleship.

2lċτ, *f*. a decree.

Bαρρι, *m*. from bα, state of being; and αρδ, high; is itself a principal root: (1) top; as, ό bυη ζο bαρρι, from bottom to top; bαρρι δο ċιηη, the top of your head; αιρ bαρρι, on top; (2) point; as, ρηάτάδ ζαη bαρρι, a needle without point; (3) head; as, ζαη bυη ζαη bαρρι, without foundation or superstruction, without head or tail; (4) the head, branches, plants, potato stalks, oats, corn, grass, crops, harvest—béaṛ-ꞃaıð aꞃ calaṁ ꞃo ðá ḃáꞃꞃ, this land will yield two crops; (5) baꞃꞃa, tops, corn, green crops, produce; (6) the oily portion of broth, grease; (7) the surface, bubbles, scum, spume—so called because always found on the surface; (8) superiority—ꞃuaıꞃ ꞃe aꞃ báꞃꞃ, he obtained the superiority; (9) excess, overplus, profit—ꞃı'l ꞃıð aıꞃ bıc aᵹaıꞃꞃ ð'a báꞃꞃ, we have nothing by it; literally, there is nothing at all to us of it, profit: cuıꞃ báꞃꞃ aıꞃ, finish it, perfect; baꞃꞃać, m. branches of trees, brushwood, tow.

Ƒeoıꞃ, f. the river Nore; gen. Ƒeoꞃać.

Ceaṁaıꞃ, f. Tara; gen. Ceaṁꞃać.

NOUNS OF THE FOURTH DECLENSION.

(1) All personal nouns ending in aıꞃe, aıð, uıð, aıᵹ; (2) derivatives from the genitive feminine of adjectives; (3) diminutives in ıꞃ.

(2) Aıᵹꞃe, f. mind, attention.

Aılcıꞃe, m. or f. a foreigner; from aıle, other, and cıꞃ, country. It is written also eılcıꞃe; from eıle, which is the usual Irish spelling of the Gaelic term for other.

Aıꞃe, f. heed, attention; of cognate meaning with ꞃaıꞃe, watch.

Aıćꞃe, f. a commandment; ca ṁeuð aıćꞃe ćuᵹ Dıa ðuıꞃꞃ? how many commandments has God given us? ćuᵹ Dıa aꞃ aıćꞃe ꞃo ðo Ⱳaoıꞃe, God gave this command to Moses.

Baılbe, f. from the genitive case fem. of the adj. Balḃ, mute; stammering, stuttering.

Baıꞃe, f. milk; from báꞃ, white.

Báıꞃıð, f. madness; ca ꞃe aıꞃ báıꞃıð, he is mad (vexed).

Cꞃapa, f. a button.

Coıᵹe, f. a province; Cuıᵹe Coꞃꞃaćca, the province of Connaught.

Cóꞃꞃa, a coffin.

Baıle, f. town, village; Latin, *villa*; plu. baılce.

Ƒeıle, f. a festival, a feast; ꞃeıle Pacꞃaıc, the festival of St. Patrick; ꞃeıle Naoıṁ Bꞃıᵹıð, the feast of St. Bridget.

Leıne, *f.* a shirt, a tunicle, an alb; léıne aıffrınn, an alb part of the priest's vestments worn while offering sacrifice.

Teıne, *f.* fire; plu. teınte.

Tuıle, *f.* a flood; plu. tuılte.

Nouns in ın of the fourth declension.

(3) Baırrın, *m.* a hat, a head-dress, a cap, a mitre; ıf buaıntear aınm de'n m-baırrın, the name is not taken from the baırrın. The term baırrın must be applied whether it be the baırrın or head-gear of dignitary or peasant.

Caıllın, a girl; the diminutive of caılle, which means a stout, able woman; from calla, a hooded cloak worn by the ancients of Gaul and Ireland; capacalla (from capa or ceıtre, *i.e.,* four, four-sided; and calla, a hood—root col, protect), the square hood—from the wearing of which the fierce son of the Emperor Severus derived his well-known name: caılleać, a woman in a hood. The calla was generally worn by the old, and hence the term caılleać came to signify an old woman, a hag. It means also a hooded religious, a nun; " caılleaća duba," black religious.

Crúır$ın, *m.* a pitcher, a cruise, a lamp, a goblet.

> $ráš mo ćroıde mo ćruır$ın,
> The love of my heart 's my pitcher.

Dreoılın, *m.* a wren, a silly person, a ninny.

Smı$ın, *m.* the chin; from smı$, the chin, a smile, mirth.

Proper names:

A$uıtın, (and Aıbırtın), Augustin.

Antonı, Anthony.

Daıbıd (*Dávee,* commonly pronounced *dáyé*) David, Mac Dabıd, Davidson.

Doımınıc, Dominick.

Felım, Feilim, or Felix.   Fraın$, Frank.

$ıollmuıre, Maurice; Gilmore, from $ıolla, a servant, or one devoted to; and Muıre, Mary.

Henrı, Henry.

Maolmuıre (pr. Maolre), Myles; from maol, bald, shaven, therefore having the tonsure, hence devoted to; and Muıre, Mary.

Ⱏaoıɾe, Moses. Ⱏaoı, and Ⱏoaᵹ, Noah.

Pılıp, Philip; Pılıpın, little Philip.

Ruaıḋɾı, Roderick. Sılḃeɾcıɾ, Silvester.

Soṁaıɾle, Charles, or Sorley; as, Soṁaıɾle Buıḋe, Sorley the Yellow, Sorley Buidhe (Mac Donnell), who fought against Shane O'Neill and Hugh.

Ualencın, Valentine. Uıɲɾeɲc, Vincent.

Aᵹaca, Agata. Aᵹɲeɾ, Agnes. Aɲɲa, Anne.

Baɾbaɾa, and contractedly Baɲba, Barbara.

Cáıclın, and Caıcɾıɲa, Catherine.

Eḃelın, and contractedly Eḃlın, Eleanor. Elıɲ, Helen.

Elıɾaḃec, Elizabeth. Elıɾa, Eliza.

Faɲɲı, Fanny.

Laɾaɲpıoɲa, Lusarina; from Laɾaıɾ, flame, and pıoɲa, of wine; gen. case of pıoɲ, wine.

Luɾı, Lucy. Ⱏaıble, Mabel. Ⱏaıɾe, Mary.

Ⱏapla, Penelope. Ⱏóɾa, Honoria. Oılıḃıa, Olivia.

Saıḋḃe, or Saḋḃ, Sabia. Soɾċa, Sarah.

Sıᵹıle, Celia. Sıɾele, Cecila. Uɲa, Wineford, Juno.

The diminutives of these names are formed by affixing ıɲ.

The ending of the genitive case is the only means by which a person can know whether a noun terminating in a vowel is of the fifth declension. If a noun of this class undergoes no inflection, it is then of the fourth. Any difficulty on this head is removed by the accompanying list of all the nouns in the language belonging to the fifth declension.

NOUNS BELONGING TO THE FIFTH DECLENSION.

Aɾa, *f.* kidney.

Alba, *f.* Scotland.

Alṁa, *f.* Allen, in Kildare.

Aɾa, *f.* the Island of Arran; plu. aıɾɲe.

Bo, a cow; gen. bo; dat. boıɲ; nom. pl. ba (dat. pl. buaıḃ).

Bɾeıċeaṁ, a judge; gen. bɾeıċeaṁaɲ; it is also of the first declension, gen. bɾeıċeıṁ.

Bɾo, *f.* a quern, a handmill; gen. bɾóɲ; dat. bɾóıɲ; plu. bɾóıɲce.

Bɾu, or bɾuıɲɲ, *f.*, a womb; gen. bɾoɲɲ; as, beaɲɲuıᵹċe coɾaḋ ɖo bɾoɲɲ, blessed is the fruit of thy womb; dat.; bɾoıɲɲ; nom. plu. bɾoɲɲa.

Ceatṗaṁa, *f.* a quarter, from ceaċaṗ, four.

Coṁuṗṗa, *f.* a neighbour, from coṁ and uṗṗa, a jamb, a support.

Cu, *f.* a hound; gen. sing. coṅ, (pronounced *kŭn*, short); dat. coiṅ; nom. plu. coiṅ.

Cuiṗle, *f.* a vein; cuiṗle ṁo ċṗoiðe, pulse of my heart.

Daileaṁ, a cup-bearer; from ðáil, a festive gathering.

Deaṗṅa, *f.* the palm of the hand.

Díle, *f.* a flood.

Duileaṁ, the Creator, from ðuil, an element.

Eaṗcu, *f.* an eel; gen. eaṗcoṅ; from eaṗ, water, and cu, a hound. See cu, above.

Ealaða, *f.* (pr. *ál-y-ah*), a science.

Ealḃa; gen. ealḃaṅ; plu. ealḃaṅa; "Pṗioṁ-ᵹeiṅċe ð ealḃaṅ—the first fruits of thy herds."—*Deuteronomy*, xii. 18, *Irish Bible by Dr. MacHale*, p. 345.

Eiṗe, Ireland; gen. Eiṗeaṅṅ; dat. Eiṗiṅṅ.

Ᵹoḃa, *m.* a smith; Ⰼacᵹoḃaṅ (smith's son), MacGowen.

Ᵹuala, *f.* a shoulder.

Fealṗaṁ, a philosopher, like bṗeiċeaṁ, is of the fifth and first.

Fiaċaṁ, *m.* a debtor; "aᵹuṗ ṁaiċ ðuiṅṅ aṗ ḃ-fiaċa ṁaṗ ṁaiċaṁuið-ṅe ð' aṗ 'ḃ-fiaċaṁṅaiḃ' ṗéiṅ, and forgive us our trespasses (debts); as we forgive our debtors."— *The Lord's Prayer.*

Fioṅṅ-ᵹuala, *f.* a woman's name. *Fionguala*, fair shoulder

Ioṅᵹa, *f.* nail (of the finger).

Ioċla, *f.* a hay-yard.

Laċa, *f.* a duck; makes the gen. sing. and gen. plu. laċaṅ, and laċaiṅ in the nom. plu.

Laṅaṁa, *f.* a married couple.

Leaca, *m.* a cheek.

Leiᵹeaṅṅ *f.* Leinster; Cuiᵹe leiᵹeaṅṅ, province of Leinster.

Luṗᵹa, *f.* the shin.

Ⰼuṁa, *f.* Munster; gen. Ⰼuṁaṅ; as, Cuiᵹe Ⰼuṁaṅ, the province of Munster. Deaṗ-Ⰼuṁaṅ, South-Munster— Desmond; Tuað-Ⰼuṁaṅ, North-Munster, Thomond; Oiṗ-Ⰼuṁaṅ, East-Munster—Ormond.

Ⰼeaṅṁa, *f.* the mind; uṗṅaiᵹe ṅa ṁeaṅṁaṅ, mental prayer, meditation.

Pearsa, *f.* a person.

Sacsain, *f.* England; gen. Sacsan; as talaṁ Sacsan land of England.

Séanga, *f.* a cormorant; from seang, lank.

Raoine, Reelion, in the county Kildare.

Taillte, *f.* Teltown, in Meath.

Teanga, *f.* a tongue; plu. teangṫa.

Teora, *m.* border, boundary, limit; Latin, *terminus.*

Uille, *f.* an elbow; Latin, *ulna ; ell,* a measure.

Ulċa, *f.* beard.

Ursa, the jamb of a door.

Braġa, shoulder, mas. and fem.; gen. braġaḋ.

Cara, *m.* a friend, makes gen. caraḋ, and dat. caraiḋ, plu. caraḋa, or caraiḋe, and contractedly cairde. Cairde is the usual form. Caraḋ, a friend, in the nom. case, is not unusual. It is then of the first declension; plu. caraiḋ.

Caora, *f.* a sheep; makes the gen. sing. and plu. caoraċ; nom. plu. caoiriġ, sheep.

Talaṁ, *f.* land, earth, makes gen.; talṁan, contractedly for talaṁan; dat. talaiṁ; plu. talṁana and tailte.

Those are the only nouns in the language that belong to the fifth declension.

EXERCISE LXXII.

An t-am imiġear an reun (1) slán le cairdib.

"When fortune begins to frown, friends will be packing."

An, time, being a noun masc., takes t for euphony after the article an, the; slan, *adj.* farewell; literally (be) save, sound; cairdib, with friends, the prepositional case, contractedly for caraḋaib.

An niḋ do ċiḋ an leanb do ġniḋ an leanb.

"What the child sees that he doeth."

leanb, a child (pr. *lednov*), gen. leinb (pr. *lynv*); ciḋ, *sees,* irr, *v.,* ġniḋ (*nee*), does.

Má 'r maiṫ leat do ṁolaḋ, fáġ bás;
Má 'r maiṫ leat do ċáineaḋ, pós.

"If you wish to be lauded, await death.
If you wish to be reviled, marry."

"*Ne laudes hominem in vitâ suâ'—tanquam
Si diceret, laudâ post vitam magnifica post consummationem.*"—
S. *Maximus Homilia,* 59.

2ψilleaɲɲ caoɲa (5) cɲeuꝺ (1).

"A sheep mars a flock."

2ψilleaɲɲ ꝺɲoċ-ċoṁluaꝺaɲ (1) ꝺeaᵹ-ḃeuɲa (3)..

"Evil communications corrupt good manners."—*St. Paul.*

2ψa cá a leaca (5) ꝼaoɲ,
Nꝼl aɲ luċc (1) aɲ a ꝼꙇacal (1).

"If his cheek is wan,
The fault rests not with his tooth."

2ψa 'ɲ mall ꙇꝼ ꝺꙇɲeaċ ꝺꙇoᵹalcaɲ (1) ꝺe.

"Though slow yet sure is God's justice" (ꝺé is gen. of ꝺꙇa, God).

"'Ειπερ γαρ τὲ καὶ αὐτίκ' Ο'λυμπιος ουκ ἐτελεσσεν
Εκ τε καὶ ὀψὲ τελεῖ."—*Book* iv., *ll.* 160, 161.

Thus rendered into Irish verse by Dr. MacHale :

Ᵹꙇꝺ 'ɲ mall aꙇᵹ cuꙇɲlꙇɲc ꝺꙇoᵹalcaɲ ceaɲc ɲa ɲ-ꝺea ;
Beꙇꝺ ꝼóɲ 'ᵹ a ꙇmꙇɲc ꝺꙇɲeaċ, 'ɲ ɲꙇ ᵹaɲ ꝼáċ.—

Lines 195-6.

"Though the mills of God grind slowly, yet they grind exceeding small ;
Though with patience He stands waiting, with exactness grinds He all."

—*Longfellow's Poetic Aphorisms.*

Na labaꙇɲ leꙇɲ ɲa coɲaꙇꝺ ċo-ꝼaꝺ a'ɲ beꙇꝺeaɲ aɲ ceaɲɲ a laċaꙇɲ.

"As long as the head is present do not speak to the feet."

Coɲaꙇꝺ, dat. plu. of coɲ, *f.*; *n.* 2nd d.; gen. coꙇɲe, plu. coɲa; ceaɲɲ, *m.* 1st d. gen. cꙇɲɲ, plur. ceaɲɲa.

Nꙇ bꙇꝺeaɲɲ ᵹoɲc (1) ᵹaɲ ꝺꙇaɲaċ (1) ꝼꙇaꝺ.
Cuꙇᵹeaꝺ caċ cꙇall (2) mo ɲaꙇɲɲ. (1 ; gen. case)
Jꝼ ceaɲc ɲeaċ aꙇɲ a m-bꙇꝺ ɲaċ (3).
Naċ m-bꙇꝺeaɲɲ ɲeaċ (3) aꙇɲ ċuꙇꝺ (3) ꝺ'a ċlaꙇɲ (2).

There is not a corn-field without a wild blade,
Let each understand the purport of my song. .
So, rarely is the man found whom fortune favors,
That a blight falls not on some of his children.

ꝺꙇaɲaċ, from ꝺꙇaɲ, a blade of corn; ꝼꙇaꝺ, wild; cꙇall, *f.* 2 gen. céꙇlle; ɲaꙇɲɲ gen. of ɲaɲɲ, a song, a poem, a stanza; ceaɲc, rare, scarce; ɲeaċ (indeclinable), an individual. Ꝼaċ, luck; ꝺɲoċ-ɲaċ, bad luck; ꝺeaᵹ-ɲaċ, good luck; ɲeaċ, pining, a blight; cá aɲ cuɲ ɲeaċca, the crop is blighted.

Cṙíoc (1) coṙóɪn (2) ɲa h-oɪḃṙe, *finis coronat opus,*

Cṙíoċ, end ; coṙóɪn, a crown ; oɪḃṙe, gen. of óḃaɪṙ, (2) work, gen óḃaɪṙe, and contractedly oḃṙe, in which ɪ, a slender vowel, must, before ḃ, be inserted to conform to the rule *slender with slender,* hence oɪḃṙe.

FORTY-FIFTH LESSON.

ADJECTIVES.

In English, adjectives remain unchanged in their terminations. The word *good,* for instance, undergoes no change in gender, number, or case, in the following : *a-good man* (*m.*) ; *a good woman* (*f.*) ; *a good house* (*n.*) ; *I see a good man* (*obj.*) ; *I see good men* (*plu. obj.*) ; *a good man's* (*poss.*) *house ; good men's* (*plu. poss.*) *houses.*

The slightest acquaintance with any foreign language will show the mere English student that the adjective is inflected like the noun with which it agrees. In French and in Italian, for example, it varies in gender and number.

French.	Italian.
Sing. *bon, m.* ; *bonne, f., good.*	*bono, m.* ; *bona, f.*
Plu. *bons, m.* ; *bonnes, f., good.*	*boni, m.* ; *bone, f.*

In other languages—say, Latin, Greek, German—it varies in gender, number, and case :

	Latin.	Greek.	German.	
Nom.	*bonus.*	ἀγαθος.	*guter.*	*good* (*man*).
Gen.	*boni.*	ἀγαθου.	*gutes.*	*of a good* (*man*).
Dat.	*bono.*	ἀγαθῳ.	*gutem.*	*to a good* (*man*).
Acc.	*bonum.*	ἀγαθον.	*guten.*	*good* (*man*).
Ab.	*bono.*	ἀγαθῳ.	*gutem.*	*with a good* (*man*)

In the singular number, masculine gender, the adjective undergoes several inflections, as is seen by the foregoing.

These remarks are in some measure necessary for the young student, who is accustomed to look upon the adjective in English as invariable. They will serve to render clear what is going to be said of the declension of adjectives in Gaelic.

Take an example of a noun and adjective:

Fear mór, *a big man.*

	Singular.	Plural.
Nom. } Acc. }	an fear mór	na fir móra
Gen.	an fir móir.	na b-fear mór.
Dat.	do 'n fear mór.	do na fearaib móra.

In this example, mór, the nominative singular, masculine, becomes móir in the genitive singular, and móra in the nominative plural:

An bean mór, *the big women.*

	Singular.	Plural.
Nom. } Acc. }	an bean mór.	na mna móra (*mora*).
Gen.	na mna móire (*moirhye*)	na m-ban mór.
Dat.	do 'n mnaoi móir.	do na mnaib móra.

Agreeing with a noun of the feminine gender, mór becomes, in the genitive singular, móire, and in the dative móir; nom. plu. móra, masculine and feminine.

An example, one in which the final vowel of the adjective is slender:

An snátad mín, *the fine needle.*

	Singular.	Plural.
Nom. } Acc. }	an snátad mín.	na snátaib míne.
Gen.	an t-snátaib mín.	na snátad mín.
Dat.	do n' t-snátad mín.	do na snátadaib míne.

Obs.—Mín is not changed in the genitive masculine, because the peculiar effect of that case is to assume a slender vowel. Now, as the vowel is already slender, the genitive cannot assume another, and therefore undergoes no change.

Adjectives are, therefore, declined like nouns of the same gender and of the same final syllable. Their inflection consequently follows the analogies of the first, second, third, and fourth declensions of nouns. Those that end in vowels are *invariable.*

Adjectives, therefore, ending in a consonant take before it a slender vowel, i, (if i be not already in the final syllable,) in the genitive masculine; and an additional syllable, e, if the noun is feminine.

The plural usually ends in a, except where the rule caol
le caol requires e and not a.

DECLENSION OF ADJECTIVES.

móp, large, great, big.

	Singular.		Plural. Mas. & Fem.
	Mas.	Fem.	
Nom. and Acc.	móp,	móp,	mópa.
Gen.	móip,	móipe,	móp.
Dat.	móp,	móip,	mópa.

mín, fine.

Nom. and Acc.	mín,	mín,	míne.
Gen.	mín,	míne,	mín.
Dat.	mín,	mín,	míne.

apo, high.

Nom. and Acc.	apo,	apo,	apoa.
Gen.	aipo,	aipoe,	apo.
Dat.	apo,	aipo,	apoa.

Adjectives ending in amail are declined after the form
the third declension of nouns; as,

Flaiċamail, princely, hospitable.

	Mas. and Fem.	Mas. and Fem.
Nom. and Acc.	flaiċamail,	flaiċamla.
Gen.	flaiċamla,	flaiċamail.
Dat.	flaiċamail,	flaiċamla.

Obs.—Whenever any word—be it adjective, noun, or
verb—of two syllables, or more than two, has a liquid letter,
l, m, n, p, terminating the last syllable, or the last but one,
should an increase take place, the liquid letter unites with
the other consonant and elides the vowel; as, in the adjective flaiċamail, just declined, nom. flaiċamail, gen. flai-
ċamala, and eliding a between m and l, flaiċamla; aluin,
beautiful, gen. fem. aluine, l and n (liquids) unite, and form
alne and then the first syllable takes i, a slender vowel, to
assimilate the slender final vowel of the first syllable with the
slender vowel of the second—thus, ailne: aoibin, delightful,

makes aoiḃine (gen. fem.), and by syncope, eliding i before n, aoiḃne; aḃainn, a river, makes aḃainne; ḃ and nn coalesce, and form aḃne, and correcting the spelling, the word becomes aiḃne, rivers; aṫair, a father, makes aiṫre (and aiṫreaċa) in the plural; bráṫair, a brother, a friar, bráiṫre; milis, sweet, makes milise; i, from the second last syllable, unites with s, and the word assumes the contracted form (nios) milse, sweeter; so dilis, fond, makes dilse.

An adjective ending in a vowel is indeclinable; as, sona, lucky; dona, unlucky; órḋa, golden (rḋ are pronounced like rr); fada, long;

Lá fada, a long day.
Laeṫe fada, long days.
Duine dona, an unlucky person.
Daoine dona, unlucky people.
Teaċ órḋa, a golden house.
Tiġṫe órḋa, golden houses.

Nouns terminate the dative plural in iḃ, adjectives do not. Agreeing with the noun, the adjective is, like it, affected by aspiration.

	Masculine.		Feminine.
	Sing.	Plu.	Sing.
Aspiration of adj. when in concord with a noun articulated.	—	Nom.	Nom. and Acc.
	Gen.	...	...
	Dat.	...	Dat.
	Voc.	Voc.	Voc.

In the articulated dative, the adjective, in the modern language, suffers only aspiration in the initial consonant, though the mutable of the noun is generally eclipsed. In modern Gaelic the termination iḃ is rarely annexed to the dative plural.

VOCABULARY.

Euluiġ, *v.* depart, separate from; d'euluiġ se, he went off.

Iasg, *m.* fish; an t-iasg, the fish; an t-iasg mor, the large fish; gen. case, éisg, nom. plur. eisg, fish; na h-éisg, the fish; na h-éisg ṁóra agus na h-éisg beaga, the large fish and the little fish.

Iasgaire, *m.* a fisherman; an t-iasgaire, the fisherman. "An tráṫ ḃiḋeas air loċ Neaċaiḋ an t-iasgaire ag siubal." "On Lough Neagh's banks as the fisherman strays."—*Moore.*

Lion, gen. lín, *m.* flax, lint, linen; ag buaint lín, pulling flax; ag bualeaḋ lín, beetling flax; lín-eudaċ, linen (cloth); brat-lín, a sheet; from brat, a covering, and lín—Latin, *linum;* Welsh, *llin.* From lion, flax, is derived,

Lion, *m.* gen. lín, a net, a fishing net, a snare; lín iasgaċ, a fishing net; lion eisirriḋ, an oyster net, a dredge.

Sleaṁnuiġ, *v.* to glide away; to slip off; from sleaṁain, slippery.

EXERCISE LXXIII.

Na h-éirg móra agus na h-éirg beaga.

Do ḃí am ann agus do ḃí iargaire aig tarraing ċum tráige, lín a ḃí lán d' éirgiḃ beaga agus móra. Do ḟleaṁnuiġḋar na h-éirg beaga tríd na poill agus d' euluiġḋar leo faoi 'n toinn; aċt na h-éirg móra do gaḃaḋ iad, agus caiṫeaḋ a ṡteaċ iad air an loing.

Is minic liġṫean do'n dream beag, boċt, treal imṫeaċt; agus gaḃṫar an muintir mór, raiḋḃir, uasal.

EXERCISE LXXIV.

An puntán óg (young crab) agus a maṫair.

Duḃairt (said) sean-puntán le ceann d'a h-ál: "cad é an faṫ, a leinḃ (O child), tá tu aig riuḃal (walking) mar ro air do ċúl?—riuḃal air d' aġaiḋ (walk forward)." "A maṫair," air (says) an puntán óg, déanfad (I shall act) mar deir tu, ma riuḃlann tu-féin romam le tair-beánaḋ ḋam an nós is cóir mo ċoir-ċeim a ḋírugaḋ.

Is fearr sompla na teagasg.

Example is better than instruction.

Si vis me flere, dolendum est primum ipsi tibi.

—*Horatius, Epistola ad Pisones.*

OBS.—The adjective is not declined whenever it forms part of the predicate; as, this man is tall, tá an fear ro 'árd'; these men are tall, táid na fir ro 'árd.' In these sentences árd remains unchanged whether the nominative or subject be singular or plural. But if it is said, these are tall men, is fir 'árda' iad ro, then the adjective árd suffers a change, to accord with the noun 'men,' 'fir,' in the nominative plural. In the latter case the adjective agrees with the noun; in the former it refers to the verb, showing that the attribute 'tallness,' is predicated of the man or of the men.

It may be quite in place to explain what the term 'predicate' means. The word is derived from *prac*, before, in public, and *dicare*, to tell, to announce; therefore, to assert, or declare of. The predicate, then, is that which is asserted of something taken as a subject; as, the man is tall; 'man' is the subject; 'is tall,' is the predicate. In logic, 'man' is the subject, 'is,' the copula or connecting link, 'tall,' the attribute. The predicate includes the adjective and the verb is, are, was, were, &c. It is thus seen that naturally and logically the attribute 'tall,' 'ᴀpᴅ,' being part of the predicate, refers to the verb, and not the noun, and that, therefore, its remaining unchanged in Irish, as it does in German, is quite correct, logical, and natural. In those languages in which the attribute varies, as in Latin, Greek, Italian, its relation extends back to the subject, either directly or indirectly. In Irish and German it does not do so, but refers to the verb.

EXERCISE LXXV.

1. Is the sky (ꞃpeuꞃ) blue, and are the stars (ꞃeulcᴀ) bright (loꞃꞃᴀċ)? 2. The sky is blue and the stars are bright. 3. Do you see (ᴀꞃ b-ꞃeꞁceᴀꞃꞃ cu) the blue sky and the bright stars (ꞃeulcᴀ loꞃꞃᴀċᴀ)? 4. I see (ꞃeꞁcꞁꞃ) the blue sky and the bright stars. 5. Are the fields green (ȝlᴀꞃ), and the pretty (ꝺeᴀꞃᴀ) blossoms white? 6. The fields are not green, but the pretty blossoms are white. 7. I say that green fields and white flowers are pretty to be seen (le ꞃeꞁcꞃꞁꞃc). 8. Are the hills in your country high, the men large, the women fair, the trees fruitful, the harvest abundant (lꞃoꞃꞃᴀꞃ)? 9. The hills are high, the land rich, the men are large, the women fair, the trees fruitful, the harvest abundant. 10. I like (ꞁꞃ ᴀꞁl lꞃoꞃ) to see high hills, tall men, fair women, fruitful trees, and the harvest abundant. 11. Have you large farms? 12. I have not large farms—I have only one small farm; my father and brother have each a large farm. 13. Has your father fat sheep (cᴀoꞃᴀꞁȝ ꞃᴀꞃᴀꞃᴀ)? 14. He has fat sheep. 15. Has your brother large stacks of corn? 16. He has, but he is able to consume twice the number (ꝺᴀ oꞁꞃeᴀꝺ). 17. Oh, I know the saying: "ꞁcᴀᴀꞃ ꞃᴀ cꞃuᴀċᴀ ꞃóꞃᴀ, ᴀȝuꞃ cꞁȝċeᴀꞃ leꞁꞃ ꞃᴀ cꞃuᴀċᴀ beᴀȝᴀ—large stacks are eaten, and small ones suffice."

FORTY-SIXTH LESSON.

DEGREES OF COMPARISON.

Adjectives express the qualities of things. An adjective may have a certain quality—say (1) whiteness, as something differing from blackness or redness—and so far indicates a state or degree, which it can in a certain sense be called; or, viewing it in relation to some other definite object, it may have the quality (2) in a higher or lower degree; or, (3) in relation to all other things of the same kind, it may possess the quality in a state which no other object possesses, and, therefore, in the highest or utmost degree. There are, then, three states called degrees, which an adjective represents: (1) the positive, (2) comparative, and (3) superlative. They are termed degrees of comparison, for, even in the superlative there is a comparison between the quality found in the special subject spoken of and the like quality as it abides in all other things, taking each singly. This view of the superlative degree is correctly expressed in Gaelic by the form of words employed.

"(a) The positive is the simple form of the adjective; as, caol, *slender*; zeaṅaṁail, *amiable*.

"(b) The comparative expresses an increase or decrease of the quality, form, or number of one thing, in respect to those that abide in some other.

"(c) The superlative shows them to exist in the highest state, either absolutely or relatively."—*College Irish Grammar.*

REGULAR COMPARISON.

Obs.—The comparative and superlative are the same as the genitive singular feminine.

Ex.: áրd, high; gráḋṁaր, affectionate; gráḋaċ, loving.

Singular.	Comparative.	Superlative.
Gen. *m.* áրd, *f.* áiրde.*	(níoр) áiրde.	(iр) áiրde.
Gen. *m.* gráḋṁaiր, *f.* gráḋṁaiրe.	(níoр) gráḋṁaiրe.	(iր) gráḋṁaiրe.
Gen. *m.* gráḋaiz, *f.* gráḋaize.	(níoр) gráḋaize.	(iր) gráḋaize.

Comparison of equality:

Ċo, as { le, *with* (as); azuр, *and* (as).

'Ċo' aṅb 'le' cṗaṅ, *as* high *as* a tree.
'Ċo' aṅb 'aᵹuṗ' iṗ ḟeⁱbⁱṗ é, *as* high *as* it is possible.

Obs. 1.—In plain narrative the terms ṅⁱoṗ and iṗ are employed. They serve then as signs of the comparative and superlative degrees; as,

Comparative. —Cȧ aṅ ᵹⁱṗⁱaṅ 'ṅⁱoṗ' loṅṗaⁱᵹe 'ṅa aṅ ᵹeallaċ, the sun is more luminous than the moon.

Ḃⁱ aṅ ceⁱṅcṗeaċ 'ṅⁱoṗ' luaⁱce 'ṅa aṅ coⁱṅaċ, the lightning was more rapid than the thunder.

Ḋo ċeaṅṅuⁱᵹ ṗé 'ṅⁱoṗ' ṗaoⁱṗe 'ṅa bⁱol ṗe, he bought more cheaply than he sold.

Superlative.—Ȧmeaṗᵹ cṗuⁱⁱṅⁱe ṅa ṗṗeuⁱṗ ṗⁱ aṅ ᵹⁱṗⁱaṅ 'iṗ' loṅṗaⁱᵹe, amidst the orbs of the heavens the sun is the most luminous.

Obs. 2.—The superlative *relative* requires the presence of the article before the noun. It is in this especially it differs from the comparative; as,

Sⁱ cⁱll Ṗeabaⁱṗ 'aṅ ceaⁱṅpal 'iṗ' aⁱṗbe ṗaṅ boⁱṅaṅ, the Church of St. Peter is *the* highest in the world.

Sé Paⁱṗⁱⁱṗ 'aṅ' baⁱle iṗ beⁱṗe be baⁱlcⁱb ṅa h-Ꝺⁱⁱoⁱṗe, Paris is *the* handsomest city of the cities of Europe—*Paris est 'la' plus belle de toutes les villes de l'Europe.*

From the foregoing examples of the relative superlative it is seen that the use of the article in Gaelic distinguishes the superlative from the comparative, as it does in the French and Italian languages. In French, Italian, English, the article precedes the adjective; in Gaelic, the *noun*. The change arises from the positions which, in these languages, the adjective holds in relation with the noun which it qualifies.

Superlative *absolute.*—The particles aṅ, very; ṗaⁱṗ, surpassingly; corresponding with the German *sehr*, ṗo, exceedingly, are employed in Gaelic to express the superlative absolute, as *very* in English, *tres* in French, *molto* Italian.

Note.—The term ṅⁱoṗ, which precedes the comparative, is derived from ṅⁱb, a thing (sometimes in old writings, written ṅⁱ), and iṗ, *is*, the third person singular of the assertive form of the verb bo beⁱċ, to be. Jⁱ, which goes before the superlative, is the assertive verb, *is*. This is immediately seen by employing the comparative or superlative form about something which requires the use of the past tense; as,

Τά 2ɲаɪɲе ' ɲɪoɼ' óɪჳe 'ɲа Bɼɪჳɪò, Mary is younger than Bridget.

Bɪ 2ɲаɪɲе ' ɲɪ b' ' óɪჳe 'ɲа Bɼɪჳɪò, Mary was younger than Bridget.

Here ' ɲɪoɼ' in the present tense becomes ' ɲɪ b' ' (for ' ɲɪ bа') in the past.

Again, in the present assertive form it is seen where ɲɪò (severed from ɪɼ) is omitted; as,

' Jɼ' óɪჳe 2ɲаɪɲе 'ɲа Bɼɪჳɪò (with emphasis), Mary is younger than Bridget.

Negative emphatic form.—Nɪ óɪჳe 2ɲаɪɲе 'ɲа Bɼɪჳɪò, Mary is not younger than Bridget.

In the assertive negative.—Nɪ óɪჳe, the verb ɪɼ is left understood.

Past tense.—Nɪ b' óɪჳe 2ɲаɪɲе 'ɲа Bɼɪჳɪò, Mary was not older than Bridget.

From the third example above—ɪɼ óɪჳe 2ɲаɪɲе 'ɲа Bɼɪჳɪò, Mary is older than Bridget—it is seen that ɪɼ, which points out the superlative, precedes also the assertive form of the comparative. The use of the article, therefore, before the noun, and other aids—such as that of a noun governed by a preposition—become necessary to distinguish the former from the latter. This very readily becomes known from the context.

EXERCISE LXXVI.

1. Here we are together—George, Joseph, and Gregory (ჳɼeჳóɪɼ). .I, George, am the youngest (аɲ ɼe ɪɼ óɪჳe), you, Joseph, are the tallest, and Gregory is the oldest (аɲ ɼe ɪɼ ɼɪɲɲe : from ɼeаɲ, old). 2. (Gregory), who is the oldest, you say? 3. You are. 4. I am not, indeed; with great respect (le uɼɼаɱ móɼ); I think you are as old yourself as I am (ċo ɼeаɲ ċu ɼéɪɲ а'ɼ ɼáɪɱ-ɼe). 5. Well, be it so— we are not women, that we should thus dispute about age. 6. Certainly we are all as old as that the youngest of us should have sense. 7. I agree with you (ɼuɪჳɪɱ leаɼ). 8. How is your family (cuɼаɱ)? 9. They are well, thank you. 10. Are your sons at home—John, Vincent, and

Alphred (Uינrenc aჳur 2ⅼꝼꞃeꝺ)? 11. They are. 12.
Which of them is the older (cⅰa aca ⁊r rⅰnne)? 13.
Vincent. 14. Which of them is the strongest (⁊r laⅰꝺⅰꞃe,
from laⅰꝺⅰꞃ, strong)? 15. Alphred. 16. Do you tell me
so? 17. Yes. 18. And is he not the youngest and the
slenderest (caol—caoⅰle)? 19. Yes (⁊r ꞃe). 20. He is a
fine fellow—buacal bꞃeaჳ, or oჳꝼeaꞃ aluⅰn—his head is
as massive (cꞃom) and as intellectual (cⅰalṁaꞃ) as Daniel
O'Connell's (le ceann Ɗoṁnaⅰl Uⅰ Connaⅰll). 21. How
is business doing (cⅰannor a b-ꝼuⅰl ჳnocaⅰꝺe aⅰჳ ꝺeanaꝺ)?
22. Fairly (ჳo mearaꞃꝺa). 23. Is wine dear? 24 It is.
25. Is meat dearer (nⅰor baoⅰꞃe) than bread ('na aꞃaⅰn)?
26. It is. 27. Are bread and meat cheaper than wine and
spirits (uⅰrჳe-beaca)? 28. Certainly. 29. Have you bought
(aꞃ ceannuⅰჳ cu) gloves (lamana)? 30. I have (ꝺo cean-
nuⅰჳear). 31. I buy cloth, and everything that I want, in
Dublin. 32. Why do you do so—do you not know that
by thus acting you injure the trade of small towns, in which
things are sold really as cheap as in large cities?

VOCABULARY.

2lⅰce (pr. *ak-ĕhé*) *m.* proximity ; ann
aⅰce, in proximity, *adv.* ; near,
close by; ann a h-aⅰce, in her
proximity, near her ; ann a aⅰce,
near him; ann a n-aⅰce, near
them.

Connaⅰꞃc (*khonnark*), saw ; past tense
of ꝼeⅰc, see, *ir. v* ; ꝼeⅰcⅰm, I see ;
ꝼeⅰcꝼⅰꝺ, I shall see ; connaⅰꞃc,
saw.

Ɗⅰon, *m.* (3rd dec.) a shelter, protection Ꝼa Ɗⅰon, under shelter.

Ɗⅰc, want.

Ɗ'a bꞃⅰჳ rⅰn (*dha vree shin*), for that
reason, therefore—literally, be

of, by ; a its, (bꞃⅰჳ) virtue, rⅰn,
that.

2Ŋaꞃ, (conj.) as, even as, like ; maꞃ
ceo, as a mist ; maꞃ blac an
macaⅰꞃe, as the flower of the
field : maꞃ rⅰn, in that (manner) ;
thus so; ꝺean maꞃ rⅰn, do so—
i.e., in that manner ; maꞃ ro, in
this manner ; maꞃ rub, in that
other manner.

2Ŋaꞃ, (prep.) for, like to ; maꞃ rⅰn, for
that—*i.e.*, then, therefore ; maꞃ
abaⅰn, like to a river.

Sceⅰlpe, *f.* (2nd declen.) a cliff, a bare
mountain ridge ; gen. of rceⅰlp.

EXERCISE LXXVII.

2ln ჳabaꞃ aჳur an maꝺaꝺ alla.

Ɗo connaⅰꞃc maꝺaꝺ alla ჳabaꞃ aⅰꞃ baꞃꞃ rceⅰlpe, aⅼ
ꞃaꞃ b' ꝼeⅰꝺⅰꞃ leⅰr ceacc ann a h-aⅰce. Ɗ'ꝼoჳaⅰꞃ maꞃ
rⅰn onnⅰ aⅰჳ ꞃaꝺ: Caꝺ e an ꝼac b-ꝼuⅰl cu ann rⅰn ꞃuar,
aⅰc lom, noccuⅰჳce, aჳur ჳo leoꞃ ꝼeuꞃ ann ro aꞃⅰ a b-
ꝼuⅰl blar aჳur blac. Ɗ'a bꞃⅰჳ rⅰn caꞃꞃ anuar." "ჳo

raiḃ maiṫ aġaḋ," ḋ' ḟreaġair an ġaḃar, "ir fearr liom
díṫ aġur díon, 'na roṫ aġur ġaḃ."

Ir fearr beaġan le roṫ 'na moran le anḟoṫ.

A little with peace and quiet is better than much with
contention.

VOCABULARY.

At last, fa ḋeiṙé.
Contention, strife, imṙear, m. 1st
  dec. gen. imṙir.
Durability, buanar, m.; from buan,
  lasting, enduring.
Fine, *adj.* breaġ, áluiṅ maireaċ,
  rġiaṁaċ, gen. fem. áluiṅe, contractedly ailne (pr. aillé); níor
  ailne, more beautiful; níor rġia-
  maiġe, níor mairiġe.
Raven, fanġ (vulture), *f.* 2nd dec.
  ruil na fainġe, the eye of the
  vulture; fiaċ, m. 1st dec. gen.
  fiaiċ, plu. fiaiċ; fiaċ duḃ, a
  raven; fiaċ fairnġe, a cormorant.
Swallow, ainleoġ, *f.* 2nd dec. gen.
  ainleoiġe; plu. ainleoġa. See
  example—nouns in óġ, *f.* of the
  second declension. Ní ḋeanann
  aon riṅeolaċ (linnets) fairṅaḋ,
  one swallow will not make a
  summer.
  „ bruaċailín (a swallow); from
  bruaċ, a bank; also called by
  some, ġaḃlan ġaoiṫe (ġaḃlan,
  fork, gable, one that moves zig-
  zag), and ġaoiṫe, of wind.

EXERCISE LXXVIII.

The Swallow and the Raven.

There was a contention between the swallow and the
raven, which of them was the finer bird. The raven at last
said: "Your beauty stands (is) for the summer alone, but
mine lasts many winters."

Ir fearr buanar 'na ailneaċt.

Durability is better than beauty.

VOCABULARY.

Cailin lán cruinne, a maid in the
  midst of a gathering.
Cu, a hound, *f.* 5th dec. gen. cun.
  (Most of these terms have been
  explained in the foregoing Lessons.)
Dealġ, a thorn, *m.* 1st dec. gen. deilġ.
Feiḋm, use, 4th dec. ġan féiḋm (*gan
  féme*), useless.
Ġéire, compar. and super. degree of
  ġeur, sharp.
Ġlún, 1st dec., knee.
Ṁná, the gen. sing. and nom. plur.
  of bean, a woman.
Ṁunlaċ, *m* 1st dec. gen. munlaiġ, mire;
  derived from loċ, a pond, &c.
Niṁniġe, super. of niṁneaċ; from
  niṁ (*niv*), poison.
Raḋarc (*rhyark*), sight, vision, the
  ken, power of seeing.
Raḋarc, sight, is applied to the power
  of seeing; amarc, sight, to the
  thing seen; tá raḋarc maiṫ
  aġam, I have good sight; ir-
  breaġ an t-amarc é, it is a
  fine sight (thing seen).
Suil, *f.* 2nd dec., an eye.
Teanġa, *f.* tongue, 5th dec.
Uile, elbow, arm; gen. uilean, 5th
  dec
(Ir) Fearr, better, best.

EXERCISE LXXIX.

COMPARATIVES AND SUPERLATIVES.

Níl níos "níos géire" 'na teanga mná.

Ná trí neiṫe "is nimhnighe" ann duine;
   fuil; glún; agus uile.

Ná trí radairc (*rhy-irk*) "is géire air bíṫ:"

Seabac air cnap; cu ann glean; cailín lán cruinne.

Ná trí neiṫe "gan féidm air bíṫ;"

Caiṫeaḋ cloc air cuan; comharlughaḋ mnaoi boirb;
   cainт le ceann gan céil.

Ná trí neiṫe "is géire air bíṫ:"

Dealg múnlaiġ, fiacal (tooth) cun, a'r focal (word)
   amadáin (of a fool).

> Is fearr mine 'na boirbe móir,
> Is fearr cóir 'na dul cum dliġe;
> Is fearr teac beag a'r ceann lón,
> 'Na teac mór a'r beagán bíoc.

FORTY-SEVENTH LESSON.

ADJECTIVES IRREGULAR IN THE MODE OF COMPARISON.

The adjectives irregular in their mode of comparison in English are:

Positive.	*Comparative.*	*Superlative.*
Good,	better,	best.
Bad, or ill,	worse,	worst.
Little,	less,	least.
Much, or many,	more,	most.

and some few others.

The adverbs also derived from these adjectives are irregular:

Well,	better,	best.

John sings well (*adv.*); James, better (*adv.* comparative); Jane, best (*adv.* superlative).

Badly,	worse,	worst.
Little,	less,	least.

In Gaelic those irregularly compared are:

Positive.	Comparative.	Superlative.
Beag, little, small,	níor luġa (pr. *lhoo*),	is luġa.
Faḋa, long; from {	„ faiḋe,	„ faiḋe.
faḋ, length, {	„ sia,	„ sia.
Furur, easy,	„ fura, ura,	„ fura, and ura.
Fogur, near; Welsh, agos; Gr. ἔγγυς,	„ foigre (for fog-re), by *Metathesis*, foirge.	„ foigre.
Gar, near,	„ goire, gaire.	„ goire.
Geárr, short,	„ giorra,	„ giorra.
Ionṁuin, dear,	„ anra,	„ anra.
Iomḋa, many,	„ lia,	„ lia.
Luaṫ, quick, fleet, {	„ luaiṫe,	„ luaiṫe.
(pr. *lhoo-ah*, in one syl.) {	„ tuirce,	„ túirce.
Maiṫ, good,	„ feárr (pr. *far*, as in English),	„ feárr.
Deaġ, good,	„ beaċ,	„ beaċ.
Minic, often,	„ mionca,	„ mionca.
Mór, greàt,	„ mó,	„ mó.
Olc, bad,	„ meara,	„ meara.
Droċ, bad,	„ dona,	„ dona.
Teiṫ, hot,	„ teo, teoiċe,	„ teo, teoiċe.

"Is luaiṫe" beiḋear euluiġṫe uaim m' annan a'r mo ḃriġ,
'Na crionfar an gleann glas úd úr ar mo ċroiḋe.

    Literally :—

"Sooner" shall have fled from me my feeling and my strength,
Than that green glen shall fade from my heart.—

                 Irish Melodies, by Dr. MacHale.

Oh! the last rays of feeling and life must depart
Ere the bloom of that valley shall fade from my heart.

     Ní tuirce faġail 'na ċaiṫeaḋ.
     No sooner got than spent.

     Ní tuirce ann 'na as.
     No sooner in it than out of it.

Tuirge is formed from an old adjective, turaċ, derived from tur, the beginning, therefore the proper radical spelling is tuirce, yet tuirge is common.

Obs.—Tuirse means sooner, in regard to time; luaiṫe, sooner, in respect to speed.

Dona, means unfortunate, unlucky, opposed to rona, lucky.

The learner knows that adjectives in Irish become adverbs by the particle ʒo preceding them; as, maiṫ, good; ʒo maiṫ, well; rona, prosperous; ʒo rona, prosperously.—(See "Easy Lessons," Part I., p. 49, Eleventh Lesson.)

It is only adjectives in the positive degree that become adverbs by the influence of the preposition ʒo. For, the comparative and superlative form of adverbs—like the words better, best, worse, worst, in English—is the same as that of the adjectives from which they are derived. That such comparatives or superlatives are adverbs can be known only from the context; as,

Ta Seorra níor fearr 'na Seirpe, George is better than Geoffry. "Níor fearr"—here is an adjective.

Labaraɳɳ Seorra níor fearr 'na Seirpe, George speaks better than Geoffry (adv.).

Ir fearr labaraɳɳ Sɣnéiḋ 'na ceaċtar aca, Jane speaks better than any of them (ir fearr, better, adv.).

EXERCISE LXXX.

In which an example of each irregular adjective is given.

Ir beaʒ eiḋir an t-olc a'r an maiṫ.
There is little between that (which) is good and bad

Ir "beaʒ" an niḋ aḋḃar na h-urcóiḋe.
It is a little thing (which is) the cause of mishap.

Ir "luʒa" (smaller) 'na frɣḋe aḋḃar na h-urcoiḋe.
Smaller than a flesh-worm is the cause of calamity.

Ʒiḋ "raḋa" lá, tiʒ oiḋce.
Though long the day, night comes.

Na téiḋ níor "raiḋe" 'na do aċṁuiɳɳe.
Do not go beyond your means.

Ir "forur" fuiɳeaḋ aɳɳ aice na míɳe.
It is "easy" to bake with meal at hand.

Ir "fura" ráḋ 'na ḋeanaḋ.
It is "easier" to say than to act.

Iſ " ꝼoiꝃꞃe" miꞃe ꝺaṁ ꝼéiṅ.
I am nearest to myself.
Ego proximus mihi.

Iſ " ꝼoiꝃꞃe" aṅ báꞃ 'ṅa ꞃaoilteaꞃ.
Death is " nearer" than is supposed.

Iſ " ꝃeaꞃꞃ" eiꝺiꞃ aṅ cṅocáṅ aꝃuꞃ aṅ aṅaċ.
" Short" is the distance between the hill and the swamp.
There is " little" between the sublime and the ridiculous.

Iſ " ꝃeaꞃꞃ" eiꝺiꞃ aṅṅ iuꝺ a'ꞃ a ṅae.
Iſ " ꝃeaꞃꞃ" ḃiꝺeaꞃ aṅ t-euꝃ a teaċt.
" Short" is the time between this day and yesterday.
" Short" does death be approaching.

Iſ " ꝃoiꞃꞃe" caḃaiꞃ Ꝺé 'ṅa aṅ ꝺoꞃuꞃ.
The assistance of God is " nigher" than (even) the door.

Ṁa'ꞃ " ioṅṁuiṅ" leat aṅ ċꞃáiṅ, iſ " ioṅṁuiṅ" leat aṅ t-ál.
Iſ " aṅꞃa" leo coiṅꝃioll a'ꞃ caiꝺe ꝃo móꞃ.
They love honour and virtue more.

Iſ " luaṫ" beaṫa aṅ ꝺuiṅe.
" Fleet" is the life of man.

Iſ " maiṫ" ꞃꝃeul ꝃo ꝺ-tiꝃ aṅ ꝺaꞃa ꞃꝃeul.
One story is " good" till another is told.

Iſ " ꝼeaꞃꞃ" aṅṅ am 'ṅa aṅṅ aṅtꞃaċ.
" Better" in season than out of season.

Iſ " ꝼeaꞃꞃ" bail 'ṅa iomaꝺ.
Good luck is " better" than abundance.

Ṅi ꝼaꝃaṅ aṅ ṁiṅic oṅóiꞃ.
" Often" does not receive honour.

Iſ " móꞃ" ꝺial ꝺꞃoċ mṅa-tiꝃe ꝺ'a cuiꝺ ꝺꞃoċḃláċaiꝃ ꝼéiṅ.
" Large" is the clotty housewife's portion of her own sour milk.

Iſ " mo" aṅ toꞃaṅ 'ṅa aṅ ollaṅ.
The noise is " greater" than the wool.

Iſ " mo" a ċoꞃt 'ṅa a ċaiꞃḃe.
Its size is " greater" than its crop. A fine show and a small crop.

Iſ olc aṅ ꝃaoṫ ṅaċ ꞃéiꝺeaṅṅ maiṫ ꝃo tìꞃ.
It is a bad wind that does not blow some good to shore.

Ꝺa ꝺoṅa Séaꞃluꞃ " iſ meaꞃa" 'ꝃ a éaꝃṁaiꞃ.
Bad as (was King) Charles, it is worse without him.

Réip aipoe úaille "ir irle" ʒɲiom.
Greatest talkers least doers—literally, according to the
  height of vaunting acts get low.

Beip opoċ-poċal, poċal ɲior "oona" 'ɲu a ōiaiʒ.
A bad word draws a worse one after it.
Qui malum dixit pejus audiet.

Ceiċ, hot—comp. ceoiċe and ceo. Aɲ ce ir cuirce aɲɲ
  a pilliɲ ir o'a ʒilléaɲ ir ceoiċe.
He who sits first in the saddle has the warmest seat; the
  man who gets possession first has comfortable quarters.

Note.—The particle ioɲa or 'ɲa, than, follows the comparative degree of
the adjective, and hence makes it clearly distinguishable from the superlative.
Ňior precedes the comparative except whenever the assertive ir, *is*, or assertive negative ɲi (ir) is employed. Therefore whenever ir or ɲi, *not* (ɲior,
not, for past tense), is expressed, ɲior cannot, of course, be used, but 'ɲa
(than) follows.

*** These idioms and proverbs should be committed to memory, or frequently repeated aloud. Every word which the memory receives or the
intellect understands is so much gained.

EXERCISE LXXXI.

IDIOMS FROM ADJECTIVES.

Translate   by

(1) more ⎫ than   ɲior mó   ⎫ 'ɲa
     less ⎭   ɲior luʒa ⎭

as much, as many ⎫ as   aɲ oireao   ⎫ aʒur
not as much, as many ⎭   ɲi...aɲ oireao ⎭

much, ʒo leoir; much money, ʒo leoir airʒio; much wine,
ʒo leoir piona.

(2) many ⎰ ʒo leoir; many people, ʒo leoir oaoiɲe;
        ⎱ iomōa (pr. *um·ee*), ioɲoual.

Many a man, ir iomōa pear—literally, it is many a man.
Iomōa is followed by a noun singular.

Ir iomōa la 'raɲ ʒ-cill oraiɲɲ.
Many a day shall we be in the tomb—literally, it is many
a day in the church-yard on us.

Creacaɲ, *m.* a skin.
Óiʒe, *f.* youth, the time of youth.

Óige is a *n. fem.* of the fourth declension. It is formed, like all abstract nouns of this class, from the gen. fem. of the adj., from which it springs; óg, for instance, makes óig in the gen. sing. mas., oige in the gen. sing. fem. The noun thus formed retains the gender of its last parent stock. In this manner are formed:

Adjective positive.	Genitive feminine.	Comparative.	Noun.
ard, high.	airde, of a high.	airde, higher.	airde, height.
bog, soft.	boige, „ soft.	boige, softer.	boige, softness.
cam, crooked.	caime, „ crooked.	caime, more crooked	caime, crookedness
geal, white, bright	gile, „ bright.	gile, brighter.	gile, brightness.
saor, free.	saoire, „ free.	saoire, freer.	saoire, freeness.
sean, old.	sinne, „ old.	sinne, older.	sinne, oldness.
trom, heavy.	troime „ heavy.	troime, heavier.	troime, heaviness.

Is iomḋa creacan a ċuireas an oige ḋi.

Many a coating does youth cast (shed) off it.

Another form—Is iomḋa blaṫ a ċuireas an oige ḋi. Many a blossoming does youth blow off it.

Is iomḋa cor ann dliġe Sacsanaiġ.

Many a twist in English law.

This is a proverb amongst our humble people, who have but too often experienced the devious windings of British law, whenever justice in redressing their wrongs has been sought.

(3) Many a time, iondual (frequently), is minic; as,

Is iondual gur b 'i an ḃo is airde géim 'san dorus is bradaiġe 's an g-coill.

Many a time it is that the cow of the loudest bellow at the door is the greatest pest in the wood.

Minic a leigeas beul na h-uaiġe rud aig beul na truaiġe.

The mouth of the grave often leaves something to the mouth of pity.

Is minic a ḃideas an ḟirine searḃ.

Truth is often bitter.

Again—Is searḃ an ḟirine, is milis an ḃreug air uairiḃ.

Truth is bitter, a lie is agreeable (sweet) at times.

(4.) At least { Air an laġad (pronounced *lhy-adh*, a noun; from luġa, smaller, smallest).
An rud is luġa de.

At most (4.)

Air an méiḋ; of the highest (kind) ḋ'a méiḋ; as,
Ní ḃ-ḟuil ġráḋ ḋ'a méiḋ, náċ ḋ-ṫaġann ḟuaṫ ḋ'a réir.
There is no love be it ever so ardent, that is not succeeded by proportionate hate.
An ruḋ 's mo ḋe.

At best (5.)

An ċaoi is fearr.
Air feaḃas; ḋ'a ḟeaḃas biaḋ is fearr ciall, though food is good sense is better.—Infinite Wisdom replied to the tempter: not by bread *alone* doth man live. Tá sé air feaḃas, it is in the best state. Is fearr marcuiġeaċt an ġaḃar 'na coisiḋeaċt ḋ'a ḟeaḃas.

(6.) The same, alike, céaḋna, an niḋ céaḋna; ionnan, identical; from ionn, for ann, in, and aon, one—i.e., in one.

Biḋeann beirt ann aon broinn is ní "h-ionnan" iaḋ.
Two persons are in the one womb and they are not alike (Jacob and Esau).

Is ionnan connraḋ a's éisteaċt.
They are the same—a compact and silence (éisteaċt *f.* from éist, hear, listen, listening, consenting).
"Silence gives consent."
Qui tacet consentire videtur.

Is "ionnan" aois, uaisle agus cumaċt ḋoiḃ air aon.
Identical is age, dignity, power, to them alike.

Is ionnan iṫe a's ól ó tá buiṋe air an g-ceannuiġeaċt.
It is the same—to eat or to drink since a person is for buying.

(7.) Too much, iomarca.

Iomarca ḋ' aon niḋ is ionnan a's gan aon niḋ.
Too much of one thing is the same as without anything.
(8.) Over and above—fearr ar bárr

Ní 'l pian, ní 'l pianaḋ, ní 'l galair ċo cruaiḋ craiḋte.
Le eug na g-caraḋ agus sgarraḋ na g-companaċ.
Carolan's lament over the grave of MacCabe: *Irish Minstrelsy*, p. 94.

FORTY-EIGHTH LESSON.

IDIOMS ARISING FROM ADJECTIVES—*continued*.

Obs.—This form of phrase; you are the better *of it*; you are the worse *of this*; he is the easier *of that*; is translated into Gaelic by annexing the prepositional pronoun ðé (of it, for ðe é) to the comparative degree of the adjective; as, ní luᵹaðé an tρócaιρe ροιnn, mercy is not the less-of-it (the fact of being) distributed. The sentence is thus analized: tρócaιρe, subject or nominative; luᵹa, less—irr. comparative of beaᵹ, little; ðe, of it, prepositional pronoun subjoined to luᵹa; ροιnn, a verbal noun, in opposition to the pronoun é, understood in ðé.

VOCABULARY.

Cumann, *m.* (from co and maon, wealth, substance; or from co and méιn, mind), according to the first derivation (not unlike that of the Latin *communis i.e., communus*), it means fellowship, company, joint share in stock and profits, therefore community of interests — hence it means what is common ; according to the latter, mutual affection, having the same views, of one mind, mutual friendship.

Comaoιn, *f.* communion, common possession. (Comaoιn is spelled also cumaoιn. It is derived, like its Latin · equivalent, from co and maoιn, although com, together, and aon, one, is very natural and striking.)

Comaoιneać, *m.* the holy communion, the body and blood of our Lord ; b-ꝼuaιρ tu comaoιneać, have you received holy communion ?

ᵹníðιρ, thou doest, 2nd pers. sing. from the verb ᵹníðιm, I do— hence ᵹníom, an act ; ðéanað also signifies to do, to act.

SHORT EXERCISE, LXXXII.

An té aιρ a b-teιðeann cáιl na moć-eιριᵹe amać ní "mιρðe" ðó a beιć 'nna ćoðlað (pr. *collou*) ᵹo meaðon lae, he of whom has spread the same for early rising is not the worse of it (the fact of) his sleeping till mid-day. Ní 'l ρᵹeul aιρ bιć naċ "ꝼeaρρ-ðé" cuιð ꝼaᵹaιl ᵹan ιnριn, there is no story at all of which it is not the better-of-it (the fact of) leaving some of it untold

      Na ðéan cumann le ꝼeaρ ᵹallða,
      Ma ᵹníðιρ ní "ꝼeaρρ-ðé" ðuιt
      Beιð ćoιðće aιρ tι ðo ṁeallta
      Aᵹ ριn comann an ꝼιρ ᵹallða ριρτ.

—See " Minstrelsy," vol. i., pp. 188, 189—the tragic story relative to Fitzgerald and O'Reilly—how the ꝼeaꞃ ꟝allꝺа robbed and murdered the confiding ꝼeaꞃ ꟝аelаċ, or native Irishman.

" Perchance," " probably," " likely," are translated by moꝺé (compounded of mó, greater [from moꞃ, great], and ꝺe, of it—*i.e.*, greater probability of it). Very likely he has not come, ꞃí móꝺe ꟝uꞃ ċаіꞃіc ꞃé; very likely he will not come, ꞃí móꝺe ꟝o ꝺ·ciocꝼаіꝺ ꞃé; perhaps you are not quite well, ꞃí móꝺe ꟝o ꝺ·ꝼuіl cu ꞃláꞃ. Ꙏóꝺe is commonly spelled móіꝺe by those who adhere strictly to the rule cаol le cаol.

Note.—That ꝺé in such sentences as those in the foregoing examples, is a prepositional pronoun, is plain to any one who analizes its meaning. The opinion of those (Stewart, Haliday,) who consider it a form of the comparative degree, is opposed to the truth deduced from analysis; to the authority of the two most distinguished writers on Irish and Celtic philology—O'Donovan and Zeuss; and is supported by conjecture and not by reason.

An adjective repeated has the same meaning as the absolute superlative, expressed in English by " very" " exceedingly." This is true likewise of adverbs: ꝼuаꞃ, ꝼuаꞃ, very cold, ceіċ ceіċ, very warm, cꞃom cꞃóm, very heavy; ꟝o cꞃom, cꞃom, very heavily, excessively; móꞃ móꞃ, very great. ꟝o moꞃ-moꞃ, exceedingly, especially, above all. This form of superlative is indeed seldom at present employed.

Note.—It is worth the learner's attention to observe a feature in some measure peculiar to the character of the native Irish people as reflected in the mirror of their language. The positive worth or merit of an object is expressed, not unusually, by asserting that it does not possess qualities of an opposite character. It is true that many examples of this style are found in the inspired writings; and that it is not uncommon; yet amongst the Irish—this peculiarity is very striking.

Ꞃí ꞃаṁаꝺаċ ꝺ' ꞃoꞃꞃꞃuі꟝ ꞃіаꝺ а ċeіle.
Not as foes did they encounter each other.

Ꞃí míꞃꝺe ꝺuіꞃe lóꞃ ꝺul аꞃꞃ аіꞃcіꞃe.
A person is not the worse of getting viatic on going a journey.

Ꞃí lіа cíꞃ 'ꞃа ꟝ꞃáꞃ.
No country (lіа) greater (in number) than a peculiar usage—*i.e.*, every country has each its own peculiar customs: *quot gentes, tot consuetudines.*

Ní mó an ịaplačt 'na a h-ịappačt.

The earldom is not greater than the calls upon it—*i.e.*, the highest position has its own proportionate share of calls and demands.

EXERCISE LXXXIII.

Ní "lịa" an ṛonaṛ 'na an donaṛ aṇn uplaịb čṛịb,

Ní "lịa" meuṛa aịṛ coṛaịb 'na cṛéịɣče (traits, turns of mind) do ṇa daoịṇịb,

Ní buan coɣad ṇa ɣ-caṛad.

Ní "h-ịonann" ɣeallad a'ṛ coịṁlịoṛad (fulfilling).

Ní b-ḟuịl coịll (wood) aịṛ bịč, ɣan a loṛɣad (burning) ḟéịn cṛịoṇaịɣ (of brushwood) ann.

Ní ḟeaṛṛ mall (late) 'na ṛo-ṁall

Ní 'l cuịle (tide, flood) "d'a ṁéịd" naċ cṛáɣann (ebbs),

Ịr ḟeáṛṛ ɣo mall 'na ɣo bṛáč,

Ịr ḟeáṛṛ ṛúịl (eye, expectation) le muịṛ 'na le cịll.

Ịr ḟeaṛṛ clú 'na conaċ (wealth, affluence).

Ịr anaṁ (seldom) čịɣ coɣad ɣan ɣoṛcad

Ịr anaṁ čịɣ oṛna ɣan doịlɣịor móṛ 'ṛ an ɣ-cṛoịde,

Ịr anaṁ čịɣ čṛáịɣ ɣan láṇ ceaċc maṛa 'ṇn a dịaịɣ.

An ce ịr ḟaịde čuaịd, ṛé ịr ɣịoṛṛa do 'n uaịɣ.

He who has advanced furthest (in age) is nighest the grave.

An Idiom that should be remembered.

OBS.—A noun in the predicate, accompanied by an adjective expressive of praise or dispraise, is nominative case, and not genitive. In English, the noun corresponding to it, is governed by the preposition *of*.

Bean bud deịṛe cṛuč, a woman *of* the fairest form.

Feaṛ ịr mó cịall, a man *of* the greatest sense.

Caṛṛuịll bud bịnne ḟonn, Carrul *of* the sweetest song.

VOCABULARY.

Amplač, *adj.* greedy, voracious, covetous; from ampal, famine, hunger.

baịneaṛ, *v.* appertains; from baịnịm, I appertain: leịr, with, usually follows it; cad é ṛịn, do'n ce ṛịn, naċ m-baịneann ṛịn do, what is that to the person to whom it does not appertain.

beịṛịm, *Irr. v.* I give; čuɣ, I gave: beịṛịm, I bear or carry, of which the perfect tense is ṛuɣ; ṛuɣar aịṛ, I seized him, I overtook him.

Cualaḃ, *v.* per. tense, heard; from *irr. v.* cluiṅ, *m.* to hear.

Foġlaṁ, *n.* learning; from foġla or foġla, learned, which comes from foġ, acquisition, booty, acquirements, physical or intellectual; hence it signifies knowledge, therefore learning.

Leoṅ, a lion; spelled also leoṁaṅ.

Raḋ, speaking, a discourse; coṁ-raḋ, a conversation; rean-raḋ, an old saying, a proverb.

Sáruiġim, *v.* I surpass, excel; from rár, very excessive; raruiġ, to act with excess, to oppress, to overcome.

Sáruġaḋ, oppression, conquest, devastation, continual annoyance.

Sáruiġeác, a pest, a bore.

Sáruiġeacc, *f.* contention; a trial for superiority.

Saoilim, *v.* I think; sometimes spelled, and commonly proncunced ríliṁ (*sheel-im*).

Seal, *m.* a while, a space of time; real ġeann, a short while.

Tuiġim, *v.* I understand.

Tuiġre, *f.* 5th dec. understanding, genius.

Tuiġrinc, *f.* 2nd dec. the same.

Tuiġrineác, *adj.*, intelligent, knowing.

Tuiġrince, *part.*-understood.

So-ċuiġrince, intelligible; comprehensible.

Do-ċuiġrince, incomprehensible.

EXERCISE LXXXIV.

IDIOMS OF THE ADJECTIVE.

1. A aṫair, ir faḋa ó ḃí aġainṅ le 'céile coṁraḋ air ṅeiċḃ a baiṅear le foġlaṁ? 2. Ir faḋa ġo ḃeirṁiṅ a leiṅḃ. 3. Caḋ fa, ro—a aṫair? 4. Ṁar naċ raiḃ tuféiṁ, ṅo ḋo ḋeaṅḃriuṅ Irabel ioṅ (fit), ṅeiċe foġlamċa ċuirġinc; ḃ'a ḃriġ riṅ ṅioṅ labair mé liḃ, óiṅ ḋeirceaṅ "ġur ioṅṅaṅ tafaiṅc (barking) ġaḋaiṅ (a beagle) aṅṅ ġleaṅṅ ġlear, a'r a ḃeiċ caiṅc le ceaṅṅ ġaṅ eolur." 5. Saoilim ġur rean-raḋ ṅa focla uḃ ḋo labair tu aṅoir? 6. Ir rean-raḋ iaḋ. 7. Ḃí fíor aġam riṅ. 8. Ciaṅṅof raiḃ fíor aġaḋ? 9. Ir miṅic ḋo ċualaḃ me m'aṫair-ṁóir 'ġ a raḋ. 10. Aṅ ċualair rean-raiċe air biċ eile uaiḋe? 11. ċualar. 12. Ca meuḋ? 13. Ir "ioṁḋa" riṅ. 14 Do ċualaḃ me-féiṅ é, a raḋ leat, ġur raḃair "ċo' crioṅa "le" beaċ "ċo ġlic le" rioṅṅaċ, aġur "ċo amplaċ le" leoṅ. 15. Ir "ioṁḋa" focal ġreaṅaṁail ḃiḋeaḋ aġaiṅṅ. Ġo cince ḃí ġo leoṅ eolur aiġe air ṅeiċḃ aġur air ḋaoiṅiḃ. 16. b-fuil aġaḋ uaiḋe coṁairle aṅ t-reaṅḋuiṅe? 17. Tá, ro í:

Ná bí caiṅceáċ a ḋ-tiġ aṅ óil,
Ná cuir aṅfíor air feaṅóir,
Ná h-aḃair naċ ṅ-ḋeaṅtar cóir,
Ná h-oḃ aġur ṅa h-iair oṅóir,

Ná bí cruaiḋ agus ná bí bog,
Ná tréig do ċaraiḋ air a ċuid,
Ná bí mí-ṁoḋaṁail, ná déan troiḋ,
A'r ná h-ob í ma'r éigin duit.

Sin duit coṁairle an t-Seanduine; nac maiṫ an coṁairle í. 18. b-ḟuil tu ann rin Jrabéil? 19. Táim. 20. Tann a leiṫ ann ro; b-ḟuil tu aig eirteaċt le do ḋearḃraṫair gan focal air biṫ a raḋ tu fein? 21. "Ní muinte go coigcrioċ;" bi re-ran real (a while, a short time) a b-Frainc agus ann Allamain, agus cad é an maiṫ muna raiḃ níor mo eoluir aige 'na tá agam-ra, a d' ḟan 'r an m-baile? 22. Tamuiḋ aiġ coṁraḋ anoir air rean-raite agus air rean-rġeultaiḃ; b-ḟuil "an oiread aca agaḋ-ra, a'r" tá aig do ḋearḃraṫair? 23. Deir re-ran go b-ḟuil fior aige níor mo 'na tá agam-ra; aċt deirim-re nac b-ḟuil. 24. (Aṫair) cuimniġ air ro, a inġin; "na mol-agus na cáin tu fein." Éirtfiḋ mire liḃ le céile, óir deirtear linn:

"Na tabair do ḃreiṫ air an g-ceuḋ rġeul,
Go m-beiriḋ an taoḃ eile ort":

'nuair eirtfiḋ le rġeul rarruiġeaċta air gaċ taoḃ, ann rin ḃearfad ḃreiṫeaṁnar "cia agaiḃ ir fearr." 25. Ir mire d' inġean air a b-ḟuil agaḋ, deir tu, gráḋ mór, agus tá aig d' inġean gráḋ mór ort, agus cuimniġ:

"Ir mac duit do mac go b-portan é,
Aċt ir inġean duit d'inġean go d-teiġ rí ra g-cré."

26. Caḋ é deir do ḋearḃraṫair leir rin. 27. Deirim gur:

"Mairg leigear a ċogar ciun
No a rún, le mnaoi baoċ;
Cogarnaċ nac ngabann rġiṫ
ó racar ó ḋir go triur."

28. ó tá riḃ anoir a dréim le céile a b-treir feara (in a trial of knowledge), beiḋ againn gnatuġaḋ eile. Aċt glac uaim-re aig imteaċt duit, an coṁairle ro a beir O'Dala Fionn d' inġean:

"Gaiḃ mo ċeagarg, a inġin finn, ná déan bán ar do ḋeilḃ.

Níoṙ b' áilne ṫu a ḟolc maṙ óṙ, na Uǧna ingíon Deiṙg;
Níoṙ b' áilne ṫu a ɣ-cṙuṫ ṙaoiṙ, 'na Deiṙḋṙe ṙa ċaoṁ
    ċṙuiṫ.
Iṙ níoṙ ḋeaṙmaḋ ĵ an t-euɣ; a ɣṙuaḋ (cheek, brow), iṙ
    ɣleɣeal 'na 'n ṙnuaḋ ṙuɣ (surge).
Eilíonóiṙ ṙa caoṁ ḋealḃ; a'ṙ Claṙiana ṙa ḋeaṙɣ ḃṙeaċ
    (features)
Súṙanna ṙa ɣeal ɣné; ḋo ċuaḋaṙ ṙo ḋ'euɣ ṙa ṙeaċ.

Na meallaḋ ṫu an ṙolṫ maṙ óṙ; an beul maṙ ṙóṙ na 'ṙ
    ɣṙuaḋ ɣlan
Na 'ṙ coṙp a ṫa ṙéiṙṁiḋe (slender) ṙeanɣ; a ṫa lan ḋe
    ɣṙeaṙ a'ṙ ḋe ɣeaṙ."   29. Ɣlaċaim an ḋeaɣ-ċoṁaiṙle
    ṙí meallṙaṙ ṁé.

VOCABULARY.

Coṙ (pr. *korh*), a crime; cóiṙ, *kóirh*,
    adj. just; justice.
Fuiṙeoɣ, a skylark.
ṁaoḃaṙ (pr. *wee-am*), from maot,
    soft, to affect, to move, to excite
    to tears.

Ṁealtoċ, for ṁealtoḋaiḃ, would be-
    guile.
Seaċṙall, from ṙeaċ, aside, apart, a
    digression, an oversight, wander-
    ing, error.
Cóiṙ, search; aiṙ cóiṙ, in search.

EXERCISE LXXXV.

BY THAT LAKE WHOSE GLOOMY SHORE.

From the "Irish Melodies" by his Grace the Archbishop of Tuam.

Fonn—"An Cailíṙ ḋonn Ciṙionnaċ."

I.

A n-ɣleann an Duḃ-loċa 'ṙ lé n-a ṫaoḃ,
'N áit naṙ ṙeinn fuiṙeoɣ ṙóṙ a ṙiaṁ,
Aiṙ ḃáṙ áṙḃ áille, oṙ cionn an ċuaiṙ,
Ċuaiḋ naoṁ Caoiṁɣeiṙ óɣ cuṙ ṙuaiṙ.
"An ḃean, ṫa aiṙ ṁo ṫóiṙ, ṙí ḃ-fuiɣiḃ
"An áit ṙo, m-béiḃiḃ me ṙeaṙḋ 'mo luiḋc."
Faṙaoṙ! iṙ beaɣ ḋo ċuiɣ ṙa ṫṙa
Sé cluaiṙ iṙ cleaṙa ṁealltoċ' mṙa.

II.

Sí Cáit óɣ, na n-ɣoṙm-ṙúl,
A ċuiṙ aiṙ teiċeaḋ, é, 'ṙ ċuṙ ṙuḃal;
Buḋ buan a ɣṙaḋ. 'ṙ níoṙ ċoiṙ léi é,
A beiṫ 'nna céile aiɣ ɣiolla Dé.

Cia ain bié aic an ġluair an naoṁ,
Cluin ré a coircéim lé n-a éaob;
Téiḃeaḋ roṁ no rian, be ló, nó b'oiḋċe
Carraḋ a rúil leir annra t-rliġe.

III.

Ain bán na creige anoir 'nn a luiḋe,
Téiḋ re cum ruairṁir a'r cum rġít.
Aig rmuaineaḋ ain neaṁ, gan cár, gan crab
Fa beit ó catugaḋ mná raoi rġát.
Aċt níl aon ċlúiḋ, no clair, fanaon!
O ġaeċiḃ mná, ca ceanaṁail, raon:
Faḋ ca 'nn a ċoḃlaḋ, feuċ 'ra cra
Cáit aig ric na n-beor lé ġraḋ.

IV.

Gan eagla gáḃa, trí creaga gorg,
Go cuar na h-aille lean rí a lorg,
Ir 'nuain bo ḃealruiġ bán an laé,
D'foilriġ rġéiṁ a ḃreaċ 'r a ġné.
Ir cruaiḋ an croiḃe, a ca aig na naoiṁ;
Óṁ b'éir a h-ainiuġaḋ lé n-a éaob,
Do léim go beiffieaċ ó n-a ráṁ.
Ir teilg lé fanaḋ í, ra t-rnáṁ.

V.

A lán bo linne, a Ġleann-bá-loċ,*
Ċuit Cáit lé glaraḋ an lae go moċ.
Do ṁaoḃam go mall é cruaiṡe bo 'n ṁnaoi,
A b'cuz tré ġraḋ 'r tre reaċṁall croiḃe—
Tra ġuiḃ b'a h-anam beaċa ruċain,
Do cloireaḋ ceol ain faḃ an ċuain,
Lé a naiḃ na cnoic 'r na gleanta binn,
'Nuain a b'éiriġ a caire ġeal ó'n tuinn.

* Glen of the two lakes.

END OF PART IV.

PART V.

FORTY-NINTH LESSON.

CONJUGATION OF A DERIVATIVE ACTIVE VERB.

Our readers must have seen in some of the Gaelic exercises that the future tense, and the conditional mood of certain verbs have been presented in a form quite different from that shown in the paradigm of the verb ṁol, *praise thou*, as is shown in the Twelfth and Thirteenth Lessons.

The fact is, there is a class of verbs which make the future tense terminate in oċaḋ, and that of the conditional in oċainn, and not in ꝼaḋ and in ꝼainn. It appears also that this class is by no means few, nay, on the contrary, that it comprises a vast number of verbs. They can, therefore, be fitly ranked under a special conjugation.

THE SECOND CONJUGATION.

' Active voice.

EXAMPLE: Beannuiġ (*beannee*), bless thou; salute. In Scotch Gaelic, beannaiċ; Fr. *benir*; *benison*, a blessing.

IMPERATIVE MOOD—PRESENT TENSE.

Singular.	Plural.
1.	1. beannuiġ-muiḋ } let us beannuiġ-muir } bless.
2. beannuiġ, *beannee*, bless thou.	2. beannuiġiḋ, bless ye.
3. beannuiġ-aḋ ꞃé, *beannee-oo she*, let him bless.	3. beannuiġ-ḋir, let them bless.

See Lessons 5, 7, 8, 10, 12, 13, in which the meanings of the tenses, and their inflections are explained.

INDICATIVE MOOD—PRESENT TENSE.

Singular.	Plural.
1. beannuiġ-im, I bless.	1. beannuiġmuiḋ, we bless.
2. beannuiġ-ir, thou blessest.	2. beannuiġċiḋ, ye bless.
3. beannuiġ-iḋ ꞃé, he blesses.	3. beannuiġiḋ, they bless.

The personal endings, (1) im, (2) ir, (3) iḋ, for the singular; (1) muiḋ, (2) ċiḋ, (3) iḋ, for the plural, are the same as the inflections of the verb mol, an example of the first conjugation. See "*Easy Lessons*," page 54.

The relative affirmative is beannuiġear; as, an te a beannuiġear, he who blesses. The habitual present, beannuiġeann; as,

beannuiġeann
- me, I am in the habit of blessing.
- tu, „
- ṙe, ṙí, „
- ṙinn, „
- ṙib, „
- ṙiad. „

IMPERFECT.

Singular.	Plural.
1. beannuiġ-inn, *vanny-inn*, I used to bless.	1. beannuiġ-muir, we used to bless.
2. beannuiġ-ċá, „	2. beannuiġ-ċí, „
3. beannuiġ-aḋ ṙe, „	3. beannuiġ-ḋir, „

PERFECT.

Singular.	Plural.
1. beannuiġ-ar, *vanny-as*, I blessed.	1. beannuiġ-mar, we blessed.
2. beannuiġ-ir, *vanny-ish*.	2. beannuiġ-bar, you blessed.
3. beannuiġ ṙe, *vanny she*.	3. beannuiġ-bar, they blessed.

FUTURE.

Singular.	Plural.
1. beannóċaḋ, *bannochadh*, I will bless.	1. beannoċamuiḋ, *beannoch-amudh*, we will bless.
2. beannóċair, *bannochairh*, thou wilt bless.	2. beannoċaiḋ, *bannochy*, you will bless.
3. beannoċaiḋ ṙe, *bannochy she*, he will bless.	3. beannoċaiḋ, *bannochidh*, they will bless.

CONDITIONAL.

Singular.	Plural.
1. beannoċainn, *vannochyn*, I would bless.	1. beannoċamuir, *vannocha-mush*, we would bless.
2. beannoċċá, *vannochá*, thou wouldst bless.	2. beannoċaiḋ, *vannochy*, you would bless.
3. beannoċaḋ ṙe, *vannochoo she*, he would bless.	3. beannoċaiḋir, *vannocha-deesh*, they would bless.

OPTATIVE MOOD.

Singular.	Plural.
1. ʒo m-beaṅṅuiʒaḃ, *go man-nyidh*, may I bless.	1. ʒo m-beaṅṅuiʒmuiḋ, *go mannymudh*, may we bless.
2. ʒo m-beaṅṅuiʒ-iṛ, *go man-nyirh*, mayest thou bless.	2. ʒo m-beaṅṅuiʒċiḋ, *go man-ny-hee*, may ye bless.
3. ʒo m-beaṅṅuiʒe ṛe, *go man-ny she*, may he bless.	3. ʒo m-beaṅṅuiʒiḋ, *go man-ny-idh*, may they bless.

With the prepositional pronoun ḋaṁ, to me (ḋuiċ, to thee; ḋó, to him; ḋi, to her; ḋuiṅṅ, to us; ḋaoiḃ, to you; ḋoiḃ, to them), this verb expresses a salutation; as, ʒo m-beaṅṅuiʒe Ḋia ḋuiċ, God save you; ʒo m-beaṅṅuiʒe Ḋia ḋaoiḃ, God save ye.

Infinitive, beaṅṅuʒaḃ, *bannoo,* to bless.
Participle, beaṅṅuʒaḃ, ,, blessing.

Note.—"A noun is a word capable of declension only. A verb is a word capable of declension and conjugation also. The fact of verbs being declined as well as conjugated must be remembered. The participle has the declension of a noun adjective; the infinitive mood, the declension of a noun substantive. Verbs of languages in general are as naturally declinable as nouns."—*The English Language, by Professor Latham,* p. 290.

The infinitive mood, in Gaelic, and the active participle, have the prepositional as well as the independent form; as—infin:

beaṅṅuʒaḃ, ţo bless.

"Le" beaṅṅuʒaḃ, "*pour*" *benir,* for the puspose of blessing.

"ḋo" beaṅṅuʒaḃ, to bless.

Participles: Aiʒ beaṅṅuʒaḃ, a blessing; iaṙ m-beaṅṅu ʒaḃ, after blessing.

VOCABULARY.

bṙeaċṅuiʒ, *v.* second conjugation from bṙeaċ, a perception, judgment; bṙeaċṅuiʒ, *v.* to judge, perceive in the mind, behold, observe.

bṙiʒ, force, power, substance; ʒaṅ bṙiʒ, without force, &c., useless; ṅuḋ ʒaṅ ḃṙiʒ, a thing of no account; bṙiʒṁaṙ, solid, good, substantial.

bṙoċaiṙe, a butcher (from bṙoċ, meat; raw, broken flesh).

Coṙaṁlaċċ, *f.* likeness; from co and raṁlaċċ, root; ṙaṁail, similar, like

Iaṙṛiaḃ, (*eer-ree*), an asking, an effort, an attempt; iaṙṛaiḋaċċ, the same; root, iaṙṛ, ask, seek after.

Spólla, *m.* (fourth dec.) a piece of meat; a fragment, a joint; broken meat; plur. ṙpollaiḃ, ṁaille leiṙ ṅa ṙpollaiḃ, together with the fragments.

EXERCISE LXXXVI.

An maḋaḋ aguṡ a ṡgáṫ.

Do ġoid maḋaḋ ṡpólla ar tiġ bróċaire, aguṡ do ḃí dul ċar aḃain a ḃaile, leiṡ, 'nuair do ḃreaṫnuiġ ṡé a ċoram-laċt ḟéin 'ṡan t-ṡruṫ. Do ṁeaṡ ṡé ġur maḋaḋ eile a ḃí ann le ġreim ḟeola: ṫainic dúil air, an dara ṡpólla a ḃeiṫ aiġe mar an g-ceaḋna. Leiṡ ṡin ṫug ṡe iarraḋ air, aċt do ċuit uaiḋe an méid ḃí ann a ḃeul, aguṡ mar ṡo do ċail an t-iomlan.

Air niḋ ġan ḃriġ cailtear ġo minic ṡub briġṁar.

VOCABULARY.

Air ḟad, entirely.

beanṫraiġ, the prep. case of bean-ṫreaċ, a widow; a contraction for bean, a woman, and ṫreiġ-eaċ, forlorn, forsaken—a woman bereft and alone; a relict.

De ġnáṫ, usually ṡguir, v. to cease, to give over, to slip or slide off; to desist.

EXERCISE LXXXVII.

Ḃí aiġ beanṫreaiġ ceaṡc a ṡuġ uḃ ġaċ maidin. Duḃairt an bean leiċe ḟéin: "Ma ḃeṡṡim ḋa oireaḋ óṡna ḋi, ḃeaṡḟaiḋ ṡí ḟa do ṡan lá." Do ṡinne ṡi aṁlaiḋ, aċt ṫarla ar, ġur ṡguir an ceaṡc ó ḃréiṫ air ḟad.

Ni mar ṁeaṡmuiḋ tuitear amaċ de ġnáṫ.

Note.—Verbs ending in ġ are derived, some from nouns, others from adjectives.

From nouns; as,

NOUNS.	VERBS.
Aċt, a decree.	Aċtuiġ, pass a decree, enact.
Alt, a height, a joint (Latin, *altus*, high).	Altuiġ, to extol, to magnify; to thank God; mile altuġaḋ le Dia, a thousand thanks to God; a prayer ever on the tongues of the Catholic Irish.
Barr, a top, a summit, a swelling tide.	Barruiġ, to come to a top, to increase, to swell; to flow like the tide. Spelled burruiġ sometimes.

NOUNS.	VERBS.

Báp, death.

Báṭuiẓ, put to death, kill, perish.

Beann, (as if biṫ ain), the felicity of life; beaṇ, a woman, is from bė, a creature, a being, and ain, fair.

Beannuiẓ, bless.

Beaṫa, life, food.

Beaṫuiẓ, feed.

Caṫ, a battle.

Caṫuiẓ, to contend, fight, to tempt; Caṫuẓaṫ, fighting, temptation.

Céim, a step.

Céimniẓ, step, move, advance, stride.

Críoṫ, end.

Críoṫnuiẓ, to bring to an end.

Criṫ, trembling.

Criṫnuiẓ, to quake, to tremble.

Cuairṫ, a round, a circuit, a visit.

Cuairṫuiẓ, to look for, to go around, to search for.

Cuimne, (co, with, meine, mind), recollection.

Cuimniẓ, recollect.

Ẓorṫ, hunger, injury.

Ẓorṫuiẓ, to hurt, injure; na ẓorṫuiẓ mė, do not hurt me.

Jomaṫ, many, a multitude.

Jomaṫuiẓ, to multiply.

Orṫ, order.

Orṫuiẓ, to order.

Pian (pr. peṭ-an, in one syl.), pain.

Piannuiẓ, to pain.

Sol, the sun; rolur, light.

Solruiẓ (and roilriẓ), to enlighten.

Tor, beginning.

Toruiẓ, commence, begin.

Treor, a lead, a guide.

Treoruiẓ, to lead, to guide, to direct, steer.

ADJECTIVES.	VERBS.

Arṫ, high.

Arṫuiẓ, elevate.

Aibiṫ, ripe; aipiṫ, same; (from ai, an element, biṫ, of food).

Aibuiẓ and apuiẓ, to ripen.

Ban, white, pale.

Banuiẓ, to make white, to lay bare, to devastate; to grow

vexed, angry, mad—because the features grow *pale* when the soul is filled with anger.

ADJECTIVES.	VERBS.
Beo, living, lively.	Beoḋuiġ, to vivify, to enliven.
Boḋaṙ (pr. *lower*), deaf; hence the common English, bother.	Boḋruiġ, to deafen.
Boġ, soft.	Boġuiġ, to soften.
Buan, lasting, enduring.	Buanuiġ, persevere, continue, make lasting.
Ciún, still, silent.	Ciúnuiġ, to pacify, to render silent.
Daoṙ, slavish, condemned.	Daoruiġ, to condemn.
Deaṙġ, red.	Deaṙġuiġ, redden, blush, incite.
Dub, black.	Dubuiġ, blacken.
Faḋa, long.	Faḋuiġ, lengthen.
Follus, apparent.	Foillriġ, reveal, make known, publish.
Fuaṙ, cold.	Fuaṙuiġ, cool.
Geuṙ, sharp, sour	Geuṙuiġ, sharpen, make sour.
Laġ, weak.	Laġuiġ, weaken.
Maol, bare, smooth, blank, mild, harmless. Welsh, *moil*; Latin, *mollis*.	Maoluiġ, to level, to sweeten, to appease.
Maṙb, dead.	Maṙbuiġ, to deaden.
Milis, sweet.	Milriġ, to sweeten.
Min, fine, minced.	Miniġ, to make fine, to explain.
Móṙ, large, great.	Móṙuiġ, enlarge, magnify.
Saoṙ, free.	Saoruiġ, to make free.
Saiḋbiṙ, rich.	Saiḋbriġ, to enrich.
Slán, safe, sound.	Slánuiġ, to save, to redeem, to render sound.
Soiṙb, prosperous.	Soiṙbuiġ, to prosper.
Tirim, dry.	Tirmiġ, to dry.
Umal, humble.	Umluiġ, to humble.

Verbs derived from adjectives have, besides the transitive, a reflective meaning, which is well exemplified in the verb derived from ᴅeaꞃᵹ, red.

ᴅeaꞃᵹuiᵹ, to redden, to en-kindle; as, ᴅeaꞃᵹuiᵹ aꞃ ceiꞃe, kindle the fire; to make red with anger, to inflame, to excite; ᴅeaꞃᵹuiᵹ é, in-cense, inflame him; to grow red; as, ᴅeaꞃᵹuiᵹeaꞃꞃ ꞃe, he blushes.

And from baꞃ, white; báꞃuiᵹ, to whiten, oꞃ to grow white—hence (1) to devastate, to make another pale with anger, to madden one; (2) to grow white, pale.

Note.—The final ᵹ of the imperative mood, second person singular, is, in many parts of Ireland, not aspirated, and is pronounced hard. The written language favours the aspirated sound.

" The pronunciation of ᵹ (hard and unaspirated) is," says Dr. O'Donovan, " one of the strongest characteristics of the Munster dialect."—p. 80.

VOCABULARY.

Cheese, cáiꞃ; 2nd dec. gen. caiꞃe (Latin, *caseus*). Cáiꞃ means also regard, love, esteem.

Crow (1) pꞃiacáꞃ, (2) ꞃioꞃꞃ, ꞃioꞃꞃóᵹ, from ꞃioꞃꞃ, fair; a hooded-crow, the *corvus cornix*— pꞃiacáꞃ; from pꞃeac, to grasp, to hold; pꞃiacáꞃ ioꞃᵹꞃac, or pꞃiacáꞃ cꞃioꞃac, a vulture; pꞃiacáꞃ ꞃa ᵹ-ceaꞃc, a kite, a ringtail; pꞃiacáꞃ ᵹeaꞃꞃ, a buzzard.

Claw, cꞃub; piur. cꞃuba.

How, ꞃac; literally, " is it not?" how fair, ꞃac beaꞃ; how beautiful, ꞃac aluiꞃ. The negative form is peculiarly Irish—it adds strength to the expression.

Piece, ᵹꞃeaꞃ, pioꞃa.

Snatch, cóiᵹ, ꞃᵹiob.

Spied, ᴅo coꞃꞃaiꞃc.

Tree, cꞃaꞃ, *m.* 1st D.

Window, ꞃuiꞃeóᵹ, *f.* 2nd D. (from ꞃeꞃ, an old Irish word signifying air); Fr. *fenetre;* Lat. *fenestra.*

Wing, ꞃᵹiacáꞃ, *m.* dim. of ꞃᵹiac, a shield—a wing spread out covers like a shield.

Wishing, aiᵹ ᴅuil (le ᴅuil, with a wish) le ꞃoꞃꞃ, with intent, pur-pose, wish.

EXERCISE LXXXVIII.

THE FOX AND THE CROW.

A crow snatched a large piece of cheese out of a window, and flew with it to the top of a tree, with intent to eat it. A fox spied her, and wishing to get the cheese, thus planned his approaches: "O, fair crow," said he, "how beautiful are thy wings, how sparkling thy eyes, how (ꞃac) graceful (beaꞃ) thy neck (moiꞃéal); thy breast (ucc) is the breast of an eagle; thy claws—I beg pardon—thy talons excel those of every beast of the field. But my sad sorrow! that thou

art dumb, and wantest only a voice!' The crow grew
elated, and wished to show that she had a sweet voice. She
opened her mouth; down dropped the cheese, which the
fox snapped up, and observed to the crow: " Whatever I
said of your beauty—of sense you have none."

Men seldom flatter without some selfish views; and they
who listen to flatterers must pay well for such alluring
strains.

FIFTIETH LESSON.

THE PASSIVE VOICE.

To conjugate a verb in the passive voice, annex to the
root of the active verb those endings which shall presently
be shown.

Take for the first conjugation, the verb

mol, praise thou:

	tar,	for the present tense,	moltar
	taidh, or ti,	imperfect tense,	moltaidh
To the	adh,	perfect tense,	moladh
root, mol,	far (fear),	future tense,	molfar
annnex	faidhe,	conditional tense,	molfaidhe
	ta, te,	for the passive	
		participle,	molta

In this manner are formed all the tenses.

Present—moltar, which is the present tense also of the
imperative, indicative, or optative, according to its position
in a sentence: moltar, me, I am praised; or, let me be
praised; go moltar me, that I may be praised—the optative formed by the use of go, *that*, like the French *que*.

OBSERVE. In the passive there is no inflection or change in the persons
of each tense. The personal pronoun or the subject must be expressed in
order to distinguish the persons, whether first, second, or third; as,

Singular.	Plural.
1. moltar mé, I am praised.	1. moltar sinn, we are praised.
2. moltar tu, thou art praised.	2. moltar sib, you are praised
3. moltar é, or i, he, or she, is praised.	3. moltar iad, they are praised

In like manner the persons of the other tenses are expressed by means of
the personal pronouns or subject after the single inflection, which is, like the
past tense in English, common to all.

In the third person singular the secondary, oᚱ aspirated, and *not* the primary form of the personal pronoun is found to represent the subject.

VOCABULARY.

Cⁱneál (from cⁱn, *of* the head, source; and ál, offspring), clan—a race, a kind, a class, a progeny, a nation; pronounced with (ⁱ) scarcely articulated—*knáwl.* It is of the second dec. and makes the gen. case cⁱnéⁱl, *knéyil.*

Cⁱuⁱnnⁱ̇ɫeaⁱⁿ, present tense, imperative of cⁱuⁱnnⁱ̇ɫ, gather, collect, root; cⁱuⁱnn, gathered, rolled together, folded; cⁱuⁱnne, the orb, world.

Ꝟoⁱⁿ, v, called.

Léⁱꞁɫeaⁱⁿ, from léⁱꞁ, let, allow, passive imperative.

ꝳaⁱⁿeaⁱⁿ, n. f. 2 dec. gen. maⁱⁿⁱⁿe; contractedly, maⁱⁿⁿe, and pronounced maⁱⁿⁿe; Latin, *mane.*

ꝳⁱⁿ-ɫeuⁱⁿ, m. 1 dec., from mⁱⁿ, fine; and ɫeuⁱⁿ, grass, soft grass, smooth grass, meadow.

Sⁱol, gen. ꞁⁱl, seed, corn, issue, race, children, clan, tribe; ꞁⁱol ꝺaⁱꞃⁱꝺ, of the race of David; ꞁⁱol Neallaⁱꝺ, of the race of the O'Neills.

Coⁱⁿaⁱꝺ, m. 1st dec., gen. coⁱⁿaⁱꝺ, produce, fruit, fruitfulness; pronounced *thoroo.* Observe how it differs in sound from Caⁱⁿꝺ (*tharw*), a bull; and from caⁱⁿꝺ and caⁱⁿꝺe, *tháirv, thairve,* gain, advantage, profit. "Iꞇ beannuⁱꞃɫe coⁱⁿaⁱꝺ ꝺo bꞃonn—Ioꞇa," blessed is the fruit of thy womb, Jesus.

EXERCISE LXXXIX.

9. Aꞁuꞇ a ꝺubaⁱꞇꞇ ꝺⁱa; " cⁱuⁱnnuⁱꞃɫaⁱⁿ" na h-uⁱꞃꞁɫe a ꞇá ɫaoⁱ neaⁱ̇ ann aon áⁱꞇ, aꞁuꞇ bⁱꝺeaꝺ an ꞇ-úⁱⁿ ꞇⁱꞃⁱⁿ le ɫeⁱcꞁⁱnꞇ. Aꞁuꞇ ꝺo bⁱ maⁱⁿ ꞁⁱn. 10. Aꞁuꞇ ꝺo ꞁoⁱⁿ ꝺⁱa ꝺe'n uⁱⁿ ꞇⁱꞃⁱⁿ, ꞇalaⁱ̇; aꞁuꞇ ꝺe cⁱuⁱnnuꞁaꝺ na n-uⁱꞃꞁe, ꝺo ꞁoⁱⁿ ꞁé, ɫaⁱꞃⁱꞃꞁe. Aꞁuꞇ ꝺo ċonnaⁱꞃc ꝺⁱa ꞁuⁱⁿ buꝺ maⁱꞇ ꞁⁱn. 11. Aꞁuꞇ ꝺubaⁱꞇꞇ ꞁe; ꞇuꞁaꝺ an ꞇalaⁱ̇ ɫeuⁱⁿ, aꞁuꞇ an luⁱb aⁱⁿ a b-ꞇⁱꞁ ꞁⁱol, aꞁuꞇ cⁱⁿan coⁱⁿaⁱꝺ a beⁱⁿeaⁱⁿ coⁱⁿaꝺ ꝺo ⁿéⁱⁿ a cⁱⁿéⁱl, a b-ɫuⁱl a ꞁⁱol ann ⁿéⁱⁿ aⁱⁿ an ꞇalaⁱ̇. Aꞁuꞇ ꝺo bⁱ maⁱⁿ ꞁⁱn. 12. Aꞁuꞇ ċuꞁ an ꞇalaⁱ̇ mⁱⁿɫeuⁱⁿ, aꞁuꞇ luⁱb a beⁱⁿeaⁱⁿ ꞁⁱol ꝺe ⁿéⁱⁿ a cⁱⁿéⁱl, aꞁuꞇ cⁱⁿan ꝺo beⁱⁿeaⁱⁿ coⁱⁿaꝺ ꝺe ⁿéⁱⁿ a cⁱⁿéⁱl. Aꞁuꞇ ꝺo ċonnaⁱꞃc ꝺⁱa ꞁuⁱⁿ buꝺ maⁱꞇ ꞁⁱn. 13. Aꞁuꞇ ꝺo ⁿⁱⁿⁿe an ⁿóⁱⁿ aꞁuꞇ an maⁱꝺⁱⁿ an ꞇꞃeaⁱⁿ lá.

PASSIVE VOICE—SECOND CONJUGATION.

Take beannuⁱꞃ, bless thou, to which annex.

—	ċaⁱⁿ,	for the present,
—	ⁱꝺe	„ imperfect,
—	aꝺ	„ perfect,
—	ꞇe	„ participle,
Change uⁱꞃ into	oċaⁱⁿ	„ future,
—	oċaⁱꝺ	„ conditional,

In the past participle ṫe, and the other tense endings, t, in the suffix is sometimes aspirated and sometimes not. The cause of this shall presently be shown.

VOCABULARY.

Coṁaṙṫa, m. a sign, a mark, a token, print, vestige, proof; coṁaṙṫa na cṙoiċe, the sign of the cross. It is derived apparently from coṁ, together, and áiṙeaṁ, to reckon, to count—because by signs or marks objects are reckoned.

Loċṙan, m. a luminary, a lamp, a light, a candle, from ló, (for) day, or lía, colour, brilliancy, and cṙan, a stand, a support.

Oiḋċe, m. fourth dec., pronounced *ee-che*, and sometimes, especially in poetry, *ee*—night, as opposed to lá, day; noċt means a special night—this night, and is in opposition in meaning to an iuḋ, to-day; be lá a'ſ d' oiḋċe, by day and night; meaḋon oiḋċe, midnight; aiṙ uaiṙ an meaḋoin oiḋċe, at the hour of midnight; meaḋon na h-oiḋċe, the middle of *the* night. This word, from its being aspirated in the middle, appears to be a derivative, and is derived probably from oṙ or aiḋ, an element, a symbol, a cause; and ce, or ceo, darkness.

Ṙiaġail, f., a rule; derived from ṙiġ, a king, and áil, a wish, desire, pleasure; and, in a secondary sense, approbation, mark, impression. From ṙiaġail is derived ṙiaġluġaḋ, to rule, to direct, to govern, to regulate; mná ṙiaġalta, religious women, nuns; from ṙiaġail, is derived (1.) ṙiaġaltóiṙ, a ruler; and (2.) ṙiaġluiġṫeoiṙ, a ruler, from ṙiaġluiġṫe, ruled; Latin, *regula*, a rule.

EXERCISE XC.

14. Aġuſ duḃaiṙt Dia: bíḋeaḋ loċṙain a ſpeuṙ neiṁe, aġuſ ṙoinneaḋ ſiaḋ eidiṙ an lá aġuſ an oiḋċe, aġuſ bíḋeaḋ ſiaḋ aiṙ ſon ċoṁaṙṫa aġuſ aiṙ ſon aimſiṙ aġuſ aiṙ ſon laeṫe aġuſ bliaḋan. 15. Aġuſ dealṙuiġeaḋ ſiaḋ a ſpeuṙ neiṁe, taḃaiṙt ſoluiſ aiṙ an talaṁ. Aġuſ do ṙinneaḋ aṁlaiḋ. 16. Aġuſ do ṙinne Dia ḋa loċṙain ṁóṙa, an loċṙan iſ mó le ṙiaġluġaḋ an lae; aġuſ an loċṙan iſ luġa do ṙiaġluġaḋ an oiḋċe: aġuſ na ṙeulta. 17. Aġuſ do ċuiṙ Dia iaḋ a ſpeuṙ neiṁe le ſoluſ a ṫaḃaiṙt aiṙ an talaṁ. 18. Aġuſ le ṙiaġluġaḋ aiṙ an ló aġuſ aiṙ an oiḋċe, aġuſ do ṙoinn eidiṙ an ſoluſ aġuſ an doṙċaḋaſ. Aġuſ do ċonnaiṙc Dia ġuṙ buḋ maiṫ ſin. 19. Aġuſ do ṙinne an nóin aġuſ an ṁaidin an ceaṫaṙṁaḋ lá.

VOCABULARY.

Ainṁiḋ, m, an animal, a brute, a beast.

Ainnéiſ, f. live or dead stock, stuff, household furniture.

Dealḃ, m, shape, image, picture, stature.

Snáiġeaċ, creeping, crawling.

Soilléiṙ, adj., clear, bright, lucid, manifest, intelligible; from ſo, easily, and leuṙ, light.

EXERCISE XCI.

20. Aguṙ ḋuḃaiṙc Dia; cuġaiḋiṙ na h-uiṙġċe amaċ an ḋuil coṙṙuiġṫeaċ ann b-ḟuil anam, aguṙ eunlaiṫ a ḟeuḋaṙ eṙiollaḋ oṙ cionn na calṁan ḟaoi ṙpeuṙ ṙoilléiṙ neiṁe. 21. Aguṙ ḋo ċṙuṫuiġ Dia miolla móṙa, aguṙ gaċ uile ḋuil beo, coṙṙuiġṫeaċ, a ḃeiṙ na h-uiṙġṫe uaṫa ḋo ṙéiṙ a ċinéil. Aguṙ ḋo ċonnaiṙc Dia guṙ buḋ ṁaiṫ ṙin. 22. Aguṙ ḋo ḃeannuiġ Dia iaḋ aig ṙáḋ: bíḋeaḋ ṙiḃ coṙṙċaċ aguṙ "leaċnuiġiḋ," aguṙ líonaiḋ uiṙġṫe na b-ḟaiṙṙgeaḋ; aguṙ "líonaḋ," an eunlaiṫ aiṙ an calaṁ. 23. Aguṙ ḋo ṙinne an nóin aguṙ an ṁaiḋin an cuigṁaḋ lá. 24. Aguṙ ḋuḃaiṙc Dia: cuġaḋ an calaṁ uaiṫċe an ḋuil beo ḋo ṙéiṙ a cinéil, áiṙneiṙ aguṙ gaċ uile niḋ a ṙnáigeaṙ aiṙ an calaṁ, aguṙ bíṫeaċa na calṁan ḋo ṙéiṙ a g-cineal.

FIFTY-FIRST LESSON.

VERBS IRREGULAR.

The number of verbs irregular in Irish is ten. They are called irregular, mainly to conform to the fashion of grammarians, who thus denominate in other languages that class of verbs which differ from the common standard of conjugation. Irish verbs differing from the regular form are defective rather than irregular; moreover, the defect is confined to one or two tenses, chiefly to the perfect. A certain very numerous class of verbs in Latin, like those defective in Gaelic, borrow the perfect from some obsolete verbs of kindred meaning, and yet they are not denominated irregular.

" It is very evident," says Robert G. Latham, " that it is in the power of the grammarian to raise the number of Etymological irregularities to any amount, by narrowing the definition of the word irregular; in other words, by framing an exclusive rule. . . . . . This is the last art (framing exclusive rules) that the philosophic grammarian is ambitious of acquiring."—*The English Language.*

These Gaelic verbs are: (1) beiṙim, I bear; (2) ḃeiṙim (*veirhim*) I give; (3) cluinim, I hear; (4) ḋeanaim, I do; (5) ḋeiṙim, I say; (6) ḟaġaim, I find; (7) ḟeicim, I see; (8) ṙiġim, I reach; (9) ṙeiḋim, I go; (10) ṙiġim, I come.

(1) Beiṙ (pr. *be-irh*, in one syl. short), Eng. bear; Anglo-Sax. *bearan*; Goth. *bairan*; Lat. *fer*; Gr. φέρω, *phero.*

The several meanings of beiṙ are : (1) bring, (2) bear, (3) carry ; as, beiṙ aɲ ṟo aɲ leaḃaṙ, bring hither the book ; beiṙ uaiɱ' aɲ leaḃaṙ, bear off this book ; (4) produce, (5) bring forth ; as, aᵹuṟ beiṙḟiḋ ṫu ɱac, and you shall bring forth a son ; applied to animals signifies (6) yean, (7) litter, &c. ; (8) to lay ; as, beiṙeaɲɲ ceaṙc ḋuḃ, uḃ ᵹeall, a black hen lays a white egg ; (9) to spawn ; (10) to obtain, to procure ; as, beiṙ buaiḋ, obtain victory, beiṙ beaɲaċṫ, obtain a blessing. It has as many meanings as the word " bear" in English. " The word ' bear' is used," says Watts, " in very different senses." Or the word " get" in the same language, which implies possession of, or at, any place or thing ; (11) with the preposition aiṙ, on, it implies seize, lay hold of, catch, overtake, beiṙ aiṙ, catch him (it) ; aɲ m-beiṙḟiḋ ɱe aiṙ, shall I overtake him ? Leiṟ (with) coming after beiṙ, gives the idea of taking away ; beiṙ leaṫ é, take it away. These are the several meanings which beiṙ has in all its moods and tenses : bṙeiṫ, birth ; ó mo ḃṙeiṫ, from my birth ; bṙeiṫ, the offspring of the mind; i. e., a judgment, sentence, decision, determination ; aiᵹ ṫaḃaiṙṫ bṙeiṫe, giving a judgment; bṙeiṫeaṁ, a judge; hence the Irish ṙeaċṫa bṙeiṫeaṁaɲ, Brehon laws; bṙeiṫeaṁɲaṟ, a judgment.

Beiṙiɱ, I give—a form of ṫaḃaiṙ, give thou.

CONJUGATION OF THE TEN IRREGULAR VERBS.

1 beiṙ
2 ḃeiṙ
3 cluiɲ
4 ḋéaɲ
5 ḃeiṙ
6 ḟaᵹ
7 ḟeic
8 ṟiᵹ
9 ṫeiḋ
10 ṫiᵹ

Active Voice.

Imperative mood.	Indicative mood.
2nd person, is the root or theme. 3rd, eaḋ. Plural—ɱuiṟ, -iḋ, -ḋiṟ.	Present tense, Singular, iɱ, -iṙ, -iḋ, (ṟe). Plu.—ɱuiḋ, -iḋ, -iḋ.

Imperfect.

Singular—iɲɲ, -ċa, -aḋ (ṟe).   Plural—ɱuiṟ, -iḋ, -ḋiṟ.

.The Imperfect of ḋéaɲ is commonly borrowed from ᵹɲiḋ, do, act ; ᵹɲiḋ-iɲ (*nhee-yin*), I used to act, do, &c.

VOCABULARY.

Caoṅa-ḟíoṅa (wine-berries), grapes; from caoṅa, the plural of caoṅ, a berry (anything red, hence it means also a coal); and ḟíoṅa, of wine, gen. case of ḟíoṅ, wine.

Oṗéiṁ. *f.* 2nd dec. contention, struggling, endeavour, attempt.

Oṗeiṁ, *v.* to climb, get up on; endeavour, emulate, attempt, struggle; ní'l aon ġaṗ aiġ oṗéiṁ leiṗ aṅ cláiḋe tá aṅṗ, there is no use endeavouring to get up on a high ditch. Hence, oṗéiṁṅe, a ladder, and oṗeiṁṅe, warfare.

O'imiġ ṗe aiṗ ṗiubal, he went away a-walking—an idiom like the English "he went his way."

Eiṗiġ, *v.* to arise; eiṗiġ ṗuaṗ, rise up, *n.* dawn; aiġ eiṗiġ aṅ lae, at the dawn of day; with le (*with*), it denotes success; ġo n-eiṗiġ

leaṫ, may it prosper with you; níoṗ eiṗiġ leiṗ, it did not prosper with him.

Fíoṅcaṅ, a vineyard; from ḟíoṅ and caṅ, land.

Ní móṗ le ṗaḋ íaḋ, an idiom—they are not worth much; literally, they are not great (le ṗaḋ) to be spoken of—le lends a passive meaning to ṗaḋ.

Tṗíopall, *m.* 1st dec. a bunch, a cluster, a festoon.

Tṗíopallaċ, *adj.* after the form of bunches or clusters; ġo tṗíopallaċ, in bunches, in festoons. It is commonly applied to a fine head of hair, or to berries on a tree. Snuṫaṅ tṗíopall ṅa ġ-caoṅ-ḟíoṅa, the torrent of the cluster of grapes.

EXERCISE XCII.

Aṅ Sioṅṅaċ aġuṗ ṅa caoṅa-ḟíoṅa.

O'euluiġ ṗoṅṅaċ a ṗteaċ a ḃ-ḟíoṅcaṅ aṅṅ aimṗiṗ aṅ foġṁaiṗ 'ṅuaiṗ ḃíḋaṗ ṅa caoṅa-ḟíoṅa ḋeaṗġ, apuiġċe aġuṗ íaḋ 'ṅṅ a ḃ-tṗíopaill ġo h-áluiṅ, ġeuġaċ, aiṗ ṅa cṗaoḃaiḃ. Iṗ íoṁḃa léiṁ aġuṗ oṗéiṁ ċuġ ṗe ṗuaṗ oṗṗċu. 'Nuaiṗ ṅaṗ éiṗiġ leiṗ o' imiġ ṗe aiṗ ṗiubal a ṗaḋ leiṗ féiṅ; "ní móṗ le ṗaḋ íaḋ." Taiḋ ṗeaṗḃ.

PERFECT TENSE.

		Singular.			Plural.	
	1	**2**	**3**	**1**	**2**	**3**
of beiṗ is	ṗuġ-aṗ,	aiṗ,	ṗuġ ṗe.	aṁaṗ,	aḃaṗ,	aḋaṗ.
... beiṗ ...	ċuġ-aṗ	...	ċuġ ṗe.	...	...	...
... cluiṗ ...	ċual-aṗ	...	aíḋ ṗe.	...	...	...
... ḋéaṅ ...	ṗiṅṅ-eaṗ	...	ṗiṅṅe ṗe	...	...	...
... beiṗ ...	buḃṗ-aṗ	...	buḃaiṗc ṗe.	...	...	...
... faġ ...	ṗuaṗ-aṗ	...	ṗuaiṗ ṗe.	...	...	...
... ḟeic ...	ċoṅṅaṗc-aṗ	coṅṅaiṗc ṗe.		...	...	...
... ṗiġ ...	ṗaṅġaṗ, ṗíaċc-aṗ	ṗíaċc ṗe ...		...	...	...
... ceíḋ ...	ċuaḋ-aṗ, ḃeaċ-aṗ	ċuaíḋ ṗe ...		...	...	...
... cíġ ...	ċaíṅíc-eaṗ	ċaíṅíc ṗé		...	...	...

FUTURE.

1 beir	
2 béir	
3 cluin	The initial consonant is aspirated.
4 déan	
5 beir	
6 faġ	
7 feic	
8 suiġ	
9 teiḋ	
10 tiġ	

1	2	3		1	2	3
fad,	fair,	faiḋ.		famuiḋ,	faiḋ,	faiḋ.

6 Faġ borrows its future from ġab, *take*, ġab-
faḋ; neg. form, ní b-fuiġeaḋ.

9 teiḋ makes racfaḋ in the future.

10 tiġ   „   tiocfaḋ.—(See 52nd and 53rd
lessons.)

CONDITIONAL.

The changeable initial consonant suffers aspiration.

beir	
beir	
cluin	
déan	
beir	
faġ	
feic	
suiġ	
teiḋ	
tiġ	

Singular.   Plural.

1	2	3		1	2	3
-fainn,	-fá,	-faḋ (re).		-amuir,	-faiḋ,	-faidír.

6 faġ makes ġab-fainn, in this tense.

9 teiḋ   „   racfainn.

10 tiġ   „   tiocfainn.

VOCABULARY.

Die, ready to die, a nucc báir.

Espied, do connairc, perf. from feic,
see.

Fly, v. eiciol; he flew with joy, d'eiciol ġo fonṁar.

Ingenuity, ruaim, *f.* ir feárr ruaim
'na neanc, ingenuity is better
than strength.

Necessity, caill, *f.* riaccánar cruaḋ-
tán.

Pebbles, min-cloca, from minn, small

(Greek, μειον, Latin, *minus*),
and cloca, stones.

Pitcher, cruircin; ġráḋ mo croiḋe
mo cruircin, the love of my
heart is my pitcher.

Stooping and straining, cromaḋ aġur
rraonaḋ: rraonaḋ is a straining or stretching which is made
by a person when tired; or in
going to walk fast, or preparing
for any effort.

To quench thirst, tart do corġ.

EXERCISE XCIII.

THE CROW AND THE PITCHER.

A crow ready to die (in the state of death) with thirst,
espied a pitcher, to which he flew with joy; but when he

came up to it and found the water so low that he could not, with all his stooping and straining, reach it, then he thought to break it or upset it, but he had not strength. At last, seeing pebbles at hand, he dropped a great many of them one by one into the pitcher, and by this means he raised the water to the brim and quenched his thirst.

Ingenuity is better than strength.

Necessity is the mother of (begets) invention.

OPTATIVE—REGULAR.

	Singular.			Plural.		
ʒo m-beiŗ	1	2	3	1	2	3
„ beiŗ	-aŏ,	-aiŗ,	-aiŏ ŗe.	-amuiŏ,	-aiŏ,	-aiŏ.
„ ʒ-cluiɲ						
„ ɲ-ŏéaɲ						
„ ɲ-beiŗ						
„ b-ŗaʒ́						
„ b-ŗeic						
„ ŗiʒ́						
„ ŏ-ceiŏ						
„ ŏ-ciʒ						

The particle ʒo thus precedes the optative, and on that account the radical initial consonant, b, for instance, is eclipsed by m; c, by ʒ, &c.

The tenses borrowed from other verbs, which now, from usage, belong to the foregoing or any of them, shall be explained in next lesson.

EXERCISE XCIV.

An ċeaŗc aʒuŗ an cac

Ɖo "ċualaiŏ" (perf. tense of cluiɲ) cac ʒo ŗaiḃ ceaŗc aiɲiŏ ciɲɲ aɲɲ a ɲeaŏ (nest): ŏo ċuʒ (perfect of beiŗ) ŗé cuaiŗc aiŗċi, aʒuŗ "ŏuḃaiŗc" (per. of beiŗ) aiʒ "ŏul" (from céiŏ) aŗceaċ ŏó; ciaɲɲoŗ a b-ŗuil cu, a ċaŗa ŏiliŗ mo ċŗoiŏe? an "ŏ-ciʒ" liom maiċ aiŗ biċ a ŏéaɲaŏ ŏuic? b-ŗuil ŏiċ aiŗ biċ oŗc? Jɲɲiŗ ŏam a "ŏ-ciʒ" liom ɲiŏ aiŗ biċ ŗaɲ ŏoiɲaiɲ a ċaḃaiŗc (inf. of beiŗ) ċuʒaŏ? Ʒlac (assume courage) miŗɲeaċ: na biŏeaŏ eaʒla aiŗ biċ oŗc." "Ʒo ŗaiḃ maiċ aʒac," aiŗŗ (aiŗ, says, def. v.; ŗ is annexed for sake of sound, see 53rd lesson) an ċeaŗc, "iŗ ŏóiʒ́ liom ʒo m-beiŏiŏ ŗlaɲ 'ɲuaiŗ imŏċaŗ cu-ŗa uaim"

Cuaiŗc ʒaɲ cuiŗeaŏ iŗ ŗeaŗŗ ʒaɲ a ċaḃaiŗc.

FIFTY-SECOND LESSON.

THE PASSIVE VOICE OF THE IRREGULAR VERBS.

RULE.—The general rule for the formation of the tenses of the passive voice is, to annex to the verbal root, for the

Present tense   ... ċaʁ (ċaʁ); of the indicative; of the
                                    imperat., optative, and subjunct.

For the Imperfect   ... ċι
    ,,   Perfect   ... aδ
    ,,   Future   ... ꝼaʁ
    ,,   Conditional... ꝼaιδe.

According to this the passive voice o

beιʁ
beιʁ   Present tense.
cluιŋ
δéaŋ   Indicative, Imperative, Optative, Subjunctive,
beιʁ
ꝼáʒ   is, (beιʁ) -ċaʁ me, ċu, é; ʁιŋŋ ʁιḃ, ιaδ.
ꝼeιc
ʁιʒ   Imperfect.
ceιδ   ċι,   ,,   ,,   ,,   ,,   ,,
cιʒ

-ċaʁ, for the present (-ċι, for the past) is annexed to each root; to which, by supplying the personal pronouns, the persons of each tense are formed.

Note.—After ŋ,-ċ of the suffix ċaʁ, ċι, is not aspirated; therefore the present tense of cluιŋ, δéaŋ, is cluιŋċaʁ, δéaŋ-ċaʁ.

Although the above rule is plain and short, it is not objectively correct; for it is not from the root precisely, so much as from the first person singular of each of the several tenses, active voice, that the indicative tenses of the passive are formed; just as in Latin—amat, amatur; amant, amantur; amabit, amabitur. The perfects of the passive then are formed each from its respective tense irregular in the active, thus:

Perfect active.	Perfect passive.
1 ʁuʒ-aʁ, I bore,	ʁuʒaδ me, was born.
2 ċuʒ-aʁ, I gave,	ċuʒaδ, was given.
3 ċuaʟ-aʁ, I heard,	cuaʟaδ, and cluιŋeaδ, regularly, was heard.

4 ꝛꙗꞃꞃ-eꝛ, I did,   ꝛꙗꞃꞃeꝛ, was done.
5 ꝺuꞁꞃ-ꝛꞃ, I said,   ꝺuꞁꞃꝛꝺ, was said.
6 ꝛuꝛꞃ-ꝛꞃ, I got,   ꝛuꝛꝛꝺ, was found.
7 coꞃꞃꝛꞁꞃc-ꝛꞃ, I saw   coꞃꞃꝛꞁꞃcꝛꝺ, from coꞃꞃꝛꞁꞃc,
                              3rd sin.; ꝛꝛcꝛꞃ, the affect-
                              ed irreg. perf. pass., was
                              seen.

The remaining three verbs are intransitive.

☞ The tenses of the passive have never the initial consonant aspirated, like those of the active.

VOCABULARY.

Fuꞁꞃꞁoꞃꞃ, plu. reg. ꝛuꞁꞃꞁoꞃꞃꝛ, contractedly ꝛuꞁꞃꞃꝛ and ꝛuꞁꞃꞃe,
(1) those that abide or belong to
a place, the original inhabitants,
the old natives of a country, (2)
the crew of a ship, (3) the inhabitants of a town or territory;
from ꝛuꞁꞃ, to abide, await, rest,
remain.

Ꞡꞃꞁꝺ, v. 2, third person sing., present
ind. from ꞡꞃꞁꝺꞁꝼ, I do, I act;
like *ago* in Latin; from it is derived ꞡꞃꞁoꝼ, an act. It is pronounced as if ꞡ were not in the
word, like the English "gnat"
(pr. "nat").

Ꞡꝛꝺꝛꞁcꝛꞃ, m. 1st dec. conquest, possession, any landed property obtained by conquest or otherwise,
from ꞡꝛꝺ, take, seize, get. At
present it signifies a "holding of
land," a farm; ꝺ-ꝛuꞁꞁ ꞡꝛꝺꝛꞁcꝛꞃ
ꝛꞡꝛꝺ, have you a farm?

Ꞡꝛꝺ (*gaw*), has many meanings, primary and secondary, (1) take;
as, ꝛꞡuꞃ ꞡꝛꝺꝛꞁꝺ me ꞃꞁꝺ ꝺꝛꝼ
ꝛéꞃꞃ ꝼꝛꞃ ꝯoꝺꝛꞁ, and I will take
you to me for a people.—*Exodus;*
(2) accept, rescue, ꞡꝛꝺ é ꞃo
uꝛꞁꝼ, accept this from me; (3)
catch; as, cꝛꞁꝺ ꝛ ꞡꝛꝺꝛꞁꞁ ꞁꝛꞃꞡ,
they are catching fish; (4) seize,
making prisoners of; ꝛꞃ ꞡꝛꝺꝛꝺ
é, was he seized; cꝛꞁꝺ ꞡꝛꝺꞁꝛ,
they are seized (caught), impri-
soned; (5) get; (6) conceive,
ꞡꝛꝺ ꞃꞁ ꝛꞃꞃ ꝛ ꝺꞃoꞁꞃꞃ, she con-

ceived in her womb ;(7) go,
come, pass by, ꞡꝛꝺ cuꞡꝛꝼ, come
to (take side with) me; in this
sense it is by some confounded
with the English word "go," as,
ꞡꝛꝺ uꝛꞁꝼ, go from me, away
from me; (8) operate, practise
it; ꞡꝛꝺ ꝛꞁꞃ, beat him; (9) perform, ꞡꝛꝺ ꝛꝺꞃꝛꞃ, sing a song.

Ꞡꝛꝺꝛꞁꞁ, *a participle:* a taking or
seizing.

Ꞡꝛꝺꝛꞁꞁ, *a noun:* a portion of land
ploughed by cattle at one yoking;
a dividing of land. From this
word and cꞁꞃꞃe, or cꞁꞃꞃ—written
in old MSS. cꞁꞃꝺ, (for ꞃꝺ—ꞃꞃ,
in sound, in Gaelic) a clan, a race,
is derived the term ꞡꝛꝺꝛꞁꞁ-cꞁꞃꞃe,
gavel-kind, the name of the law
according to which the ancient
Irish and Britons, as well as the
Caledonians and Anglo-Saxons
were wont to divide and sub-
divide the lands of the chief or
head amongst the members that
composed the cꞁꞃꞃe.

Ꞡꝛꝺꝛꞁꞁ, n. spoil, booty; (2) seizing;
a course, direction; (3) barn;
v. to bind in fetters.

Ꞡꝛꝺꝛꞃꞃ, a gaol or prison, a pound;
the term now employed for pound;
a place in which one is in cus-
tody or in fetters.

Ꞡꝛꝺꝛꞁ, (1) a fork, because with it
farmers take (ꞡꝛꝺ), or gather,
what grows on their lands; (2),
a pen, a fold; (3) a prong; (4)

a gable; (5) the rafters of a house, because like a fork; (6) the groin; (7) a descendant, a branch; (8) a lawn between two headlands, hence the names of places near lakes, called "eporṅ-ᵹabal," Adragoole.

Múċ, v. to quench, to extinguish múċ an cojnjol.

EXERCISE XCV.

(From Dr. Keating's History of Ireland.)

An te do ṫjnjö ᵹabalcar (conquest) cnjorcaṁajl, nj ṁuċann an ceanᵹa bjöear nojṁe 'r an ċnjċ (country, re-gion) cujnear (re) ᶂa n-a ·rmaċc; aᵹur jr man rjn do njnne (from bèan) Ujlljam ᵹabalcar ajn na Sacranajö; njon ṁuċ ceanᵹa na Sacranaċ de bnjᵹ ᵹun ᶂaᵹaö (perfect passive) ᶂujnjonn na ceanᵹa do ċojṁeuö 'ran cnjċ, aᵹur ᵹo ö-cajnjc de rjn (and there came of that) an ceanᵹa do bejċ ajn bun 'r an ᵹ-cnjċ ö rojn a lejċ (idiom, literally, from that time, a part—*i.e.*, ever since, without any interruption) ajᵹ Sacranaċajö.

VOCABULARY.

Djbjn, v. (derived from djċ, want absence of, and bejn, bring), in-flict, banish, drive away, expel; *inf.* djbjnc; ajᵹ djbjnc, banish-ing.

Djbjnc, n. f. gen.-e, banishment; dujl djbjnce na ᶂujnnne, a desire of the banishment of (of banishing) the inhabitants.

Fuaċṁan, *adj.* hateful; from ᶂuaċ, hate; and ṁan, as, like.

Sᵹnjor, m. destruction, ruin, devas-tation; rᵹnjör aᵹur lom ajn do naṁaö, ruin and destitution be the lot of thy enemy.

Sᵹnjoraċ, *adj.* destructive.

Sᵹnjoraö, the act of destroying.

Sᵹnjor, v. to ruin, sack, wreck, de-stroy.

Sᵹnjorca, robbed, ruined, ransacked; ca re rᵹnjorca ᵹo bnaċ, he is ruined for ever; bejö me rᵹnj-orca, I shall be undone.

Sᵹnjorcöjn, a destroyer.

Tèjrc, f. a witness, test, proof, attes-tation. This word is the root of the Latin word *testis*, a wit-ness; for which lexicographers have found no derivation. It is one of the few British words at present retained in English.

Tejrc, v. a. to try, to prove, to sound, to aver.

Tejröear, m. proof, the act of testi-fying; a certificate, testimony; tejröear Dè, the testimony of God.

Tejrmèjö, f. the last will, testament.

Ún, *adj.* means fresh; jm ún, fresh butter; noble, generous; ún-rljoċc, a noble race; as a *noun* it means (1) maiden or *fresh* earth, mould; (2) hence earth, as opposed to water, one of the four elements; (3) a valley, the green and fresh appearance of a valley; (4) a verdant aspect, such as a valley presents; (5) land newly dug; (6) a grave; (7) a border, verge or end; as, ᵹo h-ún na ᶂajnnᵹe, to the verge of the sea; (8) fire, ún-ċujl (fire-fly), a cricket.

Únlan, m. a floor; from ún, fresh earth, and lan, the midst; be-cause in houses newly built the ún within the walls was, as op-posed to that without, in the (lan) or midst.

EXERCISE XCVI.

(Selections from Dr. Geoffry Keating's "History of Ireland.")

Is gaḃalcas Paȝanca do riȝne Henȝirc, re rin, caoireaċ
na Sacsanaċ, air na Breacnacaiḃ (on the Britons) mar
ȝur rȝrios re ó h-unlár (the floor, the soil) na Bricáine
iad, aȝus ȝur ċuir fuirionn uaiḋ féin ann a n-áicib, aȝus
iar n-diḃirc caiċ ȝo h-iomlan (entirely, fully) do óiḃir an
ceanȝa leo; aȝus a rámail céadna rin ba mian le Scain-
huirc do déanaḋ air Eireannacaiḃ. Oir ni feidir an
ceanȝa do óiḃirc ȝan an fuirionn d'ar ceanȝa í do óiḃirc,
aȝus de briȝ ȝo raiḃ mian na ceanȝa do óiḃirc air, do bi
mar an ȝ-céadna, mian óiḃirce na fuirnne d'ar ceanȝa í,
air; aȝus da rein rin (according to that) do bi fuaċmar
d'Eireannacaiḃ, aȝus mar rin nior ionȝaḃca (fit to be
received) a ceirc air Eireannacaiḃ.

From the conjugation of these verbs, called in Irish Grammar irregular,
presented to the learner in this and the foregoing lessons, it is seen that they
are perfectly regular in their numbers and persons, and are irregular only in
this, that they want certain tenses.

The tenses which make any show of difficulty to the learner, are the perfect
and infinitive.

"In language itself," says Latham ('English Language,' p. 336, fourth
edition), "there is no irregularity. The word itself is only another name
for our ignorance of the processes that change words." Again, "The whole
scheme of language is analogical."

REMARKS ON EACH OF THE IRREGULAR VERBS, AND ON THE SECONDARY OR ACQUIRED TENSES.

1. Beirim, *I bear* or bring forth, wants only the perfect,
which it borrows from an obsolete verb, rugaim, formed,
very likely, from ro, very; and tugaim, I bring, give, bestow. In the future tense indicative, and that of the conditional, e of beir is long beirfad, or bearfad; future passive,
bearfar; conditional, bearfainn—passive, bearfaide; in
the infinitive or verbal noun the position of the final r (being
a liquid letter) is changed, and made to coalesce with the
initial b, thus:

Infinitive participle, breiṫ, *breh* (and not beireṫ).

2. The verb, beirim, I give, pr. *veirhim*, distinguished
from the former by the letter b being aspirated, has, as it

were, two handmaids, which supply it with tenses, not only
the imperative, perfect indicative, and infinitive, which are
found wanting, but other tenses which it does not want.
These assisting verbs are cuᵹaim and cabᵽaim (contractedly
for cabaiṗim). From cabaiṗ alone it borrows the imperative and infinitive, and along with the regular form béaṗṗaö
supplies to the future the secondary form cabaṗṗaö (pr.
thowarfadh), I shall give.

Imperative mood.

Singular.	Plural.
… …	cabṗamuiṗ, *thowramush.*
cabaiṗ, pr. *thower,*	cabṗaiö, *thowree.*
cabṗaö ṗé, *thowroo,*	cabṗaiöiṗ, *thowradeesh.*

The infinitive, cabaiṗc, *thowarth.*

Indicative Mood—Present Tense.

beiṗim, cuᵹaim, and cabṗaim; passive, present, (indicative
and imperative), beiṗceaṗ, cuᵹcaṗ, cabaṗcaṗ.

Habitual Present.

beiṗeann mé, cuᵹann mé, and cabṗann, mé.

Imperfect.

beiṗinn, and cuᵹainn.

The *perfect* is from the verb cuᵹaim alone, as shown in
last Lesson: the perfect passive is cuᵹaö, from the perfect
active.

Note.— The verb cabaiṗ, give, seems to be derived from the verb
beiṗim, itself, and a certain prefix expressive of *being, essence, a thing, a real
gift;* and appearing to be related in meaning, and very likely derived from
the old verb, cá, am, is, are, which is found in the present tense of the verb
öo beiṫ, to be—of which said cá, the infinitive, would be "caö," a *being, an
essence, a reality.* Cabeiṗim or cabaiṗṗim, then means, I give in reality, I
bestow, confer a gift, favour, or the like. With this meaning it has a certain
force and strength, which the verb beiṗim has not, and is on that account
employed solely in that mood—the imperative—in which command, entreaty,
is implied, and in the infinitive, because that mood, being a verbal noun, conveys the idea of imparting gifts, cabaṗc (cabaṗcaṗ—a gift bestowed.)

The future tense of cabaiṗ, although composed of two
syllables, receives not the suffix öċaö, but ṗaö, the future
suffix peculiar to verbs of the first-conjugation—like the
simple verb beiṗ, for derivative and compound verbs follow
in most instances the analogy of their primitives and sim-
ples.

Obs. 1.—The correct spelling is ṫaḃaiṙṙaḋ, suffixing-ṙaḋ to the root ṫaḃaiṙ, which is preserved throughout, and not the phonetic spelling ṫiuḃṙaḋ, employed by Dr. Keating, by the translators of the Protestant version of the Bible, and others.

Obs. 2.—According to Dr. Johnson the verb "give" in English has twenty-two different meanings, primary and secondary, and receives nine others additional from the accessary aid of prepositions and adverbs, such as *in*, *out*, *over*, *up*, *off*, (as, give *up*, give *over*, give *out*, &c). These several meanings—primary, secondary, and accessory—the verb ḃeiṙim (ṫaḃṙaim) in Irish receives. But it is necessary to remark that ṫaḃaiṙ, ḃeiṙ, and ṫuġ have the meaning of ḃeiṙ, bear, bring, convey, carry, along with that which signifies give; as, ṫaḃaiṙ ċuġam mo ċaṗal, bring hither to me my horse; ṫaḃaiṙ uaim aṅ ṫ-olc ṙo, take away from me the evil; ṫuġ ṙe leiṙ aṅ meuḋ a ḃi aġam, he brought with him all I had in possession. Thus the verb ṫaḃaiṙ conveys in Irish ideas apparently opposed one to the other.

VOCABULARY.

Aḃḃa, *m.* 3 dec. from aḃ, an e ement; and ḃa, in life, living, or exciting life, vitality; (1) an instrument, especially of music; (2) a habitation. fortress, palace; aḃḃa ceoil, an instrument of music; aġuṙ ṫuġ ṙe leiṙ aṅn a aḃḃa ṙéin ṙaḋ, and he brought them with him to his own dwellings.

Alloḋ, *adj.* ancient aṅn alloḋ (*adj.*), in ancient times, formerly. From this Keltic root the Latin word "allodium," freehold, ancient, or independent possession of land—a term for which there has been discovered no satisfactory derivation, appears to have been formed. Allodium is opposed in meaning to feudum, a fief, or feefarm, *i.e.*, land held from a patron, for which the client promises fidem, faith, or dutiful service. Taking feudum, or, as it was at first spelled foedum, to be derived from the Keltic ṙoḋ, the sod, turf, or earth, it means mere possession of the soil for one's use, but not to have the allodium, or original ancient right and title to it which the patron, or chief lord, enjoys.

Aoiṙ, *f.*, age.

Aoṙ, *m.* a sect, a class of people; aṅ ṫ-aoṙ óġ, the young; aṅ ṫ-aoṙ aoṙṫa, the aged; aṅ ṫ-aoṙ ceoil, musicians; aoṙ ṙeaṅma ṅa claṅṙaċ, the race of playing of the harps—*i.e.*, harpers.

Ḃiċ, gen. ḃeaṫa, life, existence; ṙaṅ ḃiċ, in the world, in existence; aiṙ ḃiċ, at all; ḃuiṅe aiṙ ḃiċ, any person at all; Welsh, byd. As a prefix it implies everlasting; as, ḃiċ-ḃeo, ever-living, eternal.

Ḃṙeiṫeaṁ, gen. ḃṙeiṫeaṁaṅ, irr. 3d d. a judge, from ḃṙeiṫ, to bear, to bring forth, therefore, to bring forth in the mind, to judge of a thing, to discern, to pass sentence.

bṗeıżeaṁnaṗ, a judgment; na ċabaıṗ (give) bṗeıżeaṁnaṗ aıṗ aon ṅeaċ, do not judge anybody.

Claṗṗaċ, f. a harp; from claṗ, a music board, and ṗıżeaċ, pacifying.

Daṅa, bold, daring; from ḃo, bad, contrary to; and aṅa, agreeable. The prefix meaṗ, is an adj. signifying foolish, wanton (English "merry" is nearly like it). From meaṗ is derived the noun meıṗe, or mıṗe, wanton folly, madness, aıṗ mıṗe, mad, in a transport. Meaṗ-ḃaṅa, therefore, means fool-hardy.

Léıżeaṗ, n. 1st d. gen. léıżıṗ, a cure, remedy, medicine, healing, act of curing. From léıż, (pr. lhey),

m. gen. leaża, a physician, English, leech; Germ. lech.

léıżım, cure, heal.

léıż (ley-ee), Scotch Gaelic, leugh, read thou; Latin, lege, read; léıżean, learning a lesson; ṗeaṗ léıżın, a man of learning.

Loċt, f. a fault; ḃo żeıḃ loċt, found fault.

Loċtaċ, adj. faulty.

Loċtuıż, v. find fault.

Loċtużaḃ, the act of blaming, censuring.

Seınm (pr. shinm), singing, playing, creating melody in any way, vocal or instrumental; eolaċ aṅn ṗeınm, skilled in music; aıż ṗeınm ażuṗ aıż ḃaṁṗa, playing and dancing.

Cuıż, v. understood.

Cıż, v. comes. (See Thirty-fifth Lesson, Vocabulary to Exercise LVI.)

EXERCISE XCVII.

(Selections from Dr. Geoffry Keating's "History of Ireland," p. lii).

Do żeıḃ (got, found) maṗ an ż-céaḃna loċt aıṗ an aoıṗ ṗeaṅma (of playing) na ż-claṗṗaċ aṅn Eıṗınn; ażuṗ a beıṗ naċ ṗaıḃ ceol aṅnta (that they were not possessed of a knowledge of music). Iṗ corṁaıl, ṅaṗ bṗeıżeaṁ é-ṗaṅ aıṗ ceol 'ṗaṅ m-bıż, ażuṗ żo h-aıṗıḃe (especially) aıṗ aṅ ż-ceol ṅżaoḃalaċ (Gaelic) ṗo na h-Eıṗeaṅn, aıṗ m-beıż aṅeolaċ 'ṗ na ṗıażlaċaıḃ beaṅaṗ (that appertain to it) leıṗ, ḃḃ. Saoılım ṅaċ aṅ ċuıż (understood) Scaṅıhuṗṗc żuṗ ab (for buḃ, was) aṁlaıḃ ḃo bı Eıṗé 'ṅn-a ṗıżeaċt, ṗa leıż (apart, separate), leı ṗéıṅ, aṁaıl ḃoṁaıṅ bıż (gen. case of beaż, small), ażuṗ na h-uaıṗle (the nobles) ażuṗ na h-ollaṁaıṅ ḃo bı ıṅnce (in her [Ireland]) aṅn allḃḃ żuṗ ċumaḃaṗ bṗeıżeaṁnaṗ, leıżıoṗ, ṗıḃeaċt, ceol, ażuṗ ṗıażlaċa cıṅnce (certain) ḃo bı aıṗ buṅ aṅn Eıṗınn, ażuṗ maṗ ṗıṅ ṅıoṗ ċneaṗḃa (honest) ḃo Scaṅıhuṗṗc bṗeıżeaṁnaṗ meaṗ-ḃaṅa ḃo ḃéanaḃ aıṗ ceol na h-Eıṗeaṅn ḃo loċtużaḃ; ażuṗ ıṗ ıoṅżnaḃ lıom (and it is [ıoṅżnaḃ] a wonder to me—Irish idiom, with me) ṅaṗ léıż Cambṗenṗıṗ. . . . . Oıṗ ṅı b-ṗuıl ṗaṅ bıż ṅıḃ ıṗ mo aṅn a ṁolaṅn Cambṗenṗıṗ

 É||peannaı̇̃ na annr an ceol Ɜaoᵭalaċ; aɜ ro maṗ a deıṗ
ran caıbıȯıl ceaᵭna (same chapter); " ann a aᵭbaıᵬ ceoıl
aṁaın ᵭo ɜeıᵬıṁ (I find) ᵭıċċıoll (the diligence) an cınıᵭ
ro (of this people) roṁolca maṗ ᵭo ᵬ-ɼuıļıᵭ caṗ an uıle
cıneaᵭ ᵭ'a ᵬ-ɼacamaṗ cļırce ɜo ᵭoṁearᵭa."

FIFTY-THIRD LESSON.

OBSERVATIONS ON THE IRREGULAR VERBS.

(3) The verb cluı̇n, hear.

The *third* in order is cluı̇n, " hear," which in the formation of its tenses is regularly formed after the model of
the first conjugation; except that (1), its regular perfect,
" cluı̇near," is commonly, by metathesis, or rather substi-
tuting l in place of ŋ, written and pronounced " cualar"
(irregular); and (2), that the infin. and part. form is " clor."
Cluı̇near, the reg. perf. is not uncommon. This verb,
cluı̇n, may therefore be safely ranked among the regular
verbs, yet it is here retained to conform to received notions,
which regard it as irregular.

With the infin., clor, the following terms in the Keltic
and foreign dialects seem to have a strong affinity :

Noun, cluar, ear, that which has (clor) hearing ;
  ... clú, report, fame, reputation—what the public
    hear of one.
Welsh, *clyw,* hearing.
Greek, κλυω, to hear on report.
Latin, *clu*eo, to be talked of, to be reputed.
Irish, clúcaċ, *adj.* renowned, famed.
Greek, κλυτος and κλυτικος, renowned, famed.
Latin, *incly*tus.

EXERCISE XCVIII.

THE TREES AND THE HATCHET.

Na cṗaın aɜur an cuaċ.

A wood-man (ɼeaṗ-aṁuıᵭ) came into a forest (coıll) to
ask the trees to give him a handle (cor) for his axe (cuaɜ).

It was not much he asked, and therefore the large trees consented .(cuz aoncuzaó) to give him the humble ash (puinrean, and puinreoz). No sooner had he fitted the handle in the axe than he began to fell (zeappaó) the noblest trees in the wood. The oak, witnessing the destruction (plaó) that was made, said in a whisper (aiz or iriol) to the cedar (reuóap), " We lost ourselves when we gave him the ash." (óo cailaman rinn péin 'nuain cuzaman óó an puinreoz.)

When the rich surrender the rights of the poor, they give a handle (to be used) against themselves.

(4) Déan. The verb óéan, " do," act, make, is in meaning like the Latin *facio*. It borrows the perfect from the verb znióim, I act; root, znioṁ, *n.* an act; and also the imperfect, znióinn, I used to do.

Perfect.

1 rizneaτ,	1 riznaman.
2 rizóir,	2 riznaóaτ.
3 rizne re,	3 riznaóaτ.

The regular perfect of znió is znióeaτ, which, with the prefix no incorporated, becomes rizneaτ (z asp). In the modern spelling z (asp) is changed into n, for sound's sake. The infinitive is óéanaó—old form, óéanaṁ. The subjunctive or secondary form of the verb after the particles, nac, ní, zo, is óeannain; as, óéin re nac nóeannain (subjunctive mood), he says that I do not do; and perf. óeannaó; óein re nac nóeannaó me an ceapc, he says that (subjunctive perfect) I did not do the-right-thing (justice).

Déan is very likely compounded of óo and znióim. That it is so, is seen more plainly from the spelling of the secondary or subjunctive form of the verb, viz.,óionznaim—zo n-óionznaim, that I do. This form is clearly derived from óo and znióim; óéan, in process of time, assumed the present form from the older, óionzaim.

(5) Dein. All the tenses of óeinim are regular, except the perfect, óubnaτ; the imperative, abaiτ; and the subjunctive, abnaim.

Dubnaτ=óo óeineaτ (óo, sign of the perfect, óeineaτ), perfect tense, from the verb óeinim, I bear, bring forth, out, &c.

Abaiτ, say,=a, an intensive particle, and óein.

Abnaim, I say, is composed of a, and óeinim. The infinitive is, óo naó, to say. The passive of abnaim is abancaτ; of óeinim, óeinceaτ; perfect, óubnaτ, active; óubnaó, passive.

EXERCISE XCIX.

An t-íolar agus an fíonnaċ.

THE EAGLE AND THE FOX.

Do bíoḋar íolar agus fíonnaċ a b-ḟad aimsir[...] ṅua ṅ-oraġ
coṁursana d'a ċeile, an t-íolar air bárr cráin áird,
agus an fíonnaċ a g-clair faoi n-a bonn. Lá áiriḋe 'nuair
do bí an fíonnaċ amuiġ faoi 'n tír, do rinne an íolair
íonnruiḋe air a cuileán óg agus do tóig leiṫe é, d'a
ṅeaḋ do faoil rí a beiṫ co áno ar beallaċ an t-fíonnaġ.
'Nuair táinic an fíonnaċ a baile do tug rí faoi 'an íolár
b-taob an bearta fealtaiġ do riġne rí, agus d'iarr d'
impiḋe an cuileán óg uaiṫe. 'Nuair do ċonnairc rí naċ
rab aon ṁaiṫ ann beiṫ aig déanaḋ impiḋe, do rgíob ann a
beul troillreán a bí a b-teine garr ḋí, agus do ċuir faoi
'n g-cráin, larair a líon an t-íolar le an-eagla ḋí féin
agus d'a h-ál, agus a ċuir d'ualaċ airṫí an cuileán a
ḋiulṫuiġ rí air ball air impiḋe, ċabairt air air.

Ní 'l an tíorán raor ó ḋíoġaltar na muintire faoi, air
a ḋeanann ré plaḋ.

Observations on the Irregular verbs—continued.

(6) Faġ. In faġ, get, find, the sixth of the irregular
verbs, the only tenses not following the normal mode of
conjugation are (fuarar), the perfect active, and (fuaraḋ:
and fríṫ), the perfect passive; with fuiġinn, *would get,* the
conditional. Geiḃim (like gaḃaim), a verb of kindred meaning, signifying *to get,* supplies, most commonly, the *imperfect,
future,* and *conditional tenses.*

Fríṫ, *was found,* although not much employed in written or spoken Irish, is still not unfrequently read and heard.

(7) Feic. The Gaelic verb, signifying *to see, to look at,*
is expressed in Irish by the term feic, see (*vide*) and cíḋim.
In the imperative mood the word amarc is usually heard,
and beirc; Gr., δέρκω.

Feicim and cíḋim are each conjugated regularly. In
the perfect, however, connarcar, I saw, is the form. This
term, connarcar, is equal to " con," *together* (Latin, *con*),
and bearcar. Connacar, I saw, is another form nearly as
common, derived from con, *go,* and feicear, regularly formed
from feic, see. The inf. is irreg. feicrin, and by the inter-

change of c and ſ—ᵹeɪſcɪn, to which c is sometimes annexed for the sake of strength, thus, ᵹeɪſcɪnc.   The perfect passive is, strangely enough, " ᵹacaſ," as well as " connaſcaḃ."

(8) The irregular features of ſɪᵹ, reach; and of (9) ceɪḃ, go, have been already shown (see p. 320).

Rɪᵹ makes its inf. ſoċcaɪn; and ceɪḃ, inf., ḃo ḃul.

(10) The conjugation of the verb cɪᵹɪm, I come, should be well known, for its use in Gaelic is very common, being employed with the compound pronoun lɪom, with me, leac, with thee, leɪſ, with him, &c., to express the English words can, could; as,

Cɪᵹ lɪom, *I can*—literally, it comes with me.

Cɪᵹ leac, *thou canst.*

Cɪᵹ leɪſ, *he can;* cɪᵹ leɪċe, *she can.*

Caɪnɪc lɪom, *I was* able, I could—literally, it came with me.

Cɪocᵹaɪḃ lɪom, *I will* be able; conditional, cɪocᵹaɪnn; infin. ḃo ċeacc.

VOCABULARY.

Aṁlear, misfortune, ill-luck; from aṁ. a negative particle, and lear, luck.

Anaċ, help, power.

ḃaſamaɪl, opinion.

Cleaċc, v. to practise, to experience, to exercise.

ḃul, a trap, a snare.

Caſᵹaɪḃeaċc, lightness, fleetness, smartness, the fact of being relieved of an incumbrance.

Fonaṁaḃ, jeering, gibing, mocking; (from ſo oᵹ ſoᵹ, respect, entertainment; namaḃ, an enemy. *i. e.*, the entertainment given a foe; mockery.)

Jaſbal, a tail; (from ɪaſ, aft, behind, and ball, a member.) It is pronounced as if ſɪabal, transposing ɪ and ſ respectively.

Socſoɪḃeaċc (from ſo, happy; and cſoɪḃe, a heart), light-heartedness, ease of mind.

EXERCISE C.

An Sɪonnaċ ᵹan ɪaſbal.

Do ᵹaḃaḃ Sɪonnaċ ann ḃul, aɪſ ᵹſeɪm ɪaſbaɪl noċ b' ᵹeaſſ leɪſ " ᵹaᵹaɪl " 'nn a ḃɪaɪᵹ 'na beɪċ ᵹabċa aɪſ ᵹaḃ. 'Nuaɪſ ḃ'éɪſɪᵹ ſe amaċ ᵹaoɪ 'n c-ſaoᵹal, ḃo " ᵹacaſ " ḃó ᵹo n-ḃéanᵹaɪḃe ᵹonaṁaḃ ᵹaoɪ. B'ᵹeaſſ leɪſ baſ 'na eaſba Jaſbaɪl; acc ó ċaſla naċ ſaḃ anaċ aɪſ, buḃ ṁɪan leɪſ an baɪl a b' ᵹeaſſ a ċuſ aɪſ a aṁlear. Uɪme ſɪn, " ċuᵹ " ſe cuɪſeaḃ ḃo na ſɪonnaɪᵹ a ċeacc ᵹo h-uɪle aɪᵹ ḃaɪl. 'Nuaɪſ bɪḃaſ uɪle cſuɪnɪᵹċe ḃo laḃaɪſ léo na bſɪaċaſa ſo. " Nɪ'l ᵹɪoſ aɪᵹ neaċ aᵹaɪḃ aɪſ bɪċ beo, caḃ é an lan ſo-ċſoɪḃeacc' aᵹuſ éaſᵹuɪḃeaċca ca oſm anoɪſ aɪſ ᵹaċ caoi. Ní beiḋeaḋ an fíos so aġam, cinnte, aċt muna an cleaċtuġaḋ "fuair" mé. Aġus leis an ceart-a raḋ, caḋ é an tairḃe anois féin ta ann iarbal. B-fuil maiṫ air biṫ do ḟionnaċ ann? Níl cinnte: is mór an t-ionġnaḋ ta orm gur ġlac siḃ leis co fada so? Le bur leas a ċur romaiḃ bi fonn anṁor orm an comraḋ so a ḋéanaḋ daoiḃ. "Feiciḋ," do "ṫug" mise rompla daoiḃ—óir is fearr rompla na teaġasg; foillriġeann an gníoṁ deaġ-intin ar te beirear an comairle. Deanaḋ mar sin, mar do riġne mise. Bainiḋ díoḃ na iarbala grána sin o 'n la so amaċ.

Air an comairle so a "clos," do "tainic" seantrionnaċ a latair aġus tug mar so freagraḋ:

"Sé mo baraṁail, a ḋuine muintriġ, naċ amlaiḋ béarfa comairle uait, ḋa m-ba féidir leat d' iarbal féin fágail air air."

In the shortest compass the fullest elucidation of the irregular as well as the regular verbs has been, in the foregoing Lessons, presented to the reader.

The irregular verbs have been grouped so as to give to the ten only the same inflection as far as possible.

Few as the number of irregular verbs is, they could well be made fewer. Some verbs in Irish form, it is true, their infinitive mood and participles differently from the regular mode, but they are not, on this account, irregular. To increase the amount of irregularities "is the last art that the philosophic grammarian is ambitious of acquiring. True etymology reduces irregularity by making the rules of grammar not exclusive but general."—*Latham on the English Language*, p. 336.

☞ The verb iṫ, *eeh*, eat (Latin, *ed-o*), changes t into s in the future and conditional tenses. Iosfaḋ, I shall eat; iosfainn, I would eat.

The change from t to s is phonetic; the use of o before it, as found in MSS., arises from collating the vowels broad with broad.

VOCABULARY.

Crane, corr.

Fat, *adj.* raṁar, meiṫ, *noun;* (fatness,) meiṫ, sult.

Goose, *f.* gé; Gr., χήν (ch and g are commutable letters); German, *gans;* Anglo-Saxon, *gós;* Latin, *anser, m.* and *f.;* Ger, *ganser.*

Get off (to), get away, hoist one's sails. get out of a place which is dangerous, is expressed by the words ardugaḋ liom, (leat, leis, leiṫe, linn, liḃ, leo); ardug, to hoist; root, ard, high; liom, with me; leat, with thee, &c.

Jeopardy, gaḃ; aimsir gaḃa, time of jeopardy, danger, commotion, distress from without, persecution.

Sportsman, fear seilge, literally, a man of hunting, seilge being gen. case of seilg.

EXERCISE CI.

Na géaḋa (pr. *gé-oó-a—a* short), agus na corra.

Lá airiḋe do ḃiḋar géaḋa agus corra aig iṫe air aon maċaire agus do ṫainic na fir reilge orra. D'Arḃuiġḋar na corra leo, óir ḃiḋar eaḋtrom; aċt na géaḋa a ḃi trom agus ramar gaḃaḋ iad.

Ann aimsir gaḃa is fosur do 'n muintir tá gan meiṫ gan maon, arḃuġaḋ leo.

VOCABULARY.

Allow, *v.* leiġ, ceaḋuiġ, beir ceaḋ, would not allow, ni leiġfaḋ; naċ ḃéarfaḋ ceaḋ.

Cur, cuillean.

Fodder, foḃar, (Ger., *fuer;* Dan., *foeder;* Anglo-Saxon, *fodher;* Eng., *fodder;* Latin, *fodrum.*) From fóḋ, the sod, earth; and ar, ploughing, springing from; hence, provender; everything that supports beasts.

Grab, *v.* to stop, to hinder, to keep all to one's self, to cram.

Grabaire, a hinderer; a mean fellow who keeps all he can, and annoys others.

Manger, mannaċ, mairréan.

Miserable, ruanaċ.

EXERCISE CII.

THE DOG IN THE MANGER.

A dog made his bed in a manger, and, lying on the provender, he would not allow the horses to touch any. "See," said one of them, "what a miserable cur ! that neither can eat it himself, nor will he allow those to eat it who can."

Never act the cur through selfishness.

Na bi do ġrabaire go deo.

IMPERSONAL VERBS.

According to the strict meaning of the term impersonal there is, in Gaelic, only one—dar liom, methinks; dar leis féin, he thinks himself, in his own opinion; dar is, perhaps, a form of beir, says.

Verbs, like the English, "it appears," *videtur* (Latin), are in as great a variety in Irish as in English. But no philosophic writer can admit that this class is impersonal, since the pronoun or sentence is, manifestly, the subject of such verbs, which are, withal, invariably found in the third person. Hence, in point of fact, such verbs are not impersonal.

DEFECTIVE VERBS.

These are more numerous. For the English "quoth he," the Irish equivalents are, " air se," and or se; ol se; ad ᵮᴀᴆ (he relates). There are others—ᵮᴀᶕᴆ, *he resigns, yields*, ᵮᶕᴅᶕᶉ, *he knows;* ᶇᶕ ᵮᴜʟᴀᶕᶉ (which is, very likely, from ᶇᶕᴆ, *a thing*, and ᵮᴜʟᴀᶕᶉ, *necessary*), *it is necessary;* ᴄᴀᶉʟᴀ, *it happened;* ᴛᴏᶉᴄᴀᶉ, *he fell.* " Ꮧᶕᶉ," *says,* takes ᶊ final, when followed by a vowel; as, ᴀᶕᶇᶊ ᴀᶇ Lᴀᴏᴄ-ᴄᴇᴏᶕl ᴈᶉᶕᶇ, " says the warrior bard."—Song, *The Minstrel Boy—Irish Melodies.*

VOCABULARY.

ᴃᶉᴇᴀᴄᶇᴜᶕᴈ (from ᴃᶉᴇᶕᴄ), perceive judge, look into, observe.	Cᶉᴇᴀᴄ, plunder, booty; ᶇᶃᴏ ᴄᶉᴇᴀᴄ, my ruin, alas! my woe!

EXERCISE CIII.

Ꮧᶇ ᵮᶕᴀᴄ-ᴆᴜᴃ ᴀᴈᴜᶊ ᶇᴀ ᶆᴀᴆᴀᶕᴆ ᴀʟʟᴀ.

THE RAVEN AND THE WOLVES.

Ꮧᶄ Jᴀᶉᶉ ᵮᶕᴀᴄ ᴀᶕᶉ ᶇᴀ ᶆᴀᴆᴀᶕᴆ ᴀʟʟᴀ ᶉᴏᶕᶇᶇ ᴆᶄ ᴀ ᴈ-ᴄᶉᴇᴀᴄ ᴜᴀᴄᴀ, ᶆᴀᶉ ᴈᴇᴀʟʟ ᴈᴜᶉ ᶉᴀᴃ ᶊᴇ 'ᶇᶇᴀ ᴈ-ᴄᴜᶕᴆᴇᴀᴄᴛ ᴀᶕᶉ ᵮᴇᴀᴆ ᴀᶇ Lᴀᴇ, ᴀᴄᴛ " ᴄᴜᴈᴀᴆᴀᶉ" ᴀᶇ ᵮᶉᴇᴀᴈᶉᴀᴆ ᶉᴏ ᴆᴆ. Nᶕ ᶉᶕᶇᶇ-ᶇᴇ, ᴀᴄᴛ ᴀᶇ ᴄᶉᴇᴀᴄ ᴆᴏ lᴇᴀᶇ ᴛᴜ; ᴀᴈᴜᶊ ᴄᴀᶕᶉᶕᶉ ᶉᶕᶇ (moreover) ᴆᴏ " ᴆᴇᴀᶇᵮᴀ" ᴄᶉᴇᴀᴄ ᴆᶕᶇᶇ ᶉᴇᶕᶇ ᴆᴀ ᴃ-ᴛᴜᶕᴄᵮᴀᶆᴜᶕᶉ (if we should have fallen).

Nᶕ ᶊᴇ ᴀᶕᶉ ᴀᶇ ᶉᴜᴃ ᴀ ᴈᶉᶕᴆᴇᴀᶊ ᴆᴜᶕᶇᴇ, ᴀᴄᴛ ᴀᶇ ᶕᶇᴛᶕᶇ lᴇ ᴀ ᴈᶉᶕᴆᴄᴇᴀᶉ ᴇ̂ ᶕᶊ ᴄᴏᶕᶉ ᴆᴜᶕᶇᶇ ᴃᶉᴇᴀᴄᶇᴜᴈᴀᴆ.

EXERCISE CIV.

THE TWO MEN AND THE HATCHET.

There were two men (ᴃᴇᶕᶉᴛ) travelling (ᶉᶕᴜᴃᴀl) together along the same road, when one of them met with a hatchet, which he took up and said, " Behold, what I have found." " Do not say ' I' (ᶆᶕᶉᴇ), says the other—say ' we' (ᶉᶕᶇᶇ-ᶇᴇ) have found.' " After a short time it happened that the party who lost the hatchet came up and seized (ᴈᴀᴃ) the man who had it, as the thief. " Oh," said he, " ' we' are undone." (ᴛᴀ ᶉᶕᶇᶇ ᴄᴀᶉᴛ). " Do not say ' we,' say ' I,' " replied his companion, " for it is not right that one should have a share in the danger (ᴈᴀᴃ) without having had a share in the profits" (ᴛᴀᶕᶉᴃᴇ).

FIFTY-FOURTH LESSON

ADVERBS.

An adverb is a word that shows the time, manner, or circumstances of an action; as, John walks hastily; John walks with haste; " with haste," or " hastily," points out the manner of John's walking. The expression " with haste" is as much an adverb as that other ending in " ly," according to Dr. Priestly, who defines adverbs to be (1) " contractions of sentences; or (2) clauses of sentences, serving to denote the manner and other circumstances of an action."

(1) In the eleventh lesson, page 49, part I., it is shown that adverbs in Irish are formed from adjectives, by employing immediately before the latter the preposition ʒo, with (equal to *con* or *cum*, Latin), as, ɲuaʓ, new; ʒo ɲuaʓ, newly, *de novo*. This class corresponds with those denominated by Dr. Priestly " contractions of sentences."

(2) There is another class which are nothing else than " clauses of sentences," composed of prepositions, nouns, pronouns. It is. of these latter the present Lesson shall treat. They are common to every language; as, wherefore, *i. e.*, *for which*; therefore, *i.e.*, *for that*; *quam-ob-rem* (Latin); *quem-ad-modum*, *scilicet* (*scire-licet*); *videlicet* (*videre-licet*); *pour-quoi* (French),

ADVERBS.

A b-ꝼaʓ, a-far; from a, in; and ꝼaʓ, length.

A b-ꝼaʓ aꞃ ꞃo, far hence (in relation to time or place).

A b-ꝼaʓ ꞃoɩṁe, long before (in time or place).

A ʒ-céɩɲ, far off (from a, in; and céɩɲ, dat. case of cꞃaɲ, remote, distant, foreign, tedious), as to time; ɩꞃ cꞃaɲ lɩoṁ ꞇá ꞇu aṁuɩʓ, I feel you are long absent; as to place; ɩꞃ ꝼaʓa o'' ɲ laṁ a ꞇá a ʒ-céɩɲ, one is far removed from the (friendly) hand that is in a foreign land; cꞃaɲ, n; plur., cꞃaɲꞇa; ꞇá ꞃe ɲa " cꞃaɲꞇa" ó ċoɲɲaꞃꞁc me ċu, it is ages since I saw you—I have not seen you this age.

A ʒ-coṁɲuɩʓe, always, continuously; from a, and coṁɲuɩʓe, abode; *i. e.*, *abidingly*.

Aṁaċ, out.

Aṁuɩʓ, without, outside. The difference between aṁaċ and aṁuɩʓ is, that the one is connected with a verb of motion; as, ꞇeɩʓ aṁaċ, go out; the other with a verb of rest; as, ꞇá me aṁuɩʓ, I am without.

Aṁaꞃaċ,   }
Aṁaɩꞃeaċ,   } to-morrow.

Lá aiṙ na maiṙeaċ, to-morrow.
Aiṙ aiṙ, back.
Aiṙ an áḋḃaṙ ṙin, therefore.
Aiṙ ball, on the spot, presently, very soon.
Aiṙ biċ, at all, in the world.
Aiṙ éigin, with difficulty.

EXERCISE CV.

An faolċu aguṙ an ṫreuḃaiḋ.

THE WOLF AND THE SHEPHERD.

Do ḃí madaḋ alla ann, a ḃí "a ḃ-faḋ" aig ḃreaṫ (watching) aiṙ treuḋ caoraiġ, aċt níoṙ ṙinne rlaḋ (slaughter) aiṙ biċ orṙa. Ḃí feaṙ an tréiḋ a "g-coṁnuiḋe" faoi aṁraṙ naċ raiḃ ann aċt gaḋaiḋ. D' fan, an madaḋ naṁaḋaċ a ḃ-faḋ aimṙine (a length of time) 'nn a ḋeaġ-ċoṁuṙrain gan égcóir aiṙ biċ a ḋeanaḋ. "Fa ḋeiṙe" (at last) do faoil an treuḃaiḋ guṙ caṙaḋ ceanṙa (gentle) é, aguṙ "aiṙ an áḋḃaṙ ṙin" (therefore) ċuiṙ ṙé, aig dul ó baile ḋó—na caoraiġ faoi n-a ċuṙam. Ní tuiṙge (no sooner) fuaiṙ ṙe faill (opportunity) 'na do ċuit aiṙ na caoraiġ boċta aguṙ ṙinne rlaḋ aguṙ creaċ (spoil) orṙa. Aig teaċt a ḃaile do 'n treaḃaiḋ ċonnaiṙc ṙe an t-áṙ móṙ a ṙinneaḋ faḋ a'ṙ ḃí ṙe "amuiġ," aguṙ ġáiṙ: ama-ḃán móṙ mé! ċuil me an meuḋ ro 'nuaiṙ ċug me cuṙam mo ċaoraiġ go biṫeaṁnaċ.

Iṙ meaṙa caṙaḋ feallṫaċ 'ná naṁaḋ folluṙaċ.

VOCABULARY.

Comaiṙc, f. 2 dec. protection, favour, patronage; as, in the Litany, cuiṙamuiḋ ṙinn fein faoi do ċomaiṙc, we put ourselves under thy protection ("we fly to thy patronage.") The word is spelled thus, comaṙaic, in many places. It is derived from com, together, with; and aṙaċ, aid, power. This latter is itself from the root aṙ, a plough, and means (1) supporting, defending, (2) the power to support and defend; aṙaṙ, a habitation, comes from the same root.

Fair, v. watch, observe, attend.
Faiṙe (far-ye), (1) watching, watchfulness; (2) a watch, hour of the night, a timepiece, or watch; (3) the vigil-hour, or dawn, "faiṙe na maiḋne," the dawn of morn; luċt faiṙe (people-of-watching), watchmen; cnoc-faiṙe, a watch-hill—a special name applied to many hills through the country; hence the word faiṙe of itself signifies (4) the top of a hill, height. "Faiṙe" is the exclamation addressed by the peasantry to one in danger,

implying "watch," "be on your guard," "take care." It is a military term also, as Dr. Keating remarks, like that of Frenchmen, "gardez." One is astonished at Stanihurst's ignorance and impudent glibness, deriving this exclamation of the Irish soldiers, in the hour of danger, from the term Pharao. King of Egypt—one instance out of the countless calumnies which ignorance of the people and of their language have given birth to.

EXERCISE CVI.

A ḋeir Stainihurst an tan bio Eirinnaig aig compac (contending in battle), no aig bualaḋ a ceile go "n-abraiḋ" mar comairc, de ġut apo Pharo! Pharo! agur raoiliḋ re-ran (and he thinks) gur ab' ó 'n b-ḟocal, Pharao, b' ainm do riġ na Egipte cleactaḋ leo, mar comairc é; giḋ ni fior ḋó rin; ir ionan é agur (for it is the same as) "faire, faire ó," aig raḋ leir an roinn eile (the other party) a beit air a g-coiṁeaḋ amail a ḋeir an Francac "gardez, gardez," an tan do ciḋ re a coiṁurḟa ann guair (danger).

ADVERBS.

Ann aice, near, nigh; aice, i.e., faice, nearness; from fccur. Welsh, agos, near.

Ann airde, on high.

Anall (=ó, an, oll, see below), over, hither, to this side; always connected with a verb of *motion*; as, tarr anall, come over. It is the opposite of anon, to the other side; as, dul anon agur anall, *going* to that side, and to this side, wavering, changing from side to side. Anon and anall convey necessarily the idea of motion. Whenever a state of rest is implied, the adverbs employed are a bur (for a b-foġur), on this side; tall, on that side; as, tá re a bur, he is on *this* side (not anall); tá re tall, he is on the opposite side (not anon).

A bur agur tall, here there, *hic, illic;* on this side and on that (when a state of rest is implied).

Anon agur anall, hither, thither, *huc, illuc;* to this side and to that (when the idea of motion to a place is conveyed).

Anon (1) is written also anoll in many instances. On this account, and because it is in meaning antithetic to anall, which ends in ll, its derivation appears to be from the preposition oll, above, superior, yonder, higher; and an, the; anon, i.e., anoll=an, the, oll, higher, yonder (taob, side, or leit, half, being understood); (2) anall, hither, to this side, is a contraction for ó, ᴀn, oil (ó *from*, ᴀn, *the*, oll, *over, above*); (3) ċᴀl is derived from the same word, oll, and c, a prepositive, like ꞅ, in ꞅuᴀꞅ, or rather the remnant of the preposition bo (omitting o, and changing b into c); (4) ᴀ buꞅ is ᴀ contracted form of ᴀ ḃ-ꞅoꞃuꞅ, *i.e.*, ᴀn (cᴀoḃ) ꞅoꞃuꞅ, the nigh side.

The particle ᴀn, the prefix to these adverbs, is considered by Z. üss to be the article, and not, as others think, the preposition.

2ᴀn ᴀlloḃ, *of yore* (for ᴀn c-ᴀm ᴀlloḃ, the old time; or for ᴀnn [ᴀm] ᴀlloḃ, *in* the olden time).

2ᴀn ḃeᴀꞅ, *southward*; or, *from the south.*

2ᴀn oꞃ, *eastward*; or, *from the east.*

2ᴀn Ꞁᴀꞃ, *westward*; or, *from the west.*

2ᴀ ḃ-cuᴀꞃċ, *northward*; or, *from the north.*

Note.—2ᴀn ḃeᴀꞅ, meaning *from* the south, is a contraction for ó ᴀn ḃeᴀꞅ; so also ᴀn oꞃ, *from* the east; for ó ᴀn oꞃ; ᴀn Ꞁᴀꞃ, from the west; ó ᴀn Ꞁᴀꞃ—ó, *from*, being omitted. 2ᴀn ḃeᴀꞅ, the south (in the nom. case), is composed of the article ᴀn, and the word ḃeᴀꞅ, south, right side; also ᴀn ḃeᴀꞅ, is for ᴀnn ḃeᴀꞅ, in the south, according to the grammatical arrangement of the context or sentence.—See "Easy Lessons," part II., p. 128, second edition.

2ᴀn noċc, *to-night*; sometimes oꞃḋċe is added; as, ᴀn oꞃḋċe noċc, this very night. Greek, *νυκτι*; Latin, *nocte*; Saxon, *nicht*; English, night.

2ᴀn Ꞁuḃ, *to-day*; ᴀn lᴀ 'n Ꞁuḃ, this very **day**; *au jour d'hui.*

2ᴀn neᴀċcᴀꞃ, *externally*; for, ᴀnn ḟeᴀċcᴀꞃ (the initial ḟ, when aspirated, being omitted); root, ꞅeᴀċ, apart, outside; ḟeᴀċcᴀꞃ, more apart.

2ᴀnn ᴀon-ḟeᴀċc, *together.*

The word uᴀꞅ means *above, high*; hence uᴀꞅᴀl (uᴀꞅ-ᴀl), high-born, noble; uᴀꞃꞅle, nobility.

So, Ꞁoꞅ means *below*; hence Ꞁꞅeᴀl, low-born, lowly, humble; ᴀn c-ᴀoꞅ Ꞁꞅeᴀl, the common people.

Whenever Irishmen wish to express the idea of motion up, or motion in a downward direction, uᴀꞅ and Ꞁoꞅ take an initial ꞅ; as, ꞅuᴀꞅ, upwards; ꞅꞀoꞅ, downwards; ꞅuᴀꞅ ᴀꞅuꞅ ꞅꞀoꞅ, up and down (active).

A state of rest above is expressed by ḟuᴀꞅ and ḟꞀoꞅ; as, cᴀꞃḃ ḟuᴀꞅ (thaid huas), they are above; cᴀꞃḃ ḟꞀoꞅ, they are below.

Motion from above is expressed by the form, ᴀn uᴀꞅ (*i. e.*, ó ᴀn uᴀꞅ); from below, by ᴀn Ꞁoꞅ (for ó ᴀn Ꞁoꞅ).

Hence, ᴀnuᴀꞅ signifies down; as, cᴀꞃꞃ ᴀnuᴀꞅ, come down; *i. e.*, come from above; ᴀnꞀoꞅ, up; cᴀꞃꞃ ᴀnꞀoꞅ, come up; *i.e.*, from below.

Oꞃ, east; ꞅoꞃ, eastward; Ꞁᴀꞃ, after, west; ꞅꞀᴀꞅ, westward; follow the same analogy. The initial ꞅ is perhaps from the preposition ᴢuꞅ, towards.

VOCABULARY.

Ceaɳɳ, *adj.*, tight, stiff, straight, terse, independent, stubborn, hopeful, strong, reliant : ɳać ceaɳɳ ću, are you not stiff? how stiff you are ; cá me ceaɳɳ, I am stiff ; cá ɼe ċo ceaɳɳ le ɼeaɼɼ ɳa bɼaża (pr. braha), he is as independent as the miller (literally, he is as independent as the man of the mill)—not in any dread of being in want of food. bɼa, bɼaż, and bɼo, is the Gaelic of hand-mill or quern. bɼa appears to be of the same root as the Irish bɼać, an arm, French, *bras*, the hand-mill being worked by the strength of the (bɼać) arm :

ʒaɳ eaʒla ʒo ɼcɼóıcɼaż aɳ Saɼaɳać "ceaɳɳ"

Aoɳ ceub aɼ bo ćɼuıc, ɳó aoɳ blaoıʒ aɼ bo ćeaɳɳ.

Nor dread that the cold-hearted (ceaɳɳ) Saxon will tear

One cord from that harp, or one lock from that hair.—Song, *Though the last glimpse of Erin.*

Ceaɳɳ, having ʒo prefixed, becomes an *adv.*, meaning stiffly, tightly, independently, &c.

Aıʒ ɼalać ɳa ɼlabɼaıże a ċɼáıż ɼıɳɳ " ʒo ceaɳɳ."

Covering the chains that galled us pressingly.—Song, *St. Patrick's day.*

Ceaɳɳ, a prefix—as, ɼać, enough, plenty ; ceaɳɳɼać, a surfeit, as much as one can eat, or drink, or possess ; ʒlac, hold, receive ; ceaɳɳ-ʒlac, tightly grasp, &c.

Ceaɳɳ, *v.*, press on, move, force, hasten, tighten, press together ; Greek, τειⱱω ; Latin, *tendo, teneo ;* Welsh, *tynnu.*

Ceaɳɳuıʒ, *v.*, cause to be tight, straight, to fill, to cram.

Ceaɳɳ, *n.*, dint, force, stiffness, pressure, le ceaɳɳ aoıɼc. from the pressure of age, from dint of age.

Ceaɳɳaż, a participal noun ; from Ceaɳɳ, to fasten, to draw near ; aıʒ ceaɳɳaż leıɼ, drawing nigh ; a surfeit, a cramming, abundance ; ıɼ maıɼʒ a ɼacaż aıɼ baɳɳaıʒ, aʒuɼ a ceaɳɳaż aıʒe ɼéıɳ, it is woful to get (money) on bail, and one self having plenty.

Ceaɳɳaćaɳ, a pincers, a vice, an instrument for tightening and squeezing.

Coɼc, *m.*, (1) a boar, a hog, "bo bıaċaż a b-coɼc," to feed their hogs ; loć Cuıɼc, Turk Lake, Killarney ; and ıɳıɼ ɳa b-Coɼc, in Loch Finvoy, county Leitrim ; (2) a whale ; hence ıɳıɼ ɳa b-Coɼc, Innishturk, near Clare Island, on the western coast ; (3) a torque, a "ring of twisted metal, generally gold, worn either on the neck, round the waist, across the breast, or on the limbs, as an armilla or finger-ring." Many such are every year dug up—golden treasures of the past.—See Dr. Wilde's *Catalogue of the Museum,* class V., p. 70 ; *metallic materials—gold ;* or "The Transactions of the Kilkenny Archæological Society."

EXERCISE CVII.

Aɳ ɼeaɳ-ċu.

'Aıʒ ɼeaɼ aıɼıże bo bı ɼeaɳ-ċu a ɼıɳɳe ɼeıɼbıɼ maıċ bó aɳɳ a h-am, ać le ceaɳɳ aoıɼe b' euluıʒ a luċ aʒuɼ a ⱱeaɼc. Aıʒ ɼeılʒ lá ɳ-aoɳ bo ɼuʒ ɼı coɼc aıɼ ʒɼéım cluaire, aċt briseaḋ a ḟiacla agus 'b' eigin ói leigin do 'n m-beiċeaċ imċeaċt. D'éis so, ċainic fear na reilge-ruar agus ċug se faoiċe go ceann: aċt ċug an t-sean-ċuuaiċe an freagraḋ so: Na leag ċo cruaiḋ sin, air do sean-foġantaċ; se earba briġ agus luċ agus ni ḃiċḃáil fonna bi orm: buḋ cóire buic ċuimnuġaḋ, ni air an nór a táim, aċt air an nór a bḋear.

Na bi doirb le deaġ-feanbroġantaiḃ ann am a aoire-agus a laiġe.

VOCABULARY.

At the same time, anns an am céaḋna.	Rub, cuimil; (aig) cuimilt, rubbing.
Groom, giolla eiċ.	The whole day long, air feaḋ an lae.
His allowance of corn, a ċo-roinn arbair.	

EXERCISE CVIII.

THE HORSE AND THE GROOM.

An t-eaċ agus an giolla.

A groom was the whole day long rubbing and fitting out his horse, while, at the same time, he was stealing and selling his allowance of corn. "If you really wish me," said the horse, "to look well, give me less of the rubbing and more of the corn."

FIFTY-FIFTH LESSON.

ADVERBS RESULTING FROM NOUNS GOVERNED BY PREPOSITIONS.

Air ball, on (the) spot, just now.

Air biċ, at all, in existence.

Air éigin, with difficulty.

Air faḋ, altogether.

Air d-tús, at first, in the beginning.

Air déire, at the end.

Arteaċ, into; artiġ, within (doors); (arteaċ, i.e., gus an teaċ, to the house; artiġ, i.e., anns an tiġ, in the house).

Air uairiḃ, at times (uairiḃ is Dat. plur. of uair, an hour).

De bṁṫ, because, by virtue of.

De ṁaċ, usually.

De laṫaṁ, presently.

De ló, by day, in the day-time.

D' óiöċe, by night, in the night-time.

Fa ċuaṁṫ, round about, in a circle.

Fa öeoiṁ, at last (pr. *yeo-igh*, in one syl.)

Fa öó, twice.

Fa ṁeaċ, by turns.

Fa ċuaṁṁṁ, conjecturally; buṁle ṁa ċuaṁṁṁ, a blow by chance (ṫuaṁ), without aim; ṫuaṁṁṁ means *about, in the direction of*, without defining the precise way.

Fa ċuaṁṁṁ is a preposition also (see lesson 56).

ó ċeṁle, asunder (ó, from, ċeṁle, a companion, from one another).

ó ṁṁ, from that time, since.

óṁ ṁṁol, lowly, in a whisper.

óṁ áṁö, above board, aloud.

VOCABULARY.

Áṁö-ṁóṁ (from áṁö, high, ṁóṁ, fashion, custom), high-life, fashion, state.

Coṁ le ṁeaċ, " as well as another," is an idiom for aṁṁ coṁ le ṁeáċ, in the same way with another; beṁöṁṁ-ṁe aṁláṁö coṁ le öuṁṁe, I would be similarly (situated) like everybody else.

Cṁoċnuṁ, v., 2nd con. to *tremble*; from cṁṁċ, trembling, shaking.

Cṁoċnuṁaö, the *act* of trembling from fear or terror; a *trembling*; being in terror and awe.

Cṁoṁceaṁ, pr. *kroykan* (gen. ṁṁ, 1st dec., plu. cṁoṁċṁṁ, like the gen. sin., but more commonly cṁoṁcne, the contracted form of cṁoṁceaṁa), the skin of any animal, the hide, pelt, peel of fruit, the rind. Cṁoṁceaṁ caóṁaṁ, a sheep's skin; cṁoṁceaṁ laoṁ, calf's skin; cṁoṁceaṁ ṫaṁṁö, a bull's hide; Welsh, *croen*; Arm. *krochen*; Greek, χρῶμα; cṁoṁceaṁ aṁṁ ṁoṁ cṁoṁċṁṁ, skin for skin. Cṁoṁceaṁ is, probably, from cṁuṁċ, figure, shape, formation; and ceaṁ, the heading or covering, *i. e.*, the coating which gives completion to the frame.

Faoṁ'ṁ ṫṁṁ, at large about the country (ṁaoṁ *under*, has, as in this instance, like its equivalent in Greek and Latin, the more extended meaning of *about, around*).

Ṁlóṁ, *m.*, 1st dec., a sound; a cry; utterance, noise like that of streams; the voice as distinguished from articulate sound; as, ṁṁ ṁṁaṁċ öo ṁlóṁ, aċṫ ṁṁ olc öo ṁuċ, thy voice is good, but thy musical powers (ṁuċ) are bad; the roar of animals. Ṁlóṁaċ, noisy, humming, ever-talking.

Ṁlóṁ, *sound*, is mas. gen. 1st dec. gen. ṁlóṁṁ; ṁlóṁṁ, *glory*, is fem. and of 2nd dec., making the gen. in e, ṁlóṁṁé.

EXERCISE CIX.

Aṅ t-Aṙal a ʒ-cṙoicean leoiṅ.

Do ċuiṙ aṙal cṙoicean leoiṅ aiṙ, aʒuṫ do ċuaiḋ amaċ ṫaoi 'n tiṙ aiʒ cuṙ eaʒla aiṙ ʒaċ beiṫeaċ (brute) a ċaṙluiʒ leiṫ. Do ṫaoil ṫe ṫaiṫċioṫ a 'cuṙ maṙ an ʒ-céaḋna aiṙ ṫionnaċ, aċt aiʒ cloṫ do 'n maḋaḋ ʒliċ ṫo a ʒlóṙ, duḃaiṙt ṫe: "Ṁaiṙe, ʒo deiṁiṅ! beiḋeaḋ cṙiċnuʒaḋ oṙmṫa, ċoṙ le ṅeaċ, muṅa ʒuṙ éiṙt mé ṫuaiṙ do ʒéiṁṅil."

Aṙḋ-ṅóṫ ṅaċ cleaċtaṙ bṙeaṫaṅṅ é-ṫéiṅ.

Ċeaṅṅa, already.

Ciḋ, although; from ciḋ, sees, i. e., seeing that.

Coiḋċe, ever, in future.

Eaḋoiṅ, to wit, viz.

Ḟóil, yet, awhile; ṫaṅ ʒo ṫóil, wait awhile.

Feaṙḋa, henceforward.

Fóṙ, yet, moreover.

Ʒiḋ, a form of ciḋ (which see).

Jlle, thenceforward; as, ó ṫiṅ ille, from that forward.

Léiṫ, entire; ʒo léiṫ, entirely.

Leoṙ, sufficient; ʒo leoṙ, sufficiently.

Ṁaṙ ṫiṅ, in that way, so so; maṙ ṫo, thus; maiṫe, well! maiṫe, ʒo deiṁiṅ, well, indeed!

Ṁiṅic, frequently.

Riaṁ,' ever, up to this, hitherto, in past time; coiḋċe means ever in time to come; ṅi ṙaḃ ṫe a ṙiaṁ aṅṅ ṫo, aʒuṫ ṅi beiḋ a coiḋċe, he was (not ever) never here, and he will not ever be.

Sul, before.

Saṁlaiḋ (same as aṁlaiḋ), in like manner; from ṫaṁail, like, similar.

VOCABULARY.

Blow, v., ṫeuḃ; blew with all his might and main, do ṫeuḃ ʒo luċ, láiḋiṙ.

Cloak, ṫallaiṅ; Latin, *pallium.*

Close, *adj.,* dluṫ; ʒo dluṫ, closely, tightly; ṅioṫ dluiċe, closer; more closely, more **tightly.**

Conquer, v., buaiḋ ṫaʒail,—buaḋuʒaḋ; also, cṙéiṫe ṫaʒail; baṙṙ cṙéiṫe; cṙéiṫe, signifies a trial of strength (from cṙeuṅ, strong, powerful); baṙṙ cṙeiṫe, is, therefore, superiority (baṙṙ) in a trial of strength.

Shower, ciḋ, *f.,* gen., ceaċa, tuaṙ ċeaċa, a rainbow—prognostic of a storm.

Sun, ʒṙian, *f.,* gen., ʒréiṅe (two syl-

lables), ﬋olur ﻧﺎ 5ﻧéﻧﻋ, the light of the sun.	Which of the two was the stronger, cﻳﺎ ﺎﻋﺎ ﺑe'ﻧ ﻣ-ﺑeﻳﻧﻋ ﺑuﺑ ﻋﻧéﻧﻋ.
Traveller, ﻓeﺎﻧ ﻧﻳuﺑﺎﻳﻝ, ﻓeﺎﻧ ﻋuﻧuﻳﻝ, coﻓﺎﻳﺑ, ﻧﻳuﺑﺎﻝﺎﻳﺑ.	Wind, 5ﺎoﻋ.
Vapour, ceo.	

EXERCISE CX.

A dispute arose between the wind and the sun, which of the two was the stronger. At last they agreed to put the point upon this issue, that whichever soonest made a traveller take off his cloak should be accounted the more powerful. The wind began, and blew briskly and strongly a blast sharp, scathing, and fierce; but the more strongly he blew, the more tightly did the wayfarer wrap his cloak about him. Then the sun shone forth. With his warm beams he expelled the storm and the vapour. The man felt the heat; and, as the sun began to shine with greater warmth, he at last sat himself down and threw his cloak on the ground. The sun gained the victory; and, from that day to this, one is subdued sooner by the warm beams of kindness than by the pelting storm of severity and violence.

Mildness is better than fierceness.

Jﻴ ﻓeﺎﻧﻧ ﻣﻳﻧe 'ﻧﺎ ﺑoﻳﻧﺑe ﻣóﻧ.

VOCABULARY.

bﻧeﻳﻋeﺎﻣ (*see* Vocabulary Exercise, XCVII); bﻧeﻳﻋeﺎﻣ ceﺎﻧﻋ coﻋﻧoﻣ ﺎﻧ ﻋ-euﺟ, death is a righteous, equitable judge.

Cuﻋullﺎﻧ, the general-in-chief of the Knights of the Red Branch, "cuﻧﺎﻳﺑe ﻧﺎ cﻧﺎoﻳﺑe Ruﺎﻳﺑe." The name seems to be formed from cu (gen. case plur.), *of heroes;* and cullﺎﻧ, *stay*, the guardian, support (root, cul, back, reserve).

Dﺎﻳﻝ, *f.*, history, meeting, the friends who meet, passing events, respite, time, friendship, the expression of it, a gift.

Dﺎﻣﺟeﺎﻧ, *adj.* (from ﺑo, difficult, and ﺟoﻳﻧ, to wound), firm, strong, protective, secure.

Déﻳﺑ, *n.*, desire, wish, longing; as, ﻧﻳ 'l ﻣe ﺎﻧﻧ déﻳﺑ ﻋﻳﻧ oﻧﻋ, I do not grudge you that—literally, I am not in any feeling of sympathy for you on that (head).

Doﻋﻋ, *adj.*, strait, narrow, close, fast; 5o ﺑoﻋﻋ, closely.

Gﺎﻣﻧﺎ, a doublet; defence, protector.

5ﺎﺑﺎﻧﻧ (*see* Vocabulary for Exercise XCV.), gets, receives, ﻧﻳ 5ﺎﺑﺎﻧﻧ ﻓe bﺎ, no ﻋﻧeuﺑ, he receives not cows nor herd; followed by leﻳﻝ, with, it implies to yield to, also to succeed—literally, to take with; as, ﻧﻳ 5ﺎﺑﺎﻧﻧ le ﻋﻧeuﻧ ﻧo le ﻋﻧuﺎﺟ, he yields not to the brave, nor base; ﻧﻳ 5ﺎﺑﺎﻧﻧ coﻣﻧﺎc leﻳﻝ ﻧo cﺎﻋ, nor contest, nor battle with him (death) succeeds.

Solﺎﻣ, Solomon.

Cﻧuﺎﺟ, *adj.* pitiable, mean, wretched.

The following piece, taken from a collection of manuscript poems formerly in the possession of Dr. Murphy, Bishop of Cork, is ascribed to

Donough Mor O'Daly, Abbot of Boyle, who flourished in the thirteenth
century. The date of the poem is A.D. 1219, twenty-five years before the
abbot's death. His poems, like those of our own Moore—"the poet of all
circles"—will continue to be admired as long as the language in which they
have been composed shall exist. His versification is easy and natural; his
thoughts dignified, often sublime, always elevating; his language, like the
manna, fair and fine, satisfies the soul at once with its sweetness and its
strength. On account of the wonderful simplicity and purity of his style he
is called the "Ovid of Ireland." In the "Transactions of the Iberno Celtic
Society," by Edward O'Reilly, author of the Irish-English Dictionary, the
names of thirty-one poems, most of which are in the possession of the present
writer, are given. The following poem, though not found amongst the collection which O'Reilly saw, appears, judging even from internal evidence, to
have been written by the abbot. How wonderfully simple and correct the
Irish Ovid has written, when these stanzas, as well as all others which he
has left us, are at the present day, after the lapse of more than six centuries,
perfectly intelligible to every Irish-speaking scholar.

EXERCISE CXI.

Bɼeiċeaṁ ceaɼᴄ, coṁċɼom aɲ ᴄ-euᴣ; ɲí ᴣabaɲɲ le ᴄɼeuɲ
   ɲo le ᴄɼuaᴣ,

Ní ᴣabaɲɲ aiɼᴣioᵭ ɲo óɼ, aᴣuɼ ɲi ᴄeiᴣ óᴣ ɲo aɼɼaiᵭ uaiᵭ,

Ní ᵭaiɲᴣeaɲ oiᵭċe aiɼ ɲo lá; ɲi ᵭaiɲᴣeaɲ ᴄɼáᴄ aiɼ aɲ
   euᴣ,

Ní ᴣabaɲɲ coṁɼaċ leiɼ ɲo caċ; ɲi ᴣabaɲɲ ɼe ba ɲo
   ᴄɼeuᵭ.

Ⱥiɼ aɲ m-báɼ maɼ ᴄuiᴣċeaɼ liɲɲ, ɲi ᵭaiɲᴣeaɲ cill ɲo
   ᴄuaċ,

Ní ᵭaiɲᴣeaɲ caiɼleáɲ aiɼ, ɲo múɼ; ɲo ᴣo ᴣ-cuɼᴄaɼ ᴄu 'ɼ
   aɲ uaiᴣ,

Ní b-ꝼuil luaᵭaiɼeaċᴄ ɲo luᴄ, ᵭo béaɼꝼaɼ ᴄu ċaɼ ᵭo ᴄɼáᴄ,

Feuċ ɲáɼ ċuṁᵭuiᴣ ɲeaɼᴄ a ċoɼɼp Samᵽɼoɲ,
   Aɲ ᵭɼaoi Ⱥ)aɲaɲɲaɲ aᴣuɼ Coɲɼaoi; aɲ b-ꝼeiċᴄeaɼ
   ᵭaoiᵭ ᴣuɼ lóɼ.

Ⱥ cleaɼa ᴣoile ᴣo léiɼ, ɲioɼ ċuṁᵭuiᴣ é aiɼ aɲ m-báɼ,
   Cuċullaɲ eaṁɲa ɲa ɲ-eaċ; ɲáɼ leiᴣeaᵭ uaiᵭ ɲeaċ ɼláɲ,

Solaṁ mac Ⱦaiᵭí ᴣeuɼ, ᴣlic; iɼ ᵭeiṁiɲ a ṁic ᴣuɼ ꝼioɼ,
   Aɲɲɼ aɲ uaiᴣ a ᴄá ᴣo ᵭoċᴄ, ᵭo cuiɼeaᵭ a ċoɼɼ ꝼa
   ᵭioɲ.

Fiɼiɲɲe ɼo ᴣiᵭ ᴣuɼ ɼeaɼᵭ; ɲi ɼiɲe ɲaɼ ᵭeaɼᵭ aɲ ᵭail,
   Iɼ ioɲaɲɲ aᴣuɼ euᴣ ᵭaɼ liɲɲ; beiċ a leiɲe luiɼm aɲ
   báɼɼ,

Ó ɲaċ ᵭam ó'ɲ euᴣ ᵭul, m' aɲaṁ ɼo ċeaᵭ a'ɼ ɼo ᵭeiᵭ,
   Ⱦo beiɼim ᵭo Ríᴣ ɲa ɲᴣɼáɼ, ᴣo ᵭ-ciᴣiᵭ aɲ báɼ ᵭo m'
   bɼeiċ.

FIFTY-SIXTH LESSON.

COMPOUND PREPOSITIONS.

Prepositions are of two kinds, simple and compound.
The simple, as, ₐ⅂ᵹ, at ; ₐⱮ, on ; ᵭo, to, &c., have received
the earliest attention in these lessons.

The compound are composed of substantives and prepositions. They are short phrases having the meaning peculiar
to single prepositional particles. In this view they are quite
easy, for phrases bearing a prepositional sense exist in every
language. But some of the Irish compound prepositions—
like ċuⱮ, towards, for the purpose of—are not in meaning
clear, being composed of nouns now obsolete, and have become, by usage, so reduced from their compound state, that
they resemble simple prepositions.

Ⰰ ⱺ-ꝼₐⱭ, in the border of, vicinity of (from ₐ, in, and
ꝼₐⱭ, a ring, a wreath, border, circle—kindred in meaning
to ꝼáⱶ, a fence, enclosure; whence ꝼáⱶₐⱮ, a cloak, covering).

Ⰰ ⱺ-ꝼₐⱭⱭₐᵭ (from ₐ, in, and ꝼₐⱭⱭₐᵭ, company, linked
in society—root, ꝼₐⱭ, same as ⱮₐⱭ, along, Ɑe, with), along
with, in company with, in comparison with; in this last
sense written ₐ ⱺ-ꝼₐⱭⱭₐⱪ; Ɑₐċ ⱱⱭeₐᵹ ₐⱭoⱭ ê, ₐ ⱺ-ꝼₐⱭⱭₐⱪ
ⱮₐⱭ ⱱⱭ ⱪê, how splendid it is now, in comparison with how
it was.

Ⰰ ⱺ-ꝼₐⱭⱭₐᵭ, Ɑⱪ ꞇⱭuₐᵹ ᵹₐⱭ oⱭᵹⱭ " 'ⱭⱭ ₐ ⱺ-ꝼₐⱭⱭₐᵭ," it
is a pity there is not an heir in their company.—Davis's
" Lament for the Milesians."

Ⰰ ⱺ-ꝼⱵₐᵭⱭuⱭⱪe (from ₐ, in, and ꝼⱵₐᵭⱭuⱭⱪe, witness, presence), in sight of, in presence of so as to witness; ᵭeⱭⱪⱭⱮ
ê ₐ ⱺ-ꝼⱵₐᵭⱭuⱭⱪe Ɖe, I say it in the presence of God; ₐⱭⱭ
Ɱ ꝼⱶₐᵭⱭuⱭⱪe, in my presence, before my face.

ꝼⱶₐⱭuⱭⱪ (i. e., ꝼⱭoⱪ, knowledge; ⱭⱭⱭⱭⱪ, tell), to declare (in
testimony) what one knows.

Ⰰ ⱺ-ꝼoⱪₐⱭⱪ, with, together with, in company ; ꝼoⱪₐⱭⱪ,
company, nearness to ; it is from the same root as ꝼoⱪuⱪ,
near.

Ⰰ ⱵₐċₐⱭⱪ (from ₐ, and ⱵₐċₐⱭⱪ, spot, presence, where one

stands), in presence of, **a láċaiṙ an Ċiġeaṙna**, in the presence of the Lord.

Oṙ coṁaiṙ (from oṙ, over, and coṁaiṙ, direction, count, aim, front face, presence), oṙ coṁaiṙ an ṁóiṙ, before the whole world.

Oṙ coiṅṅe, opposite, diagonally, face to face, *vis-a-vis*, in presence of (from oṙ, and coiṅṅe, *i. e.*, cuaiṅe, an angle, diagonally, in opposite angles or positions).

[Observe the resemblance in meaning of the five preceding prepositional phrases.]

VOCABULARY.

Aiṙceoiṙ, *m.*, a (play) actor; a jester, a showman; also a merryandrew, a jester. **beanaiṙceoiṙ**, an actress. From **aiṙceaċ**, astute, tricky, sportful, mirthful, jolly; **naċ aiṙceaċ tu?** Are not you queer (a strange fellow)? **Aiṙce**, invention, conception, a plan; Greek, ἀστεῖος, witty, clever.

beallaiġ, gen. case of **beallaċ**. *m.*, a way; **a ḃ-ḟaḋ beallaiġ**, a long way; **ṙaġ an beallaċ**, clear the way.

bṙoṙna, *n.*, a faggot, a bundle, an armful.

Cióiṙ (*cee-yish*), a mask (root, cíḋ, to see, aṙ, through); **bṙeuġ-éuḋan**, a false face; **ṙġáċ-euḋaiṅ**, a veil or cover, in general, for the face.

Cuaṙċuġaḋ ċaṙc, search all round.

Inċiṅṅ, *n.*, brains; from iṅṅ, or aṅṅ, in, and ceaṅṅ, head.

Ioṁċuṙ, *v.* (from ioṙ, for uiṅṅe, *about*, and cuiṙ, to put, send, lay), to carry; **ḋ' ioṁċuṙ**, he carried.

Leuṅ, misery, misfortune. **Aṙo leuṅ**, my sad sorrow!

Ceaṙcáil, *f.*, want, defect; **caḋ é ta ceaṙcáil uaiṫ**, what is it you want? **Ṅi'l mé a ḃ-ceaṙcáil ṅiḋ aiṙ biṫ**, I am wanting nothing.

Ceaṙcuiġiṁ, I fail, I am in want, I die. It is very commonly, in the spoken language, employed in the third persons singular or plural, with the compound pronouns, **uaiṁ**, from me; **uaiṫ**, from thee; **uaiḋ**, from him, &c.; as, **ceaṙcuiġeaṅṅ puṅca uaiṁ**, I want a pound—literally, is wanting from me a pound; **a ḃ-ceaṙcuiġeaṅṅ aiṙġeaḋ uaiṫ?** Do you want money—literally, is money wanting from you?

EXERCISE CXII.

An ṙioṅṅaċ aġuṙ an cióiṙ.

THE FOX AND THE MASK.

Ċuaiḋ ṙioṅṅaċ a ṙceaċ a ciġ aiṙceoiṙe aġuṙ aiġ cuaṙcuġaḋ ċaṙc ḋo ċoṅṅaiṙc ṙe cióiṙ ṙġiaṁaċ aṅṅ: " Iṙ bṙeaġ aṅ cloiġeaṅ é, ġo ciṅce, beiṙ ṙe, aċc mo leuṅ, naċ ḃ-ḟuil iṅċiṅṅ aṅṅ."

Iṙ beaġ iṙ ḟiu éaḋan áluiṅ ġan ceaṅ céilḋ.

EXERCISE CXIII.

Aп peaп-peaп aʒup aп bap.

THE OLD MAN AND DEATH.

Bɪ peaп-peaп a ꝺ' ɪomċuɪп "a b-paꝺ" beallaɪʒ cpom-ualaċ bpopпaɪꝺ. Ċaɪпɪc aп oɪпeaꝺ pɪп (there came so much) cuɪppe (weariness) aɪp paoɪ a ċpoɪme (its heaviness, weight) ʒup ċaɪċ pe ꝺe e, aʒup ʒup ʒlaoɪꝺ (called) pe aɪp aп m-bap a ċeaċc aʒup cpɪoċ 'cup leɪp aп m-beaċa cpuaʒ bɪ pe aɪʒ caċaꝺ (leading, spending). Nɪ cuɪpce ʒlaoɪꝺeaꝺ aɪp, 'пa ċaɪпɪc aп bap aʒup ꝺ' pɪappuɪʒ (enquired) caꝺ e bɪ ceapcaɪl uaɪꝺ. "Nɪ'l ceo," aɪp pe-paп, aċc, ma 'p pɪ ꝺo ċoɪl e (if you please) apꝺuɪʒ (raise) oɪpп aп c-ualaċ po.

Nɪ h-ɪoппaп cuɪppeaꝺ a ċup aɪp aп m-bap aʒup a ɪoппpuɪꝺe.

To invite death and to encounter his presence are not alike.

Obs.—The case which compound prepositions govern is the genitive, because the leading word in a prepositional phrase is a noun; as, ap uċc Ꝺe (imploringly), for God's sake—Ꝺe is gen. of Ꝺɪa, governed by uċc (bosom): ap uċc, for the sake of, is literally translated, out of the bosom of, for the love of—uċc being the seat of the affections. Aɪp poп pɪoċċaɪпe, for peace sake.

Ap uċc, for the sake of, *pour l'amour de.*

A ʒ-cɪoпп, a ʒ-ceaпп, at the head of, at the end of, in addition to, along with; root, ceaпп, head, end.

Op cɪoпп, over, above, at the head of; ca Ꝺɪa op cɪoпп пa ꝺomaɪп moɪp, God is above (at the head of) the entire world.

Aпп aɪpcɪp (aɪpcɪp, a meeting), in the meeting of; ceɪʒ aпп a aɪpcɪp, go to meet him.

A ʒ-cuɪппe, in order to-get, to meet, to obtain, for, ċaɪпɪċ pe a ʒ-cuɪппe aɪпʒɪꝺ, he came for (*i. e.,* in order to get, a ʒ-cuɪппe) money. This preposition is ever on the lips of the speaking Irish, implying to meet with, to get. It always follows a verb of motion. See op coɪппe.

A leɪċ (from leɪċ, half, one of two; side), to the charge of. It is an adv., and means aside, apart, hither.

A ταοb (ταοb, side), relating to, in regard to.

Ameαρ3, among, amidst (from α), and meαρc, mixing—Latin, *misceo*; Eng. *mix*, i. e., *misc.*

From α3αιb (*eye-e*) face, front, is formed the preposition αιηι α3αιb, against, which is very much in use. Le α3αιb with the (face) *view* to, intended for, τα ρe ρο le α3αιb Seαmuιρ, this is intended for James. Ó α3αιb, away from, from the face of; ғαοι α3αιb, under the eye of, in the view of.

The preposition αιρ, on, is omitted oftentimes before buη, foundation; cul, rear, back; ғαb, length; ғeαb, space; ғub, breadth; ρ3αc, shade, appearance; ροη, sake;—bo, to, is not always expressed with cum, the form, shape, the waist, circumference, position; nor with ρéιρ, will, accord. In this way these nouns have the appearance of simple prepositions. In the following list they are given in full:—

Αιρ buη, established.

Αιρ cul, behind; as, αιρ cul ηα ρleιbe, behind the mountain; αιρ cul αη boρuιρ, behind the door.

Αιρ ғαb, in length; the length of.

Αιρ ғeαb, during; as, αιρ ғeαb αη lαe, during the day.

Αιρ ғub αη bomαιη, throughout the world.

Αιρ ρ3αc, for the sake (rather, show) of, for the lucre of; αιρ ρ3αc cαιρbe, for the sake of a respite; for a little loan.

Αιρ ροη, for the sake of, through.

Αr ucτ, through, by virtue of.

Do ρéιρ, according to (ρéιρ, accord, will).

Do cum (or, cum alone), to, towards, for, for the purpose of; cum ηα ρleιbe, to the mountain; cum α beαητα, in order to do it (literally, in order to its doing).

VOCABULARY.

Αιρηeιρ, *f.* (root, αρ, ploughing, support), gen.. αιρηéιρe (the final e in these instances is always in Irish a distinct syllable, and is, therefore, to be pronounced), cattle, chattels; αιρηéιρ τι3e, household stuff; Armoric, *har-nes*; English, *harness.* Αιρηeιρ, in the spoken Irish, means, *per se*, cattle—from it is derived αιρηeαc, disease in cattle, murrain. In αιρηéιρ, cattle, α and e are pronounced long; in αιρηeιρ, chattels, short.

Cuοlαιb, birds; a noun of multitude, from euη, a bird. The ending laıð, like "ry," in the English word, "poultry," from the French, *pouletrie*, imparts to the root, eun, a collective meaning. Poulet (Fr.), a young hen; pouletrie, all kinds of fowl. See Easy Lessons, part IV., p. 256.

Ioṁaıᵹ, image, idea, idiom, figure (from ı, or aoı, an element, an outline; and ṁaıᵹ, or ṁoıᵹ, the gen. case of ṁoᵹ, the old Irish term for man, found in the Latin, ho*m*o, ne*m*o). That ıoṁaıᵹ is a compound word appears from the fact that ṁ is asp. The second part of the compound begins, therefore, with the aspirated letter ṁ. Armor., *imach;* Latin, *imago.* It is in vain one looks in a Latin dictionary for the derivation of imago; at best a quasi derivation (imago, as if imitatio) is the only one given. It is plain the Latins borrowed the term from the Keltic dialect which the Sabines spoke.

Snáıᵹ, v., to creep, to crawl, to sneak; from ɼnáıᵹ is formed ɼnáıᵹeaċ, *adj.*, creeping, crawling; *n.*, a creeper, or crawler, *i. e.*, a ser-

pent, a reptile—words which come, the one from *serpo*, Latin, to crawl; ϸϵπω, Greek, to creep.

Snaıᵹean, same; a serpent, snake.

Snáıᵹ, to creep, is pronounced snaw-y, in one syl., and is thus distinguished from ɼnaıᵹ, or ɼnáıð, snyee (ı long), to cleave, to cut, to hew, to make thin, fine, to pare. This latter should be, as it is often written, ɼnaıᵹ.

Snaᵹ, v. (ᵹ not asp.) means to creep, to crawl—hence the word snake, a serpent of the oviparous kind.

Snaᵹ, n , signifies one with a creeping gait—hence a woodpecker: ɼnaᵹ bɼeaċ (speckled) a magpie.

,, the hiccup.

Snaᵹaċ, full of woodpeckers.

,, creeping.

Snaᵹaıɼe, a sneaking fellow; a term of contempt common among the people.

Snaᵹ labaıɼ, v., to stammer. The English word " snail" appears to come from ɼnáıᵹ-aıl, a thing that creeps.

Snaṁ, v., *snawv*, to swim, is of kindred meaning with ɼnáıᵹ.

EXERCISE CXIV.

(*Continuation from page* 317.)

Aᵹuɼ do ɼıᵹne Dıa beıċıᵹ ca calṁan "do ɼéıɼ" a ᵹ-cıneál (according to their kinds) aᵹuɼ áıɼɼear, aᵹuɼ ᵹaċ níð a ɼnaıᵹeaɼ aıɼ an calaṁ "do ɼéıɼ" a ċınéıl. Aᵹuɼ do ċonnaıɼc Dıa ᵹuɼ buð ṁaıċ ɼın. Aᵹuɼ dubaıɼc ɼe: déanaṁuıɼ an duıne ann aɼ n-déılb féın, "do ɼéıɼ" aɼ ᵹ-coɼaṁlaċca féın; aᵹuɼ bıðeað cıᵹeaɼnaɼ (lordship, dominion) aıᵹe "oɼ cıonn" ıaɼᵹ na faıɼɼᵹe, aᵹuɼ "oɼ cıonn" eunlaıð an aeıɼ, aᵹuɼ "oɼ cıonn" na h-aıɼɼéıɼe aᵹuɼ na calṁan uıle, aᵹuɼ ᵹaċ uıle níð ɼnaıᵹeaċ a ɼnaıᵹeaɼ aıɼ an calaṁ. Maɼ ɼın do ċɼucuıᵹ Dıa an duıne ann a ıoṁaıᵹ féın: ann ıoṁaıᵹ De do ċɼucuıᵹ ɼé é, fıɼıonn aᵹuɼ baınıonn do ċɼucuıᵹ ɼe ıad.

Obs. 2.—The pronouns governed by these propositions (1) are *placed between* the simple preposition and the noun; and (2) are put into the *genitive* case; as,

In the midst *of us*: ⱀⱀ "ⱇ" mⱇⱃ⅁ (in *our* midst),
Before *you*:   oⱃ "ⰱⱎ" ⅁-comⱇⱃⱎ (in *your* front).
After *them*:   ⱇⱀⱀ "ⱄ" ⱀ-ⰱⱃⱇⱃ⅁ (in *their* aft); con-
                  tractedly, 'ⱀ ⱄ ⱀ-ⰱⱃⱇⱃ⅁.
Before *thee* (in your presence—where you stand): ⱇⱀⱀ "ⰱo" Lⱇⰱⱇⱃⱃ.
Before *me* (in my view, so that I can observe): ⱇⱀⱀ "mo" ⱇⱃⱇⰱⱀⱎⱃe.

That these prepositions should in this way govern the pronouns is quite natural, as is plain from their meaning. For, in English, the words "in *our* midst," is the same as "in the midst *of us*;" "in *our* presence;" "in the presence *of us*;" &c. The possessive pronoun *our* holds the place of the gen. case of the pronoun personal *of us*. Its corresponding term in Irish is, "ⱇⱃ," *of us*, or *our*.

From eⱃⱃ, a spot, a place, a track, a foot-print, come the prepositions:

Ⱇⱀⱀ eⱃⱃ, after (in the track of).

Ⰹ' eⱃⱃ, after (of the track of); ⰱ' eⱃⱃ is commonly written without the apostrophe, ⰱeⱃⱃ, after.

Ⱌⱇⱃ eⱃⱃ, after (over the track of).

From ⰱⱃⱇⱃ⅁, end, conclusion, is formed the preposition, ⱇⱀⱀ ⰱⱃⱇⱃ⅁, after; contractedly, ⱀ-ⰱⱃⱇⱃ⅁ (pr. *ney-ee*); ⱇⱀⱀ ⰱⱃⱇⱃ⅁ relates to place, or position; as, John is after James (in place), ⱌⱇ Seⱇ⅁ⱇⱀ 'ⱀ ⰱⱃⱇⱃ⅁ Seⱇmⱎⱃ.

Ⰹéⱃⰱ, with longing desire; as, ⱀⱃ'l mé ⱇⱀⱀ ⰱéⱃⰱ ⱃⱀ oⱃⱌ, I do not grudge you that.

Jⱇⱃ, after, behind (ⱃⱇⱃ, the west); ⱌⱇⱃ éⱃⱃ and ⱃⱇⱃ, relate to time; as, ⱃⱇⱃ ⱌeⱇⰱⱌ, after coming.

Joⱀⱀⱃⱇⱃⰱ (from the noun ⱃoⱀⱀⱃⱎⱃⰱ, an attack, a turning towards an approach to; ⱃⱀ, in, and ⱃⱎⱃⰱ, sit, rest); ⰱ'ⱃoⱀⱀⱃⱎⱃⰱe, towards, against; with a verb of motion it gives the idea of hostility, opposition, also of seeking refuge; ⰱⱎⱇⱃⰱ ⱃe ⱃoⱀⱀⱃⱎⱃⰱe ⱇⱀ ⱀⱇmⱇⱃⰱ, he went to encounter the enemy.

Ⱌⱃmⰱⱃoll means circuit, ambit; ⱇ ⱌⱃmⰱⱃoll, therefore, means about, around; and is usually employed without the preposition ⱇ (in).

Τυαιṗιṁ, conjecture; root, τυαṗ, a sign, a prognostic; ṗa ċuaiṗiṁ, towards, about; as, ṗa ċuaiṗiṁ ḋo ṗláinτe, towards your health; ṗa ċuaiṗiṁ na ṛleiḃe, towards, or somewhere about the mountain; *i. e.*, in the direction of, without defining that it is really so—this meaning accords with its radix, τυαṗ, guess, conjecture, sign.

Ʒo ḃ-τι, to, unto, up to.

Ʒó ṅυιʒe, until, up to.

Ʒuṛ, towards; same as ʒo, to, towards. It receives ṛ final for the sake of euphony. Whenever the article an, *the*, comes immediately after; as, ʒuṛ an m-baile ṁóṛ, *to the* large town; *i. e.*, city or town, as contra-distinguished from (baile) a village.

The word aiṛ, meaning side, border, brink (perhaps for éiṛ, track, mark), is not found in any Irish Dictionary which the writer has seen, yet it is common in the spoken language; as, le aiṛ, along, by the side of.

"Le aiṛ na τoṅnτa ʒloṛaċ' ʒéiṁṅaċ' ʒaṛʒ."

"Along by the waves, roaring, loud-resounding, raging."

EXERCISE CXV.

A DIALOGUE BETWEEN A YOUNG MAN AND A YOUNG WOMAN—
HIS COUSIN.

[The use and application of the compound proposition are here attended to.]

1. (Rose.) Oh, William, I have found you, all alone (aṅṅ ḋ' aonaṛ); what a pensive being! Here you are in the garden, like Adam in Eden, with the trees and flowers (aiṛ ḋo laṁ ḋeiṛ aʒuṛ aiṛ ḋo) on your right, and on your left, the verdant plains spread out "before you" (oṛ ḋo ċoṁaiṛ), lambkins and sheep, calves and cows, and beasts of all kinds roaming "in your view" (aṅṅ ḋo ṗiaḋnuiṛe), the cloudless sky above you (oṛ ḋo ċιoṅṅ), the running streams hard by (aṅṅ ḋ' aice), all forming a picture on which poets might love to look: for all that, you are, I find (ṗeicιṁ) alone. 2. (William.) Not so (ṅ' aṁlaιḋ τá), my dear girl (mo ċaιlιn ḋιlιn), I am not alone. 3. (Rose.) It is true you are not at present (anoιṛ), since I have come (ó ċaιnιc mιṛe). 4. You want to appear clever (ιṛ mιan leaτ a

beiċ ꝟliċ); did you take long to think so deeply and speak so sapiently (labaiṟt ċo eaȝnaċ)? 5. You do not wish, I am sure, to do me wrong (eaȝcóiṟ a ḋeanaḋ oṟm), nor to do yourself wrong! 6. Neither, my dear sir; I like you (ta cionn aȝam oṟt) as a kind friend and brother, and I confess I like myself more; so there is no fear then that I shall do you an injustice (eaȝcóiṟ); much less is there fear that I shall do injustice to myself. 7. I am glad to hear you say so; pray tell me, if you please (inṟiȝ ḋam, ma ṟ ṟi do ċoil e), whenever you view a mirror (ṟȝáċan), do you not perceive some pleasing reflections (naċ ḃ-ḟeiceann tu iomaiȝiḋ ḋeaṟa aiȝ eiṟiȝ) arise "before" you (oṟ do ċoṁaiṟ)? 8. I must be candid (ḟiṟineaċ), and admit I do (aȝuṟ a ṟaḋ ȝo ḃ-ḟeicim). 9. And am I to be less reflective than mere glass (nioṟ lḭú ḋealṟaċ 'na ȝlaine) "in your presence" (ann do laċaiṟ)? can I prevent bright images from floating across my mind when (an tṟáċ) your radiant countenance sheds (ṟȝeiċeinn do ȝnuiṟ ṟoillṟeaċ ṟmiȝiḋ aȝuṟ ṟuaiṟceiṟ) smiles and sweetness across its exterior (aiṟ a aȝaiḋ)? The very cliffs, cold and flinty ((cṟuaiḋe), would return sweet echoes to your voice, and am I to be mute (balḃ) speechless (ȝan ṟócail), in your presence (ann do laċaiṟ)? 10. You overpower me, if these be spoken in reference to me. You astonish me if you are preaching philosophy (ṟaiṟṟuiȝeann tu me, ma 'ṟ oṟm-ṟa labṟann tu maṟ ṟo, cuiṟeann tu ionȝnaḋ oṟm ma 'ṟ ḟealṟanaċt táiṟ aiȝ teaȝaṟȝ). 11. I shall speak neither flattery (blanḋaṟ) nor philosophy, although my words seem to have a share of both. "In your presence" I must have high thoughts. 12. Very well; whence do you derive your wisdom? 13. From solitude (uaiȝneaṟ). 14. That is, you love to be alone? 15. I am never alone; I am never less alone than when you perceive me alone. 16. How is that? Are you surrounded by fairies or nymphs of the woods? Is this fairyland (tíṟ na n-óȝ)? 17. It is not fairyland, though, perhaps, it is the land of fairies; yet I must say that I have never seen any fairy or sylvan nymph less real than yourself. 18. Give over (coṟȝ oṟt); just come along (taṟṟ uait). Have we got any wonderful fish in this river? 19. No; we have got only trout. 20. Oh, just see some yonder, how they bask in the sun; at our approach they dart off. 21. How fleet they move in the waters! 22. Astonishingly. 23. If you wish to see a good many, move slowly "along the" bank; look on the side of the river on which the sun sheds his warm rays. 24. Why look there? 25. Because fish love the sunshine. 26. Do fish in water receive heat from the sun's rays? 27. Certainly. 28. The sands and pebbles on the bed of the stream appear lighted up—how clearly everything in the waters and beneath them appears. 29. That, to me, is a proof (cᴀⱚrbeᴀɲᴀ̆) of how God's eye sees all creatures, as yours or mine behold the fish and the pebbles beneath the waters—nay, he sees the very thoughts of the soul (ꞃmuᴀⱚnce ᴀn ᴀnᴀmᴀ) for "all things," we are taught, " are naked and open to his eyes" (ɲoⱖcuⱚ⅁ce ᴀ⅁uꞃ oꞃ⅁ᴀⱚlce oꞃ comᴀⱚꞃ ᴀ ᵹul). The darkest abyss (ᴀⱚbeⱚꞃ ⱚꞃ ᴆoⱚꞃⱖe), the most hidden recess, becomes like the bed of the stream in the sun's light, open to His view. 30. I see you are not only philosophic (eᴀ⅁nᴀⱖ), but religious (ᴆuⱚɲe ᴆⱚᴀᴆᴀ). 31. True philosophy and true religion go together. They are like the earth and sun—the earth receives (ꝼᴀ⅁ᴀɲɲ) light and heat and steadiness in its movements from the sun—so philosophy receives all its lustre from religion, and without her influence would go adrift (ᴆul ᴀⱚꞃ ꝼᴀɲ) and perish. 32. Good bye; I shall profit by your thoughts and take a lesson from those words of wisdom.

FIFTY-SEVENTH LESSON.

CONJUNCTIONS, INTERJECTIONS—GAELIC SYNTAX.

A sentence, like a chain, cannot be formed without the collecting links of speech—conjunctions. The very first Exercise required their use, and the first word in the Vocabulary to that Exercise is a conjunctive particle. All the conjunctions in the language have, in different stages of the foregoing Lessons, been brought before the learner's notice. They are here presented in one group :—

CONJUNCTIONS.

Ꮇⱖc (1), but; (2) except, *at; ast*, Latin. Ꮇⱖ is an incorrect spelling; ᴀⱖc is found in the most ancient MSS.
Ꮇ⅁uꞃ (1), and; (2) ᴀs, like the Latin *ac, atque*, which

have both meanings, that of "and," and "as." See the
word ċo, "Easy Lessons," Part I., p. 21—Vocabulary of
Fourth Lesson.

Aᵹur, in ancient writings, ᴀccur and ocur, akin to ꝼoᵹur, near, connecting; and to ᴀɪᵹ, prep. at; British, *ac*, and; Welsh, *ag;* Latin, *ac;* Scand.
ık; by changing the palatal c (k) into t, *et*, Lat., and by altering the position of the consonant k, is obtained the Greek καɩ.

The learner will remember that its modern spelling is "ᴀᵹur," and not,
as some authorities write it, "ocur." This latter was its spelling some ten
hundred years ago.

Aᵹur is contracted into 'ᵹur, ᴀ'r, and 'r, in poetry; ᴀ'r is sometimes
but incorrectly, printed ɪr, thus confounded in its spelling with the word ɪr,
is—the assertive form of the verb *to be*, ꝺo beɪċ.

An, whether; used in asking questions in the present
tense; as, "An" ᴄu ᴄᴀ ᴀnn? Is it you who are here? Latin
same, *an*—"*án*" tu qui es?

When preceding a verb in the past tense it becomes ᴀr, whether; r is
part of the obsolete particle ro, sign of the past tense.

Ċeᴀnᴀ, before, already, even; ᴀċᴄ ċeᴀnᴀ, but, however,
moreover.

Ċo (and coṁ in composition), (1) so, (2) that, (3) until;
ċo luᴀċ "ᴀᵹur," as soon as. See p. 21, "Easy Lessons."

ᵹo, conj. *that*, to the end that; French, *que;* Erse, or
Scotch Gaelic, *gu*. (ᵹo is also a prep. *to;* and sign of the
adv., as, ᵹo mór, exceedingly.)

ᵹur, that (*i.e.*, ᵹo and ro), employed before the subjunctive tenses.

With buꝺ, may be, ᵹur forms the compound ᵹuᴀrb, that it may be—
which, in old writings, is found written thus—curb and curᴀb.

Bɪꝺ and bɪoꝺ (pr. *bee*), or bɪꝺeᴀꝺ, let it be (imperative
mood, third singular), be it so, grant it, like the Latin, *esto*,
although.

ᵹɪꝺ and ᵹɪꝺeᴀꝺ, although, yet, nevertheless, composed of
ᵹo, that, and bɪꝺeᴀꝺ.

Ce and ᵹe, although, appear to be derived (like *quod*, ii
Latin) from the pronoun cɪᴀ, cᴀ, who, what.

Cɪꝺ (pr. *kee*), seeing that, even, although, yet, perhaps;
same as ᵹɪꝺ, or from cɪꝺ, sees.

Dᴀ, *if, had it been that*, on the hypothesis *that*—precedes the conditional mood, to which, in reference to past
time, it imparts the meaning of the pluperfect subjunctive.

ꝺᴀ differs from ṁᴀ in this—that ṁᴀ precedes the *indicative* form of conjugation; ʙᴀ goes before the *conditional*, ʙᴀ ᵹ-ʙuᴀɪlꝼᴀɪɲɲ, if I should strike; and, in reference to past time, *had* I stricken, *if* I had stricken.

Ṁᴀ, if; and ṁᴀꞃ for ṁᴀ'ꞃ, or ṁᴀ ɪꞃ, *if it is.*

Ṁᴀʙ and ṁᴀꞇ, in ancient writings, are for ṁᴀ and ʙuꝺ, if it were.

Fóꞃ, yet, moreover; from fóꞃ, rest; hence, fóꞃuᵹᴀꝺ, to abide; cluᴀɲ-fóɪꞃ, *the abode of rest*—the name of St. Jarlath's church, near Tuam.

Joɲᴀ, and contractedly, 'ɲᴀ, which, is now the common form=than; ꞇᴀ ꞇuꞃᴀ ɲɪoꞃ ꝼeᴀꞃꞃ ɲᴀ ṁɪꞃe, thou art better than I.

Olꝺᴀꞃ in old writings, means literally, *is above;* from ol (same as oꞃ), above, and ɪꞃ, is; also, olʙᴀ, and olʙᴀꞇe (from ol, over, and ꞇᴀ, is. "It should also be noted," says Dr. O'Donovan, "that olʙᴀꞃ, olʙᴀꞇ, is very frequently used for joɲᴀ, in ancient writings; as, ᴀꞃ ꞃo ʙᴀ ꝺɪle leɪꞃ clᴀɲɲ. Neᴀꞇꞃᴀɪɲ olʙᴀꞇ clᴀɲɲ Neɪll, 'for the sons of Neachtan were dearer to him than the children of Nial.'"—Ann. Four Mast., A.D. 1460.

Ṁᴀꞃ, as; ṁᴀꞃ ꞃo, thus; ṁᴀꞃ ꞃɪɲ, in that way; so and so. Ṁᴀꞃ ᴀɲ ᵹ-céᴀꝺɲᴀ (ꝺɲ, pr.=*nn*), also, in like manner.

Nᴀ, *not*, like (*ne* Latin) prohibitive, ɲᴀ ꝺéᴀɲ, do not; ɲᴀꞃ, not (=ɲᴀ and ꞃo) before subjunctive tenses; ɲᴀꞃ leɪᵹɪꝺ Ðɪᴀ, God forbid.

Ṁᴀ, if, with ɲᴀ, makes ṁuɲᴀ, if not, unless, except that. Ṁuɲᴀꞃ, in the subj. tenses, and contractedly, ṁuꞃ. Before ʙuꝺ, *is, may be,* ṁuɲᴀ becomes ṁuɲᴀb and ṁuɲbᴀꝺ, *were it not, if it was not;* and also ṁuɲᴀꞃ before ʙuꝺ, with ᵹo, *that,* following. Ṁuɲᴀꞃ ʙuꝺ ᵹo, contractedly, ṁuꞃ ʙᴀ ᵹ', commonly pronounced by the people, ṁuꞃ beᴀᵹ, *were it not that,* &c.

Nɪ (1), not (*absolute* negative), ɲɪ coɪꞃ, it is not right; ɲɪ me, it is not I (2) neither, nor; ɲɪ ṁɪꞃe, ɲo ꞇuꞃᴀ, neither I nor thou; ɲɪ ṁᴀɪꞇ, ɲo olc, neither good nor evil.

Nɪ becomes in the past tense ɲɪoꞃ, absolute negative.

☞ Observe the difference between ɲɪoꞃ and ɲᴀꞃ: ɲɪoꞃ is in the direct form, as, "ɲɪoꞃ" ꞃɪɲɲe mé é, I did not do it; ɲᴀꞃ, in the indirect or subjunctive; as, ꝺeɪꞃ ꞃe "ɲᴀꞃ" ꞃɪɲɲe me é, he said that I did *not* do it.

"Nᴀꞃ" ꞃɪɲɲe, here follows the verb ꝺeɪꞃ, says, and therefore ɲᴀꞃ, and not ɲɪoꞃ, is employed.

No, or, nor.

This particle should be spelled with o and not with ᴀ, to distinguish it from 'ɲᴀ, than, ɲᴀ, not, ɲᴀ, of the (article).

Nᴀꞃ (a negative relative employed in clauses that are dependent), is not=ɲɪ, not, and ᴀꞁ, for ᴀꞇꞇ, but=not but;

 náċ maiṫ é, but is he not good? Ʒan=ʒo. na, *that not,*
in secondary or dependent clauses.

Ó, since; before verbs.

Ó ċapla, whereas. See p. 243.

Óip, for, perhaps from aip, on.

Seaḋ (*shah*), yes=ir é, it is; ni ḟeaḋ (*nee hah*), no, it
is not.

Ⱥ)aireaḋ (accent on ḟeaḋ), if it is it, if so.

Ⱥ)aireaḋ (accent on maip), pr. *maise*=well, wéll.

Sul, before that.

VOCABULARY.

Coṁ-ionann, co-equal; from coṁ,
together; and ionann, the same.

Deiṁin, indeed, true; ʒo deiṁin
truly.

Deaʒ-ḋaoine, good people; the vir-
tuous, the elect; ḋaoine maiṫe
(good people), the fairies.

Dpong, *f.* gen. ḋpoinʒe, 2nd dec., a
class, a tribe, a race. It is of
kindred meaning with the word
ḋpeam, a tribe, a family, a race,
ḋpong is used in a disparaging
sense, like the word *gang*, in
English.

Cibín-ḋealḃṫa, distinct; from eiḋin,
between, and ḋealḃṫa, formed;
ḋealḃ, frame, form.

Naḋuip,*f.*, nature; Welsh, *natur.*

The word "only" in English is
translated into Gaelic by the words
"not but;" as, there is only one
God, "ni" b-ḟuil "aċt" aon Dia
aṁain, there is not but.

EXERCISE CXVI.

This Exercise is taken from the Catechism, because in it is exemplified the
use of the conjunctions; it is withal very easy:

1. Caḋ é an ceuḋ niḋ, ir cóip do ʒaċ uile ċpiortaiʒe
(Christian) a ċpeiḋeaḋ (to believe)? 2. Ʒo b-ḟuil aon
Dia aṁain ann; ir é ro an ceuḋ aipteaʒal de 'n cpé (of
the creed). 3. Cia ḟe Dia? 4. Cpuṫuiʒṫeoip neiṁe
aʒur talṁan; aʒur apḋ-Tiʒeapna ʒaċ uile niḋ. 5. An
pab Dia ann, ʒaċ uile am? 6. Bi aʒur poiṁ ʒaċ uile
am; de ḃpiʒ ʒo b-ḟuil ḟé ʒan túr, ʒan deipeaḋ (end). 7.
Ca b-ḟuil Dia? 8. Ta ḟé aip neaṁ aʒur aip cálaṁ,
aʒur ann ʒaċ uile ball (spot, part), de 'n ḋoṁan. 9. An
b-ḟeiceann ḟé ʒaċ uile niḋ? 10. Ciḋ ḟe ʒaċ uile niḋ, ʒo
ḟiú na rmuainte ir uaiʒniʒe a ʒ-cpoiḋe an duine. 11.
Ca méiḋ Dia ann? 12. Ni b-ḟuil "aċt" aon Dia aṁain;
a beipṟear aoiḃṅeaṡ ṟiopnuiḋe do na deaʒ-ḋaoinib aʒur
pianta ṟiopnuiḋe do 'n ḋpong loċtaċ. 13. Ca méiḋ peapṟa

ann Dia? 14. Trí pearsana, eidir-ḋealḃṫa agus coṁḣ-ionann ann gaċ uile níḋ; mar ṫá an t-Aṫair, agus an Mac, agus an Spioraḋ Naoṁ. 15. An Dia an t-Aṫair? 16. "Is seaḋ" go deiṁin. 17. An Dia an Mac? 18. "Is seaḋ" go deiṁin. 19. An Dia an Spioraḋ Naoṁ? 20. "Is seaḋ" go deiṁin. 21. An trí Deiṫe iaḋ? 22. "Ní seaḋ," "aċt" aon Dia aṁáin a ḃ-trí ḃ-pearsannaiḃ; dé ḃriġ, naċ ḃ-fuil aca "aċt" aon náḋúir agus aon t-suḃstair aṁáin ḋiaḋa. 23. Caḋ is ainm do na trí pearsannaiḃ "ann aoinḟeaċt?" 24. An Trínóiḋ ro Naoṁṫa, "nó" aon Dia aṁáin a ḃ-trí ḃ-pearsannaiḃ. 25. Cia aca is sine, "nó" is óige, "nó" is cuṁaċtaiġe? 26. Is ionann aois, uaisle agus cuṁaċt ḋóiḃ araon.

INTERJECTIONS.

A, O! sign of the vocative case; O! Oh!

Oċ,
Uċ, } alas; oċōn! alas!

Éist, hush; from the verb éist, listen.

Feuċ, behold; *ecce*, from the verb.

Faraoir, alas! (fá-ar áir, the cause of our ruin).

Monuair, woe is the day! alas! (from mo, my; an, very, sad; uair, hour); my hour of woe.

Abú (a war cry), for ever; as, O'Doṁnall abú, O'Donnell for ever; Láṁ-ḋearg abu, the red hand for ever. Abu! is derived from a, in; and bu, living, ever-living; kindred to biṫ, life, and derived from the verb buḋ, may be, is, exists. With this derivation abu means" for ever;" bu is, perhaps, a contracted fòrm of buaiḋ, victory; if so, abu means, in victory, victorious; O Doṁnall abu, O'Donnell victorious!

Abu, abu, and abu, bú, oh, my! oh, fie! oh, life, life!

There remain yet to be explained in form, a few of (1) the general principles of syntactical arrangement, according to which words and phrases in Gaelic, as in other languages, unite in forming sentences; and (2) the special principles from which idioms, or peculiarities of construction and collocation, spring.

(1) The learner is supposed to know that the verb agrees with its nominative case in two points of relation (1) number, and (2) person.

(2) The agreement of adjectives with nouns in Gaelic has been pointed out in the forty-fifth lesson.

(3) Participles, like those adjectives which end in a vowel, are indeclinable. The relative pronouns, also, do not admit declension.

Many special principles of the language from which idioms flow, have in the foregoing fifty-seven lessons been explained.

In page 34, Part I., and pp. 75, 76, Part II., of " Easy Lessons." the verb is shown to have two forms of the same conjugation—the one called the synthetic, *i. e.*, in which the personal pronouns have become incorporated in the verb, which therefore admits change of ending; the other called the analytic.

Again, Obs. 1.—Whenever the nominative case is not expressed, the verb is in the synthetic form, and conforms to the general rule of agreement in number and person with its subject; as, " b-ꝼuıl" ꞃıb ꞃláɲ, are ye well? Ꞇaṁuıb (we are). " Ḃ-ꝼuıl" is the analytic, used when " ꞃıb," the nom. case is expressed; " ꞇaṁuıb," the synthetic, employed when the nominative is not expressed.

In asking questions the analytic form is more forcible, it is therefore more in use than the other; but, in replying, the synthetic is the fullest and most usual.

Obs. 2—Whenever the *nominative* case is *expressed*, the verb must be analytically conjugated, and must therefore have only the same ending in all numbers and persons.

Exception.—After nouns in the third person plural, the verb follows the general rule and agrees in number with its subject.—See seventh lesson, part I., p. 34.

EXERCISE CXVII.

Aɲ ꞇ-Aꞃal, aɲ Sıoɲɲaċ, aᵹuꞃ aɲ Leoɲ.

THE ASS, THE FOX, AND THE LION.

Ðo " ꞃıɲɲaban" (exception to Obs. 2), aꞃal aᵹuꞃ ꞃıoɲ ɲaċ coɲɲꞃab (compact) ꝼıoɲ, baıɲᵹeaɲ (firm, strong), le ceıle (together, with each other), aᵹuꞃ bo " ċuaban" (Obs. 1), amaċ ċuṁ ꞃeılᵹe. Ðo ċaꞃluıᵹ oꞃꞃa leoɲ 'ꞃ aɲ ꞇ-ꞃlıᵹe. Nuaıꞃ bo bꞃeaċ aɲ ꞃıoɲɲaċ ᵹo " ꞃababaꞃ" aɲɲ ᵹáb, bo ċuaıb ꞃe ꞃuaꞃ aıᵹ aɲ leoɲ aᵹuꞃ bo ċuᵹ coᵹaıꞃ bó (gave him a whisper) ᵹo m-beaꞃꝼab ꞃé aɲ ꞇ-aꞃal bó ꝼaoı láṁ, aċꞇ ᵹaɲ boċaıꞃ aıꞃ bıċ a beaɲab aꞃ ꝼéıɲ. Ð' aoɲꞇuıᵹ aɲ leoɲ. Maꞃ ꞃıɲ bo ꞃıɲɲe aɲ mabab ᵹlıc ꝼeıll-beaꞃꞇ aıꞃ a ċompaɲaċ aᵹuꞃ ċuᵹ ꞃuaꞃ é bo ċuṁaċꞇ a ɲaṁaıb Aɲɲ ꞃıɲ aıᵹ cuꞃ bo 'ɲ leoɲ aɲ aꞃaıl ꝼaoı bıoɲ, b' ıoɲꞃuıᵹ ꞃé (he turned) aıꞃ aɲ ꞇ-ꞃıoɲɲaċ, aᵹuꞃ ɲıoꞃ ꝼaᵹ ᵹꞃeım bé, le ceıle (and did not leave a bit of him together) aıᵹ coɲᵹbaıl (reserving) aɲ aꞃaıl ᵹo h-am eıle.

Nıoꞃ ꞃab a ꞃıaṁ aɲ ꞇ-ab aıꞃ luċꞇ ɲa ꝼeılle.

Those who betray others never yet have had success.

VOCABULARY.

Cnóḋa, *adj.* (pr. *crow-ya*), brave, hardy, valiant; ⱱⁱn cnóḋa, brave men. Ꝺull cnóḋa, the valiant Goll.

Cnóḋa, *adv.* (ᵹo cncóḋa), bravely, valiantly; ⱱéⱥn ᵹo cnóḋa, act like a man, valiantly and with courage.

Ꝺluċ, *adj.*, tight, close (ᵹo ⱱluċ, *adv.* tightly, closely); also, thick; coⁱll ⱱluċ, a thick wood; ⱱolⱦ ⱱluċ, a thick head-of-hair; ⱱluċ ⱥnn ⱱⱥⁱṁ, near in kin; ⁱⱦ ⱱluċ ⱥoⁱⱬnⱦeⱥⱦ ⱱo ⱱⱦón, joy is close upon grief; "Ours the light grief that is sister to joy."—Moore. Ꝺⱦⁱuⁱⱱ "ᵹo ⱱluċ" lⱦ ċeⁱlⱦ, move closely together.

Ꝺluċ, *n.* -mas., a confined space, a yard, an enclosure; the warp or woof of a web.

Ꝺóⁱċ, *v.*, burn, singe, scorch; ⱱoⁱċ-eⱥⱱ, per. pass., was burned.

Ɍⱥⁱⱦᵹ, *v.*, squeeze, press, wring, compress; to wring, as with wet cloth; Ⱨⱥⁱⱦᵹ, *n.*, a tie, a band, a penfold, a press. Ⱦⱥnⱱ-Ⱨⱥⁱⱦᵹ, *n.*, the tie under the chin of a dead body. Ⱦⱥnⱱ-Ⱨⱥⁱⱦᵹ onⱦ,

is a common curse. (Welsh, *fasg.*) The *adj.* Ⱨoᵹⱥⱦ, near, is of this family of words.

Ꝫoⁱn, ᵹuⁱn, *v.*, wound, hurt, sting, from ᵹⱥ, an arrow, and ⱥn, a circle, an opening—whence *annulus*, Latin. Johnson knows not the derivation of the English word "gun." In the Gaelic its root is easily found. Welsh, *gwanu*, to stab.

Luⱦ, *m.* (Welsh, *llys*; Fr., *lis*), an herb, a weed, a plant, or flower.

Luⁱⱱ, *f.*, an herb, weed, grass. Luⁱⱱ is applied to herbs in general; luⱦ, to those of special size and efficacy.

Ⱦⱥċⱥⁱⱦe, *m.*, a paddock, a field; from mⱥᵹ, a plain, and ᵹⱥⁱⱦe, nearer; or ᵹⁱoⱦⱦⱥ, shorter—a field not so large as a mⱥᵹ, or extended plain; luⁱⱱ nⱥ mⱥċⱥⁱⱦe, the herb of the field.

Neⱥnⱦóᵹ, *f.*, a nettle.

Nⁱⱦṁeⱥċ, *adj.* (from nⁱⱦṁ, poison), poisonous, envenomed, virulent, sharp, bitter in its physical and moral acceptation.

Ɍⁱnc, *v.*, to dance, to sport, to play.

EXERCISE CXVIII.

Ⱥn buⱥċⱥⁱl ⱥᵹuⱦ ⱥn neⱥnⱦóᵹ.

THE BOY AND THE NETTLE.

Ꝺo ᵹoⁱn neⱥnⱦóᵹ buⱥċⱥⁱl ⱥ ⱱⁱ ⱥⁱᵹ ⱦⁱnc 'ⱦ ⱥn mⱥċⱥⁱⱦe Ꝺo ⱱeⁱⱧⱦⁱᵹ ⱦé (he hastened) ⱥ m-bⱥⁱle ⱥnn ⱥ ṁⱥċⱥⱦ (home to his mother), ⱥᵹuⱦ ⱱ' ⁱnnⁱⱦ ⱱⁱ (and told [to] her) ᵹuⱦ ᵹoⁱn ⱥn luⱦ nⁱⱦṁeⱥċ ⱦⁱn é, ᵹⁱⱱ nⁱoⱦ nⁱᵹnⱦ ⱦé ⱥċⱦ ⱥ lⱥⁱm ⱥ leⱥᵹⱥn ⱥⁱⱦ (although he only laid his hand on it). "Sⁱn é ᵹo ⱱⁱⱦeⱥċ" (that is just—ⱱⁱⱦeⱥċ, *directly*), ⱥⁱⱦ ⱦⁱⱦe (said she) ⱥn ⱦ-ⱥⱱⱱⱥⱦ ⱥⱦ ⱱóⁱċeⱥⱱ ⱦu; 'Nuⱥⁱⱦ ⱦⱥⁱⱦ ⱥⁱᵹ buⱥⁱnⱦ neⱥnⱦóⁱᵹe, Ⱨⱥⁱⱦᵹ ᵹo ⱱluċ ⁱ (grasp it tightly) ⱥᵹuⱦ nⁱ ⱱéⱥnⱧⱥⁱⱱ ⱦⁱ ⱱoⁱlⁱᵹ onⱦ (and it will do you no mischief—hurt).

Ꝺéⱥn ᵹo cnóḋa ⱥn nⁱⱱ ⁱⱦ ⱱuⱥl ⱱuⁱⱦ ⱱéⱥnⱥⱱ.

Do with courage whate'er you are to do.

FIFTY-EIGHTH LESSON.

GOVERNMENT OF NOUNS.

The grammatical agreement, usually called "concord," between verbs and their subjects, between the adjective and noun, has, in the preceding lesson, just been shown.

The influence exercised by words on each other, causing in the noun a change of case, is called "government." This influence on nouns is produced (1) by other nouns, and adjectives taken substantively; (2) by verbs; (3) by prepositions.

The change of case may be to the (1) genitive, (2) dative, (3) accusative.

GOVERNMENT OF THE GENITIVE CASE.

Obs. 1.—The latter of two nouns coming together, when the objects of which they are names are different, is governed by the former in the genitive case; as,

Ⅿⱥc Ⅾé, God's Son.

Ⅾé is the gen. case of Ⅾⱥ, God, governed by the noun mⱥc, son, which precedes it.

Ⱥinm mⱥc, a son's name.

Ⅿⱥc is the gen. of mⱥc, governed by ⱥinm.

If instead of ⱥinm, the word leabⱥr (*lhower*), Latin, *liber*, a book, be substituted, the sentence runs thus:

Leabⱥr mⱥc, a son's book,

(and with the pronouns, or the article preceding mⱥc);

Leabⱥr mo mⱥc, my son's book;
Leabⱥr ⱥo mⱥc, thy son's book;
Leabⱥr ⱥ mⱥc, his son's book;
Leabⱥr " ⱥn" mⱥc, the son's book.

The words Ⅾé and mⱥc. are conformable to rule in the gen. case; and rightly, for they express the idea of generation, source, origin, ownership of that which is conveyed by the nouns which precede them.—See "Easy Lessons," Part IV., p. 261.

☞ In every single instance, in Irish, as is seen from the foregoing examples, it is the *latter* of the two nouns, and *never* the *former*, which is the governed word. It is not so in Latin.

Ⅿⱥc Ⅾé may be translated filius *Dei*, or *Dei* filius, the gen.. *Dei* being before or after the governing word; and in the Anglo-Saxon genitive case (that is the genitive or possessive ending in 's) it is the *former* of the two nouns, and *never* the *latter* which is the governed word; as,

God's Son, Ⅿⱥc " Ⅾé"; filius *Dei*.
The Lord's Day, Lá " ⱥn Ⅽiȝeⱥrnⱥ," dies *Domini*.

Obs. 2.—In translating from English cases like those (ending in 's) the position of the governed noun must therefore be reversed in Irish, as in the examples just presented.

But, in translating the Norman genitive, *i. e.*, genitive expressed by "*of*," into Irish, the order and position of the nouns are retained, the preposition *of*, or sign of the first oblique case omitted, while the latter noun assumes the genitive case-ending; as,

> Son (of) God, Mac Dé;
> Day (of) the Lord, Lá an Tiġeanna.

The definite article "the" is translated by "an," which, coming before tiġeanna, the genitive, is in the same case with it.

It is worth while observing that mere English students, not acquainted with Latin, or Greek, or German, regard the particle "*of*," in such instances as the foregoing, purely as a preposition, and not as a sign of the genitive case; and on this account they are, whenever learning to translate into those languages, as well as in the present instance into Irish, puzzled at the non-use of the preposition "*of*." On the other hand, they find French and Italian easy in this respect.

VOCABULARY.

Céimnuġaḋ, v. to bound, to advance in strides; from céim, a step, a bound; as in coir céim, a foot-step.

Fear reilge, a huntsman (reilge is gen. case of realg, a hunt, and fear, a man; huntsman is the same as hunt's-man).

lean, to follow; luċt leanṁuinte, pursuers, followers; luċt, a tribe, a class, a set; leanṁuinc, following; gen. case, leanṁuinte.

EXERCISE CXIX.

An Fiaḋ aiġ an Linn.

THE STAG AT THE POOL.

Lá n-aon do ṫáinic fiaḋ aiġ linn le n-a "ṫart" (acc. case coming before the infinitive) a ċorġ, aġus 'nuair do bí aiġ ól do ċonairc se a ċaire (shadow) 'san t-sruṫ. "Naċ mór, maireaċ," deir se, na aḋarca (pr. *eye-arka*) so onm, aċt oċ! naċ táir (poor) iaḋ mo ċora caola. Leir rin do ṫáinic fear-reilge leir' na cuin aġus na ġaḋair 'nna ḋiaiġ. Ni faḋa bí na cora caola a ċáin re cuiḋeaḋ leir céimnuġaḋ de léim a b-faḋ ó 'n namaḋ a lean é; aġus na aḋarca a mol ré ġo mór, do ċonġbuiġṫar é ġabṫa ġo ḋluṫ a láir "na ġ-cran" (gen. plur. on láir, midst) no ġur ṫáinicaḋar na fir reilge leir na cuin ruar, aġus ġur ṁarḃuiġḋar é.

IDIOMS OF THE INFINITIVE AND PARTICIPLES OF ACTIVE
VERBS.

Obs. 3—The infinitive mood of active verbs governs the
genitive case of those nouns which come immediately *after*
it; as,

> Do ʒráðuʒað Dé, to love God ;
> Do ðéanað oibre, to do work.

When the noun goes before the infinitive—which is the
usual vernacular form—it is governed in the accusative case,
and not in the genitive; as,

> Le "Dia" a ʒráðuʒað ;
> Le "obair" a ðéanað.

Dia and obair are in the accusative case.

After the compound preposition cum, towards, for the
purpose of, the gen. and sometimes the accusative is employed; as,

> Cum Dé a ʒráðuʒað ;
> Cum oibre a ðéanað ; or,
> Cum Dia a ʒráðuʒað ;
> Cum obair a ðéanað.

Obs. 4.—The active participle governs the genitive; as,

> Aiʒ ðéanað oibre, doing work.
> Aiʒ ʒráðuʒað Dé, loving God.
> Iar ndéanað copuir, after performing a journey.

Before the infinitive or participle, the gen. case of the
personal pronoun is the more common; as,

> Le n-"a" ʒráðuʒað, in order to love (a) him ;
> Le n-a ʒráðuʒað, in order to love (a) her ;
> 'ʒ a ʒráðuʒað, loving him ;
> 'ʒ a ʒráðuʒað, loving her ;

literally, at his (a) loving; at (her) loving; a, his, aspirates
the initial or first letter of the infinitive mood; a, her, does
not; a, their, causes eclipsis.—See Twenty-first Lesson, p.
115.

The difference in sound leads the hearer to know their
respective meanings.

Note.—The two foregoing idioms in Gaelic are founded
on the substantival character of verbs—a principle which is
true in all languages, and which is well explained in the
following words of Professor Latham, in his work—" The
English Language," p. 290 :—

" A noun is a word capable of declension only. A verb
is a word capable of declension and conjugation also. . . . . .
The infinitive mood has the declension of a noun substantive. Verbs of languages, in general, are as naturally declinable as nouns."

If the learner ask, then, why does the infinitive active and
the active participle govern in Gaelic the genitive case of
nouns immediately following them, the reason is, because
they are verbal *nouns,* and therefore come under Obs. 1,
" the latter of two nouns," &c., p. 361.

Obs. 5.—For this reason adjectives and other words, employed as nouns in a sentence, govern the genitive case.

Obs. 6.—Family names preceded by the words O or
Uᴀ, a descendant; ṁac, son, ṅɩ, or ṅɩ̇ᵹ, a daughter, are
always in the genitive case; as, Ɖoiṅɳall, Donnell, Uᴀ
Ɖoṁɳaɩll, O'Donnell (Ɖoṁɳaɩll being the gen. case of
Ɖoṁɳall); Nɩall, Neill, Uᴀ Ṅéɩll, O'Neill (Néɩll, gen. case
of Nɩall); Ceallᴀċ, Kelly, O'Ceallaɩᵹ, O'Kelly; Caɼċᴀċ,
Carthy, ƜᴀcCaɼċaɩᵹ, MacCarthy—" Nɩᵹ" Caɼċaɩᵹ, Mac
Carthy, as applied to a woman of that name.

Nɩᵹ is the feminine form of Uᴀ or Ɯᴀc, and must, therefore, with reason and with the sanction of usage, be prefixed
to the family names of women; as, Jane O'Donnell is Sɩu-
bᴀɳ " ɳɩᵹ" Ɖoṁɳaɩll (not Uᴀ, or ƜᴀcƉoṁɳaɩll); Bridget
O'Neill, Bɼɩᵹɩᵭ ɳɩ Néɩll (not Uᴀ or ƜᴀcNéɩll).

Obs. 7.—Proper names in the gen. case are aspirated,
whether preceded by the article " aɲ " or not; as, cɩll
Ƥeaᵭaɩɼ, the Church of St. Peter; aɳɳ aɩmɼɩɼ Ƥaᵭɼuɩc,
in the time of Patrick.

Nouns which are not proper names are not thus aspirated.

☞ Uᴀ and Ɯᴀc, in the nominative case, follow this latter class, and
do not aspirate the sirname, as is seen in the foregoing examples. But if
Uᴀ, O, or Ɯᴀc be governed in the case (uɩ, mɩc, genitive), *then* the family
names suffer aspiration; as, John the son of James O'Donnell, Seaᵹaɳ
Ɯᴀc Seaɳuɩɼ Uɩ Coɳɳaɩll. Seaɳuɩɼ and Uɩ are each in the genitive case,
and accordingly aspirate Coɳɳaɩll, the family name.

Obs. 8.—Níʒ causes aspiration; as, Níʒ Ċoṅnaıll, Níʒ Doṁnaıll.

VOCABULARY.

Descent (offspring), rıol, rlıoċc (race). buṅaḋ, cṅeaḃ, ʒıṅ ᴐaláċ, well descended, ó ċṅeıḃ ṁaıċ (of a good tribe).

Family (members of one house), ceaʒlaċ, *i.e.*, luċc "cıʒe," clann (children, offspring); rıol (seed), rlıoċc (race, progeny), ál, cṅeaḃ, ʒıṅealaċ, cıʒeaċar (those of one house cıʒ).

Education, oıleaṅuıṅ; (from oıl, or aıl, to feed, to train), roʒlam; (learning), cóʒaıl; (from cóʒ, to bring up); muṅaḋ, as, buıṅe ʒan muṅaḋ, a person without education or manners, ceaʒurʒ (instruction), bcur (manners).

The young man's grandfather's name, aınm aċaıṅ-móıṅ an ḟıṅ óıʒ ro. (In possessives of this kind the position of the gen. cases in Irish is the opposite of the natural arrangement in English.)

Thistle, róʒanan, the seed of the thistle, rıol "an" róʒanaṅ.

☞ *Of* in English is generally the sign of the gen. case in Irish; as, the Son *of* God, Ṁac "Dé;" the Lord *of* the Word, Cıʒeaṅna "an" boṁaıṅ.

EXERCISE CXX.

In this Exercise the government of the genitive case is shown.

1. Who is this young friend with you, my dear sir, a Ṡaoı (hwee) óılır? 2. He is John (Ua) O'Kelly, the son of Patrick O'Kelly (Seaʒan Ua Ceallaıʒ, mac Páoṅuıc Uı Ċeallaıʒ). 3. His "father's son" ought to be good (ır bual ʒo ṁac "a aċaṅ" a beıċ maıċ); there is a great deal in being well descended and of a good family. 4. I like the old saying, ʒaċ leaṅb maṅ oılceaṅ, ʒaċ oıʒe maṅ aóbaṅ, because it tells truly, that education combined with natural powers forms the man. 5. You are right; for although education is the chief means (an meaóon ır ɼeaṅṅ) to make a man good and great, natural gifts "of" mind (cabaṅcaır naóuṅóa "na" h-ıṅcıṅe) which are often connected with nobility "of" race must precede. 6. The seed "*of*" the thistle can never produce an oak (baıṅ). 7. Like the son "*of*" King David, you speak in proverbs (reaṅ-ṅaıócıḃ). 8. What is the young "man's grandfather's name"? 9. Patrick, son of Charles O'Kelly, was the name of his "father's" father; and James, the son "of" Cormac MacCarthy, was the name of his "mother's" father. 10. Where did they live? 11. They lived on the banks "of"

the Shannon. 12. What is this boy learning? 13. He is learning the sciences (a⁊ ꝼoⱷlaᵯ na ᵑ-alaóaᵰ [gen. case]). 14. Although young, he has much (ⁱomaó eoluⁱꞃ) knowledge (gen. case by Obs. 5). 15. He is a very good boy.

FIFTY-NINTH LESSON.

Observe (1), in translating compound substantives, and those followed by the preposition "*of*"—that term of the two which expresses the property, office, character, ownership, title, relation, or quality of the object pointed out by the other noun, is governed in the genitive case ; as,

Property : a house-of-gold,   ceaċ óⁱꞃ (gen. of óꞃ, gold).
   ,,   a ship-of-war.   lonⱷ coⱷaⁱó.
   ,,   a wall-of-silver,   balla aⁱꞃⱷⁱó (gen of aⁱꞃⱷeaó).
   ,,   a tin-can,   cana ꞃcáⁱn (gen. of ꞃcáᵰ).
Office : a door-keeper (porter), ꝼeaꞃ ooꞃuⁱꞃ (*dorish*, gen. of ooꞃuꞃ, *dhorus*).
   ,,   a musician (man-of-music), ꝼeaꞃ ceoⁱl.
Character : a soothsayer,   ꝼeaꞃ ꝼeaꞃa (man-of-knowledge).
Title : gate-of-heaven,   ⱷeaca ꝼlaⁱċⁱꞃ.

Note.—The second noun *specifies* the meaning of the first. For instance, in the expression ceaċ óⁱꞃ (house-of-gold) the word "gold" does not make fuller nor clearer the prominent idea conveyed by the term "house," yet it distinguishes this latter from one of silver, clay, stone, or the like.

The use, therefore, of the article "aᵰ" *of the* (" na," fem., "*of the*"), is not employed in instances like the foregoing before the noun in the genitive case.

☞ The nature and use of this last remark will be seen when compared with the coming Observations 2, 3, 4.

Obs. 2.—In translating a certain class of compound terms, and those followed by "*of*," from English into Gaelic, the article precedes the genitive, although not found in its English equivalent ; as,

Prophet-of-evils, ꝼáⁱⱷ " na " mallaċc, *i. e.*, prophet-of-*the*-curses.

Mouth-of-pity, beul " na " cꞃuaⁱⱷe, *i. e.*, mouth of *the* pity.

Pillar and ground of truth, bun ᴀᵹuꝛ pꞽléꞽꝛ " ɳᴀ" ꝼꞽꝛꞽɳɲe, *i. e.*, of *the* truth.

Father of lies, ᴀċᴀꞽꝛ " ɳᴀ" ᵯ-bꝛeuᵹ, *i. e.*, father of *the* lies.

Of course, if the definite article be found in English before the genitive, or after " *of*," its sign, it is no wonder that it be employed similarly in Irish; as,

Star of *the* sea, ꝛeulċ " ɳᴀ" ᵯᴀꝛᴀ.
Man of *the* mountain, ꝼeᴀꝛ " ᴀɲ" cɳoꞽc.
Friend of *the* affections, cᴀꝛᴀᵬ " ɳᴀ" ᵹ-cuᵯᴀɲ.

From the text of Observation 2, just given, the learner is naturally induced to ask, what *class* of terms take the article " ᴀɲ," *the*, in Gaelic, the English equivalents of which dispense with its use? The answer is contained in page 58 of Part I., which see.

VOCABULARY.

beo, *adj.*, living, lively; ᵹo beo, quickly, with life.
bꞽċeᴀꞽɲɲᴀċ, a thief.
Cᴀoꞽɲ, *v.*, to cry; cᴀoꞽɲeᴀᵬ, crying; cᴀoꞽɲe, (kueené), lamentation.
euᵹcᴀoꞽɲ (from euᵹ, death, and cᴀoꞽɲ,) crying very much.
Ꝼᴀᵬ ó, long ago (for ꝼᴀᵬ ó ꞧꞽɲ, a length since, or [ó] from, [ꞧꞽɲ] that).

Luċċ ᵹᴀbᴀlċᴀ, captors; ᵹᴀbᴀlċᴀ, of arresting; gen. case of ᵹᴀbᴀꞽl, to seize, to arrest.
Sᵹɲᴀꞽb, *v.*, to roar, to bawl.
Cꞽꞽᵹeᴀᵬ, *v.*, pass. voice, past tense, was condemned (from cꞽꞽᵹ, to turn a scale. When one is condemned, the scale in the hands of justice is turned against him).

EXERCISE CXXI.

Ⱥɲ bꞽċeᴀᵯɲᴀċ ᴀᵹuꝛ ᴀ ᵯᴀċᴀꞽꝛ.

THE THIEF AND HIS MOTHER.

Ꝺo bꞽ óᵹᴀɲᴀċ, ꝼᴀᵬ ó, ᴀɲɲ, ᴀ ᵹoꞽᵬ leᴀbᴀꝛ ó ċeᴀɲɲ " ᵬe 'ɲ" ᴀoꝛ óᵹ ᴀ bꞽ ᴀꞽꝛ ᴀoɲ ꞧcoꞽl leꞽꝛ; ᴀᵹuꝛ ᵬo ċuᵹ é ᴀ bᴀꞽle ᴀɲɲ ᴀ ᵯᴀċᴀꝛ. Ⱥɲɲ ᴀꞽċ ᴀ ꞧᵯᴀċċuᵹᴀᵬ (chastise) ꝛe ᵬo ꞧꞽɲɲe ꞧꞽ ᴀ ᵯolᴀᵬ. Ⱥċċ ꝼéꞽɲ ᵯᴀꝛ ᵬ' ꝼᴀꞧ ᴀɲ ꝼeᴀꝛ óᵹ ᵬo ꞧꞽɲɲe ꝛe ɲeꞽċe ɲꞽoꞧ luᴀċᵯᴀꝛᴀ ᴀ ᵹoꞽᵬ, ɲo ᵹuꝛ ᵹᴀbᴀᵬ (was arrested) ꝼᴀ ᵬéꞽꝛe é ᴀꞽꝛ ꞧꞽᴀᵬ ᵯóꝛ ᴀ ᵬeᴀɲᴀᵬ, ᴀᵹuꝛ ᵬo cꞽꞽᵹeᴀᵬ é ᴀɲɲ bᴀꞽꝛ. Ⱥꞽᵹ ᵬul ᵬ' ᴀꞽċ ᴀ ċꝛoċċᴀ ᵬó, ᵬo coɲɲᴀꞽꝛc ꝛe ᴀ ᵯᴀċᴀꝛ ᴀꞽᵹ ꝛꞽubᴀl lᴀɲ ᴀɲ ċ-ꞧluᴀᵹᴀ 'ɲɲ ᴀ ᵬꞽᴀꞽᵹ ᴀꞽᵹ cᴀoꞽɲeᴀᵬ ᴀᵹuꝛ ᴀꞽᵹ euᵹcᴀoꞽɲ ᵹo ᵯóꝛ. Ꝺ'Jᴀꝛꝛ ꝛe ᴀꞽꞝ luċċ ᴀ ᵹᴀbᴀlċᴀ, ceᴀᵬ ᴀoɲ ꝼocᴀꞽl ᴀᵯᴀꞽɲ ᴀ lᴀbᴀꞽꝛc ᴀ ᵹ-cluᴀꞧ

a ṁáṫair. Aig teaċt ós go beo ċuige do ċuir rí a cluas-
ruas le n-a beul le congar a Ṁic muirniġ a ċlos. Aċt
re do rinne re a fiacla a leaġan go cruaiḋ, daingean air
agus a ġearrṫaḋ ós.   Do sgraiḋ rí faoi 'n b-póir, agus do
ġlaoiḋ mac "na" mallaċt air. Is milteaċ an biṫeaṁnaċ ṫu
a rinne cleas ċo dorraċ rin air do ṁáṫair, dubairt an
pobal. Aċt re an freaġraḋ ṫug re dóiḃ: " Is rire is
aḋḃar an ṁi-áiḋ ro ann a b-fuilim, óir 'nuair do ġoiḋ me
leabar faḋ ó rin, agus ṫug me ċuici e, da bearfaḋ rí
smaċtuġaḋ maiṫ an lá rin dam, ni beiḋinn a láṁaiḃ "an"
ċroċadóra ann riḃ.

Smaċtuiġ an leanb a laeṫiḃ a óiʒe.

The defining office of the article "the" (an, m—na, *gen.*, fem.) is more
special in Gaelic than in English. This accounts for its use before those
several classes of nouns named in the first part of the present Lesson; it helps
to show also the reason of its non-use—as compared with English—before
the former and less definable term of the two, as is seen by the following :—

Obs. 3.— In rendering into Gaelic such sentences as these,
"*the* Lord of the world," "*the* light of the sun," omit the
article " *the*" before the former, and retain it with the latter
noun ; as,

> *The* Lord of the world,
> ... Tiġearna "an" doṁain.
> The light of the sun,
> ... solus "na" gréine.

It is retained only in the last of even three or more genitives ; as,

> *The* beauty of *the* daughter of the king,
> Áilneaċt ingine " an" ríg.

Note.—This specially defining use of the article, and its
non-use in Gaelic, does not differ in idiom from the English
form when the Saxon genitive is employed ; as,

> The sun's light,
> ... solus "na" gréine.
> The king's daughter's beauty,
> ... Áilneaċt ingine "an" ríg.

The Saxon and Gaelic genitives are here alike in their requiring the
presence of the definite article; but the Norman (see Obs. 3) and Gaelic are
not. For instance, in that last sentence, neither the term " beauty," no

"daughter's" has the article, while the word "king," which is the term to be specified above the rest, and its Irish equivalent, ríġ, have the article.
In the Saxon and Irish forms the position of the nouns in the one is the reverse of the order in the other, for instance :—

English : The king's daughter's beauty.
"Beauty" is the last, "king's" the first term.
Gaelic : Ailneaċt inġine "an" ríġ.
"Ríġ" (king), is the last, "ailneaċt," the first.—Obs. 2, p. 362.

EXERCISE CXXII.

THE DOCTOR AND HIS PATIENT.

An liaiġ agus an fear-tinn.

A sick man died (fuair bás) under the hands of a physician (liaiġ) who had been attending him (aig tabairt aire dó). At the funeral (aig an socraide, or, aig dul leis do'n ċill) the physician said to the relatives (luċt gaoil) *of* the deceased (marḃán), "Oh, if he had acted in this way and in that (da ndeanfaḋ sé mar sin agus mar so) not to be drinking strong drink (uisge beaṫa, biṫáilte), and to pay greater attention to himself (níos mó aire ṫabairt dó féin), he would not now be lying low" (sínte air lár). But one of the mourners (fear de luċt a ċaointe) made him this reply (freagraḋ): "There is no use speaking thus now; it was fitter for you to have given this advice to the man when he was alive. It is of no use now, for he is dead."

There is no good in the best advice when it comes (is) too late, or untimely.

Ní 'l aon ṁaiṫ san g-coṁairle is fearr air biṫ 'nuair tá sé mall, antráṫaċ.

Principiis obsta, sero medicina paratur.

Obs. 4.—The application of the article (an, *the*) and the change arising in meaning from its use and non-use, before the first, as well as before the second, or the noun governed in the genitive, is best learned by examples.

Compound nouns. { long cogaiḋ, *a* man-of-war.
{ "an" long cogaiḋ, *the* man-of-war.

Compound nouns. { fear tiġe, *a* householder.
{ "an" fear tiġe, *the* householder.

. The words loṅ̇ and ⟨feaṟ⟩ express the leading ideas—ⱅⁱ̇ᵹ̇e and coᵹⱹⁱⰔ, those of quality, character, or office. The leading term is the more definite, and hence, in such instances, has the article.

If the definite article be inserted now before coᵹⱹⁱⰔ, *of war*; and before ⱅⁱ̇ᵹ̇e, *of* house, we have loṅ̇ "an" coᵹⱹⁱⰔ, a ship of *the* war, or, *the* ship of *the* war (see Obs. 3)—meaning some *special* war, and not war in general; ⱅfeaṟ "an" ⱅⁱ̇ᵹ̇e, a (or the) man of *the* house—meaning of a *special* house, known to, or treated of by the speakers. Take another example: meaⰔⱁᾓ oⁱⰔ̇ċe, midnight; "an" meaⰔⱁᾓ oⁱⰔ̇ċe, *the* midnight; aⁱṟ uaⁱṟ "an" meaⰔⱁⁱᾓ oⁱⰔ̇ċe, the hour of (the) midnight. Now insert "an" before oⁱⰔ̇ċe, and its meaning is at once defined: meaⰔⱁᾓ "na" h-oⁱⰔ̇ċe, middle of the night, *i. e.*, of some special night named or known.

To sum up all that has been said in this lesson :—

(1) There is a Gaelic idiom which requires the use of the Art. (definite) when (Obs. 2) its presence before nouns in English of the like import is never needed; (2) the article before the governing noun in English is omitted in Irish (see Obs. 3); (3) the word which the speaker requires to define, be it the governing or the governed term, must have the article; (4) Gaelic follows the Norman and not the Saxon collocation of the genitives in the relative position of the terms.

EXERCISE CXXIII.

Na luċⱁᵹa ann Ⰱáⁱl.

Ann am áⁱ̇ṟⁱⰔ, 'nuaⁱṟ Ⰱⱁ Ⰱ̇ⁱ luċⱁᵹa ⱅaoⁱ ᵹeuṟċⱹaⰔ aⁱᵹ càⱅ, Ⰱⱁ ᵹ̇laoⁱⰔaṟ Ⰱáⁱl (council), ⁱⱁnnⱁⱅ ᵹⱁ Ⰱ-ⱅuⁱᵹⰔⁱ̇ṟ amaċ an ċaoⁱ a Ⰱ̇' ⱅfeaṟṟ ⁱaⰔ ⱅféⁱn a ċoⱅaⁱnⱅ aⁱṟ. Ⱅⁱⱅ ⁱⱁmⰁa ṟⱅ̇ⁱᵹe Ⰱⱁ ⱅṟaċⱅaⰔaṟ aⁱṟ le céⁱle ᵹan ⱅféⱁm aⁱṟ Ⰱⁱⱅ̇, uaⁱⰔe. Ⱅa Ⰱeⁱṟe, Ⰱⱁ ⱅfeaⱅ luċⱁᵹ ṟuaⱅ aᵹuⱅ Ⰱⱁ ⱅuᵹ an comaⁱṟle ṟⱁ: "ceanᵹal cloᵹ aⁱṟ ṁuⁱⱅéal an ċàⱅ̇, aᵹuⱅ ann ṟⁱⱅ aⁱṟ ⱅeaċⱅ Ⰱⱁ ann aⁱⱅ aⁱṟ Ⰱⁱⱅ̇ ⱅⁱⱅ̇ baoᵹal ⰁaoⁱⰔ, oⁱṟ Ⰱ̇eaⱅṟaⁱⰔ an cloᵹ ᵹáⁱⱅⱅⁱm, aᵹuⱅ Ⰱⱁ Ⰱ̇' ⱅfeⁱⰔⁱṟ ealuᵹaⰔ uaⁱⰔ." Ⰰⱁ ċaⁱⱅⁱṟ (pleased) ᵹⱁ h-anṁaⁱⱅ̇ an comaⁱṟle ṟⱁ leo (with them), ᵹⱁ h-uⁱⱅle. Aⱅⱅ ⰁuⰁaⁱṟⱅ aon ⱅfean-ċaⱅ amaⁱṟ—"ᵹⱁ cⁱⱅⱅe ⁱⱅ maⁱⱅ̇ é Ⰱⱁ comaⁱⱅle, ⁱⱅ ᵹⱅⁱc aᵹuⱅ ṟⱅⁱⰔ an ᵹleuⱅ coⱅaⁱⱅⱅe é, aⱅⱅ ⱅá aon ċeⁱṟⱅ amáⁱⱅ aᵹam oⱅaⁱⰔ—cⁱa aᵹaⁱⰔ, a ċuⁱṟⱅfeaⱅ an cloᵹ aⁱṟ an ᵹ-caⱅ? Ⱅⁱⱅ ⁱ̇ an Ⰱṟéⁱm.

Ⱅⁱ h-ⁱⱁnann ṟuⰁ a ṟáⰔ aᵹuⱅ a Ⰱ̇eanaⰔ.

SIXTIETH LESSON.

NOTE.—The student who knows only English should be made aware of
the several meanings which the preposition " of" in its various relations with
nouns is capable of admitting. Dr. Johnson counts twenty-three. These
can all be grouped under four heads. "·Of" denotes—
(1) Origin, cause, possession.
(2) Class, rank, partnership.
(3) *Of* has the meaning of *among, on, from.*
(4) *Of* expresses property, quality, attribute.

(1) *Of*, in the *first* sense is translated into Gaelic by the
genitive, for that case gives the idea of *origin, cause, material, possession*, &c.,

(2) *Of*, in the *second* sense, is rendered by " ꝺe," of, (same
as the French *de*), whenever it follows *numerals, adjectives,*
of the *comparative* and of the *superlative* degrees, *partitives,*
nouns denoting fullness, abundance, and the contrary, as,

One "·of" the whole, ceaṅ " ꝺe'n" ꞁomlaꞃ; full " of" wisdom, láꞃ " ꝺ' " eaᵹꞃa ; Catherine is *the fairest of* the daughters, ꞃꞁ Caꞁꞇlꞁꞃ ꞁꞃ ꝺeꞁꞃe " ꝺe" ꞃa h-ꞁꞃᵹꞁꞃꞁꝺ; *of all,* a
ḃ-ꝥuꞁl ꝺe.

'Joḃ 'ꞃ ḃ-ꝥuꞁl ꞃuaꞃ leaꞇ, " ꝺe" ꞃa Ɗeaċ ꞃꞁoꞃ-ḃeo.

Jove, and *all that* are with thee above *of* the immortal
gods.

See the prayer of Hector at the end of the present lesson, p. 376.

> " Ɗe" mꞃaꞁḃ ꝺeaꞃ' aꞃ ꝺoṁaꞁꞃ
> Jꞃ ꝺa ḃ-ꝥaᵹaꞁꞃꞃ ꞃe mo ꞃoᵹaꞃ,
>   Sꞁ Aꞃol ꝺuḃ aꞃ ᵹleaꞃa ꞁꞃ ꝥeaꞃꞃ lꞁoṁ.

Old Song.

> Aċꞇ " ꝺe" ꞃa Ꞇꞃoꞁᵹċe uꞁle aꞁꞃ ᵹaċ laoċ,
> 'Ᵹuꞃ oꞃm ᵹo h-aꞁꞃꝡꝺe ꞇá aꞃ caċ a ḃlaoċ.
> But on *each* hero of the Trojans all;
> And on me especially the contest is calling.

See exercise, p. 377.

(3) In the third, *of* signifies *among* ; as, cꞁa aᵹaꞁḃ, which
of you (See Part III., thirty-second Lesson, Obs. p. 190);
and *on* ; as, ꝺo laḃaꞁꞃ ꞃe " oꞃꞇ-ꞃa," he spoke *of* (on) you ;—·
from ; as, a man *of* France, ꝥeaꞃ " ꝺ' ꞃ" ḃ-Ꝥꞃaꞁꞃc ; he

did it *of* himself, rinne se é "uaide" féin (from, *i. e.*, it proceeded *from* him as the originator).

(4) In the fourth acceptation *of* has no equivalent in Gaelic—the mere absence of any preposition suffices—the noun remains in the nominative case; as—a man *of* the highest position and fame, fear a b' airde céim, agus clú. Trí h-uaire d' ḟeuc leis fir is airde clu, three times there attempted it, men of the highest fame.—See next exercise.

This last is a very remarkable Irish idiom. In Latin, the ablative case answers the purpose; in Greek, commonly an accusative after the adjective; but in Irish 'tis the nominative case.—See Part iv. p. 302, Obs.—*An idiom that should be remembered.*

The Exercises of these "Easy Lessons" could not have a more elegant nor a more befitting finish than the dialogue (Homer's Iliad, Book 6—translated into Irish heroic metre by Dr. MacHale) between Hector and Andromache. The tenderness and pathos which breathe through the original are infused through every line, nay, through every word, of the simple familiar Irish in which it has been rendered by the great prelate poet.

VOCABULARY.

Ablaċ, carrion, a mangled carcase (from a, not, and blaḋaċ, contractedly, blaċ, a thing having blaḋ, *i. e.*, pith, juice, force, energy, inherent vitality). Conablaċ is the common word for carcase, carrion; root, con, for dogs, and ablaċ, carrion. Conablaċ is applied to a living creature so lean that the ribs become visible—*i. e.*, to that which is, as it were dead.

Ablaċ is derived by others from ab, not, and luaċ, price, but this derivation is forced, for, the particle ab, is not a negative.

Agraim, *v.* I entreat, (from an, very, and gairim); root, gáir, cry.

Baoġal, danger, peril (from baṫ, drowning, death; gaol, kindred, connected with). Hence baoġalaċ, means dangerous, perilous.

Baoġalta, which is very like the former, means *simple, silly;* as, aig déanaḋ baoġalta glic, make the silly sapient; baoġalta in this sense, is derived from baoṫ, vain, and gaol, kindred.

Bascaḋ, to perish, to put to death; from basaċ (root, bás) causing death.

Baintreuġaċ (*i.e.*, bean, a woman, and tréigṫe, forsaken, direlict), a widow, a relict.

Dileaċta, an orphan (dí want of, leaċta, milk).

Dubron, sorrow (do, bad, brón, grief).

Faiċ (or faċ), a plain, a field; vesture, dress, heat, warmth.

Fioga, fig-tree; crann-fioga, a fig-tree.

Feaḋna, *gen.* case of feaḋna, (*gen.* regularly feaḋana, and contractedly, feaḋna), a band, a troop, a company of soldiers:—ceann na feaḋna, a captain of the guard, a general, a chieftain; a d-tig cinn feaḋna an garda, in the house of the captain of the guard.—Genesis, xl. 3. (Feaḋan from feaḋ, extent, number of; daoine, persons,)—a host.

Mairṫain, natural life; from mair, live (thou), exist, continue, endure.

Mairṫeanaċ, and marṫanaċ, *adj.*, enduring, everlasting, an beaṫa marṫanaċ.

Oiġ, a virgin; from óg, young; óiġin, a little maid.

Oiġinteaċ, a simpleton (*fem.*); from oiġin, a maiden, and teaċ, wayward, wandering; amaḋán, (a fool) is applied to a man; óiġinteaċ, to a woman.

Séirreaṅ, six (persons)=re, six, and rean, man. Món ḟeirean (the big six), seven.

Tuic, fell—participle; tuicim, falling (irreg. in its terminatious).

Urraim, respect, esteem.

Taċa, support, second; ḟear mo ṫaca, stand my support.

EXERCISE CXXIV.

ADDRESS OF ANDROMACHE TO HECTOR.

" A ḋuine ḋána ḟaraoir tá air tí,
Do ḃarcaḋ féin, gan imníḋ faoi ḃo ṁnaoi
'Gur faoi ḃo leanḃ, ciḋ gur ḋóiḃ is baoġal,
A beiṫ gan coimirc, tréigṫe air an raoġal,
Is ort-ra aṁáin, tá an namaiḋ uile, 'braċ,
Is tu-ra aṁáin, is mian leo ḟínaḋ 'g-caṫ,
Ma 'r leat tuicim 'r truaġ, mar rin, gan mé,
Roiṁ tura imṫeact, rínte ríor faoi 'n g-cre
Ma 'bióim do ḋiaiġ mo ḃainṫreuġaċ, béiḋ mo ḃiḋ,
Mar bí ó túr, faoi ḋuḃrón 'gur faoi caoi.
Gan aṫair, maṫair, braṫair, le mo ló,
Maoluġaḋ mo leaṫríoim, nó, a roiṅt liom roġ.
Tuic m' aṫair ṁuirneaċ faoi laiṁ Aċuil ġarg,
Trá rgríor a ċaṫair Teaḃ, an coṡaḋ ḋearg.
Aċt giḋ gur tuic re annr an air neaṁ-beo,
Níor ṫairbain Aċuil earḃaiḋ urraim ḋó.
Air carn aire, leaġṫa air a ḃar,
D' ḟáġ ablaċ a'r arm m' aṫar ann a lár,
'Gur ḋ' ḟar 'n a ṫiomcioll, leaṁuin air gaċ taoḃ,
Cuir óiġe Oriaḋ, inġin' aluin' Joḃ,
Monḟeirar braṫra, taca 'r ḋ éiġ 'gur blaċ
Toigeaḋ uainn go h-uile ann aoin lá;
Do ḟin iaḋ Aċuil milteaċ le n-a lann
Air ṁaġ a rababar' cumḃaċ treuḋa ann.
Mo ṁaṫair bannriġan críċ' na g-coilte duḃ,
Do ċuġ re leir, a'r cáinte triom' lé bruċ,
Aċt ceannuiġ rí a raoirire o'n geaḃal ṁór.
Airg brionaḋ moráin maoin ḋo, aġur ór.
Buḋ geárr an t-am 'n éir fileaḋ cuin a críc'
'Gur fáġ gaċ Dian i gan aon beo 'una luiḋe.

Aır ḟeaḋ do ṁarċaın, aġam beıḋır ġo braċ
Ṁar aṫaır, maṫaır, braṫaır, ceıle ġraḋaċ
Aċt ġlac ḋam ṫruaıġe, aġraıṁ ṫu, na bı
Ṁar rıocar mı-aḋ, aıġ do ṁac '~ do ṁnaoı:
Ṁıre na ḟaġ mar beanṫreuġaċ le mo ċraḋ
'Ġur é 'nn a ḋıleaċṫ ġan aon ṫac' no rġaċ
Aċt ann ro ḟan, ran áıṫ a b-ḟuıl ṫrom ġeuġ
De cran ḟıoġa, ṫabaırṫ do na Ġreuġ',
Sınṫe le balla, uaın maıṫ áġur r-ıġe
Le beaġan raoṫaır ıonnruıḋ rteaċ ra Troıġe,
Trı h-uaıre ḋ'ḟeuċ leır fır ır aıṅḋe clu,
Dır na Aıacr cumaraċ le luṫ,
'Ġur Joḋmuın 'r Tuıḋe mılṫeaċ aır a b'-ḟaıṫ
'S mac Aṫrı, Aġmon, cean na Féaḋna 'r rġaıṫ
'S a braṫaır Ṁuınlea, reolṫa le ġaeṫ' Dea
Na ar a nearṫ ḟeın muınıneaċ, ġan rġaċ."

THE ADJECTIVE.

The syntax of the adjective has been from time to time pointed out in these lessons—its position (see first and thirty-seventh lesson); its agreement with the noun (see thirty-fifth lesson, p. 286); its idioms (thirty-seventh and thirty-eighth); its governing effects (twenty-ninth and fifty-eighth).

GOVERNING POWER OF THE VERB.

That an active verb governs the objective or accusative case, every learner knows; as,.

John loves God, ġraḋuıġeann Seaġán Dıa; God loves John; ġraḋuıġeann Dıa Seaġan.

In these sentences the nominative case comes after the verb, as well as the accusative. The first (or nominative) comes immediately after; the accusative next in order after the nominative.

In old Irish writings the nominative case is found sometimes before the verb. It is employed in poetry, too, in the same manner.

4. Prepositions govern the dative—in fact prepositions govern no other case; as,

Ann ro ċarluıġ a ċaraḋ le n-a ṁnaoı
Aınoreomaċ caoṁ 'ġur ı ḋo lán de ġnaoı.

Homer, Book vi. ll. 545-6.

(Ṁnaoı is the dat. case of bean; gen. ṁna.)
Leır an m-buın, with the cow (nom. bo, gen. bó, dat. buın); the phrase,

do 'n beaṅ, is incorrect: leir aṅ ṅ-bó is also incorrect—it should be, leir aṡ ṅ-buiṅ, and the former—do'n ṫṅnaoi.

In all other nouns the dative case happens to be the same as the nominative, and therefore requires no special ending or inflection, except in nouns of the fifth declension; as,

Do 'n b-peaṁraiṅ, to the person (nom. peaṁra, gen. peaṁraṅ, dat. peaṁraiṅ.)

Regarding prepositions, see Part III. (Lessons from 25 to 35,)

VOCABULARY.

Áiṫeaṁreaċ, *adj.* reproachful, rebuking, reviling; *n,* a reviler, an abuser; .áṫaṁr, rebuke, reproach.

Carcaiṅc, *v.* slay, slaughter; *infin.* carcaiṅc; maṁ uaṅ gaṅ loċc a b'imliġeaṁ aṅ láiṁ a ċargṅaṁr é, as a harmless lamb that licks the hand which slays it.

Ceaṅṁaṁr, *m.* headship, chieftaincy; root, ceaṅ, a head.

Coraiṅc, *v.* to defend, keep of, preserve, maintain.

Foṅṅóiṁ, same as fonamaṁ, jeering, gibing, mocking. (See Lesson 53—Vocabulary.)

Láḃaċ, *adj.* gentle, polite.

Ṁuaṁraiṅ, memory, remembrance. Latin, *memoria,* from ṁéiṅ the mind, aud maṁr lives.

Riġ-laṅ, *m.* a palace; riġ, a king; and laṅ, a castle.

Sgaiṫ, the chief, the best; fioṁrrgaiṫ, the very best, the real.

Ceaṁrcaṁr (from ceaṁrc, a proof, a testimony) character, reputation; Latin, *testimoniam, testis;* Eng. test. See Lesson 52.

EXERCISE CXXV.

REPLY OF HECTOR TO ANDROMACHE.

Do freaṁgaiṁr a céile: aṁgaṁ béiṁó a ṁeamaiṁr
Do ċomaiṁrle ċaoṁ, ċuṁ cabaiṁrc uaiṁr gaċ cabaiṁr;
Aċc béiṁóeaṁó ṅa fiṁr 'r mṅá laṁóaċ' ṅa Cṁroiṁge
A rgéiṫ mo ċlu 'r mo ċeaṁrcaiṁr leir aṅ gaoṫ,
Da b-faiṅiṅn riaṁr, maṁr claṁóaiṁne aṁr aṅ gleo,
Niṁó ṅaċ m-béiṁóeaṁó caiṫneaṁaċ le mo rpiṁióob beo
'Oiṁr ṁo beiṫ calṁaċ ḃ' foġlaṁ mé go luaṫ
Á beiṫ ḃ-coiṁreaċ, 'meaṁrg fioṁr-rgaiṫ ṅa rluaṁ
Aiṁg coriṁc ceaṅṅaiṁr m' aṫaṁr maṁr buṁó cóiṁr
Aṁguṁr 'ṅa ceaṅṅ riṁn, coriṁc fóiṁr mo ġlóiṁr,
Aċc caiṁm fioraċ 'r fóiṁr, le imṅiṁó láṅ,
Go ḃ-ciocfaiṁó aṅ lá a m-beiṁóiṁó aṅ ċaṫaiṁr báṅ,
A ḃuṅ 'r a riṁg-laṅ leagṫa uiṁle aiṁr láṅ
'S aṅ riṁg 'r a ṁaoiṁne riṁnce aṅṅr aṅ áṁr.
Aċc ní goiṁleaṅṅ aiṁgaṁr luċc' ṅa Cṁroiṁge,
No, aṫaṁr, máṫaṁr, braṫaṁr, aiṁr mo ċroiṁóe,
Do béiṁóeaṁr a' cuiṁciṁm aiṁg laiṁṅn cṁroṁ ṅa ṅṁreuṁg
'Nṅa 'ṅ uiṁṁiṁr ṁóiṁr, faoṁ ċaṁrcaiṁc 'guṁr faoṁ euṁg

A'r goileas ḋ' amgar: 'nn éis ḋul ċríḃ gaċ gáḃ
Béirfar tu go críċ na nGréug mar sglaḃ
Folluingt ann, mór anaċair 'gus leun
Faoi ċuing mna eilṫriġe danarṫa 'gus béin'
Fiġeaḃ aig seol stair dólaraċ na Troiġe
No tabhairt ó an t-sruṫ miar uisge ann a tiġe,
'S aig éirteaċt le fonnóiḃ aṫaireaċ, gan truaġ:
Feuċ díol bantraiġ Hectoir móir na sluaġ.
Dubróċaiḃ an t-ainm mo ċuiṁne ann do ċroiḃe,
Agus beidir lán de dubrón 'gus de ċoiḃe
Fá é béiṫ imiġte, ċornoċaḃ tu 'ra tra
'Gus duit-se do beurfaḃ cabhair agus sgáṫ
Aċt roiṁ me feircint niḃ ċo táir, beiḃ mé
Faoi an b-fóḃ, is dóiġ liom, ríṫṫe anus an g-cré.

Homer, Book vi., Dublin—Duffy.

VOCABULARY.

Caṫḃar, a helmet; from cat, a battle; and bann, top, head, dress for the head.

buiḋeaċas, thanks, le banta buiḋeaċais, with hymns of thanks.

Cloġa, a helmet; because it is like a cloġ, or bell.

anḋoġaiḋ, will raise; for anḋocaiḋ.

Aġaiḋ, face; táis, moist, wet.

EXERCISE CXXVI.

CONTINUATION OF THE FAREWELL DISCOURSE BETWEEN HECTOR AND ANDROMACHE.

N'éir ro ráḋ, do ṡín amaċ go raṁ
Cum an t-óg do ċabairt, a ḋa láiṁ,
Do ġeit le eagla mór an leanaḃ searc,
Trá air a g-cloġaḋ uaṁanaċ, soillseaċ, dearc,
'S an eiaḃ capal guanaċ, naḃ gaċ dlaoig
Anón 'r a nál aig smlaḋ leir an gaoṫ.
Do smigḃar an dír: Sgaol Hectoir an lub teann
Bí air a ċaṫbar; 'r tóig í ó n-a ceann
'Gur leag an cloga lannaċ air an b-feur;
Rug air a leanaḃ, 'r cnoc é ruar san aer,
N'éir a pógaḋ 'r breugaḋ le mín cruṫ
A láiṁe, ċuir le impiġiḃ, ruar a ġut.
"'Job 'r b-fuil fuar leat, de na Deaṫ' síon beo,
Dearcaiḃe mo leanaḃ 'r tabraiḃe 'n g-cuimirc dó,

Tabraiḋ ḋó, siubal go céimaṁail anns a t-sliġ,
A siubalim féin mar sompla aig na Troiġṫe,
Aṁirnaṁail, calmaċ, lán de neart 's do luṫ,
'S a coisint a ṫire, toillaḋ gceann a's clú,
'S casgairt náṁaḋ filleaḋ le creaċ ṁóir,
'S le banta buiḋeacais árdoġaiḋ suas gaċ glóir
'S aig cluinst ḋ'a ṁaċair: "beir air aṫair báin,
Líonfar a croiḋe le gáirdeas ann a lár."

  Leis sin·do feaċaiḋ ḋi· an leanab óg,
Sin air a brolaċ é, 'gur tug ḋó póg,
'Smig, 'r ṫuid a smig, do bris na deor' go fuar
Silt 'nuar a leacaib, ó a suilib dears,
D'a feicsint do-san, cuimil le bos a laiṁ'
A h-aġaiḋ tair, ar labair léi go rain:
" Ṁó ceile anraċ, ġeann mo ċroiḋe, caḋ fáṫ?
B-fuil go h-antraċ, le geur brón do ḋ' ċráḋ,
Roiṁ ṫeaċt mo lae 'gur n' am, ni'l orm báoġal,
A g-cumar aon neaċ, ni'l mo ċur de 'n t-ragaol,
An t-olc 'r an ṁaiṫ, an toġa 'gur an ḋioġa,
Níor faruiġeaḋ an bar bí 'n-bán doiḃ fór a nioṁ,
Uime rin, fil a baille 'r aig an t-reol
Gabṫa, fiġeaḋ le rin agur le spól,
Nó 'rniaṁ le feanraiḋ, treoruġaḋ do ċuiḃ ban
Ann uile oiḃne láiṁe 'r stuaire, fan,
Aċt de na Troiġṫe uile air gaċ lauċ,
'Gur orm go h-ainiḋe, tá an caċ a glauċ."

  Do labair a'r ḋ' fairg a ċaṫbar air a ċeann,
Toig sire an t-sliġe a filleaḋ ċum a lann
A ḋeancaḋ rian 'r aig ornail go trom, tiuġ,
'S a silt na deora boġa, 'nna lán sruċ.
Teaċt ḋi baille, ġuil a'r ġáir na mná,
Glacaḋ poinn ḋ'a duḃrón gur ḋ' a ċráḋ,.
Aig caoineaḋ a ceile, aṁail 'r anir go h-euġ
Nár 'n-bán ḋó ṫeaċt, ó láṁ 'r ó lann na nGreuġ.

EXERCISE CXXVII.
VOCABULARY.

Deora, tears; smigeaḋ (*smigoo*), a smile, from smig, the chin, and the playful expression of the mouth; plural smigeaḋa; súl (*sool*), gen. plu. of súil (*soo-il*), eye; cuintar, is formed; measgaḋ, commingling, mixing; lonnaċ, lustrous, bright; cáire, a stream, a flow; rianr' for rianra (root, ríé) peace, happiness, prosperity; ḋuḃan, blackness, darkness (root, ḋuḃ, black).

Tirimóċan, shall be dried; root, cirim, *adj.*, dry, cirimiġ, dry up, cause to dry up, and omitting i before the liquid r, crimiġ—*fut. pass.*, trimóċan; ciun, silent, gentle; ciun-deoir, silent tear; buan (*boo-an*), lasting; ġáire, a laugh; lag, weak, languid; fa réir, in readiness (as it were, reiḋir, from réiḋ, ready).

Tuar, an omen, a presage; tuar-ceaċa, omen of a shower, a rainbow.— "The *sign* of the covenant made by God with Noah, that there shall no more be waters of a flood."—*Gen.* ix.

SONG—"ERIN, THE TEAR AND THE SMILE IN THINE EYE."

Air—Foṅn, Eibhlin a Rúin.

I.

Éire, tá deora agus smigeaḋa do fúl
Mar an bóġa-uirge cumtar ar meargaḋ na n-dúl;
  Lonnaċ tri ċáire deor,
  Bróṅaċ lán rianr' go leor,
  'Tá do ġrianta fa ḋuban mór
    Aig éiriġe gaċ lá.

II.

Éire, ní trimóċan do ċiun-deor go deo;
Éire, ní buan beiḋear do lag-ġáire beo:
  Go rab gaċ daċ fa réir,
  Ann aon-ḟeaċt lé cur go léir,
  'S aig déanaḋ mar tuar na rréir'
    Bóġa riċċair' gaċ traċ.

EXERCISE CXXVIII.

VOCABULARY.

*** The most of the following words have been explained and their derivations given in the body of this work. They are here presented to enable the young learner to understand the songs without any reference to former lessons.

Airiġ, feel, perceive, reckon.

Briscan, is broken; root, bris (*brish*).

Cáil, reputation, character; clú, fame, report, renown.

Ceo (*Keogh*), darkness; faoi ċeo, in darkness.

Ceol, (*keoghl*), song, music, gen. ceoil (*keoghil*), of music, plu. ceolta, songs, strains.

Cruit, *f.* a small harp.

Duisgan, is awakened.

Feaċt, *n.*, an army, forces, *v.*, to force, to bow, to make yield, to bend, to sever, to break down; feaċta, broken down, defeated, worsted,

Fearraḋ, a spindle, a stave, a verse; gan fearraḋ ceoil, without a stanza of song.

Fearra, a verse; this term is in common use to express a stanza, or verse.

Follur, manifest, plain; foillrugaḋ to make plain, to manifest, to reveal.

Ga, an arrow, a ray, a beam, a wave—

music, like light, is wafted to the ear in rays, as is supposed, or rather, in waves.

Ⅿol, *v.* praise; ⅿolaḋ, praising, *n.*, praise; *pl.* ⅿolca, praises.

Oiḋċe, night, is usually in poetry pronounced *ee.*

Rinn, a pointed end, a promontory, an ending of a line in poetry, rhyme, harmony, music.

Sancuiġ, coveted, yearned for.

Saoi, a sage, a gentleman, a man of letters.

Scap, scattered, shed.

Suan, rest; faoi ruan, at rest.

Ċalla, a hall; *pl.,* ċallaiḋ.

Ceaṁain, *gen.* Ceaṁna, Tara, from ceo, warm, sunny; and ⅿuṙ, a fortified place. (See note at foot of song.)

Cṙáċ, time, special time, ir anaṁ cṙáċ, it is seldom a time that.

THE HARP THAT ONCE THROUGH TARA'S HALLS.

Fonn—"Molly a Stóir."

I.

An ċṙuic, do ṙcap ċ𝑟i ċallaiḋ 'n ṙiġ
  Na ꜱaeċe ceolca binn',
Cá 'ṙ ballaiḋ Ceaṁṙa 'noiṙ 'ṙn a luiḋc
  Ꙅan feaṙṙaḋ ceoil, ṙo ṙinn:
Ⅿaṙ ṙúḋ cá 'ṙ c-aṙ, ċuaiḋ ċaṙc, faoi ceo,
  Cá 'ċáil, 'ꝛ a ċlu faoi ṙuan;
A'ꝛ cṙoiḋċe, 'ꝛancuiġ ⅿolca ceo,
  Ni aiꝛiġeann iaḋ ꝛo buan.

II.

Ni cluincaꝛ cṙuic na Ceaṁṙa cṙeun
  Ⅿeaꝛꝛ cṙuinṙiúꝛaḋ ban, ṙo faoi,
Óiꝛ, fuaꝛꝛann i beiċ feaċca, faon,
  Fuaiⅿ bꝛiꝛce ceuḋ 'ꝛa ṙ-oiḋċe!
Ⅿaꝛ ṙúḋ ꝺo 'ṙ c-ꝛaoiṙꝛaċc, 'ꝛ anaṁ cṙá
  A ꝺúꝛꝛċaꝛ i ꝛo ꝺeo,
Aċc 'ṙuaiꝛ a bꝛiꝛcaꝛ cṙoiḋe 'ꝛ a ċꝛaḋaḋ,
  Aiꝛ foiꝛṙúꝛaḋ i beiċ beo.

☞ Ceaṁaiṙ, the Irish name of Tara, Latinized *Temora,* is derived:—
(1) According to the Four Masters, from Cea, the name of the first queen who dwelt on that royal hill; and ⅿúṙ, an old Irish word signifying rampart, fortified place, palace, protected mound, hill—found in its Latin derivative *murus,* a wall: (2) From ceaġ, a house, and ⅿúṙ; (3) from ceaġ, a house; and ⅿóṙ, large.

None of those derivation is satisfactory. The last (ceaġ-ⅿóṙ) cannot be received, for it is no way special. The suffix ⅿóṙ, being the part of the compound that stamps the "residence of the Irish Kings," with special significancy, should be pronounced openly and in full, as in the compounds Cṙaiġ-ⅿóṙ, *Tramore;* Aḃaṙ-ⅿóṙ, *Avonmore;* now in the word (Ceaṁaiṙ)-ⅿaiṙ, the second syllable is pronounced curtly, and without the accent. Again ⅿóṙ as an adjective following in gramatical order the noun ceaġ, mas. ꝛender, should not be aspirated; but in Ceaṁaiṛ, it is aspirated. Summing up, then, these reasons, the weight of probability lies against supposing that the adjective móṛ, *great*, enters into the composition of the word.

Ṁuṛ and móṛ are the only terms about which there is question amongst the ancients or moderns. The nature of the place of which Ceaṁaiṛ is the name, and its history favor the conclusion that ṁúṛ is the second part of the compound term.

But is it the term ceaġ, a house; or is it Cea, the name of the Milesian queen, which is the first part of the word? It is very likely neither of them forms a component part of Ceaṁaiṛ. (2) Ceaġ-ṁuṛ, a house-stronghold, or house enclosure, does not sound well; besides Ceaṁaiṛ was the name, not of the house or palace alone, but of the entire hill.

(1) Cea, then, must be the prefix of ṁuṛ? And this opinion is strengthened by the authority of the " Annals of the Kingdom of Ireland"— "It is from her it was called, *i.e.*, from Cea, daughter of Lughaidh and wife of Eremhon, who requested of her husband a choice hill, as her dower, in whatever place she should select it, that she might be interred therein, and that her mound and her grave-stone should be thereon raised, and where every prince ever to be born of her should dwell. . . . . The hill she selected was Druim-Caein, *i.e.* Ceaṁaiṛ" (vol. I., p. 31, second edition). Cea, is not the prefix.

" This derivation is however," says Dr. O'Donovan, " legendary, for Ceaṁaiṛ was very common in Ireland as a woman's name; and it was applied to more hills than Ceaṁaiṛ in Meath; as, Teamhair Luachra, in Kerry, and Teamhair Bhrogha-Niadh, in Leinster. In Cormac's Glossary, it is stated that the Teamhair of a house means a *grianan*, *i.e.*, a bower, balcony ; and that Ceaṁaiṛ of the country means a hill commanding a pleasant prospect."— *Note*, p. 31.

(4) From this, then, it is plain that Ceaṁaiṛ means a *sunny mound*, or a sunshiny (ceo) enclosure (ṁuṛ), a fortified palace having a pleasant prospect. This being, according to, Cormac king and archbishop, and the most learned Irishman of the tenth century, the meaning of the name Ceaṁaiṛ; its derivation is plainly from ceo, *warm, sunshiny*, and ṁuṛ, *a fortified enclosure, mound, or hill.*

EXERCISE CXXIX.
VOCABULARY.

Bṛeuġ, *n.*, a lie; *v.* to cajole.	Rún, a secret, love, fond one.
cṛíc, country.	Seiṅn, to sing.
Dutċaṡ, *gen.* butċaiṛ, native country.	Suiṛiḋ (*sir-y*), a lover, a wooer.
Cuġaḋ, perishing.	Uaiṁ, grave.
Fiaṛ, slanting	Uimpiġ (from uiṁe, about, around),
Luċt cluiṅṛte, listeners.	turn round, move from.
Ṁaṛaċ, morrow.	

SHE IS FAR FROM THE LAND.
Fonn—" Foṛcaiṛ an boṛaṛ."

1.

Iṛ fad í o'n g-cṛíc, b-fuil a h-og-laoċ 'nn a luiḋe
'S gan ainb aiṛ a ṛuiṛiġíb 'g a bṛeuġaḋ.
Act uimpiġeann go fuaṛ ó ṛúilib gaċ ṛaoi,
Óiṛ tá a cṛoiḋe le n-a ceile 'g a euġaḋ.

II.

Buḋ iaḋ aḃráin ḋuṫċair a ṫír' féin ḋo ṡeinn,
  Rinn ġaċ fearṫra ḋ' an áil leis ḋo ṁeaṁaraḋ.
O 's beaġ imniḋe loċt cluinṫe a ceolta binn;
  A croiḋe beiṫ 'ġ a ḃriseaḋ ġan cáḃaraḋ.

III.

Do ṁairr se ḋ' a rún; aġus ḋ'euġ se ḋ'a ċríċ:
  So an meuḋ bi 'ġa ċeanġail air talaṁ:
Ni luaṫ 'ġaḃfas trom-ġul a ṫíre aon rġíċ,
  'S ni béiḋ 'b-faḋ ġan a ċéile an uairṁ fallaṁ.

iv.

O! ḋéan uairṁ ḋi 's an áit b-fuil na ġaeṫ' ġréine fiar,
  'Nuair ġealleann riaḋ ṁarać ġlórać:
Béiḋ roilriuġaḋ air a ruan mar rṁiġeaḋ an iar
  Ó n-a ḋil innse féin a tá brónać.

EXERCISE CXXX.
VOCABULARY.

Caoiḋean (from caoiḋ, to lament), a pelican, a barnicle; caoiḋean aonrac, a lonely pelican—a term commonly applied to one who has no friends and is quite alone.

Claoiḋtar, are subdued, broken.

Daiṅ, kindred.

Fearḋa, henceforth.

Laraḋ (from lar, to light up), to bloom.

Meaḋaḋ, to perish.

Orna, a sigh.

Seoḋ, a jewel, a precious thing.

Teilġean, v., to cast, to fling.

'TIS THE LAST ROSE OF SUMMER.

Fonn—"Coillte blaṅna."

I.

Tá rós déiġionać an t-samraiḋ leis féin air an ġ-craoḃ,
  D' éis a ċuallaċt na ṡeiṁe, beiṫ euġta air ġaċ taoḃ;
Ġan aon rós aṁáin ġaolṁar, ġan blaṫ, lé 'b-fuil daiṁ,
  Le laraḋ, no orna ċabairt air air ḋó ġo ráiṁ.

II.

Ni fáġfaḋ leat féin tú, lé meaḋaḋ air an ġeuġ,
  Ġan do ċeilġean a ċoḋlaḋ, mearġ do ġaolta ġo h-euġ:
'N áit a m-béiḋir fearta ġaċ lá a'r ġaċ oiḋċe,
  Leis na róraiḋ ġan blaṫ a'r ġan balaḋ 'do luiḋe.

III.

Ⅿaṛ ṙúḋ iṛ ḋúal iṁṫeaċṫ, 'nuaiṛ a ċṛionaṛ an ṡnaḋ,
  'S nuaiṛ éaluiṡeaṛ ó na ṛeoiḋiḃ an ṛṡéiṁ a'ṛ an blaṫ;
'Nuaiṛ a claoiḋṫaṛ na cṛoiḋṫe, ṛcaṛ ṛuaṛcaṛ a'ṛ ṛeun,
  Cia beiḋaḋ maṛ ċaoiḋean aonṛac, ṛa ṫ-ṛaoṡal ṛo leiṛ ṛéin.

EXERCISE CXXXI.

VOCABULARY.

Coiṡṛiṡeaċ, foreign.
Fleaḋ, a feast; *gen.* ṛleiḋe; buṇ na ṛleiḋe, at the feast; iompuiṡ, turn, change, around it; buṇ means bottom, foot.

Coiṇṡioll, connection, acquaintance.
Lá aiṛ ṛian, the day declining.
Siuḃlaċ (*shoolach, s.*, followed by i sounds like *sh*), a traveller, a walker; from ṛiuḃal, to walk.

AS SLOW OUR SHIP. \
ṛonn—Ⱥn cailin ḋ' ṛáṡ me 'mo ḋiaiṡ."

I.

Ⱥiṡ ṛṇaṁ ḋ'aṛ lonṡ ann aṡaiḋ ṡaoṫ ṫeann|
  Le' ṛaiḃ a ṛeolṫa lioṇṫa,
Do ċióṛeaḋ an bṛaṫ a ṛṫeaċ ó'n ṡ-cṛann
  Ċum an ċuain, 'ḋ'ṛáṡ ṛí, ṛinṫe.
Ⅿaṛ ṛuḋ iṛ mall an ṛiuḃal 'ṛ an ṫ-ṛliṡe
  Ó aṛaṛ ṡṛaḋaċ an ṡ-caiṛḋe,
Ⱥiṛ a ṇ-iompuiṡeaṇn claoṇṫa úṁal' an ṡ-cṛoiḋe,
  Ⅿaṛ an lonṡ-bṛaṫ ṛṡaoilṫe ann áiṛḋe.

II.

Ⱥiṡ meaḃṛúṡaḋ an am', ċuaiḋ ṫaṛṫ maṛ ceó
  Neaṁ-ḃṛiṡṁaṛ, 'buṇ na ṛleiḋe;
Biḋeann bṛón a'ṛ ṡaiṛḋeoċaṛ ṛioṛ-beo,
  'S a meaṛṡaḋ láṛ an ṡ-cleiḃe;
'S 'nuaiṛ ḋúṛuiṡeaṇn ceolṫa ṛlaṫ 'ṛ an b-ṛleiḋ,
  Ṡaċ caiṛḋeaċṫ óṡ a'ṛ cṛoiḋaṁaiṛ—
Ḋ'aṛ ṛan 'ṇnaṛ ṇ-ḋiaiṡ, biḋeann cuaċ aiṛ leiṫ
  'Dul ṫaṛṫ, 'ṛ 'ṡ a ól ṡo ṛaoiṫaṁaiṛ.

III.

Ⱥ ḋ-ṫiṛṫiḃ coiṡṛiṡeaċa, an ṫṛá,
  Do ċióṁuiṛ iṇnṛe 'ṛ ṡleaṇnṫa;
'S ṡaċ niḋ ṛa blaṫ, aċṫ eaṛba ṡṛaḋ
  'S an coiṇṡioll caoṁ do ṛaṇṫuiṡ;

Buḋ mór an rólar air ar g-croiḋe,
   Gur barr air aoiḃnear raoġalta,
Dá m-beiḋaḋ rúḋ againn le n-ar m-biṫ
   Ann aoin-ḟeaċt cairbe 'r gaolta.

III.

Mar riúḃlaċ roin, aig amarc rian,
   Go mall aig teaċt na h-oiḋċe,
Aig breaṫnuġaḋ air an lá air fiar
   Roiṁ euluġaḋ uaḋe ċoiḋċe:
Mar rúḋ, d' éir teilgean rian ar n-ḋearc,
   O bruaċaiḃ garr na h-uaiṁe,
Tig lóċrán geal na h-óige rearḋ
   Tre neulta aoire a'r cúṁa.

EXERCISE CXXXII.

VOCABULARY.

Aigne, mind, temper, spirit, affection.
bás-breiṫ, a death-judgment.
baoġal, danger.
brosduġaḋ, inciting.
Caiṫ-néim (from caiṫ, of battle; ném, power), triumph, glory after battle, pride of soul, jubilation.

Sinrean, sires, ancestors, progenitors, from rean, adj.,
Truailliġ, v., to pollute, disgrace, shame.
Trillrán, torch, a lamp, a lantern, a flambeau, diminutive of trillriḋ a torch, a lamp.
Trilir, bushy locks, ringlets (Eng. trellis).

OH! BLAME NOT THE BARD.

Fonn—"Caitlín Tirial."

I.

Ná tóg air an b-file, má euluigeann fá'n g-cluan,
'N a m-bíḋeann roġ-claon aig fonóiḋ faoi ard-ċuaḋ go
   buan,
Tá a ṁirneaċ gan traoċaḋ, 'r le h-uain, ní fé ir lúġa
A ḋéanfaḋ gaċ gairge, a beir céim agus clu:
An teud, tá 'noir rínte air an g-ceol-ċruit go fann,
Do feolfaḋ a g-croiḋe námaḋ an bár-ġaċ go teann;
'S an teanga, naċ rileann aċt mil-ḟruṫ na g-claon,
Buḋ tuilteaċ í aig brosduġaḋ gráḋa tíre na b-Fian—

II.

Mo nuaiṙ ḃ'a éiṙ áluinṅ tá a caiṫṙéim 'nn a luiḋe,
'S an croiḋe cróḋa buiṙte, náṙ b' féiḋiṙ a claoiḋeaḋ
Caiṫfiḋ éagcaoin a fíoṙ-ṡliocṫ beiṫ faluiġṫe ó'n t-raoġal,
Oiṙ iṙ báṙ-ḃreiṫ a coraint, 'r ní b-fuil a cumann gan
    baoġal.
Ta a claṅ gan aon ceannaṙ, muṙ n-déanfaiḋ riaḃ feall,
'S muṙ b-truailliġiḋ a riṅreaṙ aig iompóġaḋ le Ġall;
'S an truillreaṅ, tá aig laraḋ, ṡliġe céime gaċ lá,
Naċ rgiobtaṙ ó'n g-cann é, aiṙ a b-fuil Éiṙe ḋ'a craḋaḋ.

III.

Na tóg aiṙ an b-file a beiṫ aig fíoṙ-déanaḋ rann,
'S an t-olc, naċ n-dán léiġeaṙ, do óiḃreaḋ le greann:
Bíḋeaḋ aige aċt leur bóċċuiṙ, iṙ larfaiḋ go beo
A rorga tre ḃrat cúṁa maṙ an ġrian tre rlám ceo:
Déanfaiḋ íoḋḃairt do Éiṙinn de na béuraiḋ, a bíḋeann
D'a reolaḋ aiṙ meaṙball le ṙanaḋ a claon,
'S le blaoiġ na g-craoḃ glar, a tá fiġte aiṙ a ceann
Maṙ an Ġreug, aig imiṙt díoġaltaiṙ, falóċaiḋ, ré a lann

IV.

Aċt giḋ guṙ eulaiġ do ṁóṙ-céim, maṙ airling na h-oiḋċe
Béiḋiḋ ḃ'ainm ḃ'a luaḋ aig an b-file a coiḋċe
An trá iṙ mó ruaṙcar aiṙ a aigne le reun,
Béiḋiḋ aig reinnm go h-aṙd-binn do leaċtrom 'r do leun:
Cluinfiḋ an coigriġeaċ do ġaṙta-croiḋe fíoṙ,
Raċfaiḋ éagcaoin do claiṙriġe taṙ muiṙ a'r taṙ tíṙ,
'S do tiġeaṙnaiḋ, aig teannaḋ ná rlaḃraiḋe do ḋ' claoiḋ,
Silfiḋ deora na truaiġe lé teann buiṙte croiḋe.

EXERCISE CXXXIII.

VOCABULARY.

Anṙa, dear, fond, beloved.

Cruit, Welsh criodd, Lat. *Crotta*, already defined, a hump, a small harp; Clárṙaċ, a harp.—"The cruit was a six-stringed instrument, used of old in Scotland and Ireland."

"The cruit and the clárreáċ differed only in this, that the strings of the former were cat-gut, those of the latter were brass wire."

Cuing, a fetter, a bond, n chain; fuar-cuing, the cold chain.

Cuibṙaċ, fetters.

Dealb, *v.* to frame, to fashion, to twine.

Blaoiġ, a wreath.

Colgaċ, knowing, acquainted with; root, eol; knowledge; eolar, the same; neaṁ-eolgaċ, not acquainted with.

Gairgeaċ, a hero, a champion.

Luinne, mirth, melody, glee, the chorus, burden of a song.

Oiteog, f., a blast, a gust, a breeze.

Suairc, sweet, pleasant.

Suaircar, pleasanty.

Suairc-faoi, a man of sprightliness and sport.

Sugairġil, jollity, from rugaċ, jolly, merry; root, ruġ, sap.

Sunnḋaċ, adj. joyous, merry, jocund, glad, mirthful; from runnḋ or runnc, mirth, joy, as expressed in music and melody.

DEAR HARP OF MY COUNTRY.

Fonn—"Langolí,"

I.

'Ċruiṫ anra mo ċíne, ann ḋorċaḋar ḃí ṫínte,
　Ḃí fuar-ċuing na torḃa oiṫ ḟáirgṫe go teann;
Do ċoig mé ar geiḃeal, ḋ' eir ḋo ċuiḃreaċ beiṫ rgaoilte,
　Air ḋo ċeuḋaiḃ rgeiṫ gaeṫe, a'r roluir faoṫ-ṗann.
Ḃí fuaim runḋaċ feaṫa ḋo ḃ' aeraige 'r buḋ ḃinne,
　Aig ḃúraċt ḋo ċeuḃa, 'ḃí ruaṁar, ċum ceoil;
Aċt ḃjöir ċo neaṁ-eólgaċ air ruaṫcar 'r air luinne
　Go m-ḃuireann an ḃrón tri ḋo rúgaigil go fóill.

II.

Slán agur beannaċt le ḋo ḃinn-ġaeṫiḃ, 'ċruiṫ ċroim,
　So an ḋlaoiġ ḋéiġionaċ ḋánta, ḋo ḃéanfam' a ṡealḃ,-
Téiḋ, ir coḋail faoi rgáil lonnraiġ gaiṫṫe air ḋo fuan
　　trom,
　Go b-fáġaiḋ meura njor rtuama air ḋo ċeuḋaiḃ ċiun',
　　realḃ.
Má ḃí croiḋe gairgiġ treunṁair,-tír-ġráḋaiġ, nó ruanc-
　　faoi,
　'G'a g-connuġuḋ, aig eirḃeaċt lé feinnim an n-ḋann,-
Ní raiḃ annam-ra aċt oiteog neaṁ-ḃriġṁar na luaṫgaoiṫ',
　Agur uair-re ḋo ċainic an fuaim binn aṁáin.

(Original.)

I.

Dear Harp of my country! in darkness I found thee,
　The cold chain of silence had hung o'er thee long,
When proudly, my own Island Harp! I unbound thee,
　And gave all thy cords to light, freedom, and song!
The warm lay of love and the light note of gladness
　Have waken'd thy fondest, thy liveliest thrill;
But, so oft hast thou echoed the deep sigh of sadness,
　That ev'n in thy mirth it will steal from thee still.

II.

Dear Harp of my country! farewell to thy numbers,
　This sweet wreath of song is the last we shall twine;
Go, sleep with the sunshine of fame on thy slumbers,
　Till touch'd by some hand less unworthy than mine.
If the pulse of the patriot, soldier, or lover,
　Have throbb'd at our lay, 'tis thy glory alone;
I was *but* as the wind, passing heedlessly over,
　And all the wild sweetness I wak'd was thy own.

EXERCISE CXXXIV.

VOCABULARY.

Cuiſcuġaḋ, requital.
Deoṙaiḋ, an exile, from deoṙ, a tear.
Ꝼṙeaḃ, to beat, to lash severely to
　torment.

Sáṁailc, resemblance; from ṙaṁail,
　like, resembling.
Salcaṅc (from ſál, heel), treading,
　trampling.

☞ Mount Sion is called by the people Slịaḃ Sịan, (*pr. Shee-awn*);
voc. case, "O holy Sion," a Naoṁ Sịaịn, (*Sheeawin*).

THE PARALLEL; or, "YES, SAD ONE OF SION."

An coſaṁlaċc.

Ꝼonn—"Aịṙ an m-baịle ṙo cá an Cúlꝼịonn."
b' Ꝼeaṙṙ lịom 'na Cịṅc.

I.

Aḃa beiṙ ṙaṁailc bṙóna 'ᵹuṙ ṙịoṙ-cṙịce cléịbe
　Aon coṁaṙċa cịncé aịṙ daịṁ aᵹuṙ ᵹaol,
Iſ deaṙbċa ᵹuṙ uaịc-ṙe, a cṙuaᵹ-ḋeoṙaịḋ ſleịbe,
　Naoṁ Sịaịn, do ċaịnịc ſlịoċc Eịṙeann 'ᵹuṙ ſịol.

II.

Aḃan ċu, cá an ṙịᵹeaċc ꝼaoị ᵹeuṙ-ċeaṅaṙ bṙịrce,
　'Ᵹuṙ cuịce ó ᥒ-a ceann, cá an cṙóịn-ꝼleaṙᵹ 'ᥒ·a luịḋe
Cá a baịlce 'ſ a ſṙaịḋe maṙ ꝼaṙaċ bán ſᵹṙịorca,
　'Sa ᵹ-ceaṙc-láṙ an lae ꝼéịn, cá a ᵹṙịan 'ᥒ éịr dul
'ꝼaoị.*

III.

Aḃaṙ do ċlan, cá a ḋeoṙaịḋe láṙ dóċaịṙ ꝼịlleaḋ,
　Ꝼáᵹaịl baịſ ꝼad o'n m-baịle a beịṫ ann, buḋ é 'mịaṙ,
Aḃaṙ do ſlịoċc, cá a ſlịoċc-ṙan, láṙ duḃ-bṙóṙ, na cịlle,
　A meoṁṙaḋ laeċe lanṙaċcá baịċce a ᵹ-cịan.

---

* "Her sun is gone down while it is yet day."—*Jerom.*, xv. 9.

ıu.

'S oual a baıɾceaḋ "beaṅ ḟáġċe,"* maɾ ċuɾa 'ṅ am áḟɾa,
   Cá a h-uaıɾle 'ṅṅ a ɾġláḃaıḋ 'ġuɾ a cɾeuṅ-ḟıɾ ġaṅ
     búaıḋ,
'S ṅa ceolca ıɾ bıṅṅe oo ċıġ ó ṅ-a claṅɾaıġ,
   Se ıɾ ɾaṁaıl ooıḃ oɾṅaıġeal ṅa ġaoıċe aıɾ uaıṁ.

u.

Acc ꝼuaıɾ cú oo ċúıcuġaḋ, bı 'ṅ máɾaċ a ɾoılɾuġaḋ
   Do ċıġ 'ṅ-éıɾ aṅ oubċaıṅ, o'ɑ ḟaḋ í aṅ oıḋċe,
'S aṅ ɾíġ-ꝼlac oo ġɾeaḋ ċu, ꝼuaḋ aṅ ṅaṁaḋ a ɾoılɾuġaḋ
   Maɾ ġıolcaċ, cá bɾıɾce oɾ oo ċoṁaıɾ ġaṅ aoṅ bɾıġ.

uı.

Óıɾ aṅ ċuaċ ɾeaṅḃ béıɾꝼeaḋ aṅ óıɾ-ċaċaıɾc líṅce,
   Bı 'ġa ċuɾ le ṅ-a beul ꝼéṁ 'ɾ buḋ cóıɾ, ceaɾc aṅ
     cɾíoċ,
'S ċuıɾ ġaıɾḃeaɾ aıɾ ṅa oaoıṅe, ꝼaoı ṅ-a ġeuɾċeaṅaɾ
     ɾíṅce,
   Aṅ uaıl ó ṅa ċallaıḋ' 'ɾ ó ṅ-a luıṅġıɾ aṅ ɾġɾıaċ.

uıı.

ṅ-Uaıɾ oo ċuıc malacc ṅeıṁe, bı a o-caıɾġe, ġo bolaċ
   Aıɾ a ceaṅaıḋ 'ɾ aıɾ a ceaṅꝼaıɾc luċc-cɾeaċca, ġo
     cɾom,
'S ꝼaoı léıɾɾġıoɾ, ꝼa ḋeıɾe 'ɾ aıġ cṅuṁóġ ꝼaoı ḟalaċ,‡
   Bı baṅɾıġeaṅ ṅa ɾíġaċc 'ġ a ɾalcaıɾc ġo lom.§

THE PARALLEL; or, "YES, SAD ONE OF SION."

[*Original.*]

I.

Yes, sad one of Sion—if closely resembling,
   In shame and in sorrow, thy withered-up heart;
   If drinking deep, deep, of the same "cup of trembling"
   Could make us thy children—our parent thou art.

---

* "Thou shalt no more be termed forsaken."—*Isaias*, lxii. 4.
† "How hath the oppressor ceased, the golden city ceased."—*Idem.*, xiv. 4.
‡ "Thy pomp is brought down to the grave."—*Idem.*, xv. 11.
§ "Thou shalt no more be called the Lady of Kingdoms."—*Idem.*, 47, v.

II.

Like thee doth our nation lie conquer'd and broken,
   And fall'n from her head is the once royal crown;
In her streets, in her halls, Desolation hath spoken,
   And, "while it is day yet, her sun hath gone down!"

III.

Like thine doth her exile, 'mid dreams of returning,
   Die far from the home it were life to behold—
Like thine do her sons, in the day of their mourning,
   Remember the bright things that bless'd them of old.

IV.

Ah! well may we call her, like thee, "The Forsaken,"
   Her boldest are vanquished, her proudest are slaves;
And the harps of her minstrels, when gayest they waken,
   Have breathings as sad as the wind over graves.

V.

Yet hadst thou thy vengeance—yet came there the morrow,
   That shines out at last on the longest dark night,
When the sceptre that smote thee with slavery and sorrow
   Was shiver'd at once, like a reed in thy sight!

VI.

When that cup, which for others the proud Golden City
   Had brimm'd full of bitterness, drench'd her own lips,
And the world she had trampled on, heard without pity
   The howl in her halls, and the cry from her ships!

VII.

When the curse Heaven keeps for the haughty came over
   Her merchants rapacious, her rulers unjust,
And—a ruin, at last, for the earth-worm to cover—
   "The Lady of Kingdoms" lay low in the dust!

THE CELTIC TONGUE.

[These lines, taken from a beautiful piece which appeared in *The Nation* of the 1st of November, 1862, are very soul-inspiring, full of historic truth, and of power.

I.

Ay, build ye up the Celtic tongue above O'Curry's grave;
Speed the good work, ye patriot souls who long your land to save,
Who long to light the flame again on Freedom's altar dead,
Who long to call the glories back from hapless Erin fled,
Who long to gem her sadden'd brow with queenly wreath again,
And raise a warrior people up, a NATION in her train.
Speed then the work; be scorn our lot, our ancient pride is flown,
If midst the nations on the earth we stand in shame alone.

Throughout the lovely land of vines, where dwells the lively Gaul,
They speak the tongue of Charlemagne in cot, and bower, and hall.
Where Spain extends her sun-loved realms, from prince to muleteer,
The language of the mighty Cid still strikes the listening ear.
Their olden tongue still speak the tribes the Danube's banks along;
The German loves the rushing speech that swells in Schiller's song;
By Tiber's stream are uttered yet, as in the golden days,
The music-tones of Dante's lyre, of Petrarch's loving lays.
And we, who own that tongue of tongues that saints and sages spoke,
Have bowed our very minds beneath the Saxon's galling yoke,
And clothe the thoughts that make our hearts with Celtic ardour glow
In words that chill the lips they touch, like flakes of winter snow.
The Saxon tongue!   Why, we should hate this speech we love so well!
The Saxon tongue of Saxon guile its fraudful accents tell.
Oft to our trusting Irish ears it syllabled foul lies—
Methinks such tongue the Serpent spoke to Eve in Paradise.

Ah! cease that alien speech—too long its hollow sounds have rung,
And pour ye forth from Celtic lips the rushing CELTIC TONGUE.

II.

The Celtic Tongue! the Celtic Tongue! why should its voice be still,
When all its magic tones with old and golden glories thrill—
When, like an aged bard, it sings departed warriors' might—
When it was heard in kingly halls where throng'd the brave and bright—
When oft its glowing tales of war made dauntless hearts beat high—
When oft its tales of hapless love drew tears from beauty's eye?

Grand tongue of heroes! how its tones upon the gale uprose,
When great Cuchuilin's Red Branch Knights rushed down upon their foes;
And how its accents fired the brave to struggle for their rights,
When from thy lips they burst in flames, Con of the Hundred Fights!
Or when the breeze its war-cries bore across that gory plain,
Where royal Brian cheered his hosts to battle with the Dane.
Oh, who may fire *our* sluggish hearts like them to dare and do?
When shall we see thy like again, O hero-soul'd Boru?

Sweet tongue of bards! how swelled its tones in lofty flights of song,
When white-robed minstrels deftly swept the sounding chords along!
When Oisin touch'd the trembling strings to hymn the Fenian name,
When thrill'd thy lyre, fond Fionbell, with gallant Osgar's fame.
Alike 'twould tell of ladye-love and chief of princely line—
Fair Aileen now the poets sung, and now the Geraldine.
'Twas music's self—that barded tongue, till iron days began,
Then swell'd its swan-like strains, and died with thee, O'Carolan!

In dulcet tones the wide world o'er though gifted bards have sung,
Yet sweeter sounds thy minstrelsy, soul-soothing CELTIC TONGUE.

III.

The Celtic Tongue! the Celtic Tongue! no more in bower and hall
Where Rank holds sway or Beauty reigns, its liquid accents fall.

Far from the courts of Pride and Power, within the lowly cot
It finds a home—that outlaw'd tongue—the poor despise it not.
But still upon the mountain heath, or in the moonlit vale,
In that sweet speech the shepherd sings, the lover breathes his tale,
And oft times in the rustic church the _Soggarth_ knows its might
To lead the wretch from shades of vice to virtue's path of light.
Oh, on the sinner's harden'd heart it falls as dew from Heaven,
The softened soul dissolves in tears—he weeps, and is forgiven.

Thus lurks amid the simple poor, forgotten and unknown,
That ancient tongue, that royal tongue, so prized in ages flown,
Which came to make our isle its home from lands 'neath orient skies,
Which saw the wondrous pillar-shrines in graceful grandeur rise—
Which echoed in its days of pride within Emania's walls,
Through high Kincora's princely courts, through Tara's regal halls,
Which swelled in holy song to Heaven upon the morning air—
When from the Sacred Groves went up the Druid's voice of prayer.
And oft, in brighter Christian days, it rose in holier strain
From Glendalough's calm Eden shades, from Innisfallen's fane.
It breathed in vesper orison, when evening's shadows fell,
From city shrines, from abbey piles, from hermit's lonely cell,
It sped in winged accents forth, from dawn to day's last smile,
From lips of sages, saints, and kings, throughout our sacred Isle,
Ere Grecian fame, ere Latin name, from infant state had sprung,
In manhood's strength that language stood, the mighty CELTIC TONGUE!

IV.

The Celtic Tongue!—then must it die?   Say, shall our language go?
No! by Ulfadha's kingly soul! by sainted Laurence, no!
No! by the shades of saints and chiefs, of holy name and high,
Whose deeds, as they have lived with it, must die when it shall die—
No! by the memories of the Past that round our ruin twine—
No! by our evening hope of suns in coming days to shine.
It shall not go—it must not die—the language of our sires;
While Erin's glory glads our souls or freedom's name inspires,
That lingering ray from stars gone down—oh, let its light remain!
That last bright link with splendours flown—oh, snap it not in twain!

*　　*　　*　　*　　*　　*　　*　　*

THE END.